INTERNATIONAL TREATIES ON INTELLECTUAL PROPERTY

INTERNATIONAL TREATIES ON INTELLECTUAL PROPERTY

Marshall A. Leaffer
Editor

BNA BOOKS

The Bureau of National Affairs, Inc., Washington, D.C.

Library of Congress Cataloging-in-Publication Data

International treaties on intellectual property/Marshall A. Leaffer, editor.
p. cm.
Includes bibliographical references and index.
ISBN-0-87179-659-7
1. Intellectual property (International law) I. Leaffer, Marshall A., 1943- .
K1401.A35I57 1990
341.7'58—dc20 90-46683
CIP

Published by BNA Books
1231 25th St., N.W., Washington, D.C. 20037

International Standard Book Number: 0-87179-659-7
Printed in the United States of America

Preface

This book brings together in one volume the major international treaties and agreements covering intellectual property. These vary from the large, multinational treaties such as the Paris and the Berne conventions to treaties having a more limited participation such as the Trademark Registration Treaty and the Hague Agreement Concerning the International Deposit of Industrial Designs. In this compilation, I have incorporated the international treaties in a one-volume edition for the convenience of the busy practitioner (not to mention the student) who needs to make his or her way quickly around this increasingly important international dimension of intellectual property.

In putting together this book, I chose comprehensive coverage of the major international treaties and agreements currently in force. I have included two proposed treaties and a protocol to a treaty because of their current importance: the Treaty on Intellectual Property in Respect of Integrated Circuits; the Treaty on the International Registration of Audiovisual Works; and the Protocols Relating to the Madrid Agreement Concerning the International Registration of Marks. In addition, I have not incorporated certain regional agreements, e.g., African and Malagasy Union, Pan American Union, Benelux Designs Convention, and the Nordic Patent Law.

Each treaty is presented in a uniform manner. Before the text of the treaty, I have provided a short summary that situates the treaty and identifies certain important statutory features. These summaries introduce the reader to the treaty. They enable the reader to determine quickly the general subject matter, purpose, and scope of each treaty. Unless indicated otherwise the discussion in the summaries relates to the latest version of the treaty at issue.

For convenience, the treaties are divided into seven categories: industrial property, patents, trademarks, copyright and neighboring rights, industrial design, classification treaties, and international organizations. Nothing is sacrosanct or official about this organization. Patents, trademarks, and industrial design, for example, could easily have been included generally under industrial property; neighboring rights and signals transmitted by satellites could have constituted separate categories in themselves. In addition, the treaties covering international classification for patents, trademarks, and industrial designs could have been placed under the appropriate subject matter classification heading. I have chosen this organization because it seemed to be a reasonably logical breakdown that will enable the reader to make his or her way easily through the subject matter.

The appendix, bibliography, and index also will guide the researcher through the international treaties. The appendix includes a list of treaties showing the countries that adhere to it and the date on which they became a party to the treaty. The bibliography includes a compilation of books and articles in English that I have found to be helpful secondary sources. In addition, an index provides subject access to the treaties.

I would like to thank those who assisted in this book: Louise Rosenblatt Goines of BNA for her support, advice, and enthusiasm; Ruth Ann Cornfield for her insightful editing suggestions; my colleague, Richard Edwards, for reading and commenting on the manuscript; Kory Tilgner and Tom Boutall of the University of Toledo College of Law for their research assistance; and my secretary Donna Hunt for all her help, and especially to my wife Joelle Bahloul for her daily encouragement. My deepest appreciation to all.

Marshall A. Leaffer

Toledo, Ohio
May 1990

Table of Contents

Preface v

Introduction 1

Part I. Industrial Property

1. Paris Convention for the Protection of Industrial Property 17

Part II. Patents

1. International Convention for the Protection of New Varieties of Plants (UPOV) 53
2. Patent Cooperation Treaty...76
3. Budapest Treaty on the International Recognition of the Deposit of Microorganisms for the Purposes of Patent Procedure 125
4. European Patent Convention (With Protocols) 141

Part III. Trademarks

1. Madrid Agreement Concerning the International Registration of Marks (With Protocol)..........................229
2. Agreement of Madrid for the Prevention of False or Misleading Indications of Source on Goods 270

3. Lisbon Agreement for the Protection of Appellations of Origin and Their International Registration 278

4. Trademark Registration Treaty 291

Part IV. Copyrights and Neighboring Rights

1. Berne Convention for the Protection of Literary and Artistic Works 339

2. Universal Copyright Convention (And Protocols)....378

3. International Convention for the Protection of Performers, Producers of Phonograms and Broadcasting Organisations (Rome Convention) 415

4. Convention for the Protection of Producers of Phonograms Against Unauthorized Duplication of Their Phonograms (Geneva Convention)....430

5. Convention Relating to the Distribution of Programme-Carrying Signals Transmitted by Satellite (Brussels Convention) 437

6. Treaty on the International Registration of Audiovisual Works 444

7. Treaty on Intellectual Property in Respect of Integrated Circuits 455

Part V. Industrial Design

1. The Hague Agreement Concerning the International Deposit of Industrial Designs....471

Part VI. Classification Treaties

1. Nice Agreement Concerning the International Classification of Goods and Services for the Purposes of the Registration of Marks....499

2. Locarno Agreement Establishing an International Classification for Industrial Designs....513

3. Strasbourg Agreement Concerning the International Patent Classification 531

4. Vienna Agreement Establishing an International Classification of the Figurative Elements of Marks 546

Part VII. Organizations

1. Convention Establishing the World Intellectual Property Organization 563

Appendix 583

Bibliography 611

Index 623

Introduction

The International Dimension of Intellectual Property

Intellectual property law, which confers property rights on certain forms of information, has always had a significant international dimension. The flow of information, intangible by nature, is not constrained by space or national borders. Recognition of this fact is not new. The need for comprehensive international agreements governing intellectual property was already evident in the 19th century, coming to fruition with the Union of Paris for the Protection of Industrial Property (1883) and the Berne Convention for the Protection of Literary and Artistic Works (1886).

In today's world, the international dimension of intellectual property is of ever-increasing importance for three compelling reasons. First, the composition of world trade is changing. Currently, commerce in intellectual property has become an even greater component of trade between nations. The value of informational products has been enhanced greatly by the new technologies of the semiconductor chip, computer software, and biotechnology. Technologies in these new fields have greatly expanded the boundaries of intellectual property. As such, informational products, both traditional and new, have often become the most valuable assets of many companies. Similarly, for some countries such as the United States, trade in intellectual property is one bright spot in an otherwise unfavorable balance of payments.

Second, world commerce has become ever more interdependent, establishing a need for international cooperation. No longer can a single country impose its economic will on the rest of the world, as the United States was once able to do after World War II. Accordingly, countries have recognized this interdependence and have called for a broadening of international arrangements involving intellectual property. A prime example is the United States' adherence on March 1, 1988, to the Berne Convention, it being the last major Western country to join the leading international convention on copyright law.

Third, new reprographic and information storage technologies permit unauthorized copying to take place faster and more efficiently than ever, undermining the value of the creator's work. Much of this copying has taken place in the Third World. These information-poor countries justify their relaxed legal standards for the protection of intellectual property in their need for access to Western technology. The economic goals of the developing world and the rights of the intellectual property owner often conflict. Accordingly, both proprietor nations in the West and intellectual property owners everywhere have turned with renewed interest to develop world standards and institutional mechanisms for the protection of intellectual property. These include the rethinking and revision of traditional international agreements as administered by the World Intellectual Property Organization (WIPO). But the effort to reformulate the international relationships in intellectual property matters does not end there. New methods of transnational participation as manifested by the current push to incorporate an intellectual code within the General Agreement on Tariffs and Trade (GATT) are the subject of much interest and debate on the world stage.

What Is Intellectual Property?

The treaties reproduced on intellectual property[1] in this book include, in the broadest sense, all rights resulting from intellectual activity in the industrial, scientific, literary, or artistic fields.[2] Most often one thinks of property as either

---

[1]Basic terminology—"conventions," "agreements," and "arrangements": The reader of international treaties in general and intellectual property treaties specifically will encounter a specialized vocabulary. A review of the table of contents shows that some of the treaties are called "conventions," e.g., Paris Convention, Berne Convention; others are called "agreement" or "arrangement," e.g., Madrid Agreement. This difference in terminology is not of great significance but merely suggests the relative importance of the treaty. The major treaties are generally called conventions whereas smaller treaties are called agreements or arrangements.

[2]Convention Establishing the World Intellectual Property Organization, Art. 2 (viii), provides that " 'intellectual property' shall include the rights relating to (1) literary, artistic, and scientific works, (2) performances of performing artists, phonograms, and broadcasts, (3) inventions in all fields of human endeavor, (4) scientific discoveries, (5) industrial design, (6) trademarks, service marks, and commercial names and designations, (7) protection against unfair competition and all other rights resulting from intellectual activity in the industrial, scientific, literary, or artistic fields." (Full text of Convention is included in Part VII.)

movable property (e.g., a radio or a coat) or immovable property (e.g., a house or land). One characteristic of these forms of property is their tangible existence. In comparison, intellectual property law confers property rights on intangibles. Intellectual property has been characterized as

> "pieces of information which can be incorporated in tangible objects at the same time in an unlimited number of copies at different locations anywhere in the world. The property is not in those copies but in the information reflected in those copies."[3]

Intellectual property is generally broken down into two major branches: industrial property and copyright law. A term of French origin, "industrial property" (*propriete industrielle*) encompasses patents[4] (technological information), trademarks[5] (symbolic information), and industrial designs.[6] Copyright law and neighboring rights[7] (expressive information) cover artistic, musical, and literary works. The term "intellectual property" has been given official recognition by the international community with the establishment of WIPO, a specialized agency of the United Nations.

---

[3]World Intellectual Property Organization, Background Reading on Intellectual Property 3 (1988).

[4]Also included in the patent category are "utility models" and "inventors' certificates." "Utility models" are inventions in the mechanical field that require a lower standard of inventiveness than those required for a patent and whose term of protection is less than that conferred by patent. Some countries provide for utility models in their laws, e.g., Japan and Federal Republic of Germany; others do not, e.g., United States and the United Kingdom. Inventors' certificates are patents in which the state has the sole right to exploit, not the patentee. They are found in Socialist countries, e.g., Algeria and the Soviet Union.

[5]A trademark is a sign that serves to distinguish the products of one enterprise from those of others. Closely related to the trademark is the service mark, which serves the same function for services as a trademark does for products. Almost any identifying word, name, symbol, or device can function as a trademark if it meets the criteria for validity under national law.

[6]An industrial design is the ornamental aspect of a useful object that may consist of the shape, pattern, color, or a combination of one or more of these elements. The design must be reproducible by industrial means. Industrial designs are protected in many countries by special design legislation.

[7]"Neighboring rights" in the narrow sense are those rights granted to protect performers, producers of phonograms, and broadcasting organizations in the performance of their works. In the broader sense it covers all other rights similar to copyright such as the protection of photographs in some countries. The term "neighboring rights" comes from the French *droits voisins*, those rights which have developed parallel and are related to copyright. Examples of neighboring rights treaties are the International Convention for the Protection of Performers, Producers of Phonograms and Broadcasting Organisations (Rome Convention), and the Convention for the Protection of Producers of Phonograms Against the Unauthorized Duplication of Their Phonograms (Geneva Convention).

Theories of Protection

Why does the law protect intellectual property? The justification can be found under two theories. The natural rights theory would maintain that the creator is entitled to the intellectual fruits of his or her labor. A second theory, basic to Anglo-American law, would justify property rights on intangibles to encourage production of information through economic reward. These theories, natural rights and economic incentive, focus on the owner or creator as property owner. But the right of ownership is not the only interest at stake in providing legal protection on intellectual property.

When a third party infringes the rights of the intellectual property owner, another theory of protection comes into play. Infringement of intellectual property constitutes an act of unfair competition and falls under the general body of tort law. Protection against unfair competition benefits not only the intellectual property owner but also the consumer. This interest arises particularly in trademark law that prohibits the sale of products or services bearing words, names, symbols, and devices which are confusingly similar to that of the trademark owner. The protection against acts of unfair competition has been given recognition in international treaties and is embodied in Article 10 *bis* of the Paris Convention.[8]

Harmonization and Unification of Law

For those concerned with the international aspects of intellectual property law, the hope has been to construct a truly uniform supranational law. This utopian goal has never been achieved. Unification of law requires a proper mix of historical, political, and economic factors that merge at a particular moment in time. As for intellectual property law, there are simply too many nations having too many diverse laws and legal cultures for a stable comprehensive worldwide unification to take place. The field of patent, trademark, and copyright law is

[8]Article 10 *bis* para. 3 prohibits the following: (1) all acts of such a nature as to create confusion by any means whatever with the establishment, the goods, or the industrial or commercial activities of a competitor; (2) false allegations in the course of trade of such a nature as to discredit the establishment, the goods, or the industrial or commercial activities of a competitor; (3) indications or allegations the use of which in the course of trade is liable to mislead the public as to the nature, the manufacturing process, the characteristics, the suitability for their purpose, or the quantity of the goods.

varied, complicated, and ever changing. It is hardly surprising that a worldwide consensus has never been struck on anything more than certain of its basic principles.

Regionally, however, some progress has been made toward unification. For example, the Benelux Trademark Law constitutes a uniform law of trademark for three countries: the Netherlands, Belgium, and Luxembourg. Similarly, the African and Malagasy Union has done the same for patents, designs, trademarks, and appellations of origin for its members. A comparable unification has taken place for five Scandinavian countries. But on the whole the utopian vision of a multinational uniform law established by treaty has never been a realistic option.

The major treaties of comprehensive international scope attempt harmonization of law, a more modest goal than unification of law. To harmonize the law means to reconcile national legal systems, without necessarily achieving a uniform result. Generally, harmonization of law to date operates more in the domain of formalities, such as the procedures and filing of claims for intellectual property rights. Most of the treaties found in this book harmonize rather than unify national law. They were designed by their founding members to effect uniform solutions to certain international problems arising from international legal diversity.

In their attempt to harmonize the law, the Paris and the Berne conventions (the two major intellectual property treaties) have greatly influenced the other conventions concerning intellectual property. The following remarks are directed largely to these two treaties, but the principles discussed below can be applied generally to the other treaties as well.

The Paris and Berne Unions: Their Role

The Paris Convention originated from the first International Patent Congress that took place in Vienna in 1873. On March 20, 1883, the Paris Union was concluded and signed by 11 states with varying degrees of industrial development and entered into force in 1884. Its objectives were to secure legal protection for industrial property and to encourage uniformity of law. It achieved these goals by providing a truly multinational treaty with liberal rules of accession and an administrative structure that permitted further organizational development. It largely superseded a chaotic system of bilateral treaties.

The Berne Convention developed in similar fashion for many of the same reasons as the Paris Convention. It arose through the efforts of La Société des Gens de Lettres and from the Association Littéraire et Artistique Internationale (ALAI). These groups promoted the diplomatic conferences held in Geneva that ultimately concluded in the Berne Convention of 1886. The guiding principle was that all authors of works published in contracting states, irrespective of their nationality, should be treated without discrimination under the national law of a member state and without being subjected to any formalities.

The founding members, from the inception of the Paris and Berne conventions, wished to create an entity of permanent independent legal existence open to all countries. The Paris and Berne unions were designed to take into account changing world conditions and, in so doing, to revise periodically the Paris and Berne conventions. Under the auspices of the Paris and Berne unions, the Paris Convention has been revised five times and the Berne Convention has undergone two additions and five revisions.

One important function of the unions, particularly the Paris Union, is to form "special agreements." As stated in the 1883 text of the Paris Convention: "It is understood that the . . . Contracting Parties reserve the right to make separately between themselves special agreements for the protection of industrial property, insofar as these agreements do not contravene the provisions of this Convention." (Art. 15). By this provision, special agreements have been concluded. They are designed to make the international protection of industrial property rights more secure and, at the same time, easier and less expensive to obtain. Membership in the Paris Union, however, does not mean accession to the special agreements. They are distinct international treaties requiring separate accession by each state. However, to accede to a special agreement (e.g., the Patent Cooperation Treaty) requires membership in the Paris Union.[9]

[9]*See, e.g.*, Patent Cooperation Treaty Art. 62 para. 1. Similarly, to become a party to the International Convention for the Protection of Performers, Producers of Phonograms and Broadcasting Organisations (Rome Convention), membership in either the Berne Convention or the Universal Copyright Convention (UCC) is required. *See* Rome Convention Art. 23.

At this time, there are 11 special agreements under the Paris Union[10] administered by the International Bureau of WIPO. They cover the full range of intellectual property: trademarks, e.g., the Madrid Agreement; patents, e.g., the Patent Cooperation Treaty; industrial design, e.g., the Hague Agreement; and the various classification agreements, e.g., the Strasbourg Agreement Concerning the International Patent Classification. The special agreements constitute a large portion of this book.

The Principle of National Treatment

From its inception, the Union of Paris avoided a substantive law approach that would apply to all its members. Rather, a simple and politically workable *principle of national treatment* was adopted as its foundation. Article 2(1) states:

> "Nationals of any country of the Union shall, as regards the protection of industrial property, enjoy in all the other countries of the Union the advantages that their respective laws now grant, or may hereafter grant, to nationals; all without prejudice to the rights specially provided for by this Convention."

The principle of national treatment serves an important function. It avoids problems associated with reciprocity and, as a result, simplifies international relations in intellectual property among nations. Under the principle of reciprocity, country A will protect the citizens of country B in the same manner that country B protects citizens of country A. For example, if country A has a patent term of 17 years whereas

---

[10] *Patents*: the Patent Cooperation Treaty; the Budapest Treaty on the International Recognition of the Deposit of Microorganisms for the Purposes of Patent Procedure; the Strasbourg Agreement Concerning the International Patent Classification. *Trademarks*: the Madrid Agreement Concerning the International Registration of Marks; the Trademark Registration Treaty; The Nice Agreement Concerning the International Classification of Goods and Services for the Purposes of the Registration of Marks; the Vienna Agreement Establishing an International Classification of the Figurative Elements of Marks; the Madrid Agreement for the Repression of False or Deceptive Indications of Source on Goods; the Lisbon Agreement for the Protection of Appellations of Origin and Their International Registration. *Industrial Design*: the Hague Agreement Concerning the International Deposit of Industrial Designs; the Locarno Agreement Establishing an International Classification for Industrial Designs.

country B has a patent term of 20 years, A would be given no more than 17 years of protection in country B.

By comparison, the principle of national treatment eliminates the need for a reciprocity inquiry. Nationals of country A will enjoy 20 years of protection in county B, even though nationals of country B will receive only 17 years of protection in country A. The principle of national treatment applies not only to the substantive law but also to procedural law before both courts and administrative agencies. The principle of national treatment simplifies the relations between countries that no longer have to negotiate and maintain bilateral arrangements. It immediately forges industrial property relations among members of the Paris Union that differ as to law, ideology, and stage of economic development.

The international conventions have established various bases, commonly called "connecting factors," by which national treatment can be claimed. The essential connecting factor of the Paris Convention is the nationality of the claimant. For example, suppose a person wishes to claim national treatment under the patent laws of country A. Under the Paris Convention, this person would have to be a national of member country B.

Some conventions have more than one connecting factor. In addition to nationality, the Berne Convention incorporates another connecting factor on which national treatment can be claimed. It establishes the place of *publication* as an alternative basis for national treatment. Thus, under Berne, protection must be given to a work by a member country if it is first *published* in a member state irrespective of the author's nationality.[11]

Minimum Rights Principle

In addition to national treatment, the Paris and Berne conventions establish minimum substantive standards that each country must recognize in its national laws. These minimum standards serve two important functions. First, they are

[11] *See* Berne Convention Art. 3 (Paris Act). Under Art. 3, protection is accorded to any work, if unpublished or wherever published, if the work is authored by a national of a Berne country. Non-Berne authors who are habitual residents of a Berne country are to be treated as nationals of the member country.

necessary to avoid serious imbalances created by the principle of national treatment. For example, if country A provided protection for performance rights to sound recordings whereas country B did not, the result would be that nationals of country B would enjoy performance rights in country A, whereas nationals of country A would not enjoy them in country B. Thus, minimum standards avoid this kind of inequality by imposing a common denominator of legal rights shared by all member countries.

Second, minimum rights have a role to play in the eventual unification of law. The trend has been that even if a convention begins with a small number of minimum rights, later revisions continue to add others. Both the Paris and Berne conventions illustrate how each revision tends to incorporate an extended body of minimum rights.

The Berne Convention continues with each revision to add other minimum rights. Since the Rome revision of 1928, Article 6 *bis* (1) requires member countries to recognize moral rights. Additions also came about with the Brussels revision of 1948 that requires a minimum term for copyright of at least life of the author plus 50 years (Art. 7). Other important Convention minima concern protection of a work absent formalities (Art. 5 para. 2) and provisions relating to the exploitation of works (Art. 9 para. 2). Berne also declares certain rights that are not required for recognition. For example, Article 14 *ter* specifies that member states may, but are not required to, allow for a resale royalty right (*droit de suite*).[12]

Similarly, the Paris Convention establishes minimum rights that all member countries must recognize and has extended the concept with every revision. Some of these principles are broadly stated. For example, Article 10 *bis* (1) of the Paris Convention provides that nationals of parties to the Convention shall enjoy, in all the countries party to the Convention, effective protection against unfair competition, and Article 5 *quinquies* provides that industrial designs shall be protected in all countries of the Union. The Paris Convention also specifies certain minimum rights more concretely than the above examples. For instance, Article 5 *lit* provides that a

---

[12]A resale royalty right (*droit de suite*) requires a percentage of the resale price to be paid during the copyright period to the artist or his or her successors. The right is recognized in several European states, e.g., France, but generally not in the common law world.

compulsory license for failure to work or insufficient working may not be granted before the expiration of four years from the filing of patent application or three years from the granting of the patent, and such a license shall only be nonexclusive.

Territorial Scope of Protection

Rights conferred by the international conventions are territorially limited whereby national law decides both substance and procedure. Although territorially limited, certain conventions include provisions for international deposit and application that greatly facilitate the acquisition of rights in member countries. The first such treaty establishing the process is the Madrid Agreement Concerning the International Registration of Marks of 1891. Another example is the Hague Agreement Concerning the International Deposit of Industrial Designs. These treaties allow the option of a centralized application and deposit that is expedited to the designated countries. In these designated countries, the application and deposit is treated as a national application. By streamlining and lowering the cost of multinational filings, such treaties partially integrate and unify procedural matters, encouraging closer ties among countries in matters of intellectual property.

The European Patent Convention of 1973 introduces another level of territorial integration. In addition to central application and deposit, the Convention sets up procedures for the examination and issuance of the patent applications originating from participating countries. Upon issuance, the patent becomes effective as a national patent in those states party to the European Patent Convention. In each of the member states, the patent so issued is treated as though it were granted by that state as to its duration, enforcement, and other specialized rules governing patent law. For example, if the patent falls into the public domain in one state, its validity is not affected in any other state. Thus, the European Patent Convention has established a certain body of unified law beyond the traditional notions of territoriality, but falls short of a truly supranational patent.

The European Patent Convention should be compared with the proposed Common Market Patent Convention of 1975, which unifies patent law and creates a *supranational* patent for the European Community. Here the patents issued under the Common Market Patent Convention will be Community Patents and will have the same effect in all member states. A Community Patent will endure for an identical term and can only be transferred as a unit.

Adherence and Internal Applicability

For the most part, adherence to a treaty is an uncomplicated matter; its procedures are usually specified in the treaty itself. In general, a treaty becomes binding by ratification, acceptance, or approval, that is, by the deposit of the required documents. The treaty itself may fix the date it enters into force, which is usually dependent on the adherence of a minimum number of states. Once a state ratifies a treaty, and that treaty enters into force for that state, the state is bound by the obligations stated in the treaty and has a further obligation not to frustrate the purpose of the treaty. In general, the treaty remains binding on the state in perpetuity until the state denounces it according to its specific provisions or under the rules of international law.

Once a treaty becomes binding, a state is required to implement its provisions. How the provisions of the treaty are applied by the internal courts is an important issue that varies among countries. In other words, when does a treaty become *self-executing* or directly applicable? If a treaty is self-executing, its provisions become the law of the land and a party may invoke the treaty before an internal court. Under international law, a state is free to decide whether a treaty is to be self-executing according to its constitutional law. For example, the Berne Convention in the Federal Republic of Germany is self-executing and has thus superseded national law. This permits a private party to directly invoke it before a German court. Alternatively, treaties in the United Kingdom and Scandinavian countries are not regarded as self-executing. In those countries, the treaty provisions are implemented through statutory and executive measures. Thus, a claimant in the United Kingdom must invoke the appropriate national law embodying the right established by the treaty before the national court.

Reservations to a Treaty

The rights granted by certain treaties included in this book can be limited by reservations. A reservation allows a country to become bound by a treaty but without having to adhere to all of its provisions. Some conventions such as the Convention for the Protection of Producers of Phonograms Against Unauthorized Duplication of Their Phonograms (Geneva Convention) permit no reservations, whereas other conventions such as the Convention for the Protection of Performers, Producers of Phonograms and Broadcasting Organisations (Rome Convention) allow a number of reservations. A good example of a reservation is found in the Paris Convention Stockholm text (1967). Article 22 of the Paris Convention allows a member state to declare in its instrument of ratification or accession that its ratification or accession shall not apply to the substantive provisions of Articles 1 to 12 or to the administrative provisions of Articles 13 to 17.

A state that makes a reservation is subject to reciprocity by others. Suppose state A has chosen the reservation and state B has not. In this situation, state B in its relations with state A is entitled to be treated as though it had also made the reservation.

Revisions of the Treaties

Some of the treaties in this book have been revised one or more times. To revise a treaty means to introduce new provisions into it or to modify its existing provisions. In general, a revision of a treaty takes place pursuant to a diplomatic conference of representatives of the member states. Both the Paris and Berne conventions have undergone important revisions. The Paris Convention has been revised six times since it was first signed in 1883. The Berne Convention has undergone five revisions and two additions since its completion in 1886. In effect, there is no one Paris or Berne convention but a nucleus of Paris and Berne conventions that connects the 100 (Paris) and 83 (Berne) parties to each convention.[13]

Because a revision may contain significant substantive

[13]The membership figures for the Paris and Berne conventions are based on their status as of January 1, 1990.

changes, an important question arises as to which revision of the convention applies when two states are not party to the same revision. There are two basic variations on this theme. The first occurs when one state has acceded to the later version of the convention whereas another state has not. In this instance, the last version that the two states had previously shared in common will be the applicable version. For example, New Zealand acceded to the Berne Convention under the Rome Act of 1925. France, however, after having acceded to the Rome Act, now adheres to the Paris Act of 1971. Between these two countries, the Rome Act—the latest version shared by the two countries—will apply.

A second variation arises when a country newly accedes to a convention without having adhered to a previous revision. Here, the two countries have no revision of the convention in common. As for the Berne (Art. 32 para. 2) and Paris conventions (Art. 27 para. 3), the newly acceding country is required to apply the latest version of the convention in its relations with senior countries that do not adhere to the latest version. Alternatively, the senior member would apply the latest version to which it has acceded.

International Organizations

Of the several organizations that administer the international treaties, the most important is the World Intellectual Property Organization. A specialized agency of the United Nations, headquartered in Geneva, WIPO formally came into being with the Stockholm Convention of 1967. Its predecessor organizations were the international bureaus of the Paris and Berne unions, supervised by the Swiss Federal Council. These were merged into the United International Bureaus, known as Bureaux Internationaux Réunis pour la Protection de la Propriété Intellectuelle (BIRPI).

WIPO's tasks cover both administration of the international treaties, which include the Paris Convention, the special agreements, the Berne Convention, and the promotion of intellectual property worldwide. It carries out this latter task by establishing expert commissions, preparing preliminary studies, and publishing the monthly journals *Industrial Property* (*Propriété Industrielle*) and *Copyright* (*le Droit d'Auteur*).

WIPO also has been active providing developing countries with technical help, offering seminars, forming expert commissions, and preparing model laws.

Although WIPO is by far the most important international agency in promoting intellectual property, UNESCO[14] continues to play an important role in its task of administering the Universal Copyright Convention (UCC). The UCC came into being after World War II and was designed to complement the Berne Convention. UNESCO's Intergovernmental Copyright Committee collaborates with WIPO's Executive Committee of the Berne Union on such copyright matters as the effect of new technologies on copyright and the range of issues concerning developing countries. Collaboration between WIPO and UNESCO also takes place in the administration of the International Convention for the Protection of Performers, Producers of Phonograms and Broadcasting Organisations (Rome Convention). In addition to these organizations, the International Labor Office participates in administering the Convention.

Regional organizations also play a role in administering and promoting intellectual property. The European Patent Convention was created by the Council of Europe that has been active in both harmonizing and unifying intellectual property law in Europe. The Convention is overseen by the Administrative Council.

Not all international conventions are administered by WIPO; some are administered by other United Nations agencies or regional organizations. An example is the International Convention for the Protection of New Varieties of Plants (UPOV). UPOV is an independent intergovernmental organization with its own legal personality. It is, however, related to the WIPO system of special unions. Pursuant to an agreement concluded between WIPO and UPOV, the Director General of WIPO is the Secretary General of UPOV and WIPO provides administrative and financial services to UPOV.

---

[14]UNESCO is the abbreviation for the United Nations Educational Scientific and Cultural Organization.

Part I

Industrial Property

1. Paris Convention for the Protection of Industrial Property

March 20, 1883, as revised at Brussels on December 14, 1900, at Washington on June 2, 1911, at The Hague on November 6, 1925, at London on June 2, 1934, at Lisbon on October 31, 1958, and at Stockholm on July 14, 1967

The Paris Convention for the Protection of Industrial Property was concluded in Paris in 1883, and ultimately revised in Stockholm in 1967. Covering industrial property in the broadest sense, the Paris Convention includes provisions relating to inventions, trade names, trademarks, service marks, industrial designs, utility models, indications of source, appellations of origin, and the repression of unfair competition. The Paris Convention is the oldest industrial property law treaty and has the widest membership. It is the preeminent multilateral industrial property law treaty.

The member countries of the Paris Convention constitute a union for the protection of industrial property. By establishing a Union, the Paris Convention is more than a treaty; it establishes as well a legal entity under international law with administrative organs to carry out its mission. The Union has three administrative organs: the Assembly, the Executive Committee, and the International Bureau of WIPO. The Assembly, which consists of all member countries, is the chief governing body of the Union (Art. 13). The Executive Committee is a smaller body of the Union and is elected from the Assembly (Art. 14). The International Bureau of WIPO carries out the administrative tasks of the Union (Art. 15).

Within the Union of Paris is a nucleus of treaties known as the "special unions" or "special agreements," which cover a broad range of intellectual property. These special unions require membership in the Union of Paris for adherence and cannot contravene the provisions of the Paris Convention (Art. 19). Examples of the special unions are the Patent Cooperation Treaty, the Madrid Agreement of 1891, the Hague Agreement of 1925, the Trademark Registration Treaty, etc. The special unions are administered by the International Bureau.

The Paris Convention is based on three guiding principles: national treatment, right of priority, and uniform rules (convention minima).

The principle of "national treatment" requires that every member state grant the same protection to nationals of other member states as it grants to its own nationals (Arts. 2 and 3).

The principle of "right of priority" confers on any member of the Union, which has filed an application for a patent in its own state, a grace period of one year to file in other member countries. If filed within this grace period, the original filing date becomes the effective filing date in all the other member countries. This 12-month right of priority is also extended to utility models. Trademarks and industrial designs enjoy a six-month right of priority (Art. 1).

Although the Convention regards the protection of industrial property rights as a matter of domestic legislation, it establishes a set of uniform rules that must be observed by each member state to provide minimum protection for industrial property rights. For example, for patents, Article 5 sets forth limitations on compulsory licenses for failure to work a patent and on conditions of forfeiture for a patent. For industrial designs, all countries of the union require them to be protected and leave to domestic law the details (Art. 5 *quinquies*).

For trademarks, Article 6 *bis* contains provisions concerning famous marks (*Marques Notoirement Connue*). Every trademark duly registered in the country of origin must be accepted for filing and protected "as is" (*telle quelle*) in any other member country (Art. 6 *quinquies lit.* a-e). Trade names are to be protected in member countries without having to file or register them (Art. 8). A member state must provide protection against the direct or indirect use of a false indication of the source of goods or the identity of the producer, and it must also assure protection against unfair competition (Art. 10).

On January 1, 1990, the following 100 states were party to the Paris Convention:

Algeria
Argentina
Australia
Austria
Bahamas
Barbados
Belgium
Benin
Brazil
Bulgaria
Burkina Faso
Burundi
Cameroon
Canada
Central African Republic
Chad
China
Congo
Cote d'Ivoire
Cuba
Cyprus
Czechoslovakia
Democratic People's Republic of Korea
Denmark
Dominican Republic
Egypt
Finland
France
Gabon
German Democratic Republic
Federal Republic of Germany
Ghana
Greece
Guinea
Guinea-Bissau
Haiti
Holy See
Hungary
Iceland
Indonesia
Iran
Iraq
Ireland
Israel
Italy
Japan
Jordan
Kenya
Lebanon
Lesotho
Libya
Liechtenstein
Luxembourg
Madagascar
Malawi
Malaysia
Mali
Malta
Mauritania
Mauritius
Mexico
Monaco
Mongolia
Morocco
Netherlands
New Zealand
Niger
Nigeria
Norway
Philippines
Poland
Portugal
Republic of Korea
Romania
Rwanda
San Marino
Senegal
South Africa
Soviet Union
Spain
Sri Lanka
Sudan
Suriname
Sweden
Switzerland
Syria
Togo
Trinidad and Tobago
Tunisia
Turkey
Uganda
United Kingdom
United Republic of Tanzania
United States of America
Uruguay
Viet Nam
Yugoslavia
Zaire
Zambia
Zimbabwe

Paris Convention for the Protection of Industrial Property, as revised at Stockholm, 1967

Article 1

Establishment of the Union; Scope of Industrial Property

(1) The countries to which this Convention applies constitute a Union for the protection of industrial property.

(2) The protection of industrial property has as its object patents, utility models, industrial designs, trademarks, service marks, trade names, indications of source or appellations of origin, and the repression of unfair competition.

(3) Industrial property shall be understood in the broadest sense and shall apply not only to industry and commerce proper, but likewise to agricultural and extractive industries and to all manufactured or natural products, for example, wines, grain, tobacco leaf, fruit, cattle, minerals, mineral waters, beer, flowers, and flour.

(4) Patents shall include the various kinds of industrial patents recognized by the laws of the countries of the Union, such as patents of importation, patents of improvement, patents and certificates of addition, etc.

Article 2

National Treatment for Nationals of Countries of the Union

(1) Nationals of any country of the Union shall, as regards the protection of industrial property, enjoy in all the other countries of the Union the advantages that their respective laws now grant, or may hereafter grant, to nationals; all without prejudice to the rights specially provided for by this Convention. Consequently, they shall have the same protection as the latter, and the same legal remedy against any infringement of their rights, provided that the conditions and formalities imposed upon nationals are complied with.

Source: Text courtesy of the World Intellectual Property Organization (WIPO).

(2) However, no requirement as to domicile or establishment in the country where protection is claimed may be imposed upon nationals of countries of the Union for the enjoyment of any industrial property rights.

(3) The provisions of the laws of each of the countries of the Union relating to judicial and administrative procedure and to jurisdiction, and to the designation of an address for service or the appointment of an agent, which may be required by the laws on industrial property are expressly reserved.

Article 3
Same Treatment for Certain Categories of Persons as for Nationals of Countries of the Union

Nationals of countries outside the Union who are domiciled or who have real and effective industrial or commercial establishments in the territory of one of the countries of the Union shall be treated in the same manner as nationals of the countries of the Union.

Article 4
A to I. *Patents, Utility Models, Industrial Designs, Marks, Inventors' Certificates:* Right of Priority.—G. *Patents:* Division of the Application

A— (1) Any person who has duly filed an application for a patent, or for the registration of a utility model, or of an industrial design, or of a trademark, in one of the countries of the Union, or his successor in title, shall enjoy, for the purpose of filing in the other countries, a right of priority during the periods hereinafter fixed.

(2) Any filing that is equivalent to a regular national filing under the domestic legislation of any country of the Union or under bilateral or multilateral treaties concluded between countries of the Union shall be recognized as giving rise to the right of priority.

(3) By a regular national filing is meant any filing that is adequate to establish the date on which the application was filed in the country concerned, whatever may be the subsequent fate of the application.

B— Consequently, any subsequent filing in any of the other countries of the Union before the expiration of the periods referred to above shall not be invalidated by reason of any acts accomplished in the interval, in particular, another filing, the publication or exploitation of the invention, the putting on sale of copies of the design, or the use of the mark, and such acts cannot give rise to any third-party right or any right of personal possession. Rights acquired by third parties before the date of the first application that serves as the basis for the right of priority are reserved in accordance with the domestic legislation of each country of the Union.

C—— (1) The periods of priority referred to above shall be twelve months for patents and utility models, and six months for industrial designs and trademarks.

(2) These periods shall start from the date of filing of the first application; the day of filing shall not be included in the period.

(3) If the last day of the period is an official holiday, or a day when the Office is not open for the filing of applications in the country where protection is claimed, the period shall be extended until the first following working day.

(4) A subsequent application concerning the same subject as a previous first application within the meaning of paragraph (2), above, filed in the same country of the Union, shall be considered as the first application, of which the filing date shall be the starting point of the period of priority, if, at the time of filing the subsequent application, the said previous application has been withdrawn, abandoned, or refused, without having been laid open to public inspection and without leaving any rights outstanding, and if it has not yet served as a basis for claiming a right of priority. The previous application may not thereafter serve as a basis for claiming a right of priority.

D—— (1) Any person desiring to take advantage of the priority of a previous filing shall be required to make a declaration indicating the date of such filing and the country in which it was made. Each country shall determine the latest date on which such declaration must be made.

(2) These particulars shall be mentioned in the publications issued by the competent authority, and in particular in the patents and the specifications relating thereto.

(3) The countries of the Union may require any person making a declaration of priority to produce a copy of the application (description, drawings, etc.) previously filed. The copy, certified as correct by the authority which received such application, shall not require any authentication, and may in any case be filed, without fee, at any time within three months of the filing of the subsequent application. They may require it to be accompanied by a certificate from the same authority showing the date of filing, and by a translation.

(4) No other formalities may be required for the declaration of priority at the time of filing the application. Each country of the Union shall determine the consequences of failure to comply with the formalities prescribed by this Article, but such consequences shall in no case go beyond the loss of the right of priority.

(5) Subsequently, further proof may be required.

Any person who avails himself of the priority of a previous application shall be required to specify the number of that application; this number shall be published as provided for by paragraph (2), above.

E—— (1) Where an industrial design is filed in a country by virtue of a right of priority based on the filing of a utility model, the period of priority shall be the same as that fixed for industrial designs.

(2) Furthermore, it is permissible to file a utility model in a country by virtue of a right of priority based on the filing of a patent application, and vice versa.

F—— No country of the Union may refuse a priority or a patent application on the ground that the applicant claims multiple priorities, even if they originate in different countries, or on the ground that an application claiming one or more priorities contains one or more elements that were not included in the application or applications whose priority is claimed, provided that, in both cases, there is unity of invention within the meaning of the law of the country.

With respect to the elements not included in the application or applications whose priority is claimed, the filing of the subsequent application shall give rise to a right of priority under ordinary conditions.

G—— (1) If the examination reveals that an application for a patent contains more than one invention, the applicant may divide the application into a certain number of divisional applications and preserve as the date of each the date of the initial application and the benefit of the right of priority, if any.

(2) The applicant may also, on his own initiative, divide a patent application and preserve as the date of each divisional application the date of the initial application and the benefit of the right of priority, if any. Each country of the Union shall have the right to determine the conditions under which such division shall be authorized.

H—— Priority may not be refused on the ground that certain elements of the invention for which priority is claimed do not appear among the claims formulated in the application in the country of origin, provided that the application documents as a whole specifically disclose such elements.

I—— (1) Applications for inventors' certificates filed in a country in which applicants have the right to apply at their own option either for a patent or for an inventor's certificate shall give rise to the right of priority provided for by this Article, under the same conditions and with the same effects as applications for patents.

(2) In a country in which applicants have the right to apply at their own option either for a patent or for an inventor's certificate, an applicant for an inventor's certificate shall, in accordance with

the provisions of this Article relating to patent applications, enjoy a right of priority based on an application for a patent, a utility model, or an inventor's certificate.

Article 4*bis*

Patents: Independence of Patents Obtained for the Same Invention in Different Countries

(1) Patents applied for in the various countries of the Union by nationals of countries of the Union shall be independent of patents obtained for the same invention in other countries, whether members of the Union or not.

(2) The foregoing provision is to be understood in an unrestricted sense, in particular, in the sense that patents applied for during the period of priority are independent, both as regards the grounds for nullity and forfeiture, and as regards their normal duration.

(3) The provisions shall apply to all patents existing at the time when it comes into effect.

(4) Similarly, it shall apply, in the case of the accession of new countries, to patents in existence on either side at the time of accession.

(5) Patents obtained with the benefit of priority shall, in the various countries of the Union, have a duration equal to that which they would have, had they been applied for or granted without the benefit of priority.

Article 4*ter*

Patents: Mention of the Inventor in the Patent

The inventor shall have the right to be mentioned as such in the patent.

Article 4*quater*

Patents: Patentability in Case of Restrictions of Sale by Law

The grant of a patent shall not be refused and a patent shall not be invalidated on the ground that the sale of the patented product or of a product obtained by means of a patented process is subject to restrictions or limitations resulting from the domestic law.

Article 5

A. *Patents:* Importation of Articles; Failure to Work or Insufficient Working; Compulsory Licenses.—B. *Industrial Designs:* Failure to Work; Importation of Articles.—C. *Marks:* Failure to Use; Different Forms; Use by Co-proprietors.—D. *Patents, Utility Models, Marks, Industrial Designs:* Marking

A—— (1) Importation by the patentee into the country where the patent has been granted of articles manufactured in any of the countries of the Union shall not entail forfeiture of the patent.

(2) Each country of the Union shall have the right to take legislative measures providing for the grant of compulsory licenses to prevent the abuses which might result from the exercise of the exclusive rights conferred by the patent, for example, failure to work.

(3) Forfeiture of the patent shall not be provided for except in cases where the grant of compulsory licenses would not have been sufficient to prevent the said abuses. No proceedings for the forfeiture or revocation of a patent may be instituted before the expiration of two years from the grant of the first compulsory license.

(4) A compulsory license may not be applied for on the ground of failure to work or insufficient working before the expiration of a period of four years from the date of filing of the patent application or three years from the date of filing of the grant of the patent, whichever period expires last; it shall be refused if the patentee justifies his inaction by legitimate reasons. Such a compulsory license shall be non-exclusive and shall not be transferable, even in the form of the grant of a sub-license, except with that part of the enterprise or goodwill which exploits such license.

(5) The foregoing provisions shall be applicable, *mutatis mutandis,* to utility models.

B—— The protection of industrial designs shall not, under any circumstances, be subject to any forfeiture, either by reason of failure to work or by reason of the importation of articles corresponding to those which are protected.

C—— (1) If, in any country, use of the registered mark is compulsory, the registration may be cancelled only after a reasonable period, and then only if the person concerned does not justify his inaction.

(2) Use of a trademark by the proprietor in a form differing in elements which do not alter the distinctive character of the mark in the form in which it was registered in one of the countries of the Union shall not entail invalidation of the registration and shall not diminish the protection granted to the mark.

(3) Concurrent use of the same mark on identical or similar goods by industrial or commercial establishments considered as co-proprietors of the mark according to the provisions of the domestic

law of the country where protection is claimed shall not prevent registration or diminish in any way the protection granted to the said mark in any country of the Union, provided that such use does not result in misleading the public and is not contrary to the public interest.

D—— No indication or mention of the patent, of the utility model, of the registration of the trademark, or of the deposit of the industrial design, shall be required upon the goods as a condition of recognition of the right to a protection.

Article 5*bis*

All Industrial Property Rights: Period of Grace for the Payment of Fees for the Maintenance of Rights; *Patents:* Restoration

(1) A period of grace of not less than six months shall be allowed for the payment of the fees prescribed for the maintenance of industrial property rights, subject, if the domestic legislation so provides, to the payment of a surcharge.

(2) The countries of the Union shall have the right to provide for the restoration of patents which have lapsed by reason of non-payment of fees.

Article 5*ter*

Patents: Patented Devices Forming Part of Vessels, Aircraft, or Land Vehicles

In any country of the Union the following shall not be considered as infringement of the rights of a patentee:

1. the use on board vessels of other countries of the Union of devices forming the subject of his patent in the body of the vessel, in the machinery, tackle, gear and other accessories, when such vessels temporarily or accidentally enter the waters of the said country, provided that such devices are used there exclusively for the needs of the vessel;
2. the use of devices forming the subject of the patent in the construction or operation of aircraft or land vehicles of other countries of the Union, or of accessories of such aircraft or land vehicles, when those aircraft or land vehicles temporarily or accidentally enter the said country.

Article 5*quater*

Patents: Importation of Products Manufactured by a Process Patented in the Importing Country

When a product is imported into a country of the Union where there exists a patent protecting a process of manufacture of the said product, the patentee shall have all the rights, with regard to the imported product, that are accorded to him by the legislation of the country of importation, on the basis of the process patent, with respect to products manufactured in that country.

Article 5*quinquies*

Industrial Designs

Industrial designs shall be protected in all the countries of the Union.

Article 6

Marks: Conditions of Registration; Independence of Protection of Same Mark in Different Countries

(1) The conditions for the filing and registration of trademarks shall be determined in each country of the Union by its domestic legislation.

(2) However, an application for the registration of a mark filed by a national of a country of the Union in any country of the Union may not be refused, nor may a registration be invalidated, on the ground that filing, registration, or renewal, has not been effected in the country of origin.

(3) A mark duly registered in a country of the Union shall be regarded as independent of marks registered in the other countries of the Union, including the country of origin.

Article 6*bis*

Marks: Well-Known Marks

(1) The countries of the Union undertake, ex officio if their legislation so permits, or at the request of an interested party, to refuse or to cancel the registration, and to prohibit the use, of a trademark which constitutes a reproduction, an imitation, or a translation, liable to create confusion, of a mark considered by the compe-

tent authority of the country of registration or use to be well known in that country as being already the mark of a person entitled to the benefits of this Convention and used for identical or similar goods. These provisions shall also apply when the essential part of the mark constitutes a reproduction of any such well-known mark or an imitation liable to create confusion therewith.

(2) A period of at least five years from the date of registration shall be followed for requesting the cancellation of such a mark. The countries of the Union may provide for a period within which the prohibition of use must be requested.

(3) No time limit shall be fixed for requesting the cancellation or the prohibition of the use of marks registered or used in bad faith.

Article 6*ter*

Marks: Prohibitions concerning State Emblems, Official Hallmarks, and Emblems of Intergovernmental Organizations

(1) (*a*) The countries of the Union agree to refuse or to invalidate the registration, and to prohibit by appropriate measure the use, without authorization by the competent authorities, either as trademarks or as elements of trademarks, of armorial bearings, flags, and other State emblems, of the countries of the Union, official signs and hallmarks indicating control and warranty adopted by them, and any imitation from a heraldic point of view.

(*b*) The provisions of subparagraph (*a*), above, shall apply equally to armorial bearings, flags, other emblems, abbreviations, and names, of international intergovernmental organizations of which one or more countries of the Union are members, with the exception of armorial bearings, flags, other emblems, abbreviations, and names, that are already the subject of international agreements in force, intended to ensure their protection.

(*c*) No country of the Union shall be required to apply the provisions of subparagraph (*b*), above, to the prejudice of the owners of rights acquired in good faith before the entry into force, in that country, of this Convention. The countries of the Union shall not be required to apply the said provisions when the use or registration referred to in subparagraph (*a*), above, is not of such a nature as to suggest to the public that a connection exists between the organization concerned and the armorial bearings, flags, emblems, abbreviations, and names, or if such use or registration is probably not of such a nature as to mislead the public as to the existence of a connection between the user and the organization.

(2) Prohibition of the use of official signs and hallmarks indicating control and warranty shall apply solely in cases where the marks in which they are incorporated are intended to be used on goods of the same or a similar kind.

(3) (*a*) For the application of these provisions, the countries of the Union agree to communicate reciprocally, through the intermediary of the International Bureau, the list of State emblems, and official signs and hallmarks indicating control and warranty, which they desire, or may hereafter desire, to place wholly or within certain limits under the protection of this Article, and all subsequent modifications of such list. Each country of the Union shall in due course make available to the public the lists so communicated.

Nevertheless such communication is not obligatory in respect of flags of States.

(*b*) The provisions of subparagraph (*b*) of paragraph (1) of this Article shall apply only to such armorial bearings, flags, other emblems, abbreviations, and names, of international intergovernmental organizations as the latter have communicated to the countries of the Union through the intermediary of the International Bureau.

(4) Any country of the Union may, within a period of twelve months from the receipt of the notification, transmit its objections, if any, through the intermediary of the International Bureau, to the country or international intergovernmental organization concerned.

(5) In the case of State flags, the measures prescribed by paragraph (1), above, shall apply solely to marks registered after November 6, 1925.

(6) In the case of State emblems other than flags, and of official signs and hallmarks of the countries of the Union, and in the case of armorial bearings, flags, other emblems, abbreviations, and names, of international intergovernmental organizations, these provisions shall apply only to marks registered more than two months after receipt of the communication provided for in paragraph (3), above.

(7) In cases of bad faith, the countries shall have the right to cancel even those marks incorporating State emblems, signs, and hallmarks, which were registered before November 6, 1925.

(8) Nationals of any country who are authorized to make use of the State emblems, signs, and hallmarks, of their country may use them if they are similar to those of another country.

(9) The countries of the Union undertake to prohibit the unauthorized use in trade of the State armorial bearings of the other countries of the Union, when the use is of such a nature as to be misleading as to the origin of the goods.

(10) The above provisions shall prevent the countries from exercising the right given in paragraph (3) of Article 6*quinquies*, Section B, to refuse or to invalidate the registration of marks incorporating,

without authorization, armorial bearings, flags, other State emblems, or official signs and hallmarks adopted by a country of the Union, as well as the distinctive signs of international intergovernmental organizations referred to in paragraph (1), above.

Article 6^quater^
Marks: Assignment of Marks

(1) When, in accordance with the law of a country of the Union, the assignment of a mark is valid only if it takes place at the same time as the transfer of the business or goodwill to which the mark belongs, it shall suffice for the recognition of such validity that the portion of the business or goodwill located in that country be transferred to the assignee, together with the exclusive right to manufacture in the said country, or to sell therein, the goods bearing the mark assigned.

(2) The foregoing provision does not impose upon the countries of the Union any obligation to regard as valid the assignment of any mark the use of which by the assignee would, in fact, be of such a nature as to mislead the public, particularly as regards the origin, nature, or essential qualities, of the goods to which the mark is applied.

Article 6^quinquies^
Marks: Protection of Marks Registered in One Country of the Union in the Other Countries of the Union

A——(1) Every trademark duly registered in the country of origin shall be accepted for filing and protected as is in the other countries of the Union, subject to the reservations indicated in this Article. Such countries may, before proceeding to final registration, require the production of a certificate of registration in the country of origin, issued by the competent authority. No authentication shall be required for this certificate.

(2) Shall be considered the country of origin the country of the Union where the applicant has a real and effective industrial or commercial establishment, or, if he has no such establishment within the Union, the country of the Union where he has his domicile, or, if he has no domicile within the Union but is a national of a country of the Union, the country of which he is a national.

B——Trademarks covered by this Article may be neither denied registration nor invalidated except in the following cases:

1. when they are of such a nature as to infringe rights acquired by third parties in the country where protection is claimed;
2. when they are devoid of any distinctive character, or consist exclusively of signs or indications which may serve, in trade, to designate the kind, quality, quantity, intended purpose, value, place of origin, of the goods, or the time of production, or have become customary in the current language or in the bona fide and established practices of the trade of the country where protection is claimed;
3. when they are contrary to morality or public order and, in particular, of such a nature as to deceive the public. It is understood that a mark may not be considered contrary to public order for the sole reason that it does not conform to a provision of the legislation on marks, except if such provision itself relates to public order.

This provision is subject, however, to the application of Article 10bis.

C—— (1) In determining whether a mark is eligible for protection, all the factual circumstances must be taken into consideration, particularly the length of time the mark has been in use.

(2) No trademark shall be refused in the other countries of the Union for the sole reason that it differs from the mark protected in the country of origin only in respect of elements that do not alter its distinctive character and do not affect its identity in the form in which it has been registered in the said country of origin.

D—— No person may benefit from the provisions of this Article if the mark for which he claims protection is not registered in the country of origin.

E—— However, in no case shall the renewal of the registration of the mark in the country of origin involve an obligation to renew the registration in the other countries of the Union in which the mark has been registered.

F—— The benefit of priority shall remain unaffected for applications for the registration of marks filed within the period fixed by Article 4, even if registration in the country of origin is effected after the expiration of such period.

Article 6^{sexies}
Marks: Service Marks

The countries of the Union undertake to protect service marks. They shall not be required to provide for the registration of such marks.

Article 6*septies*

Marks: Registration in the Name of the Agent or Representative of the Proprietor Without the Latter's Authorization

(1) If the agent or representative of the person who is the proprietor of a mark in one of the countries of the Union applies, without such proprietor's authorization, for the registration of the mark in his own name, in one or more countries of the Union, the proprietor shall be entitled to oppose the registration applied for or demand its cancellation or, if the law of the country so allows, the assignment in his favor of the said registration, unless such agent or representative justifies his action.

(2) The proprietor of the mark shall, subject to the provisions of paragraph (1), above, be entitled to oppose the use of his mark by his agent or representative if he has not authorized such use.

(3) Domestic legislation may provide an equitable time limit within which the proprietor of a mark must exercise the rights provided for in this Article.

Article 7

Marks: Nature of the Goods to which the Mark is Applied

The nature of the goods to which a trademark is to be applied shall in no case form an obstacle to the registration of the mark.

Article 7*bis*

Marks: Collective Marks

(1) The countries of the Union undertake to accept for filing and to protect collective marks belonging to associations the existence of which is not contrary to the law of the country of origin, even if such associations do not possess an industrial or commercial establishment.

(2) Each country shall be the judge of the particular conditions under which a collective mark shall be protected and may refuse protection if the mark is contrary to the public interest.

(3) Nevertheless, the protection of these marks shall not be refused to any association the existence of which is not contrary to the law of the country of origin, on the ground that such association is not established in the country where protection is sought or is not constituted according to the law of the latter country.

Article 8
Trade Names

A trade name shall be protected in all the countries of the Union without the obligation of filing or registration, whether or not it forms part of a trademark.

Article 9
Marks, Trade Names: Seizure, on Importation, etc., of Goods Unlawfully Bearing a Mark or Trade Name

(1) All goods unlawfully bearing a trademark or trade name shall be seized on importation into those countries of the Union where such mark or trade name is entitled to legal protection.

(2) Seizure shall likewise be effected in the country where the unlawful affixation occurred or in the country into which the goods were imported.

(3) Seizure shall take place at the request of the public prosecutor, or any other competent authority, or any interested party, whether a natural person or a legal entity, in conformity with the domestic legislation of each country.

(4) The authorities shall not be bound to effect seizure of goods in transit.

(5) If the legislation of a country does not permit seizure on importation, seizure shall be replaced by prohibition of importation or by seizure inside the country.

(6) If the legislation of a country permits neither seizure on importation nor prohibition of importation nor seizure inside the country, then, until such time as the legislation is modified accordingly, these measures shall be replaced by the actions and remedies available in such cases to nationals under the law of such country.

Article 10
False Indications: Seizure, on Importation, etc., of Goods Bearing False Indications as to their Source or the Identity of the Producer

(1) The provisions of the preceding Article shall apply in cases of direct or indirect use of a false indication of the source of the goods or the identity of the producer, manufacturer, or merchant.

(2) Any producer, manufacturer, or merchant, whether a natural person or a legal entity, engaged in the production or manufacture

of or trade in such goods and established either in the locality falsely indicated as the source, or in the region where such locality is situated, or in the country falsely indicated, or in the country where the false indication of source is used, shall in any case be deemed an interested party.

Article 10bis
Unfair Competition

(1) The countries of the Union are bound to assure to nationals of such countries effective protection against unfair competition.

(2) Any act of competition contrary to honest practices in industrial or commercial matters constitutes an act of unfair competition.

(3) The following in particular shall be prohibited:

1. all acts of such a nature as to create confusion by any means whatever with the establishment, the goods, or the industrial or commercial activities, of a competitor;
2. false allegations in the course of trade of such a nature as to discredit the establishment, the goods, or the industrial or commercial activities, of a competitor;
3. indications or allegations the use of which in the course of trade is liable to mislead the public as to the nature, the manufacturing process, the characteristics, the suitability for their purpose, or the quantity, of the goods.

Article 10ter
Marks, Trade Names, False Indications, Unfair Competition: **Remedies, Right to Sue**

(1) The countries of the Union undertake to assure to nationals of the other countries of the Union appropriate legal remedies effectively to repress all the acts referred to in Articles 9, 10, and 10bis.

(2) They undertake, further, to provide measures to permit federations and associations representing interested industrialists, producers, or merchants, provided that the existence of such federations and associations is not contrary to the laws of their countries, to take action in the courts or before the administrative authorities, with a view to the repression of the acts referred to in Articles 9, 10, and 10bis, in so far as the law of the country in which protection is claimed allows such action by federations and associations of that country.

Article 11

Inventions, Utility Models, Industrial Designs, Marks: Temporary Protection at Certain International Exhibitions

(1) The countries of the Union shall, in conformity with their domestic legislation, grant temporary protection to patentable inventions, utility models, industrial designs, and trademarks, in respect of goods exhibited at official or officially recognized international exhibitions held in the territory of any of them.

(2) Such temporary protection shall not extend the periods provided by Article 4. If, later, the right of priority is invoked, the authorities of any country may provide that the period shall start from the date of introduction of the goods into the exhibition.

(3) Each country may require, as proof of the identity of the article exhibited and of the date of its introduction, such documentary evidence as it considers necessary.

Article 12

Special National Industrial Property Services

(1) Each country of the Union undertakes to establish a special industrial property service and a central office for the communication to the public of patents, utility models, industrial designs, and trademarks.

(2) This service shall publish an official periodical journal. It shall publish regularly:

(*a*) the names of the proprietors of patents granted, with a brief designation of the inventions patented;

(*b*) the reproduction of registered trademarks.

Article 13

Assembly of the Union

(1) (*a*) The Union shall have an Assembly consisting of those countries of the Union which are bound by Articles 13 to 17.

(*b*) The Government of each country shall be represented by one delegate, who may be assisted by alternate delegates, advisors, and experts.

(*c*) The expenses of each delegation shall be borne by the Government which has appointed it.

(2) (*a*) The Assembly shall:

(i) deal with all matters concerning the maintenance and development of the Union and the implementation of this Convention;

(ii) give directions concerning the preparation for conferences of revision to the International Bureau of Intellectual Property (hereinafter designated as "the International Bureau") referred to in the Convention establishing the World Intellectual Property Organization (hereinafter designated as "the Organization"), due account being taken of any comments made by those countries of the Union which are not bound by Articles 13 to 17;

(iii) review and approve the reports and activities of the Director General of the Organization concerning the Union, and give him all necessary instructions concerning matters within the competence of the Union;

(iv) elect the members of the Executive Committee of the Assembly;

(v) review and approve the reports and activities of its Executive Committee, and give instructions to such Committee;

(vi) determine the program and adopt the triennial budget of the Union, and approve its final accounts;

(vii) adopt the financial regulations of the Union;

(viii) establish such committees of experts and working groups as it deems appropriate to achieve the objectives of the Union;

(ix) determine which countries not members of the Union and which intergovernmental and international non-governmental organizations shall be admitted to its meetings as observers;

(x) adopt amendments to Articles 13 to 17;

(xi) take any other appropriate action designed to further the objectives of the Union;

(xii) perform such other functions as are appropriate under this Convention;

(xiii) subject to its acceptance, exercise such rights as are given to it in the Convention establishing the Organization.

(*b*) With respect to matters which are of interest also to other Unions administered by the Organization, the Assembly shall make its decisions after having heard the advice of the Coordination Committee of the Organization.

(3) (*a*) Subject to the provisions of subparagraph (*b*), a delegate may represent one country only.

(*b*) Countries of the Union grouped under the terms of a special agreement in a common office possessing for each of them the character of a special national service of industrial property as referred to in Article 12 may be jointly represented during discussions by one of their number.

(4) (*a*) Each country member of the Assembly shall have one vote.

(*b*) One-half of the countries members of the Assembly shall constitute a quorum.

(*c*) Notwithstanding the provisions of subparagraph (*b*), if, in any session, the number of countries represented is less than one-half but equal to or more than one-third of the countries members of the Assembly, the Assembly may make decisions but, with the exception of decisions concerning its own procedure, all such decisions shall take effect only if the conditions set forth hereinafter are fulfilled. The International Bureau shall communicate the said decisions to the countries members of the Assembly which were not represented and shall invite them to express in writing their vote or abstention within a period of three months from the date of the communication. If, at the expiration of this period, the number of countries having thus expressed their vote or abstention attains the number of countries which was lacking for attaining the quorum in the session itself, such decisions shall take effect provided that at the same time the required majority still obtains.

(*d*) Subject to the provisions of Article 17(2), the decisions of the Assembly shall require two-thirds of the votes cast.

(*e*) Abstentions shall not be considered as votes.

(5) (*a*) Subject to the provisions of subparagraph (*b*), a delegate may vote in the name of one country only.

(*b*) The countries of the Union referred to in paragraph (3)(*b*) shall, as a general rule, endeavor to send their own delegations to the sessions of the Assembly. If, however, for exceptional reasons, any such country cannot send its own delegation, it may give to the delegation of another such country the power to vote in its name, provided that each delegation may vote by proxy for one country only. Such power to vote shall be granted in a document signed by the Head of State or the competent Minister.

(6) Countries of the Union not members of the Assembly shall be admitted to the meetings of the latter as observers.

(7) (*a*) The Assembly shall meet once in every third calendar year in ordinary session upon convocation by the Director General and, in the absence of exceptional circumstances, during the same period and at the same place as the General Assembly of the Organization.

(*b*) The Assembly shall meet in extraordinary session upon convocation by the Director General, at the request of the Executive Committee or at the request of one-fourth of the countries members of the Assembly.

(8) The Assembly shall adopt its own rules of procedure.

Article 14
Executive Committee

(1) The Assembly shall have an Executive Committee.

(2) (*a*) The Executive Committee shall consist of countries elected by the Assembly from among countries members of the Assembly. Furthermore, the country on whose territory the Organization has its headquarters shall, subject to the provisions of Article 16(7)(*b*), have an ex officio seat on the Committee.

(*b*) The Government of each country member of the Executive Committee shall be represented by one delegate, who may be assisted by alternate delegates, advisors, and experts.

(*c*) The expenses of each delegation shall be borne by the Government which has appointed it.

(3) The number of countries members of the Executive Committee shall correspond to one-fourth of the number of countries members of the Assembly. In establishing the number of seats to be filled, remainders after division by four shall be disregarded.

(4) In electing the members of the Executive Committee, the Assembly shall have due regard to an equitable geographical distribution and to the need for countries party to the Special Agreements established in relation with the Union to be among the countries constituting the Executive Committee.

(5) (*a*) Each member of the Executive Committee shall serve from the close of the session of the Assembly which elected it to the close of the next ordinary session of the Assembly.

(*b*) Members of the Executive Committee may be re-elected, but only up to a maximum of two-thirds of such members.

(*c*) The Assembly shall establish the details of the rules governing the election and possible re-election of the members of the Executive Committee.

(6) (*a*) The Executive Committee shall:

(i) prepare the draft agenda of the Assembly;

(ii) submit proposals to the Assembly in respect of the draft program and triennial budget of the Union prepared by the Director General;

(iii) approve, within the limits of the program and the triennial budget, the specific yearly budgets and programs prepared by the Director General;

(iv) submit, with appropriate comments, to the Assembly the periodical reports of the Director General and the yearly audit reports on the accounts;

(v) take all necessary measures to ensure the execution of the program of the Union by the Director General, in accordance with the decisions of the Assembly and having regard to circumstances arising between two ordinary sessions of the Assembly;

(vi) perform such other functions as are allocated to it under this Convention.

(*b*) With respect to matters which are of interest also to other Unions administered by the Organization, the Executive Committee shall make its decisions after having heard the advice of the Coordination Committee of the Organization.

(7) (*a*) The Executive Committee shall meet once a year in ordinary session upon convocation by the Director General, preferably during the same period and at the same place as the Coordination Committee of the Organization.

(*b*) The Executive Committee shall meet in extraordinary session upon convocation by the Director General, either on his own initiative, or at the request of its Chairman or one-fourth of its members.

(8) (*a*) Each country member of the Executive Committee shall have one vote.

(*b*) One-half of the members of the Executive Committee shall constitute a quorum.

(*c*) Decisions shall be made by a simple majority of the votes cast.

(*d*) Abstentions shall not be considered as votes.

(*e*) A delegate may represent, and vote in the name of, one country only.

(9) Countries of the Union not members of the Executive Committee shall be admitted to its meetings as observers.

(10) The Executive Committee shall adopt its own rules of procedure.

Article 15
International Bureau

(1) (*a*) Administrative tasks concerning the Union shall be performed by the International Bureau, which is a continuation of the Bureau of the Union united with the Bureau of the Union established by the International Convention for the Protection of Literary and Artistic Works.[1]

(*b*) In particular, the International Bureau shall provide the secretariat of the various organs of the Union.

(*c*) The Director General of the Organization shall be the chief executive of the Union and shall represent the Union.

---

[1]331 UNTS 217.

(2) The International Bureau shall assemble and publish information concerning the protection of industrial property. Each country of the Union shall promptly communicate to the International Bureau all new laws and official texts concerning the protection of industrial property. Furthermore, it shall furnish the International Bureau with all the publications of its industrial property service of direct concern to the protection of industrial property which the International Bureau may find useful in its work.

(3) The International Bureau shall publish a monthly periodical.

(4) The International Bureau shall, on request, furnish any country of the Union with information on matters concerning the protection of industrial property.

(5) The International Bureau shall conduct studies, and shall provide services, designed to facilitate the protection of industrial property.

(6) The Director General and any staff member designated by him shall participate, without the right to vote, in all meetings of the Assembly, the Executive Committee, and any other committee of experts or working group. The Director General, or a staff member designated by him, shall be ex officio secretary of these bodies.

(7) (*a*) The International Bureau shall, in accordance with the directions of the Assembly and in cooperation with the Executive Committee, make the preparations for the conferences of revision of the provisions of the Convention other than Articles 13 to 17.

(*b*) The International Bureau may consult with intergovernmental and international non-governmental organizations concerning preparations for conferences of revision.

(*c*) The Director General and persons designated by him shall take part, without the right to vote, in the discussions at these conferences.

(8) The International Bureau shall carry out any other tasks assigned to it.

Article 16
Finances

(1) (*a*) The Union shall have a budget.

(*b*) The budget of the Union shall include the income and expenses proper to the Union, its contribution to the budget of expenses common to the Unions, and, where applicable, the sum made available to the budget of the Conference of the Organization.

(*c*) Expenses not attributable exclusively to the Union but also to one or more other Unions administered by the Organization shall be considered as expenses common to the Unions. The share of the Union in such common expenses shall be in proportion to the interest the Union has in them.

(2) The budget of the Union shall be established with due regard to the requirements of coordination with the budgets of the other Unions administered by the Organization.

(3) The budget of the Union shall be financed from the following sources:

(i) contributions of the countries of the Union;
(ii) fees and charges due for services rendered by the International Bureau in relation to the Union;
(iii) sale of, or royalties on, the publications of the International Bureau concerning the Union;
(iv) gifts, bequests, and subventions;
(v) rents, interests, and other miscellaneous income.

(4) (*a*) For the purpose of establishing its contribution towards the budget, each country of the Union shall belong to a class, and shall pay its annual contributions on the basis of a number of units fixed as follows:

Class I	25
Class II	20
Class III	15
Class IV	10
Class V	5
Class VI	3
Class VII	1

(*b*) Unless it has already done so, each country shall indicate, concurrently with depositing its instrument of ratification or accession, the class to which it wishes to belong. Any country may change class. If it chooses a lower class, the country must announce such change to the Assembly at one of its ordinary sessions. Any such change shall take effect at the beginning of the calendar year following the said session.

(*c*) The annual contribution of each country shall be an amount in the same proportion to the total sum to be contributed to the budget of the Union by all countries as the number of its units is to the total of the units of all contributing countries.

(*d*) Contributions shall become due on the first of January of each year.

(*e*) A country which is in arrears in the payment of its contributions may not exercise its right to vote in any of the organs of the Union of which it is a member if the amount of its arrears equals or exceeds the amount of the contributions due from it for the preceding two full years. However, any organ of the Union may allow such a country to continue to exercise its right to vote in that organ if, and as long as, it is satisfied that the delay in payment is due to exceptional and unavoidable circumstances.

(*f*) If the budget is not adopted before the beginning of a new financial period, it shall be at the same level as the budget of the previous year, as provided in the financial regulations.

(5) The amount of the fees and charges due for services rendered by the International Bureau in relation to the Union shall be established, and shall be reported to the Assembly and the Executive Committee, by the Director General.

(6) (*a*) The Union shall have a working capital fund which shall be constituted by a single payment made by each country of the Union. If the fund becomes insufficient, the Assembly shall decide to increase it.

(*b*) The amount of the initial payment of each country to the said fund or of its participation in the increase thereof shall be a proportion of the contribution of that country for the year in which the fund is established or the decision to increase it is made.

(*c*) The proportion and the terms of payment shall be fixed by the Assembly on the proposal of the Director General and after it has heard the advice of the Coordination Committee of the Organization.

(7) (*a*) In the headquarters agreement concluded with the country on the territory of which the Organization has its headquarters, it shall be provided that, whenever the working capital fund is insufficient, such country shall grant advances. The amount of these advances and the conditions on which they are granted shall be the subject of separate agreements, in each case, between such country and the Organization. As long as it remains under the obligation to grant advances, such country shall have an ex officio seat on the Executive Committee.

(*b*) The country referred to in subparagraph (*a*) and the Organization shall each have the right to denounce the obligation to grant advances, by written notification. Denunciation shall take effect three years after the end of the year in which it has been notified.

(8) The auditing of the accounts shall be effected by one or more of the countries of the Union or by external auditors, as provided in the financial regulations. They shall be designated, with their agreement, by the Assembly.

Article 17
Amendment of Articles 13 to 17

(1) Proposals for the amendment of Articles 13, 14, 15, and 16, and the present Article, may be initiated by any country member of the Assembly, by the Executive Committee, or by the Director Gen-

eral. Such proposals shall be communicated by the Director General to the member countries of the Assembly at least six months in advance of their consideration by the Assembly.

(2) Amendments to the Articles referred to in paragraph (1) shall be adopted by the Assembly. Adoption shall require three-fourths of the votes cast, provided that any amendment to Article 13, and to the present paragraph, shall require four-fifths of the votes cast.

(3) Any amendment to the Articles referred to in paragraph (1) shall enter into force one month after written notifications of acceptance, effected in accordance with their respective constitutional processes, have been received by the Director General from three-fourths of the countries members of the Assembly at the time it adopted the amendment. Any amendment to the said Articles thus accepted shall bind all the countries which are members of the Assembly at the time the amendment enters into force, or which become members thereof at a subsequent date, provided that any amendment increasing the financial obligations of countries of the Union shall bind only those countries which have notified their acceptance of such amendment.

Article 18
Revision of Articles 1 to 12 and 18 to 30

(1) This Convention shall be submitted to revision with a view to the introduction of amendments designed to improve the system of the Union.

(2) For that purpose, conferences shall be held successively in one of the countries of the Union among the delegates of the said countries.

(3) Amendments to Articles 13 to 17 are governed by the provisions of Article 17.

Article 19
Special Agreements

It is understood that the countries of the Union reserve the right to make separately between themselves special agreements for the protection of industrial property, in so far as these agreements do not contravene the provisions of this Convention.

Article 20

Ratification or Accession by Countries of the Union; Entry Into Force

(1) (*a*) Any country of the Union which has signed this Act may ratify it, and, if it has not signed it, may accede to it. Instruments of ratification and accession shall be deposited with the Director General.

(*b*) Any country of the Union may declare in its instrument of ratification or accession that its ratification or accession shall not apply:

(i) to Articles 1 to 12, or
(ii) to Articles 13 to 17.

(*c*) Any country of the Union which, in accordance with subparagraph (*b*), has excluded from the effects of its ratification or accession one of the two groups of Articles referred to in that subparagraph may at any later time declare that it extends the effects of its ratification or accession to that group of Articles. Such declaration shall be deposited with the Director General.

(2) (*a*) Articles 1 to 12 shall enter into force, with respect to the first ten countries of the Union which have deposited instruments of ratification or accession without making the declaration permitted under paragraph (1)(*b*)(i), three months after the deposit of the tenth such instrument of ratification or accession.

(*b*) Articles 13 to 17 shall enter into force, with respect to the first ten countries of the Union which have deposited instruments of ratification or accession without making the declaration permitted under paragraph (1)(*b*)(ii), three months after the deposit of the tenth such instrument of ratification or accession.

(*c*) Subject to the initial entry into force, pursuant to the provisions of subparagraphs (*a*) and (*b*), of each of the two groups of Articles referred to in paragraph (1)(*b*)(i) and (ii), and subject to the provisions of paragraph (1)(*b*), Articles 1 to 17 shall, with respect to any country of the Union, other than those referred to in subparagraphs (*a*) and (*b*), which deposits an instrument of ratification or accession or any country of the Union which deposits a declaration pursuant to paragraph (1)(*c*), enter into force three months after the date of notification by the Director General of such deposit, unless a subsequent data has been indicated in the instrument or declaration deposited. In the latter case, this Act shall enter into force with respect to that country on the date thus indicated.

(3) With respect to any country of the Union which deposits an instrument of ratification or accession, Articles 18 to 30 shall enter

into force on the earlier of the dates on which any of the groups of Articles referred to in paragraph (1)(*b*) enters into force with respect to that country pursuant to paragraph (2)(*a*), (*b*), or (*c*).

Article 21
Accession by Countries Outside the Union; Entry Into Force

(1) Any country outside the Union may accede to this Act and thereby become a member of the Union. Instruments of accession shall be deposited with the Director General.

(2) (*a*) With respect to any country outside the Union which deposits its instrument of accession one month or more before the date of entry into force of any provisions of the present Act, this Act shall enter into force, unless a subsequent date has been indicated in the instrument of accession, on the date upon which provisions first enter into force pursuant to Article 20(2) (*a*) or (*b*); provided that:

(i) if Articles 1 to 12 do not enter into force on that date, such country shall, during the interim period before the entry into force of such provisions, and in substitution therefor, be bound by Articles 1 to 12 of the Lisbon Act,

(ii) if Articles 13 to 17 do not enter into force on that date, such country shall, during the interim period before the entry into force of such provisions, and in substitution therefor, be bound by Articles 13 and 14(3), (4), and (5), of the Lisbon Act.

If a country indicates a subsequent date in its instrument of accession, this Act shall enter into force with respect to that country on the date thus indicated.

(*b*) With respect to any country outside the Union which deposits its instrument of accession on a date which is subsequent to, or precedes by less than one month, the entry into force of one group of Articles of the present Act, this Act shall, subject to the proviso of subparagraph (*a*), enter into force three months after the date on which its accession has been notified by the Director General, unless a subsequent date has been indicated in the instrument of accession. In the latter case, this Act shall enter into force with respect to that country on the date thus indicated.

(3) With respect to any country outside the Union which deposits its instrument of accession after the date of entry into force of the present Act in its entirety, or less than one month before such date, this Act shall enter into force three months after the date on which its accession has been notified by the Director General, unless a

subsequent date has been indicated in the instrument of accession. In the latter case, this Act shall enter into force with respect to that country on the date thus indicated.

Article 22
Consequences of Ratification or Accession

Subject to the possibilities of exceptions provided for in Articles 20(1)(*b*) and 28(2), ratification or accession shall automatically entail acceptance of all the clauses and admission to all the advantages of this Act.

Article 23
Accession to Earlier Acts

After the entry into force of this Act in its entirety, a country may not accede to earlier Acts of this Convention.

Article 24
Territories

(1) Any country may declare in its instrument of ratification or accession, or may inform the Director General by written notification any time thereafter, that this Convention shall be applicable to all or part of those territories, designated in the declaration or notification, for the external relations of which it is responsible.

(2) Any country which has made such a declaration or given such a notification may, at any time, notify the Director General that this Convention shall cease to be applicable to all or part of such territories.

(3) (*a*) Any declaration made under paragraph (1) shall take effect on the same date as the ratification or accession in the instrument of which it was included, and any notification given under such paragraph shall take effect three months after its notification by the Director General.

(*b*) Any notification given under paragraph (2) shall take effect 12 months after its receipt by the Director General.

Article 25
Implementation of the Convention on the Domestic Level

(1) Any country party to this Convention undertakes to adopt, in accordance with its constitution, the measures necessary to ensure the application of this Convention.

(2) It is understood that, at the time a country deposits its instrument of ratification or accession, it will be in a position under its domestic law to give effect to the provisions of this Convention.

Article 26
Denunciation

(1) This Convention shall remain in force without limitation as to time.

(2) Any country may denounce this Act by notification addressed to the Director General. Such denunciation shall constitute also denunciation of all earlier Acts and shall affect only the country making it, the Convention remaining in full force and effect as regards the other countries of the Union.

(3) Denunciation shall take effect one year after the day on which the Director General has received the notification.

(4) The right of denunciation provided by this Article shall not be exercised by any country before the expiration of five years from the date upon which it becomes a member of the Union.

Article 27
Application of Earlier Acts

(1) The present Act shall, as regards the relations between the countries to which it applies, and to the extent that it applies, replace the Convention of Paris of March 20, 1883, and the subsequent Acts of revision.

(2) (*a*) As regards the countries to which the present Act does not apply, or does not apply in its entirety, but to which the Lisbon Act of October 31, 1958, applies, the latter shall remain in force in its entirety or to the extent that the present Act does not replace it by virtue of paragraph (1).

(*b*) Similarly, as regards the countries to which neither the present Act, nor portions thereof, nor the Lisbon Act applies, the London Act of June 2, 1934, shall remain in force in its entirety or to the extent that the present Act does not replace it by virtue of paragraph (1).

(*c*) Similarly, as regards the countries to which neither the present Act, nor portions thereof, nor the Lisbon Act, nor the London Act applies, the Hague Act of November 6, 1925, shall remain in force in its entirely or to the extent that the present Act does not replace it by virtue of paragraph (1).

(3) Countries outside the Union which become party to this Act shall apply it with respect to any country of the Union not party to this Act or which, although party to this Act, has made a declaration pursuant to Article 20(1)(*b*)(i). Such countries recognize that the said country of the Union may apply, in its relations with them, the provisions of the most recent Act to which it is party.

Article 28
Disputes

(1) Any dispute between two or more countries of the Union concerning the interpretation or application of this Convention, not settled by negotiation, may, by any one of the countries concerned, be brought before the International Court of Justice by application in conformity with the Statute of the Court,[2] unless the countries concerned agree on some other method of settlement. The country bringing the dispute before the Court shall inform the International Bureau; the International Bureau shall bring the matter to the attention of the other countries of the Union.

(2) Each country may, at the time it signs this Act or deposits its instrument of ratification or accession, declare that it does not consider itself bound by the provisions of paragraph (1). With regard to any dispute between such country and any other country of the Union, the provisions of paragraph (1) shall not apply.

(3) Any country having made a declaration in accordance with the provisions of paragraph (2) may, at any time, withdraw its declaration by notification addressed to the Director General.

Article 29
Signature, Languages, Depositary Functions

(1) (*a*) This Act shall be signed in a single copy in the French language and shall be deposited with the Government of Sweden.

(*b*) Official texts shall be established by the Director General,

---

[2]TS 993; 59 Stat. 1055.

after consultation with the interested Governments, in the English, German, Italian, Portuguese, Russian and Spanish languages, and such other languages as the Assembly may designate.

(*c*) In case of differences of opinion on the interpretation of the various texts, the French text shall prevail.

(2) This Act shall remain open for signature at Stockholm until January 13, 1968.

(3) The Director General shall transmit two copies, certified by the Government of Sweden, of the signed text of this Act to the Governments of all countries of the Union and, on request, to the Government of any other country.

(4) The Director General shall register this Act with the Secretariat of the United Nations.

(5) The Director General shall notify the Governments of all countries of the Union of signatures, deposits of instruments of ratification or accession and any declarations included in such instruments or made pursuant to Article 20(1)(*c*), entry into force of any provisions of this Act, notifications of denunciation, and notifications pursuant to Article 24.

Article 30
Transitional Provisions

(1) Until the first Director General assumes office, reference in this Act to the International Bureau of the Organization or to the Director General shall be deemed to be references to the Bureau of the Union or its Director, respectively.

(2) Countries of the Union not bound by Articles 13 to 17 may, until five years after the entry into force of the Convention establishing the Organization, exercise, if they so desire, the rights provided under Articles 13 to 17 of this Act as if they were bound by those Articles. Any country desiring to exercise such rights shall give written notification to that effect to the Director General; such notification shall be effective from the date of its receipt. Such countries shall be deemed to be members of the Assembly until the expiration of the said period.

(3) As long as all the countries of the Union have not become Members of the Organization, the International Bureau of the Organization shall also function as the Bureau of the Union, and the Director General as the Director of the said Bureau.

(4) Once all the countries of the Union have become Members of the Organization, the rights, obligations, and property, of the Bureau of the Union shall devolve on the International Bureau of the Organization.

Part II
Patents

1. International Convention for the Protection of New Varieties of Plants (UPOV)

December 2, 1961, as revised at Geneva on November 10, 1972, and on October 23, 1978 (followed by two Recommendations)

The International Convention for the Protection of New Varieties of Plants (UPOV) was completed in 1961, and entered into force in 1968. Because a number of countries (namely the United States) were not members of the original convention, the Act was revised October 23, 1978, to take into account various obstacles of substantive law in the nonsignatory states.

This international Union is intended to ensure to the breeder of a new plant variety the right to a special title of protection or of a patent (Arts. 1 and 2). The purpose of UPOV is to address a long-standing problem in patent law: the patent system's relative inability to provide protection to plant breeders. The reasons traditionally have been difficulties of description, exhaustion of rights, and the manner in which plants are reproducible. Although it may take great investment to produce a new plant variety, once the variety is released publicly it is reproduced easily. The subject of plant varieties came up at the Lisbon Diplomatic Conference to revise the Paris Convention in 1958. Because of the technical problems involved, it was decided, however, that plant breeding merited a special agreement rather than trying to incorporate the field into the Paris Convention. Thus, in covering botanical plant varieties, UPOV has filled a gap left by the Paris Convention; its terms do not extend to this subject matter.

Under the revised Act, both sexually and asexually reproduced plants may be protected according to the national law of the member states (Art. 4).

UPOV does not provide for a central filing system as does the Budapest Convention for microorganisms. Accordingly, one must file a separate application in each member country to obtain protection in that country.

In addition to national protection, UPOV has established minimum standards that each member country must recognize in its national law. Each member state is required to provide protection to plant varieties through a patent or an analogous grant (Art. 2 para. 1). As to coverage, member countries have wide discretion. Each member state may limit the convention's application within a genus or species to varieties with a particular manner of reproduction or multiplication, or certain end-use (Art. 2 para. 2). Thus, because countries are required to provide protection only for a limited number of plant genera or species, UPOV countries may vary considerably as to scope of protection.

Similar to the provisions of the Paris Convention, UPOV allows a breeder who has duly filed an application in one member country to enjoy a 12-month right of priority in another member country (Art. 12 para. 1).

UPOV requires that each protected variety must be designated by a name that will become its generic designation (Art. 13 para. 1). The rights granted to a breeder are to last for limited time periods, but not for less than 15 years and not less than 18 years for vines and forest, fruit, and ornamental trees including their rootstock (Art. 8).

As of January 1, 1990, the following 19 states were party to UPOV:

Australia
Belgium
Denmark
France
Federal Republic of Germany
Hungary
Ireland
Israel
Italy
Japan
Netherlands
New Zealand
Poland
South Africa
Spain
Sweden
Switzerland
United Kingdom
United States of America

International Convention for the Protection of New Varieties of Plants. as revised at Geneva, 1978

Article 1
Purpose of the Convention; Constitution of a Union; Seat of the Union

(1) The purpose of this Convention is to recognise and to ensure to the breeder of a new plant variety or to his successor in title (both hereinafter referred to as "the breeder") a right under the conditions hereinafter defined.

(2) The States parties to this Convention (hereinafter referred to as "the member States of the Union") constitute a Union for the Protection of New Varieties of Plants.

(3) The seat of the Union and its permanent organs shall be at Geneva.

Article 2
Forms of Protection

(1) Each member State of the Union may recognise the right of the breeder provided for in this Convention by the grant either of a special title of protection or of a patent. Nevertheless, a member State of the Union whose national law admits of protection under both these forms may provide only one of them for one and the same botanical genus or species.

(2) Each member State of the Union may limit the application of this Convention within a genus or species to varieties with a particular manner of reproduction or multiplication, or a certain end-use.

Article 3
National Treatment; Reciprocity

(1) Without prejudice to the rights specially provided for in this Convention, natural and legal persons resident or having their registered office in one of the member States of the Union shall, in

---

Source: Text courtesy of the World Intellectual Property Organization (WIPO).

so far as the recognition and protection of the right of the breeder are concerned, enjoy in the other member States of the Union the same treatment as is accorded or may hereafter be accorded by the respective laws of such States to their own nationals, provided that such persons comply with the conditions and formalities imposed on such nationals.

(2) Nationals of member States of the Union not resident or having their registered office in one of those States shall likewise enjoy the same rights provided that they fulfil such obligations as may be imposed on them for the purpose of enabling the varieties which they have bred to be examined and the multiplication of such varieties to be checked.

(3) Notwithstanding the provisions of paragraphs (1) and (2), any member State of the Union applying this Convention to a given genus or species shall be entitled to limit the benefit of the protection to the nationals of those member States of the Union which apply this Convention to that genus or species and to natural and legal persons resident or having their registered office in any of those States.

Article 4
Botanical Genera and Species Which Must or May be Protected

(1) This Convention may be applied to all botanical genera and species.

(2) The member States of the Union undertake to adopt all measures necessary for the progressive application of the provisions of this Convention to the largest possible number of botanical genera and species.

(3) (*a*) Each member State of the Union shall, on the entry into force of this Convention in its territory, apply the provisions of this Convention to at least five genera or species.

(*b*) Subsequently, each member State of the Union shall apply the said provisions to additional genera or species within the following periods from the date of the entry into force of this Convention in its territory:

(i) within three years, to at least 10 genera or species in all;
(ii) within six years, to at least 18 genera or species in all;
(iii) within eight years, to at least 24 genera or species in all.

(*c*) If a member State of the Union has limited the application of this Convention within a genus or species in accordance with the provisions of Article 2(2), that genus or species shall nevertheless, for the purposes of subparagraphs (*a*) and (*b*), be considered as one genus or species.

(4) At the request of any State intending to ratify, accept, approve or accede to this Convention, the Council may, in order to take account of special economic or ecological conditions prevailing in that State, decide, for the purpose of that State, to reduce the minimum numbers referred to in paragraph (3), or to extend the periods referred to in that paragraph, or to do both.

(5) At the request of any member State of the Union, the Council may, in order to take account of special difficulties encountered by that State in the fulfillment of the obligations under paragraph (3)(*b*), decide, for the purposes of that State, to extend the periods referred to in paragraph (3)(*b*).

Article 5
Rights Protected: Scope of Protection

(1) The effect of the right granted to the breeder is that his prior authorisation shall be required for

—the production for purposes of commercial marketing

—the offering for sale

—the marketing

of the reproductive or vegetative propagating material, as such, of the variety.

Vegetative propagating material shall be deemed to include whole plants. The right of the breeder shall extend to ornamental plants or parts thereof normally marketed for purposes other than propagation when they are used commercially as propagating material in the production of ornamental plants or cut flowers.

(2) The authorisation given by the breeder may be made subject to such conditions as he may specify.

(3) Authorisation by the breeder shall not be required either for the utilisation of the variety as an initial source of variation for the purpose of creating other varieties or for the marketing of such varieties. Such authorisation shall be required, however, when the repeated use of the variety is necessary for the commercial production of another variety.

(4)Any member State of the Union may, either under its own law or by means of special agreements under Article 29, grant to breeders, in respect of certain botanical genera or species, a more extensive right than that set out in paragraph (1), extending in particular to the marketed product. A member State of the Union which grants such a right may limit the benefit of it to the nationals of member States of the Union which grant an identical right and to natural and legal persons resident or having their registered office in any of those States.

Article 6
Conditions Required for Protection

(1) The breeder shall benefit from the protection provided for in this Convention when the following conditions are satisfied:

(*a*) Whatever may be the origin, artificial or natural, of the initial variation from which it has resulted, the variety must be clearly distinguishable by one or more important characteristics from any other variety whose existence is a matter of common knowledge at the time when protection is applied for. Common knowledge may be established by reference to various factors such as: cultivation or marketing already in progress, entry in an official register of varieties already made or in the course of being made, inclusion in a reference collection, or precise description in a publication. The characteristics which permit a variety to be defined and distinguished must be capable of precise recognition and description.

(*b*) At the date on which the application for protection in a member State of the Union is filed, the variety

(i) must not—or, where the law of that State so provides, must not for longer than one year—have been offered for sale or marketed, with the agreement of the breeder, in the territory of that State, and

(ii) must not have been offered for sale or marketed, with the agreement of the breeder, in the territory of any other State for longer than six years in the case of vines, forest trees, fruit trees and ornamental trees, including, in each case, their rootstocks, or for longer than four years in the case of all other plants.

Trials of the variety not involving offering for sale or marketing shall not affect the right to protection. The fact that the variety has become a matter of common knowledge in ways other than through offering for sale or marketing shall also not affect the right of the breeder to protection.

(*c*) The variety must be sufficiently homogeneous, having regard to the particular features of its sexual reproduction or vegetative propagation.

(*d*) The variety must be stable in its essential characteristics, that is to say, it must remain true to its description after repeated reproduction or propagation or, where the breeder has defined a particular cycle of reproduction or multiplication, at the end of each cycle.

(*e*) The variety shall be given a denomination as provided in Article 13.

(2) Provided that the breeder shall have complied with the formalities provided for by the national law of the member State of the Union in which the application for protection was filed, including the payment of fees, the grant of protection may not be made subject to conditions other than those set forth above.

Article 7
Official Examination of Varieties: Provisional Protection

(1) Protection shall be granted after examination of the variety in the light of the criteria defined in Article 6. Such examination shall be appropriate to each botanical genus or species.

(2) For the purposes of such examination, the competent authorities of each member State of the Union may require the breeder to furnish all the necessary information, documents, propagating material or seeds.

(3) Any member State of the Union may provide measures to protect the breeder against abusive acts of third parties committed during the period between the filing of the application for protection and the decision thereon.

Article 8
Period of Protection

The right conferred on the breeder shall be granted for a limited period. This period may not be less than 15 years, computed from the date of issue of the title of protection. For vines, forest trees, fruit trees and ornamental trees, including, in each case, their rootstocks, the period of protection may not be less than 18 years, computed from the said date.

Article 9
Restrictions in the Exercise of Rights Protected

(1) The free exercise of the exclusive right accorded to the breeder may not be restricted otherwise than for reasons of public interest.

(2) When any such restriction is made in order to ensure the widespread distribution of the variety, the member State of the Union concerned shall take all measures necessary to ensure that the breeder receives equitable remuneration.

Article 10
Nullity and Forfeiture of the Rights Protected

(1) The right of the breeder shall be declared null and void, in accordance with the provisions of the national law of each member State of the Union, if it is established that the conditions laid down in Article 6(1)(*a*) and (*b*) were not effectively complied with at the time when the title of protection was issued.

(2) The right of the breeder shall become forfeit when he is no longer in a position to provide the competent authority with reproductive or propagating material capable of producing the variety with its characteristics as defined when the protection was granted.

(3) The right of the breeder may become forfeit if:

(*a*) after being requested to do so and within a prescribed period, he does not provide the competent authority with the reproductive or propagating material, the documents and the information deemed necessary for checking the variety, or he does not allow inspection of the measures which have been taken for the maintenance of the variety; or

(*b*) he has failed to pay within the prescribed period such fees as may be payable to keep his rights in force.

(4) The right of the breeder may not be annulled or become forfeit except on the grounds set out in this Article.

Article 11
Free Choice of the Member State in Which the First Application is Filed; Application in Other Member States; Independence of Protection in Different Member States

(1) The breeder may choose the member State of the Union in which he wishes to file his first application for protection.

(2) The breeder may apply to other member States of the Union for protection of his right without waiting for the issue to him of a title of protection by the member State of the Union in which he filed his first application.

(3) The protection applied for in different member States of the

Union by natural or legal persons entitled to benefit under this Convention shall be independent of the protection obtained for the same variety in other States whether or not such States are members of the Union.

Article 12
Right of Priority

(1) Any breeder who has duly filed an application for protection in one of the member States of the Union shall, for the purpose of filing in the other member States of the Union, enjoy a right of priority for a period of 12 months. This period shall be computed from the date of filing of the first application. The day of filing shall not be included in such period.

(2) To benefit from the provisions of paragraph (1), the further filing must include an application for protection, a claim in respect of the priority of the first application and, within a period of three months, a copy of the documents which constitute that application, certified to be a true copy by the authority which received it.

(3) The breeder shall be allowed a period of four years after the expiration of the period of priority in which to furnish, to the member State of the Union with which he has filed an application for protection in accordance with the terms of paragraph (2), the additional documents and material required by the laws and regulations of that State. Nevertheless, that State may require the additional documents and material to be furnished within an adequate period in the case where the application whose priority is claimed is rejected or withdrawn.

(4) Such matters as the filing of another application or the publication or use of the subject of the application, occurring within the period provided for in paragraph (1), shall not constitute grounds for objection to an application filed in accordance with the foregoing conditions. Such matters may not give rise to any right in favour of a third party or to any right of personal possession.

Article 13
Variety Denomination

(1) The variety shall be designated by a denomination destined to be its generic designation. Each member State of the Union shall ensure that subject to paragraph (4) no rights in the designation registered as the denomination of the variety shall hamper the free

use of the denomination in connection with the variety, even after the expiration of the protection.

(2) The denomination must enable the variety to be identified. It may not consist solely of figures except where this is an established practice for designating varieties. It must not be liable to mislead or to cause confusion concerning the characteristics, value or identity of the variety or the identity of the breeder. In particular, it must be different from every denomination which designates, in any member State of the Union, an existing variety of the same botanical species or of a closely related species.

(3) The denomination of the variety shall be submitted by the breeder to the authority referred to in Article 30(1)(*b*). If it is found that such denomination does not satisfy the requirements of paragraph (2), that authority shall refuse to register it and shall require the breeder to propose another denomination within a prescribed period. The denomination shall be registered at the same time as the title of protection is issued in accordance with the provisions of Article 7.

(4) Prior rights of third parties shall not be affected. If, by reason of a prior right, the use of the denomination of a variety is forbidden to a person who, in accordance with the provisions of paragraph (7), is obliged to use it, the authority referred to in Article 30(1)(*b*) shall require the breeder to submit another denomination for the variety.

(5) A variety must be submitted in member States of the Union under the same denomination. The authority referred to in Article 30(1)(*b*) shall register the denomination so submitted, unless it considers that denomination unsuitable in its State. In the latter case, it may require the breeder to submit another denomination.

(6) The authority referred to in Article 30(1)(*b*) shall ensure that all the other such authorities are informed of matters concerning variety denominations, in particular the submission, registration and cancellation of denominations. Any authority referred to in Article 30(1)(*b*) may address its observations, if any, on the registration of a denomination to the authority which communicated that denomination.

(7) Any person who, in a member State of the Union, offers for sale or markets reproductive or vegetative propagating material of a variety protected in that State shall be obliged to use the denomination of that variety, even after the expiration of the protection of that variety, in so far as, in accordance with the provisions of paragraph (4), prior rights do not prevent such use.

(8) When the variety is offered for sale or marketed, it shall be permitted to associate a trade mark, trade name or other similar indication with a registered variety denomination. If such an indication is so associated, the denomination must nevertheless be easily recognizable.

Article 14
Protection Independent of Measures Regulating Production, Certification and Marketing

(1) The right accorded to the breeder in pursuance of the provisions of this Convention shall be independent of the measures taken by each member State of the Union to regulate the production, certification and marketing of seeds and propagating material.

(2) However, such measures shall, as far as possible, avoid hindering the application of the provisions of this Convention

Article 15
Organs of the Union

The permanent organs of the Union shall be:

(*a*) the Council;

(*b*) the Secretariat General, entitled the Office of the International Union for the Protection of New Varieties of Plants.

Article 16
Composition of the Council; Votes

(1) The Council shall consist of the representatives of the member States of the Union. Each member State of the Union shall appoint one representative to the Council and one alternate.

(2) Representatives or alternates may be accompanied by assistants or advisors.

(3) Each member State of the Union shall have one vote in the Council.

Article 17
Observers in Meetings of the Council

(1) States not members of the Union which have signed this Act shall be invited as observers to meetings of the Council.

(2) Other observers or experts may also be invited to such meetings.

Article 18
President and Vice-President of the Council

(1) The Council shall elect a President and a first Vice-President from among its members. It may elect other Vice-Presidents. The first Vice-President shall take the place of the President if the latter is unable to officiate.

(2) The President shall hold office for three years.

Article 19
Sessions of the Council

(1) The Council shall meet upon convocation by its President.

(2) An ordinary session of the Council shall be held annually. In addition, the President may convene the Council at his discretion; he shall convene it, within a period of three months, if one-third of the member States of the Union so request.

Article 20
Rules of Procedure of the Council; Administrative and Financial Regulations of the Union

The Council shall establish its rules of procedure and the administrative and financial regulations of the Union.

Article 21
Tasks of the Council

The tasks of the Council shall be to:

(*a*) study appropriate measures to safeguard the interests and to encourage the development of the Union;

(*b*) appoint the Secretary-General and, if it finds it necessary, a Vice Secretary-General and determine the terms of appointment of each;

(*c*) examine the annual report on the activities of the Union and lay down the programme for its future work;

(*d*) give to the Secretary-General, whose functions are set out in Article 23, all necessary directions for the accomplishment of the tasks of the Union;

(*e*) examine and approve the budget of the Union and fix the contribution of each member State of the Union in accordance with the provisions of Article 26;

(*f*) examine and approve the accounts presented by the Secretary-General;

(*g*) fix, in accordance with the provisions of Article 27, the date and place of the conferences referred to in that Article and take the measures necessary for their preparation; and

(*h*) in general, take all necessary decisions to ensure the efficient functioning of the Union.

Article 22
Majorities Required for Decisions of the Council

Any decision of the Council shall require a simple majority of the votes of the members present and voting, provided that any decision of the Council under Articles 4(4), 20, 21(*e*), 26(5)(*b*), 27(1), 28(3) or 32(3) shall require three-fourths of the votes of the members present and voting. Abstentions shall not be considered as votes.

Article 23
Tasks of the Office of the Union; Responsibilities of the Secretary-General; Appointment of Staff

(1) The Office of the Union shall carry out all the duties and tasks entrusted to it by the Council. It shall be under the direction of the Secretary-General.

(2) The Secretary-General shall be responsible to the Council; he shall be responsible for carrying out the decisions of the Council. He shall submit the budget for the approval of the Council and shall be responsible for its implementation. He shall make an annual report to the Council on his administration and a report on the activities and financial position of the Union.

(3) Subject to the provisions of Article 21(*b*), the conditions of appointment and employment of the staff necessary for the efficient performance of the tasks of the Office of the Union shall be fixed in the administrative and financial regulations referred to in Article 20.

Article 24
Legal Status

(1) The Union shall have legal personality.

(2) The Union shall enjoy on the territory of each member State of the Union, in conformity with the laws of that State, such legal capacity as may be necessary for the fulfillment of the objectives of the Union and for the exercise of its functions.

(3) The Union shall conclude a headquarters agreement with the Swiss Confederation.

Article 25
Auditing of the Accounts

The auditing of the accounts of the Union shall be effected by a member State of the Union as provided in the administrative and financial regulations referred to in Article 20. Such State shall be designated, with its agreement, by the Council.

Article 26
Finances

(1) The expenses of the Union shall be met from:
—the annual contributions of the member States of the Union;
—payments received for services rendered;
—miscellaneous receipts.

(2)(*a*) The share of each member State of the Union in the total amount of the annual contributions shall be determined by reference to the total expenditure to be met from the contributions of the member States of the Union and to the number of contribution units applicable to it under paragraph (3). The said share shall be computed according to paragraph (4).

(*b*) The number of contribution units shall be expressed in whole numbers or fractions thereof, provided that such number shall not be less than one-fifth.

(3)(*a*) As far as any State is concerned which is a member State of the Union on the date on which this Act enters into force with respect to that State, the number of contribution units applicable to it shall be the same as was applicable to it, immediately before the said date, according to the Convention of 1961 as amended by the Additional Act of 1972.

(*b*) As far as any other State is concerned, that State shall, on joining the Union, indicate, in a declaration addressed to the Secretary-General, the number of contribution units applicable to it.

(*c*) Any member State of the Union may, at any time, indicate, in a declaration addressed to the Secretary-General, a number of contribution units different from the number applicable to it under subparagraph (*a*) or (*b*). Such declaration, if made during the first six months of a calendar year, shall take effect from the beginning of the subsequent calendar year; otherwise it shall take effect from the beginning of the second calendar year which follows the year in which the declaration was made.

(4)(*a*) For each budgetary period, the amount corresponding to one contribution unit shall be obtained by dividing the total amount of the expenditure to be met in that period from the contributions of the member States of the Union by the total number of units applicable to those States.

(*b*) The amount of the contribution of each member State of the Union shall be obtained by multiplying the amount corresponding to one contribution unit by the number of contribution units applicable to that State.

(5)(*a*) A member State of the Union which is in arrears in the payment of its contributions may not, subject to paragraph (*b*), exercise its right to vote in the Council if the amount of its arrears equals or exceeds the amount of the contributions due from it for the preceding two full years. The suspension of the right to vote does not relieve such State of its obligations under this Convention and does not deprive it of any other rights thereunder.

(*b*) The Council may allow the said State to continue to exercise its right to vote if, and as long as, the Council is satisfied that the delay in payment is due to exceptional and unavoidable circumstances.

Article 27
Revision of the Convention

(1) This Convention may be revised by a conference of the member States of the Union. The convocation of such conference shall be decided by the Council.

(2) The proceedings of a conference shall be effective only if at least half of the member States of the Union are represented at it. A majority of five-sixths of the member States of the Union represented at the conference shall be required for the adoption of a revised text of the Convention.

Article 28
Languages Used by the Office and in Meetings of the Council

(1) The English, French and German languages shall be used by the Office of the Union in carrying out its duties.

(2) Meetings of the Council and of revision conferences shall be held in the three languages;

(3) If the need arises, the Council may decide that further languages shall be used.

Article 29
Special Agreements for the Protection of New Varieties of Plants

Member States of the Union reserve the right to conclude among themselves special agreements for the protection of new varieties of plants, in so far as such agreements do not contravene the provisions of this Convention.

Article 30
Implementation of the Convention on the Domestic Level; Contracts on the Joint Utilisation of Examination Services

(1) Each member State of the Union shall adopt all measures necessary for the application of this Convention; in particular, it shall:

(*a*) provide for appropriate legal remedies for the effective defence of the rights provided for in this Convention;

(*b*) set up a special authority for the protection of new varieties of plants or entrust such protection to an existing authority;

(*c*) ensure that the public is informed of matters concerning such protection, including as a minimum the periodical publication of the list of titles of protection issued.

(2) Contracts may be concluded between the competent authorities of the member States of the Union, with a view to the joint utilisation of the servies of the authorities entrusted with the examination of varieties in accordance with the provisions of Article 7 and with assembling the necessary reference collections and documents.

(3) It shall be understood that, on depositing its instrument of

ratification, acceptance, approval or accession, each State must be in a position, under its own domestic law, to give effect to the provisions of this Convention.

Article 31
Signature

This Act shall be open for signature by any member State of the Union and any other State which was represented in the Diplomatic Conference adopting this Act. It shall remain open for signature until October 31, 1979.

Article 32
Ratification, Acceptance or Approval; Accession

(1) Any State shall express its consent to be bound by this Act by the deposit of:

(*a*) its instrument of ratification, acceptance or approval, if it has signed this Act; or

(*b*) its instrument of accession, if it has not signed this Act.

(2) Instruments of ratification, acceptance, approval or accession shall be deposited with the Secretary-General.

(3) Any State which is not a member of the Union and which has not signed this Act shall, before depositing its instrument of accession, ask the Council to advise it in respect of the conformity of its laws with the provisions of this Act. If the decision embodying the advice is positive, the instrument of accession may be deposited.

Article 33
Entry Into Force; Closing of Earlier Texts

(1) This Act shall enter into force one month after the following two conditions are fulfilled:

(*a*) the number of instruments of ratification, acceptance, approval or accession deposited is not less than five; and

(*b*) at least three of the said instruments are instruments deposited by States parties to the Convention of 1961.

(2) With respect to any State which deposits its instrument of ratification, acceptance, approval or accession after the conditions referred to in paragraph (1)(*a*) and (*b*) have been fulfilled, this Act

shall enter into force one month after the deposit of the instrument of the said State.

(3) Once this Act enters into force according to paragraph (1), no State may accede to the Convention of 1961 as amended by the Additional Act of 1972.

Article 34
Relations Between States Bound by Different Texts

(1) Any member State of the Union which, on the day on which this Act enters into force with respect to that State, is bound by the Convention of 1961 as amended by the Additional Act of 1972 shall, in its relations with any other member State of the Union which is not bound by this Act, continue to apply, until the present Act enters into force also with respect to that other State, the said Convention as amended by the said Additional Act.

(2) Any member State of the Union not bound by this Act ("the former State") may declare, in a notification addressed to the Secretary-General, that it will apply the Convention of 1961 as amended by the Additional Act of 1972 in its relations with any State bound by this Act which becomes a member of the Union through ratification, acceptance or approval of or accession to this Act ("the latter State"). As from the beginning of one month after the date of any such notification and until the entry into force of this Act with respect to the former State, the former State shall apply the Convention of 1961 as amended by the Additional Act of 1972 in its relations with any such latter State, whereas any such latter State shall apply this Act in its relations with the former State.

Article 35
Communications Concerning the Genera and Species Protected; Information to be Published

(1) When depositing its instrument of ratification, acceptance or approval of or accession to this Act, each State which is not a member of the Union shall notify the Secretary-General of the list of genera and species to which, on the entry into force of this Act with respect to that State, it will apply the provisions of this Convention.

(2) The Secretary-General shall, on the basis of communications received from each member State of the Union concerned, publish information on:

(*a*) the extension of the application of the provisions of this

Convention to additional genera and species after the entry into force of this Act with respect to that State;

(*b*) any use of the faculty provided for in Article 3(3);

(*c*) the use of any faculty granted by the Council pursuant to Article 4(4) or (5);

(*d*) any use of the faculty provided for in Article 5(4), first sentence, with an indication of the nature of the more extensive rights and with a specification of the genera and species to which such rights apply;

(*e*) any use of the faculty provided for in Article 5(4), second sentence;

(*f*) the fact that the law of the said State contains a provision as permitted under Article 6(1)(*b*)(i), and the length of the period permitted;

(*g*) the length of the period referred to in Article 8 if such period is longer than the 15 years and the 18 years, respectively, referred to in that Article.

Article 36
Territories

(1) Any State may declare in its instrument of ratification, acceptance, approval or accession, or may inform the Secretary-General by written notification any time thereafter, that this Act shall be applicable to all or part of the territories designated in the declaration or notification.

(2) Any State which has made such a declaration or given such a notification may, at any time, notify the Secretary-General that this Act shall cease to be applicable to all or part of such territories.

(3) (*a*) Any declaration made under paragraph (1) shall take effect on the same date as the ratification, acceptance, approval, or accession in the instrument of which it was included, and any notification given under that paragraph shall take effect three months after its notification by the Secretary-General.

(*b*) Any notification given under paragraph (2) shall take effect 12 months after its receipt by the Secretary-General.

Article 37
Exceptional Rules for Protection Under Two Forms

(1) Notwithstanding the provisions of Article 2(1), any State which, prior to the end of the period during which this Act is open for signature, provides for protection under the different forms re-

ferred to in Article 2(1) for one and the same genus or species, may continue to do so if, at the time of signing this Act or of depositing its instrument of ratification, acceptance or approval of or accession to this Act, it notifies the Secretary-General of that fact.

(2) Where, in a member State of the Union to which paragraph (1) applies, protection is sought under patent legislation, the said State may apply the patentability criteria and the period of protection of the patent legislation to the varieties protected thereunder, notwithstanding the provisions of Articles 6(1)(*a*) and (*b*) and 8.

(3) The said State may, at any time, notify the Secretary-General of the withdrawal of the notification it has given under paragraph (1). Such withdrawal shall take effect on the date which the State shall indicate in its notification of withdrawal.

Article 38
Transitional Limitation of the Requirement of Novelty

Notwithstanding the provisions of Article 6, any member State of the Union may, without thereby creating an obligation for other member States of the Union, limit the requirement of novelty laid down in that Article, with regard to varieties of recent creation existing at the date on which such State applies the provisions of this Convention for the first time to the genus or species to which such varieties belong.

Article 39
Preservation of Existing Rights

This Convention shall not affect existing rights under the national laws of member States of the Union or under agreements concluded between such States.

Article 40
Reservations

No reservations to this Convention are permitted.

Article 41
Duration and Denunciation of the Convention

(1) This Convention is of unlimited duration.

(2) Any member State of the Union may denounce this Convention by notification addressed to the Secretary-General. The Secretary-General shall promptly notify all member States of the Union of the receipt of that notification.

(3) The denunciation shall take effect at the end of the calendar year following the year in which the notification was received by the Secretary-General.

(4) The denunciation shall not affect any rights acquired in a variety by reason of this Convention prior to the date on which the denunciation becomes effective.

Article 42
Languages; Depositary Functions

(1) This Act shall be signed in a single original in the French, English and German languages, the French text prevailing in case of any discrepancy among the various texts. The original shall be deposited with the Secretary-General.

(2) The Secretary-General shall transmit two certified copies of this Act to the Governments of all States which were represented in the Diplomatic Conference that adopted it and, on request, to the Government of any other State.

(3) The Secretary-General shall, after consultation with the Governments of the interested States which were represented in the said Conference, establish official texts in the Arabic, Dutch, Italian, Japanese and Spanish languages and such other languages as the Council may designate.

(4) The Secretary-General shall register this Act with the Secretariat of the United States.

(5) The Secretary-General shall notify the Governments of the member States of the Union and of the States which, without being members of the Union, were represented in the Diplomatic Conference that adopted it of the signatures of this Act, the deposit of instruments of ratification, acceptance, approval and accession, any notification received under Articles 34(2), 36(1) and (2), 37(1) and (3) or 41(2) and any declaration made under Article 36(1).

Recommendation on Article 4*

The Diplomatic Conference on the Revision of the International Convention for the Protection of New Varieties of Plants, held in 1978,

Having regard to Article 4(2) and (3) of the International Convention for the Protection of New Varieties of Plants of December 2, 1961, as revised at Geneva on November 10, 1972, and on October 23, 1978,

Considering the fact that the Convention of 1961 contains an Annex listing a number of economically important species to which each member State of the International Union for the Protection of New Varieties of Plants had to apply that Convention within certain periods,

Considering further that the Annex has been deleted in the Convention as revised in 1978, thereby giving greater freedom of choice to the member States of the Union and to those States which are intending to become members of the Union to decide which genera and species that Convention is to be applied to,

Conscious of the fact that it is in the interest both of agriculture in general and of breeders in particular that genera and species of economic importance be eligible for protection in each State,

Recommends that each member State of the Union use its best endeavours to ensure that the genera and species eligible for protection under its national law comprise as far as possible those genera and species which are of major economic importance in that State,

Recommends further that each State intending to become a member of the Union choose the genera or species to which, as a minimum, the Convention as revised in 1978 has to be applied at the time of its entry into force in the territory of that State from genera and species of major economic importance in that State.

Recommendation on Article 5*

The Diplomatic Conference on the Revision of the International Convention for the Protection of New Varieties of Plants, held in 1978,

Having regard to Article 5(1) and (4) of the International Convention for the Protection of New Varieties of Plants of December 2, 1961, as revised at Geneva on November 10, 1972, and on October 23, 1978,

---

* These Recommendations were adopted by the Diplomatic Conference on the Revision of the International Convention for the Protection of New Varieties of Plants on October 23, 1978.

Conscious of the fact that the scope of the protection laid down in Article 5(1) may create special problems with regard to certain genera and species,

Considering it of great importance that breeders be enabled effectively to safeguard their interests,

Recognizing at the same time that an equitable balance must be struck between the interests of breeders and those of users of new varieties,

Recommends that, where, in respect of any genus or species, the granting of more extensive rights than those provided for in Article 5(1) is desirable to safeguard the legitimate interests of the breeders, the Contracting States of the said Convention take adequate measures, pursuant to Article 5(4).

2. Patent Cooperation Treaty

Done at Washington on June 19, 1970, amended on October 2, 1979, and modified on February 3, 1984

The Patent Cooperation Treaty (PCT), was completed on June 19, 1970, and entered into force on January 24, 1978.[1]

Its main purpose is to create a union for cooperation in filing, searching, and examining patent applications. The PCT does not create an international patent. Rather, it facilitates the filing of separate applications in the member countries.

The PCT is a special agreement under the Paris Union and open to any country that is a member of the Paris Union. No part of the Treaty may be construed to restrict the rights of persons protected under the Paris Convention (Art. 1 para. 2).

The PCT is designed to simplify procedures in the filing of patent applications in states party to the agreement. The PCT entitles nationals or domiciliaries of a contracting state to file an international application for patent protection (Art. 9). In this application, the applicant indicates the member states in which it wishes to obtain protection. The application is filed with the national patent office of the applicant's country of residence or nationality and must include a request, a description, one or more claims, and a designation of the contracting states where protection is sought (Arts. 3-6). A claim of priority under the Paris Union is to be stated in the request (Art. 8). If no formal defects are found in the application, the applicant's filing date becomes the date when the application was received (Art. 11).

---

[1]For the Patent Cooperation regulations as amended, *see* World Intellectual Property Organization, Industrial Property Text No. 2-007, 1984/12 and 1985/12.

The application will then undergo an international search, carried out by a competent authority, to discover the relevant prior art (Art. 15) consisting of all publicly available written disclosures that are pertinent in determining whether the claimed invention is novel and inventive. The report is sent to both the applicant and the International Bureau of WIPO. After receiving the report, the applicant may amend the claims within the appropriate time limits (Art. 19). The International Bureau then transmits both the application and search report to the designated offices and publishes the application soon after the 18-month priority date expires (Arts. 20 and 21). Within 20 months of the original filing, the applicant must furnish each office a translation of the application in the country's official language and pay the registration fee (Art. 22). The international application becomes a national application in the designated member state that will apply its own substantive patent law.

Chapter II of the PCT establishes an international preliminary examination (Arts. 31-42). Adherence to Chapter II is optional and the member states may declare themselves not bound by its provisions. Under Chapter II, applicants have the discretion to undergo an international preliminary examination and may designate the states where they want their examination sent (Art. 31 para. 4 *lit.* a). The purpose of the international preliminary examination is to produce a nonbinding opinion on the claimed invention as to its novelty, inventiveness, and industrial applicability (Art. 33 para. 1). The report is sent to the International Bureau that in turn transmits it to each designated office (Art. 36). Each designated country will then apply its own substantive patent law.

As of January 1, 1990, the following 43 countries were party to the PCT:

Australia	Central African Republic	France
Austria	Chad	Gabon
Barbados	Congo	Federal Republic of Germany
Belgium	Democratic People's Republic of Korea	Hungary
Benin	Denmark	Italy
Brazil	Finland	Japan
Bulgaria		Liechtenstein
Burkina Faso		Luxembourg
Cameroon		Madagascar
Canada		

Malawi
Mali
Mauritania
Monaco
Netherlands
Norway
Republic of Korea
Romania
Senegal
Soviet Union
Spain
Sri Lanka
Sudan
Sweden
Switzerland
Togo
United Kingdom
United States of America

Patent Cooperation Treaty

Introductory Provisions

Article 1
Establishment of a Union

(1) The States party to this Treaty (hereinafter called "the Contracting States") constitute a Union for cooperation in the filing, searching, and examination, of applications for the protection of inventions, and for rendering special technical services. The Union shall be known as the International Patent Cooperation Union.

(2) No provision of this Treaty shall be interpreted as diminishing the rights under the Paris Convention for the Protection of Industrial Property of any national or resident of any country party to that Convention.

Article 2
Definitions

For the purposes of this Treaty and the Regulations and unless expressly stated otherwise:

(i) "application" means an application for the protection of an invention; references to an "application" shall be construed as references to applications for patents for inventions, inventors' certificates, utility certificates, utility models, patents or certificates of addition, inventors' certificates of addition, and utility certificates of addition;

(ii) references to a "patent" shall be construed as references to patents for inventions, inventors' certificates, utility certificates, utility models, patents or certificates of addition, inventors' certificates of addition, and utility certificates of addition;

(iii) "national patent" means a patent granted by a national authority;

(iv) "regional patent" means a patent granted by a national or an intergovernmental authority having the power to grant patents effective in more than one State;

(v) "regional application" means an application for a regional patent;

Source: Text courtesy of the World Intellectual Property Organization (WIPO).

(vi) references to a "national application" shall be construed as references to applications for national patents and regional patents, other than applications filed under this Treaty;

(vii) "international application" means an application filed under this Treaty;

(viii) references to an "application" shall be construed as references to international applications and national applications;

(ix) references to a "patent" shall be construed as references to national patents and regional patents;

(x) references to "national law" shall be construed as references to the national law of a Contracting State or, where a regional application or a regional patent is involved, to the treaty providing for the filing of regional applications or the granting of regional patents;

(xi) "priority date," for the purposes of computing time limits, means: (*a*) where the international application contains a priority claim under Article 8, the filing date of the application whose priority is so claimed; (*b*) where the international application contains several priority claims under Article 8, the filing date of the earliest application whose priority is so claimed; (*c*) where the international application does not contain any priority claim under Article 8, the international filing date of such application;

(xii) "national Office" means the government authority of a Contracting State entrusted with the granting of patents; references to a "national Office" shall be construed as referring also to any intergovernmental authority which several States have entrusted with the task of granting regional patents, provided that at least one of those States is a Contracting State, and provided that the said States have authorized that authority to assume the obligations and exercise the powers which this Treaty and the Regulations provide for in respect of national Offices;

(xiii) "designated Office" means the national Office of or acting for the State designated by the applicant under Chapter I of this Treaty;

(xiv) "elected Office" means the national Office of or acting for the State elected by the applicant under Chapter II of this Treaty;

(xv) "receiving Office" means the national Office or the intergovernmental organization with which the international application has been filed;

(xvi) "Union" means the International Patent Cooperation Union;

(xvii) "Assembly" means the Assembly of the Union;

(xviii) "Organization" means the World Intellectual Property Organization;

(xix) "International Bureau" means the International Bureau of the Organization and, as long as it subsists, the United International Bureaux for the Protection of Intellectual Property (BIRPI);

(xx) "Director General" means the Director General of the Organization and, as long as BIRPI subsists, the Director of BIRPI.

Chapter I
International Application and International Search

Article 3
The International Application

(1) Applications for the protection of inventions in any of the Contracting States may be filed as international applications under this Treaty.

(2) An international application shall contain, as specified in this Treaty and the Regulations, a request, a description, one or more claims, one or more drawings (where required), and an abstract.

(3) The abstract merely serves the purpose of technical information and cannot be taken into account for any other purpose, particularly not for the purpose of interpreting the scope of the protection sought.

(4) The international application shall:

(i) be in a prescribed language;

(ii) comply with the prescribed physical requirements;

(iii) comply with the prescribed requirement of unity of invention;

(iv) be subject to the payment of the prescribed fees.

Article 4
The Request

(1) The request shall contain:

(i) a petition to the effect that the international application be processed according to this Treaty;

(ii) the designation of the Contracting State or States in which protection for the invention is desired on the basis of the international application ("designated States"); if for any designated State a regional patent is available and the applicant wishes to obtain a regional patent rather than a national patent, the request shall so indicate; if, under a treaty concerning a regional patent, the applicant cannot limit his application to certain of the States party to that treaty, designation of one of those States and the indication of the wish to obtain the regional patent shall be treated as designation of all the States party to that treaty; if, under the national law of the designated State, the designation of that State has the effect of an application for a regional patent, the designation of the said State shall be treated as an indication of the wish to obtain the regional patent;

(iii) the name of and other prescribed data concerning the applicant and the agent (if any);

(iv) the title of the invention;

(v) the name of and other prescribed data concerning the inventor where the national law of at least one of the designated States requires that these indications be furnished at the time of filing a national application. Otherwise, the said indications may be furnished either in the request or in separate notices addressed to each designated Office whose national law requires the furnishing of the said indications but allows that they be furnished at a time later than that of the filing of a national application.

(2) Every designation shall be subject to the payment of the prescribed fee within the prescribed time limit.

(3) Unless the applicant asks for any of the other kinds of protection referred to in Article 43, designation shall mean that the desired protection consists of the grant of a patent by or for the designated State. For the purposes of this paragraph, Article 2(ii) shall not apply.

(4) Failure to indicate in the request the name and other prescribed data concerning the inventor shall have no consequence in any designated State whose national law requires the furnishing of the said indications but allows that they be furnished at a time later than that of the filing of a national application. Failure to furnish the said indications in a separate notice shall have no consequence in any designated State whose national law does not require the furnishing of the said indications.

Article 5
The Description

The description shall disclose the invention in a manner sufficiently clear and complete for the invention to be carried out by a person skilled in the art.

Article 6
The Claims

The claim or claims shall define the matter for which protection is sought. Claims shall be clear and concise. They shall be fully supported by the description.

Article 7
The Drawings

(1) Subject to the provisions of paragraph (2)(ii), drawings shall be required when they are necessary for the understanding of the invention.

(2) Where, without being necessary for the understanding of the invention, the nature of the invention admits of illustration by drawings:

(i) the applicant may include such drawings in the international application when filed,

(ii) any designated Office may require that the applicant file such drawings with it within the prescribed time limit.

Article 8
Claiming Priority

(1) The international application may contain a declaration, as prescribed in the Regulations, claiming the priority of one or more earlier applications filed in or for any country party to the Paris Convention for the Protection of Industrial Property.

(2)(*a*) Subject to the provisions of subparagraph (*b*), the conditions for, and the effect of, any priority claim declared under paragraph (1) shall be as provided in Article 4 of the Stockholm Act of the Paris Convention for the Protection of Industrial Property.

(*b*) The international application for which the priority of one or more earlier applications filed in or for a Contracting State is claimed may contain the designation of that State. Where, in the international application, the priority of one or more national applications filed in or for a designated State is claimed, or where the priority of an international application having designated only one State is claimed, the conditions for, and the effect of, the priority claim in that State shall be governed by the national law of that State.

Article 9
The Applicant

(1) Any resident or national of a Contracting State may file an international application.

(2) The Assembly may decide to allow the residents and the nationals of any country party to the Paris Convention for the Protec-

tion of Industrial Property which is not party to this Treaty to file international applications.

(3) The concepts of residence and nationality, and the application of those concepts in cases where there are several applicants or where the applicants are not the same for all the designated States, are defined in the Regulations.

Article 10
The Receiving Office

The international application shall be filed with the prescribing receiving Office, which will check and process it as provided in this Treaty and the Regulations.

Article II
Filing Date and Effects of the International Application

(1) The receiving Office shall accord as the international filing date the date of receipt of the international application, provided that that Office has found that, at the time of receipt:

(i) the applicant does not obviously lack, for reasons of residence or nationality, the right to file an international application with the receiving Office,

(ii) the international application is in the prescribed language,

(iii) the international application contains at least the following elements: (*a*) an indication that it is intended as an international application, (*b*) the designation of at least one Contracting State, (*c*) the name of the applicant, as prescribed, (*d*) a part which on the face of it appears to be a description, (*e*) a part which on the face of it appears to be a claim or claims.

(2)(*a*) If the receiving Office finds that the international application did not, at the time of receipt, fulfill the requirements listed in paragraph (1), it shall, as provided in the Regulations, invite the applicant to file the required correction.

(*b*) If the applicant complies with the invitation, as provided in the Regulations, the receiving Office shall accord as the international filing date the date of receipt of the required correction.

(3) Subject to Article 64(4), any international application fulfilling the requirements listed in items (i) to (iii) of paragraph (1) and accorded an international filing date shall have the effect of a regular national application in each designated State as of the international filing date, which date shall be considered to be the actual filing date in each designated State.

(4) Any international application fulfilling the requirements listed in items (i) to (iii) of paragraph (1) shall be equivalent to a regular national filing within the meaning of the Paris Convention for the Protection of Industrial Property.

Article 12
Transmittal of the International Application to the International Bureau and the International Searching Authority

(1) One copy of the international application shall be kept by the receiving Office ("home copy"), one copy ("record copy") shall be transmitted to the International Bureau, and another copy ("search copy") shall be transmitted to the competent International Searching Authority referred to in Article 16, as provided in the Regulations.

(2) The record copy shall be considered the true copy of the international application.

(3) The international application shall be considered withdrawn if the record copy has not been received by the International Bureau within the prescribed time limit.

Article 13
Availability of Copy of the International Application to Designated Offices

(1) Any designated Office may ask the International Bureau to transmit to it a copy of the international application prior to the communication provided for in Article 20, and the International Bureau shall transmit such copy to the designated Office as soon as possible after the expiration of one year from the priority date.

(2)(*a*) The applicant may, at any time, transmit a copy of his international application to any designated Office.

(*b*) The applicant may, at any time, ask the International Bureau to transmit a copy of his international application to any designated Office, and the International Bureau shall transmit such copy to the designated Office as soon as possible.

(*c*) Any national Office may notify the International Bureau that it does not wish to receive copies as provided for in subparagraph (*b*), in which case that subparagraph shall not be applicable in respect of that Office.

Article 14
Certain Defects in the International Application

(1)(*a*) The receiving Office shall check whether the international application contains any of the following defects, that is to say:

(i) it is not signed as provided in the Regulations;

(ii) it does not contain the prescribed indications concerning the applicant;

(iii) it does not contain a title;

(iv) it does not contain an abstract;

(v) it does not comply to the extent provided in the Regulations with the prescribed physical requirements.

(*b*) If the receiving Office finds any of the said defects, it shall invite the applicant to correct the international application within the prescribed time limit, failing which that application shall be considered withdrawn and the receiving Office shall so declare.

(2) If the international application refers to drawings which, in fact, are not included in that application, the receiving Office shall notify the applicant accordingly and he may furnish them within the prescribed time limit and, if he does, the international filing date shall be the date on which the drawings are received by the receiving Office. Otherwise, any reference to the said drawings shall be considered non-existent.

(3)(*a*) If the receiving Office finds that, within the prescribed time limits, the fees prescribed under Article 3(4)(iv) have not been paid, or no fee prescribed under Article 4(2) has been paid in respect of any of the designated States, the international application shall be considered withdrawn and the receiving Office shall so declare.

(*b*) If the receiving Office finds that the fee prescribed under Article 4(2) has been paid in respect of one or more (but less than all) designated States within the prescribed time limit, the designation of those States in respect of which it has not been paid within the prescribed time limit shall be considered withdrawn and the receiving Office shall so declare.

(4) If, after having accorded an international filing date to the international application, the receiving Office finds, within the prescribed time limit, that any of the requirements listed in items (i) to (iii) of Article 11(1) was not complied with at that date, the said application shall be considered withdrawn and the receiving Office shall so declare.

Article 15
The International Search

(1) Each international application shall be the subject of international search.

(2) The objective of the international search is to discover relevant prior art.

(3) International search shall be made on the basis of the claims, with due regard to the description and the drawings (if any).

(4) The International Searching Authority referred to in Article 16 shall endeavor to discover as much of the relevant prior art as its facilities permit, and shall, in any case, consult the documentation specified in the Regulations.

(5)(*a*) If the national law of the Contracting State so permits, the applicant who files a national application with the national Office of or acting for such State may, subject to the conditions provided for in such law, request that a search similar to an international search ("international-type search") be carried out on such application.

(*b*) If the national law of the Contracting State so permits, the national Office of or acting for such State may subject any national application filed with it to an international-type search.

(*c*) The international-type search shall be carried out by the International Searching Authority referred to in Article 16 which would be competent for an international search if the national application were an international application and were filed with the Office referred to in subparagraphs (*a*) and (*b*). If the national application is in a language which the International Searching Authority considers it is not equipped to handle, the international-type search shall be carried out on a translation prepared by the applicant in a language prescribed for international applications and which the International Security Authority has undertaken to accept for international applications. The national application and the translation, when required, shall be presented in the form prescribed for international applications.

Article 16
The International Searching Authority

(1) International search shall be carried out by an International Searching Authority, which may be either a national Office or an intergovernmental organization, such as the International Patent Institute, whose tasks include the establishing of documentary search reports on prior art with respect to inventions which are the subject of applications.

(2) If, pending the establishment of a single International Searching Authority, there are several International Searching Authorities, each receiving Office shall, in accordance with the provisions of the applicable agreement referred to in paragraph (3)(*b*),

specify the International Searching Authority or Authorities competent for the searching of international applications filed with such Office.

(3)(*a*) International Searching Authorities shall be appointed by the Assembly. Any national Office and any intergovernmental organization satisfying the requirements referred to in subparagraph (*c*) may be appointed as International Searching Authority.

(*b*) Appointment shall be conditional on the consent of the national Office or intergovernmental organization to be appointed and the conclusion of an agreement, subject to approval by the Assembly, between such Office or organization and the International Bureau. The agreement shall specify the rights and obligations of the parties, in particular, the formal undertaking by the said Office or organization to apply and observe all the common rules of international search.

(*c*) The Regulations prescribe the minimum requirements, particularly as to manpower and documentation, which any Office or organization must satisfy before it can be appointed and must continue to satisfy while it remains appointed.

(*d*) Appointment shall be for a fixed period of time and may be extended for further periods.

(*e*) Before the Assembly makes a decision on the appointment of any national Office or intergovernmental organization, or on the extension of its appointment, or before it allows any such appointment to lapse, the Assembly shall hear the interested Office or organization and seek the advice of the Committee for Technical Cooperation referred to in Article 56 once that Committee has been established.

Article 17
Procedure Before the International Searching Authority

(1) Procedure before the International Searching Authority shall be governed by the provisions of this Treaty, the Regulations, and the agreement which the International Bureau shall conclude, subject to this Treaty and the Regulations, with the said Authority.

(2)(*a*) If the International Searching Authority considers

(i) that the international application relates to a subject matter which the International Searching Authority is not required, under the Regulations, to search, and in the particular case decides not to search, or

(ii) that the description, the claims, or the drawings, fail to comply with the prescribed requirements to such an extent that a meaningful search could not be carried out, the said Authority shall so declare and shall notify the applicant and the International Bureau that no international search report will be established.

(*b*) If any of the situations referred to in subparagraph (*a*) is found to exist in connection with certain claims only, the international search report shall so indicate in respect of such claims, whereas, for the other claims, the said report shall be established as provided in Article 18.

(3)(*a*) If the International Searching Authority considers that the international application does not comply with the requirement of unity of invention as set forth in the Regulations, it shall invite the applicant to pay additional fees. The International Searching Authority shall establish the international search report on those parts of the international application which relate to the invention first mentioned in the claims ("main invention") and, provided the required additional fees have been paid within the prescribed time limit, on those parts of the international application which relate to inventions in respect of which the said fees were paid.

(*b*) The national law of any designated State may provide that, where the national Office of that State finds the invitation, referred to in subparagraph (*a*), of the International Searching Authority justified and where the applicant has not paid all additional fees, those parts of the international application which consequently have not been searched shall, as far as effects in that State are concerned, be considered withdrawn unless a special fee is paid by the applicant to the national Office of that State.

Article 18
The International Search Report

(1) The international search report shall be established within the prescribed time limit and in the prescribed form.

(2) The international search report shall, as soon as it has been established, be transmitted by the International Searching Authority to the applicant and the International Bureau.

(3) The international search report or the declaration referred to in Article 17(2)(*a*) shall be translated as provided in the Regulations. The translations shall be prepared by or under the responsibility of the International Bureau.

Article 19
Amendment of the Claims Before the International Bureau

(1) The applicant shall, after having received the international search report, be entitled to one opportunity to amend the claims of the international application by filing amendments with the Interna-

tional Bureau within the prescribed time limit. He may, at the same time, file a brief statement, as provided in the Regulations, explaining the amendments and indicating any impact that such amendments might have on the description and the drawings.

(2) The amendments shall not go beyond the disclosure in the international application as filed.

(3) If the national law of any designated State permits amendments to go beyond the said disclosure, failure to comply with paragraph (2) shall have no consequence in that State.

Article 20
Communication to Designated Offices

(1)(*a*) The international application, together with the international search report (including any indication referred to in Article 17(2)(*b*)) or the declaration referred to in Article 17(2)(*a*), shall be communicated to each designated Office, as provided in the Regulations, unless the designated Office waives such requirement in its entirety or in part.

(*b*) The communication shall include the translation (as prescribed) of the said report or declaration.

(2) If the claims have been amended by virtue of Article 19(1), the communication shall either contain the full text of the claims both as filed and as amended or shall contain the full text of the claims as filed and specify the amendments, and shall include the statement, if any, referred to in Article 19(1).

(3) At the request of the designated Office or the applicant, the International Searching Authority shall send to the said Office or the applicant, respectively, copies of the documents cited in the international search report, as provided in the Regulations.

Article 21
International Publication

(1) The International Bureau shall publish international applications.

(2)(*a*) Subject to the exceptions provided for in subparagraph (*b*) and in Article 64(3), the international publication of the international application shall be effected promptly after the expiration of 18 months from the priority date of that application.

(*b*) The applicant may ask the International Bureau to publish his international application any time before the expiration of the time limit referred to in subparagraph (*a*). The International Bureau shall proceed accordingly, as provided in the Regulations.

(3) The international search report or the declaration referred to in Article 17(2)(*a*) shall be published as prescribed in the Regulations.

(4) The language and form of the international publication and other details are governed by the Regulations.

(5) There shall be no international publication if the international application is withdrawn or is considered withdrawn before the technical preparations for publication have been completed.

(6) If the international application contains expressions or drawings which, in the opinion of the International Bureau, are contrary to morality or public order, or if, in its opinion, the international application contains disparaging statements as defined in the Regulations, it may omit such expressions, drawings, and statements, from its publications, indicating the place and number of words or drawings omitted, and furnishing, upon request, individual copies of the passages omitted.

Article 22
Copy, Translation, and Fee, to Designated Offices

(1) The applicant shall furnish a copy of the international application (unless the communication provided for in Article 20 has already taken place) and a translation thereof (as prescribed), and pay the national fee (if any), to each designated Office not later than at the expiration of 20 months from the priority date. Where the national law of the designated State requires the indication of the name of and other prescribed data concerning the inventor but allows that these indications be furnished at a time later than that of the filing of a national application, the applicant shall, unless they were contained in the request, furnish the said indications to the national Office of or acting for the State not later than at the expiration of 20 months from the priority date.

(2)* Where the International Searching Authority makes a dec-

---

*The text of Article 22(2) ("Notwithstanding the provisions of paragraph (1), where the International Searching Authority makes a declaration, under Article 17(2)(a), that no international search report will be established, the time limit for performing the acts referred to in paragraph (1) of this Article shall be two months from the date of the notification sent to the applicant of the said declaration.") was modified by a decision taken by the Assembly of the PCT Union on February 3, 1984. In addition to that modification, the decision of the Assembly contains the following provisions:

"(2) The modification enters into force on January 1, 1985. However, as long as that time limit is incompatible with the national law applied by the designated Office, a time limit of two months from the date of the notification sent to the applicant of the said declaration shall, during that transitory period, apply with respect to that designated Office, provided that such Office has made a notification to that effect to the International Bureau.

"(3) The notification referred to in paragraph (2) shall be addressed to the International Bureau before October 1, 1984. It shall be promptly published by the International Bureau in the Gazette, and it shall become effective on January 1, 1985.

"(4) Any notification effected under paragraph (3) may be withdrawn at any time. Such withdrawal shall be promptly published by the International Bureau in the Gazette, and it shall be effective two months after its publication in the Gazette or at any later date as indicated in the notice of withdrawal."

laration, under Article 17(2)(*a*), that no international search report will be established, the time limit for performing the acts referred to in paragraph (1) of this Article shall be the same as that provided for in paragraph (1).

(3) Any national law may, for performing the acts referred to in paragraphs (1) and (2), fix time limits which expire later than the time limit provided for in those paragraphs.

Article 23
Delaying of National Procedure

(1) No designated Office shall process or examine the international application prior to the expiration of the applicable time limit under Article 22.

(2) Notwithstanding the provisions of paragraph (1), any designated Office may, on the express request of the applicant, process or examine the international application at any time.

Article 24
Possible Loss of Effect in Designated States

(1) Subject, in case (ii) below, to the provisions of Article 25, the effect of the international application provided for in Article 11(3) shall cease in any designated State with the same consequences as the withdrawal of any national application in that State:

(i) if the applicant withdraws his international application or the designation of that State;

(ii) if the international application is considered withdrawn by virtue of Articles 12(3), 14(1)(*b*), 14(3)(*a*), or 14(4), or if the designation of that State is considered withdrawn by virtue of Article 14(3)(*b*);

(iii) if the applicant fails to perform the acts referred to in Article 22 within the applicable time limit.

(2) Notwithstanding the provisions of paragraph (1), any designated Office may maintain the effect provided for in Article 11(3) even where such effect is not required to be maintained by virtue of Article 25(2).

Article 25
Review by Designated Offices

(1)(*a*) Where the receiving Office has refused to accord an international filing date or has declared that the international application is considered withdrawn, or where the International Bureau has made a finding under Article 12(3), the International Bureau shall promptly send, at the request of the applicant, copies of any document in the file to any of the designated Offices named by the applicant.

(*b*) Where the receiving Office has declared that the designation of any given State is considered withdrawn, the International Bureau shall promptly send, at the request of the applicant, copies of any document in the file to the national Office of such State.

(*c*) The request under subparagraphs (*a*) or (*b*) shall be presented within the prescribed time limit.

(2)(*a*) Subject to the provisions of subparagraph (*b*), each designated Office shall, provided that the national fee (if any) has been paid and the appropriate translation (as prescribed) has been furnished within the prescribed time limit, decide whether the refusal, declaration, or finding, referred to in paragraph (1) was justified under the provisions of this Treaty and the Regulations, and, if it finds that the refusal or declaration was the result of an error or omission on the part of the receiving Office or that the finding was the result of an error or omission on the part of the International Bureau, it shall, as far as effects in the State of the designated Office are concerned, treat the international application as if such error or omission had not occurred.

(*b*) Where the record copy has reached the International Bureau after the expiration of the time limit prescribed under Article 12(3) on account of any error or omission on the part of the applicant, the provisions of subparagraph (*a*) shall apply only under the circumstances referred to in Article 48(2).

Article 26
Opportunity to Correct before Designated Offices

No designated Office shall reject an international application on the grounds of non-compliance with the requirements of this Treaty and the Regulations without first giving the applicant the opportunity to correct the said application to the extent and according to the procedure provided by the national law for the same or comparable situations in respect of national applications.

Article 27
National Requirements

(1) No national law shall require compliance with requirements relating to the form or contents of the international application different from or additional to those which are provided for in this Treaty and the Regulations.

(2) The provisions of paragraph (1) neither affect the application of the provisions of Article 7(2) nor preclude any national law from requiring, once the processing of the international application has started in the designated Office, the furnishing:

(i) when the applicant is a legal entity, of the name of an officer entitled to represent such legal entity,

(ii) of documents not part of the international application but which constitute proof of allegations or statements made in that application, including the confirmation of the international application by the signature of the applicant when that application, as filed, was signed by his representative or agent.

(3) Where the applicant, for the purposes of any designated State, is not qualified according to the national law of that State to file a national application because he is not the inventor, the international application may be rejected by the designated Office.

(4) Where the national law provides, in respect of the form or contents of national applications, for requirements which, from the viewpoint of applicants, are more favorable than the requirements provided for by this Treaty and the Regulations in respect of international applications, the national Office, the courts and any other competent organs of or acting for the designated State may apply the former requirements, instead of the latter requirements, to international applications, except where the applicant insists that the requirements provided for by this Treaty and the Regulations be applied to his international application.

(5) Nothing in this Treaty and the Regulations is intended to be construed as prescribing anything that would limit the freedom of each Contracting State to prescribe such substantive conditions of patentability as it desires. In particular, any provision in this Treaty and the Regulations concerning the definition of prior art is exclusively for the purposes of the international procedure and, consequently, any Contracting State is free to apply, when determining the patentability of an invention claimed in an international application, the criteria of its national law in respect of prior art and other conditions of patentability not constituting requirements as to the form and contents of applications.

(6) The national law may require that the applicant furnish evidence in respect of any substantive condition of patentability prescribed by such law.

(7) Any receiving Office or, once the processing of the international application has started in the designated Office, that Office may apply the national law as far as it relates to any requirement that the applicant be represented by an agent having the right to represent applicants before the said Office and/or that the applicant have an address in the designated State for the purpose of receiving notifications.

(8) Nothing in this Treaty and the Regulations is intended to be construed as limiting the freedom of any Contracting State to apply measures deemed necessary for the preservation of its national security or to limit, for the protection of the general economic interests of that State, the right of its own residents or nationals to file international applications.

Article 28
Amendment of the Claims, the Description, and the Drawings, before Designated Offices

(1) The applicant shall be given the opportunity to amend the claims, the description, and the drawings, before each designated Office within the prescribed time limit. No designated Office shall grant a patent, or refuse the grant of a patent, before such time limit has expired except with the express consent of the applicant.

(2) The amendments shall not go beyond the disclosure in the international application as filed unless the national law of the designated State permits them to go beyond the said disclosure.

(3) The amendments shall be in accordance with the national law of the designated State in all respects not provided for in this Treaty and the Regulations.

(4) Where the designated Office requires a translation of the international application, the amendments shall be in the language of the translation.

Article 29
Effects of the International Publication

(1) As far as the protection of any rights of the applicant in a designated State is concerned, the effects, in that State, of the international publication of an international application shall, subject to the provisions of paragraphs (2) to (4), be the same as those which the national law of the designated State provides for the compulsory national publication of unexamined national applications as such.

(2) If the language in which the international publication has been effected is different from the language in which publications under the national law are effected in the designated State, the said national law may provide that the effects provided for in paragraph (1) shall be applicable only from such time as:

(i) a translation into the latter language has been published as provided by the national law, or

(ii) a translation into the latter language has been made available to the public, by laying open for public inspection as provided by the national law, or

(iii) a translation into the latter language has been transmitted by the applicant to the actual or prospective unauthorized user of the invention claimed in the international application, or

(iv) both the acts described in (i) and (iii), or both the acts described in (ii) and (iii), have taken place.

(3) The national law of any designated State may provide that, where the international publication has been effected, on the request of the applicant, before the expiration of 18 months from the priority date, the effects provided for in paragraph (1) shall be applicable only from the expiration of 18 months from the priority date.

(4) The national law of any designated State may provide that the effects provided for in paragraph (1) shall be applicable only from the date on which a copy of the international application as published under Article 21 has been received in the national Office of or acting for such State. The said Office shall publish the date of receipt in its gazette as soon as possible.

Article 30
Confidential Nature of the International Application

(1)(*a*) Subject to the provisions of subparagraph (*b*), the International Bureau and the International Searching Authorities shall not allow access by any person or authority to the international application before the international publication of that application, unless requested or authorized by the applicant.

(*b*) The provisions of subparagraph (*a*) shall not apply to any transmittal to the competent International Searching Authority, to transmittals provided for under Article 13, and to communications provided for under Article 20.

(2)(*a*) No national Office shall allow access to the international application by third parties, unless requested or authorized by the applicant, before the earliest of the following dates:

(i) date of the international publication of the international application,

(ii) date of the receipt of the communication of the international application under Article 20,

(iii) date of the receipt of a copy of the international application under Article 22.

(*b*) The provisions of subparagraph (*a*) shall not prevent any national Office from informing third parties that it has been designated, or from publishing that fact. Such information or publication may, however, contain only the following data: identification of the receiving Office, name of the applicant, international filing date, international application number, and title of the invention.

(c) The provisions of subparagraph (*a*) shall not prevent any designated Office from allowing access to the international application for the purposes of the judicial authorities.

(3) The provisions of paragraph (2)(*a*) shall apply to any receiving Office except as far as transmittals provided for under Article 12(1) are concerned.

(4) For the purposes of this Article, the term "access" covers any means by which third parties may acquire cognizance, including individual communication and general publication, provided, however, that no national Office shall generally publish an international application or its translation before the international publication or, if international publication has not taken place by the expiration of 20 months from the priority date, before the expiration of 20 months from the said priority date.

Chapter II
International Preliminary Examination

Article 31
Demand for International Preliminary Examination

(1) On the demand of the applicant, his international application shall be the subject of an international preliminary examination as provided in the following provisions and the Regulations.

(2)(*a*) Any applicant who is a resident or national, as defined in the Regulations, of a Contracting State bound by Chapter II, and whose international application has been filed with the receiving Office of or acting for such State, may make a demand for international preliminary examination.

(*b*) The Assembly may decide to allow persons entitled to file international applications to make a demand for international preliminary examination even if they are residents or nationals of a State not party to this Treaty or not bound by Chapter II.

(3) The demand for international preliminary examination shall be made separately from the international application. The demand shall contain the prescribed particulars and shall be in the prescribed language and form.

(4)(*a*) The demand shall indicate the Contracting State or States in which the applicant intends to use the results of the international preliminary examination ("elected States"). Additional Contracting States may be elected later. Election may relate only to Contracting States already designated under Article 4.

(*b*) Applicants referred to in paragraph (2)(*a*) may elect any Contracting State bound by Chapter II. Applicants referred to in paragraph (2)(*b*) may elect only such Contracting States bound by Chapter II as have declared that they are prepared to be elected by such applicants.

(5) The demand shall be subject to the payment of the prescribed fees within the prescribed time limit.

(6)(*a*) The demand shall be submitted to the competent International Preliminary Examining Authority referred to in Article 32.

(*b*) Any later election shall be submitted to the International Bureau.

(7) Each elected Office shall be notified of its election.

Article 32
The International Preliminary Examining Authority

(1) International preliminary examination shall be carried out by the International Preliminary Examining Authority.

(2) In the case of demands referred to in Article 31(2)(*a*), the receiving Office, and, in the case of demands referred to in Article 31(2)(*b*), the Assembly, shall, in accordance with the applicable agreement between the interested International Preliminary Examining Authority or Authorities and the International Bureau, specify the International Preliminary Examining Authority or Authorities competent for the preliminary examination.

(3) The provisions of Article 16(3) shall apply, *mutatis mutandis,* in respect of International Preliminary Examining Authorities.

Article 33
The International Preliminary Examination

(1) The objective of the international preliminary examination is to formulate a preliminary and non-binding opinion on the questions whether the claimed invention appears to be novel, to involve an inventive step (to be non-obvious), and to be industrially applicable.

(2) For the purposes of the international preliminary examination, a claimed invention shall be considered novel if it is not anticipated by the prior art as defined in the Regulations.

(3) For the purposes of the international preliminary examination, a claimed invention shall be considered to involve an inventive step if, having regard to the prior art as defined in the Regulations,

it is not, at the prescribed relevant date, obvious to a person skilled in the art.

(4) For the purposes of the international preliminary examination, a claimed invention shall be considered industrially applicable if, according to its nature, it can be made or used (in the technological sense) in any kind of industry. "Industry" shall be understood in its broadest sense, as in the Paris Convention for the Protection of Industrial Property.

(5) The criteria described above merely serve the purposes of international preliminary examination. Any Contracting State may apply additional or different criteria for the purpose of deciding whether, in that State, the claimed invention is patentable or not.

(6) The international preliminary examination shall take into consideration all the documents cited in the international search report. It may take into consideration any additional documents considered to be relevant in the particular case.

Article 34

Procedure before the International Preliminary Examining Authority

(1) Procedure before the International Preliminary Examining Authority shall be governed by the provisions of this Treaty, the Regulations, and the agreement which the International Bureau shall conclude, subject to this Treaty and the Regulations, with the said Authority.

(2)(*a*) The applicant shall have a right to communicate orally and in writing with the International Preliminary Examining Authority.

(*b*) The applicant shall have a right to amend the claims, the description, and the drawings, in the prescribed manner and within the prescribed time limit, before the international preliminary examination report is established. The amendment shall not go beyond the disclosure in the international application as filed.

(*c*) The applicant shall receive at least one written opinion from the International Preliminary Examining Authority unless such Authority considers that all of the following conditions are fulfilled:

(i) the invention satisfies the criteria set forth in Article 33(1),

(ii) the international application complies with the requirements of this Treaty and the Regulations in so far as checked by that Authority,

(iii) no observations are intended to be made under Article 35(2), last sentence.

(*d*) The applicant may respond to the written opinion.

(3)(*a*) If the International Preliminary Examining Authority considers that the international application does not comply with the requirement of unity of invention as set forth in the Regulations, it may invite the applicant, at his option, to restrict the claims so as to comply with the requirement or to pay additional fees.

(*b*) The national law of any elected State may provide that, where the applicant chooses to restrict the claims under subparagraph (*a*), those parts of the international application which, as a consequence of the restriction, are not to be the subject of international preliminary examination shall, as far as effects in that State are concerned, be considered withdrawn unless a special fee is paid by the applicant to the national Office of that State.

(*c*) If the applicant does not comply with the invitation referred to in subparagraph (*a*) within the prescribed time limit, the International Preliminary Examining Authority shall establish an international preliminary examination report on those parts of the international application which relate to what appears to be the main invention and shall indicate the relevant facts in the said report. The national law of any elected State may provide that, where its national Office finds the invitation of the International Preliminary Examining Authority justified, those parts of the international application which do not relate to the main invention shall, as far as effects in that State are concerned, be considered withdrawn unless a special fee is paid by the applicant to that Office.

(4)(*a*) If the International Preliminary Examining Authority considers

(i) that the international application relates to a subject matter on which the International Preliminary Examining Authority is not required, under the Regulations, to carry out an international preliminary examination, and in the particular case decides not to carry out such examination, or

(ii) that the description, the claims, or the drawings, are so unclear, or the claims are so inadequately supported by the description, that no meaningful opinion can be formed on the novelty, inventive step (non-obviousness), or industrial applicability, of the claimed invention,

the said Authority shall not go into the questions referred to in Article 33(1) and shall inform the applicant of this opinion and the reasons therefor.

(*b*) If any of the situations referred to in subparagraph (a) is found to exist in, or in connection with, certain claims only, the provisions of that subparagraph shall apply only to the said claims.

Article 35
The International Preliminary Examination Report

(1) The international preliminary examination report shall be established within the prescribed time limit and in the prescribed form.

(2) The international preliminary examination report shall not contain any statement on the question whether the claimed invention is or seems to be patentable or unpatentable according to any national law. It shall state, subject to the provisions of paragraph (3), in relation to each claim, whether the claim appears to satisfy the criteria of novelty, inventive step (non-obviousness), and industrial applicability, as defined for the purposes of the international preliminary examination in Article 33(1) to (4). The statement shall be accompanied by the citation of the documents believed to support the stated conclusion with such explanations as the circumstances of the case may require. The statement shall also be accompanied by such other observations as the Regulations provide for.

(3)(*a*) If, at the time of establishing the international preliminary examination report, the International Preliminary Examining Authority considers that any of the situations referred to in Article 34(4)(*a*) exists, that report shall state this opinion and the reasons therefor. It shall not contain any statement as provided in paragraph (2).

(*b*) If a situation under Article 34(4)(*b*) is found to exist, the international preliminary examination report shall, in relation to the claims in question, contain the statement as provided in subparagraph (*a*), whereas, in relation to the other claims, it shall contain the statement as provided in paragraph (2).

Article 36
Transmittal, Translation, and Communication, of the International Preliminary Examination Report

(1) The international preliminary examination report, together with the prescribed annexes, shall be transmitted to the applicant and to the International Bureau.

(2)(*a*) The international preliminary examination report and its annexes shall be translated into the prescribed languages.

(*b*) Any translation of the said report shall be prepared by or under the responsibility of the International Bureau, whereas any translation of the said annexes shall be prepared by the applicant.

(3)(*a*) The international preliminary examination report, together with its translation (as prescribed) and its annexes (in the original language), shall be communicated by the International Bureau to each elected Office.

(*b*) The prescribed translation of the annexes shall be transmitted within the prescribed time limit by the applicant to the elected Offices.

(4) The provisions of Article 20(3) shall apply, *mutatis mutandis*, to copies of any document which is cited in the international preliminary examination report and which was not cited in the international search report.

Article 37
Withdrawal of Demand or Election

(1) The applicant may withdraw any or all elections.

(2) If the election of all elected States is withdrawn, the demand shall be considered withdrawn.

(3)(*a*) Any withdrawal shall be notified to the International Bureau.

(*b*) The elected Offices concerned and the International Preliminary Examining Authority concerned shall be notified accordingly by the International Bureau.

(4)(*a*) Subject to the provisions of subparagraph (*b*), withdrawal of the demand or of the election of a Contracting State shall, unless the national law of that State provides otherwise, be considered to be withdrawal of the international application as far as that State is concerned.

(*b*) Withdrawal of the demand or of the election shall not be considered to be withdrawal of the international application if such withdrawal is effected prior to the expiration of the applicable time limit under Article 22; however, any Contracting State may provide in its national law that the aforesaid shall apply only if its national Office has received, within the said time limit, a copy of the international application, together with a translation (as prescribed), and the national fee.

Article 38
Confidential Nature of the International Preliminary Examination

(1) Neither the International Bureau nor the International Preliminary Examining Authority shall, unless requested or authorized by the applicant, allow access within the meaning, and with the

proviso, of Article 30(4) to the file of the international preliminary examination by any person or authority at any time, except by the elected Offices once the international preliminary examination report has been established.

(2) Subject to the provisions of paragraph (1) and Articles 36(1) and (3) and 37(3)(*b*), neither the International Bureau nor the International Preliminary Examining Authority shall, unless requested or authorized by the applicant, give information on the issuance or nonissuance of an international preliminary examination report and on the withdrawal or nonwithdrawal of the demand or of any election.

Article 39
Copy, Translation, and Fee, to Elected Offices

(1)(*a*)* If the election of any Contracting State has been effected prior to the expiration of the 19th month from the priority date, the provisions of Article 22 shall not apply to such State and the applicant shall furnish a copy of the international application (unless the communication under Article 20 has already taken place) and a translation thereof (as prescribed), and pay the national fee (if any), to each elected Office not later than at the expiration of 30 months from the priority date.

(*b*) Any national law may, for performing the acts referred to in subparagraph (*a*), fix time limits which expire later than the time limit provided for in that subparagraph.

(2) The effect provided for in Article 11(3) shall cease in the elected State with the same consequences as the withdrawal of any national application in that State if the applicant fails to perform

---

*The text of Article 39(1)(*a*) ("If the election of any Contracting State has been effected prior to the expiration of the 19th month from the priority date, the provisions of Article 22 shall not apply to such State and the applicant shall furnish a copy of the international application (unless the communication under Article 20 has already taken place) and a translation thereof (as prescribed), and pay the national fee (if any), to each elected Office not later than at the expiration of 25 months from the priority date.") was modified by a decision taken by the Assembly of the PCT Union on February 3, 1984. In addition to that modification, the decision of the Assembly contains the following provisions:

"(2) The modification enters into force on January 1, 1985. However, as long as the said time limit of 30 months is incompatible in all cases with the national law applied by the elected Office, a time limit of 25 months from the priority date shall, during that transitory period, apply with respect to that elected Office, provided that such Office has made a notification to that effect to the International Bureau.

"(3) The notification referred to in paragraph (2) shall be addressed to the International Bureau before October 1, 1984. It shall be promptly published by the International Bureau in the Gazette, and it shall become effective on January 1, 1985.

"(4) Any notification effected under paragraph (3) may be withdrawn at any time. Such withdrawal shall be promptly published by the International Bureau in the Gazette, and it shall be effective two months after its publication in the Gazette or at any later date as indicated in the notice of withdrawal."

the acts referred to in paragraph (1)(*a*) within the time limit applicable under paragraph (1)(*a*) or (*b*).

(3) Any elected Office may maintain the effect provided for in Article 11(3) even where the applicant does not comply with the requirements provided for in paragraph (1)(*a*) or (*b*).

Article 40
Delaying of National Examination and Other Processing

(1) If the election of any Contracting State has been effected prior to the expiration of the 19th month from the priority date, the provisions of Article 23 shall not apply to such State and the national Office of or acting for that State shall not proceed, subject to the provisions of paragraph (2), to the examination and other processing of the international application prior to the expiration of the applicable time limit under Article 39.

(2) Notwithstanding the provisions of paragraph (1), any elected Office may, on the express request of the applicant, proceed to the examination and other processing of the international application at any time.

Article 41
Amendment of the Claims, the Description, and the Drawings, before Elected Offices

(1) The applicant shall be given the opportunity to amend the claims, the description, and the drawings, before each elected Office within the prescribed time limit. No elected Office shall grant a patent, or refuse the grant of a patent, before such time limit has expired, except with the express consent of the applicant.

(2) The amendments shall not go beyond the disclosure in the international application as filed, unless the national law of the elected State permits them to go beyond the said disclosure.

(3) The amendments shall be in accordance with the national law of the elected State in all respects not provided for in this Treaty and the Regulations.

(4) Where an elected Office requires a translation of the international application, the amendments shall be in the language of the translation.

Article 42
Results of National Examination in Elected Offices

No elected Office receiving the international preliminary examination report may require that the applicant furnish copies, or information on the contents, of any papers connected with the examination relating to the same international application in any other elected Office.

CHAPTER III
Common Provisions

Article 43
Seeking Certain Kinds of Protection

In respect of any designated or elected State whose law provides for the grant of inventors' certificates, utility certificates, utility models, patents or certificates of addition, inventors' certificates of addition, or utility certificates of addition, the applicant may indicate, as prescribed in the Regulations, that his international application is for the grant, as far as that State is concerned, of an inventor's certificate, a utility certificate, or a utility model, rather than a patent, or that it is for the grant of a patent or certificate of addition, an inventor's certificate of addition, or a utility certificate of addition, and the ensuing effect shall be governed by the applicant's choice. For the purposes of this Article and any Rule thereunder, Article 2(ii) shall not apply.

Article 44
Seeking Two Kinds of Protection

In respect of any designated or elected State whose law permits an application, while being for the grant of a patent or one of the other kinds of protection referred to in Article 43, to be also for the grant of another of the said kinds of protection, the applicant may indicate, as prescribed in the Regulations, the two kinds of protection he is seeking, and the ensuing effect shall be governed by the applicant's indications. For the purposes of this Article, Article 2(ii) shall not apply.

Article 45
Regional Patent Treaties

(1) Any treaty providing for the grant of regional patents ("regional patent treaty"), and giving to all persons who, according to Article 9, are entitled to file international applications the right to file applications for such patents, may provide that international applications designating or electing a State party to both the regional patent treaty and the present Treaty may be filed as applications for such patents.

(2) The national law of the said designated or elected State may provide that any designation or election of such State in the international application shall have the effect of an indication of the wish to obtain a regional patent under the regional patent treaty.

Article 46
Incorrect Translation of the International Application

If, because of an incorrect translation of the international application, the scope of any patent granted on that application exceeds the scope of the international application in its original language, the competent authorities of the Contracting State concerned may accordingly and retroactively limit the scope of the patent, and declare it null and void to the extent that its scope has exceeded the scope of the international application in its original language.

Article 47
Time Limits

(1) The details for computing time limits referred to in this Treaty are governed by the Regulations.

(2)(a) All time limits fixed in Chapters I and II of this Treaty may, outside any revision under Article 60, be modified by a decision of the Contracting States.

(b) Such decisions shall be made in the Assembly or through voting by correspondence and must be unanimous.

(c) The details of the procedure are governed by the Regulations.

Article 48
Delay in Meeting Certain Time Limits

(1) Where any time limit fixed in this Treaty or the Regulations is not met because of interruption in the mail service or unavoidable loss or delay in the mail, the time limit shall be deemed to be met in the cases and subject to the proof and other conditions prescribed in the Regulations.

(2)(a) Any Contracting State shall, as far as that State is concerned, excuse, for reasons admitted under its national law, any delay in meeting any time limit.

(b) Any Contracting State may, as far as that State is concerned, excuse, for reasons other than those referred to in subparagraph (a), any delay in meeting any time limit.

Article 49
Right to Practice before International Authorities

Any attorney, patent agent, or other person, having the right to practice before the national Office with which the international application was filed, shall be entitled to practice before the International Bureau and the competent International Searching Authority and competent International Preliminary Examining Authority in respect of that application.

Chapter IV
Technical Services

Article 50
Patent Information Services

(1) The International Bureau may furnish services by providing technical and any other pertinent information available to it on the basis of published documents, primarily patents and published applications (referred to in this Article as "the information services").

(2) The International Bureau may provide these information services either directly or through one or more International Searching Authorities or other national or international specialized institutions, with which the International Bureau may reach agreement.

(3) The information services shall be operated in a way particularly facilitating the acquisition by Contracting States which are

developing countries of technical knowledge and technology, including available published know-how.

(4) The information services shall be available to Governments of Contracting States and their nationals and residents. The Assembly may decide to make these services available also to others.

(5)(a) Any service to Governments of Contracting States shall be furnished at cost, provided that, when the Government is that of a Contracting State which is a developing country, the service shall be furnished below cost if the difference can be covered from profit made on services furnished to others than Governments of Contracting States or from the sources referred to in Article 51(4).

(b) The cost referred to in subparagraph (a) is to be understood as cost over and above costs normally incident to the performance of the services of a national Office or the obligations of an International Searching Authority.

(6) The details concerning the implementation of the provisions of this Article shall be governed by decisions of the Assembly and, within the limits to be fixed by the Assembly, such working groups as the Assembly may set up for that purpose.

(7) The Assembly shall, when it considers it necessary, recommend methods of providing financing supplementary to those referred to in paragraph (5).

Article 51
Technical Assistance

(1) The Assembly shall establish a Committee for Technical Assistance (referred to in this Article as "the Committee").

(2)(a) The members of the Committee shall be elected among the Contracting States, with due regard to the representation of developing countries.

(b) The Director General shall, on his own initiative or at the request of the Committee, invite representatives of intergovernmental organizations concerned with technical assistance to developing countries to participate in the work of the Committee.

(3)(a) The task of the Committee shall be to organize and supervise technical assistance for Contracting States which are developing countries in developing their patent systems individually or on a regional basis.

(b) The technical assistance shall comprise, among other things, the training of specialists, the loaning of experts, and the supply of equipment both for demonstration and for operational purposes.

(4) The International Bureau shall seek to enter into agreements, on the one hand, with international financing organizations

and intergovernmental organizations, particularly the United Nations, the agencies of the United Nations, and the Specialized Agencies connected with the United Nations concerned with technical assistance, and, on the other hand, with the Governments of the States receiving the technical assistance, for the financing of projects pursuant to this Article.

(5) The details concerning the implementation of the provisions of this Article shall be governed by decisions of the Assembly and, within the limits to be fixed by the Assembly, such working groups as the Assembly may set up for that purpose.

Article 52
Relations with Other Provisions of the Treaty

Nothing in this Chapter shall affect the financial provisions contained in any other Chapter of this Treaty. Such provisions are not applicable to the present Chapter or to its implementation.

Chapter V
Administrative Provisions

Article 53
Assembly

(1)(a) The Assembly shall, subject to Article 57(8), consist of the Contracting States.

(b) The Government of each Contracting State shall be represented by one delegate, who may be assisted by alternate delegates, advisors, and experts.

(2)(a) The Assembly shall:

- (i) deal with all matters concerning the maintenance and development of the Union and the implementation of this Treaty;
- (ii) perform such tasks as are specifically assigned to it under other provisions of this Treaty;
- (iii) give directions to the International Bureau concerning the preparation for revision conferences;
- (iv) review and approve the reports and activities of the Director General concerning the Union, and give him all necessary instructions concerning matters within the competence of the Union;

(v) review and approve the reports and activities of the Executive Committee established under paragraph (9), and give instructions to such Committee;

(vi) determine the program and adopt the triennial* budget of the Union, and approve its final accounts;

(vii) adopt the financial regulations of the Union;

(viii) establish such committees and working groups as it deems appropriate to achieve the objectives of the Union;

(ix) determine which States other than Contracting States and, subject to the provisions of paragraph (8), which intergovernmental and international non-governmental organizations shall be admitted to its meetings as observers;

(x) take any other appropriate action designed to further the objectives of the Union and perform such other functions as are appropriate under this Treaty.

(b) With respect to matters which are of interest also to other Unions administered by the Organization, the Assembly shall make its decisions after having heard the advice of the Coordination Committee of the Organization.

(3) A delegate may represent, and vote in the name of, one State only.

(4) Each Contracting State shall have one vote.

(5)(a) One-half of the Contracting States shall constitute a quorum.

(b) In the absence of the quorum, the Assembly may make decisions but, with the exception of decisions concerning its own procedure, all such decisions shall take effect only if the quorum and the required majority are attained through voting by correspondence as provided in the Regulations.

(6)(a) Subject to the provisions of Articles 47(2)(b), 58(2)(b), 58(3) and 61(2)(b), the decisions of the Assembly shall require two-thirds of the votes cast.

(b) Abstentions shall not be considered as votes.

(7) In connection with matters of exclusive interest to States bound by Chapter II, any reference to Contracting States in paragraphs (4), (5), and (6), shall be considered as applying only to States bound by Chapter II.

(8) Any intergovernmental organization appointed as International Searching or Preliminary Examining Authority shall be admitted as observer to the Assembly.

(9) When the number of Contracting States exceeds forty, the Assembly shall establish an Executive Committee. Any reference to

*Editor's Note: Since 1980, the budget of the Union is biennial.

the Executive Committee in this Treaty and the Regulations shall be construed as references to such Committee once it has been established.

(10) Until the Executive Committee has been established, the Assembly shall approve, within the limits of the program and triennial budget, the annual programs and budgets prepared by the Director General.*

(11)(a) The Assembly shall meet in every second calendar year in ordinary session upon convocation by the Director General and, in the absence of exceptional circumstances, during the same period and at the same place as the General Assembly of the Organization.

(b) The Assembly shall meet in extraordinary session upon convocation by the Director General, at the request of the Executive Committee, or at the request of one-fourth of the Contracting States.

(12) The Assembly shall adopt its own rules of procedure.

Article 54
Executive Committee

(1) When the Assembly has established an Executive Committee, that Committee shall be subject to the provisions set forth hereinafter.

(2)(a) The Executive Committee shall, subject to Article 57(8), consist of States elected by the Assembly from among States members of the Assembly.

(b) The Government of each State member of the Executive Committee shall be represented by one delegate, who may be assisted by alternate delegates, advisors, and experts.

(3) The number of States members of the Executive Committee shall correspond to one-fourth of the number of States members of the Assembly. In establishing the number of seats to be filled, remainders after division by four shall be disregarded.

(4) In electing the members of the Executive Committee, the Assembly shall have due regard to an equitable geographical distribution.

(5)(a) Each member of the Executive Committee shall serve from the close of the session of the Assembly which elected it to the close of the next ordinary session of the Assembly.

(b) Members of the Executive Committee may be re-elected but only up to a maximum of two-thirds of such members.

(c) The Assembly shall establish the details of the rules govern-

*Editor's Note: Since 1980, the program and budget of the Union are biennial.

ing the election and possible re-election of the members of the Executive Committee.

(6)(a) The Executive Committee shall:

(i) prepare the draft agenda of the Assembly;
(ii) submit proposals to the Assembly in respect of the draft program and biennial budget of the Union prepared by the Director General;
(iii) *[deleted]*
(iv) submit, with appropriate comments, to the Assembly the periodical reports of the Director General and the yearly audit reports on the accounts;
(v) take all necessary measures to ensure the execution of the program of the Union by the Director General, in accordance with the decisions of the Assembly and having regard to circumstances arising between two ordinary sessions of the Assembly;
(vi) perform such other functions as are allocated to it under this Treaty.

(b) With respect to matters which are of interest also to other Unions administered by the Organization, the Executive Committee shall make its decisions after having heard the advice of the Coordination Committee of the Organization.

(7)(a) The Executive Committee shall meet once a year in ordinary session upon convocation by the Director General, preferably during the same period and at the same place as the Coordination Committee of the Organization.

(b) The Executive Committee shall meet in extraordinary session upon convocation by the Director General, either on his own initiative or at the request of its Chairman or one-fourth of its members.

(8)(a) Each State member of the Executive Committee shall have one vote.

(b) One-half of the members of the Executive Committee shall constitute a quorum.

(c) Decisions shall be made by a simple majority of the votes cast.

(d) Abstentions shall not be considered as votes.

(e) A delegate may represent, and vote in the name of, one State only.

(9) Contracting States not members of the Executive Committee shall be admitted to its meetings as observers, as well as any intergovernmental organization appointed as International Searching or Preliminary Examining Authority.

(10) The Executive Committee shall adopt its own rules of procedure.

Article 55
International Bureau

(1) Administrative tasks concerning the Union shall be performed by the International Bureau.

(2) The International Bureau shall provide the secretariat of the various organs of the Union.

(3) The Director General shall be the chief executive of the Union and shall represent the Union.

(4) The International Bureau shall publish a Gazette and other publications provided for by the Regulations or required by the Assembly.

(5) The Regulations shall specify the services that national Offices shall perform in order to assist the International Bureau and the International Searching and Preliminary Examining Authorities in carrying out their tasks under this Treaty.

(6) The Director General and any staff member designated by him shall participate, without the right to vote, in all meetings of the Assembly, the Executive Committee and any other committee or working group established under this Treaty or the Regulations. The Director General, or a staff member designated by him, shall be *ex officio* secretary of these bodies.

(7)(a) The International Bureau shall, in accordance with the directions of the Assembly and in cooperation with the Executive Committee, make the preparations for the revision conferences.

(b) The International Bureau may consult with intergovernmental and international non-governmental organizations concerning preparations for revision conferences.

(c) The Director General and persons designated by him shall take part, without the right to vote, in the discussions at revision conferences.

(8) The International Bureau shall carry out any other tasks assigned to it.

Article 56
Committee for Technical Cooperation

(1) The Assembly shall establish a Committee for Technical Cooperation (referred to in this Article as "the Committee").

(2)(a) The Assembly shall determine the composition of the Committee and appoints its members, with due regard to an equitable representation of developing countries.

(b) The International Searching and Preliminary Examining Authorities shall be *ex officio* members of the Committee. In the case where such an Authority is the national Office of a Contracting State, that State shall not be additionally represented on the Committee.

(c) If the number of Contracting States so allows, the total number of members of the Committee shall be more than double the number of *ex officio* members.

(d) The Director General shall, on his own initiative or at the request of the Committee, invite representatives of interested organizations to participate in discussions of interest to them.

(3) The aim of the Committee shall be to contribute, by advice and recommendations:

(i) to the constant improvement of the services provided for under this Treaty,
(ii) to the securing, so long as there are several International Searching Authorities and several International Preliminary Examination Authorities, of the maximum degree of uniformity in their documentation and working methods and the maximum degree of uniformly high quality in their reports, and
(iii) on the initiative of the Assembly or the Executive Committee, to the solution of the technical problems specifically involved in the establishment of a single International Searching Authority.

(4) Any Contracting State and any interested international organization may approach the Committee in writing on questions which fall within the competence of the Committee.

(5) The Committee may address its advice and recommendations to the Director General or, through him, to the Assembly, the Executive Committee, all or some of the International Searching and Preliminary Examining Authorities, and all or some of the receiving Offices.

(6)(a) In any case, the Director General shall transmit to the Executive Committee the texts of all the advice and recommendations of the Committee. He may comment on such texts.

(b) The Executive Committee may express its views on any advice, recommendation, or other activity of the Committee, and may invite the Committee to study and report on questions falling within its competence. The Executive Committee may submit to the Assembly, with appropriate comments, the advice, recommendations and report of the Committee.

(7) Until the Executive Committee has been established, references in paragraph (6) to the Executive Committee shall be construed as references to the Assembly.

(8) The details of the procedure of the Committee shall be governed by the decisions of the Assembly.

Article 57
Finances

(1)(a) The Union shall have a budget.

(b) The budget of the Union shall include the income and expenses proper to the Union and its contribution to the budget of expenses common to the Unions administered by the Organization.

(c) Expenses not attributable exclusively to the Union but also to one or more other Unions administered by the Organization shall be considered as expenses common to the Unions. The share of the Union in such common expenses shall be in proportion to the interest the Union has in them.

(2) The budget of the Union shall be established with due regard to the requirements of coordination with the budgets of the other Unions administered by the Organization.

(3) Subject to the provisions of paragraph (5), the budget of the Union shall be financed from the following sources:

(i) fees and charges due for services rendered by the International Bureau in relation to the Union;
(ii) sale of, or royalties on, the publications of the International Bureau concerning the Union;
(iii) gifts, bequests, and subventions;
(iv) rents, interests, and other miscellaneous income.

(4) The amounts of fees and charges due to the International Bureau and the prices of its publications shall be so fixed that they should, under normal circumstances, be sufficient to cover all the expenses of the International Bureau connected with the administration of this Treaty.

(5)(a) Should any financial year close with a deficit, the Contracting States shall, subject to the provisions of subparagraphs (b) and (c), pay contributions to cover such deficit.

(b) The amount of the contribution of each Contracting State shall be decided by the Assembly with due regard to the number of international applications which has emanated from each of them in the relevant year.

(c) If other means of provisionally covering any deficit or any part thereof are secured, the Assembly may decide that such deficit be carried forward and that the Contracting States should not be asked to pay contributions.

(d) If the financial situation of the Union so permits, the Assembly may decide that any contributions paid under subparagraph (a) be reimbursed to the Contracting States which have paid them.

(e) A Contracting State which has not paid, within two years of the due date as established by the Assembly, its contribution under subparagraph (b) may not exercise its right to vote in any of the organs of the Union. However, any organ of the Union may allow such a State to continue to exercise its right to vote in that organ so long as it is satisfied that the delay in payment is due to exceptional and unavoidable circumstances.

(6) If the budget is not adopted before the beginning of a new financial period, it shall be at the same level as the budget of the previous year, as provided in the financial regulations.

(7)(a) The Union shall have a working capital fund which shall be constituted by a single payment made by each Contracting State. If the fund becomes insufficient, the Assembly shall arrange to increase it. If part of the fund is no longer needed, it shall be reimbursed.

(b) The amount of the initial payment of each Contracting State to the said fund or of its participation in the increase thereof shall be decided by the Assembly on the basis of principles similar to those provided for under paragraph (5)(b).

(c) The terms of payment shall be fixed by the Assembly on the proposal of the Director General and after it has heard the advice of the Coordination Committee of the Organization.

(d) Any reimbursement shall be proportionate to the amounts paid by each Contracting State, taking into account the dates at which they were paid.

(8)(a) In the headquarters agreement concluded with the State on the territory of which the Organization has its headquarters, it shall be provided that, whenever the working capital fund is insufficient, such State shall grant advances. The amount of these advances and the conditions on which they are granted shall be the subject of separate agreements, in each case, between such State and the Organization. As long as it remains under the obligation to grant advances, such State shall have an *ex officio* seat in the Assembly and on the Executive Committee.

(b) The State referred to in subparagraph (a) and the Organization shall have the right to denounce the obligation to grant advances, by written notification. Denunciation shall take effect three years after the end of the year in which it has been notified.

(9) The auditing of the accounts shall be effected by one or more of the Contracting States or by external auditors, as provided in the financial regulations. They shall be designated, with their agreement, by the Assembly.

Article 58
Regulations

(1) The Regulations annexed to this Treaty provide Rules:

(i) concerning matters in respect of which this Treaty expressly refers to the Regulations or expressly provides that they are or shall be prescribed,

(ii) concerning any administration requirements, matters, or procedures,

(iii) concerning any details useful in the implementation of the provisions of this Treaty.

(2)(a) The Assembly may amend the Regulations.

(b) Subject to the provisions of paragraph (3), amendments shall require three-fourths of the votes cast.

(3)(a) The Regulations specify the Rules which may be amended

(i) only by unanimous consent, or

(ii) only if none of the Contracting States whose national Office acts as an International Searching or Preliminary Examining Authority dissents, and, where such Authority is an intergovernmental organization, if the Contracting State member of that organization authorized for that purpose by the other member States within the competent body of such organization does not dissent.

(b) Exclusion, for the future, of any such Rules from the applicable requirement shall require the fulfillment of the conditions referred to in subparagraph (a)(i) and (a)(ii), respectively.

(c) Inclusion, for the future, of any Rule in one or the other of the requirements referred to in subparagraph (a) shall require unanimous consent.

(4) The Regulations provide for the establishment, under the control of the Assembly, of Administrative Instructions by the Director General.

(5) In the case of conflict between the provisions of the Treaty and those of the Regulations, the provisions of the Treaty shall prevail.

Chapter VI
Disputes

Article 59
Disputes

Subject to Article 64(5), any dispute between two or more Contracting States concerning the interpretation or application of this Treaty or the Regulations, not settled by negotiation, may, by any one of the States concerned, be brought before the International Court of Justice by application in conformity with the Statute of the Court, unless the States concerned agree on some other method of settlement. The Contracting State bringing the dispute before the

Court shall inform the International Bureau; the International Bureau shall bring the matter to the attention of the other Contracting States.

Chapter VII
Revision and Amendment

Article 60
Revision of the Treaty

(1) This Treaty may be revised from time to time by a special conference of the Contracting States.

(2) The convocation of any revision conference shall be decided by the Assembly.

(3) Any intergovernmental organization appointed as International Searching or Preliminary Examining Authority shall be admitted as observer to any revision conference.

(4) Articles 53(5), (9) and (11), 54, 55 (4) to (8), 56, and 57, may be amended either by a revision conference or according to the provisions of Article 61.

Article 61
Amendment of Certain Provisions of the Treaty

(1)(a) Proposals for the amendment of Articles 53(5), (9) and (11), 54, 55(4) to (8), 56, and 57, may be initiated by any State member of the Assembly, by the Executive Committee, or by the Director General.

(b) Such proposals shall be communicated by the Director General to the Contracting States at least six months in advance of their consideration by the Assembly.

(2)(a) Amendments to the Articles referred to in paragraph (1) shall be adopted by the Assembly.

(b) Adoption shall require three-fourths of the votes cast.

(3)(a) Any amendment to the Articles referred to in paragraph (1) shall enter into force one month after written modifications of acceptance, effected in accordance with their respective constitutional processes, have been received by the Director General from three-fourths of the States members of the Assembly at the time it adopted the amendment.

(b) Any amendment to the said Articles thus accepted shall bind all the States which are members of the Assembly at the time the amendment enters into force, provided that any amendment increasing the financial obligations of the Contracting States shall bind only those States which have notified their acceptance of such amendment.

(c) Any amendment accepted in accordance with the provisions of subparagraph (a) shall bind all States which become members of the Assembly after the date on which the amendment entered into force in accordance with the provisions of subparagraph (a).

Chapter VIII
Final Provisions

Article 62
Becoming Party to the Treaty

(1) Any State member of the International Union for the Protection of Industrial Property may become party to this Treaty by:

(i) signature followed by the deposit of an instrument of ratification, or
(ii) deposit of an instrument of accession.

(2) Instruments of ratification or accession shall be deposited with the Director General.

(3) The provisions of Article 24 of the Stockholm Act of the Paris Convention for the Protection of Industrial Property shall apply to this Treaty.

(4) Paragraph (3) shall in no way be understood as implying the recognition or tacit acceptance by a Contracting State of the factual situation concerning a territory to which this Treaty is made applicable by another Contracting State by virtue of the said paragraph.

Article 63
Entry into Force of the Treaty

(1)(a) Subject to the provisions of paragraph (3), this Treaty shall enter into force three months after eight States have deposited their instruments of ratification or accession, provided that at least four of those States each fulfill any of the following conditions:

(i) the number of applications filed in the State has exceeded 40,000 according to the most recent annual statistics published by the International Bureau,

(ii) the nationals or residents of the State have filed at least 1,000 applications in one foreign country according to the most recent annual statistics published by the International Bureau,

(iii) the national Office of the State has received at least 10,000 applications from nationals or residents of foreign countries according to the most recent annual statistics published by the International Bureau.

(b) For the purposes of this paragraph, the term «applications» does not include applications for utility models.

(2) Subject to the provisions of paragraph (3), any State which does not become party to this Treaty upon entry into force under paragraph (1) shall become bound by this Treaty three months after the date on which such State has deposited its instrument of ratification or accession.

(3) The provisions of Chapter II and the corresponding provisions of the Regulations annexed to this Treaty shall become applicable, however, only on the date on which three States each of which fulfill at least one of the three requirements specified in paragraph (1) have become party to this Treaty without declaring, as provided in Article 64(1), that they do not intend to be bound by the provisions of Chapter II. That date shall not, however, be prior to that of the initial entry into force under paragraph (1).

Article 64
Reservations

(1)(a) Any State may declare that it shall not be bound by the provisions of Chapter II.

(b) States making a declaration under subparagraph (a) shall not be bound by the provisions of Chapter II and the corresponding provisions of the Regulations.

(2)(a) Any State not having made a declaration under paragraph (1)(a) may declare that:

(i) it shall not be bound by the provisions of Article 39(1) with respect to the furnishing of a copy of the international application and a translation thereof (as prescribed),

(ii) the obligation to delay national processing, as provided for under Article 40, shall not prevent publication, by or through its national Office, of the international application or a translation thereof, it being understood, however, that it is not exempted from the limitations provided for in Articles 30 and 38.

(b) States making such a declaration shall be bound accordingly.

(3)(a) Any State may declare that, as far as it is concerned, international publication of international applications is not required.

(b) Where, at the expiration of 18 months from the priority date, the international application contains the designation only of such States as have made declarations under subparagraph (a), the international application shall not be published by virtue of Article 21(2).

(c) Where the provisions of subparagraph (b) apply, the international application shall nevertheless be published by the International Bureau:

(i) at the request of the applicant, as provided in the Regulations,

(ii) when a national application or a patent based on the international application is published by or on behalf of the national Office of any designated State having made a declaration under subparagraph (a), promptly after such publication but not before the expiration of 18 months from the priority date.

(4)(a) Any State whose national law provides for prior art effect of its patents as from a date before publication, but does not equate for prior art purposes the priority date claimed under the Paris Convention for the Protection of Industrial Property to the actual filing date in that State, may declare that the filing outside that State of an international application designating that State is not equated to an actual filing in that State for prior art purposes.

(b) Any State making a declaration under subparagraph (a) shall to that extent not be bound by the provisions of Article 11(3).

(c) Any State making a declaration under subparagraph (a) shall, at the same time, state in writing the date from which, and the conditions under which, the prior art effect of any international application designating that State becomes effective in that State. This statement may be modified at any time by notification addressed to the Director General.

(5) Each State may declare that it does not consider itself bound by Article 59. With regard to any dispute between any Contracting State having made such a declaration and any other Contracting State, the provisions of Article 59 shall not apply.

(6)(a) Any declaration made under this Article shall be made in writing. It may be made at the time of signing this Treaty, at the time of depositing the instrument of ratification or accession, or, except in the case referred to in paragraph (5), at any later time by notification addressed to the Director General. In the case of the said notification, the declaration shall take effect six months after the day on which the Director General has received the notification, and shall not affect international applications filed prior to the expiration of the said six-month period.

(b) Any declaration made under this Article may be withdrawn at any time by notification addressed to the Director General. Such withdrawal shall take effect three months after the day on which the Director General has received the notification and, in the case of the withdrawal of a declaration made under paragraph (3), shall not affect international applications filed prior to the expiration of the said three-month period.

(7) No reservations to this Treaty other than the reservations under paragraphs (1) to (5) are permitted.

Article 65
Gradual Application

(1) If the agreement with any International Searching or Preliminary Examining Authority provides, transitionally, for limits on the number or kind of international applications that such Authority undertakes to process, the Assembly shall adopt the measures necessary for the gradual application of this Treaty and the Regulations in respect of given categories of international applications. This provision shall also apply to requests for an international-type search under Article 15(5).

(2) The Assembly shall fix the dates from which, subject to the provision of paragraph (1), international applications may be filed and demands for international preliminary examination may be submitted. Such dates shall not be later than six months after this Treaty has entered into force according to the provisions of Article 63(1), or after Chapter II has become applicable under Article 63(3), respectively.

Article 66
Denunciation

(1) Any Contracting State may denounce this Treaty by notification addressed to the Director General.

(2) Denunciation shall take effect six months after receipt of the said notification by the Director General. It shall not affect the effects of the international application in the denouncing State if the international application was filed, and, where the denouncing State has been elected, the election was made, prior to the expiration of the said six-month period.

Article 67
Signature and Languages

(1)(a) This Treaty shall be signed in a single original in the English and French languages, both texts being equally authentic.

(b) Official texts shall be established by the Director General after consultation with the interested Governments, in the German, Japanese, Portuguese, Russian and Spanish languages, and such other languages as the Assembly may designate.

(2) This Treaty shall remain open for signature at Washington until December 31, 1970.

Article 68
Depositary Functions

(1) The original of this Treaty, when no longer open for signature, shall be deposited with the Director General.

(2) The Director General shall transmit two copies, certified by him, of this Treaty and the Regulations annexed hereto to the Governments of all States party to the Paris Convention for the Protection of Industrial Property and, on request, to the Government of any other State.

(3) The Director General shall register this Treaty with the Secretariat of the United Nations.

(4) The Director General shall transmit two copies, certified by him, of any amendment to this Treaty and the Regulations to the Governments of all Contracting States and, on request, to the Government of any other State.

Article 69
Notifications

The Director General shall notify the Governments of all States party to the Paris Convention for the Protection of Industrial Property of:

(i) signatures under Article 62,

(ii) deposits of instruments of ratification or accession under Article 62,

(iii) the date of entry into force of this Treaty and the date from which Chapter II is applicable in accordance with Article 63(3),

(iv) any declarations made under Article 64(1) to (5),
(v) withdrawals of any declarations made under Article 64(6)(b),
(vi) denunciations received under Article 66, and
(vii) any declarations made under Article 31(4).

---

3. Budapest Treaty on the International Recognition of the Deposit of Microorganisms for the Purposes of Patent Procedure

Done at Budapest on April 28, 1977

The Budapest Treaty on the International Recognition of the Deposit of Microorganisms for the Purposes of Patent Procedure was concluded on April 28, 1977, and came into force in 1980.

This treaty was designed to solve the problems resulting from the lack of uniformity in national requirements for microorganism deposits. Fundamental to patent law is the requirement of a disclosure of an invention sufficient to enable one skilled in the field to reproduce it. Normally, this is done by a written disclosure, containing chemical formulas, drawings, etc. Microorganisms, however, present particularly difficult problems of disclosure because repeatability cannot always be assured by written disclosure alone.

To remedy this problem, the Treaty and its regulations provide for a series of international depository authorities (IDA), a depository institution located in a member country that has agreed to comply with certain requirements. These include the acceptance of the deposit, the period of storage, the right to redeposit, viability testing, secrecy, the furnishing of samples, and import/export restrictions (Arts. 5 and 6).

The Treaty requires that all contracting parties recognize the deposit in a single IDA (Art. 6 para. 1(a)). In addition, member countries must also recognize that the deposit was made on the indicated date and that any sample provided by an IDA is a sample of a microorganism deposited on that date (Art. 3 para. 1(a)). The Budapest Treaty is a special agreement under the Union of Paris and is administered by the International Bureau of WIPO.[1]

As of January 1, 1990, the following 24 countries were party to the Budapest Treaty:

Australia
Austria
Belgium
Bulgaria
Czechoslovakia
Denmark
Finland
France
German Democratic Republic
Federal Republic of Germany
Hungary
Italy
Japan
Liechtenstein
Netherlands
Norway
Philippines
Republic of Korea
Soviet Union
Spain
Sweden
Switzerland
United Kingdom
United States of America

[1]For regulations under the Budapest Treaty, *see* WORLD INTELLECTUAL PROPERTY ORGANIZATION, INDUSTRIAL PROPERTY Text No. 2-004, 1977/5 and 1981/4.

Budapest Treaty on the International Recognition of the Deposit of Microorganisms for the Purposes of Patent Procedure

Introductory Provisions

Article 1
Establishment of a Union

The States party to this Treaty (hereinafter called "the Contracting States") constitute a Union for the international recognition of the deposit of microorganisms for the purposes of patent procedure.

Article 2
Definitions

For the purposes of this Treaty and the Regulations:

(i) references to a "patent" shall be construed as references to patents for inventions, inventors' certificates, utility certificates, utility models, patents or certificates of addition, inventors' certificates of addition, and utility certificates of addition;

(ii) "deposit of a microorganism" means, according to the context in which these words appear, the following acts effected in accordance with this Treaty and the Regulations; the transmittal of a microorganism to an international depositary authority, which receives and accepts it, or the storage of such a microorganism by the international depositary authority, or both the said transmittal and the said storage;

(iii) "patent procedure" means any administrative or judicial procedure relating to a patent application or a patent;

(iv) "publication for the purposes of patent procedure" means the official publication, or the official laying open for public inspection, of a patent application or a patent;

(v) "intergovernmental industrial property organization" means an organization that has filed a declaration under Article 9(1);

(vi) "industrial property office" means an authority of a Con-

---

Source: Text courtesy of the World Intellectual Property Organization (WIPO).

tracting State or an intergovernmental industrial property organization competent for the grant of patents;

(vii) "depositary institution" means an institution which provides for the receipt, acceptance and storage of microorganisms and the furnishing of samples thereof;

(viii) "international depositary authority" means a depositary institution which has acquired the status of international depositary authority as provided in Article 7;

(ix) "depositor" means the natural person or legal entity transmitting a microorganism to an international depositary authority, which receives and accepts it, and any successor in title of the said natural person or legal entity;

(x) "Union" means the Union referred to in Article 1;

(xi) "Assembly" means the Assembly referred to in Article 10;

(xii) "Organization" means the World Intellectual Property Organization;

(xiii) "International Bureau" means the International Bureau of the Organization and, as long as it subsists, the United International Bureaux for the Protection of Intellectual Property (BIRPI);

(xiv) "Director General" means the Director General of the Organization;

(xv) "Regulations" means the Regulations referred to in Article 12.

Chapter I
Substantive Provisions

Article 3
Recognition and Effect of the Deposit of Microorganisms

(1)(*a*) Contracting States which allow or require the deposit of microorganisms for the purposes of patent procedure shall recognize, for such purposes, the deposit of a microorganism with any international depositary authority. Such recognition shall include the recognition of the fact and date of the deposit as indicated by the international depositary authority as well as the recognition of the fact that what is furnished as a sample is a sample of the deposited microorganism.

(*b*) Any Contracting State may require a copy of the receipt of the deposit referred to in subparagraph (*a*), issued by the international depositary authority.

(2) As far as matters regulated in this Treaty and the Regula-

tions are concerned, no Contracting State may require compliance with requirements different from or additional to those which are provided in this Treaty and the Regulations.

Article 4
New Deposit

(1)(*a*) Where the international depositary authority cannot furnish samples of the deposited microorganism for any reason, in particular,

(i) where such microorganism is no longer viable, or
(ii) where the furnishing of samples would require that they be sent abroad and the sending or the receipt of the samples abroad is prevented by export or import restrictions,

that authority shall, promptly after having noted its inability to furnish samples, notify the depositor of such inability, indicating the cause thereof, and the depositor, subject to paragraph (2) and as provided in this paragraph, shall have the right to make a new deposit of the microorganism which was originally deposited.

(*b*) The new deposit shall be made with the international depositary authority with which the original deposit was made, provided that:

(i) it shall be made with another international depositary authority where the institution with which the original deposit was made has ceased to have the status of international depositary authority, either entirely or in respect of the kind of microorganism to which the deposited microorganism belongs, or where the international depositary authority with which the original deposit was made discontinues, temporarily or definitively, the performance of its functions in respect of deposited microorganisms;

(ii) it may be made with another international depositary authority in the case referred to in subparagraph (*a*)(ii).

(*c*) Any new deposit shall be accompanied by a statement signed by the depositor alleging that the newly deposited microorganism is the same as that originally deposited. If the allegation of the depositor is contested, the burden of proof shall be governed by the applicable law.

(*d*) Subject to subparagraphs (*a*) to (*c*) and (*e*), the new deposit shall be treated as if it had been made on the date on which the original deposit was made where all the preceding statements concerning the viability of the originally deposited microorganism indicated that the microorganism was viable and where the new deposit was made within three months after the date on which the depositor received the notification referred to in subparagraph (*a*).

(*e*) Where subparagraph (*b*)(i) applies and the depositor does not receive the notification referred to in subparagraph (*a*) within six months after the date on which the termination, limitation or discontinuance referred to in subparagraph (*b*)(i) was published by the International Bureau, the three-month time limit referred to in subparagraph (*d*) shall be counted from the date of the said publication.

(2) The right referred to in paragraph (1)(*a*) shall not exist where the deposited microorganism has been transferred to another international depositary authority as long as that authority is in a position to furnish samples of such microorganism.

Article 5
Export and Import Restrictions

Each Contracting State recognizes that it is highly desirable that, if and to the extent to which the export from or import into its territory of certain kinds of microorganisms is restricted, such restriction should apply to microorganisms deposited, or destined for deposit, under this Treaty only where the restriction is necessary in view of national security or the dangers for health or the environment.

Article 6
Status of International Depositary Authority

(1) In order to qualify for the status of international depositary authority, any depositary institution must be located on the territory of a Contracting State and must benefit from assurances furnished by that State to the effect that the said institution complies and will continue to comply with the requirements specified in paragraph (2). The said assurances may be furnished also by an intergovernmental industrial property organization; in that case, the depositary institution must be located on the territory of a State member of the said organization.

(2) The depositary institution must, in its capacity of international depositary authority:

(i) have a continuous existence;

(ii) have the necessary staff and facilities, as prescribed in the Regulations, to perform its scientific and administrative tasks under this Treaty;

(iii) be impartial and objective;

(iv) be available, for the purposes of deposit, to any depositor under the same conditions;

(v) accept for deposit any or certain kinds of microorganisms, examine their viability and store them, as prescribed in the Regulations;

(vi) issue a receipt to the depositor, and any required viability statement, as prescribed in the Regulations;

(vii) comply, in respect of the deposited microorganisms, with the requirement of secrecy, as prescribed in the Regulations;

(viii) furnish samples of any deposited microorganism under the conditions and in conformity with the procedure prescribed in the Regulations.

(3) The Regulations shall provide the measures to be taken:

(i) where an international depositary authority discontinues, temporarily or definitively, the performance of its functions in respect of deposited microorganisms or refuses to accept any of the kinds of microorganisms which it should accept under the assurances furnished;

(ii) in case of the termination or limitation of the status of international depositary authority of an international depositary authority.

Article 7
Acquisition of the Status of International Depositary Authority

(1)(*a*) A depositary institution shall acquire the status of international depositary authority by virtue of a written communication addressed to the Director General by the Contracting State on the territory of which the depositary institution is located and including a declaration of assurances to the effect that the said institution complies and will continue to comply with the requirements specified in Article 6(2). The said status may be acquired also by virtue of a written communication addressed to the Director General by an intergovernmental industrial property organization and including the said declaration.

(*b*) The communication shall also contain information on the depositary institution as provided in the Regulations and may indicate the date on which the status of international depositary authority should take effect.

(2)(*a*) If the Director General finds that the communication includes the required declaration and that all the required information has been received, the communication shall be promptly published by the International Bureau.

(*b*) The status of international depositary authority shall be acquired as from the date of publication of the communication or, where a date has been indicated under paragraph (1)(*b*) and such date is later than the date of publication of the communication, as from such date.

(3) The details of the procedure under paragraphs (1) and (2) are provided in the Regulations.

Article 8
Termination and Limitation of the Status of International Depositary Authority

(1)(*a*) Any Contracting State or any intergovernmental industrial property organization may request the Assembly to terminate, or to limit to certain kinds of microorganisms, any authority's status of international depositary authority on the ground that the requirements specified in Article 6 have not been or are no longer complied with. However, such a request may not be made by a Contracting State or intergovernmental industrial property organization in respect of an international depositary authority for which it has made the declaration referred to in Article 7(1)(*a*).

(*b*) Before making the request under subparagraph (*a*), the Contracting State or the intergovernmental industrial property organization shall, through the intermediary of the Director General, notify the reasons for the proposed request to the Contracting State or the intergovernmental industrial property organization which has made the communication referred to in Article 7(1) so that that State or organization may, within six months from the date of the said notification, take appropriate action to obviate the need for making the proposed request.

(*c*) Where the Assembly finds that the request is well founded, it shall decide to terminate, or to limit to certain kinds of microorganisms, the status of international depositary authority of the authority referred to in subparagraph (*a*). The decision of the Assembly shall require that a majority of two-thirds of the votes cast be in favor of the request.

(2)(*a*) The Contracting State or intergovernmental industrial property organization having made the declaration referred to in Article 7(1)(*a*) may, by a communication addressed to the Director General, withdraw its declaration either entirely or in respect only of certain kinds of microorganisms and in any event shall do so when and to the extent that its assurances are no longer applicable.

(*b*) Such a communication shall, from the date provided for in the Regulations, entail, where it relates to the entire declaration, the termination of the status of international depositary authority or, where it relates only to certain kinds of microorganisms, a corresponding limitation of such status.

(3) The details of the procedure under paragraphs (1) and (2) are provided in the Regulations.

Article 9
Intergovernmental Industrial Property Organizations

(1)(*a*) Any intergovernmental organization to which several States have entrusted the task of granting regional patents and of which all the member States are members of the International (Paris) Union for the Protection of Industrial Property may file with the Director General a declaration that it accepts the obligation of recognition provided for in Article 3(1)(*a*), the obligation concerning the requirements referred to in Article 3(2) and all the effects of the provisions of this Treaty and the Regulations applicable to intergovernmental industrial property organizations. If filed before the entry into force of this Treaty according to Article 16(1), the declaration referred to in the preceding sentence shall become effective on the date of the said entry into force. If filed after such entry into force, the said declaration shall become effective three months after its filing unless a later date has been indicated in the declaration. In the latter case, the declaration shall take effect on the date thus indicated.

(*b*) The said organization shall have the right provided for in Article 3(1)(*b*).

(2) Where any provision of this Treaty or of the Regulations affecting intergovernmental industrial property organizations is revised or amended, any intergovernmental industrial property organization may withdraw its declaration referred to in paragraph (1) by notification addressed to the Director General. The withdrawal shall take effect:

(i) where the notification has been received before the date on which the revision or amendment enters into force, on that date;

(ii) where the notification has been received after the date referred to in (i), on the date indicated in the notification or, in the absence of such indication, three months after the date on which the notification was received.

(3) In addition to the case referred to in paragraph (2), any intergovernmental industrial property organization may withdraw its declaration referred to in paragraph (1)(*a*) by notification addressed to the Director General. The withdrawal shall take effect two years after the date on which the Director General has received

the notification. No notification of withdrawal under this paragraph shall be receivable during a period of five years from the date on which the declaration took effect.

(4) The withdrawal referred to in paragraph (2) or (3) by an intergovernmental industrial property organization whose communication under Article 7(1) has led to the acquisition of the status of international depositary authority by a depositary institution shall entail the termination of such status one year after the date on which the Director General has received the notification of withdrawal.

(5) Any declaration referred to in paragraph (1)(*a*), notification of withdrawal referred to in paragraph (2) or (3), assurances furnished under Article 6(1), second sentence, and included in a declaration made in accordance with Article 7(1)(*a*), request made under Article 8(1) and communication of withdrawal referred to in Article 8(2) shall require the express previous approval of the supreme governing organ of the intergovernmental industrial property organization whose members are all the States members of the said organization and in which decisions are made by the official representatives of the government of such States.

Chapter II
Administrative Provisions

Article 10
Assembly

(1)(*a*) The Assembly shall consist of the Contracting States.

(*b*) Each Contracting State shall be represented by one delegate, who may be assisted by alternate delegates, advisors, and experts.

(*c*) Each intergovernmental industrial property organization shall be represented by special observers in the meetings of the Assembly and any committee and working group established by the Assembly.

(*d*) Any State not member of the Union which is a member of the Organization or of the International (Paris) Union for the Protection of Industrial Property and any intergovernmental organization specialized in the field of patents other than an intergovernmental industrial property organization as defined in Article 2(v) may be represented by observers in the meetings of the Assembly and, if the Assembly so decides, in the meetings of any committee or working group established by the Assembly.

(2)(*a*) The Assembly shall:

(i) deal with all matters concerning the maintenance and development of the Union and the implementation of this Treaty;

(ii) exercise such rights and perform such tasks as are specially conferred upon it or assigned to it under this Treaty;

(iii) give directions to the Director General concerning the preparations for revision conferences;

(iv) review and approve the reports and activities of the Director General concerning the Union, and give him all necessary instructions concerning matters within the competence of the Union;

(v) establish such committees and working groups as it deems appropriate to facilitate the work of the Union;

(vi) determine, subject to paragraph (1)(*d*), which States other than Contracting States, which intergovernmental organizations other than intergovernmental industrial property organizations as defined in Article 2(v) and which international non-governmental organizations shall be admitted to its meetings as observers and to what extent international depositary authorities shall be admitted to its meetings as observers;

(vii) take any other appropriate action designed to further the objectives of the Union;

(viii) perform such other functions as are appropriate under this Treaty.

(*b*) With respect to matters which are of interest also to other Unions administered by the Organization, the Assembly shall make its decisions after having heard the advice of the Coordination Committee of the Organization.

(3) A delegate may represent, and vote in the name of, one State only.

(4) Each Contracting State shall have one vote.

(5)(*a*) One-half of the Contracting States shall constitute a quorum.

(*b*) In the absence of the quorum, the Assembly may make decisions but, with the exception of decisions concerning its own procedure, all such decisions shall take effect only if the quorum and the required majority are attained through voting by correspondence as provided in the Regulations.

(6)(*a*) Subject to Articles 8(1)(*c*), 12(4) and 14(2)(*b*), the decisions of the Assembly shall require a majority of the votes cast.

(*b*) Abstentions shall not be considered as votes.

(7)(*a*) The Assembly shall meet once in every third calendar year in ordinary session upon convocation by the Director General, preferably during the same period and at the same place as the General Assembly of the Organization.

(*b*) The Assembly shall meet in extraordinary session upon convocation by the Director General, either on his own initiative or at the request of one-fourth of the Contracting States.

(8) The Assembly shall adopt its own rules of procedure.

Article 11
International Bureau

(1) The International Bureau shall:

(i) perform the administrative tasks concerning the Union, in particular such tasks as are specifically assigned to it under this Treaty and the Regulations or by the Assembly;

(ii) provide the secretariat of revision conferences, of the Assembly, of committees and working groups established by the Assembly, and of any other meeting convened by the Director General and dealing with matters of concern to the Union.

(2) The Director General shall be the chief executive of the Union and shall represent the Union.

(3) The Director General shall convene all meetings dealing with matters of concern to the Union.

(4)(*a*) The Director General and any staff member designated by him shall participate, without the right to vote, in all meetings of the Assembly, the committees and working groups established by the Assembly, and any other meeting convened by the Director General and dealing with matters of concern to the Union.

(*b*) The Director General, or a staff member designated by him, shall be ex officio secretary of the Assembly, and of the committees, working groups and other meetings referred to in subparagraph (*a*).

(5)(*a*) The Director General shall, in accordance with the directions of the Assembly, make the preparations for revision conferences.

(*b*) The Director General may consult with intergovernmental and international non-governmental organizations concerning the preparations for revision conferences.

(*c*) The Director General and persons designated by him shall take part, without the right to vote, in the discussions at revision conferences.

(*d*) The Director General, or a staff member designated by him, shall be ex officio secretary of any revision conference.

Article 12
Regulations

(1) The Regulations provide rules concerning:

(i) matters in respect of which this Treaty expressly refers to the Regulations or expressly provides that they are or shall be prescribed;

(ii) any administrative requirements, matters or procedures;

(iii) any details useful in the implementation of this Treaty.

(2) The Regulations adopted at the same time as this Treaty are annexed to this Treaty.

(3) The Assembly may amend the Regulations.

(4)(*a*) Subject to subparagraph (*b*), adoption of any amendment of the Regulations shall require two-thirds of the votes cast.

(*b*) Adoption of any amendment concerning the furnishing of samples of deposited microorganisms by the international depositary authorities shall require that no Contracting State vote against the proposed amendment.

(5) In the case of conflict between the provisions of this Treaty and those of the Regulations, the provisions of this Treaty shall prevail.

Chapter III
Revision and Amendment

Article 13
Revision of the Treaty

(1) This Treaty may be revised from time to time by conferences of the Contracting States.

(2) The convocation of any revision conference shall be decided by the Assembly.

(3) Articles 10 and 11 may be amended either by a revision conference or according to Article 14.

Article 14
Amendment of Certain Provisions of the Treaty

(1)(*a*) Proposals under this Article for the amendment of Articles 10 and 11 may be initiated by any Contracting State or by the Director General.

(*b*) Such proposals shall be communicated by the Director General to the Contracting States at least six months in advance of their consideration by the Assembly.

(2)(*a*) Amendments to the Articles referred to in paragraph (1) shall be adopted by the Assembly.

(*b*) Adoption of any amendment to Article 10 shall require four-fifths of the votes cast; adoption of any amendment to Article 11 shall require three-fourths of the votes cast.

(3)(*a*) Any amendment to the Articles referred to in paragraph (1) shall enter into force one month after written notifications of acceptance, effected in accordance with their respective constitutional processes, have been received by the Director General from three-fourths of the Contracting States members of the Assembly at the time the Assembly adopted the amendment.

(*b*) Any amendment to the said Articles thus accepted shall bind all the Contracting States which were Contracting States at the time the amendment was adopted by the Assembly, provided that any amendment creating financial obligations for the said Contracting States or increasing such obligations shall bind only those Contracting States which have notified their acceptance of such amendment.

(*c*) Any amendment which has been accepted and which has entered into force in accordance with subparagraph (*a*) shall bind all States which become Contracting States after the date on which the amendment was adopted by the Assembly.

Chapter IV
Final Provisions

Article 15
Becoming Party to the Treaty

(1) Any State member of the International (Paris) Union for the Protection of Industrial Property may become party to this Treaty by:

(i) signature followed by the deposit of an instrument of ratification, or

(ii) deposit of an instrument of accession.

(2) Instruments of ratification or accession shall be deposited with the Director General.

Article 16
Entry Into Force of the Treaty

(1) This Treaty shall enter into force, with respect to the first five States which have deposited their instruments of ratification or accession, three months after the date on which the fifth instrument of ratification or accession has been deposited.

(2) This Treaty shall enter into force with respect to any other State three months after the date on which that State has deposited its instrument of ratification or accession unless a later date has been indicated in the instrument of ratification or accession. In the latter case, this Treaty shall enter into force with respect to that State on the date thus indicated.

Article 17
Denunciation of the Treaty

(1) Any Contracting State may denounce this Treaty by notification addressed to the Director General.

(2) Denunciation shall take effect two years after the day on which the Director General has received the notification.

(3) The right of denunciation provided for in paragraph (1) shall not be exercised by any Contracting State before the expiration of five years from the date on which it becomes party to this Treaty.

(4) The denunciation of this Treaty by a Contracting State that has made a declaration referred to in Article 7(1)(*a*) with respect to a depositary institution which thus acquired the status of international depositary authority shall entail the termination of such status one year after the day on which the Director General received the notification referred to in paragraph (1).

Article 18
Signature and Languages of the Treaty

(1)(*a*) This Treaty shall be signed in a single original in the English and French languages, both texts being equally authentic.

(*b*) Official texts of this Treaty shall be established by the Director General, after consultation with the interested Governments and within two months from the date of signature of this Treaty, in the other languages in which the Convention Establishing the World Intellectual Property Organization was signed.

(*c*) Official texts of this Treaty shall be established by the Director General, after consultation with the interested Governments, in the Arabic, German, Italian, Japanese and Portuguese languages, and such other languages as the Assembly may designate.

(2) This Treaty shall remain open for signature at Budapest until December 31, 1977.

Article 19
Deposit of the Treaty; Transmittal of Copies; Registration of the Treaty

(1) The original of this Treaty, when no longer open for signature, shall be deposited with the Director General.

(2) The Director General shall transmit two copies, certified by him, of this Treaty and the Regulations to the Governments of all

the States referred to in Article 15(1), to the intergovernmental organizations that may file a declaration under Article 9(1)(*a*) and, on request, to the Government of any other State.

(3) The Director General shall register this Treaty with the Secretariat of the United Nations.

(4) The Director General shall transmit two copies, certified by him, of any amendment to this Treaty and to the Regulations to all Contracting States, to all intergovernmental industrial property organizations and, on request, to the Government of any other State and to any other intergovernmental organization that may file a declaration under Article 9(1)(*a*).

Article 20
Notifications

The Director General shall notify the Contracting States, the intergovernmental industrial property organizations and those States not members of the Union which are members of the International (Paris) Union for the Protection of Industrial Property of:

(i) signatures under Article 18;

(ii) deposits of instruments of ratification or accession under Article 15(2);

(iii) declarations filed under Article 9(1)(*a*) and notifications of withdrawal under Article 9(2) or (3);

(iv) the date of entry into force of this Treaty under Article 16(1);

(v) the communications under Articles 7 and 8 and the decisions under Article 8;

(vi) acceptance of amendments to this Treaty under Article 14(3);

(vii) any amendment of the Regulations;

(viii) the dates on which amendments to the Treaty or the Regulations enter into force;

(ix) denunciations received under Article 17.

4. European Patent Convention (With Protocols)

October 5, 1973, as amended December 21, 1978, and Protocol on Jurisdiction and the Recognition of Decision in Respect of the Right to the Grant of a European Patent (Protocol on Recognition of October 5, 1973) and Protocol on the Centralisation of the European Patent System and on Its Introduction (Protocol on Centralisation of October 5, 1973)

The European Patent Convention (EPC) was signed on October 5, 1973, and came into force on October 7, 1977. Accession to the treaty is limited to European countries that either participated in the preparation of the treaty or that are recommended by the Administrative Council.

The Convention takes a first but significant step in unifying patent law within the European Community. It does so by establishing uniform rules as to the *issuance* (but not as to the enforcement) of patents among the member states.

The European Patent creates two administrative bodies: the Administrative Council and the European Patent Office. The Council (Arts. 26-36) is composed of representatives from the member states and oversees the European Patent Office (Art. 4). Both organizations are located in Munich with a branch office in the Hague (Art. 6).

The Convention establishes uniform standards for the granting of patents in the member countries. It sets up a uniform procedure (Arts. 90-98) for granting a patent as well as substantive rules regarding the criteria for patentability (Arts. 50-57), duration (Art. 63), conversion to national patents

(Arts. 135-137), the extent of protection, and grounds for invalidity.

To obtain a European Patent, an applicant may submit its application to the European Patent Office and must specify the countries in which protection is requested (Arts. 75-86). After the application is processed, the European Patent Office issues a patent that has national force in the designated member states (Art. 64). Once issued, national law applies and such matters as maintenance fees, licensing provisions, working requirements, and infringement are governed by the law of the member state. The Convention, however, sets forth the specific grounds for revocation and invalidation.

A European patent is separately valid in each country. Thus, invalidation in one country, e.g., France, does not automatically invalidate the patent in another, e.g., Italy.

The EPC should not be confused with a *proposed* treaty, the Common Market Patent Convention,[1] concluded in Luxembourg on December 15, 1975. Unlike the EPC, which creates a bundle of national rights, the Common Market Patent Convention would create a truly transnational patent which would have the same effect in all member states and which could only be transferred or invalidated as a whole. As of January 1, 1990, the Common Market Patent Convention had not entered into force.

As of January 1, 1990, the following 13 states were party to the European Patent Convention:

Austria	Liechtenstein
Belgium	Luxembourg
France	Netherlands
Federal Republic of Germany	Spain
Greece	Sweden
Italy	Switzerland
	United Kingdom

[1]For the text of this Convention, *see* 19 (L.17) OFFICIAL J. EUR. COMMUNITIES (1976).

European Patent Convention

Part I
General and Institutional Provisions

Chapter I
General provisions
Article 1
European law for the grant of patents

A system of law, common to the Contracting States, for the grant of patents for invention is hereby established.

Article 2
European patent

(1) Patents granted by virtue of this Convention shall be called European patents.

(2) The European patent shall, in each of the Contracting States for which it is granted, have the effect of and be subject to the same conditions as a national patent granted by that State, unless otherwise provided in this Convention.

Article 3
Territorial effect

The grant of a European patent may be requested for one or more of the Contracting States.

Source: Text courtesy of the World Intellectual Property Organization (WIPO). Reprinted with permission of the European Patent Office from *European Patent Convention* (2d ed.), EPO, Munich, June 1981.

Article 4
European Patent Organisation

(1) A European Patent Organisation, hereinafter referred to as the Organisation, is established by this Convention. It shall have administrative and financial autonomy.

(2) The organs of the Organisation shall be:

(a) a European Patent Office;

(b) an Administrative Council.

(3) The task of the Organisation shall be to grant European patents. This shall be carried out by the European Patent Office supervised by the Administrative Council.

Chapter II
The European Patent Organisation

Article 5
Legal status

(1) The Organisation shall have legal personality.

(2) In each of the Contracting States, the Organisation shall enjoy the most extensive legal capacity accorded to legal persons under the national law of that State; it may in particular acquire or dispose of movable and immovable property and may be a party to legal proceedings.

(3) The President of the European Patent Office shall represent the Organisation.

Article 6
Seat

(1) The Organisation shall have its seat at Munich.

(2) The European Patent Office shall be set up at Munich. It shall have a branch at The Hague.

Article 7
Sub-offices of the European Patent Office

By decision of the Administrative Council, sub-offices of the European Patent Office may be created if need be, for the purpose of information and liaison, in the Contracting States and with intergovernmental organisations in the field of industrial property, subject to the approval of the Contracting State or organisation concerned.

Article 8
Privileges and immunities

The Protocol on Privileges and Immunities annexed to this Convention shall define the conditions under which the Organisation, the members of the Administrative Council, the employees of the European Patent Office and such other persons specified in that Protocol as take part in the work of the Organisation, shall enjoy, in the territory of each Contracting State, the privileges and immunities necessary for the performance of their duties.

Article 9
Liability

(1) The contractual liability of the Organisation shall be governed by the law applicable to the relevant contract.

(2) The non-contractual liability of the Organisation in respect of any damage caused by it or by the employees of the European Patent Office in the performance of their duties shall be governed by the provisions of the law of the Federal Republic of Germany. Where the damage is caused by the branch at The Hague or a sub-office or employees attached thereto, the provisions of the law of the Contracting State in which such branch or sub-office is located shall apply.

(3) The personal liability of the employees of the European Patent Office towards the Organisation shall be laid down in their Service Regulations or conditions of employment.

(4) The courts with jurisdiction to settle disputes under paragraphs 1 and 2 shall be:

(a) for disputes under paragraph 1, the courts of competent jurisdiction in the Federal Republic of Germany, unless the contract concluded between the parties designates the courts of another State;

(b) for disputes under paragraph 2, either the courts of competent jurisdiction in the Federal Republic of Germany, or the courts of competent jurisdiction in the State in which the branch or sub-office is located.

Chapter III
The European Patent Office
Article 10
Direction

(1) The European Patent Office shall be directed by the President who shall be responsible for its activities to the Administrative Council.

(2) To this end, the President shall have in particular the following functions and powers:

(a) he shall take all necessary steps, including the adoption of internal administrative instructions and the publication of guidance for the public, to ensure the functioning of the European Patent Office;

(b) in so far as this Convention contains no provisions in this respect, he shall prescribe which transactions are to be carried out at the European Patent Office at Munich and its branch at The Hague respectively;

(c) he may place before the Administrative Council any proposal for amending this Convention and any proposal for general regulations or decisions which come within the competence of the Administrative Council;

(d) he shall prepare and implement the budget and any amending or supplementary budget;

(e) he shall submit a management report to the Administrative Council each year;

(f) he shall exercise supervisory authority over the personnel;

(g) subject to the provisions of Article 11, he shall appoint and promote the employees;

(h) he shall exercise disciplinary authority over the employees other than those referred to in Article 11, and may propose disciplinary action to the Administrative Council with regard to employees referred to in Article 11, paragraphs 2 and 3;

(i) he may delegate his functions and powers.

(3) The President shall be assisted by a number of Vice-Presidents. If the President is absent or indisposed, one of the Vice-Presidents shall take his place in accordance with the procedure laid down by the Administrative Council.

Article 11
Appointment of senior employees

(1) The President of the European Patent Office shall be appointed by decision of the Administrative Council.

(2) The Vice-Presidents shall be appointed by decision of the Administrative Council after the President has been consulted.

(3) The members, including the Chairmen, of the Boards of Appeal and of the Enlarged Board of Appeal shall be appointed by decision of the Administrative Council, taken on a proposal from the President of the European Patent Office. They may be re-appointed by decision of the Administrative Council after the President of the European Patent Office has been consulted.

(4) The Administrative Council shall exercise disciplinary authority over the employees referred to in paragraphs 1 to 3.

Article 12
Duties of office

The employees of the European Patent Office shall be bound, even after the termination of their employment, neither to disclose nor to make use of information which by its nature is a professional secret.

Article 13
Disputes between the Organisation and the employees of the European Patent Office

(1) Employees and former employees of the European Patent Office or their successors in title may apply to the Administrative Tribunal of the International Labour Organisation in the case of disputes with the European Patent Organisation in accordance with the Statute of the Tribunal and within the limits and subject to the conditions laid down in the Service Regulations for permanent employees or the Pension Scheme Regulations or arising from the conditions of employment of other employees.

(2) An appeal shall only be admissible if the person concerned has exhausted such other means of appeal as are available to him under the Service Regulations, the Pension Scheme Regulations or the conditions of employment, as the case may be.

Article 14
Languages of the European Patent Office

(1) The official languages of the European Patent Office shall be English, French and German. European patent applications must be filed in one of these languages.

(2) However, natural or legal persons having their residence or principal place of business within the territory of a Contracting State having a language other than English, French or German as an

official language, and nationals of that State who are resident abroad, may file European patent applications in an official language of that State. Nevertheless, a translation in one of the official languages of the European Patent Office must be filed within the time limit prescribed in the Implementing Regulations; throughout the proceedings before the European Patent Office, such translation may be brought into conformity with the original text of the application.

(3) The official language of the European Patent Office in which the European patent application is filed or, in the case referred to in paragraph 2, that of the translation, shall be used as the language of the proceedings in all proceedings before the European Patent Office concerning the application or the resulting patent, unless otherwise provided in the Implementing Regulations.

(4) The persons referred to in paragraph 2 may also file documents which have to be filed within a time limit in an official language of the Contracting State concerned. They must however file a translation in the language of the proceedings within the time limit prescribed in the Implementing Regulations; in the cases provided for in the Implementing Regulations, they may file a translation in a different official language of the European Patent Office.

(5) If any document, other than those making up the European patent application, is not filed in the language prescribed by this Convention, or if any translation required by virtue of this Convention is not filed in due time, the document shall be deemed not to have been received.

(6) European patent applications shall be published in the language of the proceedings.

(7) The specifications of European patents shall be published in the language of the proceedings; they shall include a translation of the claims in the two other official languages of the European Patent Office.

(8) There shall be published in the three official languages of the European Patent Office:

(a) the European Patent Bulletin;

(b) the Official Journal of the European Patent Office.

(9) Entries in the Register of European Patents shall be made in the three official languages of the European Patent Office. In cases of doubt, the entry in the language of the proceedings shall be authentic.

Article 15
The departments charged with the procedure

For implementing the procedures laid down in this Convention, there shall be set up within the European Patent Office:

(a) a Receiving Section;

(b) Search Divisions;
(c) Examining Divisions;
(d) Opposition Divisions;
(e) a Legal Division;
(f) Boards of Appeal;
(g) an Enlarged Board of Appeal.

Article 16
Receiving Section

The Receiving Section shall be in the branch at The Hague. It shall be responsible for the examination on filing and the examination as to formal requirements of each European patent application up to the time when a request for examination has been made or the applicant has indicated under Article 96, paragraph 1, that he desires to proceed further with his application. It shall also be responsible for the publication of the European patent application and of the European search report.

Article 17
Search Divisions

The Search Divisions shall be in the branch at The Hague. They shall be responsible for drawing up European search reports.

Article 18
Examining Divisions

(1) An Examining Division shall be responsible for the examination of each European patent application from the time when the Receiving Section ceases to be responsible.

(2) An Examining Division shall consist of three technical examiners. Nevertheless, the examination prior to a final decision shall, as a general rule, be entrusted to one member of the Division. Oral proceedings shall be before the Examining Division itself. If the Examining Division considers that the nature of the decision so requires, it shall be enlarged by the addition of a legally qualified examiner. In the event of parity of votes, the vote of the Chairman of the Division shall be decisive.

Article 19
Opposition Divisions

(1) An Opposition Division shall be responsible for the examination of oppositions against any European patent.

(2) An Opposition Division shall consist of three technical examiners, at least two of whom shall not have taken part in the proceedings for grant of the patent to which the opposition relates. An examiner who has taken part in the proceedings for the grant of the European patent shall not be the Chairman. Prior to the taking of a final decision on the opposition, the Opposition Division may entrust the examination of the opposition to one of its members. Oral proceedings shall be before the Opposition Division itself. If the Opposition Division considers that the nature of the decision so requires, it shall be enlarged by the addition of a legally qualified examiner who shall not have taken part in the proceedings for grant of the patent. In the event of parity of votes, the vote of the Chairman of the Division shall be decisive.

Article 20
Legal Division

(1) The Legal Division shall be responsible for decisions in respect of entries in the Register of European Patents and in respect of registration on, and deletion from, the list of professional representatives.

(2) Decisions of the Legal Division shall be taken by one legally qualified member.

Article 21
Boards of Appeal

(1) The Boards of Appeal shall be responsible for the examination of appeals from the decisions of the Receiving Section, Examining Divisions, Opposition Divisions and of the Legal Division.

(2) For appeals from a decision of the Receiving Section or the Legal Division, a Board of Appeal shall consist of three legally qualified members.

(3) For appeals from a decision of an Examining Division, a Board of Appeal shall consist of:

(a) two technically qualified members and one legally qualified member, when the decision concerns the refusal of a European patent application or the grant of a European patent and was taken by an Examining Division consisting of less than four members;

(b) three technically qualified members and two legally qualified members, when the decision was taken by an Examining Division consisting of four members or when the Board of Appeal considers that the nature of the appeal so requires;

(c) three legally qualified members in all other cases.

(4) For appeals from a decision of an Opposition Division, a Board of Appeal shall consist of:

(a) two technically qualified members and one legally qualified member, when the decision was taken by an Opposition Division consisting of three members;

(b) three technically qualified members and two legally qualified members, when the decision was taken by an Opposition Division consisting of four members or when the Board of Appeal considers that the nature of the appeal so requires.

Article 22
Enlarged Board of Appeal

(1) The Enlarged Board of Appeal shall be responsible for:

(a) deciding points of law referred to it by Boards of Appeal;

(b) giving opinions on points of law referred to it by the President of the European Patent Office under the conditions laid down in Article 112.

(2) For giving decisions or opinions, the Enlarged Board of Appeal shall consist of five legally qualified members and two technically qualified members. One of the legally qualified members shall be the Chairman.

Article 23
Independence of the members of the Boards

(1) The members of the Enlarged Board of Appeal and of the Boards of Appeal shall be appointed for a term of five years and may not be removed from office during this term, except if there are serious grounds for such removal and if the Administrative Council, on a proposal from the Enlarged Board of Appeal, takes a decision to this effect.

(2) The members of the Boards may not be members of the Receiving Section, Examining Divisions, Opposition Divisions or of the Legal Division.

(3) In their decisions the members of the Boards shall not be

bound by any instructions and shall comply only with the provisions of this Convention.

(4)* The Rules of Procedure of the Boards of Appeal and the Enlarged Board of Appeal shall be adopted in accordance with the provisions of the Implementing Regulations. They shall be subject to the approval of the Administrative Council.

Article 24
Exclusion and objection

(1) Members of the Boards of Appeal or of the Enlarged Board of Appeal may not take part in any appeal if they have any personal interest therein, if they have previously been involved as representatives of one of the parties, or if they participated in the decision under appeal.

(2) If, for one of the reasons mentioned in paragraph 1, or for any other reason, a member of a Board of Appeal or of the Enlarged Board of Appeal considers that he should not take part in any appeal, he shall inform the Board accordingly.

(3) Members of a Board of Appeal or of the Enlarged Board of Appeal may be objected to by any party for one of the reasons mentioned in paragraph 1, or if suspected of partiality. An objection shall not be admissible if, while being aware of a reason for objection, the party has taken a procedural step. No objection may be based upon the nationality of members.

(4) The Boards of Appeal and the Enlarged Board of Appeal shall decide as to the action to be taken in the cases specified in paragraphs 2 and 3 without the participation of the member concerned. For the purposes of taking this decision the member objected to shall be replaced by his alternate.

Article 25
Technical opinion

At the request of the competent national court trying an infringement or revocation action, the European Patent Office shall be obliged, against payment of an appropriate fee, to give a technical

---

* See the Rules of Procedure of the Boards of Appeal of June 4, 1980, which entered into force on June 6, 1980 (OFFICIAL JOURNAL OF THE EUROPEAN PATENT OFFICE 7/80, p. 171 *et seq.*).

opinion concerning the European patent which is the subject of the action. The Examining Divisions shall be responsible for the issue of such opinions.

Chapter IV
The Administrative Council
Article 26
Membership

(1) The Administrative Council shall be composed of the Representatives and the alternate Representatives of the Contracting States. Each Contracting State shall be entitled to appoint one Representative and one alternate Representative to the Administrative Council.

(2) The members of the Administrative Council may, subject to the provisions of its Rules of Procedure, be assisted by advisers or experts.

Article 27
Chairmanship

(1) The Administrative Council shall elect a Chairman and a Deputy Chairman from among the Representatives and alternate Representatives of the Contracting States. The Deputy Chairman shall ex officio replace the Chairman in the event of his being prevented from attending to his duties.

(2) The duration of the terms of office of the Chairman and the Deputy Chairman shall be three years. The terms of office shall be renewable.

Article 28
Board

(1) When there are at least eight Contracting States, the Administrative Council may set up a Board composed of five of its members.

(2) The Chairman and the Deputy Chairman of the Administrative Council shall be members of the Board ex officio; the other three members shall be elected by the Administrative Council.

(3) The term of office of the members elected by the Administra-

tive Council shall be three years. This term of office shall not be renewable.

(4) The Board shall perform the duties given to it by the Administrative Council in accordance with the Rules of Procedure.

Article 29
Meetings

(1) Meetings of the Administrative Council shall be convened by its Chairman.

(2) The President of the European Patent Office shall take part in the deliberations of the Administrative Council.

(3) The Administrative Council shall hold an ordinary meeting once each year. In addition, it shall meet on the initiative of its Chairman or at the request of one-third of the Contracting States.

(4) The deliberations of the Administrative Council shall be based on an agenda, and shall be held in accordance with its Rules of Procedure.

(5) The provisional agenda shall contain any question whose inclusion is requested by any Contracting State in accordance with the Rules of Procedure.

Article 30
Attendance of observers

(1) The World Intellectual Property Organization shall be represented at the meetings of the Administrative Council, in accordance with the provisions of an agreement to be concluded between the European Patent Organisation and the World Intellectual Property Organization.

(2) Any other inter-governmental organisation charged with the implementation of international procedures in the field of patents with which the Organisation has concluded an agreement shall be represented at the meetings of the Administrative Council in accordance with any provisions contained in such agreement.

(3) Any other inter-governmental and international non-governmental organisations exercising an activity of interest to the Organisation may be invited by the Administrative Council to arrange to be represented at its meetings during any discussion of matters of mutual interest.

Article 31
Languages of the Administrative Council

(1) The languages in use in the deliberations of the Administrative Council shall be English, French and German.

(2) Documents submitted to the Administrative Council, and the minutes of its deliberations, shall be drawn up in the three languages mentioned in paragraph 1.

Article 32
Staff, premises and equipment

The European Patent Office shall place at the disposal of the Administrative Council and any body established by it such staff, premises and equipment as may be necessary for the performance of their duties.

Article 33
Competence of the Administrative Council in certain cases

(1) The Administrative Council shall be competent to amend the following provisions of this Convention:

(a) the time limits laid down in this Convention; this shall apply to the time limit laid down in Article 94 only in the conditions laid down in Article 95;

(b) the Implementing Regulations.

(2) The Administrative Council shall be competent, in conformity with this Convention, to adopt or amend the following provisions;

(a) the Financial Regulations;

(b) the Service Regulations for permanent employees and the conditions of employment of other employees of the European Patent Office, the salary scales of the said permanent and other employees, and also the nature, and rules for the grant, of any supplementary benefits;

(c) the Pension Scheme Regulations and any appropriate increases in existing pensions to correspond to increases in salaries;

(d) the Rules relating to Fees;

(e) its Rules of Procedure.

(3) Notwithstanding Article 18, paragraph 2, the Administrative Council shall be competent to decide, in the light of experience,

that in certain categories of cases Examining Divisions shall consist of one technical examiner. Such decision may be rescinded.

(4) The Administrative Council shall be competent to authorise the President of the European Patent Office to negotiate and, with its approval, to conclude agreements on behalf of the European Patent Organisation with States, with inter-governmental organisations and with documentation centres set up by virtue of agreements with such organisation.

Article 34
Voting rights

(1) The right to vote in the Administrative Council shall be restricted to the Contracting States.

(2) Each Contracting State shall have one vote, subject to the application of the provisions of Article 36.

Article 35
Voting rules

(1) The Administrative Council shall take its decisions other than those referred to in paragraph 2 by a simple majority of the Contracting States represented and voting.

(2) A majority of three-quarters of the votes of the Contracting States represented and voting shall be required for the decisions which the Administrative Council is empowered to take under Article 7, Article 11, paragraph 1, Article 33, Article 39, paragraph 1, Article 40, paragraphs 2 and 4, Article 46, Article 87, Article 95, Article 134, Article 151, paragraph 3, Article 154, paragraph 2, Article 155, paragraph 2, Article 156, Article 157, paragraphs 2 to 4, Article 150, paragraph 1, second sentence, Article 162, Article 163, Article 166, Article 167 and Article 172.

(3) Abstentions shall not be considered as votes.

Article 36
Weighting of votes

(1) In respect of the adoption or amendment of the Rules relating to Fees and, if the financial contribution to be made by the Contracting States would thereby be increased, the adoption of the budget of the Organisation and of any amending or supplementary budget,

any Contracting State may require, following a first ballot in which each Contracting State shall have one vote, and whatever the result of this ballot, that a second ballot be taken immediately, in which votes shall be given to the States in accordance with paragraph 2. The decision shall be determined by the result of this second ballot.

(2) The number of votes that each Contracting State shall have in the second ballot shall be calculated as follows:

(a) the percentage obtained for each Contracting State in respect of the scale for the special financial contributions, pursuant to Article 40, paragraphs 3 and 4, shall be multiplied by the number of Contracting States and divided by five;

(b) the number of votes thus given shall be rounded upwards to the next higher whole number;

(c) five additional votes shall be added to this number;

(d) nevertheless no Contracting State shall have more than 30 votes.

Chapter V
Financial provisions
Article 37
Cover for expenditure

The expenditure of the Organisation shall be covered:

(a) by the Organisation's own resources;

(b) by payments made by the Contracting States in respect of renewal fees for European patents levied in these States;

(c) where necessary, by special financial contributions made by the Contracting States;

(d) where appropriate, by the revenue provided for in Article 146.

Article 38
The Organisation's own resources

The Organisation's own resources shall be the yield from the fees laid down in this Convention, and also all receipts, whatever their nature.

Article 39

Payments by the Contracting States in respect of renewal fees for European patents

(1) Each Contracting State shall pay to the Organisation in respect of each renewal fee received for a European patent in that State an amount equal to a proportion of that fee, to be fixed by the Administrative Council; the proportion shall not exceed 75 per cent and shall be the same for all Contracting States. However, if the said proportion corresponds to an amount which is less than a uniform minimum amount fixed by the Administrative Council, the Contracting State shall pay that minimum to the Organisation.

(2) Each Contracting State shall communicate to the Organisation such information as the Administrative Council considers to be necessary to determine the amount of its payments.

(3) The due dates for these payments shall be determined by the Administrative Council.

(4) If a payment is not remitted fully by the due date, the Contracting State shall pay interest from the due date on the amount remaining unpaid.

Article 40

Level of fees and payments— Special financial contributions

(1) The amounts of the fees referred to under Article 38 and the proportion referred to under Article 39 shall be fixed at such a level as to ensure that the revenue in respect thereof is sufficient for the budget of the Organisation to be balanced.

(2) However, if the Organisation is unable to balance its budget under the conditions laid down in paragraph 1, the Contracting States shall remit to the Organisation special financial contributions, the amount of which shall be determined by the Administrative Council for the accounting period in question.

(3) These special financial contributions shall be determined in respect of any Contracting State on the basis of the number of patent applications filed in the last year but one prior to that of entry into force of this Convention, and calculated in the following manner:

(a) one half in proportion to the number of patent applications filed in that Contracting State;

(b) one half in proportion to the second highest number of patent applications filed in the other Contracting States by natural or legal persons having their residence or principal place of business in that Contracting State.

However, the amounts to be contributed by States in which the number of patent applications filed exceeds 25,000 shall then be taken as a whole and a new scale drawn up determined in proportion to the total number of patent applications filed in these States.

(4) Where, in respect of any Contracting State, its scale position cannot be established in accordance with paragraph 3, the Administrative Council shall, with the consent of that State, decide its scale position.

(5) Article 39, paragraphs 3 and 4, shall apply *mutatis mutandis* to the special financial contributions.

(6) The special financial contributions shall be repaid together with interest at a rate which shall be the same for all Contracting States. Repayments shall be made in so far as it is possible to provide for this purpose in the budget; the amount thus provided shall be distributed among the Contracting States in accordance with the scale mentioned in paragraphs 3 and 4 above.

(7) The special financial contributions remitted in any accounting period shall be wholly repaid before any such contributions or parts thereof remitted in any subsequent accounting period are repaid.

Article 41
Advances

(1) At the request of the President of the European Patent Office, the Contracting States shall make advances to the Organisation, on account of their payments and contributions, within the limit of the amount fixed by the Administrative Council. Such advances shall be apportioned in proportion to the amounts due by the Contracting States for the accounting period in question.

(2) Article 39, paragraphs 3 and 4, shall apply *mutatis mutandis* to the advances.

Article 42
Budget

(1) Income and expenditure of the Organisation shall form the subject of estimates in respect of each accounting period and shall be shown in the budget. If necessary, there may be amending or supplementary budgets.

(2) The budget shall be balanced as between income and expenditure.

(3) The budget shall be drawn up in the unit of account fixed in the Financial Regulations.

Article 43
Authorisation for expenditure

(1) The expenditure entered in the budget shall be authorised for the duration of one accounting period, unless any provisions to the contrary are contained in the Financial Regulations.

(2) Subject to the conditions to be laid down in the Financial Regulations, any appropriations, other than those relating to staff costs, which are unexpended at the end of the accounting period may be carried forward, but not beyond the end of the following accounting period.

(3) Appropriations shall be set out under different headings according to type and purpose of the expenditure and subdivided, as far as necessary, in accordance with the Financial Regulations.

Article 44
Appropriations for unforeseeable expenditure

(1) The budget of the Organisation may contain appropriations for unforeseeable expenditure.

(2) The employment of these appropriations by the Organisation shall be subject to the prior approval of the Administrative Council.

Article 45
Accounting period

The accounting period shall commence on 1 January and end on 31 December.

Article 46
Preparation and adoption of the budget

(1) The President of the European Patent Office shall lay the draft budget before the Administrative Council not later than the date prescribed in the Financial Regulations.

(2) The budget and any amending or supplementary budget shall be adopted by the Administrative Council.

Article 47
Provisional budget

(1) If, at the beginning of the accounting period, the budget has not been adopted by the Administrative Council, expenditures may be effected on a monthly basis per heading or other division of the budget, according to the provisions of the Financial Regulations, up to one-twelfth of the budget appropriations for the preceding accounting period, provided that the appropriations thus made available to the President of the European Patent Office shall not exceed one-twelfth of those provided for in the draft budget.

(2) The Administrative Council may, subject to the observance of the other provisions laid down in paragraph 1, authorise expenditure in excess of one-twelfth of the appropriations.

(3) The payments referred to in Article 37, subparagraph (b), shall continue to be made, on a provisional basis, under the conditions determined under Article 39 for the year preceding that to which the draft budget relates.

(4) The Contracting States shall pay each month, on a provisional basis and in accordance with the scale referred to in Article 40, paragraphs 3 and 4, any special financial contributions necessary to ensure implementation of paragraphs 1 and 2 above. Article 39, paragraph 4, shall apply *mutatis mutandis* to these contributions.

Article 48
Budget implementation

(1) The President of the European Patent Office shall implement the budget and any amending or supplementary budget on his own responsibility and within the limits of the allocated appropriations.

(2) Within the budget, the President of the European Patent Office may, subject to the limits and conditions laid down in the Financial Regulations, transfer funds as between the various headings or sub-headings.

Article 49
Auditing of accounts

(1) The income and expenditure account and a balance sheet of the Organisation shall be examined by auditors whose independence is beyond doubt, appointed by the Administrative Council for a period of five years, which shall be renewable or extensible.

(2) The audit, which shall be based on vouchers and shall take place, if necessary, in *situ,* shall ascertain that all income has been received and all expenditure effected in a lawful and proper manner and that the financial management is sound. The auditors shall draw up a report after the end of each accounting period.

(3) The President of the European Patent Office shall annually submit to the Administrative Council the accounts of the preceding accounting period in respect of the budget and the balance sheet showing the assets and liabilities of the Organisation together with the report of the auditors.

(4) The Administrative Council shall approve the annual accounts together with the report of the auditors and shall give the President of the European Patent Office a discharge in respect of the implementation of the budget.

Article 50
Financial Regulations

The Financial Regulations shall in particular establish:

(a) the procedure relating to the establishment and implementation of the budget and for the rendering and auditing of accounts;

(b) the method and procedure whereby the payments and contributions provided for in Article 37 and the advances provided for in Article 41 are to be made available to the Organisation by the Contracting States;

(c) the rules concerning the responsibilities of accounting and paying officers and the arrangements for their supervision;

(d) the rates of interest provided for in Articles 39, 40 and 47;

(e) the method of calculating the contributions payable by virtue of Article 146;

(f) the composition of and duties to be assigned to a Budget and Finance Committee which should be set up by the Administrative Council.

Article 51
Rules relating to Fees

The Rules relating to Fees shall determine in particular the amounts of the fees and the ways in which they are to be paid.

Part II
Substantive Patent Law

Chapter I
Patentability

Article 52
Patentable inventions

(1) European patents shall be granted for any inventions which are susceptible of industrial application, which are new and which involve an inventive step.

(2) The following in particular shall not be regarded as inventions within the meaning of paragraph 1:

(a) discoveries, scientific theories and mathematical methods;

(b) aesthetic creations;

(c) schemes, rules and methods for performing mental acts, playing games or doing business, and programs for computers;

(d) presentations of information.

(3) The provisions of paragraph 2 shall exclude patentability of the subject-matter or activities referred to in that provision only to the extent to which a European patent application or European patent relates to such subject-matter or activities as such.

(4) Methods for treatment of the human or animal body by surgery or therapy and diagnostic methods practised on the human or animal body shall not be regarded as inventions which are susceptible of industrial application within the meaning of paragraph 1. This provision shall not apply to products, in particular substances or compositions, for use in any of these methods.

Article 53
Exceptions to patentability

European patents shall not be granted in respect of:

(a) inventions the publication or exploitation of which would be contrary to "ordre public" or morality, provided that the exploitation shall not be deemed to be so contrary merely because it is prohibited by law or regulation in some or all of the Contracting States;

(b) plant or animal varieties or essentially biological processes for the production of plants or animals; this provision does not apply to microbiological processes or the products thereof.

Article 54
Novelty

(1) An invention shall be considered to be new if it does not form part of the state of the art.

(2) The state of the art shall be held to comprise everything made available to the public by means of a written or oral description, by use, or in any other way, before the date of filing of the European patent application.

(3) Additionally, the content of European patent applications as filed, of which the dates of filing are prior to the date referred to in paragraph 2 and which were published under Article 93 on or after that date, shall be considered as comprised in the state of the art.

(4) Paragraph 3 shall be applied only in so far as a Contracting State designated in respect of the later application, was also designated in respect of the earlier application as published.

(5) The provisions of paragraphs 1 to 4 shall not exclude the patentability of any substance or composition, comprised in the state of the art, for use in a method referred to in Article 52, paragraph 4, provided that its use for any method referred to in that paragraph is not comprised in the state of the art.

Article 55
Non-prejudicial disclosures

(1) For the application of Article 54 a disclosure of the invention shall not be taken into consideration if it occurred no earlier than six months preceding the filing of the European patent application and if it was due to, or in consequence of:

(a) an evident abuse in relation to the applicant or his legal predecessor, or

(b) the fact that the applicant or his legal predecessor has displayed the invention at an official, or officially recognised, international exhibition falling within the terms of the Convention on international exhibitions signed at Paris on 22 November 1928 and last revised on 30 November 1972.

(2) In the case of paragraph 1(b), paragraph 1 shall apply only if the applicant states, when filing the European patent application, that the invention has been so displayed and files a supporting certificate within the period and under the conditions laid down in the Implementing Regulations.

Article 56
Inventive step

An invention shall be considered as involving an inventive step if, having regard to the state of the art, it is not obvious to a person skilled in the art. If the state of the art also includes documents within the meaning of Article 54, paragraph 3, these documents are not to be considered in deciding whether there has been an inventive step.

Article 57
Industrial application

An invention shall be considered as susceptible of industrial application if it can be made or used in any kind of industry, including agriculture.

Chapter II
Persons entitled to apply for and obtain European patents—Mention of the inventor

Article 58
Entitlement to file a European patent application

A European patent application may be filed by any natural or legal person, or any body equivalent to a legal person by virtue of the law governing it.

Article 59
Multiple applicants

A European patent application may also be filed either by joint applicants or by two or more applicants designating different Contracting States.

Article 60
Right to a European patent

(1) The right to a European patent shall belong to the inventor or his successor in title. If the inventor is an employee the right to the European patent shall be determined in accordance with the law of the State in which the employee is mainly employed; if the State

in which the employee is mainly employed cannot be determined, the law to be applied shall be that of the State in which the employer has his place of business to which the employee is attached.

(2) If two or more persons have made an invention independently of each other, the right to the European patent shall belong to the person whose European patent application has the earliest date of filing; however, this provision shall apply only if this first application has been published under Article 93 and shall only have effect in respect of the Contracting States designated in that application as published.

(3) For the purposes of proceedings before the European Patent Office, the applicant shall be deemed to be entitled to exercise the right to the European patent.

Article 61
European patent applications by persons not having the right to a European patent

(1) If by a final decision it is adjudged that a person referred to in Article 60, paragraph 1, other than the applicant, is entitled to the grant of a European patent, that person may, within a period of three months after the decision has become final, provided that the European patent has not yet been granted, in respect of those Contracting States designated in the European patent application in which the decision has been taken or recognised, or has to be recognised on the basis of the Protocol on Recognition annexed to this Convention:

(a) prosecute the application as his own application in place of the applicant,

(b) file a new European patent application in respect of the same invention, or

(c) request that the application be refused.

(2) The provisions of Article 76, paragraph 1, shall apply *mutatis mutandis* to a new application filed under paragraph 1.

(3) The procedure to be followed in carrying out the provisions of paragraph 1, the special conditions applying to a new application filed under paragraph 1 and the time limit for paying the filing, search and designation fees on it are laid down in the Implementing Regulations.

Article 62
Right of the inventor to be mentioned

The inventor shall have the right, *vis-à-vis* the applicant for or proprietor of a European patent, to be mentioned as such before the European Patent Office.

Chapter III
Effects of the European patent and the European patent application

Article 63
Term of the European patent

(1) The term of the European patent shall be 20 years as from the date of filing of the application.

(2) Nothing in the preceding paragraph shall limit the right of a Contracting State to extend the term of a European patent under the same conditions as those applying to its national patents, in order to take into account a state of war or similar emergency conditions affecting that State.

Article 64
Rights conferred by a European patent

(1) A European patent shall, subject to the provisions of paragraph 2, confer on its proprietor from the date of publication of the mention of its grant, in each Contracting State in respect of which it is granted, the same rights as would be conferred by a national patent granted in that State.

(2) If the subject-matter of the European patent is a process, the protection conferred by the patent shall extend to the products directly obtained by such process.

(3) Any infringement of a European patent shall be dealt with by national law.

Article 65
Translation of the specification of the European patent

(1) Any Contracting State may prescribe that if the text, in which the European Patent Office intends to grant a European patent or maintain a European patent as amended for that State, is not drawn up in one of its official languages, the applicant for or proprietor of the patent shall supply to its central industrial property office a translation of this text in one of its official languages at his option or, where that State has prescribed the use of one specific official language, in that language. The period for supplying the translation shall be three months after the start of the time limit referred to in

Article 97, paragraph 2(b), or Article 102, paragraph 3(b), unless the State concerned prescribes a longer period.

(2) Any Contracting State which has adopted provisions pursuant to paragraph 1 may prescribe that the applicant for or proprietor of the patent must pay all or part of the costs of publication of such translation within a period laid down by that State.

(3) Any Contracting State may prescribe that in the event of failure to observe the provisions adopted in accordance with paragraphs 1 and 2, the European patent shall be deemed to be void *ab initio* in that State.

Article 66
Equivalence of European filing with national filing

A European patent application which has been accorded a date of filing shall, in the designated Contracting States, be equivalent to a regular national filing, where appropriate with the priority claimed for the European patent application.

Article 67
Rights conferred by a European patent application after publication

(1) A European patent application shall, from the date of its publication under Article 93, provisionally confer upon the applicant such protection as is conferred by Article 64, in the Contracting States designated in the application as published.

(2) Any Contracting State may prescribe that a European patent application shall not confer such protection as is conferred by Article 64. However, the protection attached to the publication of the European patent application may not be less than that which the laws of the State concerned attach to the compulsory publication of unexamined national patent applications. In any event, every State shall ensure at least that, from the date of publication of a European patent application, the applicant can claim compensation reasonable in the circumstances from any person who has used the invention in the said State in circumstances where that person would be liable under national law for infringement of a national patent.

(3) Any Contracting State which does not have as an official language the language of the proceedings, may prescribe that provisional protection in accordance with paragraphs 1 and 2 above shall not be effective until such time as a translation of the claims in one of its official languages at the option of the applicant or, where that

State has prescribed the use of one specific official language, in that language:

(a) has been made available to the public in the manner prescribed by national law, or

(b) has been communicated to the person using the invention in the said State.

(4) The European patent application shall be deemed never to have had the effects set out in paragraphs 1 and 2 above when it has been withdrawn, deemed to be withdrawn or finally refused. The same shall apply in respect of the effects of the European patent application in a Contracting State the designation of which is withdrawn or deemed to be withdrawn.

Article 68
Effect of revocation of the European patent

The European patent application and the resulting patent shall be deemed not to have had, as from the outset, the effects specified in Articles 64 and 67, to the extent that the patent has been revoked in opposition proceedings.

Article 69*
Extent of protection

(1) The extent of the protection conferred by a European patent or a European patent application shall be determined by the terms of the claims. Nevertheless, the description and drawings shall be used to interpret the claims.

(2) For the period up to grant of the European patent, the extent of the protection conferred by the European patent application shall be determined by the latest filed claims contained in the publication under Article 93. However, the European patent as granted or as

*See Protocol on the Interpretation of Article 69 of the Convention, adopted at the Munich Diplomatic Conference for the setting up of a European System for the Grant of Patents on 5 October 1973, as set out below:

"Article 69 should not be interpreted in the sense that the extent of the protection conferred by a European patent is to be understood as that defined by the strict, literal meaning of the wording used in the claims, the description and drawings being employed only for the purpose of resolving an ambiguity found in the claims. Neither should it be interpreted in the sense that the claims serve only as a guideline and that the actual protection conferred may extend to what from a consideration of the description and drawings by a person skilled in the art, the patentee has contemplated. On the contrary, it is to be interpreted as defining a position between these extremes which combines a fair protection for the patentee with a reasonable degree of certainty for third parties."

(The Protocol shall be an integral part of the Convention pursuant to Article 164, paragraph 1.)

amended in opposition proceedings shall determine retroactively the protection conferred by the European patent application, in so far as such protection is not thereby extended.

Article 70
Authentic text of a European patent application or European patent

(1) The text of a European patent application or a European patent in the language of the proceedings shall be the authentic text in any proceedings before the European Patent Office and in any Contracting State.

(2) However, in the case referred to in Article 14, paragraph 2, the original text shall, in proceedings before the European Patent Office, constitute the basis for determining whether the subject-matter of the application or patent extends beyond the content of the application as filed.

(3) Any Contracting State may provide that a translation, as provided for in this Convention, in an official language of that State, shall in that State be regarded as authentic, except for revocation proceedings, in the event of the application or patent in the language of the translation conferring protection which is narrower than that conferred by it in the language of the proceedings.

(4) Any Contracting State which adopts a provision under paragraph 3:

(a) must allow the applicant for or proprietor of the patent to file a corrected translation of the European patent application or European patent. Such corrected translation shall not have any legal effect until any conditions established by the Contracting State under Article 65, paragraph 2, and Article 67, paragraph 3, have been complied with *mutatis mutandis*;

(b) may prescribe that any person who, in that State, in good faith is using or has made effective and serious preparations for using an invention the use of which would not constitute infringement of the application or patent in the original translation may, after the corrected translation takes effect, continue such use in the course of his business or for the needs thereof without payment.

Chapter IV
The European patent application as an object of property

Article 71
Transfer and constitution of rights

A European patent application may be transferred or give rise to rights for one or more of the designated Contracting States.

Article 72
Assignment

An assignment of a European patent application shall be made in writing and shall require the signature of the parties to the contract.

Article 73
Contractual licensing

A European patent application may be licensed in whole or in part for the whole or part of the territories of the designated Contracting States.

Article 74
Law applicable

Unless otherwise specified in this Convention, the European patent application as an object of property shall, in each designated Contracting State and with effect for such State, be subject to the law applicable in that State to national patent applications.

Part III
Application for European Patents

Chapter I
Filing and requirements of the European patent application

Article 75
Filing of the European patent application

(1) A European patent application may be filed:

(a) at the European Patent Office at Munich or its branch at The Hague, or

(b) if the law of a Contracting State so permits, at the central industrial property office or other competent authority of that State. An application filed in this way shall have the same effect as if it had been filed on the same date at the European Patent Office.

(2) The provisions of paragraph 1 shall not preclude the applica-

tion of legislative or regulatory provisions which, in any Contracting State:

(a) govern inventions which, owing to the nature of their subject-matter may not be communicated abroad without the prior authorisation of the competent authorities of that State, or

(b) prescribe that each application is to be filed initially with a national authority or make direct filing with another authority subject to prior authorisation.

(3) No Contracting State may provide for or allow the filing of European divisional applications with an authority referred to in paragraph 1(b).

Article 76
European divisional applications

(1) A European divisional application must be filed directly with the European Patent Office at Munich or its branch at The Hague. It may be filed only in respect of subject-matter which does not extend beyond the content of the earlier application as filed; in so far as this provision is complied with, the divisional application shall be deemed to have been filed on the date of filing of the earlier application and shall have the benefit of any right to priority.

(2) The European divisional application shall not designate Contracting States which were not designated in the earlier application.

(3) The procedure to be followed in carrying out the provisions of paragraph 1, the special conditions to be complied with by a divisional application and the time limit for paying the filing, search and designation fees are laid down in the Implementing Regulations.

Article 77
Forwarding of European patent applications

(1) The central industrial property office of a Contracting State shall be obliged to forward to the European Patent Office, in the shortest time compatible with the application of national law concerning the secrecy of inventions in the interests of the State, any European patent applications which have been filed with that office or with other competent authorities in that State.

(2) The Contracting States shall take all appropriate steps to ensure that European patent applications, the subject of which is obviously not liable to secrecy by virtue of the law referred to in paragraph 1, shall be forwarded to the European Patent Office within six weeks after filing.

(3) European patent applications which require further examination as to their liability to secrecy shall be forwarded in such manner as to reach the European Patent Office within four months after filing, or, where priority has been claimed, fourteen months after the date of priority.

(4) A European patent application, the subject of which has been made secret, shall not be forwarded to the European Patent Office.

(5) European patent applications which do not reach the European Patent Office before the end of the fourteenth month after filing or, if priority has been claimed, after the date of priority, shall be deemed to be withdrawn. The filing, search and designation fees shall be refunded.

Article 78
Requirements of the European patent application

(1) A European patent application shall contain;

(a) a request for the grant of a European patent;

(b) a description of the invention;

(c) one or more claims;

(d) any drawings referred to in the description or the claims;

(e) an abstract.

(2) A European patent application shall be subject to the payment of the filing fee and the search fee within one month after the filing of the application.

(3) A European patent application must satisfy the conditions laid down in the Implementing Regulations.

Article 79
Designation of Contracting States

(1) The request for the grant of a European patent shall contain the designation of the Contracting State or States in which protection for the invention is desired.

(2) The designation of a Contracting State shall be subject to the payment of the designation fee. The designation fees shall be paid within twelve months after filing the European patent application or, if priority has been claimed, after the date of priority; in the latter case, payment may still be made up to the expiry of the period specified in Article 78, paragraph 2, if that period expires later.

(3) The designation of a Contracting State may be withdrawn at any time up to the grant of the European patent. Withdrawal of

the designation of all the Contracting States shall be deemed to be a withdrawal of the European patent application. Designation fees shall not be refunded.

Article 80
Date of filing

The date of filing of a European patent application shall be the date on which documents filed by the applicant contain:

(a) an indication that a European patent is sought;

(b) the designation of at least one Contracting State;

(c) information identifying the applicant;

(d) a description and one or more claims in one of the languages referred to in Article 14, paragraphs 1 and 2, even though the description and the claims do not comply with the other requirements of this Convention.

Article 81
Designation of the inventor

The European patent application shall designate the inventor. If the applicant is not the inventor or is not the sole inventor, the designation shall contain a statement indicating the origin of the right to the European patent.

Article 82
Unity of invention

The European patent application shall relate to one invention only or to a group of inventions so linked as to form a single general inventive concept.

Article 83
Disclosure of the invention

The European patent application must disclose the invention in a manner sufficiently clear and complete for it to be carried out by a person skilled in the art.

Article 84
The claims

The claims shall define the matter for which protection is sought. They shall be clear and concise and be supported by the description.

Article 85
The abstract

The abstract shall merely serve for use as technical information; it may not be taken into account for any other purpose, in particular not for the purpose of interpreting the scope of the protection sought nor for the purpose of applying Article 54, paragraph 3.

Article 86
Renewal fees for European patent applications

(1) Renewal fees shall be paid to the European Patent Office in accordance with the Implementing Regulations in respect of European patent applications. These fees shall be due in respect of the third year and each subsequent year, calculated from the date of filing of the application.

(2) When a renewal fee has not been paid on or before the due date, the fee may be validly paid within six months of the said date, provided that the additional fee is paid at the same time.

(3) If the renewal fee and any additional fee have not been paid in due time the European patent application shall be deemed to be withdrawn. The European Patent Office alone shall be competent to decide this.

(4) The obligation to pay renewal fees shall terminate with the payment of the renewal fee due in respect of the year in which the mention of the grant of the European patent is published.

Chapter II
Priority

Article 87
Priority right

(1) A person who has duly filed in or for any State party to the Paris Convention for the Protection of Industrial Property, an application for a patent or for the registration of a utility model or

for a utility certificate or for an inventor's certificate, or his successors in title, shall enjoy, for the purpose of filing a European patent application in respect of the same invention, a right of priority during a period of twelve months from the date of filing of the first application.

(2) Every filing that is equivalent to a regular national filing under the national law of the State where it was made or under bilateral or multilateral agreements, including this Convention, shall be recognised as giving rise to a right of priority.

(3) By a regular national filing is meant any filing that is sufficient to establish the date on which the application was filed, whatever may be the outcome of the application.

(4) A subsequent application for the same subject-matter as a previous first application and filed in or in respect of the same State shall be considered as the first application for the purposes of determining priority, provided that, at the date of filing the subsequent application, the previous application has been withdrawn, abandoned or refused, without being open to public inspection and without leaving any rights outstanding, and has not served as a basis for claiming a right of priority. The previous application may not thereafter serve as a basis for claiming a right of priority.

(5) If the first filing has been made in a State which is not a party to the Paris Convention for the Protection of Industrial Property, paragraphs 1 to 4 shall apply only in so far as that State, according to a notification published by the Administrative Council, and by virtue of bilateral or multilateral agreements, grants on the basis of a first filing made at the European Patent Office as well as on the basis of a first filing made in or for any Contracting State and subject to conditions equivalent to those laid down in the Paris Convention, a right of priority having equivalent effect.

Article 88
Claiming priority

(1) An applicant for a European patent desiring to take advantage of the priority of a previous application shall file a declaration of priority, a copy of the previous application and, if the language of the latter is not one of the official languages of the European Patent Office, a translation of it in one of such official languages. The procedure to be followed in carrying out these provisions is laid down in the Implementing Regulations.

(2) Multiple priorities may be claimed in respect of a European patent application, notwithstanding the fact that they originated in different countries. Where appropriate, multiple priorities may be

claimed for any one claim. Where multiple priorities are claimed, time limits which run from the date of priority shall run from the earliest date of priority.

(3) If one or more priorities are claimed in respect of a European patent application, the right of priority shall cover only those elements of the European patent application which are included in the application or applications whose priority is claimed.

(4) If certain elements of the invention for which priority is claimed do not appear among the claims formulated in the previous application, priority may nonetheless be granted, provided that the documents of the previous application as a whole specifically disclose such elements.

Article 89
Effect of priority right

The right of priority shall have the effect that the date of priority shall count as the date of filing of the European patent application for the purposes of Article 54, paragraphs 2 and 3, and Article 60, paragraph 2.

Part IV
Procedure up to Grant

Article 90
Examination on filing

(1) The Receiving Section shall examine whether:

(a) the European patent application satisfies the requirements for the accordance of a date of filing;

(b) the filing fee and the search fee have been paid in due time;

(c) in the case provided for in Article 14, paragraph 2, the translation of the European patent application in the language of the proceedings has been filed in due time.

(2) If a date of filing cannot be accorded, the Receiving Section shall give the applicant an opportunity to correct the deficiencies in accordance with the Implementing Regulations. If the deficiencies are not remedied in due time, the application shall not be dealt with as a European patent application.

(3) If the filing fee and the search fee have not been paid in due time or, in the case provided for in Article 14, paragraph 2, the

translation of the application in the language of the proceedings has not been filed in due time, the application shall be deemed to be withdrawn.

Article 91
Examination as to formal requirements

(1) If a European patent application has been accorded a date of filing, and is not deemed to be withdrawn by virtue of Article 90, paragraph 3, the Receiving Section shall examine whether:

(a) the requirements of Article 133, paragraph 2, have been satisfied;

(b) the application meets the physical requirements laid down in the Implementing Regulations for the implementation of this provision;

(c) the abstract has been filed;

(d) the request for the grant of a European patent satisfies the mandatory provisions of the Implementing Regulations concerning its content and, where appropriate, whether the requirements of this Convention concerning the claim to priority have been satisfied;

(e) the designation fees have been paid;

(f) the designation of the inventor has been made in accordance with Article 81;

(g) the drawings referred to in Article 78, paragraph 1(d), were filed on the date of filing of the application.

(2) Where the Receiving Section notes that there are deficiencies which may be corrected, it shall give the applicant an opportunity to correct them in accordance with the Implementing Regulations.

(3) If any deficiencies noted in the examination under paragraph 1(a) to (d) are not corrected in accordance with the Implementing Regulations, the application shall be refused; where the provisions referred to in paragraph 1(d) concern the right of priority, this right shall be lost for the application.

(4) Where, in the case referred to in paragraph 1(e), the designation fee has not been paid in due time in respect of any designated State, the designation of that State shall be deemed to be withdrawn.

(5) Where, in the case referred to in paragraph 1(f), the omission of the designation of the inventor is not, in accordance with the Implementing Regulations and subject to the exceptions laid down therein, corrected within 16 months after the date of filing of the European patent application or, if priority is claimed, after the date of priority, the application shall be deemed to be withdrawn.

(6) Where, in the case referred to in paragraph 1(g), the drawings were not filed on the date of filing of the application and no steps

have been taken to correct the deficiency in accordance with the Implementing Regulations, either the application shall be re-dated to the date of filing of the drawings or any reference to the drawings in the application shall be deemed to be deleted, according to the choice exercised by the applicant in accordance with the Implementing Regulations.

Article 92
The drawing up of the European search report

(1) If a European patent application has been accorded a date of filing and is not deemed to be withdrawn by virtue of Article 90, paragraph 3, the Search Division shall draw up the European search report on the basis of the claims, with due regard to the description and any drawings, in the form prescribed in the Implementing Regulations.

(2) Immediately after it has been drawn up, the European search report shall be transmitted to the applicant together with copies of any cited documents.

Article 93
Publication of a European patent application

(1) A European patent application shall be published as soon as possible after the expiry of a period of eighteen months from the date of filing or, if priority has been claimed, as from the date of priority. Nevertheless, at the request of the applicant the application may be published before the expiry of the period referred to above. It shall be published simultaneously with the publication of the specification of the European patent when the grant of the patent has become effective before the expiry of the period referred to above.

(2) The publication shall contain the description, the claims and any drawings as filed and, in an annex, the European search report and the abstract, in so far as the latter are available before the termination of the technical preparations for publication. If the European search report and the abstract have not been published at the same time as the application, they shall be published separately.

Article 94
Request for examination

(1) The European Patent Office shall examine, on written request, whether a European patent application and the invention to which it relates meet the requirements of this Convention.

(2) A request for examination may be filed by the applicant up to the end of six months after the date on which the European Patent Bulletin mentions the publication of the European search report. The request shall not be deemed to be filed until after the examination fee has been paid. The request may not be withdrawn.

(3) If no request for examination has been filed by the end of the period referred to in paragraph 2, the application shall be deemed to be withdrawn.

Article 95
Extension of the period within which requests for examination may be filed

(1) The Administrative Council may extend the period within which requests for examination may be filed if it is established that European patent applications cannot be examined in due time.

(2) If the Administrative Council extends the period, it may decide that third parties will be entitled to make requests for examination. In such cases, it shall determine the appropriate rules in the Implementing Regulations.

(3) Any decision of the Administrative Council to extend the period shall apply only in respect of applications filed after the publication of such decision in the Official Journal of the European Patent Office.

(4) If the Administrative Council extends the period, it must lay down measures with a view to restoring the original period as soon as possible.

Article 96
Examination of the European patent application

(1) If the applicant for a European patent has filed the request for examination before the European search report has been transmitted to him, the European Patent Office shall invite him after the transmission of the report to indicate, within a period to be determined, whether he desires to proceed further with the European patent application.

(2) If the examination of a European patent application reveals that the application or the invention to which it relates does not meet the requirements of this Convention, the Examining Division shall invite the applicant, in accordance with the Implementing Regulations and as often as necessary, to file his observations within a period to be fixed by the Examining Division.

(3) If the applicant fails to reply in due time to any invitation under paragraph 1 or paragraph 2, the application shall be deemed to be withdrawn.

Article 97
Refusal or grant

(1) The Examining Division shall refuse a European patent application if it is of the opinion that such application or the invention to which it relates does not meet the requirements of this Convention, except where a different sanction is provided for by this Convention.

(2) If the Examining Division is of the opinion that the application and the invention to which it relates meet the requirements of this Convention, it shall decide to grant the European patent for the designated Contracting States provided that:

(a) it is established, in accordance with the provisions of the Implementing Regulations, that the applicant approves the text in which the Examining Division intends to grant the patent;

(b) the fees for grant and printing are paid within the time limit prescribed in the Implementing Regulations;

(c) the renewal fees and any additional fees already due have been paid.

(3) If the fees for grant and printing are not paid in due time, the application shall be deemed to be withdrawn.

(4) The decision to grant a European patent shall not take effect until the date on which the European Patent Bulletin mentions the grant. This mention shall be published at least 3 months after the start of the time limit referred to in paragraph 2(b).

(5) Provision may be made in the Implementing Regulations for the applicant to file a translation, in the two official languages of the European Patent Office other than the language of the proceedings, of the claims appearing in the text in which the Examining Division intends to grant the patent. In such case, the period laid down in paragraph 4 shall be at least five months. If the translation has not been filed in due time, the application shall be deemed to be withdrawn.

Article 98
Publication of a specification of the European patent

At the same time as it publishes the mention of the grant of the European patent, the European Patent Office shall publish a specification of the European patent containing the description, the claims and any drawings.

Part V
Opposition Procedure

Article 99
Opposition

(1) Within nine months from the publication of the mention of the grant of the European patent, any person may give notice to the European Patent Office of opposition to the European patent granted. Notice of opposition shall be filed in a written reasoned statement. It shall not be deemed to have been filed until the opposition fee has been paid.

(2) The opposition shall apply to the European patent in all the Contracting States in which that patent has effect.

(3) An opposition may be filed even if the European patent has been surrendered or has lapsed for all the designated States.

(4) Opponents shall be parties to the opposition proceedings as well as the proprietor of the patent.

(5) Where a person provides evidence that in a Contracting State, following a final decision, he has been entered in the patent register of such State instead of the previous proprietor, such person shall, at his request, replace the previous proprietor in respect of such State. By derogation from Article 118, the previous proprietor and the person making the request shall not be deemed to be joint proprietors unless both so request.

Article 100
Grounds for opposition

Opposition may only be filed on the grounds that:

(a) the subject-matter of the European patent is not patentable within the terms of Articles 52 to 57;

(b) the European patent does not disclose the invention in a manner sufficiently clear and complete for it to be carried out by a person skilled in the art;

(c) the subject-matter of the European patent extends beyond the content of the application as filed, or, if the patent was granted on a divisional application or on a new application filed in accordance with Article 61, beyond the content of the earlier application as filed.

Article 101
Examination of the opposition

(1) If the opposition is admissible, the Opposition Division shall examine whether the grounds for opposition laid down in Article 100 prejudice the maintenance of the European patent.

(2) In the examination of the opposition, which shall be conducted in accordance with the provision of the Implementing Regulations, the Opposition Division shall invite the parties, as often as necessary, to file observations, within a period to be fixed by the Opposition Division, on communications from another party or issued by itself.

Article 102
Revocation or maintenance of the European patent

(1) If the Opposition Division is of the opinion that the grounds for opposition mentioned in Article 100 prejudice the maintenance of the European patent, it shall revoke the patent.

(2) If the Opposition Division is of the opinion that the grounds for opposition mentioned in Article 100 do not prejudice the maintenance of the patent unamended, it shall reject the opposition.

(3) If the Opposition Division is of the opinion that, taking into consideration the amendments made by the proprietor of the patent during the opposition proceedings, the patent and the invention to which it relates meet the requirements of this Convention, it shall decide to maintain the patent as amended, provided that:

(a) it is established, in accordance with the provisions of the Implementing Regulations, that the proprietor of the patent approves the text in which the Opposition Division intends to maintain the patent;

(b) the fee for the printing of a new specification of the European patent is paid within the time limit prescribed in the Implementing Regulations.

(4) If the fee for the printing of a new specification is not paid in due time, the patent shall be revoked.

(5) Provision may be made in the Implementing Regulations for the proprietor of the patent to file a translation of any amended claims in the two official languages of the European Patent Office other than the language of the proceedings. If the translation has not been filed in due time the patent shall be revoked.

Article 103
Publication of a new specification of the European patent

If a European patent is amended under Article 102, paragraph 3, the European Patent Office shall, at the same time as it publishes the mention of the opposition decision, publish a new specification of the European patent containing the description, the claims and any drawings, in the amended form.

Article 104
Costs

(1) Each party to the proceedings shall meet the costs he has incurred unless a decision of an Opposition Division or Board of Appeals, for reasons of equity, orders, in accordance with the Implementing Regulations, a different apportionment of costs incurred during taking of evidence or in oral proceedings.

(2) On request, the registry of the Opposition Division shall fix the amount of the costs to be paid under a decision apportioning them. The fixing of the costs by the registry may be reviewed by a decision of the Opposition Division on a request filed within the period laid down in the Implementing Regulations.

(3) Any final decision of the European Patent Office fixing the amount of costs shall be dealt with, for the purpose of enforcement in the Contracting States, in the same way as a final decision given by a civil court of the State in the territory of which enforcement is to be carried out. Verification of such decision shall be limited to its authenticity.

Article 105
Intervention of the assumed infringer

(1) In the event of an opposition to a European patent being filed, any third party who proves that proceedings for infringement of the same patent have been instituted against him may, after the opposition period has expired, intervene in the opposition proceedings, if he gives notice of intervention within three months of the date on which the infringement proceedings were instituted. The same shall apply in respect of any third party who proves both that the proprietor of the patent has requested that he cease alleged infringement of the patent and that he has instituted proceedings for a court ruling that he is not infringing the patent.

(2) Notice of intervention shall be filed in a written reasoned statement. It shall not be deemed to have been filed until the opposition fee has been paid. Thereafter the intervention shall, subject to any exceptions laid down in the Implementing Regulations, be treated as an opposition.

Part VI
Appeals Procedure

Article 106
Decisions subject to appeal

(1) An appeal shall lie from decisions of the Receiving Section, Examining Divisions, Opposition Divisions and the Legal Division. It shall have suspensive effect.

(2) An appeal may be filed against the decision of the Opposition Division even if the European patent has been surrendered or has lapsed for all the designated States.

(3) A decision which does not terminate proceedings as regards one of the parties can only be appealed together with the final decision, unless the decision allows separate appeal.

(4) The apportionment of costs of opposition proceedings cannot be the sole subject of an appeal.

(5) A decision fixing the amount of costs of opposition proceedings cannot be appealed unless the amount is in excess of that laid down in the Rules relating to Fees.

Article 107
Persons entitled to appeal and to be parties to appeal proceedings

Any party to proceedings adversely affected by a decision may appeal. Any other parties to the proceedings shall be parties to the appeal proceedings as of right.

Article 108
Time limit and form of appeal

Notice of appeal must be filed in writing at the European Patent Office within two months after the date of notification of the decision appealed from. The notice shall not be deemed to have been filed until after the fee for appeal has been paid. Within four months after the date of notification of the decision, a written statement setting out the grounds of appeal must be filed.

Article 109
Interlocutory revision

(1) If the department whose decision is contested considers the appeal to be admissible and well founded, it shall rectify its decision. This shall not apply where the appellant is opposed by another party to the proceedings.

(2) If the appeal is not allowed within one month after receipt of the statement of grounds, it shall be remitted to the Board of Appeal without delay, and without comment as to its merit.

Article 110
Examination of appeals

(1) If the appeal is admissible, the Board of Appeal shall examine whether the appeal is allowable.

(2) In the examination of the appeal, which shall be conducted in accordance with the provisions of the Implementing Regulations, the Board of Appeal shall invite the parties, as often as necessary, to file observations, within a period to be fixed by the Board of Appeal, on communications from another party or issued by itself.

(3) If the applicant fails to reply in due time to an invitation under paragraph 2, the European patent application shall be deemed to be withdrawn, unless the decision under appeal was taken by the Legal Division.

Article 111
Decision in respect of appeals

(1) Following the examination as to the allowability of the appeal, the Board of Appeal shall decide on the appeal. The Board of Appeal may either exercise any power within the competence of the department which was responsible for the decision appealed or remit the case to that department for further prosecution.

(2) If the Board of Appeal remits the case for further prosecution to the department whose decision was appealed, that department shall be bound by the *ratio decidendi* of the Board of Appeal, in so far as the facts are the same. If the decision which was appealed emanated from the Receiving Section, the Examining Division shall similarly be bound by the *ratio decidendi* of the Board of Appeal.

Article 112
Decision or opinion of the Enlarged Board of Appeal

(1) In order to ensure uniform application of the law, or if an important point of law arises:

(a) the Board of Appeal shall, during proceedings on a case and either of its own motion or following a request from a party to the appeal, refer any question to the Enlarged Board of Appeal if it considers that a decision is required for the above purposes. If the Board of Appeal rejects the request, it shall give the reasons in its final decision;

(b) the President of the European Patent Office may refer a point of law to the Enlarged Board of Appeal where two Boards of Appeal have given different decisions on that question.

(2) In the cases covered by paragraph 1(a) the parties to the appeal proceedings shall be parties to the proceedings before the Enlarged Board of Appeal.

(3) The decision of the Enlarged Board of Appeal referred to in paragraph 1(a) shall be binding on the Board of Appeal in respect of the appeal in question.

Part VII
Common Provisions

Chapter I
Common provisions governing procedure

Article 113
Basis of decisions

(1) The decisions of the European Patent Office may only be based on grounds or evidence on which the parties concerned have had an opportunity to present their comments.

(2) The European Patent Office shall consider and decide upon the European patent application or the European patent only in the text submitted to it, or agreed, by the applicant for or proprietor of the patent.

Article 114
Examination by the European Patent Office of its own motion

(1) In proceedings before it, the European Patent Office shall examine the facts of its own motion; it shall not be restricted in this examination to the facts, evidence and arguments provided by the parties and the relief sought.

(2) The European Patent Office may disregard facts or evidence which are not submitted in due time by the parties concerned.

Article 115
Observations by third parties

(1) Following the publication of the European patent application, any person may present observations concerning the patentability of the invention in respect of which the application has been filed. Such observations must be filed in writing and must include a statement of the grounds on which they are based. That person shall not be a party to the proceedings before the European Patent Office.

(2) The observations referred to in paragraph 1 shall be communicated to the applicant for or proprietor of the patent who may comment on them.

Article 116
Oral proceedings

(1) Oral proceedings shall take place either at the instance of the European Patent Office if it considers this to be expedient or at the request of any party to the proceedings. However, the European Patent Office may reject a request for further oral proceedings before the same department where the parties and the subject of the proceedings are the same.

(2) Nevertheless, oral proceedings shall take place before the Receiving Section at the request of the applicant only where the Receiving Section considers this to be expedient or where it envisages refusing the European patent application.

(3) Oral proceedings before the Receiving Section, the Examining Divisions and the Legal Division shall not be public.

(4) Oral proceedings, including delivery of the decision, shall be public, as regards the Boards of Appeal and the Enlarged Board of Appeal, after publication of the European patent application, and also before the Opposition Divisions, in so far as the department before which the proceedings are taking place does not decide otherwise in cases where admission of the public could have serious and unjustified disadvantages, in particular for a party to the proceedings.

Article 117
Taking of evidence

(1) In any proceedings before an Examining Division, an Opposition Division, the Legal Division or a Board of Appeal the means of giving or obtaining evidence shall include the following:

(a) hearing the parties;
(b) requests for information;
(c) the production of documents;
(d) hearing the witnesses;
(e) opinions by experts;
(f) inspection;
(g) sworn statements in writing.

(2) The Examining Division, Opposition Division or Board of Appeal may commission one of its members to examine the evidence adduced.

(3) If the European Patent Office considers it necessary for a party, witness or expert to give evidence orally, it shall either:

(a) issue a summons to the person concerned to appear before it, or

(b) request, in accordance with the provisions of Article 131, paragraph 2, the competent court in the country of residence of the person concerned to take such evidence.

(4) A party, witness or expert who is summoned before the European Patent Office may request the latter to allow his evidence to be heard by a competent court in his country of residence. On receipt of such a request, or if there has been no reply to the summons by the expiry of a period fixed by the European Patent Office in the summons, the European Patent Office may, in accordance with the provisions of Article 131, paragraph 2, request the competent court to hear the person concerned.

(5) If a party, witness or expert gives evidence before the European Patent Office, the latter may, if it considers it advisable for the evidence to be given on oath or in an equally binding form, request the competent court in the country of residence of the person concerned to re-examine his evidence under such conditions.

(6) When the European Patent Office requests a competent court to take evidence, it may request the court to take the evidence on oath or in an equally binding form and to permit a member of the department concerned to attend the hearing and question the party, witness or expert either through the intermediary of the court or directly.

Article 118

Unity of the European patent application or European patent

Where the applicants for or proprietors of a European patent are not the same in respect of different designated Contracting States, they shall be regarded as joint applicants or proprietors for the purposes of proceedings before the European Patent Office. The unity of the application or patent in these proceedings shall not be affected; in particular the text of the application or patent shall be uniform for all designated Contracting States unless otherwise provided for in this Convention.

Article 119
Notification

The European Patent Office shall, as a matter of course, notify those concerned of decisions and summonses, and of any notice or other communication from which a time limit is reckoned, or of which those concerned must be notified under other provisions of this Convention, or of which notification has been ordered by the President of the European Patent Office. Notifications may, where exceptional circumstances so require, be given through the intermediary of the central industrial property offices of the Contracting States.

Article 120
Time limits

The Implementing Regulations shall specify:

(a) the manner of computation of time limits and the conditions under which such time limits may be extended, either because the European Patent Office or the authorities referred to in Article 75, paragraph 1(b), are not open to receive documents or because mail is not delivered in the localities in which the European Patent Office or such authorities are situated or because postal services are generally interrupted or subsequently dislocated;

(b) the minima and maxima for time limits to be determined by the European Patent Office.

Article 121
Further processing of the European patent application

(1) If the European patent application is to be refused or is refused or deemed to be withdrawn following failure to reply within a time limit set by the European Patent Office, the legal consequence provided for shall not ensue or, if it has already ensued, shall be

retracted if the applicant requests further processing of the application.

(2) The request shall be filed in writing within two months of the date on which either the decision to refuse the application or the communication that the application is deemed to be withdrawn was notified. The omitted act must be completed within this time limit. The request shall not be deemed to have been filed until the fee for further processing has been paid.

(3) The department competent to decide on the omitted act shall decide on the request.

Article 122
Restitutio in integrum

(1) The applicant for or proprietor of a European patent who, in spite of all due care required by the circumstances having been taken, was unable to observe a time limit *vis-à-vis* the European Patent Office shall, upon application, have his rights reestablished if the non-observance in question has the direct consequence, by virtue of this Convention, of causing the refusal of the European patent application, or of a request, or the deeming of the European patent application to have been withdrawn, or the revocation of the European patent, or the loss of any other right or means of redress.

(2) The application must be filed in writing within two months from the removal of the cause of non-compliance with the time limit. The omitted act must be completed within this period. The application shall only be admissible within the year immediately following the expiry of the unobserved time limit. In the case of non-payment of a renewal fee, the period specified in Article 86, paragraph 2, shall be deducted from the period of one year.

(3) The application must state the grounds on which it is based, and must set out the facts on which it relies. It shall not be deemed to be filed until after the fee for re-establishment of rights has been paid.

(4) The department competent to decide on the omitted act shall decide upon the application.

(5) The provisions of this Article shall not be applicable to the time limits referred to in paragraph 2 of this Article, Article 61, paragraph 3, Article 76, paragraph 3, Article 78, paragraph 2, Article 79, paragraph 2, Article 87, paragraph 1, and Article 94, paragraph 2.

(6) Any person who, in a designated Contracting State, in good faith has used or made effective and serious preparations for using an invention which is the subject of a published European patent

application or a European patent in the course of the period between the loss of rights referred to in paragraph 1 and publication of the mention of re-establishment of those rights, may without payment continue such use in the course of his business or for the needs thereof.

(7) Nothing in this Article shall limit the right of a Contracting State to grant *restitutio in integrum* in respect of time limits provided for in this Convention and to be observed *vis-à-vis* the authorities of such State.

Article 123
Amendments

(1) The conditions under which a European patent application or a European patent may be amended in proceedings before the European Patent Office are laid down in the Implementing Regulations. In any case, an applicant shall be allowed at least one opportunity of amending the description, claims and drawings of his own volition.

(2) A European patent application or a European patent may not be amended in such a way that it contains subject-matter which extends beyond the content of the application as filed.

(3) The claims of the European patent may not be amended during opposition proceedings in such a way as to extend the protection conferred.

Article 124
Information concerning national patent applications

(1) The Examining Division or the Board of Appeal may invite the applicant to indicate, within a period to be determined by it, the States in which he has made applications for national patents for the whole or part of the invention to which the European patent application relates, and to give the reference numbers of the said applications.

(2) If the applicant fails to reply in due time to an invitation under paragraph 1, the European patent application shall be deemed to be withdrawn.

Article 125
Reference to general principles

In the absence of procedural provisions in this Convention, the European Patent Office shall take into account the principles of procedural law generally recognised in the Contracting States.

Article 126
Termination of financial obligations

(1) Rights of the Organisation to the payment of a fee to the European Patent Office shall be extinguished after four years from the end of the calendar year in which the fee fell due.

(2) Rights against the Organisation for the refunding by the European Patent Office of fees or sums of money paid in excess of a fee shall be extinguished after four years from the end of the calendar year in which the right arose.

(3) The period laid down in paragraphs 1 and 2 shall be interrupted in the case covered by paragraph 1 by a request for payment of the fee and in the case covered by paragraph 2 by a reasoned claim in writing. On interruption it shall begin again immediately and shall end at the latest six years after the end of the year in which it originally began, unless, in the meantime, judicial proceedings to enforce the right have begun; in this case the period shall end at the earliest one year after the judgement enters into force.

Chapter II
Information to the public or official authorities

Article 127
Register of European Patents

The European Patent Office shall keep a register, to be known as the Register of European Patents, which shall contain those particulars the registration of which is provided for by this Convention. No entry shall be made in the Register prior to the publication of the European patent application. The Register shall be open to public inspection.

Article 128
Inspection of files

(1) The files relating to European patent applications, which have not yet been published, shall not be made available for inspection without the consent of the applicant.

(2) Any person who can prove that the applicant for a European patent has invoked the rights under the application against him may obtain inspection of the files prior to the publication of that application and without the consent of the applicant.

(3) Where a European divisional application or a new European patent application filed under Article 61, paragraph 1, is published, any person may obtain inspection of the files of the earlier application prior to the publication of that application and without the consent of the relevant applicant.

(4) Subsequent to the publication of the European patent application, the files relating to such application and the resulting European patent may be inspected on request, subject to the restrictions laid down in the Implementing Regulations.

(5) Even prior to the publication of the European patent application, the European Patent Office may communicate the following bibliographic data to third parties or publish them:

(a) the number of the European patent application;

(b) the date of filing of the European patent application and, where the priority of a previous application is claimed, the date, State and file number of the previous application;

(c) the name of the applicant;

(d) the title of the invention;

(e) the Contracting States designated.

Article 129
Periodical publications

The European Patent Office shall periodically publish:

(a) a European Patent Bulletin containing entries made in the Register of European Patents, as well as other particulars the publication of which is prescribed by this Convention;

(b) an Official Journal of the European Patent Office, containing notices and information of a general character issued by the President of the European Patent Office, as well as any other information relevant to this Convention or its implementation.

Article 130
Exchanges of information

(1) The European Patent Office and, subject to the application of the legislative or regulatory provisions referred to in Article 75, paragraph 2, the central industrial property office of any Contracting State shall, on request, communicate to each other any useful information regarding the filing of European or national patent applications and regarding any proceedings concerning such applications and the resulting patents.

(2) The provisions of paragraph 1 shall apply to the communication of information by virtue of working agreements between the European Patent Office and:

(a) the central industrial property office of any State which is not a party to this Convention;

(b) any inter-governmental organisation entrusted with the task of granting patents;

(c) any other organisation.

(3) The communications under paragraphs 1 and 2(a) and (b) shall not be subject to the restrictions laid down in Article 128. The Administrative Council may decide that communications under paragraph 2(c) shall not be subject to such restrictions, provided that the organisation concerned shall treat the information communicated as confidential until the European patent application has been published.

Article 131
Administrative and legal co-operation

(1) Unless otherwise provided in this Convention or in national laws, the European Patent Office and the courts or authorities of Contracting States shall on request give assistance to each other by communicating information or opening files for inspection. Where the European Patent Office lays files open to inspection by courts, Public Prosecutors' Offices or central industrial property offices, the inspection shall not be subject to the restrictions laid down in Article 128.

(2) Upon receipt of letters rogatory from the European Patent Office, the courts or other competent authorities of Contracting States shall undertake, on behalf of that Office and within the limits of their jurisdiction, any necessary enquiries or other legal measures.

Article 132
Exchange of publications

(1) The European Patent Office and the central industrial property offices of the Contracting States shall despatch to each other on request and for their own use one or more copies of their respective publications free of charge.

(2) The European Patent Office may conclude agreements relating to the exchange or supply of publications.

Chapter III
Representation

Article 133
General principles of representation

(1) Subject to the provisions of paragraph 2, no person shall be compelled to be represented by a professional representative in proceedings established by this Convention.

(2) Natural or legal persons not having either a residence or their principal place of business within the territory of one of the Contracting States must be represented by a professional representative and act through him in all proceedings established by this Convention, other than in filing the European patent application; the Implementing Regulations may permit other exceptions.

(3) Natural or legal persons having their residence or principal place of business within the territory of one of the Contracting States may be represented in proceedings established by this Convention by an employee, who need not be a professional representative but who must be authorised in accordance with the Implementing Regulations. The Implementing Regulations may provide whether and under what conditions an employee of such a legal person may also represent other legal persons which have their principal place of business within the territory of one of the Contracting States and which have economic connections with the first legal person.

(4) The Implementing Regulations may prescribe special provisions concerning the common representation of parties acting in common.

Article 134
Professional representatives

(1) Professional representation of natural or legal persons in proceedings established by this Convention may only be undertaken by professional representatives whose names appear on a list maintained for this purpose by the European Patent Office.

(2) Any natural person who fulfills the following conditions may be entered on the list of professional representatives:

(a) he must be a national of one of the Contracting States;

(b) he must have his place of business or employment within the territory of one of the Contracting States;

(c) he must have passed the European qualifying examination.

(3) Entry shall be effected upon request, accompanied by certificates which must indicate that the conditions laid down in paragraph 2 are fulfilled.

(4) Persons whose names appear on the list of professional representatives shall be entitled to act in all proceedings established by this Convention.

(5) For the purpose of acting as a professional representative, any person whose name appears on the list referred to in paragraph 1 shall be entitled to establish a place of business in any Contracting State in which proceedings established by this Convention may be conducted, having regard to the Protocol on Centralisation annexed to this Convention. The authorities of such State may remove that entitlement in individual cases only in application of legal provisions adopted for the purpose of protecting public security and law and order. Before such action is taken, the President of the European Patent Office shall be consulted.

(6) The President of the European Patent Office may, in special circumstances, grant exemption from the requirement of paragraph 2(a).

(7) Professional representation in proceedings established by this Convention may also be undertaken, in the same way as by a professional representative, by any legal practitioner qualified in one of the Contracting States and having his place of business within such State, to the extent that he is entitled, within the said State, to act as a professional representative in patent matters. Paragraph 5 shall apply *mutatis mutandis*.

(8) The Administrative Council may adopt provisions governing:

(a)* the qualifications and training required of a person for

---

*See Regulation on the European qualifying examination for professional representatives before the European Patent Office of October 21, 1977 (OFFICIAL J. OF THE EPO 2/78, p. 101 *et seq.*).

admission to the European qualifying examination and the conduct of such examination;

(b)** the establishment or recognition of an institute constituted by the persons entitled to act as professional representatives by virtue of either the European qualifying examination or the provisions of Article 163, paragraph 7;

(c)*** any disciplinary power to be exercised by that institute or the European Patent Office on such persons.

Part VIII
Impact on National Law

Chapter I
Conversion into a national patent application

Article 135
Request for the application of national procedure

(1) The central industrial property office of a designated Contracting State shall apply the procedure for the grant of a national patent only at the request of the applicant for or proprietor of a European patent, and in the following circumstances:

(a) when the European patent application is deemed to be withdrawn pursuant to Article 77, paragraph 5, or Article 162, paragraph 4;

(b) in such other cases as are provided for by the national law in which the European patent application is refused or withdrawn or deemed to be withdrawn, or the European patent is revoked under this Convention.

(2) The request for conversion shall be filed within three months after the European patent application has been withdrawn or after notification has been made that the application is deemed to be withdrawn, or after a decision has been notified refusing the application or revoking the European patent. The effect referred to in Article 66 shall lapse if the request is not filed in due time.

**See Regulation on the establishment of an Institute of Professional Representatives before the European Patent Office of October 21, 1977 (OFFICIAL J. OF THE EPO 2/78, p. 85 *et seq.*).

***See Regulation on discipline for professional representatives of October 21, 1977 (Official J. of the EPO 2/78, p. 91 *et seq.*).

Article 136

Submission and transmission of the request

(1) A request for conversion shall be filed with the European Patent Office and shall specify the Contracting States in which application of the procedure for the grant of a national patent is desired. The request shall not be deemed to be filed until the conversion fee has been paid. The European Patent Office shall transmit the request to the central industrial property offices of the Contracting States specified therein, accompanied by a copy of the files relating to the European patent application of the European patent.

(2) However, if the applicant is notified that the European patent application has been deemed to be withdrawn pursuant to Article 77, paragraph 5, the request shall be filed with the central industrial property office with which the application has been filed. That office shall, subject to the provisions of national security, transmit the request, together with a copy of the European patent application, directly to the central industrial property offices of the Contracting States specified by the applicant in the request. The effect referred to in Article 66 shall lapse if such transmission is not made within twenty months after the date of filing or, if a priority has been claimed, after the date of priority.

Article 137

Formal requirements for conversion

(1) A European patent application transmitted in accordance with Article 136 shall not be subjected to formal requirements of national law which are different from or additional to those provided for in this Convention.

(2) Any central industrial property office to which the application is transmitted may require that the applicant shall, within not less than two months:

(a) pay the national application fee;

(b) file a translation in one of the official languages of the State in question of the original text of the European patent application and, where appropriate, of the text, as amended during proceedings before the European Patent Office, which the applicant wishes to submit to the national procedure.

Chapter II
Revocation and prior rights

Article 138
Grounds for revocation

(1) Subject to the provisions of Article 139, a European patent may only be revoked under the law of a Contracting State, with effect for its territory, on the following grounds:

(a) if the subject-matter of the European patent is not patentable within the terms of Articles 52 to 57;

(b) if the European patent does not disclose the invention in a manner sufficiently clear and complete for it to be carried out by a person skilled in the art;

(c) if the subject-matter of the European patent extends beyond the content of the application as filed or, if the patent was granted on a divisional application or on a new application filed in accordance with Article 61, beyond the content of the earlier application as filed;

(d) if the protection conferred by the European patent has been extended;

(e) if the proprietor of the European patent is not entitled under Article 60, paragraph 1.

(2) If the grounds for revocation only affect the European patent in part, revocation shall be pronounced in the form of a corresponding limitation of the said patent. If the national law so allows, the limitation may be effected in the form of an amendment to the claims, the description or the drawings.

Article 139
Rights of earlier date or the same date

(1) In any designated Contracting State a European patent application and a European patent shall have with regard to a national patent application and a national patent the same prior right effect as a national patent application and a national patent.

(2) A national patent application and a national patent in a Contracting State shall have with regard to a European patent in which that Contracting State is designated the same prior right effect as they have with regard to a national patent.

(3) Any Contracting State may prescribe whether and on what terms an invention disclosed in both a European patent application or patent and a national application or patent having the same date of filing or, where priority is claimed, the same date of priority, may be protected simultaneously by both applications or patents.

Chapter III
Miscellaneous effects

Article 140
National utility models and utility certificates

Article 66, Article 124, Articles 135 to 137 and Article 139 shall apply to utility models and utility certificates and to applications for utility models and utility certificates registered or deposited in the Contracting States whose laws make provision for such models or certificates.

Article 141
Renewal fees for European patents

(1) Renewal fees in respect of a European patent may only be imposed for the years which follow that referred to in Article 86, paragraph 4.

(2) Any renewal fees falling due within two months after the publication of the mention of the grant of the European patent shall be deemed to have been validly paid if they are paid within that period. Any additional fee provided for under national law shall not be charged.

Part IX
Special Agreements

Article 142
Unitary patents

(1) Any group of Contracting States, which has provided by a special agreement that a European patent granted for those States has a unitary character throughout their territories, may provide that a European patent may only be granted jointly in respect of all those States.

(2) Where any group of Contracting States has availed itself of the authorisation given in paragraph 1, the provisions of this Part shall apply.

Article 143
Special departments of the European Patent Office

(1) The group of Contracting States may give additional tasks to the European Patent Office.

(2) Special departments common to the Contracting States in the group may be set up within the European Patent Office in order to carry out the additional tasks. The President of the European Patent Office shall direct such special departments; Article 10, paragraphs 2 and 3, shall apply *mutatis mutandis*.

Article 144
Representation before special departments

The group of Contracting States may lay down special provisions to govern representation of parties before the departments referred to in Article 143, paragraph 2.

Article 145
Select committee of the Administrative Council

(1) The group of Contracting States may set up a select committee of the Administrative Council for the purpose of supervising the activities of the special departments set up under Article 143, paragraph 2; the European Patent Office shall place at its disposal such staff, premises and equipment as may be necessary for the performance of its duties. The President of the European Patent Office shall be responsible for the activities of the special departments to the select committee of the Administrative Council.

(2) The composition, powers and functions of the select committee shall be determined by the group of Contracting States.

Article 146
Cover for expenditure for carrying out special tasks

Where additional tasks have been given to the European Patent Office under Article 143, the group of Contracting States shall bear the expenses incurred by the Organisation in carrying out these tasks. Where special departments have been set up in the European

Patent Office to carry out these additional tasks, the group shall bear the expenditure on staff, premises and equipment chargeable in respect of these departments. Article 39, paragraphs 3 and 4, Article 41 and Article 47 shall apply *mutatis mutandis*.

Article 147
Payments in respect of renewal fees for unitary patents

If the group of Contracting States has fixed a common scale of renewal fees in respect of European patents the proportion referred to in Article 39, paragraph 1, shall be calculated on the basis of the common scale; the minimum amount referred to in Article 39, paragraph 1, shall apply to the unitary patent. Article 39, paragraphs 3 and 4, shall apply *mutatis mutandis*.

Article 148
The European patent application as an object of property

(1) Article 74 shall apply unless the group of Contracting States has specified otherwise.

(2) The group of Contracting States may provide that a European patent application for which these Contracting States are designated may only be transferred, mortgaged or subjected to any legal means of execution in respect of all the Contracting States of the group and in accordance with the provisions of the special agreement.

Article 149*
Joint designation

(1) The group of Contracting States may provide that these States may only be designated jointly, and that the designation of one or some only of such States shall be deemed to constitute the designation of all the States of the group.

(2) Where the European Patent Office acts as a designated Office under Article 153, paragraph 1, paragraph 1 shall apply if the applicant has indicated in the international application that he wishes to obtain a European patent for one or more of the designated States of

*See the Treaty between the Swiss Confederation and the Principality of Liechtenstein on Patent Protection of December 22, 1978 (*Industrial Property Laws and Treaties*, Bilateral Treaties Text 2-001).

the group. The same shall apply if the applicant designates in the international application one of the Contracting States in the group, whose national law provides that the designation of that State shall have the effect of the application being for a European patent.

Part X
International Application Pursuant to the Patent Cooperation Treaty

Article 150
Application of the Patent Cooperation Treaty

(1) The Patent Cooperation Treaty of 19 June 1970, hereinafter referred to as the Cooperation Treaty, shall be applied in accordance with the provisions of this Part.

(2) International applications filed under the Cooperation Treaty may be the subject of proceedings before the European Patent Office. In such proceedings, the provisions of that Treaty shall be applied, supplemented by the provisions of this Convention. In case of conflict, the provisions of the Cooperation Treaty shall prevail. In particular, for an international application the time limit within which a request for examination must be filed under Article 94, paragraph 2, of this Convention shall not expire before the time prescribed by Article 22 or Article 39 of the Cooperation Treaty as the case may be.

(3) An international application, for which the European Patent Office acts as designated Office or elected Office, shall be deemed to be a European patent application.

(4) Where reference is made in this Convention to the Cooperation Treaty, such reference shall include the Regulations under that Treaty.

Article 151
The European Patent Office as a receiving Office

(1) The European Patent Office may act as a receiving Office within the meaning of Article 2(xv) of the Cooperation Treaty if the applicant is a resident or national of a Contracting State to this Convention in respect of which the Cooperation Treaty has entered into force.

(2) The European Patent Office may also act as a receiving Office if the applicant is a resident or national of a State which is not a

Contracting State to this Convention, but which is a Contracting State to the Cooperation Treaty and which has concluded an agreement with the Organisation whereby the European Patent Office acts as a receiving Office in accordance with the provisions of the Cooperation Treaty, in place of the national office of that State.

(3) Subject to the prior approval of the Administrative Council, the European Patent Office may also act as a receiving Office for any other applicant, in accordance with an agreement concluded between the Organisation and the International Bureau of the World Intellectual Property Organization.

Article 152
Filing and transmittal of the international application

(1) If the applicant chooses the European Patent Office as a receiving Office for his international application, he shall file it directly with the European Patent Office. Article 75, paragraph 2, shall nevertheless apply *mutatis mutandis*.

(2) In the event of an international application being filed with the European Patent Office through the intermediary of the competent central industrial property office, the Contracting State concerned shall take all necessary measures to ensure that the application is transmitted to the European Patent Office in time for the latter to be able to comply in due time with the conditions for transmittal under the Cooperation Treaty.

(3)* Each international application shall be subject to the payment of the transmittal fee, which shall be payable within one month after receipt of the application.

Article 153
The European Patent Office as a designated Office

(1) The European Patent Office shall act as a designated Office within the meaning of Article 2(xiii) of the Cooperation Treaty for those Contracting States to this Convention in respect of which the Cooperation Treaty has entered into force and which are designated in the international application if the applicant informs the receiving Office in the international application that he wishes to obtain a European patent for these States. The same shall apply if, in the

---

*Amended by decision of the Administrative Council of December 21, 1978, which entered into force on March 1, 1979 (OFFICIAL J. OF THE EPO).

international application, the applicant designates a Contracting State of which the national law provides that designation of that State shall have the effect of the application being for a European patent.

(2) When the European Patent Office acts as a designated Office, the Examining Division shall be competent to take decisions which are required under Article 25, paragraph 2(a), of the Cooperation Treaty.

Article 154
The European Patent Office as an International Searching Authority

(1)* The European Patent Office shall act as an International Searching Authority within the meaning of Chapter I of the Cooperation Treaty for applicants who are residents or nationals of a Contracting State in respect of which the Cooperation Treaty has entered into force, subject to the conclusion of an agreement between the Organisation and the International Bureau of the World Intellectual Property Organization.

(2) Subject to the prior approval of the Administrative Council, the European Patent Office shall also act as an International Searching Authority for any other applicant, in accordance with an agreement concluded between the Organisation and the International Bureau of the World Intellectual Property Organization.

(3) The Boards of Appeal shall be responsible for deciding on a protest made by an applicant against an additional fee charged by the European Patent Office under the provisions of Article 17, paragraph 3(a), of the Cooperation Treaty.

Article 155
The European Patent Office as an International Preliminary Examining Authority

(1)** The European Patent Office shall act as an International Preliminary Examining Authority within the meaning of Chapter II of the Cooperation Treaty for applicants who are residents or nationals of a Contracting State bound by that Chapter, subject to

---

*See Agreement between WIPO and EPO under the PCT of April 11, 1978 (PCT GAZETTE, 1978, p. 107 *et seq.*).

**See Agreement between WIPO and EPO under the PCT of April 11, 1978 (PCT GAZETTE, 1978, p. 107 *et seq.*).

the conclusion of an agreement between the Organisation and the International Bureau of the World Intellectual Property Organization.

(2) Subject to the prior approval of the Administrative Council, the European Patent Office shall also act as an International Preliminary Examining Authority for any other applicant, in accordance with an agreement concluded between the Organisation and the International Bureau of the World Intellectual Property Organization.

(3) The Boards of Appeal shall be responsible for deciding on a protest made by an applicant against an additional fee charged by the European Patent Office under the provisions of Article 34, paragraph 3(a), of the Cooperation Treaty.

Article 156
The European Patent Office as an elected Office

The European Patent Office shall act as an elected Office within the meaning of Article 2(xiv) of the Cooperation Treaty if the applicant has elected any of the designated States referred to in Article 153, paragraph 1, or Article 149, paragraph 2, for which Chapter II of that Treaty has become binding. Subject to the prior approval of the Administrative Council, the same shall apply where the applicant is a resident or national of a State which is not a party to that Treaty or which is not bound by Chapter II of that Treaty, provided that he is one of the persons whom the Assembly of the International Patent Cooperation Union has decided to allow, pursuant to Article 31, paragraph 2(b), of the Cooperation Treaty, to made a demand for international preliminary examination.

Article 157
International search report

(1) Without prejudice to the provisions of paragraphs 2 to 4, the international search report under Article 18 of the Cooperation Treaty or any declaration under Article 17, paragraph 2(a), of that Treaty and their publication under Article 21 of that Treaty shall take the place of the European search report and the mention of its publication in the European Patent Bulletin.

(2) Subject to the decisions of the Administrative Council referred to in paragraph 3:

(a) a supplementary European search report shall be drawn up in respect of all international applications;

(b) the applicant shall pay the search fee, which shall be paid at the same time as the national fee provided for in Article 22, paragraph 1, or Article 39, paragraph 1, of the Cooperation Treaty. If the search fee is not paid in due time the application shall be deemed to be withdrawn.

(3) The Administrative Council may decide under what conditions and to what extent:

(a) the supplementary European search report is to be dispensed with;

(b) the search fee is to be reduced.

(4) The Administrative Council may at any time rescind the decisions taken pursuant to paragraph 3.

Article 158
Publication of the international application and its supply to the European Patent Office

(1) Publication under Article 21 of the Cooperation Treaty of an international application for which the European Patent Office is a designated Office shall, subject to paragraph 3, take the place of the publication of a European patent application and shall be mentioned in the European Patent Bulletin. Such an application shall not however be considered as comprised in the state of the art in accordance with Article 54, paragraph 3, if the conditions laid down in paragraph 2 are not fulfilled.

(2) The international application shall be supplied to the European Patent Office in one of its official languages. The applicant shall pay to the European Patent Office the national fee provided for in Article 22, paragraph 1, or Article 39, paragraph 1, of the Cooperation Treaty.

(3) If the international application is published in a language other than one of the official languages of the European Patent Office, that Office shall publish the international application, supplied as specified in paragraph 2. Subject to the provisions of Article 67, paragraph 3, the provisional protection in accordance with Article 67, paragraphs 1 and 2, shall be effective from the date of that publication.

Part XI
Transitional Provisions

Article 159
Administrative Council during a transitional period

(1) The States referred to in Article 169, paragraph 1, shall appoint their representatives to the Administrative Council; on the

invitation of the Government of the Federal Republic of Germany, the Administrative Council shall meet no later than two months after the entry into force of this Convention, particularly for the purpose of appointing the President of the European Patent Office.

(2) The duration of the term of office of the first Chairman of the Administrative Council appointed after the entry into force of this Convention shall be four years.

(3) The term of office of two of the elected members of the first Board of the Administrative Council set up after the entry into force of this Convention shall be five and four years respectively.

Article 160
Appointment of employees during a transitional period

(1) Until such time as the Service Regulations for permanent employees and the conditions of employment of other employees of the European Patent Office have been adopted, the Administrative Council and the President of the European Patent Office, each within their respective powers, shall recruit the necessary employees and shall conclude short-term contracts to that effect. The Administrative Council may lay down general principles in respect of recruitment.

(2) During a transitional period, the expiry of which shall be determined by the Administrative Council, the Administrative Council, after consulting the President of the European Patent Office, may appoint as members of the Enlarged Board of Appeal or of the Boards of Appeal technically or legally qualified members of national courts and authorities of Contracting States who may continue their activities in their national courts or authorities. They may be appointed for a term of less than five years, though this shall not be less than one year, and may be reappointed.

Article 161
First accounting period

(1) The first accounting period of the Organisation shall extend from the date of entry into force of this Convention to 31 December of the same year. If that date falls within the second half of the year, the accounting period shall extend until 31 December of the following year.

(2) The budget for the first accounting period shall be drawn up as soon as possible after the entry into force of this Convention. Until

contributions provided for in Article 40 due in accordance with the first budget are received by the Organisation, the Contracting States shall, upon the request of and within the limit of the amount fixed by the Administrative Council, make advances which shall be deducted from their contributions in respect of that budget. The advances shall be determined in accordance with the scale referred to in Article 40. Article 39, paragraphs 3 and 4, shall apply *mutatis mutandis* to the advances.

Article 162
Progressive expansion of the field of activity of the European Patent Office

(1) European patent applications may be filed with the European Patent Office from the date fixed by the Administrative Council on the recommendation of the President of the European Patent Office.

(2) The Administrative Council may, on the recommendation of the President of the European Patent Office, decide that, as from the date referred to in paragraph 1, the processing of European patent applications may be restricted. Such restriction may be in respect of certain areas of technology. However, examination shall in any event be made as to whether European patent applications can be accorded a date of filing.

(3) If a decision has been taken under paragraph 2, the Administrative Council may not subsequently further restrict the processing of European patent applications.

(4) Where, as a result of the procedure being restricted under paragraph 2, a European patent application cannot be further processed, the European Patent Office shall communicate this to the applicant and shall point out that he may make a request for conversion. The European patent application shall be deemed to be withdrawn on receipt of such communication.

Article 163
Professional representatives during a transitional period*

(1) During a transitional period, the expiry of which shall be determined by the Administrative Council, notwithstanding the provisions of Article 134, paragraph 2, any natural person who fulfills

*Expiry of transitional period: October 7, 1981.

the following conditions may be entered on the list of professional representatives:

(a) he must be a national of a Contracting State;

(b) he must have his place of business or employment within the territory of one of the Contracting States;

(c) he must be entitled to represent natural or legal persons in patent matters before the central industrial property office of the Contracting State in which he has his place of business or employment.

(2) Entry shall be effected upon request, accompanied by a certificate, furnished by the central industrial property office, which must indicate that the conditions laid down in paragraph 1 are fulfilled.

(3) When, in any Contracting State, the entitlement referred to in paragraph 1(c) is not conditional upon the requirement of special professional qualifications, persons applying to be entered on the list who act in patent matters before the central industrial property office of the said State must have habitually so acted for at least five years. However, persons whose professional qualification to represent natural or legal persons in patent matters before the central industrial property office of one of the Contracting States is officially recognised in accordance with the regulations laid down by such State shall not be subject to the condition of having exercised the profession. The certificate furnished by the central industrial property office must indicate that the applicant satisfies one of the conditions referred to in the present paragraph.

(4) The President of the European Patent Office may grant exemption from:

(a) the requirement of paragraph 3, first sentence, if the applicant furnishes proof that he has acquired the requisite qualification in another way;

(b) the requirement of paragraph 1(a) in special circumstances.

(5) The President of the European Patent Office shall grant exemption from the requirement of paragraph 1(a) if on 5 October 1973 the applicant fulfilled the requirements of paragraph 1(b) and (c).

(6) Persons having their places of business or employment in a State which acceded to this Convention less than one year before the expiry of the transitional period referred to in paragraph 1 or after the expiry of the transitional period may, under the conditions laid down in paragraphs 1 to 5, during a period of one year calculated from the date of entry into force of the accession of that State, be entered on the list of professional representatives.

(7) After the expiry of the transitional period, any person whose name was entered on the list of professional representatives during that period shall, without prejudice to any disciplinary measures

taken under Article 134, paragraph 8(c), remain thereon or, on request, be restored thereto, provided that he then fulfills the requirement of paragraph 1(b).

Part XII
Final Provisions

Article 164
Implementing Regulations and Protocols

(1) The Implementing Regulations, the Protocol on Recognition, the Protocol on Privileges and Immunities, the Protocol on Centralisation and the Protocol on the Interpretation of Article 69 shall be integral parts of this Convention.

(2) In the case of conflict between the provisions of this Convention and those of the Implementing Regulations, the provisions of this Convention shall prevail.

Article 165
Signature—Ratification

(1) This Convention shall be open for signature until 5 April 1974 by the States which took part in the Inter-Governmental Conference for the setting up of a European System for the Grant of Patents or were informed of the holding of that conference and offered the option of taking part therein.

(2) This Convention shall be subject to ratification; instruments of ratification shall be deposited with the Government of the Federal Republic of Germany.

Article 166
Accession

(1) This Convention shall be open to accession by:

(a) the States referred to in Article 165, paragraph 1;

(b) any other European State at the invitation of the Administrative Council.

(2) Any State which has been a party to the Convention and has

ceased so to be as a result of the application of Article 172, paragraph 4, may again become a party to the Convention by acceding to it.

(3) Instruments of accession shall be deposited with the Government of the Federal Republic of Germany.

Article 167
Reservations

(1) Each Contracting State may, at the time of signature or when depositing its instrument of ratification or accession, make only the reservations specified in paragraph 2.

(2) Each Contracting State may reserve the right to provide that:

(a) European patents, in so far as they confer protection on chemical, pharmaceutical or food products, as such, shall, in accordance with the provisions applicable to national patents, be ineffective or revocable; this reservation shall not affect protection conferred by the patent in so far as it involves a process of manufacture or use of a chemical product or a process of manufacture of a pharmaceutical or food product;

(b) European patents, in so far as they confer protection on agricultural or horticultural processes other than those to which Article 53, subparagraph (b), applies, shall, in accordance with the provisions applicable to national patents, be ineffective or revocable;

(c) European patents shall have a term shorter then twenty years, in accordance with the provisions applicable to national patents;

(d) it shall not be bound by the Protocol on Recognition.

(3) Any reservation made by a Contracting State shall have effect for a period of not more than ten years from the entry into force of this Convention. However, where a Contracting State has made any of the reservations referred to in paragraph 2(a) and (b), the Administrative Council may, in respect of such State, extend the period by not more than five years for all or part of any reservation made, if that State submits, at the latest one year before the end of the 10-year period, a reasoned request which satisfies the Administrative Council that the State is not in a position to dispense with that reservation by the expiry of the 10-year period.

(4) Any Contracting State that has made a reservation shall withdraw this reservation as soon as circumstances permit. Such withdrawal shall be made by notification addressed to the Government of the Federal Republic of Germany and shall take effect one month from the date of receipt of such notification.

(5) Any reservation made in accordance with paragraph 2(a),

(b) or (c) shall apply to European patents granted on European patent applications filed during the period in which the reservation has effect. The effect of the reservation shall continue for the term of the patent.

(6) Without prejudice to paragraphs 4 and 5, any reservation shall cease to have effect on expiry of the period referred to in paragraph 3, first sentence, or, if the period is extended, on expiry of the extended period.

Article 168
Territorial field of application

(1) Any Contracting State may declare in its instrument of ratification or accession, or may inform the Government of the Federal Republic of Germany by written notification any time thereafter, that this Convention shall be applicable to one or more of the territories for the external relations of which it is responsible. European patents granted for that Contracting State shall also have effect in the territories for which such a declaration has taken effect.

(2) If the declaration referred to in paragraph 1 is contained in the instrument of ratification or accession, it shall take effect on the same date as the ratification or accession; if the declaration is made in a notification after the deposit of the instrument of ratification or accession, such notification shall take effect six months after the date of its receipt by the Government of the Federal Republic of Germany.

(3) Any Contracting State may at any time declare that the Convention shall cease to apply to some or to all of the territories in respect of which it has given a notification pursuant to paragraph 1. Such declaration shall take effect one year after the date on which the Government of the Federal Republic of Germany received notification thereof.

Article 169
Entry into force*

(1) This Convention shall enter into force three months after the deposit of the last instrument of ratification or accession by six States on whose territory the total number of patent applications filed in 1970 amounted to at least 180,000 for all the said States.

---

*For Belgium, Federal Republic of Germany, France, Luxembourg, Netherlands, Switzerland and United Kingdom: October 7, 1977; Sweden: May 1, 1978; Italy: December 1, 1978; Austria: May 1, 1979; Liechtenstein: April 1, 1980.

(2) Any ratification or accession after the entry into force of this Convention shall take effect on the first day of the third month after the deposit of the instrument of ratification or accession.

Article 170
Initial contribution

(1) Any State which ratifies or accedes to this Convention after its entry into force shall pay to the Organisation an initial contribution, which shall not be refunded.

(2) The initial contribution shall be 5% of an amount calculated by applying the percentage obtained for the State in question, on the date on which ratification or accession takes effect, in accordance with the scale provided for in Article 40, paragraphs 3 and 4, to the sum of the special financial contributions due from the other Contracting States in respect of the accounting periods preceding the date referred to above.

(3) In the event that special financial contributions were not required in respect of the accounting period immediately preceding the date referred to in paragraph 2, the scale of contributions referred to in that paragraph shall be the scale that would have been applicable to the State concerned in respect of the last year for which financial contributions were required.

Article 171
Duration of the Convention

The present Convention shall be of unlimited duration.

Article 172
Revision

(1) This Convention may be revised by a Conference of the Contracting States.

(2) The Conference shall be prepared and convened by the Administrative Council. The Conference shall not be deemed to be validly constituted unless at least three-quarters of the Contracting States are represented at it. In order to adopt the revised text there must be a majority of three-quarters of the Contracting States represented and voting at the Conference. Abstentions shall not be considered as votes.

(3) The revised text shall enter into force when it has been ratified or acceded to by the number of Contracting States specified by the Conference, and at the time specified by that Conference.

(4) Such States as have not ratified or acceded to the revised text of the Convention at the time of its entry into force shall cease to be parties to this Convention as from that time.

Article 173
Disputes between Contracting States

(1) Any dispute between Contracting States concerning the interpretation or application of the present Convention which is not settled by negotiation shall be submitted, at the request of one of the States concerned, to the Administrative Council, which shall endeavour to bring about agreement between the States concerned.

(2) If such agreement is not reached within six months from the date when the Administrative Council was seized of the dispute, any one of the States concerned may submit the dispute to the International Court of Justice for a binding decision.

Article 174
Denunciation

Any Contracting State may at any time denounce this Convention. Notification of denunciation shall be given to the Government of the Federal Republic of Germany. Denunciation shall take effect one year after the date of receipt of such notification.

Article 175
Preservation of acquired rights

(1) In the event of a State ceasing to be party to this Convention in accordance with Article 172, paragraph 4, or Article 174, rights already acquired pursuant to this Convention shall not be impaired.

(2) A European patent application which is pending when a designated State ceases to be party to the Convention shall be processed by the European Patent Office, in so far as that State is concerned, as if the Convention in force thereafter were applicable to that State.

(3) The provisions of paragraph 2 shall apply to European pa-

tents in respect of which, on the date mentioned in that paragraph, an opposition is pending or the opposition period has not expired.

(4) Nothing in this Article shall affect the right of any State that has ceased to be a party to this Convention to treat any European patent in accordance with the text to which it was a party.

Article 176
Financial rights and obligations of a former Contracting State

(1) Any State which has ceased to be a party to this Convention in accordance with Article 172, paragraph 4, or Article 174, shall have the special financial contributions which it has paid pursuant to Article 40, paragraph 2, refunded to it by the Organisation only at the time and under the conditions where by the Organisation refunds special financial contributions paid by other States during the same accounting period.

(2) The State referred to in paragraph 1 shall, even after ceasing to be a party to this Convention, continue to pay the proportion pursuant to Article 39 of renewal fees in respect of European patents remaining in force in that State, at the rate current on the date on which it ceased to be a party.

Article 177
Languages of the Convention

(1) This Convention, drawn up in a single original, in the English, French and German languages, shall be deposited in the archives of the Government of the Federal Republic of Germany, the three texts being equally authentic.

(2) The texts of this Convention drawn up in official languages of Contracting States other than those referred to in paragraph 1 shall, if they have been approved by the Administration Council, be considered as official texts. In the event of conflict on the interpretation of the various texts, the texts referred to in paragraph 1 shall be authentic.

Article 178
Transmission and notifications

(1) The Government of the Federal Republic of Germany shall draw up certified true copies of this Convention and shall transmit them to the Governments of all signatory or acceding States.

(2) The Government of the Federal Republic of Germany shall notify to the Governments of the States referred to in paragraph 1:

(a) any signature;

(b) the deposit of any instrument of ratification or accession;

(c) any reservation or withdrawal of reservation pursuant to the provisions of Article 167;

(d) any declaration or notification received pursuant to the provisions of Article 168;

(e) the date of entry into force of this Convention;

(f) any denunciation received pursuant to the provisions of Article 174 and the date on which such denunciation comes into force.

(3) The Government of the Federal Republic of Germany shall register this Convention with the Secretariat of the United Nations.

European Patent Convention (Protocols)

Protocol on the Centralisation of the European Patent System and on its Introduction (Protocol on Centralisation)

Section I

(1)(a) Upon entry into force of the Convention, States parties thereto which are also members of the International Patent Institute set up by the Hague Agreement of 6 June 1947 shall take all necessary steps to ensure the transfer to the European Patent Office no later than the date referred to in Article 162, paragraph 1, of the Convention of all assets and liabilities and all staff members of the International Patent Institute. Such transfer shall be effected by an agreement between the International Patent Institute and the European Patent Organisation. The above States and the other States parties to the Convention shall take all necessary steps to ensure that that agreement shall be implemented no later than the date referred to in Article 162, paragraph 1, of the Convention. Upon implementation of the agreement, those Member States of the International Patent Institute which are also parties to the Convention further undertake to terminate their participation in the Hague Agreement.

(b) The States parties to the Convention shall take all necessary steps to ensure that all the assets and liabilities and all the staff members of the International Patent Institute are taken into the European Patent Office in accordance with the agreement referred to in sub-paragraph (a). After the implementation of that agreement the tasks incumbent upon the International Patent Institute at the date on which the Convention is opened for signature, and in particular those carried out *vis-à-vis* its Member States, whether or not they become parties to the Convention, and such tasks as it has undertaken at the time of the entry into force of the Convention to carry out *vis-à-vis* States which, at that date, are both members of the International Patent Institute and parties to the Convention, shall be assumed by the branch located at The Hague. In addition, the Administrative Council of the European Patent Organisation may allocate further duties in the field of searching to that branch.

(c) The above obligations shall also apply *mutatis mutandis* to the sub-office set up under the Hague Agreement under the conditions set out in the agreement between the International Patent Institute and the Government of the Contracting State concerned. This Government hereby undertakes to make a new agreement with the European Patent Organisation in place of the one already made with the International Patent Institute to harmonise the clauses concerning the organisation, operation and financing of the sub-office with the provisions of this Protocol.

(2) Subject to the provisions of Section III, the States parties to the Convention shall, on behalf of their central industrial property offices, renounce in favour of the European Patent Office any activities as International Searching Authorities under the Patent Cooperation Treaty as from the date referred to in Article 162, paragraph 1, of the Convention.

(3)(a) A sub-office of the European Patent Office for searching European patent applications shall be set up in Berlin (West) as from the date referred to in Article 162, paragraph 1, of the Convention. It shall operate under the direction of the branch at The Hague.

(b) The Administrative Council shall determine the duties to be allocated to the sub-office in Berlin in the light of general considerations and of the requirements of the European Patent Office with regard to searching.

(c) At least at the beginning of the period following the progressive expansion of the field of activity of the European Patent Office, the amount of work assigned to that sub-office shall be sufficient to enable the examining staff of the Berlin Annex of the German Patent Office, as it stands at the date on which the Convention is opened for signature, to be fully employed.

(d) The Federal Republic of Germany shall bear any additional costs incurred by the European Patent Organisation in setting up and maintaining the sub-office in Berlin.

Section II

Subject to the provisions of Section III and IV, the States parties to the Convention shall, on behalf of their central industrial property offices, renounce in favour of the European Patent Office any activities as International Preliminary Examining Authorities under the Patent Cooperation Treaty. This obligation shall apply only to the extent to which the European Patent Office may examine European patent applications in accordance with Article 162, paragraph 2, of the Convention and shall not apply until two years after the date on which the European Patent Office has begun examining activities in the areas of technology concerned, on the basis of a five-year plan which shall progressively extend the activities of the European Patent Office to all areas of technology and which may be amended only by decision of the Administrative Council. The procedures for implementing this obligation shall be determined by decision of the Administrative Council.

Section III

(1) The central industrial property office of any State party to the Convention in which the official language is not one of the official languages of the European Patent Office, shall be authorised to act as an International Searching Authority and as an International Preliminary Examining Authority under the Patent Cooperation Treaty. Such authorisation shall be subject to an undertaking by the State concerned to restrict such activities to international applications filed by nationals or residents of such State and by nationals or residents of States parties to the Convention which are adjacent to that State. The Administrative Council may decide to authorise the central industrial property office of any State party to the Convention to extend such activities to cover such international applications as may be filed by nationals or residents of any non-Contracting State having the same official language as the Contracting State in question and drawn up in that language.

(2) For the purpose of harmonising search activities under the Patent Cooperation Treaty within the framework of the European system for the grant of patents, co-operation shall be established between the European Patent Office and any central industrial property office authorised under this Section. Such co-operation shall be based on a special agreement which may cover e.g. search procedures and methods, qualifications required for the recruitment and training of examiners, guidelines for the exchange of search and other services between the offices as well as other measures needed to establish the required control and supervision.

Section IV*

(1)*(a) For the purpose of facilitating the adaptation of the national patent offices of the States parties to the Convention to the European patent system, the Administrative Council may, if it

---

*The following "Declaration concerning Section IV, paragraph 1, of the Protocol on Centralisation" was adopted on 5 October 1973 at the Munich Diplomatic Conference for the setting up of a European System for the Grant of Patents:

"The Contracting States intend that the agreement between the Organisation and the central industrial property office of any State entrusted with tasks under Section IV, paragraph 1, of the Protocol on Centralisation will provide for suitable guarantees that such tasks shall be carried out in accordance with the law and procedure established by the Convention and that the conclusions reached by the examiners of that office shall be treated in the same way as those reached by the examiners of the European Patent Office.

Furthermore, it is intended that the amount of work entrusted to any national office shall be of sufficient quantity to alleviate to a substantial extent staffing difficulties arising in that office from the introduction of the European system for the grant of patents, it being understood that that office will itself take all reasonable measures open to it to restrict such difficulties, including the release of examiners to the European Patent Office, and that regard may be had to the number of nationals of the State in question at the European Patent Office."

considers it desirable, and subject to the conditions set out below, entrust the central industrial property offices of such of those States in which it is possible to conduct the proceedings in one of the official languages of the European Patent Office with tasks concerning the examination of European patent applications drawn up in that language which, pursuant to Article 18, paragraph 2, of the Convention, shall, as a general rule, be entrusted to a member of the Examining Division. Such tasks shall be carried out within the framework of the proceedings for grant laid down in the Convention; decisions on such applications shall be taken by the Examining Division composed in accordance with Article 18, paragraph 2.

(b) Tasks entrusted under sub-paragraph (a) shall not be in respect of more than 40% of the total number of European patent applications filed; tasks entrusted to any one State shall not be in respect of more than one-third of the total number of European patent applications filed. These tasks shall be entrusted for a period of 15 years from the opening of the European Patent Office and shall be reduced progressively (in principle by 20% a year) to zero during the last 5 years of the period.

(c) The Administrative Council shall decide, while taking into account the provisions of sub-paragraph (b), upon the nature, origin and number of the European patent applications in respect of which examining tasks may be entrusted to the central industrial property office of each of the Contracting States mentioned above.

(d) The above implementing procedures shall be set out in a special agreement between the central industrial property office of the Contracting State concerned and the European Patent Organisation.

(e) An office with which such a special agreement has been concluded may act as an International Preliminary Examining Authority under the Patent Cooperation Treaty, until the expiry of the period of 15 years.

(2)(a) If the Administrative Council considers that it is compatible with the proper functioning of the European Patent Office, and in order to alleviate the difficulties which may arise for certain Contracting States from the application of Section I, paragraph 2, it may entrust searching in respect of European patent applications to the central industrial property offices of those States in which the official language is one of the official languages of the European Patent Office, provided that these offices possess the necessary qualifications for appointment as an International Searching Authority in accordance with the conditions laid down in the Patent Cooperation Treaty.

(b) In carrying out such work, undertaken under the responsibility of the European Patent Office, the central industrial property offices concerned shall adhere to the guidelines applicable to the drawing up of the European search report.

(c) The provisions of paragraph 1(b), second sentence, and subparagraph (d) of this Section shall apply to this paragraph.

Section V

(1) The sub-office referred to in Section 1, paragraph 1(c), shall be authorised to carry out searches, among the documentation which is at its disposal and which is in the official language of the State in which the sub-office is located, in respect of European patent applications filed by nationals and residents of that State. This authorisation shall be on the understanding that the procedure for the grant of European patents will not be delayed and that additional costs will not be incurred for the European Patent Organisation.

(2) The sub-office referred to in paragraph 1 shall be authorised to carry out, at the option of an applicant for a European patent and at his expense, a search on his patent application among the documentation referred to in paragraph 1. This authorisation shall be effective until the search provided for in Article 92 of the Convention has been extended, in accordance with Section VI, to cover such documentation and shall be on the understanding that the procedure for the grant of European patents will not be delayed.

(3) The Administrative Council may also extend the authorisations provided for in paragraphs 1 and 2, under the conditions of those paragraphs, to the central industrial property office of a Contracting State which does not have as an official language one of the official languages of the European Patent Office.

Section VI

The search provided for in Article 92 of the Convention shall, in principle, be extended, in respect of all European patent applications, to published patents, published patent applications and other relevant documents not included in the search documentation of the European Patent Office on the date referred to in Article 162, paragraph 1, of the Convention. The extent, conditions and timing of any such extension shall be determined by the Administrative Council on the basis of a study concerning particularly the technical and financial aspects.

Section VII

The provisions of this Protocol shall prevail over any contradictory provisions of the Convention.

Section VIII

The decisions of the Administrative Council provided for in this Protocol shall require a three-quarters majority (Article 35, paragraph 2, of the Convention). The provisions governing the weighing of votes (Article 36 of the Convention) shall apply.

Protocol on Jurisdiction and the Recognition of Decision in Respect of the Right to the Grant of a European Patent (Protocol on Recognition)

Section I
Jurisdiction
Article 1

(1) The courts of the Contracting States shall, in accordance with Articles 2 to 6, have jurisdiction to decide claims, against the applicant, to the right to the grant of a European patent in respect of one or more of the Contracting States designated in the European Patent application.

(2) For the purposes of this Protocol, the term "courts" shall include authorities which, under the national law of a Contracting State, have jurisdiction to decide the claims referred to in paragraph 1. Any Contracting State shall notify the European Patent Office of the identity of any authority on which such a jurisdiction is conferred, and the European Patent Office shall inform the other Contracting States accordingly.

(3) For the purposes of this Protocol, the term "Contracting State" refers to a Contracting State which has not excluded application of this Protocol pursuant to Article 167 of the Convention.

Article 2

Subject to Articles 4 and 5, if an applicant for a European patent has his residence or principal place of business within one of the Contracting States, proceedings shall be brought against him in the courts of that Contracting State.

Article 3

Subject to Articles 4 and 5, if an applicant for a European patent has his residence or principal place of business outside the Contracting States, and if the party claiming the right to the grant of the European patent has his residence or principal place of business within one of the Contracting States, the courts of the latter State shall have exclusive jurisdiction.

Article 4

Subject to Article 5, if the subject-matter of a European patent application is the invention of an employee, the courts of the Contracting State, if any, whose law determines the right to the European patent pursuant to Article 60, paragraph 1, second sentence, of the Convention, shall have exclusive jurisdiction over proceedings between the employee and the employer.

Article 5

(1) If the parties to a dispute concerning the right to the grant of a European patent have concluded an agreement, either in writing or verbally with written confirmation, to the effect that a court or the courts of a particular Contracting State shall decide on such a dispute, the court or courts of that State shall have exclusive jurisdiction.

(2) However, if the parties are an employee and his employer, paragraph 1 shall only apply in so far as the national law governing the contract of employment allows the agreement in question.

Article 6

In cases where neither Articles 2 to 4 nor Article 5, paragraph 1, apply, the courts of the Federal Republic of Germany shall have exclusive jurisdiction.

Article 7

The courts of Contracting States before which claims referred to in Article 1 are brought shall of their own motion decide whether or not they have jurisdiction pursuant to Articles 2 to 6.

Article 8

(1) In the event of proceedings based on the same claim and between the same parties being brought before courts of different Contracting States, the court to which a later application is made

shall of its own motion decline jurisdiction in favour of the court to which an earlier application was made.

(2) In the event of the jurisdiction of the court to which an earlier application is made being challenged, the court to which a later application is made shall stay the proceedings until the other court takes a final decision.

Section II
Recognition
Article 9

(1) Subject to the provisions of Article 11, paragraph 2, final decisions given in any Contracting State on the right to the grant of a European patent in respect of one or more of the Contracting States designated in the European patent application shall be recognised without requiring a special procedure in the other Contracting States.

(2) The jurisdiction of the court whose decision is to be recognised and the validity of such decision may not be reviewed.

Article 10

Article 9, paragraph 1, shall not be applicable where:

(a) an applicant for a European patent who has not contested a claim proves that the document initiating the proceedings was not notified to him regularly and sufficiently early for him to defend himself; or

(b) an applicant proves that the decision is incompatible with another decision given in a Contracting State in proceedings between the same parties which were started before those in which the decision to be recognised was given.

Article 11

(1) In relations between any Contracting States the provisions of this Protocol shall prevail over any conflicting provisions of other agreements on jurisdiction or the recognition of judgments.

(2) This Protocol shall not affect the implementation of any agreement between a Contracting State and a State which is not bound by the Protocol.

Part III

Trademarks

1. Madrid Agreement Concerning the International Registration of Marks (With Protocol)

April 14, 1891, as revised at Brussels on December 14, 1900, at Washington on June 2, 1911, at The Hague on November 6, 1925, at London on June 2, 1934, at Nice on June 15, 1957, and at Stockholm on July 14, 1967, and as amended on October 2, 1979, and Protocol Relating to the Madrid Agreement Concerning the International Registration of Marks at Madrid on June 28, 1989

The Madrid Agreement Concerning the International Registration of Marks entered into force on April 14, 1891. It is a special union within the Union of Paris administered by WIPO's International Bureau, and is open only to states party to the Paris Convention. The Madrid Agreement has been revised five times, the latest being at Stockholm on July 14, 1967.

The Madrid Agreement is designed to simplify the procedures for the filing of trademarks and service marks in different countries. It provides for the international registration of an approved trademark by a single filing in one language and a payment of one fee, through the International Bureau. Consequently, it eliminates the need for a trademark owner to submit an application to every member state to receive protection under the prevailing law of that member state. As such, the Agreement reduces the cost of a multicountry trademark filing.

The Agreement requires registration in the country of

origin as a prerequisite for international deposit. For this reason, the Agreement is said to favor those countries that have the least demanding requirements for registration, such as a brief examination period. Accordingly, some countries (e.g., the United States and Canada) that have more elaborate trademark examining procedures than do other countries have declined to join the Agreement.

Nationals of any member country can obtain protection for their mark registered in the country of origin by filing the mark directly at the International Bureau or through the intermediary of the country of origin (Art. 1 para. 2).

Registration of the mark in the country of origin is a prerequisite for international deposit. The country of origin is the country where the applicant has a real and effective industrial or commercial establishment. For applicants having no such establishment the country of origin is the one where they are domiciled. If the applicant has no domicile in a country of the special union, the country of origin will be the country of the special union where the applicant is a national (Art. 1 para. 3).

The International Registration is published in the *Les Marques Internaionales* by the International Bureau of WIPO, which sends a copy to each member country designated by the applicant for protection.

From the date of registration at the International Bureau, the protection of the mark in each of the contracting countries shall be the same as if the mark had been filed with them directly (Art. 4). The trademark is automatically registered if the relevant national trademark office has not exercised its right to reject the application within 12 months of its registration. For the first five years, protection under international registration depends on the national mark that remains in effect only as long as the trademark owner is protected in the country of origin. After five years from the date of international registration, such registration shall become independent of the national mark registered earlier in the country of origin unless the national mark has ceased to enjoy protection in the country of origin (Art. 6 paras. 2-3). Registration of a mark at the International Bureau remains in effect for 20 years (Art. 6 para. 1) with the possibility of renewal for another 20-year term (Art. 7).

As of January 1, 1990, the following 29 states were party to the Madrid Agreement:

Algeria
Austria
Belgium
Bulgaria
China
Cuba
Czechoslovakia
Democratic People's Republic of Korea
Egypt
France
German Democratic Republic
Federal Republic of Germany
Hungary
Italy
Liechtenstein
Luxembourg
Monaco
Mongolia
Morocco
Netherlands
Portugal
Romania
San Marino
Soviet Union
Spain
Sudan
Switzerland
Viet Nam
Yugoslavia

Protocol Relating to the Madrid Agreement

The Protocol Relating to the Madrid Agreement Concerning the International Registration of Marks was signed at Madrid on June 28, 1989. **As of January 1, 1990, it had not entered into force.** The Protocol is designed to harmonize the Madrid Agreement with regional trademark systems, the most important being the future European Community system. In addition, the Protocol tries to meet the long-standing objections about the Madrid system of certain non-adhering countries. The important changes effected by the Protocol are: the possibility of basing an international registration not on a national registration but on a national application (Protocol Art. 2), a refusal period of 18 months rather than one year (Protocol Art. 5 para. 2(b-c)), an allowance for a cancelled international registration to be transformed into national applications where the international registration had effect (Protocol Art. 9 *quinquies*), and an allowance for national offices to receive more than the uniform fee fixed by the Madrid Union (Protocol Art. 8). Under a safeguard clause, the substantive changes in the Madrid system effected by the Protocol are not applicable in the relations between countries party to the Madrid Agreement, even if such countries have adhered to the Protocol (Protocol Art. 9 *sexies*).

Madrid Agreement Concerning the International Registration of Marks*

Article 1

Establishment of a Special Union. Filing of Marks at International Bureau. Definition of Country of Origin

(1) The countries to which this Agreement applies constitute a Special Union for the international registration of marks.

(2) Nationals of any of the contracting countries may, in all the other countries party to this Agreement, secure protection for their marks applicable to goods or services, registered in the country of origin, by filing the said marks at the International Bureau of Intellectual Property (hereinafter designated as "the International Bureau") referred to in the Convention Establishing the World Intellectual Property Organization (hereinafter designated as "the Organization"), through the intermediary of the Office of the said country of origin.

(3) Shall be considered the country of origin the country of the Special Union where the applicant has a real and effective industrial or commercial establishment; if he has no such establishment in a country of the Special Union, the country of the Special Union where he has his domicile; if he has no domicile within the Special Union but is a national of a country of the Special Union, the country of which he is a national.

Article 2

Reference to Article 3 of Paris Convention (Same Treatment for Certain Categories of Persons as for Nationals of Countries of the Union)

Nationals of countries not having acceded to this Agreement who, within the territory of the Special Union constituted by the said Agreement, satisfy the conditions specified in Article 3 of the Paris Convention for the Protection of Industrial Property shall be treated in the same manner as nationals of the contracting countries.

---

*As of January 1990, this Protocol had not entered into force.
Source: Text courtesy of the World Intellectual Property Organization (WIPO).

Article 3
Contents of Application for International Registration

(1) Every application for international registration must be presented on the form prescribed by the Regulations; the Office of the country of origin of the mark shall certify that the particulars appearing in such application correspond to the particulars in the national register, and shall mention the dates and numbers of the filing and registration of the mark in the country of origin and also the date of the application for international registration.

(2) The applicant must indicate the goods or services in respect of which protection of the mark is claimed and also, if possible, the corresponding class or classes according to the classification established by the Nice Agreement Concerning the International Classification of Goods and Services for the Purposes of the Registration of Marks. If the applicant does not give such indication, the International Bureau shall classify the goods or services in the appropriate classes of the said Classification. The indication of classes given by the applicant shall be subject to control by the International Bureau, which shall exercise the said control in association with the national Office. In the event of disagreement between the national Office and the International Bureau, the opinion of the latter shall prevail.

(3) If the applicant claims color as a distinctive feature of his mark, he shall be required:

1. to state the fact, and to file with his application a notice specifying the color or the combination of colors claimed;
2. to append to his application copies in color of the said mark, which shall be attached to the notification given by the International Bureau. The number of such copies shall be fixed by the Regulations.

(4) The International Bureau shall register immediately the marks filed in accordance with Article 1. The registration shall bear the data of the application for international registration in the country of origin, provided that the application has been received by the International Bureau within a period of two months from that date. If the application has not been received within that period, the International Bureau shall record it as at the date on which it received the said application. The International Bureau shall notify such registration without delay to the Offices concerned. Registered marks shall be published in a periodical journal issued by the International Bureau, on the basis of the particulars contained in the application for registration. In the case of marks comprising a figurative element or a special form of writing, the Regulations shall

determine whether a printing block must be supplied by the applicant.

(5) With a view to the publicity to be given in the contracting countries to registered marks, each Office shall receive from the International Bureau a number of copies of the said publication free of charge and a number of copies at a reduced price, in proportion to the number of units mentioned in Article 16(4)*(a)* of the Paris Convention for the Protection of Industrial Property, under the conditions fixed by the Regulations. Such publicity shall be deemed in all the contracting countries to be sufficient, and no other publicity may be required of the applicant.

Article 3*bis*
"Territorial Limitation"

(1) Any contracting country may, at any time, notify the Director General of the Organization (hereinafter designated as "the Director General") in writing that the protection resulting from the international registration shall extend to that country only at the express request of the proprietor of the mark.

(2) Such notification shall not take effect until six months after the date of the communication thereof by the Director General to the other contracting countries.

Article 3*ter*
Request for "Territorial Extension"

(1) Any request for extension of the protection resulting from the international registration to a country which has availed itself of the right provided for in Article 3*bis* must be specially mentioned in the application referred to in Article 3(1).

(2) Any request for territorial extension made subsequently to the international registration must be presented through the intermediary of the Office of the country of origin on a form prescribed by the Regulations. It shall be immediately registered by the International Bureau, which shall notify it without delay to the Office or Offices concerned. It shall be published in the periodical journal issued by the International Bureau. Such territorial extension shall be effective from the date on which it has been recorded in the International Register; it shall cease to be valid on the expiration of the international registration of the mark to which it relates.

Article 4
Effects of International Registration

(1) From the date of the registration so effected at the International Bureau in accordance with the provisions of Articles 3 and 3*ter*, the protection of the mark in each of the contracting countries concerned shall be the same as if the mark had been filed therein direct. The indication of classes of goods or services provided for in Article 3 shall not bind the contracting countries with regard to the determination of the scope of the protection of the mark.

(2) Every mark which has been the subject of an international registration shall enjoy the right of priority provided for by Article 4 of the Paris Convention for the Protection of Industrial Property, without requiring compliance with the formalities prescribed in Section D of that Article.

Article 4*bis*
Substitution of International Registration for Earlier National Registrations

(1) When a mark already filed in one or more of the contracting countries is later registered by the International Bureau in the name of the same proprietor or his successor in title, the international registration shall be deemed to have replaced the earlier national registrations, without prejudice to any rights acquired by reason of such earlier registrations.

(2) The national Office shall, upon request, be required to take note in its registers of the international registration.

Article 5
Refusal by National Offices

(1) In countries where the legislation so authorizes, Offices notified by the International Bureau of the registration of a mark or of a request for extension of protection made in accordance with Article 3*ter* shall have the right to declare that protection cannot be granted to such mark in their territory. Any such refusal can be based only on the grounds which would apply, under the Paris Convention for the Protection of Industrial Property, in the case of a mark filed for national registration. However, protection may not be refused, even partially, by reason only that national legislation would not permit registration except in a limited number of classes or for a limited number of goods or services.

(2) Offices wishing to exercise such right must give notice of their refusal to the International Bureau, together with a statement of all grounds, within the period prescribed by their domestic law and, at the latest, before the expiration of one year from the date of the international registration of the mark or of the request for extension of protection made in accordance with Article 3*ter*.

(3) The International Bureau shall, without delay, transmit to the Office of the country of origin and to the proprietor of the mark, or to his agent if an agent has been mentioned to the Bureau by the said Office, one of the copies of the declaration of refusal so notified. The interested party shall have the same remedies as if the mark had been filed by him direct in the country where protection is refused.

(4) The grounds for refusing a mark shall be communicated by the International Bureau to any interested party who may so request.

(5) Offices which, within the aforesaid maximum period of one year, have not communicated to the International Bureau any provisional or final decision of refusal with regard to the registration of a mark or a request for extension of protection shall lose the benefit of the right provided for in paragraph (1) of this Article with respect to the mark in question.

(6) Invalidation of an international mark may not be pronounced by the competent authorities without the proprietor of the mark having, in good time, been afforded the opportunity of defending his rights. Invalidation shall be notified to the International Bureau.

Article 5*bis*
Documentary Evidence of Legitimacy of Use of Certain Elements of Mark

Documentary evidence of the legitimacy of the use of certain elements incorporated in a mark, such as armorial bearings, escutcheons, portraits, honorary distinctions, titles, trade names, names of persons other than the name of the applicant, or other like inscriptions, which might be required by the Offices of the contracting countries shall be exempt from any legalization or certification other than that of the Office of the country of origin.

Article 5*ter*
Copies of Entries in International Register. Searches for Anticipation. Extracts from International Register

(1) The International Bureau shall issue to any person applying therefor, subject to a fee fixed by the Regulations, a copy of the entries in the Register relating to a specific mark.

(2) The International Bureau may also, upon payment, undertake searches for anticipation among international marks.

(3) Extracts from the International Register requested with a view to their production in one of the contracting countries shall be exempt from all legalization.

Article 6
Period of Validity of International Registration. Independence of International Registration. Termination of Protection in Country of Origin

(1) Registration of a mark at the International Bureau is effected for twenty years, with the possibility of renewal under the conditions specified in Article 7.

(2) Upon expiration of a period of five years from the date of the international registration, such registration shall become independent of the national mark registered earlier in the country of origin, subject to the following provisions.

(3) The protection resulting from the international registration, whether or not it has been the subject of a transfer, may no longer be invoked, in whole or in part, if, within five years from the date of the international registration, the national mark, registered earlier in the country of origin in accordance with Article 1, no longer enjoys, in whole or in part, legal protection in that country. This provision shall also apply when legal protection has later ceased as the result of an action begun before the expiration of the period of five years.

(4) In the case of voluntary or ex officio cancellation, the Office of the country of origin shall request the cancellation of the mark at the International Bureau, and the latter shall effect the cancellation. In the case of judicial action, the said Office shall send to the International Bureau, ex officio or at the request of the plaintiff, a copy of the complaint or any other documentary evidence that an action has begun, and also of the final decision of the court; the Bureau shall enter notice thereof in the International Register.

Article 7
Renewal of International Registration

(1) Any registration may be renewed for a period of twenty years from the expiration of the preceding period, by payment only of the basic fee and, where necessary, of the supplementary and complementary fees provided for in Article 8(2).

(2) Renewal may not include any change in relation to the previous registration in its latest form.

(3) The first renewal effected under the provisions of the Nice Act of June 15, 1957, or of this Act, shall include an indication of the classes of the International Classification to which the registration relates.

(4) Six months before the expiration of the term of protection, the International Bureau shall, by sending an unofficial notice, remind the proprietor of the mark and his agent of the exact date of expiration.

(5) Subject to the payment of a surcharge fixed by the Regulations, a period of grace of six months shall be granted for renewal of the international registration.

Article 8

National Fee. International Fee. Division of Excess Receipts, Supplementary Fees, and Complementary Fees

(1) The Office of the country of origin may fix, at its own discretion, and collect, for its own benefit, a national fee which it may require from the proprietor of the mark in respect of which international registration or renewal is applied for.

(2) Registration of a mark at the International Bureau shall be subject to the advance payment of an international fee which shall include:

(*a*) a basic fee;
(*b*) a supplementary fee for each class of the International Classification, beyond three, into which the goods or services to which the mark is applied will fall;
(*c*) a complementary fee for any request for extension of protection under Article 3*ter*.

(3) However, the supplementary fee specified in paragraph (2)(*b*) may, without prejudice to the date of registration, be paid within a period fixed by the Regulations if the number of classes of goods or services has been fixed or disputed by the International Bureau. If, upon expiration of the said period, the supplementary fee has not been paid or the list of goods or services has not been reduced to the required extent by the applicant, the application for international registration shall be deemed to have been abandoned.

(4) The annual returns from the various receipts from international registration, with the exception of those provided for under *(b)* and *(c)* of paragraph (2), shall be divided equally among the countries party to this Act by the International Bureau, after deduc-

tion of the expenses and charges necessitated by the implementation of the said Act. If, at the time this Act enters into force, a country has not yet ratified or acceded to the said Act, it shall be entitled, until the date on which its ratification or accession becomes effective, to a share of the excess receipts calculated on the basis of that earlier Act which is applicable to it.

(5) The amounts derived from the supplementary fees provided for in paragraph (2)(*b*) shall be divided at the expiration of each year among the countries party to this Act or to the Nice Act of June 15, 1957, in proportion to the number of marks for which protection has been applied for in each of them during that year, this number being multiplied in the case of countries which make a preliminary examination, by a coefficient which shall be determined by the Regulations. If, at the time this Act enters into force, a country has not yet ratified or acceded to the said Act, it shall be entitled, until the date on which its ratification or accession becomes effective, to a share of the amounts calculated on the basis of the Nice Act.

(6) The amounts derived from the complementary fees provided for in paragraph (2)(*c*) shall be divided according to the requirements of paragraph (5) among the countries availing themselves of the right provided for in Article 3*bis*. If, at the time this Act enters into force, a country has not yet ratified or acceded to the said Act, it shall be entitled, until the date on which its ratification or accession becomes effective, to a share of the amounts calculated on the basis of the Nice Act.

Article 8*bis*
Renunciation in Respect of One or More Countries

The person in whose name the international registration stands may at any time renounce protection in one or more of the contracting countries by means of a declaration filed with the Office of his own country, for communication to the International Bureau, which shall notify accordingly the countries in respect of which renunciation has been made. Renunciation shall not be subject to any fee.

Article 9
Changes in National Registers also Affecting International Registration. Reduction of List of Goods and Services Mentioned in International Registration. Additions to that List. Substitutions in that List

(1) The Office of the country of the person in whose name the international registration stands shall likewise notify the International Bureau of all annulments, cancellations, renunciations, trans-

fers, and other changes made in the entry of the mark in the national register, if such changes also effect the international registration.

(2) The Bureau shall record those changes in the International Register, shall notify them in turn to the Offices of the contracting countries, and shall publish them in its journal.

(3) A similar procedure shall be followed when the person in whose name the international registration stands requests a reduction of the list of goods or services to which the registration applies.

(4) Such transactions may be subject to a fee, which shall be fixed by the Regulations.

(5) The subsequent addition of new goods or services to the said list can be obtained only by filing a new application as prescribed in Article 3.

(6) The substitution of one of the goods or services for another shall be treated as an addition.

Article 9*bis*

Transfer of International Mark Entailing Change in Country of Proprietor

(1) When a mark registered in the International Register is transferred to a person established in a contracting country other than the country of the person in whose name the international registration stands, the transfer shall be notified to the International Bureau by the Office of the latter country. The International Bureau shall record the transfer, shall notify the other Offices thereof, and shall publish it in its journal. If the transfer has been effected before the expiration of a period of five years from the international registration, the International Bureau shall seek the consent of the Office of the country of the new proprietor, and shall publish, if possible, the date and registration number of the mark in the country of the new proprietor.

(2) No transfer of a mark registered in the International Register for the benefit of a person who is not entitled to file an international mark shall be recorded.

(3) When it has not been possible to record a transfer in the International Register, either because the country of the new proprietor has refused its consent or because the said transfer has been made for the benefit of a person who is not entitled to apply for international registration, the Office of the country of the former proprietor shall have the right to demand that the International Bureau cancel the mark in its Register.

Article 9*ter*

Assignment of International Mark for Part Only of Registered Goods or Services or for Certain Contracting Countries. Reference to Article 6*quater* of Paris Convention (Assignment of Mark)

(1) If the assignment of an international mark for part only of the registered goods or services is notified to the International Bureau, the Bureau shall record it in its Register. Each of the contracting countries shall have the right to refuse to recognize the validity of such assignment if the goods or services included in the part so assigned are similar to those in respect of which the mark remains registered for the benefit of the assignor.

(2) The International Bureau shall likewise record the assignment of an international mark in respect of one or several of the contracting countries only.

(3) If, in the above cases, a change occurs in the country of the proprietor, the Office of the country to which the new proprietor belongs shall, if the international mark has been transferred before the expiration of a period of five years from the international registration, give its consent as required by Article 9*bis*.

(4) The provisions of the foregoing paragraphs shall apply subject to Article 6*quater* of the Paris Convention for the Protection of Industrial Property.

Article 9*quater*

Common Office for Several Contracting Countries. Request by Several Contracting Countries to Be Treated as a Single Country

(1) If several countries of the Special Union agree to effect the unification of their domestic legislations on marks, they may notify the Director General:

(*a*) that a common Office shall be substituted for the national Office of each of them, and
(*b*) that the whole of their respective territories shall be deemed to be a single country for the purposes of the application of all or part of the provisions preceding this Article.

(2) Such notification shall not take effect until six months after the date of the communication thereof by the Director General to the other contracting countries.

Article 10
Assembly of the Special Union

(1)(*a*) The Special Union shall have an Assembly consisting of those countries which have ratified or acceded to this Act.

(*b*) The Government of each country shall be represented by one delegate, who may be assisted by alternate delegates, advisors, and experts.

(*c*) The expenses of each delegation shall be borne by the Government which has appointed it, except for the travel expenses and the subsistence allowance of one delegate for each member country, which shall be paid from funds of the Special Union.

(2)(*a*) The Assembly shall:

(i) deal with all matters concerning the maintenance and development of the Special Union and the implementation of this Agreement;

(ii) give directions to the International Bureau concerning the preparation for conferences of revision, due account being taken of any comments made by those countries of the Special Union which have not ratified or acceded to this Act;

(iii) modify the Regulations, including the fixation of the amounts of the fees referred to in Article 8(2) and other fees relating to international registration;

(iv) review and approve the reports and activities of the Director General concerning the Special Union, and give him all necessary instructions concerning matters within the competence of the Special Union;

(v) determine the program and adopt the biennial budget of the Special Union, and approve its final accounts;

(vi) adopt the financial regulations of the Special Union;

(vii) establish such committees of experts and working groups as it may deem necessary to achieve the objectives of the Special Union;

(viii) determine which countries not members of the Special Union and which intergovernmental and international non-governmental organizations shall be admitted to its meetings as observers;

(ix) adopt amendments to Articles 10 to 13;

(x) take any other appropriate action designed to further the objectives of the Special Union;

(xi) perform such other functions as are appropriate under this Agreement.

(2)(*b*) With respect to matters which are of interest also to other Unions administered by the Organization, the Assembly shall make its decisions after having heard the advice of the Coordination Committee of the Organization.

(3)(*a*) Each country member of the Assembly shall have one vote.

(*b*) One half of the countries members of the Assembly shall constitute a quorum.

(*c*) Notwithstanding the provisions of subparagraph (*b*), if, in any session, the number of countries represented is less than one half but equal to or more than one third of the countries members of the Assembly, the Assembly may make decisions but, with the exception of decisions concerning its own procedure, all such decisions shall take effect only if the conditions set forth hereinafter are fulfilled. The International Bureau shall communicate the said decisions to the countries members of the Assembly which were not represented and shall invite them to express in writing their vote or abstention within a period of three months from the date of the communication. If, at the expiration of this period, the number of countries having thus expressed their vote or abstention attains the number of countries which was lacking for attaining the quorum in the session itself, such decisions shall take effect provided that at the same time the required majority still obtains.

(*d*) Subject to the provisions of Article 13(2), the decisions of the Assembly shall require two thirds of the votes cast.

(*e*) Abstentions shall not be considered as votes.

(*f*) A delegate may represent, and vote in the name of, one country only.

(*g*) Countries of the Special Union not members of the Assembly shall be admitted to the meetings of the latter as observers.

(4)(*a*) The Assembly shall meet once in every second calendar year in ordinary session upon convocation by the Director General and, in the absence of exceptional circumstances, during the same period and at the same place as the General Assembly of the Organization.

(*b*) The Assembly shall meet in extraordinary session upon convocation by the Director General, at the request of one fourth of the countries members of the Assembly.

(*c*) The agenda of each session shall be prepared by the Director General.

(5) The Assembly shall adopt its own rules of procedure.

Article 11
International Bureau

(1)(*a*) International registration and related duties, as well as all other administrative tasks concerning the Special Union, shall be performed by the International Bureau.

(*b*) In particular, the International Bureau shall prepare the meetings and provide the secretariat of the Assembly and of such committees of experts and working groups as may have been established by the Assembly.

(*c*) The Director General shall be the chief executive of the Special Union and shall represent the Special Union.

(2) The Director General and any staff member designated by him shall participate, without the right to vote, in all meetings of the Assembly and of such committees of experts or working groups as may have been established by the Assembly. The Director General, or a staff member designated by him, shall be ex officio secretary of those bodies.

(3)(*a*) The International Bureau shall, in accordance with the directions of the Assembly, make the preparations for the conferences of revision of the provisions of the Agreement other than Articles 10 to 13.

(*b*) The International Bureau may consult with intergovernmental and international non-governmental organizations concerning preparations for conferences of revision.

(*c*) The Director General and persons designated by him shall take part, without the right to vote, in the discussions at those conferences.

(4) The International Bureau shall carry out any other tasks assigned to it.

Article 12
Finances

(1)(*a*) The Special Union shall have a budget.

(*b*) The budget of the Special Union shall include the income and expenses proper to the Special Union, its contribution to the budget of expenses common to the Unions, and, where applicable, the sum made available to the budget of the Conference of the Organization.

(*c*) Expenses not attributable exclusively to the Special Union but also to one or more other Unions administered by the Organization shall be considered as expenses common to the Unions. The share of the Special Union in such common expenses shall be in proportion to the interest the Special Union has in them.

(2) The budget of the Special Union shall be established with due regard to the requirements of coordination with the budgets of the other Unions administered by the Organization.

(3) The budget of the Special Union shall be financed from the following sources:

(i) international registration fees and other fees and charges due for other services rendered by the International Bureau in relation to the Special Union;
(ii) sale of, or royalties on, the publications of the International Bureau concerning the Special Union;
(iii) gifts, bequests, and subventions;
(iv) rents, interests, and other miscellaneous income.

(4)(*a*) The amounts of the fees referred to in Article 8(2) and other fees relating to international registration shall be fixed by the Assembly on the proposal of the Director General.

(*b*) The amounts of such fees shall be so fixed that the revenues of the Special Union from fees, other than the supplementary and complementary fees referred to in Article 8(2)(*b*) and (*c*), and other sources shall be at least sufficient to cover the expenses of the International Bureau concerning the Special Union.

(*c*) If the budget is not adopted before the beginning of a new financial period, it shall be at the same level as the budget of the previous year, as provided in the financial regulations.

(5) Subject to the provisions of paragraph (4)(*a*), the amount of fees and charges due for other services rendered by the International Bureau in relation to the Special Union shall be established, and shall be reported to the Assembly, by the Director General.

(6)(*a*) The Special Union shall have a working capital fund which shall be constituted by a single payment made by each country of the Special Union. If the fund becomes insufficient, the Assembly shall decide to increase it.

(*b*) The amount of the initial payment of each country to the said fund or of its participation in the increase thereof shall be a proportion of the contribution of that country as a member of the Paris Union for the Protection of Industrial Property to the budget of the said Union for the year in which the fund is established or the decision to increase it is made.

(*c*) The proportion and the terms of payment shall be fixed by the Assembly on the proposal of the Director General and after it has heard the advice of the Coordination Committee of the Organization.

(*d*) As long as the Assembly authorizes the use of the reserve fund of the Special Union as a working capital fund, the Assembly may suspend the application of the provisions of subparagraphs (*a*), (*b*), and (*c*).

(7)(*a*) In the headquarters agreement concluded with the country on the territory of which the Organization has its headquarters, it shall be provided that, whenever the working capital fund is insufficient, such country shall grant advances. The amount of those advances and the conditions on which they are granted shall be the subject of separate agreements, in each case, between such country and the Organization.

(*b*) The country referred to in subparagraph (*a*) and the Organization shall each have the right to denounce the obligation to grant advances, by written notification. Denunciation shall take effect three years after the end of the year in which it has been notified.

(8) The auditing of the accounts shall be effected by one or more of the countries of the Special Union or by external auditors, as provided in the financial regulations. They shall be designated, with their agreement, by the Assembly.

Article 13
Amendment of Articles 10 to 13

(1) Proposals for the amendment of Articles 10, 11, 12, and the present Article, may be initiated by any country member of the Assembly, or by the Director General. Such proposals shall be communicated by the Director General to the member countries of the Assembly at least six months in advance of their consideration by the Assembly.

(2) Amendments to the Articles referred to in paragraph (1) shall be adopted by the Assembly. Adoption shall require three fourths of the votes cast, provided that any amendment to Article 10, and to the present paragraph, shall require four fifths of the votes cast.

(3) Any amendments to the Articles referred to in paragraph (1) shall enter into force one month after written notifications of acceptance, effected in accordance with their respective constitutional processes, have been received by the Director General from three fourths of the countries members of the Assembly at the time it adopted the amendment. Any amendment to the said Articles thus accepted shall bind all the countries which are members of the Assembly at the time the amendment enters into force, or which become members thereof at a subsequent date.

Article 14
Ratification and Accession. Entry into Force. Accession to Earlier Acts. Reference to Article 24 of Paris Convention (Territories)

(1) Any country of the Special Union which has signed this Act may ratify it, and, if it has not signed it, may accede to it.

(2)(*a*) Any country outside the Special Union which is party to the Paris Convention for the Protection of Industrial Property may accede to this Act and thereby become a member of the Special Union.

(*b*) As soon as the International Bureau is informed that such a country has acceded to this Act, it shall address to the Office of that country, in accordance with Article 3, a collective notification of the marks which, at that time, enjoy international protection.

(*c*) Such notification shall, of itself, ensure to the said marks the benefits of the foregoing provisions in the territory of the said country, and shall mark the commencement of the period of one year during which the Office concerned may make the declaration provided for in Article 5.

(*d*) However, any such country may, in acceding to this Act, declare that, except in the case of international marks which have already been the subject in that country of an earlier identical national registration still in force, and which shall be immediately recognized upon the request of the interested parties, application of this Act shall be limited to marks registered from the date on which its accession enters into force.

(*e*) Such declaration shall dispense the International Bureau from making the collective notification referred to above. The International Bureau shall notify only those marks in respect of which it receives, within a period of one year from the accession of the new country, a request, with the necessary particulars, to take advantage of the exception provided for in subparagraph (*d*).

(*f*) The International Bureau shall not make the collective notification to such countries as declare, in acceding to this Act, that they are availing themselves of the right provided for in Article 3*bis*. The said countries may also declare at the same time that the application of this Act shall be limited to marks registered from the day on which their accessions enter into force; however, such limitation shall not affect international marks which have already been the subject of an earlier identical national registration in those countries, and which could give rise to requests for extension of protection made and notified in accordance with Articles 3*ter* and 8(2)(*c*).

(*g*) Registrations of marks which have been the subject of one of the notifications provided for in this paragraph shall be regarded as replacing registrations effected direct in the new contracting country before the date of entry into force of its accession.

(3) Instruments of ratification and accession shall be deposited with the Director General.

(4)(*a*) With respect to the first five countries which have deposited their instruments of ratification or accession, this Act shall enter into force three months after the deposit of the fifth such instrument.

(*b*) With respect to any other country, this Act shall enter into force three months after the date on which its ratification or accession has been notified by the Director General, unless a subsequent date has been indicated in the instrument of ratification or accession. In the latter case, this Act shall enter into force with respect to that country on the date thus indicated.

(5) Ratification or accession shall automatically entail acceptance of all the clauses and admission to all the advantages of this Act.

(6) After the entry into force of this Act, a country may accede to the Nice Act of June 15, 1957, only in conjunction with ratification of, or accession to, this Act. Accession to Acts earlier than the Nice Act shall not be permitted, not even in conjunction with ratification of, or accession to, this Act.

(7) The provisions of Article 24 of the Paris Convention for the Protection of Industrial Property shall apply to this Agreement.

Article 15
Denunciation

(1) This Agreement shall remain in force without limitation as to time.

(2) Any country may denounce this Act by notification addressed to the Director General. Such denunciation shall constitute also denunciation of all earlier Acts and shall affect only the country making it, the Agreement remaining in full force and effect as regards the other countries of the Special Union.

(3) Denunciation shall take effect one year after the day on which the Director General has received the notification.

(4) The right of denunciation provided for by this Article shall not be exercised by any country before the expiration of five years from the date upon which it becomes a member of the Special Union.

(5) International marks registered up to the date on which denunciation becomes effective, and not refused within the period of one year provided for in Article 5, shall continue, throughout the period of international protection, to enjoy the same protection as if they had been filed direct in the denouncing country.

Article 16
Application of Earlier Acts

(1)(*a*) This Act shall, as regards the relations between the countries of the Special Union by which it has been ratified or acceded to, replace, as from the day on which it enters into force with respect to them, the Madrid Agreement of 1891, in its texts earlier than this Act.

(*b*) However, any country of the Special Union which has ratified or acceded to this Act shall remain bound by the earlier texts which it has not previously denounced by virtue of Article 12(4) of the Nice Act of June 15, 1957, as regards its relations with countries which have not ratified or acceded to this Act.

(2) Countries outside the Special Union which become party to this Act shall apply it to international registrations effected at the International Bureau through the intermediary of the national Office of any country of the Special Union not party to this Act, provided that such registrations satisfy, with respect to the said countries, the requirements of this Act. With regard to international registrations effected at the International Bureau through the intermediary of the national Offices of the said countries outside the Special Union which become party to this Act, such countries recognize that the aforesaid country of the Special Union may demand compliance with the requirements of the most recent Act to which it is party.

Article 17
Signature, Languages, Depositary Functions

(1)(*a*) This Act shall be signed in a single copy in the French language and shall be deposited with the Government of Sweden.

(*b*) Official texts shall be established by the Director General, after consultation with the interested Governments, in such other languages as the Assembly may designate.

(2) This Act shall remain open for signature at Stockholm until January 13, 1968.

(3) The Director General shall transmit two copies, certified by the Government of Sweden, of the signed text of this Act to the Governments of all countries of the Special Union and, on request, to the Government of any other country.

(4) The Director General shall register this Act with the Secretariat of the United Nations.

(5) The Director General shall notify the Governments of all countries of the Special Union of signatures, deposits of instruments of ratification or accession and any declarations included in such instruments, entry into force of any provisions of this Act, notifications of denunciation, and notifications pursuant to Articles 3*bis*, 9*quater*, 13, 14(7), and 15(2).

Article 18
Transitional Provisions

(1) Until the first Director General assumes office, references in this Act to the International Bureau of the Organization or to the Director General shall be construed as references to the Bureau of the Union established by the Paris Convention for the Protection of Industrial Property or its Director, respectively.

(2) Countries of the Special Union not having ratified or acceded to this Act may, until five years after the entry into force of the Convention establishing the Organization, exercise, if they so desire, the rights provided for under Articles 10 to 13 of this Act as if they were bound by those Articles. Any country desiring to exercise such rights shall give written notification to that effect to the Director General; such notification shall be effective from the date of its receipt. Such countries shall be deemed to be members of the Assembly until the expiration of the said period.

Protocol Relating to the Madrid Agreement Concerning the International Registration of Marks

Article 1
Membership in the Madrid Union

The States party to this Protocol (hereinafter referred to as "the Contracting States"), even where they are not party to the Madrid Agreement Concerning the International Registration of Marks as revised at Stockholm in 1967 and as amended in 1979 (hereinafter referred to as "the Madrid (Stockholm) Agreement"), and the organizations referred to in Article 14(1)(*b*) which are party to this Protocol (hereinafter referred to as "the Contracting Organizations") shall be members of the same Union of which countries party to the Madrid (Stockholm) Agreement are members. Any reference in this Protocol to "Contracting Parties" shall be construed as a reference to both Contracting States and Contracting Organizations.

Article 2
Securing Protection Through International Registration

(1) Where an application for the registration of a mark has been filed with the Office of a Contracting Party, or where a mark has been registered in the register of the Office of a Contracting Party, the person in whose name that application (hereinafter referred to as "the basic application") or that registration (hereinafter referred to as "the basic registration") stands may, subject to the provisions of this Protocol, secure protection for his mark in the territory of the Contracting Parties, by obtaining the registration of that mark in the register of the International Bureau of the World Intellectual Property Organization (hereinafter referred to as "the international registration," "the International Register," "the International Bureau" and "the Organization," respectively), provided that,

(i) where the basic application has been filed with the Office of a Contracting State or where the basic registration has been made by such an Office, the person in whose name that application or registration stands is a national of that Con-

---

Source: Text courtesy of the World Intellectual Property Organization (WIPO).

tracting State, or is domiciled, or has a real and effective industrial or commercial establishment, in the said Contracting State,

(ii) where the basic application has been filed with the Office of a Contracting Organization or where the basic registration has been made by such an Office, the person in whose name that application or registration stands is a national of a State member of that Contracting Organization, or is domiciled, or has a real and effective industrial or commercial establishment, in the territory of the said Contracting Organization.

(2) The application for international registration (hereinafter referred to as "the international application") shall be filed with the International Bureau through the intermediary of the Office with which the basic application was filed or by which the basic registration was made (hereinafter referred to as "the Office of origin"), as the case may be.

(3) Any reference in the Protocol to an "Office" or an "Office of a Contracting Party" shall be construed as a reference to the office that is in charge, on behalf of a Contracting Party, of the registration of marks, and any reference in this Protocol to "marks" shall be construed as a reference to trademarks and service marks.

(4) For the purposes of this Protocol, "territory of a Contracting Party" means, where the Contracting Party is a State, the territory of that State and, where the Contracting Party is an intergovernmental organization, the territory in which the constituting treaty of that intergovernmental organization applies.

Article 3
International Application

(1) Every international application under this Protocol shall be presented on the form prescribed by the Regulations. The Office of origin shall certify that the particulars appearing in the international application correspond to the particulars appearing, at the time of the certification, in the basic application or basic registration, as the case may be. Furthermore, the said Office shall indicate,

(i) in the case of a basic application, the date and number of that application,

(ii) in the case of a basic registration, the date and number of that registration as well as the date and number of the application from which the basic registration resulted.

The Office of origin shall also indicate the date of the international application.

(2) The applicant must indicate the goods and services in respect of which protection of the mark is claimed and also, if possible, the corresponding class or classes according to the classification established by the Nice Agreement Concerning the International Classification of Goods and Services for the Purposes of the Registration of Marks. If the applicant does not give such indication, the International Bureau shall classify the goods and services in the appropriate classes of the said classification. The indication of classes given by the applicant shall be subject to control by the International Bureau, which shall exercise the said control in association with the Office of origin. In the event of disagreement between the said Office and the International Bureau, the opinion of the latter shall prevail.

(3) If the applicant claims color as a distinctive feature of his mark, he shall be required

(i) to state the fact, and to file with his international application a notice specifying the color or the combination of colors claimed;

(ii) to append to his international application copies in color of the said mark, which shall be attached to the notifications given by the International Bureau; the number of such copies shall be fixed by the Regulations.

(4) The International Bureau shall register immediately the marks filed in accordance with Article 2. The international registration shall bear the date on which the international application was received in the Office of origin, provided that the international application has been received by the International Bureau within a period of two months from that date. If the international application has not been received within that period, the international registration shall bear the date on which the said international application was received by the International Bureau. The International Bureau shall notify the international registration without delay to the Offices concerned. Marks registered in the International Register shall be published in a periodical gazette issued by the International Bureau, on the basis of the particulars contained in the international application.

(5) With a view to the publicity to be given to marks registered in the International Register, each Office shall receive from the International Bureau a number of copies of the said gazette free of charge and a number of copies at a reduced price, under the conditions fixed by the Assembly referred to in Article 10 (hereinafter referred to as "the Assembly"). Such publicity shall be deemed to be

sufficient for the purposes of all the Contracting Parties, and no other publicity may be required of the holder of the international registration.

Article 3*bis*
Territorial Effect

The protection resulting from the international registration shall extend to any Contracting Party only at the request of the person who files the international application or who is the holder of the international registration. However, no such request can be made with respect to the Contracting Party whose Office is the Office of origin.

Article 3*ter*
Request for "Territorial Extension"

(1) Any request for extension of the protection resulting from the international registration to any Contracting Party shall be specially mentioned in the international application.

(2) A request for territorial extension may also be made subsequently to the international registration. Any such request shall be presented on the form prescribed by the Regulations. It shall be immediately recorded by the International Bureau, which shall notify such recordal without delay to the Office or Offices concerned. Such recordal shall be published in the periodical gazette of the International Bureau. Such territorial extension shall be effective from the date on which it has been recorded in the International Register; it shall cease to be valid on the expiry of the international registration to which it relates.

Article 4
Effects of International Registration

(1)*(a)* From the date of the registration or recordal effected in accordance with the provisions of Articles 3 and 3*ter*, the protection of the mark in each of the Contracting Parties concerned shall be the same as if the mark had been deposited direct with the Office of that Contracting Party. If no refusal has been notified to the International Bureau in accordance with Article 5(1) and (2) or if a refusal notified in accordance with the said Article has been withdrawn subsequently, the protection of the mark in the Contracting Party concerned shall, as from the said date, be the same as if the mark had been registered by the Office of that Contracting Party.

(b) The indication of classes of goods and services provided for in Article 3 shall not bind the Contracting Parties with regard to the determination of the scope of the protection of the mark.

(2) Every international registration shall enjoy the right of priority provided for by Article 4 of the Paris Convention for the Protection of Industrial Property, without it being necessary to comply with the formalities prescribed in Section D of that Article.

Article 4*bis*
Replacement of a National or Regional Registration by an International Registration

(1) Where a mark that is the subject of a national or regional registration in the Office of a Contracting Party is also the subject of an international registration and both registrations stand in the name of the same person, the international registration is deemed to replace the national or regional registration, without prejudice to any rights acquired by virtue of the latter, provided that

(i) the protection resulting from the international registration extends to the said Contracting Party under Article 3*ter*(1) or (2),

(ii) all the goods and services listed in the national or regional registration are also listed in the international registration in respect of the said Contracting Party,

(iii) such extension takes effect after the date of the national or regional registration.

(2) The Office referred to in paragraph (1) shall, upon request, be required to take note in its register of the international registration.

Article 5
Refusal and Invalidation of Effects of International Registration in Respect of Certain Contracting Parties

(1) Where the applicable legislation so authorizes, any Office of a Contracting Party which has been notified by the International Bureau of an extension to that Contracting Party, under Article 3*ter*(1) or (2), of the protection resulting from the international registration shall have the right to declare in a notification of refusal that protection cannot be granted in the said Contracting Party to the

mark which is the subject of such extension. Any such refusal can be based only on the grounds which would apply, under the Paris Convention for the Protection of Industrial Property, in the case of a mark deposited direct with the Office which notifies the refusal. However, protection may not be refused, even partially, by reason only that the applicable legislation would permit registration only in a limited number of classes or for a limited number of goods or services.

(2)(*a*) Any Office wishing to exercise such right shall notify its refusal to the International Bureau, together with a statement of all grounds, within the period prescribed by the law applicable to that Office and at the latest, subject to subparagraphs (*b*) and (*c*), before the expiry of one year from the date on which the notification of the extension referred to in paragraph (1) has been sent to that Office by the International Bureau.

(*b*) Notwithstanding subparagraph (*a*), any Contracting Party may declare that, for international registrations made under this Protocol, the time limit of one year referred to in subparagraph (*a*) is replaced by 18 months.

(*c*) Such declaration may also specify that, when a refusal of protection may result from an opposition to the granting of protection, such refusal may be notified by the Office of the said Contracting Party to the International Bureau after the expiry of the 18-month time limit. Such an Office may, with respect to any given international registration, notify a refusal of protection after the expiry of the 18-month time limit, but only if

(i) it has, before the expiry of the 18-month time limit, informed the International Bureau of the possibility that oppositions may be filed after the expiry of the 18-month time limit, and

(ii) the notification of the refusal based on an opposition is made within a time limit of not more than seven months from the date on which the opposition period begins; if the opposition period expires before this time limit of seven months, the notification must be made within a time limit of one month from the expiry of the opposition period.

(*d*) Any declaration under subparagraphs (*b*) or (*c*) may be made in the instruments referred to in Article 14(2), and the effective date of the declaration shall be the same as the date of entry into force of this Protocol with respect to the State or intergovernmental organization having made the declaration. Any such declaration may also be made later, in which case the declaration shall have effect three months after its receipt by the Director General of the organization (hereinafter referred to as "the Director General"), or at any later date indicated in the declaration, in respect of any international registration whose date is the same as or is later than the effective date of the declaration.

(*e*) Upon the expiry of a period of ten years from the entry into force of this Protocol, the Assembly shall examine the operation of the system established by subparagraphs (*a*) to (*d*). Thereafter, the provisions of the said subparagraphs may be modified by a unanimous decision of the Assembly.

(3) The International Bureau shall, without delay, transmit one of the copies of the notification of refusal to the holder of the international registration. The said holder shall have the same remedies as if the mark had been deposited by him direct with the Office which has notified its refusal. Where the International Bureau has received information under paragraph (2)(*c*)(i), it shall, without delay, transmit the said information to the holder of the international registration.

(4) The grounds for refusing a mark shall be communicated by the International Bureau to any interested party who may so request.

(5) Any Office which has not notified, with respect to a given international registration, any provisional or final refusal to the International Bureau in accordance with paragraphs (1) and (2) shall, with respect to that international registration, lose the benefit of the right provided for in paragraph (1).

(6) Invalidation, by the competent authorities of a Contracting Party, of the effects, in the territory of that Contracting Party, of an international registration may not be pronounced without the holder of such international registration having, in good time, been afforded the opportunity of defending his rights. Invalidation shall be notified to the International Bureau.

Article 5*bis*

Documentary Evidence of Legitimacy of Use of Certain Elements of the Mark

Documentary evidence of the legitimacy of the use of certain elements incorporated in a mark, such as armorial bearings, escutcheons, portraits, honorary distinctions, titles, trade names, names of persons other than the name of the applicant, or other like inscriptions, which might be required by the Offices of the Contracting Parties shall be exempt from any legalization as well as from any certification other than that of the Office of origin.

Article 5*ter*
Copies of Entries in International Register; Searches for Anticipations; Extracts from International Register

(1) The International Bureau shall issue to any person applying therefor, upon the payment of a fee fixed by the Regulations, a copy of the entries in the International Register concerning a specific mark.

(2) The International Bureau may also, upon payment, undertake searches for anticipations among marks that are the subject of international registrations.

(3) Extracts from the International Register requested with a view to their production in one of the Contracting Parties shall be exempt from any legalization.

Article 6
Period of Validity of International Registration; Dependence and Independence of International Registration

(1) Registration of a mark at the International Bureau is effected for ten years, with the possibility of renewal under the conditions specified in Article 7.

(2) Upon expiry of a period of five years from the date of the international registration, such registration shall become independent of the basic application or the registration resulting therefrom, or of the basic registration, as the case may be, subject to the following provisions.

(3) The protection resulting from the international registration, whether or not it has been the subject of a transfer, may no longer be invoked if, before the expiry of five years from the date of the international registration, the basic application or the registration resulting therefrom, or the basic registration, as the case may be, has been withdrawn, has lapsed, has been renounced or has been the subject of a final decision of rejection, revocation, cancellation or invalidation, in respect of all or some of the goods and services listed in the international registration. The same applies if

(i) an appeal against a decision refusing the effects of the basic application,

(ii) an action requesting the withdrawal of the basic application or the revocation, cancellation or invalidation of the registration resulting from the basic application or of the basic registration, or

(iii) an opposition to the basic application

results, after the expiry of the five-year period, in a final decision of rejection, revocation, cancellation or invalidation, or ordering the withdrawal, of the basic application, or the registration resulting therefrom, or the basic registration, as the case may be, provided that such appeal, action or opposition had begun before the expiry of the said period. The same also applies if the basic application is withdrawn, or the registration resulting from the basic application or the basic registration is renounced, after the expiry of the five-year period, provided that, at the time of the withdrawal or renunciation, the said application or registration was the subject of a proceeding referred to in item (i), (ii) or (iii) and that such proceeding had begun before the expiry of the said period.

(4) The Office of origin shall, as prescribed in the Regulations, notify the International Bureau of the facts and decisions relevant under paragraph (3), and the International Bureau shall, as prescribed in the Regulations, notify the interested parties and effect any publication accordingly. The Office of origin shall, where applicable, request the International Bureau to cancel, to the extent applicable, the international registration, and the International Bureau shall proceed accordingly.

Article 7
Renewal of International Registration

(1) Any international registration may be renewed for a period of ten years from the expiry of the preceding period, by the mere payment of the basic fee and, subject to Article 8(7), of the supplementary and complementary fees provided for in Article 8(2).

(2) Renewal may not bring about any change in the international registration in its latest form.

(3) Six months before the expiry of the term of protection, the International Bureau shall, by sending an unofficial notice, remind the holder of the international registration and his representative, if any, of the exact date of expiry.

(4) Subject to the payment of a surcharge fixed by the Regulations, a period of grace of six months shall be allowed for renewal of the international registration.

Article 8
Fees for International Application and Registration

(1) The Office of origin may fix, at its own discretion, and collect, for its own benefit, a fee which it may require from the applicant for international registration or from the holder of the international

registration in connection with the filing of the international application or the renewal of the international registration.

(2) Registration of a mark at the International Bureau shall be subject to the advance payment of an international fee which shall, subject to the provisions of paragraph (7)(*a*), include,

(i) a basic fee;
(ii) a supplementary fee for each class of the International Classification, beyond three, into which the goods or services to which the mark is applied will fall;
(iii) a complementary fee for any request for extension of protection under Article 3*ter*.

(3) However, the supplementary fee specified in paragraph (2)(ii) may, without prejudice to the date of the international registration, be paid within the period fixed by the Regulations if the number of classes of goods or services has been fixed or disputed by the International Bureau. If, upon expiry of the said period, the supplementary fee has not been paid or the list of goods or services has not been reduced to the required extent by the applicant, the international application shall be deemed to have been abandoned.

(4) The annual product of the various receipts from international registration, with the exception of the receipts derived from the fees mentioned in paragraph (2)(ii) and (iii), shall be divided equally among the Contracting Parties by the International Bureau, after deduction of the expenses and charges necessitated by the implementation of this Protocol.

(5) The amounts derived from the supplementary fees provided for in paragraph (2)(ii) shall be divided, at the expiry of each year, among the interested Contracting Parties in proportion to the number of marks for which protection has been applied for in each of them during that year, this number being multiplied, in the case of Contracting Parties which make an examination, by a coefficient which shall be determined by the Regulations.

(6) The amounts derived from the complementary fees provided for in paragraph (2)(iii) shall be divided according to the same rules as those provided for in paragraph (5).

(7)(*a*) Any Contracting Party may declare that, in connection with each international registration in which it is mentioned under Article 3*ter*, and in connection with the renewal of any such international registration, it wants to receive, instead of a share in the revenue produced by the supplementary and complementary fees, a fee (hereinafter referred to as "the individual fee") whose amount shall be indicated in the declaration, and can be changed in further declarations, but may not be higher than the equivalent of the amount which the said Contracting Party's Office would be entitled to receive from an applicant for a ten-year renewal of that registration, of the mark in the register of the said Office, the said amount being diminished by the savings resulting from the international procedure. Where such an individual fee is payable,

(i) no supplementary fees referred to in paragraph (2)(ii) shall be payable if only Contracting Parties which have made a declaration under this subparagraph are mentioned under Article 3*ter*, and

(ii) no complementary fee referred to in paragraph (2)(iii) shall be payable in respect of any Contracting Party which has made a declaration under this subparagraph.

(*b*) Any declaration under subparagraph (*a*) may be made in the instruments referred to in Article 14(2), and the effective date of the declaration shall be the same as the date of entry into force of this Protocol with respect to the State or intergovernmental organization having made the declaration. Any such declaration may also be made later, in which case the declaration shall have effect three months after its receipt by the Director General, or at any later date indicated in the declaration, in respect of any international registration whose date is the same as or is later than the effective date of the declaration.

Article 9
Recordal of Change in the Ownership of an International Registration

At the request of the person in whose name the international registration stands, or at the request of an interested Office made ex officio or at the request of an interested person, the International Bureau shall record in the International Register any change in the ownership of that registration, in respect of all or some of the Contracting Parties in whose territories the said registration has effect and in respect of all or some of the goods and services listed in the registration, provided that the new holder is a person who, under Article 2(1), is entitled to file international applications.

Article 9*bis*
Recordal of Certain Matters Concerning an International Registration

The International Bureau shall record in the International Register

(i) any change in the name or address of the holder of the international registration,
(ii) the appointment of a representative of the holder of the international registration and any other relevant fact concerning such representative,
(iii) any limitation, in respect of all or some of the Contracting Parties, of the goods and services listed in the international registration,
(iv) any renunciation, cancellation or invalidation of the international registration in respect of all or some of the Contracting Parties,
(v) any other relevant fact, identified in the Regulations, concerning the rights in a mark that is the subject of an international registration.

Article 9*ter*
Fees for Certain Recordals

Any recordal under Article 9 or under Article 9*bis* may be subject to the payment of a fee.

Article 9*quater*
Common Office of Several Contracting States

(1) If several Contracting States agree to effect the unification of their domestic legislations on marks, they may notify the Director General

(i) that a common Office shall be substituted for the national Office of each of them, and
(ii) that the whole of their respective territories shall be deemed to be a single State for the purposes of the application of all or part of the provisions preceding this Article as well as the provisions of Articles 9*quinquies* and 9*sexies*.

(2) Such notification shall not take effect until three months after the date of the communication thereof by the Director General to the other Contracting Parties.

Article 9*quinquies*
Transformation of an International Registration into National or Regional Applications

Where, in the event that the international registration is cancelled at the request of the Office of origin under Article 6(4), in respect of all or some of the goods and services listed in the said registration, the person who was the holder of the international registration files an application for the registration of the same mark with the Office of any of the Contracting Parties in the territory of which the international registration had effect, that application shall be treated as if it had been filed on the date of the international registration according to Article 3(4) or on the date of recordal of the territorial extension according to Article 3*ter*(2) and, if the international registration enjoyed priority, shall enjoy the same priority, provided that

(i) such application is filed within three months from the date on which the international registration was cancelled,

(ii) the goods and services listed in the application are in fact covered by the list of goods and services contained in the international registration in respect of the Contracting Party concerned, and

(iii) such application complies with all the requirements of the applicable law, including the requirements concerning fees.

Article 9*sexies*
Safeguard of the Madrid (Stockholm) Agreement

(1) Where, with regard to a given international application or a given international registration, the Office of origin is the Office of a State that is party to both this Protocol and the Madrid (Stockholm) Agreement, the provisions of this Protocol shall have no effect in the territory of any other State that is also party to both this Protocol and the Madrid (Stockholm) Agreement.

(2) The Assembly may, by a three-fourths majority, repeal paragraph (1), or restrict the scope of paragraph (1), after the expiry of a period of ten years from the entry into force of this Protocol, but not before the expiry of a period of five years from the data on which the majority of the countries party to the Madrid (Stockholm) Agreement have become party to this Protocol. In the vote of the Assembly, only those States which are party to both the said Agreement and this Protocol shall have the right to participate.

Article 10
Assembly

(1)(*a*) The Contracting Parties shall be members of the same Assembly as the countries party to the Madrid (Stockholm) Agreement.

(*b*) Each Contracting Party shall be represented in that Assembly by one delegate, who may be assisted by alternate delegates, advisors, and experts.

(*c*) The expenses of each delegation shall be borne by the Contracting Party which has appointed it, except for the travel expenses and the subsistence allowance of one delegate for each Contracting Party, which shall be paid from the funds of the Union.

(2) The Assembly shall, in addition to the functions which it has under the Madrid (Stockholm) Agreement, also

(i) deal with all matters concerning the implementation of this Protocol;
(ii) give directions to the International Bureau concerning the preparation for conferences of revision of this Protocol, due account being taken of any comments made by those countries of the Union which are not party to this Protocol;
(iii) adopt and modify the provisions of the Regulations concerning the implementation of this Protocol;
(iv) perform such other functions as are appropriate under this Protocol.

(3)(*a*) Each Contracting Party shall have one vote in the Assembly. On matters concerning only countries that are party to the Madrid (Stockholm) Agreement, Contracting Parties that are not party to the said Agreement shall not have the right to vote, whereas, on matters concerning only Contracting Parties, only the latter shall have the right to vote.

(*b*) One-half of the members of the Assembly which have the right to vote on a given matter shall constitute the quorum for the purposes of the vote on that matter.

(*c*) Notwithstanding the provisions of subparagraph (*b*), if, in any session, the number of the members of the Assembly having the right to vote on a given matter which are represented is less than one-half but equal to or more than one-third of the members of the Assembly having the right to vote on that matter, the Assembly may make decisions but, with the exception of decisions concerning its own procedure, all such decisions shall take effect only if the conditions set forth hereinafter are fulfilled. The International Bureau shall communicate the said decisions to the members of the Assembly having the right to vote on the said matter which were not represented and shall invite them to express in writing their vote or abstention within a period of three months from the date of the communication. If, at the expiry of this period, the number of such members having thus expressed their vote or abstention attains the number of the members which was lacking for attaining the quorum in the session itself, such decisions shall take effect provided that at the same time the required majority still obtains.

(*d*) Subject to the provisions of Articles 5(2)(*e*), 9*sexies*(2), 12 and 13(2), the decisions of the Assembly shall require two-thirds of the votes cast.

(*e*) Abstentions shall not be considered as votes.

(*f*) A delegate may represent, and vote in the name of, one member of the Assembly only.

(4) In addition to meeting in ordinary sessions and extraordinary sessions as provided for by the Madrid (Stockholm) Agreement, the Assembly shall meet in extraordinary session upon convocation by the Director General, at the request of one-fourth of the members of the Assembly having the right to vote on the matters proposed to be included in the agenda of the session. The agenda of such an extraordinary session shall be prepared by the Director General.

Article 11
International Bureau

(1) International registration and related duties, as well as all other administrative tasks, under or concerning this Protocol, shall be performed by the International Bureau.

(2)(*a*) The International Bureau shall, in accordance with the directions of the Assembly, make the preparations for the conferences of revision of this Protocol.

(*b*) The International Bureau may consult with intergovernmental and international non-governmental organizations concerning preparations for such conferences of revision.

(*c*) The Director General and persons designated by him shall take part, without the right to vote, in the discussions at such conferences of revision.

(3) The International Bureau shall carry out any other tasks assigned to it in relation to this Protocol.

Article 12
Finances

As far as Contracting Parties are concerned, the finances of the Union shall be governed by the same provisions as those contained in Article 12 of the Madrid (Stockholm) Agreement, provided that any reference to Article 8 of the said Agreement shall be deemed to be a reference to Article 8 of this Protocol. Furthermore, for the purposes of Article 12(6)(*b*) of the said Agreement, Contracting Organizations shall, subject to a unanimous decision to the contrary by the Assembly, be considered to belong to contribution class I (one) under the Paris Convention for the Protection of Industrial Property.

Article 13
Amendment of Certain Articles of the Protocol

(1) Proposals for the amendment of Articles 10, 11, 12, and the present Article, may be initiated by any Contracting Party, or by the Director General. Such proposals shall be communicated by the Director General to the Contracting Parties at least six months in advance of their consideration by the Assembly.

(2) Amendments to the Articles referred to in paragraph (1) shall be adopted by the Assembly. Adoption shall require three-fourths of the votes cast, provided that any amendment to Article 10, and to the present paragraph, shall require four-fifths of the votes cast.

(3) Any amendment to the Articles referred to in paragraph (1) shall enter into force one month after written notifications of acceptance, effected in accordance with their respective constitutional processes, have been received by the Director General from three-fourths of those States and intergovernmental organizations which, at the time the amendment was adopted, were members of the Assembly and had the right to vote on the amendment. Any amendment to the said Articles thus accepted shall bind all the States and intergovernmental organizations which are Contracting Parties at the time the amendment enters into force, or which become Contracting Parties at a subsequent date.

Article 14
Becoming Party to the Protocol; Entry into Force

(1)(*a*) Any State that is a party to the Paris Convention for the Protection of Industrial Property may become party to this Protocol.

(*b*) Furthemore, any intergovernmental organization may also become party to this Protocol where the following conditions are fulfilled:

(i) at least one of the member States of that organization is a party to the Paris Convention for the Protection of Industrial Property;

(ii) that organization has a regional Office for the purposes of registering marks with effect in the territory of the organization, provided that such Office is not the subject of a notification under Article 9*quater*.

(2) Any State or organization referred to in paragraph (1) may sign this Protocol. Any such State or organization may, if it has signed this Protocol, deposit an instrument of ratification, acceptance or approval of this Protocol or, if it has not signed this Protocol, deposit an instrument of accession to this Protocol.

(3) The instruments referred to in paragraph (2) shall be deposited with the Director General.

(4)(*a*) This Protocol shall enter into force three months after four instruments of ratification, acceptance, approval or accession have been deposited, provided that at least one of those instruments has been deposited by a country party to the Madrid (Stockholm) Agreement and at least one other of those instruments has been deposited by a State not party to the Madrid (Stockholm) Agreement or by any of the organizations referred to in paragraph (1)(*b*).

(*b*) With respect to any other State or organization referred to in paragraph (1), this Protocol shall enter into force three months after the date on which its ratification, acceptance, approval or accession has been notified by the Director General.

(5) Any State or organization referred to in paragraph (1) may, when depositing its instrument of ratification, acceptance or approval of, or accession to, this Protocol, declare that the protection resulting from any international registration effected under this Protocol before the date of entry into force of this Protocol with respect to it cannot be extended to it.

Article 15
Denunciation

(1) This Protocol shall remain in force without limitation as to time.

(2) Any Contracting Party may denounce this Protocol by notification addressed to the Director General.

(3) Denunciation shall take effect one year after the day on which the Director General has received the notification.

(4) The right of denunciation provided for by this Article shall not be exercised by any Contracting Party before the expiry of five

years from the date upon which this Protocol entered into force with respect to that Contracting Party.

(5)(*a*) Where a mark is the subject of an international registration having effect in the denouncing State or intergovernmental organization at the date on which the denunciation becomes effective, the holder of such registration may file an application for the registration of the same mark with the Office of the denouncing State or intergovernmental organization, which shall be treated as if it had been filed on the date of the international registration according to Article 3(4) or on the date of recordal of the territorial extension according to Article 3*ter*(2) and, if the international registration enjoyed priority, enjoy the same priority provided that

(i) such application is filed within two years from the date on which the denunciation became effective,

(ii) the goods and services listed in the application are in fact covered by the list of goods and services contained in the international registration in respect of the denouncing State or intergovernmental organization, and

(iii) such application complies with all the requirements of the applicable law, including the requirements concerning fees.

(*b*) The provisions of subparagraph (*a*) shall also apply in respect of any mark that is the subject of an international registration having effect in Contracting Parties other than the denouncing State or intergovernmental organization at the date on which denunciation becomes effective and whose holder, because of the denunciation, is no longer entitled to file international applications under Article 2(1).

Article 16
Signature; Languages; Depositary Functions

(1)(*a*) This Protocol shall be signed in a single copy in the English, French and Spanish languages, and shall be deposited with the Director General when it ceases to be open for signature at Madrid. The texts in the three languages shall be equally authentic.

(*b*) Official texts of this Protocol shall be established by the Director General, after consultation with the interested governments and organizations, in the Arabic, Chinese, German, Italian, Japanese, Portuguese and Russian languages, and in such other languages as the Assembly may designate.

(2) This Protocol shall remain open for signature at Madrid until December 31, 1989.

(3) The Director General shall transmit two copies, certified by the Government of Spain, of the signed texts of this Protocol to all States and intergovernmental organizations that may become party to this Protocol.

(4) The Director General shall register this Protocol with the Secretariat of the United Nations.

(5) The Director General shall notify all States and international organizations that may become or are party to this Protocol of signatures, deposits of instruments of ratification, acceptance, approval or accession, the entry into force of this Protocol and any amendment thereto, any notification of denunciation and any declaration provided for in this Protocol

2. Agreement of Madrid for the Prevention of False or Misleading Indications of Source on Goods

April 14, 1891, revised at Washington on June 2, 1911, at The Hague on November 6, 1925, at London on June 2, 1934, and at Lisbon on October 31, 1958, and the additional Act of Stockholm of July 14, 1967

The Madrid Agreement for the Repression of False or Deceptive Indications of Source on Goods was concluded at Madrid in 1891, and has been revised four times and supplemented by the additional Act of Stockholm in 1967. The Madrid Agreement is intended to protect consumers against persons using false indications of source on goods. An indication of source is a geographic designation indicating the place where the goods came from, e.g., Paris perfume.

The Madrid Agreement played a more important role in protecting indications of source before the Lisbon revision of the Paris Convention in 1958. Before the Lisbon revision, Article 10 of The Hague (1925) and London (1934) texts of the Paris Convention protected indications of source only if *fraudulent intent* could be proved. The Madrid Agreement was drafted to prohibit all false indications of source regardless of the user's intent. Since the Lisbon revision (1958) of the Paris Convention, Article 10 extends protection to indications of source without the fraud requirement. Accordingly, the continuing need for the Madrid Agreement has been thrown in doubt.

The Madrid Agreement requires seizure or import prohibition of all goods bearing a false or misleading indication by whichever one of the member countries or a place located therein that is directly or indirectly indicated as the country or place of origin (Art. 1 para. 1).

The Madrid Agreement does not require protection for all indications of origin. It allows the tribunals of each member country to decide whether an indication of origin has become generic (Art. 4). This provision applies to all manner of goods except for regional appellations for wine, which cannot be declared generic.

As of January 1, 1990, the following 32 states were party to the Madrid Agreement:

- Algeria
- Brazil
- Bulgaria
- Cuba
- Czechoslovakia
- Dominican Republic
- Egypt
- France
- German Democratic Republic
- Federal Republic of Germany
- Hungary
- Ireland
- Israel
- Italy
- Japan
- Lebanon
- Liechtenstein
- Monaco
- Morocco
- New Zealand
- Poland
- Portugal
- San Marino
- Spain
- Sri Lanka
- Sweden
- Switzerland
- Syria
- Tunisia
- Turkey
- United Kingdom
- Viet Nam

Agreement of Madrid for the Prevention of False or Misleading Indications of Source on Goods, as revised at Lisbon, 1958

Article 1

(1) All goods bearing a false or misleading indication, by which one of the countries to which this Agreement applies, or a place situated therein, is directly or indirectly indicated as being the country or place of origin, shall be seized on importation into any of the said countries.

(2) Seizure shall take place either in the country where the false or misleading indication of source has been applied, or in the country into which the goods bearing the false or misleading indication have been imported.

(3) If the law of a country does not permit seizure on importation, such seizure shall be replaced by prohibition of importation.

(4) If the law of a country permits neither seizure upon importation, nor prohibition of importation, nor seizure within the country, then, until such time as the law is modified accordingly, these measures shall be replaced by the actions and remedies available in such cases to nationals under the law of such country.

(5) In the absence of any special sanctions ensuring the prevention of false or misleading indications of source, the sanctions provided by the corresponding stipulations of the laws relating to marks or trade names shall be applicable.

Article 2

(1) Seizure shall be effected by the Customs Authorities, who shall immediately inform the interested party, whether an individual person or a legal entity, in order that such person may, if he so desires, take appropriate steps to confirm the seizure effected as a conservatory measure. Nevertheless, the Public Prosecutor or any other competent authority may demand seizure either at the request

---

Source: Text courtesy of the World Intellectual Property Organization (WIPO).

of the injured party or ex officio; the procedure shall then follow its normal course.

(2) The Authorities are not bound to effect seizure in transit.

Article 3

These provisions shall not prevent the vendor from indicating his name or address upon goods coming from a country other than that in which the sale takes place; but in such case the address or the name must be accompanied by a clear indication in legible characters of the country or place of manufacture or production, or by some other indication sufficient to avoid any error as to the true source of the goods.

Article 3*bis*

The countries to which this Agreement applies similarly undertake to prohibit the use, in connection with the sale or display or offering for sale of any goods, of all indications in the nature of publicity capable of deceiving the public as to the source of the goods, and appearing on signs, advertisements, invoices, wine lists, business letters or papers or any other commercial communication.

Article 4

The tribunals of each country shall decide what appellations, on account of their generic character, do not fall within the provisions of this Agreement, regional appellations concerning the source of products of the vine being, however, excluded from the reserve specified by this Article.

Article 5

(1) Countries belonging to the Union for the Protection of Industrial Property, which have not acceded to this Agreement, shall be allowed to accede at their request in the manner prescribed by Article 16 of the General Convention.

(2) The provisions of Articles 16*bis* and 17*bis* of the General Convention are applicable to this Agreement.

Article 6

(1) This Act shall be ratified and the instruments of ratification deposited in Berne not later than May 1, 1963. It shall come into force, between the countries in whose names it has been ratified, one month after that date. However, if before that date it has been ratified in the name of at least six countries, it shall come into force, between those countries, one month after the deposit of the sixth ratification has been notified to them by the Government of the Swiss Confederation, and, in the case of countries in whose names it has been ratified at a later date, one month after the notification of each of such ratifications.

(2) Countries in whose names the instrument of ratification has not been deposited within the period provided for in the preceding paragraph shall be permitted to accede under the terms of Article 16 of the General Convention.

(3) This Act shall, as regards the relations between the countries to which it applies, replace the Agreement concluded at Madrid on April 14, 1891, and the subsequent acts of revision.

(4) As regards the countries to which this Act does not apply, but to which the Agreement of Madrid revised at London in 1934 applies, the latter shall remain in force.

(5) Similarly, as regards the countries to which neither this Act nor the agreement of Madrid revised at London applies, the Agreement of Madrid revised at The Hague in 1925 shall remain in force.

(6) Similarly, as regards the countries to which neither this Act nor the Agreement of Madrid revised at London nor the Agreement of Madrid revised at The Hague applies, the Agreement of Madrid revised at Washington in 1911 shall remain in force.

Additional Act of Stockholm, of July 14, 1967, to the Madrid Agreement for the Repression of False or Deceptive Indications of Source on Goods

Article 1
Transfer of Depositary Functions in Respect of the Madrid Agreement

Instruments of accession to the Madrid Agreement for the Repression of False or Deceptive Indications of Source on Goods, of April 14, 1891 (hereinafter designated as "the Madrid Agreement"), as revised at Washington on June 2, 1911, at The Hague on November 6, 1925, at London on June 2, 1934, and at Lisbon on October 31, 1958 (hereinafter designated as "the Lisbon Act"), shall be deposited with the Director General of the World Intellectual Property Organization (hereinafter designated as "the Director General"), who shall notify such deposits to the countries party to the Agreement.

Article 2
Adaptation of References in the Madrid Agreement to Certain Provisions of the Paris Convention

References in Articles 5 and 6(2) of the Lisbon Act to Articles 16, 16*bis*, and 17*bis*, of the General Convention shall be construed as references to those provisions of the Stockholm Act of the Paris Convention for the Protection of Industrial Property which correspond to the said Articles.

Article 3
Signature and Ratification of, and Accession to, the Additional Act

(1) This Additional Act may be signed by any country party to the Madrid Agreement and may be ratified or acceded to by any country which has ratified or acceded to the Lisbon Act.

(2) Instruments of ratification or accession shall be deposited with the Director General.

Article 4
Automatic Acceptance of Articles 1 and 2 by Countries Acceding to the Lisbon Act

Any country which has not ratified or acceded to the Lisbon Act shall become bound also by Articles 1 and 2 of this Additional Act from the date on which its accession to the Lisbon Act enters into force, provided, however, that, if on the said date this Additional Act has not yet entered into force pursuant to Article 5(1), then, such country shall become bound by Articles 1 and 2 of this Additional Act only from the date of entry into force of this Additional Act pursuant to Article 5(1).

Article 5
Entry into Force of the Additional Act

(1) This Additional Act shall enter into force on the date on which the Stockholm Convention of July 14, 1967, establishing the World Intellectual Property Organization has entered into force, provided, however, that, if by that date at least two ratifications or accessions to this Additional Act have not been deposited, then, this Additional Act shall enter into force on the date on which two ratifications or accessions to this Additional Act have been deposited.

(2) With respect to any country which deposits its instrument of ratification or accession after the date on which this Additional Act has entered into force pursuant to the foregoing paragraph, this Additional Act shall enter into force three months after the date on which its ratification or accession has been notified by the Director General.

Article 6
Signature, etc., of the Additional Act

(1) This Additional Act shall be signed in a single copy in the French language and shall be deposited with the Government of Sweden.

(2) This Additional Act shall remain open for signature at Stockholm until the date of its entry into force pursuant to Article 5(1).

(3) The Director General shall transmit two copies, certified by the Government of Sweden, of the signed text of this Additional Act to the Governments of all countries party to the Madrid Agreement and, on request, to the Government of any other country.

(4) The Director General shall register this Additional Act with the Secretariat of the United Nations.

(5) The Director General shall notify the Governments of all countries party to the Madrid Agreement of signatures, deposits of instruments of ratification or accession, entry into force, and other relevant notifications.

Article 7
Transitional Provision

Until the first Director General assumes office, references in this Additional Act to him shall be construed as references to the Director of the United International Bureaux for the Protection of Intellectual Property.

3. Lisbon Agreement for the Protection of Appellations of Origin and Their International Registration

October 31, 1958, revised at Stockholm on July 14, 1967, and amended 1979

The Lisbon Agreement for the Protection of Appellations of Origin and Their International Registration was concluded in 1958 and was revised at Stockholm in 1967. The Agreement protects appellations of origin, defined as the geographical name of a country, region, or locality, which serves to designate a product originating therein having quality and characteristics due exclusively or essentially to the geographical environment, including natural or human factors (Art. 2). Examples of appellations of origin could be Limoges (china) or Roquefort (cheese).

The Lisbon Agreement for the Protection of Appellations of Origin should be compared with the Madrid Agreement on indications of source. The two terms "indications of source" and "appellations of origin" are closely related. An indication of source is merely a geographic designation indicating where the goods came from, e.g., Paris perfume. The primary goal of the Madrid Agreement is to protect the consumer from being mislead. By contrast "appellations of origin," which relate to product characteristics or quality because of their production in a specific geographic location, goes beyond protection of the consumer interest. Accordingly, manufacturers of these products concerned also are protected against the misuse of the appellation by persons not entitled to their use, even though the consumer may not be deceived about the nature or origin of the product.

Under Article 1 of the Lisbon Agreement, contracting parties must protect the appellations of origin of other contracting parties recognized and protected in the country of origin and registered at the International Bureau of WIPO. Registration of the appellation of origin with the International Bureau is a prerequisite of protection (Art. 1 para. 1). Registration may be requested only by the administration of the country on behalf of the persons who own the appellation under national law (Art. 5 para. 1). The international registration effected by the country of origin is transmitted by the International Bureau to the appropriate organization in each member country (Art. 5 para. 2). Within one year of receipt of notification, administrations of member countries may inform the International Bureau of the reasons why they cannot ensure protection of the registered appellation (Art. 5 para. 3). The International Bureau will apprise the country of origin promptly of a declaration of nonprotection of the appellation.

Member countries must ensure protection of the registered appellation against any usurpation or imitation, even if the product's true origin is indicated or if the appellation is used in translated form or accompanied by terms such as kind, type, make, imitation, or the like (Art. 3).

As of January 1, 1990, the following 16 states were party to the Lisbon Agreement:

Algeria	Haiti
Bulgaria	Hungary
Burkina Faso	Israel
Congo	Italy
Cuba	Mexico
Czechoslovakia	Portugal
France	Togo
Gabon	Tunisia

Lisbon Agreement for the Protection of Appellations of Origin and Their International Registration, as revised at Stockholm, 1967

Article 1

(1) The countries to which this Agreement applies constitute a Special Union within the framework of the Union for the Protection of Industrial Property.

(2) They undertake to protect on their territories, in accordance with the terms of this Agreement, the appellations of origin of products of the other countries of the Special Union, recognized and protected as such in the country of origin and registered at the International Bureau of Intellectual Property (hereinafter designated as "the International Bureau" or "the Bureau") referred to in the Convention establishing the World Intellectual Property Organization (hereinafter designated as "the Organization").

Article 2

(1) In this Agreement, "appellation of origin" means the geographical name of a country, region, or locality, which serves to designate a product originating therein, the quality and characteristics of which are due exclusively or essentially to the geographical environment, including natural and human factors.

(2) The country of origin is the country whose name, or the country in which is situated the region or locality whose name, constitutes the appellation of origin which has given the product its reputation.

Article 3

Protection shall be ensured against any usurpation or imitation, even if the true origin of the product is indicated or if the appellation is used in translated form or accompanied by terms such as "kind", "type", "make", "imitation", or the like.

Source: Text courtesy of the World Intellectual Property Organization (WIPO).

Article 4

The provisions of this Agreement shall in no way exclude the protection already granted to appellations of origin in each of the countries of the Special Union by virtue of other international instruments, such as the Paris Convention of March 20, 1883, for the Protection of Industrial Property and its subsequent revisions, and the Madrid Agreement of April 14, 1891, for the Repression of False or Deceptive Indications of Source on Goods and its subsequent revisions, or by virtue of national legislation or court decisions.

Article 5

(1) The registration of appellations of origin shall be effected at the International Bureau, at the request of the Offices of the countries of the Special Union, in the name of any natural persons or legal entities, public or private, having, according to their national legislation, a right to use such appellations.

(2) The International Bureau shall, without delay, notify the Offices of the various countries of the Special Union of such registrations, and shall publish them in a periodical.

(3) The Office of any country may declare that it cannot ensure the protection of an appellation of origin whose registration has been notified to it, but only in so far as its declaration is notified to the International Bureau, together with an indication of the grounds therefor, within a period of one year from the receipt of the notification of registration, and provided that such declaration is not detrimental, in the country concerned, to the other forms of protection of the appellation which the owner thereof may be entitled to claim under Article 4, above.

(4) Such declaration may not be opposed by the Offices of the countries of the Union after the expiration of the period of one year provided for in the foregoing paragraph.

(5) The International Bureau shall, as soon as possible, notify the Office of the country of origin of any declaration made under the terms of paragraph (3) by the Office of another country. The interested party, when informed by his national Office of the declaration made by another country, may resort, in that other country, to all the judicial and administrative remedies open to the nationals of that country.

(6) If an appellation which has been granted protection in a given country pursuant to notification of its international registration has already been used by third parties in that country from a date prior to such notification, the competent Office of the said coun-

try shall have the right to grant to such third parties a period not exceeding two years to terminate such use, on condition that it advise the International Bureau accordingly during the three months following the expiration of the period of one year provided for in paragraph (3), above.

Article 6

An appellation which has been granted protection in one of the countries of the Special Union pursuant to the procedure under Article 5 cannot, in that country, be deemed to have become generic, as long as it is protected as an appellation of origin in the country of origin.

Article 7

(1) Registration effected at the International Bureau in conformity with Article 5 shall ensure, without renewal, protection for the whole of the period referred to in the foregoing Article.

(2) A single fee shall be paid for the registration of each appellation of origin.

Article 8

Legal action required for ensuring the protection of appellations or origin may be taken in each of the countries of the Special Union under the provisions of the national legislation:

1. at the instance of the competent Office or at the request of the public prosecutor;
2. by any interested party, whether a natural person or a legal entity, whether public or private.

Article 9

(1)(*a*) The Special Union shall have an Assembly consisting of those countries which have ratified or acceded to this Act.

(*b*) The Government of each country shall be represented by one delegate, who may be assisted by alternate delegates, advisors, and experts.

(*c*) The expenses of each delegation shall be borne by the Government which has appointed it.

(2)(*a*) The Assembly shall:

(i) deal with all matters concerning the maintenance and development of the Special Union and the implementation of this Agreement;

(ii) give directions to the International Bureau concerning the preparation for conferences of revision, due account being taken of any comments made by those countries of the Special Union which have not ratified or acceded to this Act;

(iii) modify the Regulations, including the fixation of the amount of the fee referred to in Article 7(2) and other fees relating to international registration;

(iv) review and approve the reports and activities of the Director General of the Organization (hereinafter designated as "the Director General") concerning the Special Union, and give him all necessary instructions concerning matters within the competence of the Special Union;

(v) determine the program and adopt the biennial budget of the Special Union, and approve its final accounts;

(vi) adopt the financial regulations of the Special Union;

(vii) establish such committees of experts and working groups as it may deem necessary to achieve the objectives of the Special Union;

(viii) determine which countries not members of the Special Union and which intergovernmental and international non-governmental organizations shall be admitted to its meetings as observers;

(ix) adopt amendments to Articles 9 to 12;

(x) take any other appropriate action designed to further the objectives of the Special Union;

(xi) perform such other functions as are appropriate under this Agreement.

(*b*) With respect to matters which are of interest also to other Unions administered by the Organization, the Assembly shall make its decisions after having heard the advice of the Coordination Committee of the Organization.

(3)(*a*) Each country member of the Assembly shall have one vote.

(*b*) One-half of the countries members of the Assembly shall constitute a quorum.

(*c*) Notwithstanding the provisions of subparagraph (*b*), if, in any session, the number of countries represented is less than one-half but equal to or more than one-third of the countries members of the Assembly, the Assembly may make decisions but, with the exception of decisions concerning its own procedure, all such decisions shall take effect only if the conditions set forth hereinafter are fulfilled. The International Bureau shall communicate the said decisions to the countries members of the Assembly which were not represented and shall invite them to express in writing their vote or abstention within a period of three months from the date of the communication. If, at the expiration of this period, the number of countries having thus expressed their vote or abstention attains the number of countries which was lacking for attaining the quorum in the session itself, such decisions shall take effect provided that at the same time the required majority still obtains.

(*d*) Subject to the provisions of Article 12(2), the decisions of the Assembly shall require two-thirds of the votes cast.

(*e*) Abstentions shall not be considered as votes.

(*f*) A delegate may represent, and vote in the name of, one country only.

(*g*) Countries of the Special Union not members of the Assembly shall be admitted to the meetings of the latter as observers.

(4)(*a*) The Assembly shall meet once in every second calendar year in ordinary session upon convocation by the Director General and, in the absence of exceptional circumstances, during the same period and at the same place as the General Assembly of the Organization.

(*b*) The Assembly shall meet in extraordinary session upon convocation by the Director General, at the request of one-fourth of the countries members of the Assembly.

(*c*) The agenda of each session shall be prepared by the Director General.

(5) The Assembly shall adopt its own rules of procedure.

Article 10

(1)(*a*) International registration and related duties, as well as all other administrative tasks concerning the Special Union, shall be performed by the International Bureau.

(*b*) In particular, the International Bureau shall prepare the meetings and provide the secretariat of the Assembly and of such committees of experts and working groups as may have been established by the Assembly.

(*c*) The Director General shall be the chief executive of the Special Union and shall represent the Special Union.

(2) The Director General and any staff member designated by him shall participate, without the right to vote, in all meetings of the Assembly and of such committees of experts or working groups as may have been established by the Assembly. The Director Gen-

eral, or a staff member designated by him, shall be ex officio secretary of those bodies.

(3)(*a*) The International Bureau shall, in accordance with the directions of the Assembly, make the preparations for the conferences of revision of the provisions of the Agreement other than Articles 9 to 12.

(*b*) The International Bureau may consult with intergovernmental and international non-governmental organizations concerning preparations for conferences of revision.

(*c*) The Director General and persons designated by him shall take part, without the right to vote, in the discussions at those conferences.

(4) The International Bureau shall carry out any other tasks assigned to it.

Article 11

(1)(*a*) The Special Union shall have a budget.

(*b*) The budget of the Special Union shall include the income and expenses proper to the Special Union, its contribution to the budget of expenses common to the Unions, and, where applicable, the sum made available to the budget of the Conference of the Organization.

(*c*) Expenses not attributable exclusively to the Special Union but also to one or more other Unions administered by the Organization shall be considered as expenses common to the Unions. The share of the Special Union in such common expenses shall be in proportion to the interest the Special Union has in them.

(2) The budget of the Special Union shall be established with due regard to the requirements of coordination with the budgets of the other Unions administered by the Organization.

(3) The budget of the Special Union shall be financed from the following sources:

(i) international registration fees collected under Article 7(2) and other fees and charges due for other services rendered by the International Bureau in relation to the Special Union;

(ii) sale of, or royalties on, the publications of the International Bureau concerning the Special Union;

(iii) gifts, bequests, and subventions;

(iv) rents, interests, and other miscellaneous income;

(v) contributions of the countries of the Special Union, if and to the extent to which receipts from the sources indicated in items (i) to (iv) do not suffice to cover the expenses of the Special Union.

(4)(*a*) The amount of the fee referred to in Article 7(2) shall be fixed by the Assembly on the proposal of the Director General.

(*b*) The amount of the said fee shall be so fixed that the revenue of the Special Union should, under normal circumstances, be sufficient to cover the expenses of the International Bureau for maintaining the international registration service, without requiring payment of the contributions referred to in paragraph (3)(v), above.

(5)(*a*) For the purpose of establishing its contribution referred to in paragraph (3)(v), each country of the Special Union shall belong to the same class as it belongs to in the Paris Union for the Protection of Industrial Property, and shall pay its annual contributions on the basis of the same number of units as is fixed for that class in that Union.

(*b*) The annual contribution of each country of the Special Union shall be an amount in the same proportion to the total sum to be contributed to the budget of the Special Union by all countries as the number of its units is to the total of the units of all contributing countries.

(*c*) The date on which contributions are to be paid shall be fixed by the Assembly.

(*d*) A country which is in arrears in the payment of its contributions may not exercise its right to vote in any of the organs of the Special Union if the amount of its arrears equals or exceeds the amount of the contributions due from it for the preceding two full years. However, any organ of the Union may allow such a country to continue to exercise its right to vote in that organ if, and as long as, it is satisfied that the delay in payment is due to exceptional and unavoidable circumstances.

(*e*) If the budget is not adopted before the beginning of a new financial period, it shall be at the same level as the budget of the previous year, as provided in the financial regulations.

(6) Subject to the provisions of paragraph (4)(*a*), the amount of fees and charges due for other services rendered by the International Bureau in relation to the Special Union shall be established, and shall be reported to the Assembly, by the Director General.

(7)(*a*) The Special Union shall have a working capital fund which shall be constituted by a single payment made by each country of the Special Union. If the fund becomes insufficient, the Assembly shall decide to increase it.

(*b*) The amount of the initial payment of each country to the said fund or of its participation in the increase thereof shall be a proportion of the contribution of that country as a member of the Paris Union for the Protection of Industrial Property to the budget of the said Union for the year in which the fund is established or the decision to increase it is made.

(*c*) The proportion and the terms of payment shall be fixed by the Assembly on and after it has heard the advice of the Coordination Committee of the Organization.

(8)(*a*) In the headquarters agreement concluded with the country on the territory of which the Organization has its headquarters, it shall be provided that, whenever the working capital fund is insufficient, such country shall grant advances. The amount of those advances and the conditions on which they are granted shall be the subject of separate agreements, in each case, between such country and the Organization.

(*b*) The country referred to in subparagraph (*a*) and the Organization shall each have the right to denounce the obligation to grant advances, by written notification. Denunciation shall take effect three years after the end of the year in which it has been notified.

(9) The auditing of the accounts shall be effected by one or more of the countries of the Special Union or by external auditors, as provided in the financial regulations. They shall be designated, with their agreement, by the Assembly.

Article 12

(1) Proposals for the amendment of Articles 9, 10, 11, and the present Article, may be initiated by any country member of the Assembly, or by the Director General. Such proposals shall be communicated by the Director General to the member countries of the Assembly at least six months in advance of their consideration by the Assembly.

(2) Amendments to the Articles referred to in paragraph (1) shall be adopted by the Assembly. Adoption shall require three-fourths of the votes cast, provided that any amendment to Article 9, and to the present paragraph, shall require four-fifths of the votes cast.

(3) Any amendment to the Articles referred to in paragraph (1) shall enter into force one month after written notifications of acceptance, effected in accordance with their respective constitutional processes, have been received by the Director General from three-fourths of the countries members of the Assembly at the time it adopted the amendment. Any amendment to the said Articles thus accepted shall bind all the countries which are members of the Assembly at the time the amendment enters into force, or which become members thereof at a subsequent date, provided that any amendment increasing the financial obligations of countries of the Special Union shall bind only those countries which have notified their acceptance of such amendment.

Article 13

(1) The details for carrying out this Agreement are fixed in the Regulations.

(2) This Agreement may be revised by conferences held between the delegates of the countries of the Special Union.

Article 14

(1) Any country of the Special Union which has signed this Act may ratify it, and, if it has not signed it, may accede to it.

(2)(*a*) Any country outside the Special Union which is party to the Paris Convention for the Protection of Industrial Property may accede to this Act and thereby become a member of the Special Union.

(*b*) Notification of accession shall, of itself, ensure, in the territory of the acceding country, the benefits of the foregoing provisions to appellations of origin which, at the time of accession, are the subject of international registration.

(*c*) However, any country acceding to this Agreement may, within a period of one year, declare in regard to which appellations of origin, already registered at the International Bureau, it wishes to exercise the right provided for in Article 5(3).

(3) Instruments of ratification and accession shall be deposited with the Director General.

(4) The provisions of Article 24 of the Paris Convention for the Protection of Industrial Property shall apply to this Agreement.

(5)(*a*) With respect to the first five countries which have deposited their instruments of ratification or accession, this Act shall enter into force three months after the deposit of the fifth such instrument.

(*b*) With respect to any other country, this Act shall enter into force three months after the date on which its ratification or accession has been notified by the Director General, unless a subsequent date has been indicated in the instrument of ratification or accession. In the latter case, this Act shall enter into force with respect to that country on the date thus indicated.

(6) Ratification or accession shall automatically entail acceptance of all the clauses and admission to all the advantages of this Act.

(7) After the entry into force of this Act, a country may accede to the original Act of October 31, 1958, of this Agreement only in conjunction with ratification of, or accession to, this Act.

Article 15

(1) This Agreement shall remain in force as long as five countries at least are party to it.

(2) Any country may denounce this Act by notification addressed to the Director General. Such denunciation shall constitute also denunciation of the original Act of October 31, 1958, of this Agreement and shall affect only the country making it, the Agreement remaining in full force and effect as regards the other countries of the Special Union.

(3) Denunciation shall take effect one year after the day on which the Director General has received the notification.

(4) The right of denunciation provided for by this Article shall not be exercised by any country before the expiration of five years from the date upon which it becomes a member of the Special Union.

Article 16

(1) This Act shall, as regards the relations between the countries of the Special Union by which it has been ratified or acceded to, replace the original Act of October 31, 1958.

(2) However, any country of the Special Union which has ratified or acceded to this Act shall be bound by the original Act of October 31, 1958, as regards its relations with countries of the Special Union which have not ratified or acceded to this Act.

(3) Countries outside the Special Union which become party to this Act shall apply it to international registrations of appellations of origin effected at the International Bureau at the request of the Office of any country of the Special Union not party to this Act, provided that such registrations satisfy, with respect to the said countries, the requirements of this Act. With regard to international registrations effected at the International Bureau at the request of the Offices of the said countries outside the Special Union which become party to this Act, such countries recognize that the aforesaid country of the Special Union may demand compliance with the requirements of the original Act of October 31, 1958.

Article 17

(1)(*a*) This Act shall be signed in a single copy in the French language and shall be deposited with the Government of Sweden.

(*b*) Official texts shall be established by the Director General, after consultation with the interested Governments, in such other languages as the Assembly may designate.

(2) This Act shall remain open for signature at Stockholm until January 13, 1968.

(3) The Director General shall transmit two copies, certified by the Government of Sweden, of the signed text of this Act to the Governments of all countries of the Special Union and, on request, to the Government of any other country.

(4) The Director General shall register this Act with the Secretariat of the United Nations.

(5) The Director General shall notify the Governments of all countries of the Special Union of signatures, deposits of instruments of ratification or accession, entry into force of any provisions of this Act, denunciations, and declarations pursuant to Article 14(2)(*c*) and (4).

Article 18

(1) Until the first Director General assumes office, references in this Act to the International Bureau of the Organization or to the Director General shall be construed as references to the Bureau of the Union established by the Paris Convention for the Protection of Industrial Property or its Director, respectively.

(2) Countries of the Special Union not having ratified or acceded to this Act may, until five years after the entry into force of the Convention establishing the Organization, exercise, if they so desire, the rights provided for under Articles 9 to 12 of this Act as if they were bound by those Articles. Any country desiring to exercise such rights shall give written notification to that effect to the Director General; such notification shall be effective from the date of its receipt. Such countries shall be deemed to be members of the Assembly until the expiration of the said period.

4. Trademark Registration Treaty

Done at Vienna, on June 12, 1973, and amended in 1980

The Trademark Registration Treaty (TRT) was concluded on June 12, 1973, and entered into effect on August 7, 1980. Unlike the Madrid Arrangement, the TRT allows for an international registration that is not dependent on the mark's registration in the country of origin. The TRT thus avoids the major objection to the Madrid Agreement which is said to favor those countries that pose the least hurdles to registration, such as a brief or cursory examination of the application for trademark.

Administered by the International Bureau of WIPO, the TRT is a special agreement under the Union of Paris. Only members of the Paris Union may join the TRT.

A resident or national of a member state may file an international application (Art. 4 para. 1) that may be filed with the International Bureau (Art. 5 para. 2) or through the intermediary of its national office (Art. 5 para. 3). At the International Bureau, the mark is examined for formal requirements. If these are met, it will be published and communicated to each member state.

The effect of registration in each designated country is as though the mark had been registered in the national register of that country (Art. 11). Once registered, a member state may not refuse or cancel the mark for nonuse during a three-year grace period. However, any member state may require the owners to declare their intentions to use the mark and permit a suit for infringement only after actual use has taken place. After three years of nonuse of the mark in a member country, the mark may be canceled if the national law so allows (Art. 19 para. 3).

International registration confers an initial term of 10 years that may be renewed for subsequent 10-year terms upon payment of the required fees (Art. 17).

As of January 1, 1990, the following five states were party to the TRT:

Burkina Faso	Soviet Union
Congo	Togo
Gabon	

Trademark Registration Treaty

Introductory Provisions

Article 1
Establishment of a Union

The States party to this Treaty (hereinafter called "the Contracting States") constitute a Union for the international registration of marks.

Article 2
Abbreviated Expressions

For the purposes of this Treaty and the Regulations and unless expressly stated otherwise:

(i) "international registration" means a registration effected under this Treaty by the International Bureau in the International Register of Marks;

(ii) "international application" means an application filed for international registration;

(iii) "applicant" means the natural person who or legal entity which files the international application;

(iv) "owner of the international registration" means the natural person or the legal entity in whose name the international registration stands in respect of all or fewer than all the designated States and in respect of all or some only of the goods and/or services listed in that registration;

(v) "mark" means both a trademark and a service mark; it also includes a collective mark within the meaning of Article 7*bis* of the Stockholm (1967) Act of the Paris Convention for the Protection of Industrial Property and a certification mark whether or not such certification mark is a collective mark within the said meaning;

(vi) "national mark" means a mark registered by a government authority of a Contracting State having the power to grant registrations with effect in that State; references to a *national mark* shall not be construed as references also to regional marks;

(vii) "regional mark" means a mark registered by an intergov-

---

Source: Text courtesy of the World Intellectual Property Organization (WIPO).

ernmental authority other than the International Bureau having the power to grant registrations with effect in more than one State;

(viii) references to any *final* decision or *final* refusal shall be construed as references to a decision or refusal against which there is no remedy, or against which all remedies have been exhausted, or where the time limit for asking for a remedy against the refusal or decision has expired;

(ix) references to any *publication by the International Bureau* shall be construed as references to publications effected in the official Gazette of that Bureau;

(x) references to the *date of the publication* of the international registration or to the *date of the publication* of the recording of the later designation shall be construed as references to the date of that issue of the official Gazette of the International Bureau in which the international registration or the recording of the later designation, as the case may be, has been published;

(xi) references to any *recording by the International Bureau* shall be construed as references to recordings made in the International Register of Marks;

(xii) "designated State" means any Contracting State in which the applicant or the owner of the international registration desires that such registration produce the effects provided for in this Treaty and which has been identified for that purpose in the international application or any request for the recording of later designations;

(xiii) "national Office" means the government authority of a Contracting State entrusted with the registration of marks; references to a *national Office* shall be construed as referring also to any intergovernmental authority which several States have entrusted with the task of registering regional marks, provided that at least one of those States is a Contracting State, and provided that such authority has been empowered to assume the obligations and exercise the powers which this Treaty and the Regulations provide for in respect of national Offices;

(xiv) "national register of marks" means the register of marks kept by a national Office in which national and/or regional marks are registered;

(xv) "designated Office" means the national Office of the designated State;

(xvi) references to *national law* shall be construed as references to the national law of a Contracting State and, where a regional mark is involved, to the regional treaty providing for the registration of regional marks;

(xvii) "Madrid Agreement" means the Madrid Agreement Concerning the International Registration of Marks;

(xviii) "Union" means the Union referred to in Article 1;

(xix) "Assembly" means the Assembly of the Union;

(xx) "Organization" means the World Intellectual Property Organization;

(xxi) "International Bureau" means the International Bureau of the Organization and, as long as it subsists, the United International Bureaux for the Protection of Intellectual Property (BIRPI); and where any provision refers to the receiving of documents, or of payments, by the International Bureau, it also includes any agency of that Bureau established under Article 32(2)(*a*)(ix);

(xxii) "Director General" means the Director General of the Organization;

(xxiii) "International Classification" means the classification established under the Nice Agreement Concerning the International Classification of Goods and Services for the Purposes of the Registration of Marks;

(xxiv) "Regulations" means the Regulations referred to in Article 35.

Chapter I
Substantive Provisions

Article 3
International Register of Marks

(1) The International Bureau shall register marks in the International Register of Marks according to the provisions of this Treaty and the Regulations.

(2) International registrations shall be effected on the basis of international applications.

Article 4
Right to File International Applications and to Own International Registrations

(1)(*a*) Any resident or national of a Contracting State may file international applications and may own international registrations.

(*b*) If there are several applicants, they shall have the right to file an international application only if all of them are residents or nationals of Contracting States.

(*c*) If there are several owners of an international registration, they shall have the right to own such a registration only if all of them are residents or nationals of Contracting States.

(2)(*a*) Any natural person shall be regarded as a resident of a Contracting State if:

(i) according to the national law of that State, he is a resident of that State, or

(ii) he has a real and effective industrial or commercial establishment in that State.

(*b*) Any natural person shall be regarded as a national of a Contracting State if, according to the national law of that State, he has the nationality of that State.

(3)(*a*) Any legal entity shall be regarded as a resident of a Contracting State if it has a real and effective industrial or commercial establishment in that State.

(*b*) Any legal entity shall be regarded as a national of a Contracting State if it is constituted according to the national law of that State.

(4) If the State of the residence and the State of the nationality of the applicant or owner of the international registration are different, and only one of those States is a Contracting State, the Contracting State alone shall be considered for the purposes of this Treaty and the Regulations.

(5) Where under the national law of any Contracting State an association of natural persons or legal entities may own marks notwithstanding the fact that it is not a legal entity, it shall be entitled to file international applications and to own international registrations, provided it is a resident or national of that State within the meaning of paragraph (3).

(6)(*a*) The national law of any Contracting State may provide that, where the applicant is both a resident and a national of that State, an international application may be filed only if the mark that is the subject of the international application is, at the time of the filing of that application, the subject of an application for registration, in the name of the said applicant, in the national register of marks of that State in respect of at least those goods and/or services listed in the international application.

(*b*) Subparagraph (*a*) shall not apply where, at the time of the filing of the international application, the mark that is the subject of the international application is already registered in the name of the applicant in the national register of marks of the said State in respect of the said goods and/or services.

Article 5
The International Application

(1)(*a*) The international application shall contain, as specified in this Treaty and the Regulations:

(i) an indication that it is filed under this Treaty,

(ii) indications concerning the applicant's identity, residence, nationality, and address,

(iii) a reproduction of the mark,

(iv) a list of goods and/or services in which the terms are grouped under the applicable classes of the International Classification and in which each term is comprehensible, permits classification in one class only of that Classification, and, as far as possible, is one that appears in the alphabetical list of goods and/or services of the said Classification,

(v) the identification of the designated State or States,

(vi) in respect of any designated State in which the effects provided for in this Treaty are available either as if the mark had been applied for and registered as a national mark or as if the mark had been applied for and registered as a regional mark, an indication of the choice between the two,

(vii) in respect of any designated State in which the effects provided for in this Treaty are desired as for a collective mark or a certification mark, an indication to that effect.

(*b*) The international application may contain a declaration, as provided in the Regulations, claiming the priority of one or more earlier applications filed in or for any country party to the Paris Convention for the Protection of Industrial Property. Furthermore, the international application may contain such additional indications as are provided for in other provisions of this Treaty and in the Regulations.

(*c*) The international application shall be in a prescribed language and in the prescribed form, shall be signed as provided in the Regulations, and shall be subject to the payment of the prescribed fees.

(2) International applications shall be filed direct with the International Bureau.

(3)(*a*) Notwithstanding paragraph (2) but subject to subparagraph (*c*), the national law of any Contracting State may provide that international applications of residents of that State may be filed through the intermediary of the national Office of the said State.

(*b*) Where the international application is filed through the intermediary of a national Office competent under subparagraph (*a*), that Office shall indicate on the international application the date on which it received that application and shall promptly transmit the same to the International Bureau, as provided in the Regulations.

(*c*) Any Contracting State on whose territory an agency of the International Bureau, established under Article 32(2)(*a*)(ix), is functioning shall, at least for the time such agency functions, suspend the application of any provision of its national law referred to in subparagraph (*a*) and Article 6(3)(*a*).

Article 6
Later Designation

(1) Any Contracting State not designated in the international application or whose designation has ceased to have the effects provided for in Article 11 may be designated by the applicant or, once the international registration has been effected, by the owner of the international registration, as provided in the Regulations ("later designation").

(2)(*a*) Any later designation shall be the subject of a request for the recording of later designations. Several States may be designated in the same request. The request shall be filed direct with the International Bureau and shall contain, as specified in the Regulations:

(i) an indication that it is for the recording of later designations under this Treaty,

(ii) indications concerning the identity, residence, nationality and address of the applicant or, where the international registration has already been effected, of the owner of the international registration,

(iii) the identification of the international application or, where the international registration has already been effected, of such registration,

(iv) the identification of the later designated State or States,

(v) in respect of any later designated State in which the effects provided for in this Treaty are available either as if the mark had been applied for and registered as a national mark or as if the mark had been applied for and registered as a regional mark, an indication of the choice between the two,

(vi) in respect of any later designated State in which the effects provided for in this Treaty are desired as for a collective mark or a certification mark, an indication to that effect.

(*b*) The request may contain a declaration, as provided in the Regulations, claiming the priority of one or more earlier applications filed in or for any country party to the Paris Convention for the Protection of Industrial Property. Furthermore, the request may contain in respect of any State designated therein a list of goods and/or services, provided that, if that list is different from the list of goods and/or services included in the international registration as published, or, if the international registration has not yet been published, from the list of goods and/or services included in the international application after any limitation under Article 7(4), it shall conform with the formal concept of limitation as defined in the Regulations. Finally, the request may contain such additional indications as are provided for in other provisions of this Treaty and in the Regulations.

(*c*) The request shall be in a prescribed language and in the prescribed form, shall be signed as provided in the Regulations, and shall be subject to the payment of the prescribed fees.

(3)(*a*) Notwithstanding paragraph (2)(*a*) but subject to Article 5(3)(*c*), the national law of any Contracting State may provide that requests for the recording of later designations by residents of that State may be filed through the intermediary of the national Office of the said State.

(*b*) Where the request for the recording of later designations is filed through the intermediary of a national Office competent under subparagraph (*a*), that Office shall indicate on the request the date on which it received that request and shall promptly transmit the same to the International Bureau, as provided in the Regulations.

Article 7
International Registration or Declining of the International Application

(1) Subject to paragraphs (2) to (5), the International Bureau shall promptly effect the international registration as applied for, and the date under which such registration shall be effected ("international registration date") shall be the date on which the international application was received by the International Bureau or, in the case of an international application filed through the intermediary of a national Office under Article 5(3), the date on which it was received by that Office provided that the said application is received by the International Bureau before the expiration of 45 days from that date. The International Bureau shall issue to the owner of the international registration a certificate of international registration.

(2)(*a*) Where the International Bureau finds any of the following defects, that is to say, where:

(i) the international application does not contain an indication that it is filed under this Treaty,

(ii) the international application is in a language other than one of the prescribed languages,

(iii) the international application contains no indications concerning the residence or nationality of the applicant or only such indications as do not permit the conclusion that he has the right to file international applications,

(iv) the international application contains no indications concerning the applicant's identity and address or only such indications as do not permit him to be identified and reached by mail,

(v) the international application does not include the reproduction of the mark,

(vi) the international application does not contain a list of goods and/or services,

(vii) the international application does not designate any Contracting State,

(viii) no fees have been received by the International Bureau on or before the date on which the international application is received by that Bureau or, where the international application is filed through the intermediary of a national Office under Article 5(3), no fees have been received by the International Bureau within 45 days from the date on which that Office received the international application,

(ix) the amount of the fees received by the International Bureau by the date referred to in item (viii) does not attain the amount ("minimum amount") fixed in the Regulations,

it shall invite the applicant to correct the defect; however, where the defect referred to in item (iv) makes it unlikely for the invitation to reach the applicant, the International Bureau is not required to send such invitation.

(*b*) If the defect is not corrected within three months from the date on which the International Bureau received the international application, the International Bureau shall decline that application.

(*c*) If the defect is corrected within the time limit referred to in subparagraph (*b*) and unless the international application is declined under paragraph (3)(*b*), the International Bureau shall effect the international registration, and the international registration date shall be the date on which that Bureau received the required correction or the prescribed amount of the fees, unless a later date is applicable under paragraph (3)(*d*).

(3)(*a*) Where the International Bureau finds any of the following defects, that is to say, where:

(i) the amount of the fees received by the International Bureau by the date referred to in paragraph (2)(*a*)(viii) is less than the amount prescribed but attains the minimum amount,

(ii) the international application does not contain, in respect of any designated State to which Article 5(1)(*a*)(vi) applies, the indication of the choice referred to in the said provision,

(iii) the international application is not signed,

it shall invite the applicant to correct the defect.

(*b*) If the defect is not corrected within three months from the date on which the International Bureau received the international application, the International Bureau shall decline that application or, if the only defect which is not corrected within the said time limit is the defect referred to in subparagraph (*a*)(ii), the International Bureau shall decline to record the State concerned as a designated State.

(*c*) If the defect is corrected before the expiration of one month from the date of the invitation referred to in subparagraph (*a*) and unless the international application is declined under subparagraph (*b*) or paragraph (2)(*b*), the International Bureau shall effect the international registration, and the international registration date shall be the date referred to in paragraph (1), unless a later date is applicable under paragraph (2)(*c*).

(*d*) If the defect is corrected later than at the expiration of one month from the date of the invitation referred to in subparagraph (*a*) but earlier than at the expiration of three months from the date on which the International Bureau received the international application, and unless the international application is declined under paragraph (2)(*b*), the International Bureau shall effect the international registration, and the international registration date shall be the date on which that Bureau received the required correction or payment, unless a later date is applicable under paragraph (2)(*c*).

(4)(*a*) Where the International Bureau finds that, by classifying any of the terms appearing in the list of goods and/or services in or also in a class or classes of the International Classification in which such term was not classified in the international application as filed, the amount of the fees required is higher than if that term had not been so classified, the invitation referred to in paragraph (2)(*a*) or (3)(*a*) shall contain appropriate explanations and shall indicate that the applicant may limit the list of goods and/or services.

(*b*) If, within three months from the date on which the International Bureau received the international application, it receives from the applicant a statement which limits the list of goods and/or services in conformity with the formal concept of limitation as defined in the Regulations, the International Bureau shall modify the list of goods and/or services accordingly and, if such modification entails a change in the prescribed amount of the fees, such change shall be taken into account by the International Bureau in determining that amount and in applying paragraph (2)(*b*), (2)(*c*), (3)(*b*), (3)(*c*), or (3)(*d*), as the case may be.

(5)(*a*) The Regulations shall provide for the details of the procedure under paragraphs (1) to (4).

(*b*) Failure to send or receive any invitation referred to in paragraphs (2) to (4), or any delay in dispatching or receiving it, or any error therein, shall not extend the time limits fixed in those paragraphs and shall not affect any obligation to decline the international application.

(*c*) Where the international application is declined, the International Bureau shall reimburse to the applicant such amounts as are specified in the Regulations.

(6) Where the international application filed through the intermediary of a national Office under Article 5(3):

(i) does not indicate that the applicant is a resident of the State through the intermediary of whose national Office the international application was filed, or
(ii) does not contain a statement by the said national Office indicating the date on which that Office received the international application, or
(iii) contains the said statement indicating a date which precedes by more than 45 days the date on which the International Bureau received the international application,

that application shall be treated as if it had been filed direct with the International Bureau on the date it reached that Bureau.

Article 8
Recording or Declining of Later Designations

(1) Subject to paragraph (2), the International Bureau shall promptly effect the recording of any later designation as requested, and the date under which such recording shall be effected ("recording date of the later designation") shall be the date on which the request for the recording of the later designation was received by the International Bureau or, in the case of a request filed through the intermediary of a national Office under Article 6(3), the date on which it was received by that Office, provided that the said request is received by the International Bureau before the expiration of 45 days from that date. The International Bureau shall issue to the owner of the international registration a certificate of the recording of the later designation.

(2)(*a*) The provisions of Article 7(2) to (6) shall apply, *mutatis mutandis*, to the recording of later designations and declining of requests for the recording of later designations, provided that, once the international registration has been effected, any reference to the applicant shall be considered a reference to the owner of the international registration.

(*b*) Notwithstanding subparagraph (*a*), items (v) and (vi) of Article 7(2)(*a*) shall be considered to have been replaced by the following:

"(v) the request does not identify the international application or, once the international registration has been effected, such registration."

(*c*) Notwithstanding subparagraph (*a*), Article 7(3)(*a*) shall be considered to have been completed by the following:

"(iv) any list of goods and/or services contained in the request does not conform with the requirements of Article 6(2)(*b*), second sentence."

Article 9
Avoiding the Effects of Declining

(1) Where the International Bureau has declined the international application or a request for the recording of later designation, the applicant or the owner of the international registration may, within two months from the date of the notification of the declining, file with the national Office of any State designated in the declined international application or declined request:

(i) a petition for the purpose of requesting the International Bureau to proceed, in respect of that State, where the international application was declined, with the international registration and the recording of the designation of the said State or, where the request for the recording of the later designation was declined, with the recording of the designation of that State, or

(ii) an application for the registration, in the national register of marks ("national application"), of the mark that is the subject of the declined international application or declined request, in respect of all or some of the goods and/or services indicated in the said international application or the said request, such application complying with all the requirements of the national law of the said State for the filing of applications for the registration of marks in the national register of marks.

(2) If the national Office or any other competent authority of the said State finds that the declining, by the International Bureau, of the international application or of the request for the recording of the later designation of that State was unjustified under this Treaty or the Regulations, or that the declining was based on the fact that there was a delay in meeting a time limit which must be excused by virtue of Article 29(1), then:

(i) where a petition has been filed under paragraph (1)(i), the said national Office shall request the International Bureau to proceed as provided in that paragraph, and the International Bureau shall proceed as requested, and the international registration date or the recording date of the later designation shall be the same as if the declining had not taken place,

(ii) where a national application has been filed under paragraph (1)(ii), that application shall, provided it complies with all the requirements of the national law of the said State for the filing of applications for the registration of marks in the national register of marks, be treated as if it had been filed on the date which would have been the international registration date or the recording date of the later designation had the declining not taken place.

(3) The applicant or the owner of the international registration who files a petition under paragraph (1)(i) shall, at the time of filing the petition, transmit a copy of that petition to the International Bureau. If the petition relates to a mark which is already registered in the International Register of Marks, the International Bureau shall, as provided in the Regulations, record and publish the fact that it has received a copy of such petition; otherwise it shall keep the said copy in its files.

Article 10
Publication and Notification

(1) International registrations and recordings of later designations shall be promptly published by the International Bureau, as provided in the Regulations.

(2) International registrations and recordings of later designations shall be promptly notified by the International Bureau to the national Offices of each designated State, as provided in the Regulations.

Article 11
Effects of International Registration and of Recording of Later Designation

(1) The international registration of a mark and the recording of any later designation, published and notified as provided in Article 10, shall have the same effect in each designated State as if an application for the registration of the mark in the national register of marks had been filed with the national Office of that State on the international registration date or on the recording date of the later designation, as the case may be.

(2) Furthermore, the said international registration and recording shall, subject to Articles 12 and 13, have the same effect in each designated State as if the mark had been registered in the national register of marks of that State; such effect shall come into existence in any designated State:

(i) where no refusal or notice that a refusal may eventually be pronounced ("notice of possible refusal") has been notified by the national Office of that State within the time limit fixed in Article 12(2)(*a*)(i), at the expiration of the said time limit or on such earlier date as may be prescribed by the national law of that State,

(ii) where a refusal or a notice of possible refusal has been notified by the national Office of that State within the time limit fixed in Article 12(2)(*a*)(i), if and when, and to the extent to which, the refusal is reversed by a final decision or the final decision taken in the proceedings referred to in the notice of possible refusal results in acceptance of the effect provided for in this paragraph,

and shall be deemed to have started as of the international registration date or the recording date of the later designation, as the case may be.

(3) Where, in any designated State, there is more than one national register of marks or the national register of marks has several parts, the reference in paragraphs (1) and (2) to the national register of marks shall be construed as a reference to that national register or that part of the national register which affords the highest degree of protection, unless another register or part of the register is indicated in the international application or the request for the recording of the later designation. In the case of such indication, the reference in paragraphs (1) and (2) to the national register of marks shall be construed as a reference to the register or part of the register so indicated.

Article 12
Refusal of the Effects Provided for in Article 11

(1) Subject to paragraph (2) and Articles 19, 21(3) and 22(3), the effects provided for in Article 11 may, in respect of any designated State, be refused by the competent authorities of that State:

(i) on the same grounds and to the same extent as those in respect of which applications for the registration of marks in the national register of marks may be refused under the national law of the said State, provided that such grounds are not incompatible with this Treaty and the Regulations or the most recent provisions of the Paris Convention for the Protection of Industrial Property by which that State is bound, and provided that Article 6*quinquies* of the Stockholm (1967) Act of the said Convention shall apply also to marks registered under this Treaty, the international registration taking the place, for the purposes of the said Article 6*quinquies*, of registration in the country of origin,

(ii) on the ground that the owner of the international registration is not entitled to own international registrations or that the applicant was not entitled to file international applications.

(2)(*a*) Any refusal under paragraph (1) shall be effective only:

(i) if the refusal or notice of possible refusal is notified, as provided in the Regulations, by the national Office of the designated State to the International Bureau so that the latter receives it within 15 months or, in the case of a certification mark, 18 months from the date of the publication of the international registration, or, in the case of a later designation, of the publication of the recording of the later designation of such State, and

(ii) in the case of a refusal, if the grounds for the refusal are specified, and provided, where such refusal is not final, that the grounds given in the final decision of refusal include at least one of the grounds specified in the said refusal and the final decision is or is also based on at least one of the grounds specified in the said refusal,

(iii) in the case of a notice of possible refusal followed by a refusal, if the notice specifies, as provided in the Regulations, the grounds on which a refusal may eventually be pronounced, and provided that the grounds given in the final decision of refusal include at least one of the grounds specified in the said notice and the final decision is or is also based on at least one of the grounds specified in the said notice.

(*b*) The proviso of subparagraph (*a*)(ii) and the proviso of subparagraph (*a*)(iii) shall not apply where the final decision is that of a court or other independent review authority.

(*c*) Subparagraph (*a*) shall not apply where the refusal is based on lack of compliance with the requirements of the national law of the designated State permitted by Article 19(3).

(3) The owner of the international registration shall, with reasonable time limits, have in any designated State the same remedies against any decision of refusal and the same procedural and substantive rights in connection with any intended refusal, whether ex officio or based on the opposition of a third party, as have applicants who apply for the registration of marks in the national register of marks of the State in question.

(4)(*a*) The International Bureau shall record any notification received under paragraph (2)(*a*) and publish a corresponding notice.

(*b*) Where the decision of refusal is final, the national Office of the designated State shall notify the International Bureau accordingly, and that Bureau shall record the final decision, cancel the designation of that State, or, in a case where the final decision relates to some only of the goods and/or services listed, cancel in respect of the said State those goods and/or services to which the said decision relates, and publish such cancellation.

(*c*) Where a refusal which is not final or a notice of possible refusal has been notified under paragraph (2)(*a*) and the final decision results in acceptance of the effect referred to in Article 11(2), the national Office of the designated State shall notify the International Bureau accordingly, and the International Bureau shall record the notification received and publish a corresponding notice.

(*d*) The details of the procedures referred to in subparagraphs (*a*) to (*c*) are provided in the Regulations.

Article 13
Cancellation of the Effect Acquired Under Article 11(2)

(1) Subject to Article 19, the effect acquired under Article 11(2) may, in respect of any designated State, be cancelled by the competent authorities of that State:

(i) on the same grounds, to the same extent and subject to the same procedure as those in respect of which registrations of marks in the national register of marks may be cancelled under the national law of the said State, provided that such grounds and such procedure are not incompatible with this Treaty and the Regulations or the most recent provisions of the Paris Convention for the Protection of Industrial Property by which that State is bound, and provided that Article 6*quinquies* of the Stockholm (1967) Act of the Paris Convention for the Protection of Industrial Property shall apply also to marks registered under this Treaty, the international registration taking the place, for the purposes of the said Article 6*quinquies*, of registration in the country of origin,

(ii) on the ground that the owner of the international registration is not entitled to own international registrations or that the applicant was not entitled to file international applications.

(2) The competent authorities of the designated State shall give, with reasonable advance notice, an opportunity to the owner of the international registration to defend his rights in any cancellation proceeding and such owner shall have the same remedies against any decision of cancellation as have owners of marks registered in the national register of marks of the said State.

(3) If the decision of cancellation is final, the national Office of the designated State shall notify the International Bureau accordingly, and that Bureau shall record that decision, cancel the designation of the said State or, in a case where the cancellation relates to some only of the goods and/or services listed, cancel—in respect of that State—those goods and/or services to which the said decision relates, and publish such cancellation.

Article 14
Change in the Ownership of the International Registration

(1)(*a*) Where the ownership of any international registration changes so that the new owner has become the owner in respect of all or fewer than all of the designated States and in respect of all or some only of the goods and/or services, the change in ownership shall, on request, subject to paragraph (2), be recorded by the International Bureau.

(*b*) The request shall contain, as provided in the Regulations:

(i) an indication to the effect that the recording by the International Bureau of a change in ownership is requested,

(ii) the international registration number of the international registration,

(iii) indications concerning the name, residence, nationality and address of the new owner,

(iv) the identification of those of the designated States in respect of which the new owner has acquired ownership and the identification, in respect of each of those States, of those of the goods and/or services for which the new owner has acquired ownership.

(*c*) The request shall be signed by the person who, pursuant to the change in ownership, ceases to own the international registration in respect of all or fewer than all of the designated States and in respect of all or some only of the goods and/or services ("earlier owner") or, where the earlier owner is unable to sign, by the new owner, provided that if it is signed by the new owner the request shall also contain an appropriate attestation, as provided in the Regulations, by the national Office of the Contracting State of which the earlier owner was, at the time of the change of ownership, a national or, if at that time the earlier owner was not a national of a Contracting State, by the national Office of the Contracting State of which, at the said time, the earlier owner was a resident.

(*d*) The request shall be subject to the payment of a fee to the International Bureau, and the recording shall be published by that Bureau and notified by it to the earlier owner and the new owner and to the interested designated Offices, as provided in the Regulations.

(2)(*a*) In any of the following cases, the International Bureau shall decline the request and shall notify accordingly the person who has signed it:

(i) where the request does not contain the indication referred to in paragraph (1)(*b*)(i),

(ii) where the request does not contain the number referred to in paragraph (1)(*b*)(ii),

(iii) where the request contains no indications concerning the residence or nationality of the new owner, or only such indications as do not permit the conclusion that he is entitled to own international registrations,

(iv) where the request contains no indications concerning the identify and address of the person who has signed it or only such indications as do not permit him to be identified and reached by mail,

(v) where the request does not identify any designated State in respect of which the new owner has acquired ownership,

(vi) where the request does not identify, as provided in the Regulations, any goods and/or services in respect of each of the designated States for which the new owner has acquired ownership,

(vii) where the request is not signed and, if it is signed by the new owner, where it does not contain the attestation, as provided in the Regulations, referred to in paragraph (1)(*c*),

(viii) where the prescribed fee has not been received.

(*b*) Where the request has the defect referred to in subparagraph (*a*)(iv) to the extent that it makes it unlikely for the notification referred to in subparagraph (*a*) to reach the person who signed the request, the International Bureau is not required to send such a notification.

(3) Subject to paragraph (4), any recording effected under paragraph (1) shall, from the date of such recording, have the same effect as if it had been effected in the national register of marks, or any other related register, of each of the designated States to which the request relates.

(4)(*a*) The competent authorities of any designated State may, as far as that State is concerned, deny the effect referred to in paragraph (3) on grounds which, according to its national law, do not allow of changes in ownership or on the ground that the new owner is not entitled to own international registrations.

(*b*) The national law of any Contracting State may provide that the effect referred to in paragraph (3) may, as far as such State is concerned, be denied if, within three months from the date of the publication referred to in paragraph (1)(*d*) or, where that national law provides for a longer period, within that period, evidence is not adduced before its national Office which satisfies the conditions of the national law as regards changes in ownership. Any national office may collect the fee prescribed by its national law in connection with the examination of the said evidence adduced before it.

(*c*) Where the competent authorities of any designated State deny the effect referred to in paragraph (3), the national Office of that State shall promptly notify the International Bureau accordingly, and that Bureau shall record the denial and effect the corresponding notifications and publication. The details of the procedure are provided in the Regulations.

(5) Where there is a change in ownership other than by contract between the earlier owner and the new owner, and where the new

owner is a person who is not entitled to file international applications but is entitled under the national law of any designated State to file applications for the registration of marks in the national register of marks of that State, the new owner may file an application for the registration, in the said national register, of the mark which is registered, and in respect of all or some of the goods and/or services which are listed, in the International Register of Marks in respect of that State. If, within two years from the change in ownership and prior to six months after the expiration of the initial term of the international registration or the then running term of renewal, as the case may be, the new owner files such an application, that application shall be treated in the said State as if it had been filed at the time when the designation of that State took effect.

Article 15

Change in the Name of the Owner of the International Registration

(1) Where the owner of the international registration changes his name, such change in the name of the owner shall, on his request, be recorded by the International Bureau.

(2)(*a*) Any request may relate to several international registrations of the same owner.

(*b*) The request shall contain, as provided in the Regulations:

(i) an indication to the effect that the recording by the International Bureau of a change in the name of the owner of the international registration is requested,

(ii) a declaration to the effect that the change in name does not amount to a change in the ownership of the international registration,

(iii) the international registration number of the international registration,

(iv) an indication of the former name and of the new name of the owner of the international registration.

(*c*) The request shall be signed with the new name of the owner of the international registration.

(*d*) The request shall be subject to the payment of a fee to the International Bureau.

(3) The recording shall be published by the International Bureau and shall be notified to the designated Offices, as provided in the Regulations.

(4) In any of the following cases, the International Bureau shall decline the request and shall notify accordingly the owner:

(i) where the request does not contain the indications referred to in paragraph (2)(*b*),

(ii) where the request is not signed as provided in paragraph (2)(*c*),

(iii) where the prescribed fee has not been received.

(5) Subject to paragraph (6), any recording effected under paragraph (1) shall, from the date of such recording, have the same effect as if it had been effected in the national register of marks, or any other related register, of each of the designated States.

(6)(*a*) The national law of any Contracting State may provide that the effect referred to in paragraph (5) may, as far as such State is concerned, be denied if, within three months from the date of the publication referred to in paragraph (3) or, where that national law provides for a longer period, within that period, evidence is not adduced before its national Office which proves that the natural person or legal entity designated by the former name and the new name is the same.

(*b*) Where the competent authorities of any designated State deny the effect referred to in paragraph (5), the national Office of that State shall promptly notify the International Bureau accordingly, and that Bureau shall record the denial and effect the corresponding notifications and publication. The details of the procedure are provided in the Regulations.

Article 16
Limitation of the List of Goods and/or Services

(1) On the request of the owner of the international registration, the International Bureau shall record, in respect of any designated State, any limitation of the list of goods and/or services which conforms with the formal concept of limitation as defined in the Regulations.

(2) The request for recording shall be subject to the payment of a fee to the International Bureau, and the recording shall be published by that Bureau and notified to all the interested designated States, as provided in the Regulations.

(3) The International Bureau shall decline the recording of any change in the list of goods and/or services which does not conform with the said formal concept of limitation or other requirements of the request, and shall notify the owner of the international registration accordingly, as provided in the Regulations.

(4) Subject to paragraph (5), any recording effected under paragraph (1) shall, from the date of such recording, have the same effect

as if it had been effected in the national register of marks of each of the designated States to which the request relates.

(5)(*a*) If the national Office or other competent authority of a designated State finds that the limitation requested by the owner of the international registration in respect of that State but declined by the International Bureau is, in fact, a limitation in the sense that the terms proposed in the request relate only to goods and/or services which are covered by the terms appearing in the international registration, the national Office of that State, upon petition by the owner, shall, as provided in the Regulations, invite the International Bureau to record the limitation in respect of that State.

(*b*) If the national Office or other competent authority of a designated State finds that the limitation requested by the owner of the international registration and recorded by the International Bureau is, in fact, not a limitation in the sense indicated in subparagraph (*a*), the national Office of that State may, as provided in the Regulations and after having heard the owner, invite the International Bureau to reinstate, in respect of that State, wholly or in part, the list of goods and/or services as it was prior to the limitation in question.

(*c*) The International Bureau shall proceed as invited and effect, as provided in the Regulations, the corresponding recording, publication and notifications.

Article 17

Term and Renewal of the International Registration

(1) The initial term of any international registration shall be ten years from the international registration date.

(2)(*a*) Any international registration may be renewed in respect of any designated State by its owner for terms of ten years.

(*b*) Renewal shall prolong the effects provided for in Article 11 in each designated State for the term of the renewal.

(*c*) Each term of renewal shall start on the day following the day on which the initial term of the international registration or the term of the last renewal expires.

(3)(*a*) Renewal shall be the subject of a demand presented to the International Bureau as provided in the Regulations, and shall be subject to the payment of fees, as provided in the Regulations. The demand shall not be presented and the fees shall not be paid earlier than six months before, or later than six months after, the starting date of the term of renewal. If the demand is presented or the fees are received after the starting date of the term of renewal, renewal shall be subject to the payment of an additional fee ("renewal surcharge"), as provided in the Regulations, which shall be paid before the expiration of six months after the starting date of the term of renewal.

(*b*) The International Bureau shall record and publish the renewal and shall notify each designated Office accordingly, as provided in the Regulations.

Article 18
Fees

(1)(*a*) The International Bureau shall be entitled to fees in connection with the filing of each international application, request for recording of later designations, demand for renewal, and such other operations and services as are subject, according to this Treaty or the Regulations, to the payment of fees.

(*b*) The Regulations fix the amounts of the fees referred to in subparagraph (*a*).

(2) Each Contracting State shall be entitled to fees ("State fees") in connection with each designation and each renewal concerning it. The State fees shall be either "individual" or "standard," according to the choice of the Contracting State. The choice shall be exercised and applied as provided in the Regulations and shall apply to all designations and renewals concerning the Contracting State.

(3)(*a*) Subject to subparagraphs (*b*) to (*f*), the amounts of individual State fees applicable to any State shall be determined by such State.

(*b*) The amounts of the individual State fees shall be communicated by the national Office of the Contracting State to the International Bureau in the currency and within the time limits specified in the Regulations. They shall remain applicable for the periods specified in the Regulations.

(*c*) The amounts of the individual State fees may vary only according to the number of classes to which the goods and/or services listed in respect of that State belong under the International Classification and according to whether the mark is or is not a collective mark or a certification mark.

(*d*) Any individual State fee shall belong to the designated State in respect of which it was paid and shall be transferred to its national Office as provided in the Regulations.

(*e*) The amount of the individual State fee to which the Contracting State is entitled in connection with each designation concerning it ("individual State designation fee") shall not exceed the total amount of any filing, class, examination, registration and publication fees which that State prescribes in connection with an application for registration in the national register of marks.

(*f*) The amount of the individual State fee to which the Contracting State is entitled in connection with each renewal concerning it ("individual State renewal fee") shall not exceed the amount of the renewal fee which that State prescribes for the renewal of a registration in the national register of marks, provided that, if the latter amount relates to a period which is longer or shorter than ten years, the said limit shall be proportionately reduced or proportionately increased, as the case may be.

(4)(*a*) The amounts of the standard State designation fee and of the standard State renewal fee shall be fixed in the Regulations.

(*b*) The standard State fees shall belong to the States which have chosen standard State fees. The total amount of such fees collected by the International Bureau for any given calendar year shall be distributed and transferred in the course of the following year to the national Offices of the Contracting States to which the standard State fees apply in proportion to the number of designations and renewals concerning each of them, provided that the number resulting for each Office shall be first multiplied by a coefficient, as fixed in the Regulations, based on the extent of the examination which the national law provides.

(5) The Regulations give further details concerning fees and provide for the total or partial reimbursement of certain fees in certain circumstances.

Article 19
Certain National Requirements

(1) Subject to Article 14(4)(*b*), no national Office of any designated State shall, unless acting as an independent review authority, require the payment of any fee by the applicant or the owner of the international registration in connection with the obtaining and renewing of the effects, in the said State, of international applications, international registrations, and recordings concerning such applications and registrations.

(2) No designated State may refuse or cancel the effects provided for in Article 11 merely on the grounds that its national law allows the registration of marks only in respect of a limited number of classes or a limited number of goods and/or services.

(3)(*a*) The national law of any Contracting State may impose the same conditions as are applicable to marks whose registration is applied for or which are registered in the national register of marks in that State in respect of any requirement that the owner of an international registration use the mark in that State or in any other place, provided that such State shall not refuse under Article 12, cancel under Article 13, or otherwise fail to accord the effects of the international registration as defined in Article 11, on the ground that the mark has not been used at any time prior to the expiration of three years counted from the international registration date or the recording date of the later designation, as the case may be. However, the national law of any Contracting State may provide that any action for infringement based upon an international registration may be started only after the owner of such international registration has commenced the continuing use of the mark in the said State and that any remedy resulting from such action shall relate only to the period after such use has commenced.

(*b*) Where, at the expiration of the three-year time limit referred to in subparagraph (*a*), the final decision referred to in Article 11(2)(ii) has not been made, the said time limit shall be extended until the expiration of one year counted from the date on which the effect provided for in Article 11(2) does, in fact, come into existence, provided that in no case shall any Contracting State be required to extend the said three-year time limit by more than two years. This subparagraph shall not apply to any Contracting State whose national law does not permit of such extension. Any such State shall notify the International Bureau of the provisions of its national law in this regard at the time it deposits its instrument of ratification or accession. Each Contracting State shall notify the International Bureau whenever its national law changes in regard to this subparagraph.

(*c*) Where prior to the international registration date or the recording date of the later designation, as the case may be, the mark has been registered, in the name of the person who is the owner of the international registration, in the national register of marks of any designated State, or has been the subject on the part of the said person of an application for registration in that register, the proviso of subparagraph (*a*) and the first sentence of subparagraph (*b*) shall not apply to the extent that the said registration or application relates to the same goods and/or services as are listed in respect of such State in the international registration. However, where the application for registration in the national register was filed less than three years before the international registration date or the recording date of the later designation, as the case may be, the proviso of subparagraph (*a*) shall apply, but only during the period between such date and the expiration of the third year counted from the date on which the said application was filed. Where the three-year time limit is extended under subparagraph (*b*), the preceding sentence shall be applied accordingly. The present subparagraph shall also apply where the earlier registration is one effected in the international register under the Madrid Agreement or the present Treaty.

(*d*) Where one of the conditions of the national law of the designated State referred to in subparagraph (*a*) consists of a requirement, general in the sense that it is applicable to all marks registered in the national register of marks of that State, that a declaration stating that the mark is or is still in use in that State must be filed with its national Office at certain points in time or in connection with each renewal or other specific event ("routine declaration"), such declaration may, in the form prescribed by the national law of that State or in the form prescribed in the Regulations, be filed with the International Bureau and shall have the same effect as if it had been filed with the national Office of that State on the date on which it was received by the International Bureau. Such declaration shall be promptly forwarded by the International Bureau to the said national Office. The said effect shall not be denied on the ground that the declaration was not accompanied by any required supporting evidence, or that the evidence accompanying it was insufficient, without the said national Office's giving the owner of the international registration an opportunity to adduce or complete before it any required evidence within not less than three months after having notified the said owner or his duly appointed representative that evidence or additional evidence is required. The present subparagraph shall not apply in inter partes and other proceedings in which the requirement is not a general one in the sense indicated above ("ad hoc requirement").

(*e*) No requirement referred to in subparagraph (*d*) shall be applicable prior to the expiration of the time limit under the proviso of subparagraph (*a*), subject, where applicable, to subparagraph (*b*), or subparagraph (*c*).

(4)(*a*) Any Contracting State may apply its national law requiring that applicants file a declaration with its national Office to the effect that they intend to use the mark, provided that such requirement shall be considered to have been complied with if a declaration in the form specified in the Regulations to the effect that the applicant or the owner of an international registration intends to use the mark in that State is contained in the international application or request for the recording of the later designation, as the case may be.

(*b*) The International Bureau shall, as provided in the Regulations, notify the national Office of any designated State in respect of which a declaration under subparagraph (*a*) was filed with that Bureau of such declaration.

(5) Whenever paragraphs (3) and (4) refer to use of the mark by the applicant or the owner of the international registration, use by a person whose use, under the applicable national law, inures to the benefit of the applicant or the owner shall be sufficient for invoking the benefits provided for in the said paragraphs.

(6) Any Contracting State may apply its national law requiring that where the mark is a collective mark or a certification mark the owner thereof must adduce before its national Office certain supporting documents and other evidence, including in particular the bylaws of the association or other entity owning such mark and the rules concerning the control exercised over the use of such mark.

(7) No designated State shall require that the applicant or the owner of the international registration be represented by any natural person or legal entity located in that State or that, for the purpose of serving notices on such applicant or owner, an address in that State be indicated, except where, in respect of or based on the mark which is the subject of the international application or the international registration, the applicant or owner institutes or defends a proceeding before the national authorities of the said State.

(8)(*a*) The national law of any Contracting State may provide that proceedings before a national authority, including a court, in that State may, for the cancellation in that State pursuant to Article 13 of the effect provided for in Article 11(2), and for no other matter, validly be commenced against the owner of the international registration by means of service of a notification addressed to him at the International Bureau.

(*b*) The International Bureau shall promptly forward the said notification to the owner of the international registration by registered airmail accompanied by a postal receipt form *(avis de réception, Rückschein)*.

(*c*) Promptly upon return to the International Bureau of the receipt form, that Bureau shall send to the party instituting the proceeding a copy, certified by that Bureau, of the said receipt form.

(*d*) If the receipt form showing receipt by the said owner is not received by the International Bureau within one month from the date of its having mailed the notification, the International Bureau shall promptly publish the notification.

(*e*) Any national law referred to in subparagraph (*a*) shall provide for a reasonable time limit for the owner of the international registration to respond to the notification and defend his rights in the proceedings. This time limit shall not be less than three months from the date of the notification.

(9) Article 4(5) shall be without prejudice to the application of the national law in any designated State. However, no such State shall refuse or cancel the effects provided for in Article 11 on the ground that the applicant or the owner of the international registration is an association of the kind referred to in Article 4(5) if, within two months from the date of an invitation addressed to it by the designated Office, the said association files with that Office a list of the names and addresses of all the natural persons or legal entities who or which comprise it, together with a declaration that its members are engaged in

a joint enterprise. The said State may, in such a case, consider the said persons or entities as the owners of the international registration standing in the name of the said association.

(10) Where any document issued by the International Bureau bears the seal of that Bureau and the signature of the Director General or a person acting on his behalf, no authority of any Contracting State shall require authentication, legalization or any other certification of such document, seal or signature, by any other person or authority.

Article 20
Recordings Effected by National Offices

(1) The national Office of any Contracting State which effects any recording in its own register of marks or in any other related register in respect of matters that may be recorded in the International Register of Marks with regard to any mark which is registered in the International Register of Marks and for which that State is a designated State shall, at the time of effecting such recording and as provided in the Regulations, notify the International Bureau of the said recording unless the recording has been effected pursuant to a notification by the International Bureau to that national Office.

(2) The International Bureau shall, as provided in the Regulations, make the appropriate annotation in the International Register of Marks and publish a notice concerning such annotation.

(3)(*a*) Until the said annotation and publication are effected, any recording referred to in paragraph (1) shall not be effective in respect of any third party unless such third party was actually aware of the subject matter of the said recording.

(*b*) Notwithstanding subparagraph (*a*), the national law of any Contracting State may provide that recordings in its own register referred to in paragraph (1) shall be effective in respect of the residents of that State even before the annotation and publication referred to in subparagraph (*a*) are effected.

Article 21
Preservation of Rights Acquired Through National Registration

(1) If, at the international registration date or the recording date of the later designation, as the case may be, the owner of the international registration of a mark owns, in any designated State, a registration of the same mark in the national register of marks ("national registration"), his rights under this treaty shall be deemed

to include in respect of that State all rights, particularly any priority right, existing under the national registration, and, subject to paragraph (4), shall be deemed to continue to include them even where the national registration subsequently expires. The foregoing provision shall apply to the extent that the goods and/or services referred to in respect of the said State in the international registration are, in fact, covered by the list of goods and/or services referred to in the said national registration.

(2) The applicant or the owner of the international registration of a mark may, as provided in the Regulations, make a declaration stating that he owns national registrations of the same mark in certain designated States and identifying such registrations. The declaration may be included in the international application or the request for the recording of later designations or it may be filed separately. It shall, as provided in the Regulations, be accompanied by a certified copy of each national registration referred to in the declaration. The International Bureau shall record and publish the declaration and shall notify the interested designated Offices accordingly, as provided in the Regulations. Those Offices shall refer to the declaration in their respective national registers of marks in connection with the said national registrations.

(3)(*a*) Where a declaration under paragraph (2) has been notified to the designated Office and the conditions referred to in paragraph (1) are complied with, and to the extent that they are complied with, the effects provided for in Article 11 may not, subject to subparagraph (*b*), be refused under Article 12.

(*b*) Where, in any designated State, there is more than one national register of marks or the national register of marks has several parts and the national registration referred to in paragraph (1) exists in a national register or a part of that register which affords less than the highest degree of protection, subparagraph (*a*) shall apply only if the declaration under paragraph (2) relates to a registration in the same national register or in the same part of that register.

(4) Where the national registration referred to in paragraph (1) expires, the rights under this Treaty shall be deemed to continue to include the rights which existed under the said national registration only where a declaration referred to in paragraph (2) has been filed not later than within one year from the expiration of the said national registration.

Article 22
Preservation of Rights Acquired Through International Registration Under the Madrid Agreement

(1) If, at the international registration date or the recording date of the later designation, as the case may be, the owner of the international registration of a mark effected under this Treaty owns,

in respect of any designated State, an international registration of the same mark effected under the Madrid Agreement ("Madrid registration"), his rights under this Treaty shall be deemed to include in respect of that State all rights, particularly any priority right, existing under that Madrid registration and, subject to paragraph (4), shall be deemed to continue to include them even where the Madrid registration subsequently expires. The foregoing provision shall apply to the extent that the goods and/or services referred to in respect of the said State in the international registration under this Treaty are, in fact, covered by the list of goods and/or services referred to in respect of the said State in the Madrid registration.

(2) The applicant seeking the international registration of a mark under this Treaty, or the owner of the international registration of a mark under this Treaty, may, as provided in the Regulations, make a declaration stating that he owns a Madrid registration of the same mark in respect of certain designated States and identifying such registration. The declaration may be included in the international application or the request for the recording of later designations or it may be filed separately. The International Bureau shall record and publish the declaration, as provided in the Regulations.

(3) Where a declaration under paragraph (2) has been notified to the designated Office and the conditions referred to in paragraph (1) are complied with, and to the extent that they are complied with, the effects provided for in Article 11 may not be refused under Article 12, unless protection under the Madrid Agreement has been refused or as long as refusal under that Agreement is still possible.

(4) Where the Madrid registration referred to in paragraph (1) expires, the rights under this Treaty shall be deemed to continue to include the rights which existed under the Madrid Agreement only where a declaration referred to in paragraph (2) has been filed not later than within one year from the expiration of the said Madrid registration.

Article 23
Preservation of the Right to Use the Madrid Agreement

Where any natural person or legal entity has the right to seek international registration under the Madrid Agreement or to renew his or its international registration under that Agreement, such right shall not be affected by this Treaty in any Contracting State party also to the Madrid Agreement.

Article 24
National Registrations Based on International Registrations

(1) The owner of the international registration of a mark having the effect provided for in Article 11(2) in any Contracting State may, at any time and with reference to such international registration, apply for the registration of the same mark in the national register of marks of that State, and such national registration shall, provided the requirements of the national law are complied with, be granted in that State, and the rights of the said owner under such national registration shall be deemed to include all rights, particularly any priority right, existing under the said international registration in the said State, even where the international registration subsequently expires in respect of that State. The foregoing provision shall apply to the extent that the goods and/or services listed in the said application are in fact covered by the list of goods and/or services referred to in the said international registration in respect of the said State.

(2) Until the expiration of the effect referred to in paragraph (1), Article 20(1) and (2) shall apply also in connection with any national registration effected under that paragraph.

Article 25
Regional Marks

(1)(*a*) Where the residents or nationals of all Contracting States are given the right under a treaty providing for the registration of regional marks ("regional treaty") to file applications and obtain registrations under such regional treaty by way of this Treaty, any Contracting State party to such regional treaty may declare, as provided in the Regulations, that its designation under this Treaty shall have the same effect as if the mark had been applied for as a regional mark effective in that State.

(*b*) Where the international application is for a regional mark and, under the regional treaty, the applicant cannot limit his application to some only of the States party to that treaty, designation of one or more of those States shall be treated as designation of all the States party to that treaty, and withdrawal of the designation, or renunciation of the recording of the designation, or cancellation of the designation for any other reason, of any such State shall have the effect of withdrawal, renunciation or cancellation with respect to the designation of all such States.

(2) Where the use of this Treaty results in effects under a re-

gional treaty, Article 18(2) to (5) shall apply *mutatis mutandis* and subject to the following provisions:

(i) The beneficiary of the fees referred to in Article 18(2) shall be the intergovernmental authority administering the regional treaty.

(ii) The choice referred to in Article 18(2) shall be exercised by the intergovernmental authority administering the regional treaty.

(iii) Where, under a regional treaty, fees vary according to the number of the States to which the effect of the regional registration extends, the amounts of individual fees may vary not only according to Article 18(3)(*c*) but also according to the number of the designated States party to the said regional treaty, provided that the total amount referred to in Article 18(3)(*e*) and the amount of the renewal fee referred to in Article 18(3)(*f*) shall be that of the fees prescribed in the regional treaty with respect to as many States as are designated States.

Article 26
Representation Before the International Bureau

(1) Applicants and owners of international registrations may, as provided in the Regulations, be represented before the International Bureau by any natural person or legal entity empowered by them to that effect (hereinafter referred to as "the duly appointed representative").

(2) Any invitation, notification or other communication addressed by the International Bureau to the duly appointed representative shall have the same effect as if it had been addressed to the applicant or the owner of the international registration. Any application, request, demand, declaration or other document whose signature by the applicant or the owner of the international registration is required in proceedings before the International Bureau, except the document appointing the representative or revoking his appointment, may be signed by his duly appointed representative, and any communication from the duly appointed representative to the International Bureau shall have the same effect as if it had been effected by the applicant or the owner of the international registration.

(3)(*a*) Where there are several applicants, they shall appoint a common representative. In the absence of such appointment, the applicant first named in the international application shall be considered the duly appointed representative of all the applicants.

(*b*) Where there are several owners of the international registration, they shall appoint a common representative. In the absence of such appointment, the natural person or legal entity first named among the said owners in the International Register of Marks shall be considered the duly appointed representative of all the owners of the international registration.

(*c*) Subparagraph (*b*) shall not apply to the extent that the owners own the international registration in respect of different designated States, or in respect of different goods and/or services, or in respect of different States and different goods and/or services.

Article 27
Conditions for and Effect of Priority Claim Contained in the International Application or in the Request for the Recording of Later Designations

The conditions for and the effect of any priority claimed in the international application or in the request for the recording of later designations shall be as provided for in respect of marks in Article 4 of the Stockholm (1967) Act of the Paris Convention for the Protection of Industrial Property.

Article 28
International Application as Possible Basis of Priority Claim

(1) Any international application which is regular shall be equivalent to a regular national filing within the meaning of Article 4 of the Stockholm (1967) Act of the Paris Convention for the Protection of Industrial Property and shall be recognized as the basis of a priority claim as provided for in that Act.

(2) For the purposes of paragraph (1), an international application shall be regarded as regular if it is adequate to establish the date on which it was filed with the International Bureau or, where it was filed through the intermediary of a national Office, with that Office.

Article 29
Delay in Meeting Time Limits

(1) Subject to paragraph (3), any Contracting State shall, as far as that State is concerned, excuse, for reasons admitted under its national law, any delay in meeting any time limit fixed in this Treaty or the Regulations.

(2) Subject to paragraph (3), any Contracting State may, as far as that State is concerned, excuse, for reasons other than those admitted under its national law, any delay in meeting any time limit fixed in this Treaty or the Regulations.

(3) Paragraphs (1) and (2) shall not apply to any delay in meeting any time limit provided for in Article 7(1), Article 7(6)(iii), Article 8(1) and Article 12(2)(*a*)(i).

(4) The International Bureau shall not excuse delays by applicants, owners of international registrations or national Offices in meeting any time limit fixed in this Treaty and the Regulations.

Article 30
Correction of Errors of the International Bureau

(1) Subject to Article 9, where, in the opinion of the applicant or the owner of the international registration, the International Bureau has, in applying the provisions of this Treaty and the Regulations, made an error which may affect the interests of such applicant or owner in respect of any designated State, the said applicant or owner may, within the time limit fixed in the Regulations, file with the national Office of such State a petition for the purpose of requesting the International Bureau to correct the error in respect of the said State.

(2) If the national Office or any other competent authority of the said State finds that the International Bureau has in fact made the error which is the subject of the petition, the said national Office shall request the International Bureau to correct that error in respect of that State and the International Bureau shall proceed as requested.

(3) The applicant or the owner of the international registration who files a petition under paragraph (1) shall, at the time of filing the petition, transmit a copy of that petition to the International Bureau. If the petition relates to a mark which is already registered in the International Register of Marks, the International Bureau shall, as provided in the Regulations, record and publish the fact that it received a copy of such petition; otherwise it shall keep the said copy in its files.

(4) Where the correction requires a corresponding modification of the International Register of Marks, the International Bureau shall modify that Register accordingly. Furthermore, where the correction affects any information which has been the subject of a publication by the International Bureau, that Bureau shall publish the correction.

Article 31
Notification of Owner of International Registration

Any matter recorded by the International Bureau in respect of an international registration shall be the subject of a corresponding notification to the owner of the international registration. Details may be provided in the Regulations.

Chapter II
Administrative Provisions

Article 32
Assembly

(1)(*a*) The Assembly shall consist of the Contracting States.

(*b*) The Government of each Contracting State shall be represented by one delegate, who may be assisted by alternate delegates, advisors, and experts.

(2)(*a*) The Assembly shall:

(i) deal with all matters concerning the maintenance and development of the Union and the Implementation of this Treaty;

(ii) exercise such rights and perform such tasks as are specially conferred upon it or assigned to it under this treaty;

(iii) give directions to the Director General concerning the preparation for revision conferences;

(iv) review and approve the reports and activities of the Director General concerning the Union, and give him all necessary instructions concerning matters within the competence of the Union;

(v) determine the program and adopt the budget of the Union, and approve its final accounts;

(vi) adopt the financial regulations of the Union;

(vii) establish such committees and working groups as it deems appropriate to facilitate the work of the Union and of its organs;

(viii) determine which States other than Contracting States and which intergovernmental and international non-governmental organizations shall be admitted to its meetings as observers;

(ix) decide upon the establishment of any agency of the International Bureau in any place outside Geneva (Switzerland) for the purposes of receiving documents and payments under this Treaty and the Regulations with the same effect as if they had been received by the International Bureau in Geneva;

(x) take any other appropriate action designed to further the objectives of the Union and perform such other functions as are appropriate under this Treaty.

(*b*) With respect to matters which are of interest also to other Unions administered by the Organization, the Assembly shall make its decisions after having heard the advice of the Coordination Committee of the Organization.

(3) A delegate may represent, and vote in the name of, one State only.

(4) Each Contracting State shall have one vote.

(5)(*a*) One-half of the Contracting States shall constitute a quorum.

(*b*) In the absence of the quorum, the Assembly may make decisions but, with the exception of decisions concerning its own procedure, all such decisions shall take effect only if the quorum and the required majority are attained through voting by correspondence as provided in the Regulations.

(6)(*a*) Subject to Article 34(5)(*f*), Article 35(2)(*b*) and (*c*), and Article 38(2)(*b*), the decisions of the Assembly shall require a majority of the votes cast.

(*b*) Abstentions shall not be considered as votes.

(7)(*a*) The Assembly shall meet once in every second calendar year in ordinary session upon convocation by the Director General, preferably during the same period and at the same place as the Coordination Committee of the Organization.

(*b*) The Assembly shall meet in extraordinary session upon convocation by the Director General, either on the Director General's own initiative or at the request of one-fourth of the Contracting States.

(8) The Assembly shall adopt its own rules of procedure.

Article 33
International Bureau

(1) The International Bureau shall:

(i) perform the administrative tasks concerning the Union; in particular, it shall perform such tasks as are specially assigned to it under this Treaty or by the Assembly;

(ii) provide the secretariat of revision conferences, of the Assembly, of the committees and working groups established by the Assembly, and of any other meeting convened by the Director General and dealing with matters of concern to the Union.

(2) The Director General shall be the chief executive of the Union and shall represent the Union.

(3) The Director General shall convene any committee and working group established by the Assembly and all other meetings dealing with matters of concern to the Union.

(4)(*a*) The Director General and any staff member designated by him shall participate, without the right to vote, in all meetings of the Assembly, the committees and working groups established by the Assembly, and any other meeting convened by the Director General and dealing with matters of concern to the Union.

(*b*) The Director General or a staff member designated by him shall be ex officio secretary of the Assembly, and of the committees, working groups and other meetings referred to in subparagraph (*a*).

(5)(*a*) The Director General shall, in accordance with the directions of the Assembly, make the preparations for revision conferences.

(*b*) The Director General may consult with intergovernmental and international non-governmental organizations concerning the said preparations.

(*c*) The Director General and persons designated by him shall take part, without the right to vote, in the discussions at revision conferences.

(*d*) The Director General or a staff member designated by him shall be ex officio secretary of any revision conference.

(6) The Regulations may specify the services that national Offices shall render in order to assist the International Bureau in carrying out its tasks under this Treaty.

Article 34
Finances

(1)(*a*) The Union shall have a budget.

(*b*) The budget of the Union shall include the income and expenses proper to the Union, its contribution to the budget of expenses common to the Unions, and any sum made available to the budget of the Conference of the Organization.

(*c*) Expenses not attributable exclusively to the Union but also to one or more other Unions administered by the organization shall be considered as expenses common to the Unions. The share of the Union in such common expenses shall be in proportion to the interest the Union has in them.

(2) The budget of the Union shall be established with due regard to the requirements of coordination with the budgets of the other Unions administered by the Organization.

(3) The budget of the Union shall be financed from the following sources:

(i) fees and other charges due for services rendered by the International Bureau in relation to the Union;

(ii) sale of, or royalties on, the publications of the International Bureau concerning the Union;

(iii) gifts, bequests, and subventions;

(iv) rents, interests, and other miscellaneous income.

(4)(*a*) The amounts of fees and charges due to the International Bureau and the prices of its publications shall be so fixed that they should, under normal circumstances, be sufficient to cover the expenses of the International Bureau connected with the administration of this Treaty.

(*b*) If the budget is not adopted before the beginning of a new financial period, it shall be at the same level as the budget of the previous year, as provided in the financial regulations. If the income exceeds the expenses, the difference shall be credited to a reserve fund.

(5)(*a*) The Union shall have a working capital fund which shall be constituted by a single payment made by each Contracting State. If the fund becomes insufficient, the Assembly shall arrange to increase it. If part of the fund is no longer needed, it shall be reimbursed.

(*b*) The amount of the initial payment of each Contracting State to the said fund or of its participation shall be proportionate to the number of international applications which, among the total number of such applications, it is estimated that its residents will file. The participations of all Contracting States in the fund may be revised from time to time by the Assembly to make them correspond to the number of international applications actually filed by the residents of the various States since the date of the initial payments or the last such revision.

(*c*) The proportion and the terms of payment shall be fixed by the Assembly on the proposal of the Director General and after it has heard the advice of the Coordination Committee of the Organization.

(*d*) If loans from the reserve fund permit the constitution of a working capital fund that is sufficient, the Assembly may suspend the application of subparagraphs (*a*), (b) and (*c*).

(*e*) Any reimbursement under subparagraph (*a*) shall be proportionate to the amounts paid by each Contracting State, taking into account the dates at which they were paid.

(*f*) Any decision under subparagraphs (*a*) to (*d*) shall require two-thirds of the votes cast.

(6)(*a*) In the headquarters agreement concluded with the State on the territory of which the Organization has its headquarters, it shall be provided that, whenever the working capital fund is insufficient, such State shall grant advances. The amount of those advances and the conditions on which they are granted shall be the subject of separate agreements, in each case, between such State and the Organization. As long as it remains under the obligation to grant advances, such State shall have an ex officio seat in the Assembly if it is not a Contracting State.

(*b*) The State referred to in subparagraph (*a*) and the Organization shall each have the right to denounce the obligation to grant advances, by written notification. Denunciation shall take effect three years after the end of the year in which it has been notified.

(7) The auditing of the accounts shall be effected by one or more of the Contracting States or by external auditors, as provided in the financial regulations. They shall be designated, with their agreement, by the Assembly.

Article 35
Regulations

(1) The Regulations adopted at the same time as this Treaty are annexed to this Treaty.

(2)(*a*) The Assembly may amend the Regulations. Amendments may consist also of new provisions added to the Regulations concerning:

(i) matters in respect of which this Treaty expressly refers to the Regulations or expressly provides that they are or shall be prescribed,

(ii) any administrative requirements, matters or procedures,

(iii) any details useful in the implementation of this Treaty.

(*b*) Subject to subparagraphs (*c*) and (*d*), the amendment of the Regulations shall require two-thirds of the votes cast.

(*c*) The amendment of any provision of the Regulations affecting the amount of the fees referred to in Article 18(2), as well as the distribution among the national Offices and the transfer to them of such fees, shall require three-fourths of the votes cast. Where the amendment relates to fees referred to in Article 18(2) but those fees are fees to which only some of the Contracting States are entitled, only the Contracting States entitled thereto shall, for the purposes of the quorum, be considered Contracting States, and only they shall have the right to vote.

(*d*) The amendment of any provisions of the Regulations concerning declarations of intent to use the mark and declarations of actual use of the mark shall require that it be accepted by a majority of two-thirds of the votes cast and that no Contracting State whose national law allows or requires the filing of such declarations vote against the proposed amendment.

(3) In the case of conflict between the provisions of this Treaty and those of the Regulations, the former shall prevail.

Article 36
Search Service

(1) The International Bureau shall maintain a Service whose task shall be to search for anticipations among marks registered under this Treaty, and, to the extent authorized by the Assembly, other marks as well.

(2) Searches shall be made on request and shall be subject to the payment of fees fixed under the Regulations. The Service shall be at the disposal of any Government, national Office, other legal entity, or natural person.

(3) The amounts of the fees referred to in paragraph (2) shall be so fixed that they should be sufficient to cover the expenses of the International Bureau connected with the Service.

Chapter III
Revision and Amendment

Article 37
Revision of the Treaty

(1) This Treaty may be revised from time to time by conferences of the Contracting States.

(2) The convocation of any revision conference shall be decided by the Assembly.

(3) The provisions referred to in Article 38(1)(*a*) may be amended either by a revision conference or according to Article 38.

Article 38
Amendment of Certain Provisions of the Treaty

(1)(*a*) Proposals for the amendment of the length of any time limit fixed in Chapter I of this Treaty, other than those referred to in Articles 12(2) and 19(3), or for any amendment to Articles 32(5) and (7), 33, 34 and 36, may be initiated by any Contracting State or by the Director General.

(*b*) Such proposals shall be communicated by the Director General to the Contracting States at least six months in advance of their consideration by the Assembly.

(2)(*a*) Amendments to the provisions referred to in paragraph (1) shall be adopted by the Assembly.

(*b*) Adoption shall require three-fourths of the votes cast, provided that adoption of any amendment of the length of the time limit fixed in Articles 7(1), 7(3)(*c*), 7(6)(iii) and 8(1) shall require that no Contracting State vote against the proposed amendment.

(3)(*a*) Any amendment to the provisions referred to in paragraph (1) shall enter into force one month after written notifications of acceptance, effected in accordance with their respective constitutional processes, have been received by the Director General from three-fourths of the Contracting States members of the Assembly at the time the Assembly adopted the amendment.

(*b*) Any amendment to the said Articles thus accepted shall bind all the Contracting States which were Contracting States at the time the amendment was adopted by the Assembly, provided that any amendment increasing the financial obligations of the said Contracting States shall bind only those which have notified their acceptance of such amendment.

(*c*) Any amendment which has been accepted and which has entered into force in accordance with subparagraph (*a*) shall bind all States which become Contracting States after the date on which the amendment was adopted by the Assembly.

Chapter IV
Final Provisions

Article 39
Becoming Party to the Treaty

(1) Any State member of the International Union for the Protection of Industrial Property may become party to this Treaty by:

(i) signature followed by the deposit of an instrument of ratification, or

(ii) deposit of an instrument of accession.

(2) Instruments of ratification or accession shall be deposited with the Director General.

(3)(*a*) Any instrument of ratification or accession may be accompanied by a declaration to the effect that it shall be considered to have been deposited only when another State, or either one of two other States, or both of two other States, specified by name, shall have deposited instruments of ratification or accession. The instrument of ratification or accession of any State having made such a declaration shall be considered to have been deposited

(i) on the day on which the specified State, or one of the two specified States, or the second specified State, as the case may be, deposits its instrument of ratification or accession,

(ii) where the instrument of ratification or accession of any specified State itself is accompanied by a declaration concerning other States, on the day on which the instrument of ratification or accession of the said specified State is to be considered to have been deposited.

(*b*) Any declaration made under subparagraph (*a*) may be withdrawn at any time or, if it was made in respect of two States, may be limited to one of them. The instrument of ratification or accession of any State withdrawing its declaration shall be considered to have been deposited on the day on which the withdrawal is notified to the Director General, whereas the instrument of ratification or accession of any State limiting its declaration shall be considered to have been deposited on the day on which the remaining State deposits its instrument of ratification or accession. If the instrument of ratification or accession of the remaining State has already been deposited, the instrument of ratification or accession of the State limiting its declaration shall be considered to have been deposited on the day on which the limitation is notified to the Director General.

(4)(*a*) The provisions of Article 24 of the Stockholm (1967) Act of the Paris Convention for the Protection of Industrial Property shall apply to this Treaty.

(*b*) Subparagraph (*a*) shall in no way be understood as implying the recognition or tacit acceptance by a Contracting State of the factual situation concerning a territory to which this Treaty is made applicable by another Contracting State by virtue of the said subparagraph.

Article 40
Transitional Provisions

(1) Any State party to the Paris Convention for the Protection of Industrial Property but not party to this Treaty which, in conformity with the established practice of the General Assembly of the United Nations, is regarded as a developing country may make a declaration addressed to the Director General stating that it wishes to avail itself of the right provided for in paragraph (2) and that it intends to become party to this Treaty at the latest within two years from the date on which that right, according to the applicable provisions of paragraphs (5) to (8), ceases to be effective in respect of that State.

(2) Residents and nationals of any State having made a declaration according to paragraph (1) shall, notwithstanding Article 4(1), have the right to file international applications and to own international registrations under this Treaty.

(3) The declaration referred to in paragraph (1) shall be filed with the Director General at any time before June 12, 1978.

(4) If filed before the entry into force of this Treaty according to Article 41(1), the declaration referred to in paragraph (3) shall become effective on the date of the said entry into force. If filed after such entry into force, the said declaration shall become effective three months after the date of its filing.

(5) Subject to paragraphs (6) to (8), the right provided for in paragraph (2) shall be effective until the expiration of whichever of the following two periods expires later:

(i) a period of 10 years from the date (June 12, 1973) of the signature of this Treaty,

(ii) a period of five years from the entry into force of this Treaty according to Article 41(1).

(6)(*a*) The period referred to in paragraph (5) may be prolonged twice for periods of five years each by decisions of the Special Conference as defined in subparagraph (*b*) in respect of those States having made the declaration referred to in paragraph (1) whose residents or nationals have filed an average of not more than 200 international applications per year during the three consecutive years, as defined in subparagraph (*d*).

(*b*) The Special Conference shall consist of the States which, at the time it meets, are Contracting States and those States having made a declaration under paragraph (1) which fulfill, in respect of the number of international applications, the conditions set forth in subparagraph (*a*).

(*c*) The decision of the Special Conference shall require a simple majority of the votes cast. The said Conference shall meet upon convocation by the Director General during the year preceding the year in which:

(i) the period referred to in paragraph (5) expires, and

(ii) the first five-year period referred to in subparagraph (*a*) expires if prolongation for that period had been decided.

(*d*) The three consecutive years referred to in subparagraph (*a*) shall, in respect of each of the two possible decisions, be the fourth, third and second calendar years before the year in which the decision is made.

(7) The Assembly, in exceptional cases and upon request, may decide to prolong for two further periods of five years each the application of the right under paragraph (2) in respect of any State which, at the time the decision is made, benefits from the said right and which is then regarded as one of the least developed among the developing countries.

(8) Notwithstanding paragraphs (4) to (7), the right provided for in paragraph (2) shall cease to exist on the last day of the calendar year which follows the year in which any State having made a declaration under paragraph (1):

(i) ceases to be regarded as a developing country in conformity with the established practice of the General Assembly of the United Nations, or

(ii) denounces the Paris Convention for the Protection of Industrial Property.

Article 41
Entry Into Force of the Treaty

(1) This Treaty shall enter into force six months after five States have deposited their instruments of ratification or accession.

(2) Any State which is not among those referred to in paragraph (1) shall become bound by this Treaty three months after the date on which it has deposited its instrument of ratification or accession.

Article 42
Reservations to the Treaty

Subject to Article 46(2), no reservations to this Treaty are permitted.

Article 43
Denunciation of the Treaty

(1) Any Contracting State may denounce this Treaty by notification addressed to the Director General.

(2) Denunciation shall take effect one year after the day on which the Director General has received the notification.

(3) The right of denouncing this treaty provided for in paragraph (1) shall not be exercised by any Contracting State before the expiration of five years from the date on which it becomes bound by this Treaty.

(4)(*a*) The effects of this Treaty on any mark enjoying the benefits of this Treaty on the day preceding the day on which the denunciation by any Contracting State takes effect shall continue in that State until the expiration of the initial or renewal term which was running on that date.

(*b*) Where the right to own the international registration of a mark is based on the owner's being a resident or national of the Contracting State referred to in subparagraph (*a*), the benefits of this Treaty shall, in all designated States, continue until the day on which the period referred to in subparagraph (*a*) expires in respect of that mark.

Article 44
Signature and Languages of the Treaty

(1) This Treaty shall be signed in a single original in the English and French languages, both texts being equally authentic.

(2) Official texts shall be established by the Director General, after consultation with the interested Governments, in the German, Italian, Japanese, Portuguese, Russian and Spanish languages, and such other languages as the Assembly may designate.

(3) This Treaty shall remain open for signature at Vienna until December 31, 1973.

Article 45
Depositary Functions

(1) The original of this Treaty, when no longer open for signature, shall be deposited with the Director General.

(2) The Director General shall transmit two copies, certified by him, of this Treaty to the Governments of the States party to the Paris Convention for the Protection of Industrial Property and, on request, to the Government of any other State.

(3) The Director General shall register this Treaty with the Secretariat of the United Nations.

(4) The Director General shall transmit two copies, certified by him, of any amendment to this Treaty to the Governments of the Contracting States and, on request to the Government of any other State.

Article 46
Settlement of Disputes

(1) Any dispute between two or more Contracting States concerning the interpretation or application of this Treaty or the Regulations, not settled by negotiation, may, by any one of the States concerned, be brought before the International Court of Justice by application in conformity with the Statute of the Court, unless the States concerned agree on some other method of settlement. The

Contracting State bringing the dispute before the Court shall inform the International Bureau; the International Bureau shall bring the matter to the attention of the other Contracting States.

(2) Each Contracting State may, at the time it signs this Treaty or deposits its instrument of ratification or accession, declare by notification deposited with the Director General that it does not consider itself bound by paragraph (1). With regard to any dispute between any Contracting State having made such a declaration and any other Contracting State, paragraph (1) shall not apply.

(3) Any Contracting State having made a declaration in accordance with paragraph (2) may, at any time, withdraw its declaration by notification addressed to the Director General.

Article 47
Notifications

The Director General shall notify the Governments of the States party to the Paris Convention for the Protection of Industrial Property of:

(i) signatures under Article 44;

(ii) deposits of instruments of ratification or accession under Article 39(2) and of any declaration accompanying them under Article 39(3)(*a*) and any withdrawal or limitation of such declarations made under Article 39(3)(*b*);

(iii) the date of entry into force of this Treaty under Article 41(1) and any amendment under Article 38(3)(*a*);

(iv) denunciations received under Article 43;

(v) declarations received under Articles 40(1) and 46(2) and (3).

Part IV

Copyrights and Neighboring Rights

1. Berne Convention for the Protection of Literary and Artistic Works

September 9, 1886, completed at Paris on May 4, 1896, revised at Berlin on November 13, 1908, completed at Berne on March 20, 1914, revised at Rome on June 2, 1928, at Brussels on June 26, 1948, at Stockholm on July 14, 1967, and at Paris on July 24, 1971, and amended in 1979

The International Union for the Protection of Literary and Artistic Works (known as the Berne Union or Berne Convention) was first established in 1886 in Berne, Switzerland. It entered into force on December 5, 1887, has been revised five times with two additions, and is administered by WIPO. The current text is that of the Paris revision of 1971.

The substantive provisions of Berne are found in the first 20 articles, followed by administrative provisions and an appendix incorporating special provisions for developing countries. These substantive provisions include both specific and general obligations imposed on its membership. Other rules are optional. The Berne Convention is based on national treatment and compliance with convention minima.

Under the Berne Convention, the scope of subject matter is broad, encompassing "literary and artistic works [that] shall include every production in the literary, scientific and artistic domain, whatever may be the mode or form of its expression . . ." (Art. 2 para. 1). Article 2 provides an illustrative list of such works as choreography, painting, and architecture. Compilations and derivative works are to be given protection as well (Art. 2 paras. 2 and 5). The Convention expressly excludes from obligatory protection news of the day or miscellaneous facts having the character of mere items of press information (Art. 2 para. 8). Protection of industrial design is optional and is left to national law (Art. 2 para. 7).

The Berne Convention requires that protection be given to published or unpublished works of an author who is a national of a member state. Berne protection is also required for a work of a non-national of a member state if the work is first published in a member state or is simultaneously published in a nonmember and member state. Beginning with the Brussels revision (1948) of the Berne Convention, a work is published simultaneously if it is published in a member country within 30 days of its first publication in a nonmember country (Paris text, Art. 3 para. 4).

The Berne Convention requires that the work be protected without formalities outside the country of origin. Thus, if a work originates from a member country it must be protected in all Berne countries without being subjected to any formalities as prerequisite to copyright protection (Art. 5 para. 2). The Convention does not govern protection of works within a member's own country of origin. This means that formalities can be imposed on works within their own country of origin.

The Convention has established a minimum term of protection of life plus 50 years or an alternative of 50 years from publication for anonymous and pseudonymous works (Art. 7 paras. 1 and 3).

The Convention requires that certain exclusive rights be protected under national law (Arts. 8,9,11, and 12). Berne also recognizes certain limitations to the exclusive rights such as a fair use privilege and a possible limitation on the right of recording of musical works (Arts. 9 and 10). In addition to these exclusive economic rights, Berne requires that the author's moral right be recognized and endure beyond the life of the author (Art. 6 *bis*).

Beginning with the Stockholm revision of 1967, special privileges are given to developing countries. Similar privileges are found in an appendix to the Paris text of 1971.

As of January 1, 1990, the following 84 states were party to the Berne Convention:

Argentina	Bahamas	Benin
Australia	Barbados	Brazil
Austria	Belgium	Bulgaria

Burkina Faso
Cameroon
Canada
Central African Republic
Chad
Chile
Colombia
Congo
Costa Rica
Cote d'Ivoire
Cyprus
Czechoslovakia
Denmark
Egypt
Fiji
Finland
France
Gabon
German Democratic Republic
Federal Republic of Germany
Greece
Guinea
Holy See
Honduras
Hungary
Iceland
India
Ireland
Israel
Italy
Japan
Lebanon
Lesotho
Liberia
Libya
Liechtenstein
Luxembourg
Madagascar
Mali
Malta
Mauritania
Mauritius
Mexico
Monaco
Morocco
Netherlands
New Zealand
Niger
Norway
Pakistan
Peru
Philippines
Poland
Portugal
Romania
Rwanda
Senegal
South Africa
Spain
Sri Lanka
Suriname
Sweden
Switzerland
Thailand
Togo
Trinidad and Tobago
Tunisia
Turkey
United Kingdom
United States of America
Uruguay
Venezuela
Yugoslavia
Zaire
Zimbabwe

Berne Convention for the Protection of Literary and Artistic Works, as revised at Paris, 1971

Article 1

The countries to which this Convention applies constitute a Union for the protection of the rights of authors in their literary and artistic works.

Article 2

(1) The expression "literary and artistic works" shall include every production in the literary, scientific and artistic domain, whatever may be the mode or form of its expression, such as books, pamphlets and other writings; lectures, addresses, sermons and other works of the same nature; dramatic or dramatico-musical works; choreographic works and entertainments in dumb show; musical compositions with or without words; cinematographic works to which are assimilated works expressed by a process analogous to cinematography; works of drawing, painting, architecture, sculpture, engraving and lithography; photographic works to which are assimilated works expressed by a process analogous to photography; works of applied art; illustrations, maps, plans, sketches and three-dimensional works relative to geography, topography, architecture or science.

(2) It shall, however, be a matter for legislation in the countries of the Union to prescribe that works in general or any specified categories of works shall not be protected unless they have been fixed in some material form.

(3) Translations, adaptations, arrangements of music and other alterations of a literary or artistic work shall be protected as original works without prejudice to the copyright in the original work.

(4) It shall be a matter for legislation in the countries of the Union to determine the protection to be granted to official texts of a legislative, administrative and legal nature, and to official translations of such texts.

(5) Collections of literary or artistic works such as encyclopedias

---

Source: Reprinted from *Copyright Laws and Treaties of the World,* 15 Supplement, © 1972, BNA Books, Washington, D.C.

and anthologies which, by reason of the selection and arrangement of their contexts, constitute intellectual creations shall be protected as such, without prejudice to the copyright in each of the works forming part of such collections.

(6) The works mentioned in this Article shall enjoy protection in all countries of the Union. This protection shall operate for the benefit of the author and his successors in title.

(7) Subject to the provisions of Article 7(4) of this Convention, it shall be a matter for legislation in the countries of the Union to determine the extent of the application of their laws to works of applied art and industrial designs and models, as well as the conditions under which such works, designs and models shall be protected. Works protected in the country of origin solely as designs and models shall be entitled in another country of the Union only to such special protection as is granted in that country to designs and models; however, if no such special protection is granted in that country, such works shall be protected as artistic works.

(8) The protection of this Convention shall not apply to news of the day or to miscellaneous facts having the character of mere items of press information.

Article 2*bis*

(1) It shall be a matter for legislation in the countries of the Union to exclude, wholly or in part, from the protection provided by the preceding Article political speeches and speeches delivered in the course of legal proceedings.

(2) It shall also be a matter for legislation in the countries of the Union to determine the conditions under which lectures, addresses and other works of the same nature which are delivered in public may be reproduced by the press, broadcast, communicated to the public by wire and made the subject of public communication as envisaged in Article II*bis*(1) of this Convention, when such use is justified by the informatory purpose.

(3) Nevertheless, the author shall enjoy the exclusive right of making a collection of his works mentioned in the preceding paragraphs.

Article 3

(1) The protection of this Convention shall apply to:

(*a*) authors who are nationals of one of the countries of the Union, for their works, whether published or not;

(b) authors who are not nationals of one of the countries of the Union, for their work first published in one of those countries, or simultaneously in a country outside the Union and in a country of the Union.

(2) Authors who are not nationals of one of the countries of the Union but who have their habitual residence in one of them shall, for the purposes of this Convention, be assimilated to nationals of that country.

(3) The expression "published works" means works published with the consent of their authors, whatever may be the means of manufacture of the copies, provided that the availability of such copies has been such as to satisfy the reasonable requirements of the public, having regard to the nature of the work. The performance of a dramatic, dramatico-musical, cinematographic or musical work, the public recitation of a literary work, the communication by wire or the broadcasting of literary or artistic works, the exhibition of a work of art and the construction of a work of architecture shall not constitute publication.

(4) A work shall be considered as having been published simultaneously in several countries if it has been published in two or more countries within 30 days of its first publication.

Article 4

The protection of this Convention shall apply, even if the conditions of Article 3 are not fulfilled, to:

(*a*) authors of cinematographic works the maker of which has his headquarters or habitual residence in one of the countries of the Union;

(*b*) authors of works of architecture erected in a country of the Union or of other artistic works incorporated in a building or other structure located in a country of the Union.

Article 5

(1) Authors shall enjoy, in respect of works for which they are protected under this Convention, in countries of the Union other than the country of origin, the rights which their respective laws do now or may hereafter grant to their nationals, as well as the rights specially granted by this Convention.

(2) The enjoyment and the exercise of these rights shall not be subject to any formality; such enjoyment and such exercise shall be

independent of the existence of protection in the country of origin of the work. Consequently, apart from the provisions of this Convention, the extent of protection, as well as the means of redress afforded to the author to protect his rights, shall be governed exclusively by the laws of the country where protection is claimed.

(3) Protection in the country of origin is governed by domestic law. However, when the author is not a national of the country of origin of the work for which he is protected under this Convention, he shall enjoy in that country the same rights as national authors.

(4) The country of origin shall be considered to be:

(a) in the case of works first published in a country of the Union, that country; in the case of works published simultaneously in several countries of the Union which grant different terms of protection, the country whose legislation grants the shortest term of protection;

(b) in the case of works published simultaneously in a country outside the Union and in a country of the Union, the latter country;

(c) in the case of unpublished works or of works first published in a country outside the Union, without simultaneous publication in a country of the Union, the country of the Union of which the author is a national, provided that:

(i) when these are cinematographic works the maker of which has his headquarters or his habitual residence in a country of the Union, the country of origin shall be that country, and

(ii) when these are works of architecture erected in a country of the Union or other artistic works incorporated in a building or other structure located in a country of the Union, the country of origin shall be that country.

Article 6

(1) Where any country outside the Union fails to protect in an adequate manner the works of authors who are nationals of one of the countries of the Union, the latter country may restrict the protection given to the works of authors who are, at the date of the first publication thereof, nationals of the other country and are not habitually resident in one of the countries of the Union. If the country of first publication avails itself of this right, the other countries of the Union shall not be required to grant to works thus subjected to special treatment a wider protection than that granted to them in the country of first publication.

(2) No restrictions introduced by virtue of the preceding paragraph shall affect the rights which an author may have acquired in respect of a work published in a country of the Union before such restrictions were put into force.

(3) The countries of the Union which restrict the grant of copyright in accordance with this Article shall give notice thereof to the Director General of the World Intellectual Property Organization (hereinafter designated as "the Director General") by a written declaration specifying the countries in regard to which protection is restricted, and the restrictions to which rights of authors who are nationals of those countries are subjected. The Director General shall immediately communicate this declaration to all the countries of the Union.

Article 6*bis*

(1) Independently of the author's economic rights, and even after the transfer of the said rights, the author shall have the right to claim authorship of the work and to object to any distortion, mutilation or other modification of, or other derogatory action in relation to, the said work, which would be prejudicial to his honor or reputation.

(2) The rights granted to the author in accordance with the preceding paragraph shall, after his death, be maintained, at least until the expiry of the economic rights, and shall be exercisable by the persons or institutions authorized by the legislation of the country where protection is claimed. However, those countries whose legislation, at the moment of their ratification of or accession to this Act, does not provide for the protection after the death of the author of all the rights set out in the preceding paragraph may provide that some of these rights may, after his death, cease to be maintained.

(3) The means of redress for safeguarding the rights granted by this Article shall be governed by the legislation of the country where protection is claimed.

Article 7

(1) The term of protection granted by this Convention shall be the life of the author and 50 years after his death.

(2) However, in the case of cinematographic works, the countries of the Union may provide that the term of protection shall expire 50 years after the work has been made available to the public with the consent of the author, or, failing such an event within 50 years from the making of such a work, 50 years after the making.

(3) In the case of anonymous or pseudonymous works, the term of protection granted by this Convention shall expire 50 years after the work has been lawfully made available to the public. However, when the pseudonym adopted by the author leaves no doubt as to his

identity, the term of protection shall be that provided in paragraph (1). If the author of an anonymous or pseudonymous work discloses his identity during the above-mentioned period, the term of protection applicable shall be that provided in paragraph (1). The countries of the Union shall not be required to protect anonymous or pseudonymous works in respect of which it is reasonable to presume that their author has been dead for 50 years.

(4) It shall be a matter for legislation in the countries of the Union to determine the term of protection of photographic works and that of works of applied art in so far as they are protected as artistic works; however, this term shall last at least until the end of a period of 25 years from the making of such a work.

(5) The term of protection subsequent to the death of the author and the terms provided by paragraphs (2), (3) and (4) shall run from the date of death or of the event referred to in those paragraphs, but such terms shall always be deemed to begin on the first of January of the year following the death or such event.

(6) The countries of the Union may grant a term of protection in excess of those provided by the preceding paragraphs.

(7) Those countries of the Union bound by the Rome Act of this Convention which grant, in their national legislation in force at the time of signature of the present Act, shorter terms of protection than those provided for in the preceding paragraphs shall have the right to maintain such terms when ratifying or acceding to the present Act.

(8) In any case, the term shall be governed by the legislation of the country where protection is claimed; however, unless the legislation of that country otherwise provides, the term shall not exceed the term fixed in the country of origin of the work.

Article 7*bis*

The provisions of the preceding Article shall also apply in the case of a work of joint authorship, provided that the terms measured from the death of the author shall be calculated from the death of the last surviving author.

Article 8

Authors of literary and artistic works protected by this Convention shall enjoy the exclusive right of making and of authorizing the translation of their works throughout the term of protection of their rights in the original works.

Article 9

(1) Authors of literary and artistic works protected by this Convention shall have the exclusive right of authorizing the reproduction of these works, in any manner or form.

(2) It shall be a matter for legislation in the countries of the Union to permit the reproduction of such works in certain special cases, provided that such reproduction does not conflict with a normal exploitation of the work and does not unreasonably prejudice the legitimate interests of the author.

(3) Any sound or visual recording shall be considered as a reproduction for the purposes of this Convention.

Article 10

(1) It shall be permissible to make quotations from a work which has already been lawfully made available to the public, provided that their making is compatible with fair practice, and their extent does not exceed that justified by the purpose, including quotations from newspaper articles and periodicals in the form of press summaries.

(2) It shall be a matter for legislation in the countries of the Union, and for special agreements existing or to be concluded between them, to permit the utilization, to the extent justified by the purpose, of literary or artistic works by way of illustration in publications, broadcasts or sound or visual recordings for teaching, provided such utilization is compatible with fair practice.

(3) Where use is made of works in accordance with the preceding paragraphs of this Article, mention shall be made of the source, and of the name of the author if it appears thereon.

Article 10*bis*

(1) It shall be a matter for legislation in the countries of the Union to permit the reproduction by the press, the broadcasting or the communication to the public by wire of articles published in newspapers or periodicals on current economic, political or religious topics, and of broadcast works of the same character, in cases in which the reproduction, broadcasting or such communication thereof is not expressly reserved. Nevertheless, the source must always be clearly indicated; the legal consequences of a breach of this obligation shall be determined by the legislation of the country where protection is claimed.

(2) It shall also be a matter for legislation in the countries of the Union to determine the conditions under which, for the purpose of reporting current events by means of photography, cinematography, broadcasting or communication to the public by wire, literary or artistic works seen or heard in the course of the event may, to the extent justified by the informatory purpose, be reproduced and made available to the public.

Article 11

(1) Authors of dramatic dramatico-musical and musical works shall enjoy the exclusive right of authorizing:

(i) the public performance of their works, including such public performance by any means or process;
(ii) any communication to the public of the performance of their works.

(2) Authors of dramatic or dramatico-musical works shall enjoy, during the full term of their rights in the original works, the same rights with respect to translations thereof.

Article 11*bis*

(1) Authors of literary and artistic works shall enjoy the exclusive right of authorizing:

(i) the broadcasting of their works or the communication thereof to the public by any other means of wireless diffusion of signs, sounds or images;
(ii) any communication to the public by wire or by rebroadcasting of the broadcast of the work, when this communication is made by an organization other than the original one;
(iii) the public communication by loudspeaker or any other analogous instrument transmitting, by signs, sounds or images, the broadcast of the work.

(2) It shall be a matter for legislation in the countries of the Union to determine the conditions under which the rights mentioned in the preceding paragraphs may be exercised, but these conditions shall apply only in the countries where they have been prescribed. They shall not in any circumstances be prejudicial to the moral rights of the author, nor to his right to obtain equitable remuneration which, in the absence of agreement, shall be fixed by competent authority.

(3) In the absence of any contrary stipulation, permission granted in accordance with paragraph (1) of this Article shall not imply permission to record, by means of instruments recording sounds or images, the work broadcast. It shall, however, be a matter for legislation in the countries of the Union to determine the regulations for ephemeral recordings made by a broadcasting organization by means of its own facilities and used for its own broadcasts. The preservation of these recordings in official archives may, on the ground of their exceptional documentary character, be authorized by such legislation.

Article 11*ter*

(1) Authors of literary works shall enjoy the exclusive right of authorizing:

(i) the public recitation of their works, including such public recitation by any means or process;

(ii) any communication to the public of the recitation of their works.

(2) Authors of literary works shall enjoy, during the full terms of their rights in the original works, the same rights with respect to translations thereof.

Article 12

Authors of literary or artistic works shall enjoy the exclusive right of authorizing adaptations, arrangements and other alterations of their works.

Article 13

(1) Each country of the Union may impose for itself reservations and conditions on the exclusive right granted to the author of a musical work and to the author of any words, the recording of which together with the musical work has already been authorized by the latter, to authorize the sound recording of that musical work, together with such words, if any; but all such reservations and conditions shall apply only in the countries which have imposed them and shall not, in any circumstances, be prejudicial to the rights of these authors to obtain equitable remuneration which, in the absence of agreement, shall be fixed by competent authority.

(2) Recordings of musical works made in a country of the Union in accordance with Article 13(3) of the Conventions signed at Rome on June 2, 1928, and at Brussels on June 26, 1948, may be reproduced in that country without the permission of the author of the musical work until a date two years after that country becomes bound by this Act.

(3) Recordings made in accordance with paragraphs (1) and (2) of this Article and imported without permission from the parties concerned into a country where they are treated as infringing recordings shall be liable to seizure.

Article 14

(1) Authors of literary or artistic works shall have the exclusive right of authorizing:

(i) the cinematographic adaptation and reproduction of these works, and the distribution of the works thus adapted or reproduced;
(ii) the public performance and communication to the public by wire of the works thus adapted or reproduced.

(2) The adaptation into any other artistic form of a cinematographic production derived from literary or artistic works shall, without prejudice to the authorization of the author of the cinematographic production, remain subject to the authorization of the authors of the original works.

(3) The provisions of Article 13(1) shall not apply.

Article 14*bis*

(1) Without prejudice to the copyright in any work which may have been adapted or reproduced, a cinematographic work shall be protected as an original work. The owner of copyright in a cinematographic work shall enjoy the same rights as the author of an original work, including the rights referred to in the preceding Article.

(2) (*a*) Ownership of copyright in a cinematographic work shall be a matter for legislation in the country where protection is claimed.

(*b*) However, in the countries of the Union which, by legislation, include among the owners of copyright in a cinematographic work authors who have brought contributions to the making of the work, such authors, if they have undertaken to bring such contributions, may not, in the absence of any contrary or special stipulation, object to the reproduction, distribution, public performance, communication to the public by wire, broadcasting or any other communication to the public, or to the subtitling or dubbing of texts, of the work.

(*c*) The question whether or not the form of the undertaking referred to above should, for the application of the preceding subparagraph (*b*), be in a written agreement or a written act of the same effect shall be a matter for the legislation of the country where the maker of the cinematographic work has his headquarters or habitual residence. However, it shall be a matter for the legislation of the country of the Union where protection is claimed to provide that the said undertaking shall be in a written agreement or a written act of the same effect. The countries whose legislation so provides shall notify the Director General by means of a written declaration, which will be immediately communicated by him to all the other countries of the Union.

(*d*) By "contrary or special stipulation" is meant any restrictive condition which is relevant to the aforesaid undertaking.

(3) Unless the national legislation provides to the contrary, the provisions of paragraph (2)(*b*) above shall not be applicable to authors of scenarios, dialogues and musical works created for the making of the cinematographic work, or to the principal director thereof. However, those countries of the Union whose legislation does not contain rules providing for the application of the said paragraph (2)(*b*) to such director shall notify the Director General by means of a written declaration, which will be immediately communicated by him to all the other countries of the Union.

Article 14*ter*

(1) The author, or after his death the persons or institutions authorized by national legislation, shall, with respect to original works of art and original manuscripts of writers and composers, enjoy the inalienable right to an interest in any sale of the work subsequent to the first transfer by the author of the work.

(2) The protection provided by the preceding paragraph may be claimed in a country of the Union only if legislation in the country to which the author belongs so permits, and to the extent permitted by the country where this protection is claimed.

(3) The procedure for collection and the amounts shall be matters for determination by national legislation.

Article 15

(1) In order that the author of a literary or artistic work protected by this Convention shall, in the absence of proof to the contrary, be regarded as such, and consequently be entitled to institute

infringement proceedings in the countries of the Union, it shall be sufficient for his name to appear on the work in the usual manner. This paragraph shall be applicable even if this name is a pseudonym, where the pseudonym adopted by the author leaves no doubt as to his identity.

(2) The person or body corporate whose name appears on a cinematographic work in the usual manner shall, in the absence of proof to the contrary, be presumed to be the maker of the said work.

(3) In the case of anonymous and pseudonymous works, other than those referred to in paragraph (1) above, the publisher whose name appears on the work shall, in the absence of proof to the contrary, be deemed to represent the author, and in this capacity he shall be entitled to protect and enforce the author's rights. The provisions of this paragraph shall cease to apply when the author reveals his identity and establishes his claim to authorship of the work.

(4)(*a*) In the case of unpublished works where the identity of the author is unknown, but where there is every ground to presume that he is a national of a country of the Union, it shall be a matter for legislation in that country to designate the competent authority which shall represent the author and shall be entitled to protect and enforce his rights in the countries of the Union.

(*b*) Countries of the Union which make such designation under the terms of this provision shall notify the Director General by means of a written declaration giving full information concerning the authority thus designated. The Director General shall at once communicate this declaration to all other countries of the Union.

Article 16

(1) Infringing copies of a work shall be liable to seizure in any country of the Union where the work enjoys legal protection.

(2) The provisions of the preceding paragraph shall also apply to reproductions coming from a country where the work is not protected, or has ceased to be protected.

(3) The seizure shall take place in accordance with the legislation of each country.

Article 17

The provisions of this Convention cannot in any way affect the right of the Government of each country of the Union to permit, to control, or to prohibit, by legislation or regulation, the circulation, presentation, or exhibition of any work or production in regard to which the competent authority may find it necessary to exercise that right.

Article 18

(1) This Convention shall apply to all works which, at the moment of its coming into force, have not yet fallen into the public domain in the country of origin through the expiry of the term of protection.

(2) If, however, through the expiry of the term of protection which was previously granted, a work has fallen into the public domain of the country where protection is claimed, that work shall not be protected anew.

(3) The application of this principle shall be subject to any provisions contained in special conventions to that effect existing or to be concluded between countries of the Union. In the absence of such provisions, the respective countries shall determine, each in so far as it is concerned, the conditions of application of this principle.

(4) The preceding provisions shall also apply in the case of new accessions to the Union and to cases in which protection is extended by the application of Article 7 or by the abandonment of reservations.

Article 19

The provisions of this Convention shall not preclude the making of a claim to the benefit of any greater protection which may be granted by legislation in a country of the Union.

Article 20

The Governments of the countries of the Union reserve the right to enter into special agreements among themselves, in so far as such agreements grant to authors more extensive rights than those granted by the Convention, or contain other provisions not contrary to this Convention. The provisions of existing agreements which satisfy these conditions shall remain applicable.

Article 21

(1) Special provisions regarding developing countries are included in the Appendix.

(2) Subject to the provisions of Article 29(1)(*b*), the Appendix forms an integral part of this Act.

Article 22

(1)(*a*) The Union shall have an Assembly consisting of those countries of the Union which are bound by Articles 22 to 26.

(*b*) The Government of each country shall be represented by one delegate, who may be assisted by alternate delegates, advisors, and experts.

(*c*) The expenses of each delegation shall be borne by the Government which has appointed it.

(2)(*a*) The Assembly shall:

(i) deal with all matters concerning the maintenance and development of the Union and the implementation of this Convention;

(ii) give directions concerning the preparation for conferences of revision to the International Bureau of Intellectual Property (hereinafter designated as "the International Bureau") referred to in the Convention Establishing the World Intellectual Property Organization (hereinafter designated as "the Organization"), due account being taken of any comments made by those countries of the Union which are not bound by Articles 22 to 26;

(iii) review and approve the reports and activities of the Director General of the Organization concerning the Union, and give him all necessary instructions concerning matters within the competence of the Union;

(iv) elect the members of the Executive Committee of the Assembly;

(v) review and approve the reports and activities of its Executive Committee, and give instructions to such Committee;

(vi) determine the program and adopt the triennial budget of the Union, and approve its final accounts;

(vii) adopt the financial regulations of the Union;

(viii) establish such committees of experts and working groups as may be necessary for the work of the Union;

(ix) determine which countries not members of the Union and which intergovernmental and international non-governmental organizations shall be admitted to its meetings as observers;

(x) adopt amendments to Articles 22 to 26;

(xi) take any other appropriate action designed to further the objectives of the Union;

(xii) exercise such other functions as are appropriate under this Convention;

(xiii) subject to its acceptance, exercise such rights as are given to it in the Convention establishing the Organization.

(*b*) With respect to matters which are of interest also to other Unions administered by the Organization, the Assembly shall make its decisions after having heard the advice of the Coordination Committee of the Organization.

(3)(*a*) Each country member of the Assembly shall have one vote.

(*b*) One-half of the countries members of the Assembly shall constitute a quorum.

(*c*) Notwithstanding the provisions of subparagraph (*b*), if, in any section, the number of countries represented is less than one-half but equal to or more than one-third of the countries members of the Assembly, the Assembly may make decisions but, with the exception of decisions concerning its own procedure, all such decisions shall take effect only if the following conditions are fulfilled. The International Bureau shall communicate the said decisions to the countries members of the Assembly which were not represented and shall invite them to express in writing their vote or abstention within a period of three months from the date of the communication. If, at the expiration of this period, the number of countries having thus expressed their vote or abstention attains the number of countries which was lacking for attaining the quorum in the session itself, such decisions shall take effect provided that at the same time the required majority still obtains.

(*d*) Subject to the provisions of Article 26(2), the decisions of the Assembly shall require two-thirds of the votes cast.

(*e*) Abstentions shall not be considered as votes.

(*f*) A delegate may represent, and vote in the name of, one country only.

(*g*) Countries of the Union not members of the Assembly shall be admitted to its meetings as observers.

(4)(*a*) The Assembly shall meet once in every third calendar year in ordinary session upon convocation by the Director General and, in the absence of exceptional circumstances, during the same period and at the same place as the General Assembly of the Organization.

(*b*) The Assembly shall meet in extraordinary session upon

convocation by the Director General, at the request of the Executive Committee or at the request of one-fourth of the countries members of the Assembly.

(5) The Assembly shall adopt its own rules of procedure.

Article 23

(1) The Assembly shall have an Executive Committee.

(2) (*a*) The Executive Committee shall consist of countries elected by the Assembly from among countries members of the Assembly. Furthermore, the country on whose territory the Organization has its headquarters shall, subject to the provisions of Article 25(7)(*b*), have an ex officio seat on the Committee.

(*b*) The Government of each country member of the Executive Committee shall be represented by one delegate, who may be assisted by alternate delegates, advisers, and experts.

(*c*) The expenses of each delegation shall be borne by the Government which has appointed it.

(3) The number of countries members of the Executive Committee shall correspond to one-fourth of the number of countries members of the Assembly. In establishing the number of seats to be filled, remainders after division by four shall be disregarded.

(4) In electing the members of the Executive Committee, the Assembly shall have due regard to an equitable geographical distribution and to the need for countries party to the Special Agreements which might be established in relation with the Union to be among the countries constituting the Executive Committee.

(5)(*a*) Each member of the Executive Committee shall serve from the close of the session of the Assembly which elected it to the close of the next ordinary session of the Assembly.

(*b*) Members of the Executive Committee may be re-elected, but not more than two-thirds of them.

(*c*) The Assembly shall establish the details of the rules governing the election and possible re-election of the members of the Executive Committee.

(6)(*a*) The Executive Committee shall:

(i) prepare the draft agenda of the Assembly;
(ii) submit proposals to the Assembly respecting the draft program and triennial budget of the Union prepared by the Director General;
(iii) approve, within the limits of the program and the triennial budget, the specific yearly budgets and programs prepared by the Director General;

(iv) submit, with appropriate comments, to the Assembly the periodic reports of the Director General and the yearly audit reports on the accounts;

(v) in accordance with the decisions of the Assembly and having regard to circumstances arising between two ordinary sessions of the Assembly, take all necessary measures to ensure the execution of the program of the Union by the Director General;

(vi) perform such other functions as are allocated to it under this Convention.

(*b*) With respect to matters which are of interest also to other Unions administered by the Organization, the Executive Committee shall make its decisions after having heard the advice of the Coordination Committee of the Organization.

(7)(*a*) The Executive Committee shall meet once a year in ordinary session upon convocation by the Director General, preferably during the same period and at the same place as the Coordination Committee of the Organization.

(*b*) The Executive Committee shall meet in extraordinary session upon convocation by the Director General, either on his own initiative, or at the request of its Chairman or one-fourth of its members.

(8)(*a*) Each country member of the Executive Committee shall have one vote.

(*b*) One-half of the members of the Executive Committee shall constitute a quorum.

(*c*) Decisions shall be made by a simple majority of the votes cast.

(*d*) Abstentions shall not be considered as votes.

(*e*) A delegate may represent, and vote in the name of, one country only.

(9) Countries of the Union not members of the Executive Committee shall be admitted to its meetings as observers.

(10) The Executive Committee shall adopt its own rules of procedure.

Article 24

(1)(*a*) The administrative tasks with respect to the Union shall be performed by the International Bureau, which is a continuation of the Bureau of the Union united with the Bureau of the Union established by the International Convention for the Protection of Industrial Property.

(*b*) In particular, the International Bureau shall provide the secretariat of the various organs of the Union.

(*c*) The Director General of the Organization shall be the chief executive of the Union and shall represent the Union.

(2) The International Bureau shall assemble and publish information concerning the protection of copyright. Each country of the Union shall promptly communicate to the International Bureau all new laws and official texts concerning the protection of copyright.

(3) The International Bureau shall publish a monthly periodical.

(4) The International Bureau shall, on request, furnish information to any country of the Union on matters concerning the protection of copyright.

(5) The International Bureau shall conduct studies, and shall provide services, designed to facilitate the protection of copyright.

(6) The Director General and any staff member designated by him shall participate, without the right to vote, in all meetings of the Assembly, the Executive Committee and any other committee of experts or working group. The Director General, or a staff member designated by him, shall be ex officio secretary of these bodies.

(7) (*a*) The International Bureau shall, in accordance with the directions of the Assembly and in cooperation with the Executive Committee, make the preparations for the conferences of revision of the provisions of the Convention other than Articles 22 to 26.

(*b*) The International Bureau may consult with intergovernmental and international non-governmental organizations concerning preparations for conferences of revision.

(*c*) The Director General and persons designated by him shall take part, without the right to vote, in the discussions at these conferences.

(8) The International Bureau shall carry out any other tasks assigned to it.

Article 25

(1) (*a*) The Union shall have a budget.

(*b*) The budget of the Union shall include the income and expenses proper to the Union, its contribution to the budget of expenses common to the Unions, and, where applicable, the sum made available to the budget of the Conference of the Organization.

(*c*) Expenses not attributable exclusively to the Union but also to one or more other Unions administered by the Organization shall be considered as expenses common to the Unions. The share of the

Union in such common expenses shall be in proportion to the interest the Union has in them.

(2) The budget of the Union shall be established with due regard to the requirements of coordination with the budgets of the other Unions administered by the Organization.

(3) The Budget of the Union shall be financed from the following sources:

(i) contributions of the countries of the Union;
(ii) fees and charges due for services performed by the International Bureau in relation to the Union;
(iii) sale of, or royalties on, the publications of the International Bureau concerning the Union;
(iv) gifts, bequests, and subventions;
(v) rents, interests, and other miscellaneous income.

(4) (*a*) For the purpose of establishing its contribution towards the budget, each country of the Union shall belong to a class, and shall pay its annual contributions on the basis of a number of units fixed as follows:

Class I	25
Class II	20
Class III	15
Class IV	10
Class V	5
Class VI	3
Class VII	1

(*b*) Unless it has already done so, each country shall indicate, concurrently with depositing its instrument of ratification or accession, the class to which it wishes to belong. Any country may change class. If it chooses a lower class, the country must announce it to the Assembly at one of its ordinary sessions. Any such change shall take effect at the beginning of the calendar year following the session.

(*c*) The annual contribution of each country shall be an amount in the same proportion to the total sum to be contributed to the annual budget of the Union by all countries as the number of its units is to the total of the units of all contributing countries.

(*d*) Contributions shall become due on the first of January of each year.

(*e*) A country which is in arrears in the payment of its contributions shall have no vote in any of the organs of the Union of which it is a member if the amount of its arrears equals or exceeds the amount of the contributions due from it for the preceding two full years. However, any organ of the Union may allow such a country to continue to exercise its vote in that organ if, and as long as, it is satisfied that the delay in payment is due to exceptional and unavoidable circumstances.

(*f*) If the budget is not adopted before the beginning of a new financial period, it shall be at the same level as the budget of the previous year, in accordance with the financial regulations.

(5) The amount of the fees and charges due for services rendered by the International Bureau in relation to the Union shall be established, and shall be reported to the Assembly and the Executive Committee, by the Director General.

(6) (*a*) The Union shall have a working capital fund which shall be constituted by a single payment made by each country of the Union. If the fund becomes insufficient, an increase shall be decided by the Assembly.

(*b*) The amount of the initial payment of each country to the said fund or of its participation in the increase thereof shall be a proportion of the contribution of that country for the year in which the fund is established or the increase decided.

(*c*) The proportion and the terms of payment shall be fixed by the Assembly on the proposal of the Director General and after it has heard the advice of the Coordination Committee of the Organization.

(7) (*a*) In the headquarters agreement concluded with the country on the territory of which the Organization has its headquarters, it shall be provided that, whenever the working capital fund is insufficient, such country shall grant advances. The amount of these advances and the conditions on which they are granted shall be the subject of separate agreements, in each case, between such country and the Organization. As long as it remains under the obligation to grant advances, such country shall have an ex officio seat on the Executive Committee.

(*b*) The country referred to in subparagraph (*a*) and the Organization shall each have the right to denounce the obligation to grant advances, by written notification. Denunciation shall take effect three years after the end of the year in which it has been notified.

(8) The auditing of the accounts shall be effected by one or more of the countries of the Union or by external auditors, as provided in the financial regulations. They shall be designated, with their agreement, by the Assembly.

Article 26

(1) Proposals for the amendment of Articles 22, 23, 24, 25, and the present Article, may be initiated by any country member of the Assembly, by the Executive Committee, or by the Director General. Such proposals shall be communicated by the Director General to

the member countries of the Assembly at least six months in advance of their consideration by the Assembly.

(2) Amendments to the Articles referred to in paragraph (1) shall be adopted by the Assembly. Adoption shall require three-fourths of the votes cast, provided that any amendment of Article 22, and of the present paragraph, shall require four-fifths of the votes cast.

(3) Any amendment to the Articles referred to in paragraph (1) shall enter into force one month after written notifications of acceptance, effected in accordance with their respective constitutional processes, have been received by the Director General from three-fourths of the countries members of the Assembly at the time it adopted the amendment. Any amendment to the said Articles thus accepted shall bind all the countries which are members of the Assembly at the time the amendment enters into force, or which become members thereof as a subsequent date, provided that any amendment increasing the financial obligations of countries of the Union shall bind only those countries which have notified their acceptance of such amendment.

Article 27

(1) This Convention shall be submitted to revision with a view to the introduction of amendments designed to improve the system of the Union.

(2) For this purpose, conferences shall be held successively in one of the countries of the Union among the delegates of the said countries.

(3) Subject to the provisions of Article 26 which apply to the amendment of Articles 22 to 26, any revision of this Act, including the Appendix, shall require the unanimity of the votes cast.

Article 28

(1) (*a*) Any country of the union which has signed this Act may ratify it, if it has not signed it, may accede to it. Instruments of ratification or accession shall be deposited with the Director General.

(*b*) Any country of the Union may declare in its instrument of ratification or accession that its ratification or accession shall not apply to Articles 1 to 21 and the Appendix, provided that, if such country has previously made a declaration under Article VI(1) of the Appendix, then it may declare in the said instrument only that its ratification or accession shall not apply to Articles 1 to 20.

(*c*) Any country of the Union which, in accordance with subparagraph (*b*), has excluded provisions therein referred to from the effects of its ratification or accession may at any later time declare that it extends the effects of its ratification or accession to those provisions. Such declaration shall be deposited with the Director General.

(2) (*a*) Articles 1 to 21 and the Appendix shall enter into force three months after both of the following two conditions are fulfilled:

(i) at least five countries of the Union have ratified or acceded to this Act without making a declaration under paragraph (1) (*b*),

(ii) France, Spain, the United Kingdom of Great Britain and Northern Ireland, and the United States of America, have become bound by the Universal Copyright Convention as revised at Paris on July 24, 1971.

(*b*) The entry into force referred to in subparagraph (*a*) shall apply to those countries of the Union which, at least three months before the said entry into force, have deposited instruments of ratification or accession not containing a declaration under paragraph (1) (*b*).

(*c*) With respect to any country of the Union not covered by subparagraph (*b*) and which ratifies or accedes to this Act without making a declaration under paragraph (1) (*b*), Articles 1 to 21 and the Appendix shall enter into force three months after the date on which the Director General has notified the deposit of the relevant instrument of ratification or accession, unless a subsequent date has been indicated in the instrument deposited. In the latter case, Articles 1 to 21 and the Appendix shall enter into force with respect to that country on the date thus indicated.

(*d*) The provisions of subparagraphs (*a*) to (*c*) do not affect the application of Article VI of the Appendix.

(3) With respect to any country of the Union which ratifies or accedes to this Act with or without a declaration made under paragraph (1) (*b*), Articles 22 to 38 shall enter into force three months after the date on which the Director General has notified the deposit of the relevant instrument of ratification or accession, unless a subsequent date has been indicated in the instrument deposited. In the latter case, Articles 22 to 38 shall enter into force with respect to that country on the date thus indicated.

Article 29

(1) Any country outside the Union may accede to this Act and thereby become party to this Convention and a member of the Union. Instruments of accession shall be deposited with the Director General.

(2) (*a*) Subject to subparagraph (*b*), this Convention shall enter into force with respect to any country outside the Union three months after the date on which the Director General has notified the deposit of its instrument of accession, unless a subsequent date has been indicated in the instrument deposited. In the latter case, this Convention shall enter into force with respect to that country on the date thus indicated.

(*b*) If the entry into force according to subparagraph (*a*) precedes the entry into force of Articles 1 to 21 and the Appendix according to Article 28(2) (*a*), the said country shall, in the meantime, be bound, instead of by Articles 1 to 21 and the Appendix, by Articles 1 to 20 of the Brussels Act of this Convention.

Article 29*bis*

Ratification of or accession to this Act by any country not bound by Articles 22 to 38 of the Stockholm Act of this Convention shall, for the sole purposes of Article 14(2) of the Convention establishing the Organization, amount to ratification of or accession to the said Stockholm Act with the limitation set forth in Article 28(1)(*b*)(i) thereof.

Article 30

(1) Subject to the exceptions permitted by paragraph (2) of this Article, by Article 28(1)(*b*), by Article 33(2), and by the Appendix, ratification or accession shall automatically entail acceptance of all the provisions and admission to all the advantages of this Convention.

(2) (*a*) Any country of the Union ratifying or acceding to this Act may, subject to Article V(2) of the Appendix, retain the benefit of the reservations it has previously formulated on condition that it makes a declaration to that effect at the time of the deposit of its instrument of ratification or accession.

(*b*) Any country outside the Union may declare, in acceding to this Convention and subject to Article V(2) of the Appendix, that it intends to substitute, temporarily at least, for Article 8 of this Act concerning the right of translation, the provisions of Article 5 of the Union Convention of 1886, as completed at Paris in 1896, on the clear understanding that the said provisions are applicable only to translations into a language in general use in the said country. Subject to Article I(6)(*b*) of the Appendix, any country has the right to apply, in relation to the right of translation of works whose country of origin is a country availing itself of such a reservation, a protection which is equivalent to the protection granted by the latter country.

(*c*) Any country may withdraw such reservations at any time by notification addressed to the Director General.

Article 31

(1) Any country may declare in its instrument of ratification or accession, or may inform the Director General by written notification at any time thereafter, that this Convention shall be applicable to all or part of those territories, designated in the declaration or notification, for the external relations of which it is responsible.

(2) Any country which has made such a declaration or given such a notification may, at any time, notify the Director General that this Convention shall cease to be applicable to all or part of such territories.

(3) (*a*) Any declaration made under paragraph (1) shall take effect on the same date as the ratification or accession in which it was included, and any notification given under that paragraph shall take effect three months after its notification by the Director General.

(*b*) Any notification given under paragraph (2) shall take effect twelve months after its receipt by the Director General.

(4) This Article shall in no way be understood as implying the recognition or tacit acceptance by a country of the Union of the factual situation concerning a territory to which this Convention is made applicable by another country of the Union by virtue of a declaration under paragraph (1).

Article 32

(1) This Act shall, as regards relations between the countries of the Union, and to the extent that it applies, replace the Berne Convention of September 9, 1886, and the subsequent Acts of revision. The Acts previously in force shall continue to be applicable, in their entirety or to the extent that this Act does not replace them by virtue of the preceding sentence, in relations with countries of the Union which do not ratify or accede to this Act.

(2) Countries outside the Union which become party to this Act shall, subject to paragraph (3), apply it with respect to any country of the Union not bound by this Act or which, although bound by this Act, has made a declaration pursuant to Article 28(1)(*b*). Such

countries recognize that the said country of the Union, in its relations with them:

(i) may apply the provisions of the most recent Act by which it is bound, and
(ii) subject to Article I(6) of the Appendix, has the right to adapt the protection to the level provided for by this Act.

(3) Any country which has availed itself of any of the faculties provided for in the Appendix may apply the provisions of the Appendix relating to the faculty or faculties of which it has availed itself in its relations with any other country of the Union which is not bound by this Act, provided that the latter country has accepted the application of the said provisions.

Article 33

(1) Any dispute between two or more countries of the Union concerning the interpretation or application of this Convention, not settled by negotiation, may, by any one of the countries concerned, be brought before the International Court of Justice by application in conformity with the Statute of the Court, unless the countries concerned agree on some other method of settlement. The country bringing the dispute before the Court shall inform the International Bureau; the International Bureau shall bring the matter to the attention of the other countries of the Union.

(2) Each country may, at the time it signs this Act or deposits its instrument of ratification or accession, declare that it does not consider itself bound by the provisions of paragraph (1). With regard to any dispute between such country and any other country of the Union, the provisions of paragraph (1) shall not apply.

(3) Any country having made a declaration in accordance with the provisions of paragraph (2) may, at any time, withdraw its declaration by notification addressed to the Director General.

Article 34

(1) Subject to Article 29*bis,* no country may ratify or accede to earlier Acts of this Convention once Articles 1 to 21 and the Appendix have entered into force.

(2) Once Articles 1 to 21 and the Appendix have entered into force, no country may make a declaration under Article 5 of the Protocol Regarding Developing Countries attached to the Stockholm Act.

Article 35

(1) This Convention shall remain in force without limitation as to time.

(2) Any country may denounce this Act by notification addressed to the Director General. Such denunciation shall constitute also denunciation of all earlier Acts and shall affect only the country making it, the Convention remaining in full force and effect as regards the other countries of the Union.

(3) Denunciation shall take effect one year after the day on which the Director General has received the notification.

(4) The right of denunciation provided by this Article shall not be exercised by any country before the expiration of five years from the date upon which it becomes a member of the Union.

Article 36

(1) Any country party to this Convention undertakes to adopt, in accordance with its constitution, the measures necessary to ensure the application of this Convention.

(2) It is understood that, at the time a country becomes bound by this Convention, it will be in a position under its domestic law to give effect to the provisions of this Convention.

Article 37

(1) (*a*) This Act shall be signed in a single copy in the French and English languages and, subject to paragraph (2), shall be deposited with the Director General.

(*b*) Official texts shall be established by the Director General, after consultation with the interested Governments, in the Arabic, German, Italian, Portuguese and Spanish languages, and such other languages as the Assembly may designate.

(*c*) In cases of differences of opinion on the interpretation of the various texts, the French text shall prevail.

(2) This Act shall remain open for signature until January 31, 1972. Until that date, the copy referred to in paragraph (1)(*a*) shall be deposited with the Government of the French Republic.

(3) The Director General shall certify and transmit two copies of the signed text of this Act to the Governments of all countries of the Union and, on request, to the Government of any other country.

(4) The Director General shall register this Act with the Secretariat of the United Nations.

(5) The Director General shall notify the Governments of all countries of the Union of signatures, deposits of instruments of ratification or accession and any declarations included in such instruments or made pursuant to Articles 28(1)(*c*), 30(2)(*a*) and (*b*), and 33(2), entry into force of any provisions of this Act, notifications of denunciation, and notifications pursuant to Articles 30(2)(*c*), 31(1) and (2), 33(3), and 38(1), as well as the Appendix.

Article 38

(1) Countries of the Union which have not ratified or acceded to this Act and which are not bound by Articles 22 to 26 of the Stockholm Act of this Convention may, until April 26, 1975, exercise, if they so desire, the rights provided under the said Articles as if they were bound by them. Any country desiring to exercise such rights shall give written notification to this effect to the Director General; this notification shall be effective on the date of its receipt. Such countries shall be deemed to be members of the Assembly until the said date.

(2) As long as all the countries of the Union have not become Members of the Organization, the International Bureau of the Organization shall also function as the Bureau of the Union, and the Director General as the Director of the said Bureau.

(3) Once all the countries of the Union have become Members of the Organization, the rights, obligations, and property, of the Bureau of the Union shall devolve on the International Bureau of the Organization.

Appendix
Article I

(1) Any country regarded as a developing country in conformity with the established practice of the General Assembly of the United Nations which ratifies or accedes to this Act, of which this Appendix forms an integral part, and which, having regard to its economic situation and its social or cultural needs, does not consider itself immediately in a position to make provision for the protection of all the rights as provided for in this Act, may, by a notification deposited with the Director General at the time of depositing its instrument of ratification or accession or, subject to Article V(1)(*c*), at any time thereafter, declare that it will avail itself of the faculty provided for in Article II, or of the faculty provided for in Article III, or of both of those faculties. It may, instead of availing itself of the faculty pro-

vided for in Article II, make a declaration according to Article V(1)(*a*).

(2) (*a*) Any declaration under paragraph (1) notified before the expiration of the period of 10 years from the entry into force of Articles 1 to 21 and this Appendix according to Article 28(2) shall be effective until the expiration of the said period. Any such declaration may be renewed in whole or in part for period of 10 years each by a notification deposited with the Director General not more than 15 months and not less than 3 months before the expiration of the 10-year period then running.

(*b*) Any declaration under paragraph (1) notified after the expiration of the period of 10 years from the entry into force of Articles 1 to 21 and this Appendix according to Article 28(2) shall be effective until the expiration of the 10-year period then running. Any such declaration may be renewed as provided for in the second sentence of subparagraph (*a*).

(3) Any country of the Union which has ceased to be regarded as a developing country as referred to in paragraph (1) shall no longer be entitled to renew its declaration as provided in paragraph (2), and, whether or not it formally withdraws its declaration, such country shall be precluded from availing itself of the faculties referred to in paragraph (1) from the expiration of the 10-year period then running or from the expiration of a period of 3 years after it has ceased to be regarded as a developing country, whichever period expires later.

(4) Where, at the time when the declaration made under paragraph (1) or (2) ceases to be effective, there are copies in stock which were made under a license granted by virtue of this Appendix, such copies may continue to be distributed until their stock is exhausted.

(5) Any country which is bound by the provisions of this Act and which has deposited a declaration or a notification in accordance with Article 31(1) with respect to the application of this Act to a particular territory, the situation of which can be regarded as analogous to that of the countries referred to in paragraph (1), may, in respect of such territory, make the declaration referred to in paragraph (1) and the notification of renewal referred to in paragraph (2). As long as such declaration or notification remains in effect, the provisions of this Appendix shall be applicable to the territory in respect of which it was made.

(6) (*a*) The fact that a country avails itself of any of the faculties referred to in paragraph (1) does not permit another country to give less protection to works of which the country of origin is the former country than it is obliged to grant under Articles 1 to 20.

(*b*) The right to apply reciprocal treatment provided for in Article 30(2)(*b*), second sentence, shall not, until the date on which the period applicable under Article I(3) expires, be exercised in respect of works the country of origin of which is a country which has made a declaration according to Article V(1)(*a*).

Article II

(1) Any country which has declared that it will avail itself of the faculty provided for in this Article shall be entitled, so far as works published in printed or analogous forms of reproduction are concerned, to substitute for the exclusive right of translation provided for in Article 8 a system of non-exclusive and non-transferable licenses, granted by the competent authority under the following conditions and subject to Article IV.

(2) (*a*) Subject to paragraph (3), if, after the expiration of a period of three years, or of any longer period determined by the national legislation of the said country, commencing on the date of the first publication of the work, a translation of such work has not been published in a language in general use in that country by the owner of the right of translation, or with his authorization, any national of such country may obtain a license to make a translation of the work in the said language and publish the translation in printed or analogous forms of reproduction.

(*b*) A license under the conditions provided for in this Article may also be granted if all the editions of the translation published in the language concerned are out of print.

(3) (*a*) In the case of translations into a language which is not in general use in one or more developed countries which are members of the Union, a period of one year shall be substituted for the period of three years referred to in paragraph (2)(*a*).

(*b*) Any country referred to in paragraph (1) may, with the unanimous agreement of the developed countries which are members of the Union and in which the same language is in general use, substitute, in the case of translations into that language, for the period of three years referred to in paragraph (2)(*a*) a shorter period as determined by such agreement but not less than one year. However, the provisions of the foregoing sentence shall not apply where the language in question in English, French or Spanish. The Director General shall be notified of any such agreement by the Governments which have concluded it.

(4) (*a*) No license obtainable after three years shall be granted under this Article until a further period of six months has elapsed, and no license obtainable after one year shall be granted under this Article until a further period of nine months has elapsed

(i) from the date on which the applicant complies with the requirements mentioned in Article IV(1), or

(ii) where the identity or the address of the owner of the right of translation is unknown, from the date on which the applicant sends, as provided for in Article IV(2), copies of his application submitted to the authority competent to grant the license.

(*b*) If, during the said period of six or nine months, a translation in the language in respect of which the application was made is published by the owner of the right of translation or with his authorization, no license under this Article shall be granted.

(5) Any license under this Article shall be granted only for the purpose of teaching, scholarship or research.

(6) If a translation of a work is published by the owner of the right of translation or with his authorization at a price reasonably related to that normally charged in the country for comparable works, any license granted under this Article shall terminate if such translation is in the same language and with substantially the same content as the translation published under the license. Any copies already made before the license terminates may continue to be distributed until their stock is exhausted.

(7) For works which are composed mainly of illustrations, a license to make and publish a translation of the text and to reproduce and publish the illustrations may be granted only if the conditions of Article III are also fulfilled.

(8) No license shall be granted under this Article when the author has withdrawn from circulation all copies of his work.

(9) (*a*) A license to make a translation of a work which has been published in printed or analogous forms of reproduction may also be granted to any broadcasting organization having its headquarters in a country referred to in paragraph (1), upon an application made to the competent authority of that country by the said organization, provided that all of the following conditions are met:

(i) the translation is made from a copy made and acquired in accordance with the laws of the said country;

(ii) the translation is only for use in broadcasts intended exclusively for teaching or for the dissemination of the results of specialized technical or scientific research to experts in a particular profession;

(iii) the translation is used exclusively for the purposes referred to in condition (ii) through broadcasts made lawfully and intended for recipients on the territory of the said country, including broadcasts made through the medium of sound or visual recordings lawfully and exclusively made for the purpose of such broadcasts;

(iv) all uses made of the translation are without any commercial purpose.

(*b*) Sound or visual recordings of a translation which was made by a broadcasting organization under a license granted by virtue of this paragraph may, for the purposes and subject to the conditions referred to in subparagraph (*a*) and with the agreement of that organization, also be used by any other broadcasting organization having its headquarters in the country whose competent authority granted the license in question.

(*c*) Provided that all of the criteria and conditions set out in subparagraph (*a*) are met, a license may also be granted to a broadcasting organization to translate any text incorporated in an audiovisual fixation where such fixation was itself prepared and published for the sole purpose of being used in connection with systematic instructional activities.

(*d*) Subject to subparagraphs (*a*) to (*c*), the provisions of the preceding paragraphs shall apply to the grant and exercise of any license granted under this paragraph.

Article III

(1) Any country which has declared that it will avail itself of the faculty provided for in this Article shall be entitled to substitute for the exclusive right of reproduction provided for in Article 9 a system of non-exclusive and non-transferable licenses, granted by the competent authority under the following conditions and subject to Article IV.

(2) (*a*) If, in relation to a work to which this Article applies by virtue of paragraph (7), after the expiration of

(i) the relevant period specified in paragraph (3), commencing on the date of first publication of a particular edition of the work, or
(ii) any longer period determined by national legislation of the country referred to in paragraph (1), commencing on the same date,

copies of such edition have not been distributed in that country to the general public or in connection with systematic instructional activities, by the owner of the right of reproduction or with his authorization, at a price reasonably related to that normally charged in the country for comparable works, any national of such country may obtain a license to reproduce and publish such edition at that or a lower price for use in connection with systematic instructional activities.

(*b*) A license to reproduce and publish an edition which has been distributed as described in subparagraph (*a*) may also be granted under the conditions provided for in this Article if, after the expiration of the applicable period, no authorized copies of that edition have been on sale for a period of six months in the country concerned to the general public or in connection with systematic instructional activities at a price reasonably related to that normally charged in the country for comparable works.

(3) The period referred to in paragraph (2)(*a*)(i) shall be five years, except that

(i) for works of the natural and physical sciences, including mathematics, and of technology, the period shall be three years;
(ii) for works of fiction, poetry, drama and music, and for art books, the period shall be seven years.

(4) (*a*) No license obtainable after three years shall be granted under this Article until a period of six months has elapsed

(i) from the date on which the applicant complies with the requirements mentioned in Article IV(1), or
(ii) where the identity or the address of the owner of the right of reproduction is unknown, from the date on which the applicant sends, as provided for in Article IV(2), copies of his application submitted to the authority competent to grant the license.

(*b*) Where licenses are obtainable after other periods and Article IV(2) is applicable, no license shall be granted until a period of three months has elapsed from the date of the dispatch of the copies of the application.

(*c*) If, during the period of six or three months referred to in subparagraphs (*a*) and (*b*), a distribution as described in paragraph (2)(*a*) has taken place, no license shall be granted under this Article.

(*d*) No license shall be granted if the author has withdrawn from circulation all copies of the edition for the reproduction and publication of which the license has been applied for.

(5) A license to reproduce and publish a translation of a work shall not be granted under this Article in the following cases:

(i) where the translation was not published by the owner of the right of translation or with his authorization, or
(ii) where the translation is not in a language in general use in the country in which the license is applied for.

(6) If copies of an edition of a work are distributed in the country referred to in paragraph (1) to the general public or in connection

with systematic instructional activities, by the owner of the right of reproduction or with his authorization, at a price reasonably related to that normally charged in the country for comparable works, any license granted under this Article shall terminate if such edition is in the same language and with substantially the same content as the edition which was published under the said license. Any copies already made before the license terminates may continue to be distributed until their stock is exhausted.

(7) (*a*) Subject to subparagraph (*b*), the works to which this Article applies shall be limited to works published in printed or analogous forms of reproduction.

(b) This Article shall also apply to the reproduction in audio-visual form of lawfully made audio-visual fixations including any protected works incorporated therein and to the translation of any incorporated text into a language in general use in the country in which the license is applied for, always provided that the audio-visual fixations in question were prepared and published for the sole purpose of being used in connection with systematic instructional activities.

Article IV

(1) A license under Article II or Article III may be granted only if the applicant, in accordance with the procedure of the country concerned, establishes either that he has requested, and has been denied, authorization by the owner of the right to make and publish the translation or to reproduce and publish the edition, as the case may be, or that, after due diligence on his part, he was unable to find the owner of the right. At the same time as making the request, the applicant shall inform any national or international information center referred to in paragraph (2).

(2) If the owner of the right cannot be found, the applicant for a license shall send, by registered airmail, copies of his application, submitted to the authority competent to grant the license, to the publisher whose name appears on the work and to any national or international information center which may have been designated, in a notification to that effect deposited with the Director General, by the Government of the country in which the publisher is believed to have his principal place of business.

(3) The name of the author shall be indicated on all copies of the translation or reproduction published under a license granted under Article II or Article III. The title of the work shall appear on all such copies. In the case of a translation, the original title of the work shall appear in any case on all the said copies.

(4) (*a*) No license granted under Article II or Article III shall extend to the export of copies, and any such license shall be valid only for publication of the translation or of the reproduction, as the case may be, in the territory of the country in which it has been applied for.

(*b*) For the purposes of subparagraph (*a*), the notion of export shall include the sending of copies from any territory to the country which, in respect of that territory, has made a declaration under Article I(5).

(*c*) Where a governmental or other public entity of a country which has granted a license to make a translation under Article II into a language other than English, French or Spanish sends copies of a translation published under such license to another country, such sending of copies shall not, for the purposes of subparagraph (*a*), be considered to constitute export if all of the following conditions are met:

(i) the recipients are individuals who are nationals of the country whose competent authority has granted the license, or organizations grouping such individuals;
(ii) the copies are to be used only for the purpose of teaching, scholarship or research;
(iii) the sending of the copies and their subsequent distribution to recipients is without any commercial purpose; and
(iv) the country to which the copies have been sent has agreed with the country whose competent authority has granted the license to allow the receipt, or distribution, or both, and the Director General has been notified of the agreement by the Government of the country in which the license has been granted.

(5) All copies published under a license granted by virtue of Article II or Article III shall bear a notice in the appropriate language stating that the copies are available for distribution only in the country or territory to which the said license applies.

(6) (*a*) Due provision shall be made at the national level to ensure

(i) that the license provides, in favour of the owner of the right of translation or of reproduction, as the case may be, for just compensation that is consistent with standards of royalties normally operating on licenses freely negotiated between persons in the two countries concerned, and
(ii) payment and transmittal of the compensation: should national currency regulations intervene, the competent authority shall make all efforts, by the use of international

machinery, to ensure transmittal in internationally convertible currency or its equivalent.

(*b*) Due provision shall be made by national legislation to ensure a correct translation of the work, or an accurate reproduction of the particular edition, as the case may be.

Article V

(1) (*a*) Any country entitled to make a declaration that it will avail itself of the faculty provided for in Article II may, instead, at the time of ratifying or acceding to this Act:

(i) if it is a country to which Article 30(2) (*a*) applies, make a declaration under that provision as far as the right of translation is concerned;
(ii) if it is a country to which Article 30(2) (*a*) does not apply, and even if it is not a country outside the Union, make a declaration as provided for in Article 30(2)(*b*), first sentence.

(*b*) In the case of a country which ceases to be regarded as a developing country as referred to in Article I(1), a declaration made according to this paragraph shall be effective until the date on which the period applicable under Article I(3) expires.

(*c*) Any country which has made a declaration according to this paragraph may not subsequently avail itself of the faculty provided for in Article II even if it withdraws the said declaration.

(2) Subject to paragraph (3), any country which has availed itself of the faculty provided for in Article II may not subsequently make a declaration according to paragraph (1).

(3) Any country which has ceased to be regarded as a developing country as referred to in Article I(1) may, not later than two years prior to the expiration of the period applicable under Article I(3), make a declaration to the effect provided for in Article 30(2)(*b*), first sentence, notwithstanding the fact that it is not a country outside the Union. Such declaration shall take effect at the date on which the period applicable under Article I(3) expires.

Article VI

(1) Any country of the Union may declare, as from the date of this Act, and at any time before becoming bound by Articles 1 to 21 and this Appendix:

(i) if it is a country which, were it bound by Articles 1 to 21 and this Appendix, would be entitled to avail itself of the faculties referred to in Article I(1), that it will apply the provisions of Article II or of Article III or of both to works whose country of origin is a country which, pursuant to (ii) below, admits the application of those Articles to such works, or which is bound by Articles 1 to 21 and this Appendix; such declaration may, instead of referring to Article II, refer to Article V;

(ii) that it admits the application of this Appendix to works of which it is the country of origin by countries which have made a declaration under (i) above or a notification under Article I.

(2) Any declaration made under paragraph (1) shall be in writing and shall be deposited with the Director General. The declaration shall become effective from the date of its deposit.

2. Universal Copyright Convention (And Protocols)

Adopted at Geneva (1952), revised at Paris (1971)

The Universal Copyright Convention (UCC) was signed and entered into force on September 6, 1952, and was revised at Paris in 1971. Although the Berne Convention has been the mainstay of international copyright, certain major countries (United States, Soviet Union, and China) did not join Berne. The UCC was developed as an alternative to Berne to allow participation of these countries in an international agreement. The UCC is administered by UNESCO.

The basis of the UCC is "national treatment," which requires all member countries to accord the same protection to foreign works eligible under the UCC as is granted to its own nationals. In addition, the Convention specifies certain minimum legal obligations for each contracting state. The contracting states must provide adequate and effective protection of the rights of authors and other copyright proprietors (Art. 1).

The published works of nationals of a contracting state must receive the same protection as the contracting state accords to works of its nationals first published in its own territory. The same applies for unpublished works (Art. 2). The Convention is not retroactive and those works of a contracting state in the public domain remain there.

The Convention limits the formalities that can be required of works first published outside the territory of a member state. For such works, the only formalities allowed are that all the copies of the work bear the symbol © accompanied by the copyright proprietor's name and the year of first publication placed in such manner and location as to give reasonable notice of claim of copyright (Art. 3 para. 1). A member state may, however, require additional formalities, such as deposit, registration, and manufacturing requirements for works first published within its territory by foreign nationals or for works of its own nationals, wherever they may be published (Art. 3 para. 2).

Member states must grant a minimum copyright term of 25 years from publication, or life of the author plus 25 years (Art. 4). They must also grant exclusive rights to foreign authors of other member states for at least seven years. After this term expires, a compulsory licensing arrangement can be instituted (Art. 5).

The UCC contains a "Berne Safeguard Clause," which prohibits a Berne Convention country from denouncing Berne and relying on the UCC in its copyright relations with members of the Berne Convention (Art. 17 and Appendix Declaration relating to Art. 17).

The UCC was revised in Paris in 1971, in response to demands made by developing countries. Special provisions allow developing countries to obtain compulsory licenses under certain conditions to translate copyrighted works for teaching, scholarship, and research purposes. It also allows reproduction of copyrighted works for use in systematic instructional activities.

The Paris revision strengthened Convention minima for adequate and effective protection by adding basic rights that ensure an author's economic interest. In addition, the Berne Safeguard Clause was suspended for developing countries, permitting them to withdraw from Berne and adhere to the UCC (Appendix Declaration relating to Art. 17).

As of January 1, 1990, the following 81 states were party to the UCC:

Algeria	Belize	Czechoslovakia
Andorra	Brazil	Democratic Kampuchea
Argentina	Bulgaria	Denmark
Australia	Cameroon	Dominican Republic
Austria	Canada	Ecuador
Bahamas	Chile	El Salvador
Bangladesh	Colombia	Fiji
Barbados	Costa Rica	
Belgium	Cuba	

Finland
France
German Democratic Republic
Federal Republic of Germany
Ghana
Greece
Guatemala
Guinea
Haiti
Holy See
Hungary
Iceland
India
Ireland
Israel
Italy
Japan
Kenya
Laos
Lebanon
Liberia
Liechtenstein
Luxembourg
Malawi
Malta
Mauritius
Mexico
Monaco
Morocco
Netherlands
New Zealand
Nicaragua
Nigeria
Norway
Pakistan
Panama
Paraguay
Peru
Philippines
Poland
Portugal
Republic of Korea
Saint Vincent and the Grenadines
Senegal
Soviet Union
Spain
Sri Lanka
Sweden
Switzerland
Trinidad and Tobago
Tunisia
United Kingdom
United States of America
Venezuela
Yugoslavia
Zambia

Universal Copyright Convention and Protocols Annexed Thereto, Geneva, 1952

Article I

Each Contracting State undertakes to provide for the adequate and effective protection of the rights of authors and other copyright proprietors in literary, scientific and artistic works, including writings, musical, dramatic and cinematographic works, and paintings, engravings and sculpture.

Article II

1. Published works of nationals of any Contracting State and works first published in that State shall enjoy in each other Contracting State the same protection as that other State accords to works of its nationals first published in its own territory.

2. Unpublished works of nationals of each Contracting State shall enjoy in each other Contracting State the same protection as that other State accords to unpublished works of its own nationals.

3. For the purpose of this Convention any Contracting State may, by domestic legislation, assimilate to its own nationals any person domiciled in that State.

Article III

1. Any Contracting State which, under its domestic law, requires as a condition of copyright, compliance with formalities such as deposit, registration, notice, notarial certificates, payment of fees or manufacture or publication in that Contracting State, shall regard these requirements as satisfied with respect to all works protected in accordance with this Convention and first published outside its territory and the author of which is not one of its nationals, if from the time of the first publication all the copies of the work published with the authority of the author or other copyright proprietor bear the symbol © accompanied by the name of the copyright proprietor

---

Source: Reprinted from *Copyright Laws and Treaties of the World,* 14 Supplement, © 1971, BNA Books, Washington, D.C.

and the year of first publication placed in such manner and location as to give reasonable notice of claim of copyright.

2. The provisions of paragraph 1 of this Article shall not preclude any Contracting State from requiring formalities or other conditions for the acquisition and enjoyment of copyright in respect of works first published in its territory or works of its nationals wherever published.

3. The provisions of paragraph 1 of this Article shall not preclude any Contracting State from providing that a person seeking judicial relief must, in bringing the action, comply with procedural requirements, such as that the complainant must appear through domestic counsel or that the complainant must deposit with the court or an administrative office, or both, a copy of the work involved in the litigation; provided that failure to comply with such requirements shall not affect the validity of the copyright, nor shall any such requirement be imposed upon a national of another Contracting State if such requirement is not imposed on nationals of the State in which protection is claimed.

4. In each Contracting State there shall be legal means of protecting without formalities the unpublished works of nationals of other Contracting States.

5. If a Contracting State grants protection for more than one term of copyright and the first term is for a period longer than one of the minimum periods prescribed in Article IV, such State shall not be required to comply with the provisions of paragraph 1 of this Article III in respect of the second or any subsequent term of copyright.

Article IV

1. The duration of protection of a work shall be governed, in accordance with the provisions of Article II and this Article, by the law of the Contracting State in which protection is claimed.

2. The term of protection for works protected under this Convention shall not be less than the life of the author and 25 years after his death.

However, any Contracting State which, on the effective date of this Convention in that State, has limited this term for certain classes of works to a period computed from the first publication of the work, shall be entitled to maintain these exceptions and to extend them to other classes of works. For all these classes the term of protection shall not be less than 25 years from the date of first publication.

Any Contracting State which, upon the effective date of this

Convention in that State, does not compute the term of protection upon the basis of the life of the author, shall be entitled to compute the term of protection from the date of the first publication of the work or from its registration prior to publication, as the case may be, provided the term of protection shall not be less than 25 years from the date of first publication or from its registration prior to publication, as the case may be.

If the legislation of a Contracting State grants two or more successive terms of protection, the duration of the first term shall not be less than one of the minimum periods specified above.

3. The provisions of paragraph 2 of this Article shall not apply to photographic works or to works of applied art; provided, however, that the term of protection in those Contracting States which protect photographic works, or works of applied art in so far as they are protected as artistic works, shall not be less than 10 years for each of said classes of works.

4. No Contracting State shall be obliged to grant protection to a work for a period longer than that fixed for the class of works to which the work in question belongs, in the case of unpublished works by the law of the Contracting State of which the author is a national, and in the case of published works by the law of the Contracting State in which the work has been first published.

For the purposes of the application of the preceding provision, if the law of any Contracting State grants two or more successive terms of protection, the period of protection of that State shall be considered to be the aggregate of those terms. However, if a specified work is not protected by such State during the second or any subsequent term for any reason, the other Contracting States shall not be obliged to protect it during the second or any subsequent term.

5. For the purposes of the application of paragraph 4 of this Article, the work of a national of a Contracting State, first published in a non-Contracting State, shall be treated as though first published in the Contracting State of which the author is a national.

6. For the purposes of the application of paragraph 4 of this Article, in case of simultaneous publication in two or more Contracting States, the work shall be treated as though first published in the State which affords the shortest term; any work published in two or more Contracting States within 30 days of its first publication shall be considered as having been published simultaneously in said Contracting States.

Article V

1. Copyright shall include the exclusive right of the author to make, publish, and authorize the making and publication of translations of works protected under this Convention.

2. However, any Contracting State may, by its domestic legislation, restrict the right of translation of writings, but only subject to the following provisions:

If, after the expiration of a period of seven years from the date of the first publication of a writing, a translation of such writing has not been published in the national language or languages, as the case may be, of the Contracting State, by the owner of the right of translation or with his authorization, any national of such Contracting State may obtain a non-exclusive license from the competent authority thereof to translate the work and publish the work so translated in any of the national languages in which it has not been published; provided that such national, in accordance with the procedure of the State concerned, establishes either that he has requested, and been denied, authorization by the proprietor of the right to make and publish the translation, or that, after due diligence on his part, he was unable to find the owner of the right. A license may also be granted on the same conditions if all previous editions of a translation in such language are out of print.

If the owner of the right of translation cannot be found, then the applicant for a license shall send copies of his application to the publisher whose name appears on the work and, if the nationality of the owner of the right of translation is known, to the diplomatic or consular representative of the State of which such owner is a national, or to the organization which may have been designated by the government of that State. The license shall not be granted before the expiration of a period of two months from the date of the dispatch of the copies of the application.

Due provision shall be made by domestic legislation to assure to the owner of the right of translation a compensation which is just and conforms to international standards, to assure payment and transmittal of such compensation, and to assure a correct translation of the work.

The original title and the name of the author of the work shall be printed on all copies of the published translation. The license shall be valid only for publication of the translation in the territory of the Contracting State where it has been applied for. Copies so published may be imported and sold in another Contracting State if one of the national languages of such other State is the same language as that into which the work has been so translated, and if the domestic law in such other State makes provision for such licences and does not prohibit such importation and sale. Where the foregoing conditions do not exist, the importation and sale of such copies in a Contracting State shall be governed by its domestic law and its agreements. The licence shall not be transferred by the licensee.

The licence shall not be granted when the author has withdrawn from circulation all copies of the work.

Article VI

"Publication", as used in this Convention, means the reproduction in tangible form and the general distribution to the public of copies of a work from which it can be read or otherwise visually perceived.

Article VII

This Convention shall not apply to works or rights in works which, at the effective date of the Convention in a Contracting State where protection is claimed, are permanently in the public domain in the said Contracting State.

Article VIII

1. This Convention, which shall bear the date of 6 September 1952, shall be deposited with the Director-General of the United Nations Educational, Scientific and Cultural Organization and shall remain open for signature by all States for a period of 120 days after that date. It shall be subject to ratification or acceptance by the signatory States.
2. Any State which has not signed this Convention may accede thereto.
3. Ratification, acceptance or accession shall be effected by the deposit of an instrument to that effect with the Director-General of the United Nations Educational, Scientific and Cultural Organization.

Article IX

1. This Convention shall come into force three months after the deposit of twelve instruments of ratification, acceptance or accession, among which there shall be those of four States which are not members of the International Union for the Protection of Literary and Artistic Works.
2. Subsequently, this Convention shall come into force in respect of each State three months after that State has deposited its instrument of ratification, acceptance or accession.

Article X

1. Each State party to this Convention undertakes to adopt, in accordance with its Constitution, such measures as are necessary to ensure the application of this Convention.

2. It is understood, however, that at the time an instrument of ratification, acceptance or accession is deposited on behalf of any State, such State must be in a position under its domestic law to give effect to the terms of this Convention.

Article XI

1. An Inter-governmental Committee is hereby established with the following duties:

(*a*) to study the problems concerning the application and operation of this Convention;

(*b*) to make preparation for periodic revisions of this Convention;

(*c*) to study any other problems concerning the international protection of copyright, in co-operation with the various interested international organizations, such as the United Nations Educational, Scientific and Cultural Organization, the International Union for the Protection of Literary and Artistic Works and the Organization of American States;

(*d*) to inform the Contracting States as to its activities.

2. The Committee shall consist of the representatives of twelve Contracting States to be selected with due consideration to fair geographical representation and in conformity with the Resolution relating to this article, annexed to this Convention.

The Director-General of the United Nations Educational, Scientific and Cultural Organization, the Director of the Bureau of the International Union for the Protection of Literary and Artistic Works and the Secretary-General of the Organization of American States, or their representatives, may attend meetings of the Committee in an advisory capacity.

Article XII

The Inter-Governmental Committee shall convene a conference for revision of this Convention whenever it deems necessary, or at the request of at least 10 Contracting States, or of a majority of the Contracting States if there are less than 20 Contracting States.

Article XIII

Any Contracting State may, at the time of deposit of its instrument of ratification, acceptance or accession, or at any time thereafter, declare by notification addressed to the Director-General of the United Nations Educational, Scientific and Cultural Organization that this Convention shall apply to all or any of the countries or territories for the international relations of which it is responsible and this Convention shall thereupon apply to the countries or territories named in such notification after the expiration of the term of three months provided for in Article IX. In the absence of such notification, this Convention shall not apply to any such country or territory.

Article XIV

1. Any Contracting State may denounce this Convention in its own name or on behalf of all or any of the countries or territories as to which a notification has been given under Article XIII. The denunciation shall be made by notification addressed to the Director-General of the United Nations Educational, Scientific and Cultural Organization.
2. Such denunciation shall operate only in respect of the State or of the country or territory on whose behalf it was made and shall not take effect until 12 months after the date of receipt of the notification.

Article XV

A dispute between two or more Contracting States concerning the interpretation or application of this Convention, not settled by negotiation, shall, unless the States concerned agree on some other method of settlement, be brought before the International Court of Justice for determination by it.

Article XVI

1. This Convention shall be established in English, French and Spanish. The three texts shall be signed and shall be equally authoritative.
2. Official texts of this Convention shall be established in German, Italian and Portuguese.

Any Contracting State or group of Contracting States shall be entitled to have established by the Director-General of the United Nations Educational, Scientific and Cultural Organization other texts in the language of its choice by arrangement with the Director-General.

All such texts shall be annexed to the signed texts of this Convention.

Article XVII

1. This Convention shall not in any way affect the provisions of the Berne Convention for the Protection of Literary and Artistic Works or membership in the Union created by that Convention.

2. In application of the foregoing paragraph, a Declaration has been annexed to the present article. This Declaration is an integral part of this Convention for the States bound by the Berne Convention on January 1, 1951, or which have or may become bound to it at a later date. The signature of this Convention by such States shall also constitute signature of the said Declaration, and ratification, acceptance or accession by such States shall include the Declaration as well as the Convention.

Article XVIII

This Convention shall not abrogate multilateral or bilateral copyright conventions or arrangements that are or may be in effect exclusively between two or more American Republics. In the event of any difference either between the provisions of such existing conventions or arrangements and the provisions of this Convention, or between the provisions of this Convention and those of any new convention or arrangement which may be formulated between two or more American Republics after this Convention comes into force, the convention or arrangement most recently formulated shall prevail between the parties thereto. Rights in works acquired in any Contracting State under existing conventions or arrangements before the date of this Convention comes into force in such State shall not be affected.

Article XIX

This Convention shall not abrogate multilateral or bilateral conventions or arrangements in effect between two or more Contracting States. In the event of any difference between the provisions of such existing conventions or arrangements and the provisions of this Convention, the provisions of this Convention shall prevail. Rights in works acquired in any Contracting State under existing conventions or arrangements before the date on which this Convention comes into force in such State shall not be affected. Nothing in this article shall affect provisions of Articles XVII and XVIII of this Convention.

Article XX

Reservations to this Convention shall not be permitted.

Article XXI

The Director-General of the United Nations Educational, Scientific and Cultural Organization shall send duly certified copies of this Convention to the States interested, to the Swiss Federal Council and to the Secretary-General of the United Nations for registration by him.[1]

He shall also inform all interested States of the ratifications, acceptances and accessions which have been deposited, the date on which this Convention comes into force, the notifications under Article XIII of this Convention, and denunciations under Article XIV.

Appendix Declaration relating to Article XVII

The States which are members of the International Union for the Protection of Literary and Artistic Works, and which are signatories to the Universal Copyright Convention,

Desiring to reinforce their mutual relations on the basis of the said Union and to avoid any conflict which might result from the coexistence of the Convention of Berne and the Universal Convention,

Have, by common agreement, accepted the terms of the following declaration:

(*a*) Works which, according to the Berne Convention, have as their country of origin a country which has withdrawn from the International Union created by the said Convention, after January 1, 1951, shall not be protected by the Universal Copyright Convention in the countries of the Berne Union;

---

[1]Registered on September 27, 1955, under No. 2937 (Statement of Treaties and International Agreements, United Nations, September 1955).

(*b*) The Universal Copyright Convention shall not be applicable to the relationships among countries of the Berne Union insofar as it relates to the protection of works having as their country of origin, within the meaning of the Berne Convention, a country of the International Union created by the said Convention.

Resolution concerning Article XI
The Inter-governmental Copyright Conference

Having considered the problems relating to the Inter-governmental Committee provided for in Article XI of the Universal Copyright Convention, resolves

1. The first members of the Committee shall be representatives of the following twelve States, each of those States designating one representative and an alternate: Argentina, Brazil, France, Germany, India, Italy, Japan, Mexico, Spain, Switzerland, United Kingdom, and United States of America.

2. The Committee shall be constituted as soon as the Convention comes into force in accordance with Article XI of this Convention.

3. The Committee shall elect its chairman and one vice-chairman. It shall establish its rules of procedure having regard to the following principles:

(*a*) the normal duration of the term of office of the representatives shall be six years; with one-third retiring every two years;

(*b*) before the expiration of the term of office of any members, the Committee shall decide which States shall cease to be represented on it and which States shall be called upon to designate representatives; the representatives of those States which have not ratified, accepted or acceded shall be the first to retire;

(*c*) the different parts of the world shall be fairly represented; and expresses the wish that the United Nations Educational, Scientific and Cultural Organization provide its secretariat.

In faith whereof the undersigned, having deposited their respective full powers, have signed this Convention.

Done at Geneva, this sixth day of September, 1952 in a single copy.

Protocol 1

Annexed to the Universal Copyright Convention concerning the application of that Convention to the works of stateless persons and refugees

The States parties hereto, being also parties to the Universal Copyright Convention (hereinafter referred to as the "Convention"),

Have accepted the following provisions:

1. Stateless persons and refugees who have their habitual residence in a State party to this Protocol shall, for the purposes of the Convention, be assimilated to the nationals of that State.

2. (*a*) This Protocol shall be signed and shall be subject to ratification or acceptance, or may be acceded to, as if the provisions of Article VIII of the Convention applied hereto.

(*b*) This Protocol shall enter into force in respect of each State, on the date of deposit of the instrument of ratification, acceptance or accession of the State concerned or on the date of entry into force of the Convention with respect to such State, whichever is the later.

In faith whereof the undersigned, being duly authorized thereto, have signed this Protocol.

Done at Geneva this sixth day of September 1952, in the English, French and Spanish languages, the three texts being equally authoritative, in a single copy which shall be deposited with the Director-General of Unesco. The Director-General shall send certified copies to the signatory States, to the Swiss Federal Council, and to the Secretary-General of the United Nations for registration.

Signatory States of Protocol 1: Andorra (signed on its behalf by the representatives of the French Government), Argentine Republic, Australia, Austria, Belgium, Brazil, Canada, Cuba, Denmark, El Salvador, France, German Federal Republic, Guatemala, Haiti, Holy See, Honduras, India, Ireland, Israel, Italy, Japan, Liberia, Luxemburg, Monaco, Nicaragua, Norway, Peru, Portugal, San Marino, Sweden, Switzerland, United Kingdom, United States of America, Uruguay and Yugoslavia.

Protocol 2

Annexed to the Universal Copyright Convention concerning the application of that Convention to the works of certain international organizations

The States parties hereto, being also parties to the Universal Copyright Convention (hereinafter referred to as the "Convention"),

Have accepted the following provisions:

1. (*a*) The protection provided for in Article II(1) of the Convention shall apply to works published for the first time by the United Nations, by the Specialized Agencies in relationship therewith, or by the Organization of American States;

(b) Similarly, Article II(2) of the Convention shall apply to the said organization or agencies.

2. (*a*) This Protocol shall be signed and shall be subject to ratification or acceptance, or may be acceded to, as if the provisions of Article VIII of the Convention applied hereto.

(*b*) This Protocol shall enter into force for each State on the date of deposit of the instrument of ratification, acceptance or accession of the State concerned or on the date of entry into force of the Convention with respect to such State, whichever is the later.

In faith whereof the undersigned, being duly authorized thereto, have signed this Protocol.

Done at Geneva, this sixth day of September 1952, in the English, French and Spanish languages, the three texts being equally authoritative, in a single copy which shall be deposited with the Director-General of Unesco.

The Director-General shall send certified copies to the signatory States, to the Swiss Federal Council, and to the Secretary-General of the United Nations for registration.

Signatory States of Protocol 2: Andorra (signed on its behalf by the representatives of the French and Spanish Governments), Argentine Republic, Australia, Austria, Belgium, Brazil, Canada, Chile, Cuba, Denmark, El Salvador, Finland, France, German Federal Republic, Guatemala, Haiti, Holy See, Honduras, India, Ireland, Israel, Italy, Japan, Liberia, Luxemburg, Mexico, Monaco, Nicaragua, Norway, Peru, Portugal, San Marino, Spain, Sweden, Switzerland, United Kingdom, United States of America, Uruguay, and Yugoslavia.

Protocol 3

Annexed to the Universal Copyright Convention concerning the effective date of instruments of ratification or acceptance of or accession to that Convention

States parties hereto,

Recognizing that the application of the Universal Copyright Convention (hereinafter referred to as the "Convention") to States participating in all the international copyright systems already in force will contribute greatly to the value of the Convention;

Have agreed as follows:

1. Any State party hereto may, on depositing its instrument of ratification or acceptance of or accession to the Convention, notify the Director-General of the United Nations Educational, Scientific and Cultural Organization (hereinafter referred to as "Director-General") that that instrument shall not take effect for the purposes of Article IX of the Convention until any other State named in such notification shall have deposited its instrument.

2. The notification referred to in paragraph 1 above shall accompany the instrument to which it relates.

3. The Director-General shall inform all States signatory or which have then acceded to the Convention of any notifications received in accordance with this Protocol.

4. The Protocol shall bear the same date and shall remain open for signature for the same period as the Convention.

5. It shall be subject to ratification or acceptance by the signatory States. Any State which has not signed this Protocol may accede thereto.

6. (*a*) Ratification or acceptance or accession shall be effected by the deposit of an instrument to that effect with the Director-General.

(*b*) This Protocol shall enter into force on the date of deposit of not less than four instruments of ratification or acceptance or accession. The Director-General shall inform all interested States of this date. Instruments deposited after such date shall take effect on the date of their deposit.

Signatory States of Protocol 3: Andorra (signed on its behalf by the representatives of the French Government), Australia, Austria, Belgium, Brazil, Canada, Denmark, El Salvador, Finland, France, German Federal Republic, Guatemala, Haiti, Holy See, Honduras, Ireland, Israel, Italy, Japan, Luxemburg, Netherlands, Nicaragua, Norway, Peru, Portugal, San Marino, Sweden, United Kingdom, United States of America, Uruguay and Venezuela.

In faith whereof the undersigned, being duly authorized thereto, have signed this Protocol.

Done at Geneva, the sixth day of September 1952, in the English, French and Spanish languages, the three texts being equally authoritative, in a single copy which shall be annexed to the original copy of the Convention. The Director-General shall send certified copies to the signatory States, to the Swiss Federal Council, and to the Secretary-General of the United Nations for registration.

Universal Copyright Convention as Revised at Paris and Protocols Annexed Thereto, Paris, 1971

Article I

Each Contracting State undertakes to provide for the adequate and effective protection of the rights of authors and other copyright proprietors in literary, scientific and artistic works, including writings, musical, dramatic and cinematographic works, and paintings, engravings and sculpture.

Article II

1. Published works of nationals of any Contracting State and works first published in that State shall enjoy in each other Contracting State the same protection as that other State accords to works of its nationals first published in its own territory, as well as the protection specially granted by this Convention.

2. Unpublished works of nationals of each Contracting State shall enjoy in each other Contracting State the same protection as that other State accords to unpublished works of its own nationals, as well as the protection specially granted by this Convention.

3. For the purpose of this Convention any Contracting State may, by domestic legislation, assimilate to its own nationals any person domiciled in that State.

Article III

1. Any Contracting State which, under its domestic law, requires as a condition of copyright, compliance with formalities such as deposit, registration, notice, notarial certificates, payment of fees or manufacture or publication in that Contracting State, shall regard these requirements as satisfied with respect to all works protected in accordance with this Convention and first published outside its territory and the author of which is not one of its nationals, if from the time of the first publication all the copies of the work published

---

Source: Reprinted from *Copyright Laws and Treaties of the World,* 15 Supplement, © 1972, BNA Books, Washington, D.C.

with the authority of the author or other copyright proprietor bear the symbol © accompanied by the name of the copyright proprietor and the year of first publication placed in such manner and location as to give reasonable notice of claim of copyright.

2. The provisions of paragraph 1 shall not preclude any Contracting State from requiring formalities or other conditions for the acquisition and enjoyment of copyright in respect of works first published in its territory or works of its nationals wherever published.

3. The provisions of paragraph 1 shall not preclude any Contracting State from providing that a person seeking judicial relief must, in bringing the action, comply with procedural requirements, such as that the complainant must appear through domestic counsel or that the complainant must deposit with the court or an administrative office, or both, a copy of the work involved in the litigation; provided that failure to comply with such requirements shall not affect the validity of the copyright, nor shall any such requirement be imposed upon a national of another Contracting State if such requirement is not imposed on nationals of the State in which protection is claimed.

4. In each Contracting State there shall be legal means of protecting without formalities the unpublished works of nationals of other Contracting States.

5. If a Contracting State grants protection for more than one term of copyright and the first term is for a period longer than one of the minimum periods prescribed in Article IV, such State shall not be required to comply with the provisions of paragraph 1 of this Article in respect of the second or any subsequent term of copyright.

Article IV

1. The duration of protection of a work shall be governed, in accordance with the provisions of Article II and this Article, by the law of the Contracting State in which protection is claimed.

2. (*a*) The term of protection for works protected under this Convention shall not be less than the life of the author and twenty-five years after his death. However, any Contracting State which, on the effective date of this Convention in that State, has limited this term for certain classes of works to a period computed from the first publication of the work, shall be entitled to maintain these exceptions and to extend them to other classes of works. For all these classes the term of protection shall not be less than 25 years from the date of first publication.

(*b*) Any Contracting State which, upon the effective date of this Convention in that State, does not compute the term of protection upon the basis of the life of the author, shall be entitled to compute the term of protection from the date of the first publication of the work or from its registration prior to publication, as the case may be, provided the term of protection shall not be less than 25 years from the date of first publication of from its registration prior to publication, as the case may be.

(*c*) If the legislation of a Contracting State grants two or more successive terms of protection, the duration of the first term shall not be less than one of the minimum periods specified in sub-paragraphs (*a*) and (*b*).

3. The provisions of paragraph 2 shall not apply to photographic works or to works of applied art; provided, however, that the term of protection in those Contracting States which protect photographic works, or works of applied art in so far as they are protected as artistic works, shall not be less than 10 years for each of said classes of works.

4. (*a*) No Contracting State shall be obliged to grant protection to a work for a period longer than that fixed for the class of works to which the work in question belongs, in the case of unpublished works by the law of the Contracting State of which the author is a national, and in the case of published works by the law of the Contracting State in which the work has been first published.

(*b*) For the purposes of the application of sub-paragraph (*a*), if the law of any Contracting State grants two or more successive terms of protection, the period of protection of that State shall be considered to be the aggregate of those terms. However, if a specified work is not protected by such State during the second or any subsequent term for any reason, the other Contracting States shall not be obliged to protect it during the second or any subsequent term.

5. For the purposes of the application of paragraph 4, the work of a national of a Contracting State, first published in a non-Contracting State, shall be treated as though first published in the Contracting State of which the author is a national.

6. For the purposes of the application of paragraph 4, in case of simultaneous publication in two or more Contracting States, the work shall be treated as though first published in the State which affords the shortest term; any work published in two or more Contracting States within 30 days of its first publication shall be considered as having been published simultaneously in said Contracting States.

Article IV*bis*

1. The rights referred to in Article I shall include the basic rights ensuring the author's economic interests, including the exclusive right to authorize reproduction by any means, public perfor-

mance and broadcasting. The provisions of this Article shall extend to works protected under this Convention either in their original form or in any form recognizably derived from the original.

2. However, any Contracting State may, by its domestic legislation, make exceptions that do not conflict with the spirit and provisions of this Convention, to the rights mentioned in paragraph 1 of this Article. Any State whose legislation so provides, shall nevertheless accord a reasonable degree of effective protection to each of the rights to which exception has been made.

Article V

1. The rights referred to in Article I shall include the exclusive right of the author to make, publish and authorize the making and publication of translations of works protected under this Convention.

2. However, any Contracting State may, by its domestic legislation, restrict the right of translation of writings, but only subject to the following provisions:

(*a*) If, after the expiration of a period of seven years from the date of the first publication of a writing, a translation of such writing has not been published in a language in general use in the Contracting State, by the owner of the right of translation or with his authorization, any national of such Contracting State may obtain a non-exclusive licence from the competent authority thereof to translate the work into that language and publish the work so translated.

(*b*) Such national shall in accordance with the procedure of the State concerned, establish either that he has requested, and been denied, authorization by the proprietor of the right to make and publish the translation, or that, after due diligence on his part, he was unable to find the owner of the right. A licence may also be granted on the same conditions if all previous editions of a translation in a language in general use in the Contracting State are out of print.

(*c*) If the owner of the right of translation cannot be found, then the applicant for a licence shall send copies of his application to the publisher whose name appears on the work and, if the nationality of the owner of the right of translation is known, to the diplomatic or consular representative of the State of which such owner is a national, or to the organization which may have been designated by the government of that State. The licence shall not be granted before the expiration of a period of two months from the date of the dispatch of the copies of the application.

(*d*) Due provision shall be made by domestic legislation to ensure to the owner of the right of translation a compensation which is just and conforms to international standards, to ensure payment and transmittal of such compensation, and to ensure a correct translation of the work.

(*e*) The original title and the name of the author of the work shall be printed on all copies of the published translation. The licence shall be valid only for publication of the translation in the territory of the Contracting State where it has been applied for. Copies so published may be imported and sold in another Contracting State if a language in general use in such other State is the same language as that into which the work has been so translated, and if the domestic law in such other State makes provision for such licences and does not prohibit such importation and sale. Where the foregoing conditions do not exist, the importation and sale of such copies in a Contracting State, shall be governed by its domestic law and its agreements. The licence shall not be transferred by the licensee.

(*f*) The licence shall not be granted when the author has withdrawn from circulation all copies of the work.

Article V*bis*

1. Any Contracting State regarded as a developing country in conformity with the established practice of the General Assembly of the United Nations may, by a notification deposited with the Director-General of the United Nations Educational, Scientific and Cultural Organization (hereinafter called "the Director-General") at the time of its ratification, acceptance or accession or thereafter, avail itself of any or all of the exceptions provided for in Articles V*ter* and V*quater*.

2. Any such notification shall be effective for 10 years from the date of coming into force of this Convention, or for such part of that 10-year period as remains at the date of deposit of the notification, and may be renewed in whole or in part for further periods of 10 years each if, not more than 15 or less than 3 months before the expiration of the relevant 10-year period, the Contracting State deposits a further notification with the Director-General. Initial notifications may also be made during these further periods of 10 years in accordance with the provisions of this Article.

3. Notwithstanding the provisions of paragraph 2, a Contracting State that has ceased to be regarded as a developing country as referred to in paragraph 1 shall no longer be entitled to renew its notification made under the provisions of paragraph 1 or 2, and whether or not it formally withdraws the notification such State shall be precluded from availing itself of the exceptions provided for in Articles V*ter* and V*quater* at the end of the current ten-year period,

or at the end of the three years after it has ceased to be regarded as a developing country, whichever period expires later.

4. Any copies of a work already made under the exceptions provided for in Articles V*ter* and V*quater* may continue to be distributed after the expiration of the period for which notifications under this Article were effective until their stock is exhausted.

5. Any Contracting State that has deposited a notification in accordance with Article XIII with respect to the application of this Convention to a particular country or territory, the situation of which can be regarded as analogous to that of the States referred to in paragraph 1 of this Article, may also deposit notifications and renew them in accordance with the provisions of this Article with respect to any such country or territory. During the effective period of such notifications, the provisions of Articles V*ter* and V*quater* may be applied with respect to such country or territory. The sending of copies from the country or territory to the Contracting State shall be considered as export within the meaning of Articles V*ter* and V*quater*.

Article V*ter*

1. (*a*) Any Contracting State to which Article V*bis* (1) applies may substitute for the period of seven years provided for in Article V (2) a period of three years or any longer period prescribed by its legislation. However, in the case of a translation into a language not in general use in one or more developed countries that are party to this Convention or only the 1952 Convention, the period shall be one year instead of three.

(*b*) A Contracting State to which Article V*bis* (1) applies may, with the unanimous agreement of the developed countries party to this Convention or only the 1952 Convention and in which the same language is in general use, substitute, in the case of translation into that language, for the period of three years provided for in sub-paragraph (*a*) another period as determined by such agreement but not shorter than one year. However, this sub-paragraph shall not apply where the language in question is English, French or Spanish. Notification of any such agreement shall be made to the Director-General.

(*c*) The licence may only be granted if the applicant, in accordance with the procedure of the State concerned, establishes either that he has requested, and been denied, authorization by the owner of the right of translation, or that, after due diligence on his part, he was unable to find the owner of the right. At the same time as he makes his request he shall inform either the international copyright information centre established by the United Nations Educational, Scientific and Cultural Organization or any national or regional information centre which may have been designated in a notification to that effect deposited with the Director-General by the government of the State in which the publisher is believed to have his principal place of business.

(*d*) If the owner of the right of translation cannot be found, the applicant for a licence shall send, by registered airmail, copies of his application to the publisher whose name appears on the work and to any national or regional information centre as mentioned in sub-paragraph (*c*). If no such centre is notified he shall also send a copy to the international copyright information centre established by the United Nations Educational, Scientific and Cultural Organization.

2. (*a*) Licences obtainable after three years shall not be granted under this Article until a further period of six months has elapsed and licences obtainable after one year until a further period of nine months has elapsed. The further period shall begin either from the date of the request for permission to translate mentioned in paragraph 1 (*c*) or, if the identity or address of the owner of the right of translation is not known, from the date of dispatch of the copies of the application for a licence mentioned in paragraph 1 (*d*).

(*b*) Licences shall not be granted if a translation has been published by the owner of the right of translation or with his authorization during the said period of six or nine months.

3. Any licence under this Article shall be granted only for the purpose of teaching, scholarship or research.

4. (*a*) Any licence granted under this Article shall not extend to the export of copies and shall be valid only for publication in the territory of the Contracting State where it has been applied for.

(*b*) Any copy published in accordance with a licence granted under this Article shall bear a notice in the appropriate language stating that the copy is available for distribution only in the Contracting State granting the licence. If the writing bears the notice specified in Article III (1) the copies shall bear the same notice.

(*c*) The prohibition of export provided for in sub-paragraph (*a*) shall not apply where a governmental or other public entity of a State which has granted a licence under this Article to translate a work into a language other than English, French or Spanish sends copies of a translation prepared under such licence to another country if:

(i) the recipients are individuals who are nationals of the Contracting State granting the licence, or organizations grouping such individuals;

(ii) the copies are to be used only for the purpose of teaching, scholarship or research;

(iii) the sending of the copies and their subsequent distribution to recipients is without the object of commercial purpose; and
(iv) the country to which the copies have been sent has agreed with the Contracting State to allow the receipt, distribution or both and the Director-General has been notified of such agreement by any one of the governments which have concluded it.

5. Due provision shall be made at the national level to ensure:

(*a*) that the licence provides for just compensation that is consistent with standards of royalties normally operating in the case of licences freely negotiated between persons in the two countries concerned; and
(*b*) payment and transmittal of the compensation; however, should national currency regulations intervene, the competent authority shall make all efforts, by the use of international machinery, to ensure transmittal in internationally convertible currency or its equivalent.

6. Any licence granted by a Contracting State under this Article shall terminate if a translation of the work in the same language with substantially the same content as the edition in respect of which the licence was granted is published in the said State by the owner of the right of translation or with his authorization, at a price reasonably related to that normally charged in the same State for comparable works. Any copies already made before the licence is terminated may continue to be distributed until their stock is exhausted.

7. For works which are composed mainly of illustrations a licence to translate the text and to reproduce the illustrations may be granted only if the conditions of Article V*quater* are also fulfilled.

8. (*a*) A licence to translate a work protected under this Convention, published in printed or analogous forms of reproduction, may also be granted to a broadcasting organization having its headquarters in a Contracting State to which Article V*bis* (1) applies, upon an application made in that State by the said organization under the following conditions:

(i) the translation is made from a copy made and acquired in accordance with the laws of the Contracting State;
(ii) the translation is for use only in broadcasts intended exclusively for teaching or for the dissemination of the results of specialized technical or scientific research to experts in a particular profession;
(iii) the translation is used exclusively for the purposes set out in condition (ii), through broadcasts lawfully made which

are intended for recipients on the territory of the Contracting State, including broadcasts made through the medium of sound or visual recordings lawfully and exclusively made for the purpose of such broadcasts;

(iv) sound or visual recordings of the translation may be exchanged only between broadcasting organizations having their headquarters in the Contracting State granting the licence; and

(v) all uses made of the translation are without any commercial purpose.

(*b*) Provided all of the criteria and conditions set out in sub-paragraph (*a*) are met, a licence may also be granted to a broadcasting organization to translate any text incorporated in an audio-visual fixation which was itself prepared and published for the sole purpose of being used in connexion with systematic instructional activities.

(*c*) Subject to sub-paragraphs (*a*) and (*b*), the other provisions of this Article shall apply to the grant and exercise of the licence.

9. Subject to the provisions of this Article, any licence granted under this Article shall be governed by the provisions of Article V, and shall continue to be governed by the provisions of Article V and of this Article, even after the seven-year period provided for in Article V (2) has expired. However, after the said period has expired, the licensee shall be free to request that the said licence be replaced by a new licence governed exclusively by the provisions of Article V.

Article V*quater*

1. Any Contracting State to which Article V*bis* (1) applies may adopt the following provisions:

(*a*) If, after the expiration of

(i) the relevant period specified in sub-paragraph (*c*) commencing from the date of first publication of a particular edition of a literary, scientific or artistic work referred to in paragraph 3, or

(ii) any longer period determined by national legislation of the State,

copies of such edition have not been distributed in that State to the general public or in connexion with systematic instructional activities at a price reasonably related to that normally charged in the State for comparable works, by the owner of the right of reproduction or with his authorization, any national of such State may obtain a non-exclusive licence from the competent authority to publish such edition at that or a lower price for use in connexion with systematic instructional activities. The licence may only be granted if such national, in accordance with the procedure of the State concerned, establishes either that he has requested, and been denied, authorization by the proprietor of the right to publish such work, or that, after due diligence on his part, he was unable to find the owner of the right. At the same time as he makes his request he shall inform either the international copyright information centre established by the United Nations Educational, Scientific and Cultural Organization or any national or regional information centre referred to in sub-paragraph (*d*).

(*b*) A licence may also be granted on the same conditions if, for a period of six months, no authorized copies of the edition in question have been on sale in the State concerned to the general public or in connexion with systematic instructional activities at a price reasonably related to that normally charged in the State for comparable works.

(*c*) The period referred to in sub-paragraph (*a*) shall be five years except that:

- (i) for works of the natural and physical sciences, including mathematics, and of technology, the period shall be three years;
- (ii) for works of fiction, poetry, drama and music, and for art books, the period shall be seven years.

(*d*) If the owner of the right of reproduction cannot be found, the applicant for a licence shall send, by registered air mail, copies of his application to the publisher whose name appears on the work and to any national or regional information centre identified as such in a notification deposited with the Director-General by the State in which the publisher is believed to have his principal place of business. In the absence of any such notification, he shall also send a copy to the international copyright information centre established by the United Nations Educational, Scientific and Cultural Organization. The licence shall not be granted before the expiration of a period of three months from the date of dispatch of the copies of the application.

(*e*) Licences obtainable after three years shall not be granted under this Article,

- (i) until a period of six months has elapsed from the date of the request for permission referred to in sub-paragraph (*a*) or, if the identity or address of the owner of the right of reproduction is unknown, from the date of the dispatch of the copies of the application for a licence referred to in sub-paragraph (*d*);

(ii) if any such distribution of copies of the edition as is mentioned in sub-paragraph (*a*) has taken place during that period.

(*f*) The name of the author and the title of the particular edition of the work shall be printed on all copies of the published reproduction. The licence shall not extend to the export of copies and shall be valid only for publication in the territory of the Contracting State where it has been applied for. The licence shall not be transferable by the licensee.

(*g*) Due provision shall be made by domestic legislation to ensure an accurate reproduction of the particular edition in question.

(*h*) A licence to reproduce and publish a translation of a work shall not be granted under this Article in the following cases:

(i) where the translation was not published by the owner of the right of translation or with his authorization;
(ii) where the translation is not in a language in general use in the State with power to grant the licence.

2. The exceptions provided for in paragraph 1 are subject to the following additional provisions:

(*a*) Any copy published in accordance with a licence granted under this Article shall bear a notice in the appropriate language stating that the copy is available for distribution only in the Contracting State to which the said licence applies. If the edition bears the notice specified in Article III (1), the copies shall bear the same notice.

(*b*) Due provision shall be made at the national level to ensure:

(i) that the licence provides for just compensation that is consistent with standards of royalties normally operating in the case of licences freely negotiated between persons in the two countries concerned; and
(ii) payment and transmittal of the compensation; however, should national currency regulations intervene, the competent authority shall make all efforts, by the use of international machinery, to ensure transmittal in internationally convertible currency or its equivalent.

(*c*) Whenever copies of an edition of a work are distributed in the Contracting State to the general public or in connexion with systematic instructional activities, by the owner of the right of reproduction or with his authorization, at a price reasonably related to that normally charged in the State for comparable works, any licence granted under this Article shall terminate if such edition is in the same language and is substantially the same in content as the edition published under the licence. Any copies already made before the licence is terminated may continue to be distributed until their stock is exhausted.

(*d*) No licence shall be granted when the author has withdrawn from circulation all copies of the edition in question.

3. (*a*) Subject to sub-paragraph (*b*), the literary, scientific or artistic works to which this Article applies shall be limited to works published in printed or analogous forms of reproduction.

(*b*) The provisions of this Article shall also apply to reproduction in audio-visual form of lawfully made audio-visual fixations including any protected works incorporated therein and to the translation of any incorporated text into a language in general use in the State with power to grant the licence; always provided that the audio-visual fixations in question were prepared and published for the sole purpose of being used in connexion with systematic instructional activities.

Article VI

"Publication", as used in this Convention, means the reproduction in tangible form and the general distribution to the public of copies of a work from which it can be read or otherwise visually perceived.

Article VII

This Convention shall not apply to works or rights in works which, at the effective date of this Convention in a Contracting State where protection is claimed, are permanently in the public domain in the said Contracting State.

Article VIII

1. This Convention, which shall bear the date of 24 July 1971, shall be deposited with the Director-General and shall remain open for signature by all States party to the 1952 Convention for a period of 120 days after the date of this Convention. It shall be subject to ratification or acceptance by the signatory States.

2. Any State which has not signed this Convention may accede thereto.

3. Ratification, acceptance or accession shall be effected by the deposit of an instrument to that effect with the Director-General.

Article IX

1. This Convention shall come into force three months after the deposit of 12 instruments of ratification, acceptance or accession.

2. Subsequently, this Convention shall come into force in respect of each State three months after that State has deposited its instrument of ratification, acceptance or accession.

3. Accession to this Convention by a State not Party to the 1952 Convention shall also constitute accession to that Convention; however, if its instrument of accession is deposited before this Convention comes into force, such State may make its accession to the 1952 Convention conditional upon the coming into force of this Convention. After the coming into force of this Convention, no State may accede solely to the 1952 Convention.

4. Relations between States party to this Convention and States that are party only to the 1952 Convention, shall be governed by the 1952 Convention. However, any State party only to the 1952 Convention may, by a notification deposited with the Director-General, declare that it will admit the application of the 1971 Convention to works of its nationals or works first published in its territory by all States party to this Convention.

Article X

1. Each Contracting State undertakes to adopt, in accordance with its Constitution, such measures as are necessary to ensure the application of this Convention.

2. It is understood that at the date this Convention comes into force in respect of any State, that State must be in a position under its domestic law to give effect to the terms of this Convention.

Article XI

1. An Intergovernmental Committee is hereby established with the following duties:

(*a*) to study the problems concerning the application and operation of the Universal Copyright Convention;

(*b*) to make preparation for periodic revisions of this Convention;

(*c*) to study any other problems concerning the international protection of copyright, in co-operation with the various interested international organizations, such as the United Nations Educational, Scientific and Cultural Organization, the International Union for the Protection of Literary and Artistic Works and the Organization of American States;

(*d*) to inform States party to the Universal Copyright Convention as to its activities.

2. The Committee shall consist of the representatives of 18 States party to this Convention or only to the 1952 Convention.

3. The Committee shall be selected with due consideration to a fair balance of national interests on the basis of geographical location, population, languages and stage of development.

4. The Director-General of the United Nations Educational, Scientific and Cultural Organization, the Director-General of the World Intellectual Property Organization and the Secretary-General of the Organization of American States, or their representatives, may attend meetings of the Committee in an advisory capacity.

Article XII

The Intergovernmental Committee shall convene a conference for revision whenever it deems necessary, or at the request of at least 10 States party to this Convention.

Article XIII

1. Any Contracting State may, at the time of deposit of its instrument of ratification, acceptance or accession, or at any time thereafter, declare by notification addressed to the Director-General that this Convention shall apply to all or any of the countries or territories for the international relations of which it is responsible and this Convention shall thereupon apply to the countries or territories named in such notification after the expiration of the term of three months provided for in Article IX. In the absence of such notification, this Convention shall not apply to any such country or territory.

2. However, nothing in this Article shall be understood as implying the recognition or tacit acceptance by a Contracting State of the factual situation concerning a country or territory to which this Convention is made applicable by another Contracting State in accordance with the provisions of this Article.

Article XIV

1. Any Contracting State may denounce this Convention in its own name or on behalf of all or any of the countries or territories with respect to which a notification has been given under Article

XIII. The denunciation shall be made by notification addressed to the Director-General. Such denunciation shall also constitute denunciation of the 1952 Convention.

2. Such denunciation shall operate only in respect of the State or of the country or territory on whose behalf it was made and shall not take effect until 12 months after the date of receipt of the notification.

Article XV

A dispute between two or more Contracting States concerning the interpretation or application of this Convention, not settled by negotiation, shall, unless the States concerned agree on some other method of settlement, be brought before the International Court of Justice for determination by it.

Article XVI

1. This Convention shall be established in English, French and Spanish. The three texts shall be signed and shall be equally authoritative.

2. Official texts of this Convention shall be established by the Director-General, after consultation with the governments concerned, in Arabic, German, Italian and Portuguese.

3. Any Contracting State or group of Contracting States shall be entitled to have established by the Director-General other texts in the language of its choice by arrangement with the Director-General.

4. All such texts shall be annexed to the signed texts of this Convention.

Article XVII

1. This Convention shall not in any way affect the provisions of the Berne Convention for the Protection of Literary and Artistic Works or membership in the Union created by that Convention.

2. In application of the foregoing paragraph, a declaration has been annexed to the present Article. This declaration is an integral part of this Convention for the States bound by the Berne Conventions on 1 January 1951, or which have or may become bound to it at a later date. The signature of this Convention by such States shall

also constitute signature of the said declaration, and ratification, acceptance or accession by such States shall include the declaration, as well as this Convention.

Article XVIII

This Convention shall not abrogate multilateral or bilateral copyright conventions or arrangements that are or may be in effect exclusively between two or more American Republics. In the event of any difference either between the provisions of such existing conventions or arrangements and the provisions of this Convention, or between the provisions of this Convention and those of any new convention or arrangement which may be formulated between two or more American Republics after this Convention comes into force, the convention or arrangement most recently formulated shall prevail between the parties thereto. Rights in works acquired in any Contracting State under existing conventions or arrangements before the date this Convention comes into force in such State shall not be affected.

Article XIX

This Convention shall not abrogate multilateral or bilateral conventions or arrangements in effect between two or more Contracting States. In the event of any difference between the provisions of such existing conventions or arrangements and the provisions of this Convention, the provisions of this Convention shall prevail. Rights in works acquired in any Contracting State under existing conventions or arrangements before the date on which this Convention comes into force in such State shall not be affected. Nothing in this Article shall affect the provisions of Articles XVII and XVIII.

Article XX

Reservations to this Convention shall not be permitted.

Article XXI

1. The Director-General shall send duly certified copies of this Convention to the States interested and to the Secretary-General of the United Nations for registration by him.

2. He shall also inform all interested States of the ratifications,

acceptances and accessions which have been deposited, the date on which this Convention comes into force, the notifications under this Convention and denunciations under Article XIV.

Appendix Declaration relating to Article XVII

The States which are members of the International Union for the Protection of Literary and Artistic Works (hereinafter called "the Berne Union") and which are signatories to this Convention,

Desiring to reinforce their mutual relations on the basis of the said Union and to avoid any conflict which might result from the co-existence of the Berne Convention and the Universal Copyright Convention,

Recognizing the temporary need of some States to adjust their level of copyright protection in accordance with their stage of cultural, social and economic development,

Have, by common agreement, accepted the terms of the following declaration:

(*a*) Except as provided by paragraph (*b*), works which, according to the Berne Convention, have as their country of origin a country which has withdrawn from the Berne Union after 1 January 1951, shall not be protected by the Universal Copyright Convention in the countries of the Berne Union;

(*b*) Where a Contracting State is regarded as a developing country in conformity with the established practice of the General Assembly of the United Nations, and has deposited with the Director-General of the United Nations Educational, Scientific and Cultural Organization, at the time of its withdrawal from the Berne Union, a notification to the effect that it regards itself as a developing country, the provisions of paragraph (*a*) shall not be applicable as long as such State may avail itself of the exceptions provided for by this Convention in accordance with Article V*bis;*

(*c*) The Universal Copyright Convention shall not be applicable to the relationships among countries of the Berne Union in so far as it relates to the protection of works having as their country of origin, within the meaning of the Berne Convention, a country of the Berne Union.

Resolution Concerning Article XI

The Conference for Revision of the Universal Copyright Convention,

Having considered the problems relating to the Intergovernmental Committee provided for in Article XI of this Convention, to which this resolution is annexed,

Resolves that,

1. At its inception, the Committee shall include representatives of the twelve States members of the Intergovernmental Committee established under Article XI of the 1952 Convention and the resolution annexed to it, and, in addition, representatives of the following States: Algeria, Australia, Japan, Mexico, Senegal and Yugoslavia.

2. Any States that are not party to the 1952 Convention and have not acceded to this Convention before the first ordinary session of the Committee following the entry into force of this Convention shall be replaced by other States to be selected by the Committee at its first ordinary session in conformity with the provisions of Article XI(2) and (3).

3. As soon as this Convention comes into force the Committee as provided for in paragraph 1 shall be deemed to be constituted in accordance with Article XI of this Convention.

4. A session of the Committee shall take place within one year after the coming into force of this Convention; thereafter the Committee shall meet in ordinary session at intervals of not more than two years.

5. The Committee shall elect its Chairman and two Vice-Chairmen. It shall establish its Rules of Procedure having regard to the following principles:

(*a*) The normal duration of the term of office of the members represented on the Committee shall be six years with one-third retiring every two years, it being however understood that, of the original terms of office, one-third shall expire at the end of the Committee's second ordinary session which will follow the entry into force of this Convention, a further third at the end of its third ordinary session, and the remaining third at the end of its fourth ordinary session;

(*b*) The rules governing the procedure whereby the Committee shall fill vacancies, the order in which terms of membership expire, eligibility for re-election, and election procedures, shall be based upon a balancing of the needs for continuity of membership and rotation of representation, as well as the considerations set out in Article XI(3).

Expresses the wish that the United Nations Educational, Scientific and Cultural Organization provide its Secretariat.

In faith whereof the undersigned, having deposited their respective full powers, have signed this Convention.

Done at Paris, this twenty-fourth day of July 1971, in a single copy.

Protocol 1

Annexed to the Universal Copyright Convention as revised at Paris on 24 July 1971 concerning the application of that Convention to works of Stateless persons and refugees

The States party hereto, being also party to the Universal Copyright Convention as revised at Paris on 24 July 1971 (hereinafter called "the 1971 Convention"),

Have accepted the following provisions:

1. Stateless persons and refugees who have their habitual residence in a State party to this Protocol shall, for the purposes of the 1971 Convention, be assimilated to the nationals of that State.

2. (*a*) This Protocol shall be signed and shall be subject to ratification or acceptance, or may be acceded to, as if the provisions of Article VIII of the 1971 Convention applied hereto.

(*b*) This Protocol shall enter into force in respect of each State, on the date of deposit of the instrument of ratification, acceptance or accession of the State concerned or on the date of entry into force of the 1971 Convention with respect to such State, whichever is the later.

(*c*) On the entry into force of this Protocol in respect of a State not party to Protocol 1 annexed to the 1952 Convention, the latter Protocol shall be deemed to enter into force in respect of such State.

In faith whereof the undersigned, being duly authorized thereto, have signed this Protocol.

Done at Paris this twenty-fourth day of July 1971, in the English, French and Spanish languages, the three texts being equally authoritative, in a single copy which shall be deposited with the Director-General of the United Nations Educational, Scientific and Cultural Organization. The Director-General shall send certified copies to the signatory States, and to the Secretary-General of the United Nations for registration.

Signatory States of Protocol 1: Belgium (28 July 1971), Brazil, Costa Rica, Denmark, Finland (20 Nov. 1971), France, German Federal Republic, Guatemala, Holy See, India, Israel, Italy, Japan (22 Oct. 1971), Kenya, Lebanon, Liberia, Liechtenstein, Mexico, Monaco, Netherlands, Norway (20 Nov. 1971), Spain, Sweden, Switzerland, Tunisia, United Kingdom, United States of America and Yugoslavia.

Protocol 2

Annexed to the Universal Copyright Convention as revised at Paris on 24 July 1971 concerning the application of that Convention to the works of certain international organizations

The States party hereto, being also party to the Universal Copyright Convention as revised at Paris on 24 July 1971 (hereinafter called "the 1971 Convention"),

Have accepted the following provisions:

1. (*a*) The protection provided for in Article II(1) of the 1971 Convention shall apply to works published for the first time by the United Nations, by the Specialized Agencies in relationship therewith, or by the Organization of American States.

(*b*) Similarly, Article II(2) of the 1971 Convention shall apply to the said organization or agencies.

2. (*a*) This Protocol shall be signed and shall be subject to ratification or acceptance, or may be acceded to, as if the provisions of Article VIII of the 1971 Convention applied hereto.

(*b*) This Protocol shall enter into force for each State on the date of deposit of the instrument of ratification, acceptance or accession of the State concerned or on the date of entry into force of the 1971 Convention with respect to such state, whichever is the later.

In faith whereof the undersigned, being duly authorized thereto, have signed this Protocol.

Done at Paris, this twenty-fourth day of July 1971, in the English, French and Spanish languages, the three texts being equally authoritative, in a single copy which shall be deposited with the Director-General of the United Nations Educational, Scientific and Cultural Organization. The Director-General shall send certified copies to the signatory States, and to the Secretary-General of the United Nations for registration.

Signatory States of Protocol 2: Belgium (28 July 1971), Brazil, Costa Rica, Denmark, Finland (20 Nov. 1971), France, German Federal Republic, Guatemala, Holy See, Hungary, India, Israel, Italy, Japan (22 Oct. 1971), Kenya, Lebanon, Liberia, Liechtenstein, Mauritius, Mexico, Monaco, Netherlands, Norway (20 Nov. 1971), Spain, Sweden, Switzerland, Tunisia, United Kingdom, United States of America and Yugoslavia.

3. International Convention for the Protection of Performers, Producers of Phonograms and Broadcasting Organisations (Rome Convention)

October 26, 1961

The International Convention for the Protection of Performers, Producers of Phonograms and Broadcasting Organisations, known as the Rome Convention was completed on October 26, 1961, and entered into force on May 18, 1964. This Convention provides international protection for performing artists, the producers of phonograms (sound recordings), and broadcasting organizations. The rights protected in the convention are known as *droits voisins* or neighboring rights.

The Convention is based on national treatment and establishes minimum rights. The beneficiaries of the Convention are performers, producers of phonograms, and broadcasters. The Convention grants protection to performers if their performance takes place in another contracting state, is incorporated in a phonogram that is protected by the Convention, or if not fixed on a phonogram, is carried by a broadcast protected by the Convention (Art. 4). Each contracting state shall grant national treatment to producers of phonograms if any of the following conditions is met: the producer of the phonogram is a national of another member state, or the first fixation of the sound was made in another contracting state, or the phonogram was first published in another member state (Art. 5). Broadcasters are protected under the Convention if the headquarters of the broadcasting organization is situated in another contracting state or if the broadcast was transmitted from a transmitter situated in another member state (Art. 6).

The Convention establishes minimum rights that must be conferred for performers and producers of phonograms. These are set forth in Articles 7 through 13. Performers are protected against the unauthorized broadcast of their public performances and enjoy the right to a first fixation of their performance. Producers of phonograms enjoy the right to authorize or prohibit the direct or indirect reproduction of their phonograms (Art. 10). Article 12 establishes a duty on a user to pay a single equitable remuneration to artists or producers for a public performance of a phonogram. It leaves to domestic law the conditions by which this remuneration is to be shared between the parties.

Broadcasting organizations shall enjoy the right to the fixation, reproduction, and rebroadcast of their broadcasts (Art. 13), subject to certain limitations under domestic law (Arts. 13(d) and (15)).

Protection is granted for a 20-year term, computed from the end of the year when the fixation was made for phonograms and performances incorporated therein. However, if the performance is not incorporated in a phonogram, the term will be computed from the end of the year when the performance took place. For broadcasts, the year when the broadcast took place will determine the duration of protection (Art. 14).

To participate in the Rome Convention, a state must belong either to the Berne Convention or to the Universal Copyright Convention (Art. 24).

As of January 1, 1990, the following 32 states were party to the Rome Convention:

Austria	Ecuador	Mexico
Barbados	El Salvador	Monaco
Brazil	Fiji	Niger
Burkina Faso	Finland	Norway
Chile	France	Panama
Colombia	Federal Republic of Germany	Paraguay
Congo	Guatemala	Peru
Costa Rica	Ireland	Philippines
Czechoslovakia	Italy	Sweden
Denmark	Luxembourg	United Kingdom
Dominican Republic		Uruguay

International Convention for the Protection of Performers, Producers of Phonograms and Broadcasting Organisations

Article 1

Protection granted under this Convention shall leave intact and shall in no way affect the protection of copyright in literary and artistic works. Consequently, no provision of this Convention may be interpreted as prejudicing such protection.

Article 2

1. For the purpose of this Convention, national treatment shall mean the treatment accorded by the domestic law of the Contracting State in which protection is claimed:

(*a*) to performers who are its nationals, as regards performances taking place, broadcast, or first fixed, on its territory;

(*b*) to producers of phonograms who are its nationals as regards phonograms first fixed or first published on its territory;

(*c*) to broadcasting organisations which have their headquarters on its territory, as regards broadcasts transmitted from transmitters situated on its territory.

2. National treatment shall be subject to the protection specifically guaranteed, and the limitations specifically provided for, in this Convention.

Article 3

For the purposes of this Convention:

(*a*) "Performers" means actors, singers, musicians, dancers, and other persons who act, sing, deliver, declaim, play in, or otherwise perform literary or artistic works;

(*b*) "Phonogram" means any exclusively aural fixation of sounds of a performance or of other sounds;

Source: Reprinted from *Copyright Laws and Treaties of the World,* 5 Supplement, © 1962, BNA Books, Washington, D.C.

(*c*) "Producer of phonograms" means the person who, or the legal entity which, first fixes the sounds of a performance or other sounds;

(*d*) "Publication" means the offering of copies of a phonogram to the public in reasonable quantity;

(*e*) "Reproduction" means the making of a copy or copies of a fixation;

(*f*) "Broadcasting" means the transmission by wireless means for public reception of sounds or of images and sounds;

(*g*) "Rebroadcasting" means the simultaneous broadcasting by one broadcasting organisation of the broadcast of another broadcasting organisation.

Article 4

Each Contracting State shall grant national treatment to performers if any of the following conditions is met:

(*a*) the performance takes place in another Contracting State;

(*b*) the performance is incorporated in a phonogram which is protected under Article 5 of this Convention;

(*c*) the performance, not being fixed on a phonogram, is carried by a broadcast which is protected by Article 6 of this Convention.

Article 5

1. Each Contracting State shall grant national treatment to producers of phonograms if any of the following conditions is met:

(*a*) the producer of the phonogram is a national of another Contracting State (criterion of nationality);

(*b*) the first fixation of the sound was made in another Contracting State (criterion of fixation);

(*c*) the phonogram was first published in another Contracting State (criterion of publication).

2. If a phonogram was first published in a non-contracting State but if it was also published, within 30 days of its first publication, in a Contracting State (simultaneous publication), it shall be considered as first published in the Contracting State.

3. By means of a notification deposited with the Secretary-General of the United Nations, any Contracting State may declare that it will not apply the criterion of publication or, alternatively, the criterion of fixation. Such notification may be deposited at the time of ratification, acceptance or accession, or at any time thereafter; in the last case, it shall become effective six months after it has been deposited.

Article 6

1. Each Contracting State shall grant national treatment to broadcasting organisations if either of the following conditions is met:

(*a*) the headquarters of the broadcasting organisation is situated in another Contracting State;

(*b*) the broadcast was transmitted from a transmitter situated in another Contracting State.

2. By means of a notification deposited with the Secretary-General of the United Nations, any Contracting State may declare that it will protect broadcasts only if the headquarters of the broadcasting organisation is situated in another Contracting State and the broadcast was transmitted from a transmitter situated in the same Contracting State. Such notification may be deposited at the time of ratification, acceptance or accession, or at any time thereafter; in the last case, it shall become effective six months after it has been deposited.

Article 7

1. The protection provided for performers by this Convention shall include the possibility of preventing:

(*a*) the broadcasting and the communication to the public, without their consent, of their performance, except where the performance used in the broadcasting or the public communication is itself already a broadcast performance or is made from a fixation;

(*b*) the fixation, without their consent, of their unfixed performance;

(*c*) the reproduction, without their consent, of a fixation of their performance:

(i) if the original fixation itself was made without their consent;

(ii) if the reproduction is made for purposes different from those for which the performers gave their consent;

(iii) if the original fixation was made in accordance with the provisions of Article 15, and the reproduction is made for purposes different from those referred to in those provisions.

2. (1) If broadcasting was consented to by the performers, it shall be a matter for the domestic law of the Contracting State where protection is claimed to regulate the protection against rebroadcasting, fixation for broadcasting purposes, and the reproduction of such fixation for broadcasting purposes.

(2) The terms and conditions governing the use by broadcasting organisations of fixations made for broadcasting purposes shall be

determined in accordance with the domestic law of the Contracting State where protection is claimed.

(3) However, the domestic law referred to in sub-paragraphs (1) and (2) of this paragraph shall not operate to deprive performers of the ability to control, by contract, their relations with broadcasting organisations.

Article 8

Any Contracting State may, by its domestic laws and regulations, specify the manner in which performers will be represented in connection with the exercise of their rights if several of them participate in the same performance.

Article 9

Any Contracting State may, by its domestic laws and regulations, extend the protection provided for in this Convention to artists who do not perform literary or artistic works.

Article 10

Producers of phonograms shall enjoy the right to authorize or prohibit the direct or indirect reproduction of their phonograms.

Article 11

If, as a condition of protecting the rights of producers of phonograms, or of performers, or both, in relation to phonograms, a Contracting State, under its domestic law, requires compliance with formalities, these shall be considered as fulfilled if all the copies in commerce of the published phonogram or their containers bear a notice consisting of the symbol p, accompanied by the year date of the first publication, placed in such a manner as to give reasonable notice of claim of protection; and if the copies or their containers do not identify the producer or the licensee of the producer (by carrying his name, trade mark or other appropriate designation), the notice shall also include the name of the owner of the rights of the producer; and, furthermore, if the copies or their containers do not identify the principal performers, the notice shall also include the name of the person who, in the country in which the fixation was effected, owns the rights of such performers.

Article 12

If a phonogram published for commercial purposes, or a reproduction of such phonogram, is used directly for broadcasting or for any communication to the public, a single equitable remuneration shall be paid by the user to the performers, or to the producers of the phonograms, or to both. Domestic law may, in the absence of agreement between these parties, lay down the conditions as to the sharing of this remuneration.

Article 13

Broadcasting organisations shall enjoy the right to authorize or prohibit:

(*a*) the rebroadcasting of their broadcasts;

(*b*) the fixation of their broadcasts;

(*c*) the reproduction:

(i) of fixations, made without their consent, of their broadcasts;

(ii) of fixations, made in accordance with the provisions of Article 15, of their broadcasts, if the reproduction is made for purposes different from those referred to in those provisions;

(*d*) the communication to the public of their television broadcasts if such communication is made in places accessible to the public against payment of an entrance fee; it shall be a matter for the domestic law of the State where protection of this right is claimed to determine the conditions under which it may be exercised.

Article 14

The term of protection to be granted under this Convention shall last at least until the end of a period of 20 years computed from the end of the year in which:

(*a*) the fixation was made—for phonograms and for performances incorporated therein;

(*b*) the performance took place—for performances not incorporated in phonograms;

(*c*) the broadcast took place—for broadcasts.

Article 15

1. Any Contracting State may, in its domestic laws and regulations, provide for exceptions to the protection guaranteed by this Convention as regards:

(*a*) private use;

(*b*) use of short excerpts in connection with the reporting of current events;

(*c*) ephemeral fixation by a broadcasting organisation by means of its own facilities and for its own broadcasts;

(*d*) use solely for the purposes of teaching or scientific research.

2. Irrespective of paragraph 1 of this Article, any Contracting State may, in its domestic laws and regulations, provide for the same kinds of limitations with regard to the protection of performers, producers of phonograms and broadcasting organisations, as it provides for, in its domestic laws and regulations, in connection with the protection of copyright in literary and artistic works. However, compulsory licenses may be provided for only to the extent to which they are compatible with this Convention.

Article 16

1. Any State, upon becoming party to this Convention, shall be bound by all the obligations and shall enjoy all the benefits thereof. However, a State may at any time, in a notification deposited with the Secretary-General of the United Nations, declare that:

(*a*) as regards Article 12:

(i) it will not apply the provisions of that Article;

(ii) it will not apply the provisions of that Article in respect of certain uses;

(iii) as regards phonograms the producer of which is not a national of another Contracting State, it will not apply that Article;

(iv) as regards phonograms the producer of which is a national of another Contracting State, it will limit the protection provided for by that Article to the extent to which, and to the term for which the latter State grants protection to phonograms first fixed by a national of the State making the declaration; however, the fact that the Contracting State of which the producer is a national does not grant the protection to the same beneficiary or beneficiaries as the State making the declaration shall not be considered as a difference in the extent of the protection;

(*b*) as regards Article 13, it will not apply item (*d*) of that Article; if a Contracting State makes such a declaration, the other Contracting States shall not be obliged to grant the right referred to in Article 13, item (*d*), to broadcasting organizations whose headquarters are in that State.

2. If the notification referred to in paragraph 1 of this Article is made after the date of the deposit of the instrument of ratification, acceptance or accession, the declaration will become effective six months after it has been deposited.

Article 17

Any State which, on October 26, 1961, grants protection to producers of phonograms solely on the basis of the criterion of fixation may, by a notification deposited with the Secretary-General of the United Nations at the tine of ratification, acceptance or accession, declare that it will apply, for the purposes of Article 5, the criterion of fixation alone and, for the purposes of paragraph 1 (*a*) (iii) and (iv) of Article 16, the criterion of fixation instead of the criterion of nationality.

Article 18

Any State which has deposited a notification under paragraph 3 of Article 5, paragraph 2 of Article 6, paragraph 1 of Article 16 or Article 17, may, by a further notification deposited with the Secretary-General of the United Nations, reduce its scope or withdraw it.

Article 19

Notwithstanding anything in this Convention, once a performer has consented to the incorporation of his performance in a visual or audio-visual fixation, Article 7 shall have no further application.

Article 20

1. This Convention shall not prejudice rights acquired in any Contracting State before the date of coming into force of this Convention for that State.

2. No Contracting State shall be bound to apply the provisions of this Convention to performances or broadcasts which took place, or to phonograms which were fixed, before the date of coming into force of this Convention for that State.

Article 21

The protection provided for in this Convention shall not prejudice any protection otherwise secured to performers, producers of phonograms and broadcasting organisations.

Article 22

Contracting States reserve the right to enter into special agreements among themselves in so far as such agreements grant to performers, producers of phonograms or broadcasting organisations more extensive rights than those granted by this Convention or contain other provisions not contrary to this Convention.

Article 23

This Convention shall be deposited with the Secretary-General of the United Nations. It shall be open until June 30, 1962 for signature by any State invited to the Diplomatic Conference on the International Protection of Performers, Producers of Phonograms and Broadcasting Organisations which is a party to the Universal Copyright Convention or a member of the International Union for the Protection of Literary and Artistic Works.

Article 24

1. This Convention shall be subject to ratification or acceptance by the signatory States.
2. This Convention shall be open for accession by any State invited to the Conference referred to in Article 23, and by any State Member of the United Nations, provided that in either case such State is a party to the Universal Copyright Convention or a member of the International Union for the Protection of Literary and Artistic Works.
3. Ratification, acceptance or accession shall be effected by the deposit of an instrument to that effect with the Secretary-General of the United Nations.

Article 25

1. This Convention shall come into force three months after the date of deposit of the sixth instrument of ratification, acceptance or accession.

2. Subsequently, this Convention shall come into force in respect of each state three months after the date of deposit of its instrument of ratification, acceptance or accession.

Article 26

1. Each Contracting State undertakes to adopt, in accordance with its Constitution, the measures necessary to ensure the application of this Convention.

2. At the time of deposit of its instrument of ratification, acceptance or accession, each State must be in a position under its domestic law to give effect to the terms of this Convention.

Article 27

Any State may, at the time of ratification, acceptance or accession, or at any time thereafter, declare by notification addressed to the Secretary-General of the United Nations that this Convention shall extend to all or any of the territories for whose international relations it is responsible, provided that the Universal Copyright Convention or the International Convention for the Protection of Literary and Artistic Works applies to the territory or territories concerned. This notification shall take effect three months after the date of its receipt.

2. The notification referred to in paragraph 3 of Article 5, paragraph 2 of Article 6, paragraph 1 of Article 16 and Articles 17 and 18, may be extended to cover all or any of the territories referred to in paragraph 1 of this Article.

Article 28

1. Any Contracting State may denounce this Convention, on its own behalf, or on behalf of all or any of the territories referred to in Article 27.

2. The denunciation shall be effected by a notification addressed to the Secretary-General of the United Nations and shall take effect 12 months after the date of receipt of the notification.

3. The right of denunciation shall not be exercised by a Contracting State before the expiry of a period of five years from the date on which the Convention came into force with respect to that State.

4. A Contracting State shall cease to be a party to this Convention from that time when it is neither a party to the Universal Copyright Convention nor a member of the International Union for the Protection of Literary and Artistic Works.

5. This Convention shall cease to apply to any territory referred to in Article 27 from that time when neither the Universal Copyright Convention nor the International Convention for the Protection of Literary and Artistic Works applies to that territory.

Article 29

After this Convention has been in force for five years, any Contracting State may, by notification addressed to the Secretary-General of the United Nations, request that a conference be convened for the purpose of revising the Convention. The Secretary-General shall notify all Contracting States of this request. If, within a period of six months following the date of notification by the Secretary-General of the United Nations, not less than one half of the Contracting States notify him of their concurrence with the request, the Secretary-General shall inform the Director-General of the International Labour Office, the Director-General of the United Nations Educational, Scientific and Cultural Organization and the Director of the Bureau of the International Union for the Protection of Literary and Artistic Works, who shall convene a revision conference in co-operation with the Intergovernmental Committee provided for in Article 32.

2. The adoption of any revision of this Convention shall require an affirmative vote by two-thirds of the States attending the revision conference, provided that this majority includes two-thirds of the States which, at the time of the revision conference, are parties to the Convention.

3. In the event of adoption of a Convention revising this Convention in whole or in part, and unless the revising Convention provides otherwise:

(*a*) this Convention shall cease to be open to ratification, acceptance or accession as from the date of entry into force of the revising Convention;

(*b*) this Convention shall remain in force as regards relations between or with Contracting States which have not become parties to the revising Convention.

Article 30

Any dispute which may arise between two or more Contracting States concerning the interpretation or application of this Convention and which is not settled by negotiation shall, at the request of any one of the parties to the dispute, be referred to the International Court of Justice for decision, unless they agree to another mode of settlement.

Article 31

Without prejudice to the provisions of paragraph 3 of Article 5, paragraph 2 of Article 6, paragraph 1 of Article 16 and Article 17, no reservation may be made to this Convention.

Article 32

1. An Intergovernmental Committee is hereby established with the following duties:

(*a*) to study questions concerning the application and operation of this Convention; and

(*b*) to collect proposals and to prepare documentation for possible revision of this Convention.

2. The Committee shall consist of representatives of the Contracting States, chosen with due regard to equitable geographical distribution. The number of members shall be 6 if there are 12 Contracting States or less, 9 if there are 13 to 18 Contracting States and 12 if there are more than 18 Contracting States.

3. The Committee shall be constituted twelve months after the Convention comes into force by an election organized among the Contracting States, each of which shall have one vote, by the Director-General of the International Labour Office, the Director-General of the United Nations Educational, Scientific and Cultural Organization and the Director of the Bureau of the International Union for the Protection of Literary and Artistic Works, in accordance with rules previously approved by a majority of all Contracting States.

4. The Committee shall elect its Chairman and officers. It shall establish its own rules of procedure. These rules shall in particular provide for the future operation of the Committee and for a method of selecting its members for the future in such a way as to ensure rotation among the various Contracting States.

5. Officials of the International Labour Office, the United Nations Educational, Scientific and Cultural Organization and the Bu-

reau of the International Union for the Protection of Literary and Artistic Works, designated by the Directors-General and the Director thereof, shall constitute the Secretariat of the Committee.

6. Meetings of the Committee, which shall be convened whenever a majority of its members deems it necessary, shall be held successively at the headquarters of the International Labour Office, the United Nations Educational, Scientific and Cultural Organization and the Bureau of the International Union for the Protection of Literary and Artistic Works.

7. Expenses of members of the Committee shall be borne by their respective Governments.

Article 33

1. The present Convention is drawn up in English, French and Spanish, the three texts being equally authentic.

2. In addition, official texts of the present Convention shall be drawn up in German, Italian, and Portuguese.

Article 34

1. The Secretary-General of the United Nations shall notify the States invited to the Conference referred to in Article 23 and every State Member of the United Nations, as well as the Director-General of the International Labour Office, the Director-General of the United Nations Educational, Scientific and Cultural Organization and the Director of the Bureau of the International Union for the Protection of Literary and Artistic Works:

(*a*) of the deposit of each instrument of ratification, acceptance or accession;

(*b*) of the date of entry into force of the Convention;

(*c*) of all notifications, declarations or communications provided for in this Convention;

(*d*) if any of the situations referred to in paragraphs 4 and 5 of Article 28 arise.

2. The Secretary-General of the United Nations shall also notify the Director-General of the International Labour Office, the Director-General of the United Nations Educational, Scientific and Cultural Organization and the Director of the Bureau of the International Union for the Protection of Literary and Artistic Works of the requests communicated to him in accordance with Article 29, as well as of any communication received from the Contracting States concerning the revision of the Convention.

In faith whereof, the undersigned, being duly authorized thereto, have signed this Convention.

Done at Rome, this twenty-sixth day of October 1961, in a single copy in the English, French and Spanish languages. Certified true copies shall be delivered by the Secretary-General of the United Nations to all the States invited to the Conference referred to in Article 23 and to every State Member of the United Nations, as well as to the Director-General of the International Labour Office, the Director-General of the United Nations Educational, Scientific and Cultural Organization and the Director of the Bureau of the International Union for the Protection of Literary and Artistic Works.

4. Convention for the Protection of Producers of Phonograms Against Unauthorized Duplication of Their Phonograms (Geneva Convention)

October 29, 1971

The Convention for the Protection of Producers of Phonograms Against Unauthorized Duplication of Their Phonograms, known as the Geneva Convention, was opened for signature on October 29, 1971. Its purpose was to fight the ever-growing practice of record and tape piracy spawned by new reproductive technologies. Although the International Convention for the Protection of Performers, Producers of Phonograms and Broadcasting Organisations (Rome Convention) already covered the same ground, many states that did not recognize neighboring rights, e.g., the United States, refused to adhere to the Rome Convention.

Unlike the Rome Convention, the Geneva Convention does not create substantive rights in the protection of phonograms. As long as phonograms are protected, the mode of protection is left to domestic law: whether by copyright, unfair competition, or by penal sanctions (Art. 3). Producers of phonograms who are nationals of other contracting states can claim protection under the convention (Art. 2).

The Convention allows a contracting state to require a notice on all publicly distributed copies of the phonogram. Such notice shall consist of the symbol "P" accompanied by the year date of first publication and the name of the producer. It must be placed in such manner as to give reasonable notice of a claim of protection (Art. 5).

The duration of protection given to a phonogram is left to domestic law. However, if domestic law prescribes a specific duration for the protection, that duration shall not be less than 20 years from the end either of the year in which the sounds embodied in the phonogram were first fixed or the year in which the phonogram was first published (Art. 4).

As of January 1, 1990, the following 43 states were party to the Geneva Convention:

Argentina	Federal Republic of Germany	Norway
Australia	Guatemala	Panama
Austria	Honduras	Paraguay
Barbados	Holy See	Peru
Brazil	Hungary	Republic of Korea
Burkina Faso	India	Spain
Chile	Israel	Sweden
Costa Rica	Italy	Trinidad and Tobago
Czechoslovakia	Japan	United Kingdom
Denmark	Kenya	United States of America
Ecuador	Luxembourg	Uruguay
Egypt	Mexico	Venezuela
El Salvador	Monaco	Zaire
Fiji	New Zealand	
Finland		
France		

Convention for the Protection of Producers of Phonograms Against Unauthorized Duplication of Their Phonograms (Geneva Convention)

Article 1

For the purposes of this Convention:

(*a*) "phonogram" means any exclusively aural fixation of sounds of a performance or of other sounds;

(*b*) "producer of phonograms" means the person who, or the legal entity which, first fixes the sounds of a performance or other sounds;

(*c*) "duplicate" means an article which contains sounds taken directly or indirectly from a phonogram and which embodies all or a substantial part of the sounds fixed in that phonogram;

(*d*) "distribution to the public" means any act by which duplicates of a phonogram are offered, directly or indirectly, to the general public or any section thereof.

Article 2

Each Contracting State shall protect producers of phonograms who are nationals of other Contracting States against the making of duplicates without the consent of the producer and against the importation of such duplicates, provided that any such making or importation is for the purpose of distribution to the public, and against the distribution of such duplicates to the public.

Article 3

The means by which this Convention is implemented shall be a matter for the domestic law of each Contracting State and shall include one or more of the following: protection by means of the grant of a copyright or other specific right; protection by means of the law relating to unfair competition; protection by means of penal sanctions.

Source: Reprinted from *Copyright Laws and Treaties of the World,* 15 Supplement, © 1972, BNA Books, Washington, D.C.

Article 4

The duration of the protection given shall be a matter for the domestic law of each Contracting State. However, if the domestic law prescribes a specific duration for the protection, that duration shall not be less than 20 years from the end either of the year in which the sounds embodied in the phonogram were first fixed or the year in which the phonogram was first published.

Article 5

If, as a condition of protecting the producers of phonograms, a Contracting State, under its domestic law, requires compliance with formalities, these shall be considered as fulfilled if all the authorized duplicates of the phonogram distributed to the public or their containers bear a notice consisting of the symbol P, accompanied by the year date of the first publication, placed in such manner as to give reasonable notice of claim of protection; and, if the duplicates or their containers do not identify the producer, his successor in title or the exclusive licensee (by carrying his name, trademark or other appropriate designation), the notice shall also include the name of the producer, his successor in title or the exclusive licensee.

Article 6

Any Contracting State which affords protection by means of copyright or other specific right, or protection by means of penal sanctions, may in its domestic law provide, with regard to the protection of producers of phonograms, the same kinds of limitations as are permitted with respect to the protection of authors of literary and artistic works. However, no compulsory licenses may be permitted unless all of the following conditions are met:

(*a*) the duplication is for use solely for the purpose of teaching or scientific research;

(*b*) the license shall be valid for duplication only within the territory of the Contracting State whose competent authority has granted the license and shall not extend to the export of duplicates;

(*c*) the duplication made under the license gives rise to an equitable remuneration fixed by the said authority taking into account, *inter alia*, the number of duplicates which will be made.

Article 7

(1) This Convention shall in no way be interpreted to limit or prejudice the protection otherwise secured to authors, to performers, to producers of phonograms or to broadcasting organizations under any domestic law or international agreement.

(2) It shall be a matter for the domestic law of each Contracting State to determine the extent, if any, to which performers whose performances are fixed in a phonogram are entitled to enjoy protection and the conditions for enjoying any such protection.

(3) No Contracting State shall be required to apply the provisions of this Convention to any phonogram fixed before this Convention entered into force with respect to that State.

(4) Any Contracting State which, on October 29, 1971, affords protection to producers of phonograms solely on the basis of the place of first fixation may, by a notification deposited with the Director General of the World Intellectual Property Organization, declare that it will apply this criterion instead of the criterion of the nationality of the producer.

Article 8

(1) The International Bureau of the World Intellectual Property Organization shall assemble and publish information concerning the protection of phonograms. Each Contracting State shall promptly communicate to the International Bureau all new laws and official texts on this subject.

(2) The International Bureau shall, on request, furnish information to any Contracting State on matters concerning this Convention, and shall conduct studies and provide services designed to facilitate the protection provided for therein.

(3) The International Bureau shall exercise the functions enumerated in paragraphs (1) and (2) above in cooperation, for matters within their respective competence, with the United Nations Educational, Scientific and Cultural Organization and the International Labour Organization.

Article 9

(1) This Convention shall be deposited with the Secretary-General of the United Nations. It shall be open until April 30, 1972, for signature by any State that is a member of the United Nations, any of the Specialized Agencies brought into relationship with the United

Nations, or the International Atomic Energy Agency, or is a party to the Statute of the International Court of Justice.

(2) This Convention shall be subject to ratification or acceptance by the signatory States. It shall be open for accession by any State referred to in paragraph (1) of this Article.

(3) Instruments of ratification, acceptance or accession shall be deposited with the Secretary-General of the United Nations.

(4) It is understood that, at the time a State becomes bound by this Convention, it will be in a position in accordance with its domestic law to give effect to the provisions of the Convention.

Article 10

No reservations to this Convention are permitted.

Article 11

(1) This Convention shall enter into force three months after deposit of the fifth instrument of ratification, acceptance or accession.

(2) For each State ratifying, accepting or acceding to this Convention after the deposit of the fifth instrument of ratification, acceptance or accession, the Convention shall enter into force three months after the date on which the Director General of the World Intellectual Property Organization informs the States, in accordance with Article 13, paragraph (4), of the deposit of its instrument.

(3) Any State may, at the time of ratification, acceptance or accession or at any later date, declare by notification addressed to the Secretary-General of the United Nations that this Convention shall apply to all or any one of the territories for whose international affairs it is responsible. This notification will take effect three months after the date on which it is received.

(4) However, the preceding paragraph may in no way be understood as implying the recognition or tacit acceptance by a Contracting State of the factual situation concerning a territory to which this Convention is made applicable by another Contracting State by virtue of the said paragraph.

Article 12

(1) Any Contracting State may denounce this Convention, on its own behalf or on behalf of any of the territories referred to in Article 11, paragraph (3), by written notification addressed to the Secretary-General of the United Nations.

(2) Denunciation shall take effect twelve months after the date on which the Secretary-General of the United Nations has received the notification.

Article 13

(1) This Convention shall be signed in a single copy in English, French, Russian and Spanish, the four texts being equally authentic.

(2) Official texts shall be established by the Director General of the World Intellectual Property Organization, after consultation with the interested Governments, in the Arabic, Dutch, German, Italian and Portuguese languages.

(3) The Secretary-General of the United Nations shall notify the Director General of the World Intellectual Property Organization, the Director-General of the United Nations Educational, Scientific and Cultural Organization and the Director-General of the International Labour Office of:

(*a*) signatures to this Convention;
(*b*) the deposit of instruments of ratification, acceptance or accession;
(c) the date of entry into force of this Convention;
(d) any declaration notified pursuant to Article 11, paragraph (3);
(*e*) the receipt of notifications of denunciation.

(4) The Director General of the World Intellectual Property Organization shall inform the States referred to in Article 9, paragraph (1), of the notifications received pursuant to the preceding paragraph and of any declarations made under Article 7, paragraph (4). He shall also notify the Director-General of the United Nations Educational, Scientific and Cultural Organization and the Director-General of the International Labour Office of such declarations.

(5) The Secretary-General of the United Nations shall transmit two certified copies of this Convention to the States referred to in Article 9, paragraph (1).

In witness whereof, the undersigned, being duly authorized, have signed this Convention.

Done at Geneva, this twenty-ninth day of October, 1971.

5. Convention Relating to the Distribution of Programme-Carrying Signals Transmitted by Satellite (Brussels Convention)

Signed at Brussels on May 21, 1974

The Convention Relating to the Distribution of Programme-Carrying Signals Transmitted by Satellite, known as the Brussels Convention, was signed on May 21, 1974. The purpose of the Convention is to combat the misappropriation of satellite signals on an international level. The need for a special international agreement covering satellite transmission was apparent from its inadequate treatment in the major international copyright conventions. Both the UCC (Art. 4 *bis*) and the Berne Convention (Art. 11 *bis*) provide for an exclusive right to broadcast, but it is unclear whether these conventions cover satellite transmissions.

The Convention creates no new rights for programs transmitted by satellite. Implementation of the treaty is left to the contracting states, which agree to provide adequate protection against satellite signal piracy (Art. 2).

The Convention is limited in scope, focusing on the unauthorized distribution of signals, not their unauthorized reception. It is designed to prevent the distribution on or from its territory of any programme-carrying signal by any distributor for whom the signal emitted to or passing through the satellite was not intended (Art. 2). Thus, the private reception of signals for private use is not a violation of the Convention. Moreover, the signal is the object of protection, not the content of the material sent by the signal. The Convention is designed to protect the emitter or carrier, not the copyright owner of the material transmitted by satellite.

As of January 1, 1990, the following 12 states were party to the Brussels Convention:

- Austria
- Federal Republic of Germany
- Italy
- Kenya
- Mexico
- Morocco
- Nicaragua
- Panama
- Peru
- Soviet Union
- United States of America
- Yugoslavia

Convention Relating to the Distribution of Programme-Carrying Signals Transmitted by Satellite (Brussels Convention)

Article 1

For the purposes of this Convention:

(i) "signal" is an electronically-generated carrier capable of transmitting programmes;
(ii) "programme" is a body of live or recorded material consisting of images, sounds or both, embodied in signals emitted for the purpose of ultimate distribution;
(iii) "satellite" is any device in extraterrestrial space capable of transmitting signals;
(iv) "emitted signal" or "signal emitted" is any programme-carrying signal that goes to or passes through a satellite;
(v) "derived signal" is a signal obtained by modifying the technical characteristics of the emitted signal, whether or not there have been one or more intervening fixations;
(vi) "originating organization" is the person or legal entity that decides what programme the emitted signals will carry;
(vii) "distributor" is the person or legal entity that decides that the transmission of the derived signals to the general public or any section thereof should take place;
(viii) "distribution" is the operation by which a distributor transmits derived signals to the general public or any section thereof.

Article 2

(1) Each Contracting State undertakes to take adequate measures to prevent the distribution on or from its territory of any programme-carrying signal by any distributor for whom the signal emitted to or passing through the satellite is not intended. This obligation shall apply where the originating organization is a na-

---

Source: Reprinted from *Copyright Laws and Treaties of the World,* 17 Supplement,

tional of another Contracting State and where the signal distributed is a derived signal.

(2) In any Contracting State in which the application of the measures referred to in paragraph (1) is limited in time, the duration thereof shall be fixed by its domestic law. The Secretary-General of the United Nations shall be notified in writing of such duration at the time of ratification, acceptance or accession, or if the domestic law comes into force or is changed thereafter, within six months of the coming into force of that law or of its modifications.

(3) The obligation provided for in paragraph (1) shall not apply to the distribution of derived signals taken from signals which have already been distributed by a distributor for whom the emitted signals were intended.

Article 3

This Convention shall not apply where the signals emitted by or on behalf of the originating organization are intended for direct reception from the satellite by the general public.

Article 4

No Contracting State shall be required to apply the measures referred to in Article 2(1) where the signal distributed on its territory by a distributor for whom the emitted signal is not intended

(i) carries short excerpts of the programme carried by the emitted signal, consisting of reports of current events, but only to the extent justified by the informatory purpose of such excerpts, or

(ii) carries, as quotations, short excerpts of the programme carried by the emitted signals, provided that such quotations are compatible with fair practice and are justified by the informatory purpose of such quotations, or

(iii) carries, where the said territory is that of a Contracting State regarded as a developing country in conformity with the established practice of the General Assembly of the United Nations, a programme carried by the emitted signal, provided that the distribution is solely for the purpose of teaching, including teaching in the framework of adult education, or scientific research.

Article 5

No Contracting State shall be required to apply this Convention with respect to any signal emitted before this Convention entered into force for that State.

Article 6

This Convention shall in no way be interpreted to limit or prejudice the protection secured to authors, performers, producers of phonograms, or broadcasting organizations, under any domestic law or international agreement.

Article 7

This Convention shall in no way be interpreted as limiting the right of any Contracting State to apply its domestic law in order to prevent abuses of monopoly.

Article 8

(1) Subject to paragraphs (2) and (3), no reservation to this Convention shall be permitted.

(2) Any Contracting State whose domestic law, on May 21, 1974, so provides may, by a written notification deposited with the Secretary-General of the United Nations, declare that, for its purposes, the words "where the originating organization is a national of another Contracting State" appearing in Article 2(1) shall be considered as if they were replaced by the words "where the signal is emitted from the territory of another Contracting State."

(3)(a) Any Contracting State which, on May 21, 1974, limits or denies protection with respect to the distribution of programme-carrying signals by means of wires, cable or other similar communications channels to subscribing members of the public may, by a written notification deposited with the Secretary-General of the United Nations, declare that, to the extent that and as long as its domestic law limits or denies protection, it will not apply this Convention to such distributions.

(b) Any State that has deposited a notification in accordance with subparagraph (a) shall notify the Secretary-General of the United Nations in writing, within six months of their coming into force, of any changes in its domestic law whereby the reservation under that subparagraph becomes inapplicable or more limited in scope.

Article 9

(1) This Convention shall be deposited with the Secretary-General of the United Nations. It shall be open until March 31, 1975, for signature by any State that is a member of the United Nations, any of the Specialized Agencies brought into relationship with the United Nations, or the International Atomic Energy Agency, or is a party to the Statute of the International Court of Justice.

(2) This Convention shall be subject to ratification or acceptance by the signatory States. It shall be open for accession by any State referred to in paragraph (1).

(3) Instruments of ratification, acceptance or accession shall be deposited with the Secretary-General of the United Nations.

(4) It is understood that, at the time a State becomes bound by this Convention, it will be in a position in accordance with its domestic law to give effect to the provisions of the Convention.

Article 10

(1) This Convention shall enter into force three months after the deposit of the fifth instrument of ratification, acceptance or accession.

(2) For each State ratifying, accepting or acceding to this Convention after the deposit of the fifth instrument of ratification, acceptance or accession, this Convention shall enter into force three months after the deposit of its instrument.

Article 11

(1) Any Contracting State may denounce this Convention by written notification deposited with the Secretary-General of the United Nations.

(2) Denunciation shall take effect twelve months after the date on which the notification referred to in paragraph (1) is received.

Article 12

(1) This Convention shall be signed in a single copy in English, French, Russian and Spanish, the four texts being equally authentic.

(2) Official texts shall be established by the Director-General of the United Nations Educational, Scientific and Cultural Organization and the Director General of the World Intellectual Property Organization, after consultation with the interested Governments, in the Arabic, Dutch, German, Italian and Portuguese languages.

(3) The Secretary-General of the United Nations shall notify the States referred to in Article 9(1), as well as the Director-General of the United Nations Educational, Scientific and Cultural Organization, the Director General of the World Intellectual Property Organization, the Director-General of the International Labour Office and the Secretary-General of the International Telecommunication Union, of

(i) signatures to this Convention;
(ii) the deposit of instruments of ratification, acceptance or accession;
(iii) the date of entry into force of this Convention under Article 10(1);
(iv) the deposit of any notification relating to Article 2(2) or Article 8(2) or (3), together with its text;
(v) the receipt of notifications of denunciation.

(4) The Secretary-General of the United Nations shall transmit two certified copies of this Convention to all States referred to in Article 9(1).

In witness whereof, the undersigned, being duly authorized, have signed this Convention.

Done at Brussels, this twenty-first day of May, 1974.

6. Treaty on the International Registration of Audiovisual Works

Done at Geneva, on April 20, 1989

The Treaty on the International Registration of Audiovisual Works was concluded at Geneva on April 20, 1989. **As of January 1, 1990, it had not entered into force.** It has been signed by 17 countries.

The Treaty establishes an International Register for audiovisual works, administered by WIPO's International Bureau, for the purpose of recording statements concerning rights in such works (Art. 3 para. 1). The register was established primarily to keep track of who owns what rights (reproduction, distribution, and performance) on a particular work, where these rights are effective, and what limitations attach to these rights, e.g., tax liens or bank loans.

The registration of any statement in the International Register is based on an application filed to that effect as prescribed by the regulations under the Treaty[1] (Art. 3 para. 4).

Beneficiaries of the Treaty who may file applications may be nationals of a contracting state, those having a domicile or having an habitual residence in a contracting state, or those who have a real and effective commercial establishment in a contracting state (Art. 3 para. 5).

As of January 1, 1990, the following 17 states had signed the Treaty:

Austria	Canada
Brazil	Chile
Burkina Faso	Egypt

[1]*See Regulations Under the Treaty on the International Registration of Audiovisual Works*, COPYRIGHT Text 1-01 (June 1989).

France
Greece
Guinea
Hungary
India
Mexico
Philippines
Poland
Senegal
United States of America
Yugoslavia

Treaty on the International Registration of Audiovisual Works

Chapter I
Substantive Provisions

Article 1
Establishment of the Union

The States party to this Treaty (hereinafter called "the Contracting States") constitute a Union for the international registration of audiovisual works (hereinafter referred to as "the Union").

Article 2
"Audiovisual Work"

For the purposes of this Treaty, "audiovisual work" means any work that consists of a series of fixed related images, with or without accompanying sound, susceptible of being made visible and, where accompanied by sound, susceptible of being made audible.

Article 3
The International Register

(1) The International Register of Audiovisual Works (hereinafter referred to as "the International Register") is hereby established for the purpose of the registration of statements concerning audiovisual works and rights in such works, including, in particular, rights relating to their exploitation.

(2) The International Registry of Audiovisual Works (hereinafter referred to as "the International Registry") is hereby set up for the purpose of keeping the International Register. It is an administrative unit of the International Bureau of the World Intellectual Property Organization (hereinafter referred to as "the International Bureau" and "the Organization," respectively).

(3) The International Registry shall be located in Austria as

---

Source: Text courtesy of the World Intellectual Property Organization (WIPO).

long as a treaty to that effect between the Republic of Austria and the Organization is in force. Otherwise, it shall be located in Geneva.

(4) The registration of any statement in the International Register shall be based on an application filed to this effect, with the prescribed contents, in the prescribed form and subject to the payment of the prescribed fee, by a natural person or legal entity entitled to file an application.

(5)(*a*) Subject to subparagraph (*b*), the following shall be entitled to file an application:

(i) any natural person who is a national of, is domiciled in, has his habitual residence in, or has a real and effective industrial or commercial establishment in, a Contracting State;
(ii) any legal entity which is organized under the laws of, or has a real and effective industrial or commercial establishment in, a Contracting State.

(*b*) If the application concerns a registration already effected, it may also be filed by a natural person or legal entity not satisfying the conditions referred to in subparagraph (*a*).

Article 4
Legal Effect of the International Register

(1) Each Contracting State undertakes to recognize that a statement recorded in the International Register shall be considered as true until the contrary is proved, except

(i) where the statement cannot be valid under the copyright law, or any other law concerning intellectual property rights in audiovisual works, of that State, or
(ii) where the statement is contradicted by another statement recorded in the International Register.

(2) No provision of this Treaty shall be interpreted as affecting the copyright law, or any other law concerning intellectual property rights in audiovisual works, of any Contracting State or, if that State is party to the Berne Convention for the Protection of Literary and Artistic Works or any other treaty concerning intellectual property rights in audiovisual works, the rights and obligations of the said State under the said Convention or treaty.

Chapter II
Administrative Provisions

Article 5
Assembly

(1)(*a*) The Union shall have an Assembly that shall consist of the Contracting States.

(*b*) The Government of each Contracting State shall be represented by one delegate, who may be assisted by alternate delegates, advisors and experts.

(2) The expenses of each delegation shall be borne by the Government which has appointed it, except for the travel expenses and the subsistence allowance of one delegate for each Contracting State, which shall be paid from the funds of the Union.

(3)(*a*) The Assembly shall:

(i) deal with all matters concerning the maintenance and development of the Union and the implementation of this Treaty;

(ii) exercise such tasks as are specially assigned to it under this Treaty;

(iii) give directions to the Director General of the Organization (hereinafter referred to as "the Director General"), concerning the preparation for revision conferences;

(iv) review and approve the reports and activities of the Director General concerning the Union, and give him all necessary instructions concerning matters within the competence of the Union;

(v) determine the program and adopt the biennial budget of the Union, and approve its final accounts;

(vi) adopt the financial regulations of the Union;

(vii) establish, and decide from time to time the membership of, a consultative committee consisting of representatives of interested non-governmental organizations and such other committees and working groups as it deems appropriate to facilitate the work of the Union and of its organs;

(viii) control the system and amounts of the fees determined by the Director General;

(ix) determine which States other than Contracting States and which intergovernmental and non-governmental organizations shall be admitted to its meetings as observers;

(x) take any other appropriate action designed to further the objectives of the Union and perform such other functions as are appropriate under this Treaty.

(*b*)With respect to matters which are of interest also to other Unions administered by the Organization, the Assembly shall make its decisions after having heard the advice of the Coordination Committee of the Organization.

(4) A delegate may represent, and vote in the name of, one State only.

(5) Each Contracting State shall have one vote.

(6)(*a*) One-half of the Contracting States shall constitute a quorum.

(*b*) In the absence of the quorum, the Assembly may make decisions but, with the exception of the decisions concerning its own procedure, all such decisions shall take effect only if the quorum and the required majority are attained through voting by correspondence.

(7)(*a*) Subject to Article 8(2)(*b*) and Article 10(2)(*b*), the decisions of the Assembly shall require a majority of the votes cast.

(*b*) Abstentions shall not be considered as votes.

(8)(*a*) The Assembly shall meet once in every second calender year in ordinary session upon convocation by the Director General and, in the absence of exceptional circumstances, during the same period and at the same place as the General Assembly of the Organization.

(*b*) The Assembly shall meet in extraordinary session upon convocation by the Director General, either at the request of one-fourth of the Contracting States or on the Director General's own initiative.

(9) The Assembly shall adopt its own rules of procedure.

Article 6
International Bureau

(1) The International Bureau shall:

(i) perform, through the International Registry, all the tasks related to the keeping of the International Register;

(ii) provide the secretariat of revision conferences, of the Assembly, of the committees and working groups established by the Assembly, and of any other meeting convened by the Director General and dealing with matters of concern to the Union;

(iii) perform all other tasks specially assigned to it under this Treaty and the Regulations referred to in Article 8 or by the Assembly.

(2) The Director General shall be the chief executive of the Union and shall represent the Union.

(3) The Director General shall convene any committee and working group established by the Assembly and all other meetings dealing with matters of concern to the Union.

(4)(*a*) The Director General and any staff member designated by him shall participate, without the right to vote, in all meetings of the Assembly, the committees and working groups established by the Assembly, and any other meeting convened by the Director General and dealing with matters of concern to the Union.

(*b*) The Director General or a staff member designated by him shall be ex officio secretary of the Assembly, and of the committees, working groups and other meetings referred to in subparagraph (*a*).

(5)(*a*) The Director General shall, in accordance with the directions of the Assembly, make the preparations for revision conferences.

(*b*) The Director General may consult with intergovernmental and non-governmental organizations concerning the said preparations.

(*c*) The Director General and staff members designed by him shall take part, without the right to vote, in the discussions at revision conferences.

(*d*) The Director General or a staff member designated by him shall be ex officio secretary of any revision conference.

Article 7
Finances

(1) (*a*) The Union shall have a budget.

(*b*) The budget of the Union shall include the income and expenses proper to the Union, and its contribution to the budget of expenses common to the Unions administered by the Organization.

(*c*) Expenses not attributable exclusively to the Union but also to one or more other Unions administered by the Organization shall be considered as expenses common to the Unions. The share of the Union in such common expenses shall be in proportion to the interest the Union has in them.

(2) The budget of the Union shall be established with due regard to the requirements of coordination with the budgets of the other Unions administered by the Organization.

(3) The budget of the Union shall be financed from the following sources:

(i) fees due for registrations and other services rendered by the International Registry;

(ii) sale of, or royalties on, the publications of the International Registry;
(iii) donations, particularly by associations of rights holders in audiovisual works;
(iv) gifts, bequests, and subventions;
(v) rents, interests, and other miscellaneous income.

(4) The amounts of fees due to the International Registry and the prices of its publications shall be so fixed that they, together with any other income, shall be sufficient to cover the expenses connected with the administration of this Treaty.

(5) If the budget is not adopted before the beginning of a new financial period, it shall be at the same level as the budget of the previous period, as provided in the financial regulations. If the income exceeds the expenses, the difference shall be credited to a reserve fund.

(6) The Union shall have a working capital fund which shall be constituted from the income of the Union.

(7) The auditing of the accounts shall be effected by one or more of the Contracting States or by external auditors, as provided in the financial regulations. They shall be designated, with their agreement, by the Assembly.

Article 8
Regulations

(1) The Regulations adopted at the same time as this Treaty are annexed to this Treaty.

(2)(*a*) The Assembly may amend the Regulations.

(*b*) Any amendment of the Regulations shall require two-thirds of the votes cast.

(3) In the case of conflict between the provisions of this Treaty and those of the Regulations, the former shall prevail.

(4) The Regulations provide for the establishment of Administrative Instructions.

Chapter III
Revision and Amendment

Article 9
Revision of the Treaty

(1) This Treaty may be revised by a conference of the Contracting States.

(2) The convocation of any revision conference shall be decided by the Assembly.

(3) The provisions referred to in Article 10(1)(*a*) may be amended either by a revision conference or according to Article 10.

Article 10
Amendment of Certain Provisions of the Treaty

(1)(*a*) Proposals for the amendment of Article 5(6) and (8), Article 6(4) and (5) and Article 7(1) to (3) and (5) to (7) may be initiated by any Contracting State or by the Director General.

(*b*) Such proposals shall be communicated by the Director General to the Contracting States at least six months in advance of their consideration by the Assembly.

(2) (*b*) Amendments to the provisions referred to in paragraph (1) shall be adopted by the Assembly.

(*b*) Adoption shall required three-fourths of the votes cast.

(3)(*a*) Any amendment to the provisions referred to in paragraph (1) shall enter into force one month after written notifications of acceptance, effected in accordance with their respective constitutional processes, have been received by the Director General from three-fourths of the Contracting States members of the Assembly at the time the Assembly adopted the amendment.

(*b*) Any amendment to the said Articles thus accepted shall bind all the Contracting States which were Contracting States at the time the amendment was adopted by the Assembly.

(*c*) Any amendment which has been accepted and which has entered into force in accordance with subparagraph (*a*) shall bind all States which become Contracting States after the date on which the amendment was adopted by the Assembly.

Chapter IV
Final Provisions

Article 11
Becoming Party to the Treaty

(1) Any State member of the Organization may become party to this Treaty by:

(i) signature followed by the deposit of an instrument of ratification, acceptance or approval, or
(ii) the deposit of an instrument of accession.

(2) The instruments referred to in paragraph (1) shall be deposited with the Director General.

Article 12
Entry Into Force of the Treaty

(1) This Treaty shall enter into force, with respect to the first five States which have deposited their instruments of ratification, acceptance, approval or accession, three months after the date on which the fifth instrument of ratification, acceptance, approval or accession has been deposited.

(2) This Treaty shall enter into force with respect to any State not covered by paragraph (1) three months after the date on which that State has deposited its instrument of ratification, acceptance, approval or accession unless a later date has been indicated in the instrument of ratification, acceptance, approval or accession. In the latter case, this Treaty shall enter into force with respect to the said State on the date thus indicated.

Article 13
Reservations to the Treaty

(1) Subject to paragraph (2), no reservation may be made to this Treaty.

(2) Any State, upon becoming party to this Treaty, may, in a notification deposited with the Director General, declare that it will not apply the provisions of Article 4(1) in respect of statements which do not concern the exploitation of intellectual property rights in audiovisual works. Any State that has made such a declaration may, by a notification deposited with the Director General, withdraw it.

Article 14
Denunciation of the Treaty

(1) Any Contracting State may denounce this Treaty by notification addressed to the Director General.

(2) Denunciation shall take effect one year after the day on which the Director General has received the notification.

(3) The right of denouncing this Treaty provided for in paragraph (1) shall not be exercised by any Contracting State before the expiration of five years from the date on which this Treaty enters into force with respect to it.

Article 15
Signature and Languages of the Treaty

(1) This Treaty shall be signed in a single original in the English and French languages, both texts being equally authentic.

(2) Official texts shall be established by the Director General, after consultation with the interested Governments, in the Arabic, German, Italian, Japanese, Portuguese, Russian and Spanish languages, and such other languages as the Assembly may designate.

(3) This Treaty shall remain open for signature at the International Bureau until December 31, 1989.

Article 16
Depositary Functions

(1) The original of this Treaty and the Regulations shall be deposited with the Director General.

(2) The Director General shall transmit two copies, certified by him, of this Treaty and the Regulations, to the Governments of States entitled to sign this Treaty.

(3) The Director General shall register this Treaty with the Secretariat of the United Nations.

(4) The Director General shall transmit two copies, certified by him, of any amendment to this Treaty and the Regulations to the Governments of the Contracting States and, on request, to the Government of any other State.

Article 17
Notifications

The Director General shall notify the Governments of the States members of the Organization of any of the events referred to in Articles 8(2), 10(2) and (3), 11, 12, 13 and 14.

7. Treaty on Intellectual Property in Respect of Integrated Circuits

Done at Washington D.C., on May 26, 1989

The Treaty on Intellectual Property in Respect of Integrated Circuits was done at Washington, D.C., on May 26, 1989. **As of January 1, 1990, it had not entered into force.** The Treaty was prepared in response to laws enacted in several countries—such as the United States' Semiconductor Chip Protection Act of 1984—that provide protection for layout designs of integrated circuits (Art. 2), or "mask works" as they are called under U.S. law. Japan and members of the European Community also have enacted similar laws, which confer *sui generis* protection on integrated circuits.

The Treaty requires the contracting parties to confer protection on layout-designs (topographies) in accordance with its provisions. (Art. 3 para. 1). This obligation applies only to layout-designs that are original, in the sense that they are the result of their creator's own intellectual effort and are not commonplace (Art. 3 para. 2).

The contracting parties are given much flexibility in implementing treaty obligations. They may do so through special laws on layout-designs or through their laws on copyright, patent, utility model, industrial designs, unfair competition or any other law or a combination of any of those laws (Art. 4). Protection must be conferred on the basis of national treatment (Art. 5).

Article 6 sets forth the scope of protection that the contracting parties must provide for layout-designs. The act of reproducing the original aspects of a protected layout-design shall be deemed unlawful (Art. 6 para. 1), except when the act of reproduction is performed for the sole purpose of evaluation, analysis, research, or teaching (Art. 6 para. 2). The Treaty allows member states to provide for nonvoluntary licenses in their national laws (Art. 6 para. 3). Member states may exonerate the innocent infringer in their national laws (Art. 6 para. 4). Under Article 7, contracting states may require registration as a prerequisite for protection. Protection shall last at least eight years (Art. 8).

The contracting parties of the Treaty constitute a union (Art. 1) that shall have an assembly consisting of the member states (Art. 9). The International Bureau of WIPO performs the administrative tasks concerning the union as well as any tasks specially assigned to it by the assembly (Art. 10).

Article 14 contains provisions on dispute settlement whereby contracting parties may request consultations with each other as to disputes arising out of the interpretation or implementation of the Treaty. If a dispute cannot be resolved amicably through consultations within a reasonable period of time, the Assembly, at the written request of either party, convenes a panel of three members to examine the matter.

The United States and Japan, by far the world's largest producers of integrated circuits, have refused to sign the Treaty. Their objections have focused on the broad compulsory licensing provisions, the short term of protection, the lack of compensation for innocent infringement, the failure to adequately address the issue of importation of products that contain infringing chips, and the dispute-resolution process that they consider to be too "politicized."

As of January 1, 1990, the following six states had signed the treaty:

Egypt
Ghana
Guatemala
Liberia
Yugoslavia
Zambia

Treaty on Intellectual Property in Respect of Integrated Circuits

Article 1
Establishment of a Union

The Contracting Parties constitute themselves into a Union for the purposes of this Treaty.

Article 2
Definitions

For the purposes of this Treaty:

(i) "integrated circuit" means a product, in its final form or an intermediate form, in which the elements, at least one of which is an active element, and some or all of the interconnections are integrally formed in and/or on a piece of material and which is intended to perform an electronic function,

(ii) "layout-design (topography)" means the three-dimensional disposition, however expressed, of the elements, at least one of which is an active element, and of some or all of the interconnections of an integrated circuit, or such a three-dimensional disposition prepared for an integrated circuit intended for manufacture,

(iii) "holder of the right" means the natural person who, or the legal entity which, according to the applicable law, is to be regarded as the beneficiary of the protection referred to in Article 6,

(iv) "protected layout-design (topography)" means a layout-design (topography) in respect of which the conditions of protection referred to in this Treaty are fulfilled,

(v) "Contracting Party" means a State, or an Intergovernmental Organization meeting the requirements of item (x), party to this Treaty,

(vi) "territory of a Contracting Party" means, where the Contracting Party is a State, the territory of that State, and where the Contracting Party is an Intergovernmental Or-

---

Source: Text courtesy of the World Intellectual Property Organization (WIPO).

ganization, the territory in which the constituting treaty of that Intergovernmental Organization applies,

(vii) "Union" means the Union referred to in Article 1,

(viii) "Assembly" means the Assembly referred to in Article 9,

(ix) "Director General" means the Director General of the World Intellectual Property Organization,

(x) "Intergovernmental Organization" means an organization constituted by, and composed of, States of any region of the world, which has competence in respect of matters governed by this Treaty, has its own legislation providing for intellectual property protection in respect of layout-designs (topographies) and binding on all its member States, and has been duly authorized, in accordance with its internal procedures, to sign, ratify, accept, approve or accede to this Treaty.

Article 3
The Subject Matter of the Treaty

(1)(*a*) Each Contracting Party shall have the obligation to secure, throughout its territory, intellectual property protection in respect of layout-designs (topographies) in accordance with this Treaty. It shall, in particular, secure adequate measures to ensure the prevention of acts considered unlawful under Article 6 and appropriate legal remedies where such acts have been committed.

(*b*) The right of the holder of the right in respect of an integrated circuit applies whether or not the integrated circuit is incorporated in an article.

(*c*) Notwithstanding Article 2(i), any Contracting Party whose law limits the protection of layout-designs (topographies) to layout-designs (topographies) of semi-conductor integrated circuits shall be free to apply that limitation as long as its law contains such limitation.

(2)(*a*) The obligation referred to in paragraph (1)(*a*) shall apply to layout-designs (topographies) that are original in the sense that they are the result of their creators' own intellectual effort and are not commonplace among creators of layout-designs (topographies) and manufacturers of integrated circuits at the time of their creation.

(*b*) A layout-design (topography) that consists of a combination of elements and interconnections that are commonplace shall be protected only if the combination, taken as a whole, fulfills the conditions referred to in subparagraph (*a*).

Article 4
The Legal Form of the Protection

Each Contracting Party shall be free to implement its obligations under this Treaty through a special law on layout-designs (topographies) or its law on copyright, patents, utility models, industrial designs, unfair competition or any other law or a combination of any of those laws.

Article 5
National Treatment

(1) Subject to compliance with its obligation referred to in Article 3(1)(*a*), each Contracting Party shall, in respect of the intellectual property protection of layout-designs (topographies), accord, within its territory.

(i) to natural persons who are nationals of, or are domiciled in the territory of, any of the other Contracting Parties, and
(ii) to legal entities which or natural persons who, in the territory of any of the other Contracting Parties, have a real and effective establishment for the creation of layout-designs (topographies) or the production of integrated circuits,

the same treatment that it accords to its own nationals.

(2) Notwithstanding paragraph (1), any Contracting Party is free not to apply national treatment as far as any obligations to appoint an agent or to designate an address for service are concerned or as far as the special rules applicable to foreigners in court proceedings are concerned.

(3) Where the Contracting Party is an Intergovernmental Organization, "nationals" in paragraph (1) means nationals of any of the States members of that Organization.

Article 6
The Scope of the Protection

(1)(*a*) Any Contracting Party shall consider unlawful the following acts if performed without the authorization of the holder of the right:

(i) the act of reproducing, whether by incorporation in an integrated circuit or otherwise, a protected layout-design (topography) in its entirety or any part thereof, except the act of reproducing any part that does not comply with the requirement of originality referred to in Article 3(2),

(ii) the act of importing, selling or otherwise distributing for commercial purposes a protected layout-design (topography) or an integrated circuit in which a protected layout-design (topography) is incorporated.

(*b*) Any Contracting Party shall be free to consider unlawful also acts other than those specified in subparagraph (*a*) if performed without the authorization of the holder of the right.

(2)(*a*) Notwithstanding paragraph (1), no Contracting Party shall consider unlawful the performance, without the authorization of the holder of the right, of the act of reproduction referred to in paragraph (1)(*a*)(i) where that act is performed by a third party for private purposes or for the sole purpose of evaluation, analysis, research or teaching.

(*b*) Where the third party referred to in subparagraph (*a*), on the basis of evaluation or analysis of the protected layout-design (topography) ("the first layout-design (topography)"), creates a layout-design (topography) complying with the requirement of originality referred to in Article 3(2) ("the second layout-design (topography)"), that third party may incorporate the second layout-design (topography) in an integrated circuit or perform any of the acts referred to in paragraph (1) in respect of the second layout-design (topography) without being regarded as infringing the rights of the holder of the right in the first layout-design (topography).

(*c*) The holder of the right may not exercise his right in respect of an identical original layout-design (topography) that was independently created by a third party.

(3)(*a*) Notwithstanding paragraph (1), any Contracting Party may, in its legislation, provide for the possibility of its executive or judicial authority granting a non-exclusive license, in circumstances that are not ordinary, for the performance of any of the acts referred to in paragraph (1) by a third party without the authorization of the holder of the right ("non-voluntary license"), after unsuccessful efforts, made by the said third party in line with normal commercial practices, to obtain such authorization, where the granting of the non-voluntary license is found, by the granting authority, to be necessary to safeguard a national purpose deemed to be vital by that authority; the non-voluntary license shall be available for exploitation only in the territory of that country and shall be subject to the payment of an equitable remuneration by the third party to the holder of the right.

(*b*) The provisions of this Treaty shall not affect the freedom of any Contracting Party to apply measures, including the granting, after a formal proceeding by its executive or judicial authority, of a non-voluntary license, in application of its laws in order to secure free competition and to prevent abuses by the holder of the right.

(*c*) The granting of any non-voluntary license referred to in subparagraph (*a*) or subparagraph (*b*) shall be subject to judicial review. Any non-voluntary license referred to in subparagraph (*a*) shall be revoked when the conditions referred to in that subparagraph cease to exist.

(4) Notwithstanding paragraph (1)(*a*)(ii), no Contracting Party shall be obliged to consider unlawful the performance of any of the acts referred to in that paragraph in respect of an integrated circuit incorporating an unlawfully reproduced layout-design (topography) where the person performing or ordering such acts did not know and had no reasonable ground to know, when acquiring the said integrated circuit, that it incorporates an unlawfully reproduced layout-design (topography).

(5) Notwithstanding paragraph (1)(*a*)(ii), any Contracting Party may consider lawful the performance, without the authorization of the holder of the right, of any of the acts referred to in that paragraph where the act is performed in respect of a protected layout-design (topography), or in respect of an integrated circuit in which such a layout-design (topography) is incorporated, that has been put on the market by, or with the consent of, the holder of the right.

Article 7
Exploitation; Registration, Disclosure

(1) Any Contracting Party shall be free not to protect a layout-design (topography) until it has been ordinarily commercially exploited, separately or as incorporated in an integrated circuit, somewhere in the world.

(2)(*a*) Any Contracting Party shall be free not to protect a layout-design (topography) until the layout-design (topography) has been the subject of an application for registration, filed in due form with the competent public authority, or of a registration with that authority; it may be required that the application be accompanied by the filing of a copy or drawing of the layout-design (topography) and, where the integrated circuit has been commercially exploited, of a sample of that integrated circuit, along with information defining the electronic function which the integrated circuit is intended to perform; however, the applicant may exclude such parts of the copy or drawing that relate to the manner of manufacture of the integrated circuit, provided that the parts submitted are sufficient to allow the identification of the layout-design (topography).

(*b*) Where the filing of an application for registration according to subparagraph (*a*) is required, the Contracting Party may require that such filing be effected within a certain period of time from the date on which the holder of the right first exploits ordinarily commercially anywhere in the world the layout-design (topography) of an integrated circuit; such period shall not be less than two years counted from the said date.

(*c*) Registration under subparagraph (*a*) may be subject to the payment of a fee.

Article 8
The Duration of the Protection

Protection shall last at least eight years.

Article 9
Assembly

(1)(*a*) The Union shall have an Assembly consisting of the Contracting Parties.

(*b*) Each Contracting Party shall be represented by one delegate who may be assisted by alternate delegates, advisors and experts.

(*c*) Subject to subparagraph (*d*), the expenses of each delegation shall be borne by the Contracting Party that has appointed the delegation.

(*d*) The Assembly may ask the World Intellectual Property Organization to grant financial assistance to facilitate the participation of delegations of Contracting Parties that are regarded as developing countries in conformity with the established practice of the General Assembly of the United Nations.

(2)(*a*) The Assembly shall deal with matters concerning the maintenance and development of the Union and the application and operation of this Treaty.

(*b*) The Assembly shall decide the convocation of any diplomatic conference for the revision of this Treaty and give the necessary instructions to the Director General for the preparation of such diplomatic conference.

(*c*) The Assembly shall perform the functions allocated to it under Article 14 and shall establish the details of the procedures provided for in that Article, including the financing of such procedures.

(3)(*a*) Each Contracting Party that is a State shall have one vote and shall vote only in its own name.

(*b*) Any Contracting Party that is an Intergovernmental Organization shall exercise its right to vote, in place of its member States, with a number of votes equal to the number of its member States which are party to this Treaty and which are present at the time the vote is taken. No such Intergovernmental Organization shall exercise its right to vote if any of its member States participates in the vote.

(4) The Assembly shall meet in ordinary session once every two years upon convocation by the Director General.

(5) The Assembly shall establish its own rules of procedure, including the convocation of extraordinary sessions, the requirements of a quorum and, subject to the provisions of this Treaty, the required majority for various kinds of decisions.

Article 10
International Bureau

(1)(*a*) The International Bureau of the World Intellectual Property Organization shall:

(i) perform the administrative tasks concerning the Union, as well as any tasks specially assigned to it by the Assembly;

(ii) subject to the availability of funds, provide technical assistance, on request, to the Governments of Contracting Parties that are States and are regarded as developing countries in conformity with the established practice of the General Assembly of the United Nations.

(*b*) No Contracting Party shall have any financial obligations; in particular, no Contracting Party shall be required to pay any contributions to the International Bureau on account of its membership in the Union.

(2) The Director General shall be the chief executive of the Union and shall represent the Union.

Article 11
Amendment of Certain Provisions of the Treaty

(1) The Assembly may amend the definitions contained in Article 2(i) and (ii), as well as Articles 3(1)(*c*), 9(1)(*c*) and (*d*), 9(4), 10(1)(*a*) and 14.

(2)(*a*) Proposals under this Article for amendment of the provisions of this Treaty referred to in paragraph (1) may be initiated by any Contracting Party or by the Director General.

(*b*) Such proposals shall be communicated by the Director General to the Contracting Parties at least six months in advance of their consideration by the Assembly.

(*c*) No such proposal shall be made before the expiration of five years from the date of entry into force of this Treaty under Article 16(1).

(3) Adoption by the Assembly of any amendment under paragraph (1) shall require four-fifths of the votes cast.

(4)(*a*) Any amendment to the provisions of this Treaty referred to in paragraph (1) shall enter into force three months after written notifications of acceptance, effected in accordance with their respective constitutional processes, have been received by the Director General from three-fourths of the Contracting Parties members of the Assembly at the time the Assembly adopted the amendment. Any amendment to the said provisions thus accepted shall bind all States and Intergovernmental Organizations that were Contracting Parties at the time the amendment was adopted by the Assembly or that become Contracting Parties thereafter, except Contracting Parties which have notified their denunciation of this Treaty in accordance with Article 17 before the entry into force of the amendment.

(*b*) In establishing the required three-fourths referred to in subparagraph (*a*), a notification made by an Intergovernmental Organization shall only be taken into account if no notification has been made by any of its member States.

Article 12
Safeguard of Paris and Berne Conventions

This Treaty shall not affect the obligations that any Contracting Party may have under the Paris Convention for the Protection of Industrial Property or the Berne Convention for the Protection of Literary and Artistic Works.

Article 13
Reservations

No reservations to this Treaty shall be made.

Article 14
Settlement of Disputes

(1)(*a*) Where any dispute arises concerning the interpretation or implementation of this Treaty, a Contracting Party may bring the matter to the attention of another Contracting Party and request the latter to enter into consultations with it.

(*b*) The Contracting Party so requested shall provide promptly an adequate opportunity for the requested consultations.

(*c*) The Contracting Parties engaged in consultations shall attempt to reach, within a reasonable period of time, a mutually satisfactory solution of the dispute.

(2) If a mutually satisfactory solution is not reached within a reasonable period of time through the consultations referred to in paragraph (1), the parties to the dispute may agree to resort to other means designed to lead to an amicable settlement of their dispute, such as good offices, conciliation, mediation and arbitration.

(3)(*a*) If the dispute is not satisfactorily settled through the consultations referred to in paragraph (1), or if the means referred to in paragraph (2) are not resorted to, or do not lead to an amicable settlement within a reasonable period of time, the Assembly, at the written request of either of the parties to the dispute, shall convene a panel of three members to examine the matter. The members of the panel shall not, unless the parties to the dispute agree otherwise, be from either party to the dispute. They shall be selected from a list of designated governmental experts established by the Assembly. The terms of reference for the panel shall be agreed upon by the parties to the dispute. If such agreement is not achieved within three months, the Assembly shall set the terms of reference for the panel after having consulted the parties to the dispute and the members of the panel. The panel shall give full opportunity to the parties to the dispute and any other interested Contracting Parties to present to it their views. If both parties to the dispute so request, the panel shall stop its proceedings.

(*b*) The Assembly shall adopt rules for the establishment of the said list of experts, and the manner of selecting the members of the panel, who shall be governmental experts of the Contracting Parties, and for the conduct of the panel proceedings, including provisions to safeguard the confidentiality of the proceedings and of any material designated as confidential by any participant in the proceedings.

(*c*) Unless the parties to the dispute reach an agreement between themselves prior to the panel's concluding its proceedings, the panel shall promptly prepare a written report and provide it to the parties to the dispute for their review. The parties to the dispute shall have a reasonable period of time, whose length will be fixed by the panel, to submit any comments on the report to the panel, unless they agree to a longer time in their attempts to reach a mutually satisfactory resolution to their dispute. The panel shall take into account the comments and shall promptly transmit its report to the Assembly. The report shall contain the facts and recommendations for the resolution of the dispute, and shall be accompanied by the written comments, if any, of the parties to the dispute.

(4) The Assembly shall give the report of the panel prompt

consideration. The Assembly shall, by consensus, make recommendations to the parties to the dispute, based upon its interpretation of this Treaty and the report of the panel.

Article 15
Becoming Party to the Treaty

(1)(*a*) Any State member of the World Intellectual Property Organization or of the United Nations may become party to this Treaty.

(*b*) Any Intergovernmental Organization which meets the requirements of Article 2(x) may become party to this Treaty. The Organization shall inform the Director General of its competence, and any subsequent changes in its competence, with respect to the matters governed by this Treaty. The Organization and its member States may, without, however, any derogation from the obligations under this Treaty, decide on their respective responsibilities for the performance of their obligations under this Treaty.

(2) A State or Intergovernmental Organization shall become party to this Treaty by:

(i) signature followed by the deposit of an instrument of ratification, acceptance or approval, or
(ii) the deposit of an instrument of accession.

(3) The instruments referred to in paragraph (2) shall be deposited with the Director General.

Article 16
Entry Into Force of the Treaty

(1) This Treaty shall enter into force, with respect to each of the first five States or Intergovernmental Organizations which have deposited their instruments of ratification, acceptance, approval or accession, three months after the date on which the fifth instrument of ratification, acceptance, approval or accession has been deposited.

(2) This Treaty shall enter into force with respect to any State or Intergovernmental Organization not covered by paragraph (1) three months after the date on which that State or Intergovernmental Organization has deposited its instrument of ratification, acceptance, approval or accession unless a later date has been indicated in the instrument; in the latter case, this Treaty shall enter into force with respect to the said State or Intergovernmental Organization on the date thus indicated.

(3) Any Contracting Party shall have the right not to apply this Treaty to any layout-design (topography) that exists at the time this Treaty enters into force in respect of that Contracting Party, provided that this provision does not affect any protection that such layout-design (topography) may, at that time, enjoy in the territory of that Contracting Party by virtue of international obligations other than those resulting from this Treaty or the legislation of the said Contracting Party.

Article 17
Denunciation of the Treaty

(1) Any Contracting Party may denounce this Treaty by notification addressed to the Director General.

(2) Denunciation shall take effect one year after the day on which the Director General has received the notification of denunciation.

Article 18
Texts of the Treaty

(1) This Treaty is established in a single original in the English, Arabic, Chinese, French, Russian and Spanish languages, all texts being equally authentic.

(2) Official texts shall be established by the Director General, after consultation with the interested Governments, in such other languages as the Assembly may designate.

Article 19
Depositary

The Director General shall be the depositary of this Treaty.

Article 20
Signature

This Treaty shall be open for signature between May 26, 1989, and August 25, 1989, with the Government of the United States of America, and between August 26, 1989, and May 25, 1990, at the headquarters of WIPO.

Part V
Industrial Design

1. The Hague Agreement Concerning the International Deposit of Industrial Designs

November 6, 1925, revised at London on June 2, 1934, and at The Hague on November 28, 1960, supplemented by the Additional Act of Monaco of November 28, 1961, the Complementary Act of Stockholm of July 14, 1967, as amended on October 2, 1979, and the Protocol of Geneva of August 29, 1975

The Hague Agreement Concerning the International Deposit of Industrial Designs of November 6, 1925, was revised at London (1934) and at the Hague (1960). The Hague revision entered into force on August 1, 1984, and, simultaneously the Protocol of Geneva of 1975 ceased to have effect. The majority of contracting states adhere to the Hague revision of 1960, which is discussed below.

Beginning with the Hague revision of 1960, the contracting states constitute a separate union for the international deposit for industrial designs. Only states that are members of the Union of Paris may become members of the Hague Union.

The primary purpose of the Hague Agreement is to facilitate the international protection of industrial designs. It does this by providing for a single deposit with the International Bureau of WIPO to secure protection in other member states. Nationals of contracting states and persons who have a real and effective industrial establishment may make an international deposit.The deposit can be made directly in the International Bureau or through an intermediary of the national office if the law of the state allows.

The international deposit consists of an application, one or more photographs or a graphic representation of the design, and payment of the prescribed fee (Art. 5 para. 1). Applicants must designate the contracting states in which they wish the international deposit to be effective (Art. 5 para. 2). The International Bureau publishes each deposit in a periodical bulletin that is sent to the national offices. Publication of the deposit may be deferred at the applicant's request, but the deferral period may not exceed 12 months from the date of deposit (Art. 6 para. 4a).

The international deposit registered at the International Bureau has the same effect in the contracting states designated by the applicant as though all the formalities required by the national law for the grant of protection were complied with (Art. 7 para. 1). Substantive requirements, however, are still governed by national law (Art. 7 para. 1). These might include novelty, distinctiveness, and priority judged under the various national standards. Contracting states having a preliminary examination must notify the International Bureau of a refusal to register within six months after receiving the periodical bulletin in which the registration was published (Art. 8 para. 2).

An international deposit is protected for a first term of five years and is renewable every five years upon payment of the prescribed fees (Art. 11). The Hague Agreement requires that national law confer a minimum term of protection not less than ten years from the date of the international deposit if the deposit has been renewed, or five years from the international deposit without a renewal (Art. 11 para. 1a).

As of January 1, 1990, the following 21 states were party to the Hague Agreement:

Belgium	Holy See	Netherlands
Benin	Hungary	Senegal
Egypt	Indonesia	Spain
France	Italy	Suriname
German Democratic Republic	Liechtenstein	Switzerland
Federal Republic of Germany	Luxembourg	Tunisia
	Monaco	Viet Nam
	Morocco	

The Hague Agreement Concerning the International Deposit of Industrial Designs, as revised at The Hague, 1960

Article 1

(1) The contracting States constitute a Special Union for the international deposit of industrial designs.

(2) Only States members of the International Union for the Protection of Industrial Property may become party to this Agreement.

Article 2

For the purposes of this Agreement:

"1925 Agreement" shall mean the Hague Agreement concerning the International Deposit of Industrial Designs of November 6, 1925;

"1934 Agreement" shall mean the Hague Agreement concerning the International Deposit of Industrial Designs of November 6, 1925, as revised at London on June 2, 1934;

"this Agreement" or "the present Agreement" shall mean the Hague Agreement concerning the International Deposit of Industrial Designs as established by the present Act;

"Regulations" shall mean the Regulations for carrying out this Agreement;

"International Bureau" shall mean the Bureau of the International Union for the Protection of Industrial Property;

"international deposit" shall mean a deposit made at the International Bureau;

"national deposit" shall mean a deposit made at the national Office of a contracting State;

"multiple deposit" shall mean a deposit including several designs;

"State of origin of an international deposit" shall mean the contracting State in which the applicant has a real and effective industrial or commercial establishment or, if the applicant has such establishments in several contracting States, the contracting State which he has indicated in his application; if the applicant has no

---

Source: Text courtesy of the World Intellectual Property Organization (WIPO).

such establishment in any contracting State, the contracting State in which he has his domicile; if he has no domicile in a contracting State, the contracting State of which he is a national;

"State having a novelty examination" shall mean a contracting State the domestic law of which provides for a system which involves a preliminary ex officio search and examination by its national Office as to the novelty of each deposited design.

Article 3

Nationals of contracting States and persons who, without being nationals of any contracting State, are domiciled or have a real and effective industrial or commercial establishment in the territory of a contracting State may deposit designs at the International Bureau.

Article 4

(1) International deposit may be made at the International Bureau:

1. direct, or
2. through the intermediary of the national Office of a contracting State if the law of that State so permits.

(2) The domestic law of any contracting State may require that international deposits of which it is deemed to be the State of origin shall be made through its national Office. Noncompliance with this requirement shall not prejudice the effects of the international deposit in the other contracting States.

Article 5

(1) The international deposit shall consist of an application and one or more photographs or other graphic representations of the design, and shall involve payment of the fees prescribed by the Regulations.

(2) The application shall contain:

1. a list of the contracting States in which the applicant requests that the international deposit shall have effect;
2. the designation of the article or articles in which it is intended to incorporate the design;

3. if the applicant wishes to claim the priority provided for in Article 9, an indication of the date, the State, and the number of the deposit giving rise to the right of priority;
4. such other particulars as the Regulations may prescribe.

(3) (*a*) In addition, the application may contain:

1. a short description of characteristic features of the design;
2. a declaration as to who is the true creator of the design;
3. a request for deferment of publication as provided in Article 6(4).

(*b*) The application may be accompanied also by samples or models of the article or articles incorporating the design.

(4) A multiple deposit may include several designs intended to be incorporated in articles included in the same class of the International Design Classification referred to in Article 21(2), item 4.

Article 6

(1) The International Bureau shall maintain the International Design Register and shall register international deposits therein.

(2) The international deposit shall be deemed to have been made on the date on which the International Bureau received the application in due form, the fees payable with the application, and the photograph or photographs or other graphic representations of the design, or, if the International Bureau received them on different dates, on the last of these dates. The registration shall bear the same date.

(3)(*a*) For each international deposit, the International Bureau shall publish in a periodical bulletin:

1. reproductions in black and white or, at the request of the applicant, in color of the deposited photographs or other graphic representations;
2. the date of the international deposit;
3. the particulars prescribed by the Regulations.

(*b*) The International Bureau shall send the periodical bulletin to the national Offices as soon as possible.

(4)(*a*) The publication referred to in paragraph (3)(*a*) shall, at the request of the applicant, be deferred for such period as he may request. The said period may not exceed 12 months from the date of the international deposit. However, if priority is claimed, the starting date of such period shall be the priority date.

(*b*) At any time during the period referred to in subparagraph (*a*), the applicant may request immediate publication or may withdraw his deposit. Withdrawal of the deposit may be limited to one or a few only of the contracting States and, in the case of a multiple deposit, to some only of the designs included therein.

(*c*) If the applicant fails to pay within the proper time the fees payable before the expiration of the period referred to in subparagraph (*a*), the International Bureau shall cancel the deposit and shall not effect the publication referred to in paragraph (3)(*a*).

(*d*) Until the expiration of the period referred to in subparagraph (*a*), the International Bureau shall keep in confidence the registration of deposits made subject to deferred publication, and the public shall have no access to any documents or articles concerning such deposits. These provisions shall apply without limitation as to time if the applicant has withdrawn his deposit before the expiration of the said period.

(5) Except as provided in paragraph (4), the Register and all documents and articles filed with the International Bureau shall be open to inspection by the public.

Article 7

(1)(*a*) A deposit registered at the International Bureau shall have the same effect in each of the contracting States designated by the applicant in his application as if all the formalities required by the domestic law for the grant of protection had been complied with by the applicant and as if all administrative acts required to that end had been accomplished by the Office of such State.

(*b*) Subject to the provisions of Article 11, the protection of designs the deposit of which has been registered at the International Bureau is governed in each contracting State by those provisions of the domestic law which are applicable in that State to designs for which protection has been claimed on the basis of a national deposit and in respect of which all formalities and administrative acts have been complied with and accomplished.

(2) An international deposit shall have no effect in the State of origin if the laws of that State so provide.

Article 8

(1) Notwithstanding the provisions of Article 7, the national Office of a contracting State whose domestic law provides that the national Office may, on the basis of an administrative ex officio examination or pursuant to an opposition by a third party, refuse protection shall, in case of refusal, notify the International Bureau

within six months that the design does not meet the requirements of its domestic law other than the formalities and administrative acts referred to in Article 7(1). If no such refusal is notified within a period of six months the international deposit shall become effective in that State as from the date of that deposit. However, in a contracting State having a novelty examination, the international deposit, while retaining its priority, shall, if no refusal is notified within a period of six months, become effective from the expiration of the said period unless the domestic law provides for an earlier date for deposits made with its national Office.

(2) The period of six months referred to in paragraph (1) shall be computed from the date on which the national Office receives the issue of the periodical bulletin in which the registration of the international deposit has been published. The national Office shall communicate that date to any person so requesting.

(3) The applicant shall have the same remedies against the refusal of the national Office referred to in paragraph (1) as if he had deposited his design in that Office; in any case, the refusal shall be subject to a request for re-examination or appeal. Notification of such refusal shall indicate:

1. the reasons for which it has been found that the design does not meet the requirements of the domestic law;
2. the date referred to in paragraph (2);
3. the time allowed for a request for re-examination or appeal;
4. the authority to which such request or appeal may be addressed.

(4)(*a*) The national Office of a contracting State whose domestic law contains provisions of the kind referred to in paragraph (1) requiring a declaration as to who is the true creator of the design or a description of the design may provide that, upon request and within a period of not less than sixty days from the dispatch of such a request by the said Office, the applicant shall file in the language of the application filed with the International Bureau:

1. a declaration as to who is the true creator of the design;
2. a short description emphasizing the essential characteristic features of the design as shown by the photographs or other graphic representations.

(*b*) No fees shall be charged by a national Office in connection with the filing of such declarations or descriptions, or for their possible publication by that national Office.

(5)(*a*) Any contracting State whose domestic law contains provisions of the kind referred to in paragraph (1) shall notify the International Bureau accordingly.

(*b*) If, under its legislation, a contracting State has several systems for the protection of designs one of which provides for novelty examination, the provisions of this Agreement concerning States having a novelty examination shall apply only to the said system.

Article 9

If the international deposit of a design is made within six months of the first deposit of the same design in a State member of the International Union for the Protection of Industrial Property, and if priority is claimed for the international deposit, the priority date shall be that of the first deposit.

Article 10

(1) An international deposit may be renewed every five years by payment only, during the last year of each period of five years, of the renewal fees prescribed by the Regulations.

(2) Subject to the payment of a surcharge fixed by the Regulations, a period of grace of six months shall be granted for renewal of the international deposit.

(3) At the time of paying the renewal fees, the international deposit number must be indicated and also, if renewal is not to be effected for all the contracting States for which the deposit is about to expire, those of the contracting States for which the renewal is to be effected.

(4) Renewal may be limited to some only of the designs included in a multiple deposit.

(5) The International Bureau shall record and publish renewals.

Article 11

(1)(*a*) The term of protection granted by a contracting State to designs which have been the subject of an international deposit shall not be less than:

1. ten years from the date of the international deposit if the deposit has been renewed;
2. five years from the date of the international deposit in the absence of renewal.

(*b*) However, if, under the provisions of the domestic law of a contracting State having a novelty examination, protection commences at a date later than that of the international deposit, the minimum terms provided for in subparagraph (*a*) shall be computed from the date at which protection commences in that State. The fact that the international deposit is not renewed or is renewed only once shall in no way affect the minimum terms of protection thus defined.

(2) If the domestic law of a contracting State provides, in respect of designs which have been the subject of a national deposit, for protection whose duration, with or without renewal, is longer than ten years, protection of the same duration shall, on the basis of the international deposit and its renewals, be granted in that State to designs which have been the subject of an international deposit.

(3) A contracting State may, under its domestic law, limit the term of protection of designs which have been the subject of an international deposit to the terms provided for in paragraph (1).

(4) Subject to the provisions of paragraph (1)(*b*), protection in a contracting State shall terminate at the date of expiration of the international deposit, unless the domestic law of that State provides that protection shall continue after the date of expiration of the international deposit.

Article 12

(1) The International Bureau shall record and publish changes affecting ownership of a design which is the subject of an international deposit in force. It is understood that transfer of ownership may be limited to the rights arising from the international deposit in one or a few only of the contracting States and, in the case of a multiple deposit, to some only of the designs included therein.

(2) The recording referred to in paragraph (1) shall have the same effect as if it had been made in the national Offices of the contracting States.

Article 13

(1) The owner of an international deposit may, by means of a declaration addressed to the International Bureau, renounce his rights in respect of all or some only of the contracting States and, in the case of a multiple deposit, in respect of some only of the designs included therein.

(2) The International Bureau shall record and publish such declaration.

Article 14

(1) No contracting State may, as a condition of recognition of the right to protection, require that the article incorporating the design bear a sign or notice concerning the deposit of the design.

(2) If the domestic law or a contracting State provides for a notice on the article for any other purpose, such State shall regard such requirement as satisfied if all the articles offered to the public with the authorization of the owner of the rights in the design, or the tags attached to such articles, bear the international design notice.

(3) The international design notice shall consist of the symbol Ⓓ (a capital D in a circle) accompanied by:

1. the year of the international deposit and the name, or the usual abbreviation of the name, of the depositor, or
2. the number of the international deposit.

(4) The mere appearance of the international design notice on the article or the tags shall in no case be interpreted as implying a waiver of protection by virtue of copyright or on any other grounds, whenever, in the absence of such notice, such protection may be claimed.

Article 15

(1) The fees prescribed by the Regulations shall consist of:

1. fees for the International Bureau;
2. fees for the contracting States designated by the applicant, namely:

(*a*) a fee for each contracting State;
(*b*) a fee for each contracting State having a novelty examination and requiring the payment of a fee of such examination.

(2) Any fees paid in respect of one and the same deposit for a contracting State under paragraph (1), item 2(*a*), shall be deducted from the amount of the fee referred to in paragraph (1), item 2(*b*), if the latter fee becomes payable for the same State.

Article 16

(1) The fees for contracting States referred to in Article 15(1), item 2, shall be collected by the International Bureau and paid over annually to the contracting States designated by the applicant.

(2)(*a*) Any contracting State may notify the International Bureau that it waives its right to the supplementary fees referred to in Article 15(1), item 2(*a*), in respect of international deposits of which any other contracting State making a similar waiver is deemed to be the State of origin.

(*b*) Such State may make a similar waiver in respect of international deposits of which it is itself deemed to be the State of origin.

Article 17

The Regulations shall govern the details concerning the implementation of this Agreement and in particular:

1. the languages and the number of copies in which the application for deposit must be filed, and the data to be supplied in the application;
2. the amounts and the dates and method of payment of the fees for the International Bureau and for the States, including the limits imposed on the fee for contracting States having a novelty examination;
3. the number, size, and other characteristics, of the photographs or other graphic representations of each design deposited;
4. the length of the description of characteristic features of the design;
5. the limits within which and conditions under which samples or models of the articles incorporating the design may accompany the application;
6. the number of designs that may be included in a multiple deposit and other conditions governing multiple deposits;
7. all matters relating to the publication and distribution of the periodical bulletin referred to in Article 6(3)(*a*), including the number of copies of the bulletin which shall be given free of charge to the national Offices and the number of copies which may be sold at a reduced price to such Offices;
8. the procedure for notification by contracting States of any refusal provided for under Article 8(1), and the procedure for communication and publication of such refusals by the International Bureau;
9. the conditions for recording and publication by the International Bureau of the changes affecting the ownership of a design referred to in Article 12(1), and for the renunciations referred to in Article 13;
10. the disposal of documents and articles concerning deposits for which the possibility of renewal has ceased to exist.

Article 18

The provisions of this Agreement shall not preclude the making of a claim to the benefit of any greater protection which may be granted by domestic legislation in a contracting State, nor shall they affect in any way the protection accorded to works of art and works of applied art by international copyright treaties and conventions.

Article 19

The fees of the International Bureau for services provided for by this Agreement shall be fixed in such a manner:

(*a*) that the proceeds therefrom cover all the expenses of the International Design Service and all those necessitated by the preparation and holding of meetings of the International Design Committee or conferences for the revision of this Agreement;

(*b*) that they allow for the maintenance of the reserve fund referred to in Article 20.

Article 20

(1) There shall be a reserve fund of 250,000 Swiss francs. The amount of the reserve fund may be modified by the International Design Committee referred to in Article 21.

(2) The reserve fund shall be replenished by the surplus receipts of the International Design Service.

(3)(*a*) However, at the time of the entry into force of this Agreement, the reserve fund shall be constituted by a single contribution paid by each contracting State and computed in proportion to the number of units corresponding to the class to which it belongs by virtue of Article 13(8) of the Paris Convention for the Protection of Industrial Property.

(*b*) States which become party to this Agreement after it enters into force shall also pay a single contribution. The contribution shall be computed according to the principles formulated in the preceding subparagraph, so that all States, whatever the date of their becoming party to the Agreement, shall pay the same contribution per unit.

(4) When the amount of the reserve fund exceeds the fixed ceiling, the surplus shall be periodically distributed among the contracting States, in proportion to the single contribution paid by each, up to the maximum amount of that contribution.

(5) When the single contributions have been fully reimbursed, the International Design Committee may decide that States subsequently becoming party to the Agreement shall not be required to pay the single contribution.

Article 21

(1) There shall be an International Design Committee consisting of representatives of all the contracting States.

(2) The Committee shall have the following duties and powers:

1. to draw up its own rules of procedure;
2. to amend the Regulations;
3. to modify the ceiling of the reserve fund referred to in Article 20;
4. to establish the International Design Classification;
5. to study matters concerning the application and possible revision of this Agreement;
6. to study all other matters concerning the international protection of designs;
7. to approve the yearly management reports of the International Bureau and to give general instructions to the International Bureau concerning the discharge of the duties assigned to it under this Agreement;
8. to draw up a report on the foreseeable expenditure of the International Bureau for each triennial period to come.

(3) The decisions of the Committee shall require four-fifths of the votes of its members present or represented and voting in the case of paragraph (2), items 1, 2, 3, and 4, and a simple majority in all other cases. Abstentions shall not be considered as votes.

(4) The Committee shall be convened by the Director of the International Bureau:

1. at least once every three years;
2. at any time at the request of one-third of the contracting States, or, if deemed necessary, upon the initiative of the Director of the International Bureau or the Government of the Swiss Confederation.

(5) The travel expenses and subsistence allowances of members of the Committee shall be borne by their respective Governments.

Article 22

(1) The Regulations may be amended either by the Committee as prescribed in Article 21(2), item 2, or in accordance with the written procedure provided for in paragraph (2), below.

(2) In the case of written procedure, amendments shall be proposed by the Director of the International Bureau in a circular letter addressed to the Government of each contracting State. The amendments shall be regarded as adopted if, within one year from their communication, no contracting State has raised an objection.

Article 23

(1) This Agreement shall remain open for signature until December 31, 1961.

(2) It shall be ratified and the instruments of ratification shall be deposited with the Government of the Netherlands.

Article 24

(1) States members of the International Union for the Protection of Industrial Property which have not signed this Agreement may accede thereto.

(2) Such accessions shall be notified through diplomatic channels to the Government of the Swiss Confederation, and by the latter to the Governments of all contracting States.

Article 25

(1) Each contracting State undertakes to provide for the protection of industrial designs and to adopt, in accordance with its constitution, the measures necessary to ensure the application of this Agreement.

(2) At the time a contracting State deposits its instrument of ratification or accession, it must be in a position under its domestic law to give effect to the provisions of this Agreement.

Article 26

(1) This Agreement shall enter into force one month after the date on which the Government of the Swiss Confederation has dispatched a notification to the contracting States of the deposit of ten

instruments of ratification or accession, at least four of which are those of States which, at the date of the present Agreement, are not party either to the 1925 Agreement or to the 1934 Agreement.

(2) Thereafter, the deposit of instruments of ratification and accession shall be notified to the contracting States by the Government of the Swiss Confederation. Such ratifications and accessions shall become effective one month after the date of the dispatch of such notification unless, in the case of accession, a later date is indicated in the instrument of accession.

Article 27

Any contracting State may at any time notify the Government of the Swiss Confederation that this Agreement shall also apply to all or part of those territories for the external relations of which it is responsible. Thereupon, the Government of the Swiss Confederation shall communicate such notification to the contracting States and the Agreement shall apply also to the said territories one month after the dispatch of the communication by the Government of the Swiss Confederation to the contracting States unless a later date is indicated in the notification.

Article 28

(1) Any contracting State may, by notification addressed to the Government of the Swiss Confederation, denounce this Agreement in its own name and on behalf of all or part of the territories designated in the notification under Article 27. Such notification shall take effect one year after its receipt by the Government of the Swiss Confederation.

(2) Denunciation shall not relieve any contracting State of its obligations under this Agreement in respect of designs deposited at the International Bureau prior to the date on which the denunciation takes effect.

Article 29

(1) This Agreement shall be submitted to periodical revision with a view to the introduction of amendments designed to improve the protection resulting from the international deposit of designs.

(2) Revision conferences shall be called at the request of the International Design Committee or of not less than one-half of the contracting States.

Article 30

(1) Two or more contracting States may at any time notify the Government of the Swiss Confederation that, subject to the conditions indicated in the notification:

1. a common Office shall be substituted for the national Office of each of them;
2. they shall be deemed to be a single State for the purposes of the application of Articles 2 to 17 of this Agreement.

(2) Such notification shall not take effect until six months after the date of dispatch of the communication thereof by the Government of the Swiss Confederation to the other contracting States.

Article 31

(1) This Agreement alone shall be applicable as regards the mutual relations of States party to both the present Agreement and the 1925 Agreement or the 1934 Agreement. However, such States shall, in their mutual relations, apply the 1925 Agreement or the 1934 Agreement, as the case may be, to designs deposited at the International Bureau prior to the date on which the present Agreement becomes applicable as regards their mutual relations.

(2)(*a*) Any State party to both the present Agreement and the 1925 Agreement shall continue to apply the 1925 Agreement in its relations with States party only to the 1925 Agreement, unless the said State has denounced the 1925 Agreement.

(*b*) Any State party to both the present Agreement and the 1934 Agreement shall continue to apply the 1934 Agreement in its relations with States party only to the 1934 Agreement, unless the said State has denounced the 1934 Agreement.

(3) States party to the present Agreement only shall not be bound to States which, without being party to the present Agreement, are party to the 1925 Agreement or the 1934 Agreement.

Article 32

(1) Signature and ratification of, or accession to, the present Agreement by a State party, at the date of this Agreement, to the 1925 Agreement or the 1934 Agreement shall be deemed to include

signature and ratification of, or accession to, the Protocol annexed to the present Agreement, unless such State makes an express declaration to the contrary at the time of signing or depositing its instrument of accession.

(2) Any contracting State having made the declaration referred to in paragraph (1), or any other contracting State not party to the 1925 Agreement or the 1934 Agreement, may sign or accede to the Protocol annexed to this Agreement. At the time of signing or depositing its instrument of accession, it may declare that it does not consider itself bound by the provisions of paragraphs (2)(*a*) or (2)(*b*) of the Protocol; in such case, the other States party to the Protocol shall be under no obligation to apply, in their relations with that State, the provisions mentioned in such declaration. The provisions of Articles 23 to 28 inclusive shall apply by analogy.

Article 33

This Act shall be signed in a single copy which shall be deposited in the archives of the Government of the Netherlands. A certified copy shall be transmitted by the latter to the Government of each State which has signed or acceded to this Agreement.

PROTOCOL*

States party to this Protocol have agreed as follows:

(1) The provisions of this Protocol shall apply to designs which have been the subject of an international deposit and of which one of the States party to this Protocol is deemed to be the State of origin.

(2) In respect of designs referred to in paragraph (1), above:

(*a*) the term of protection granted by States party to this Protocol to the designs referred to in paragraph (1) shall not be less than 15 years from the date provided for in paragraphs (1)(*a*) or (1)(*b*), as the case may be, of Article 11;

(*b*) the appearance of a notice on the articles incorporating the designs or on the tags attached thereto shall in no case be required by the States party to this Protocol, either for the exercise in their territories of rights arising from the international deposit, or for any other purpose.

---

*This protocol is not yet in force.

The Hague Agreement Concerning the International Deposit of Industrial Designs, of November 6, 1925. Complementary Act of Stockholm of July 14, 1967

Article 1
Definitions

For the purposes of this Complementary Act:

"1934 Act" shall mean the Act signed at London on June 2, 1934, of the Hague Agreement concerning the International Deposit of Industrial Designs;

"1960 Act" shall mean the Act signed at The Hague on November 28, 1960, of the Hague Agreement concerning the International Deposit of Industrial Designs;

"1961 Additional Act" shall mean the Act signed at Monaco on November 18, 1961, additional to the 1934 Act;

"Organization" shall mean the World Intellectual Property Organization;

"International Bureau" shall mean the International Bureau of Intellectual Property;

"Director General" shall mean the Director General of the Organization;

"Special Union" shall mean the Hague Union established by the Hague Agreement of November 6, 1925, concerning the International Deposit of Industrial Designs, and maintained by the 1934 and 1960 Acts by the 1961 Additional Act, and by this Complementary Act.

Article 2
Assembly

(1)(*a*) The Special Union shall have an Assembly consisting of those countries which have ratified or acceded to this Complementary Act.

(*b*) The Government of each country shall be represented by one delegate, who may be assisted by alternate delegates, advisors, and experts.

Source: Text courtesy of the World Intellectual Property Organization (WIPO).

(*c*) The expenses of each delegation shall be borne by the Government which has appointed it.

(2)(*a*) The Assembly shall:

(i) deal with all matters concerning the maintenance and development of the Special Union and the implementation of this Agreement;

(ii) give directions to the International Bureau concerning the preparation for conferences of revision, due account being taken of any comments made by those countries of the Special Union which have not ratified or acceded to this Complementary Act;

(iii) modify the Regulations, including the fixation of the amounts of the fees relating to the international deposit of industrial designs;

(iv) review and approve the reports and activities of the Director General concerning the Special Union, and give him all necessary instructions concerning matters within the competence of the Special Union;

(v) determine the program and adopt the biennial budget of the Special Union, and approve its final accounts;

(vi) adopt the financial regulations of the Special Union;

(vii) establish such committees of experts and working groups as it may deem necessary to achieve the objectives of the Special Union;

(viii) determine which countries not members of the Special Union and which intergovernmental and international non-governmental organizations shall be admitted to its meetings as observers;

(ix) adopt amendments to Articles 2 to 5;

(x) take any other appropriate action designed to further the objectives of the Special Union;

(xi) perform such other functions as are appropriate under this Complementary Act.

(*b*) With respect to matters which are of interest also to other Unions administered by the Organization, the Assembly shall make its decisions after having heard the advice of the Coordination Committee of the Organization.

(3)(*a*) Each country member of the Assembly shall have one vote.

(*b*) One-half of the countries members of the Assembly shall constitute a quorum.

(*c*) Notwithstanding the provisions of subparagraph (*b*), if, in any session, the number of countries represented is less than one-half but equal to or more than one-third of the countries members of the Assembly, the Assembly may make decisions but, with the exception of decisions concerning its own procedure, all such decisions shall take effect only if the conditions set forth hereinafter are fulfilled. The International Bureau shall communicate the said decisions to the countries members of the Assembly which were not represented and shall invite them to express in writing their vote or abstention within a period of three months from the date of the communication. If, at the expiration of this period, the number of countries having thus expressed their vote or abstention attains the number of countries which was lacking for attaining the quorum in the session itself, such decisions shall take effect provided that at the same time the required majority still obtains.

(*d*) Subject to the provisions of Article 5(2), the decisions of the Assembly shall require two-thirds of the votes cast.

(*e*) Abstentions shall not be considered as votes.

(*f*) A delegate may represent, and vote in the name of, one country only.

(*g*) Countries of the Special Union not members of the Assembly shall be admitted to the meetings of the latter as observers.

(4)(*a*) The Assembly shall meet once in every second calendar year in ordinary session upon convocation by the Director General and, in the absence of exceptional circumstances, during the same period and at the same place as the General Assembly of the Organization.

(*b*) The Assembly shall meet in extraordinary session upon convocation by the Director General, at the request of one-fourth of the countries members of the Assembly.

(*c*) The agenda of each session shall be prepared by the Director General.

(5) The Assembly shall adopt its own rules of procedure.

Article 3
International Bureau

(1)(*a*) International deposit of industrial designs and related duties, as well as all other administrative tasks concerning the Special Union, shall be performed by the International Bureau.

(*b*) In particular, the International Bureau shall prepare the meetings and provide the secretariat of the Assembly and of such committees of experts and working groups as may have been established by the Assembly.

(*c*) The Director General shall be the chief executive of the Special Union and shall represent the Special Union.

(2) The Director General and any staff member designated by him shall participate, without the right to vote, in all meetings of

the Assembly and of such committees of experts or working groups as may have been established by the Assembly. The Director General, or a staff member designed by him, shall be ex officio secretary of those bodies.

(3)(*a*) The International Bureau shall, in accordance with the direction of the Assembly, make the preparations for the conferences of revision of the provisions of the Agreement.

(*b*) The International Bureau may consult with intergovernmental and international non-governmental organizations concerning preparations for conferences of revision.

(*c*) The Director General and persons designated by him shall take part, without the right to vote, in the discussions at those conferences.

(4) The International Bureau shall carry out any other tasks assigned to it.

Article 4
Finances

(1)(*a*) The Special Union shall have a budget.

(*b*) The budget of the Special Union shall include the income and expenses proper to the Special Union, its contribution to the budget of expenses common to the Unions, and, where applicable, the sum made available to the budget of the Conference of the Organization.

(*c*) Expenses not attributable exclusively to the Special Union but also to one or more other Unions administered by the Organization shall be deemed to be expenses common to the Unions. The share of the Special Union in such common expenses shall be in proportion to the interest the Special Union has in them.

(2) The budget of the Special Union shall be established with due regard to the requirements of coordination with the budgets of the other Unions administered by the Organization,

(3) The budget of the Special Union shall be financed from the following sources:

(i) international deposit fees and other fees and charges due for other services rendered by the International Bureau in relation to the Special Union;
(ii) sale of, or royalties on, the publications of the International Bureau concerning the Special Union;
(iii) gifts, bequests, and subventions;
(iv) rents, interests, and other miscellaneous income.

(4)(*a*) The amounts of the fees referred to in paragraph (3)(i) shall be fixed by the Assembly on the proposal of the Director General.

(*b*) The amounts of such fees shall be so fixed that the revenues of the Special Union from fees and other sources shall be at least sufficient to cover the expenses of the International Bureau concerning the Special Union.

(*c*) If the budget is not adopted before the beginning of a new financial period, it shall be at the same level as the budget of the previous year, as provided in the financial regulations.

(5) Subject to the provisions of paragraph (4)(*a*), the amount of the fees and charges due for other services rendered by the International Bureau in relation to the Special Union shall be established, and shall be reported to the Assembly, by the Director General.

(6)(*a*) The Special Union shall have a working capital fund which shall be constituted by the excess receipts and, if such excess does not suffice, by a single payment made by each country of the Special Union. If the fund becomes insufficient, the Assembly shall decide to increase it.

(*b*) The amount of the initial payment of each country to the said fund or of its participation in the increase thereof shall be a proportion of the contribution of that country as a member of the Paris Union for the Protection of Industrial Property to the budget of the said Union for the year in which the fund is established or the decision to increase it is made.

(*c*) The proportion and the terms of payment shall be fixed by the Assembly on the proposal of the Director General and after it has heard the advice of the Coordination Committee of the Organization.

(7)(*a*) In the headquarters agreement concluded with the country on the territory of which the Organization has its headquarters, it shall be provided that, whenever the working capital fund is insufficient, such country shall grant advances. The amount of those advances and the conditions on which they are granted shall be the subject of separate agreements, in each case, between such country and the Organization.

(*b*) The country referred to in subparagraph (*a*) and the Organization shall each have the right to denounce the obligation to grant advances, by written notification. Denunciation shall take effect three years after the end of the year in which it has been notified.

(8) The auditing of the accounts shall be effected by one or more of the countries of the Special Union or by external auditors, as provided in the financial regulations. They shall be designated, with their agreement, by the Assembly.

Article 5
Amendment of Articles 2 to 5

(1) Proposals for the amendment of this Complementary Act may be initiated by any country member of the Assembly, or by the Director General. Such proposals shall be communicated by the

Director General to the member countries of the Assembly at least six months in advance of their consideration by the Assembly.

(2) Amendments referred to in paragraph (1) shall be adopted by the Assembly. Adoption shall require three-fourths of the votes cast, provided that any amendment to Article 2, and to the present paragraph, shall require four-fifths of the votes cast.

(3) Any amendment referred to in paragraph (1) shall enter into force one month after written notifications of acceptance, effected in accordance with their respective constitutional processes, have been received by the Director General from three-fourths of the countries members of the Assembly at the time it adopted the amendment. Any amendment thus accepted shall bind all the countries which are members of the Assembly at the time the amendment enters into force, or which become members thereof at a subsequent date.

Article 6
Amendment of the 1934 Act and the 1961 Additional Act

(1)(*a*) References in the 1934 Act to "the International Bureau of Industrial Property at Berne," to "the Berne International Bureau," or to "the International Bureau," shall be construed as references to the International Bureau as defined in Article 1 of this Complementary Act.

(*b*) Article 15 of the 1934 Act is repealed.

(*c*) Any amendment of the Regulations referred to in Article 20 of the 1934 Act shall be effected in accordance with the procedure prescribed under Article 2(2)(*a*)(iii) and (3)(*d*).

(*d*) In Article 21 of the 1934 Act, for the words "revised in 1928" there shall be substituted the words "for the Protection of Literary and Artistic Works."

(*e*) References in Article 22 of the 1934 Act to Articles 16, 16*bis,* and 17*bis,* of the "General Convention" shall be construed as references to those provisions of the Stockholm Act of the Paris Convention for the Protection of Industrial Property which, in the said Stockholm Act, correspond to Articles 16, 16*bis,* and 17*bis,* of the earlier Acts of the Paris Convention.

(2)(*a*) Any modification of the fees referred to in Article 3 of the 1961 Additional Act shall be effected in accordance with the procedure prescribed under Article 2(2)(*a*)(iii) and (3)(*d*).

(*b*) Paragraph (1) of Article 4 of the 1961 Additional Act, and the words "When the reserve fund has reached this amount" in paragraph (2), are repealed.

(*c*) References in Article 6(2) of the 1961 Additional Act to Articles 16 and 16*bis* of the Paris Convention for the Protection of Industrial Property shall be construed as references to those provisions of the Stockholm Act of the said Convention which, in the Stockholm Act, correspond to Articles 16 and 16*bis* of the earlier Acts of the Paris Convention.

(*d*) References in paragraphs (1) and (3) of Article 7 of the 1961 Additional Act to the Government of the Swiss Confederation shall be construed as references to the Director General.

Article 7
Amendment of the 1960 Act

(1) References in the 1960 Act to "the Bureau of the International Union for the Protection of Industrial Property" or to "the International Bureau" shall be construed as references to the International Bureau as defined in Article 1 of this Complementary Act.

(2) Articles 19, 20, 21, and 22, of the 1960 Act are repealed.

(3) References in the 1960 Act to the Government of the Swiss Confederation shall be construed as references to the Director General.

(4) In Article 29 of the 1960 Act, the words "periodical" (paragraph (1)) and "of the International Design Committee or" (paragraph (2)) are deleted.

Article 8
Ratification of, and Accession to, the Complementary Act

(1)(*a*) Countries which, before January 13, 1968, have ratified the 1934 Act or the 1960 Act, and countries which have acceded to at least one of those Acts, may sign this Complementary Act and ratify it, or may accede to it.

(*b*) Ratification of, or accession to, this Complementary Act by a country which is bound by the 1934 Act without being bound also by the 1961 Additional Act shall automatically entail ratification of, or accession to, the 1961 Additional Act.

(2) Instruments of ratification and accession shall be deposited with the Director General.

Article 9
Entry Into Force of the Complementary Act

(1) With respect to the first five countries which have deposited their instruments of ratification or accession, this Complementary Act shall enter into force three months after the deposit of the fifth such instrument of ratification or accession.

(2) With respect to any other country, this Complementary Act shall enter into force three months after the date on which its ratification or accession has been notified by the Director General, unless a subsequent date has been indicated in the instrument of ratification or accession. In the latter case, this Complementary Act shall enter into force with respect to that country on the date thus indicated.

Article 10
Automatic Acceptance of Certain Provisions by Certain Countries

(1) Subject to the provisions of Article 8 and the following paragraph, any country which has not ratified or acceded to the 1934 Act shall become bound by the 1961 Additional Act and by Articles 1 to 6 of this Complementary Act from the date on which its accession to the 1934 Act enters into force, provided that, if on the said date this Complementary Act has not yet entered into force pursuant to Article 9(1), then, such country shall become bound by the said Articles of this Complementary Act only from the date of entry into force of the Complementary Act pursuant to Article 9(1).

(2) Subject to the provisions of Article 8 and the foregoing paragraph, any country which has not ratified or acceded to the 1960 Act shall become bound by Articles 1 to 7 of this Complementary Act from the date on which its ratification of, or accession to, the 1960 Act enters into force, provided that, if on the said date this Complementary Act has not yet entered into force pursuant to Article 9(1), then, such country shall become bound by the said Articles of this Complementary Act only from the date of entry into force of the Complementary Act pursuant to Article 9(1).

Article 11
Signature, etc., of the Complementary Act

(1)(*a*) This Complementary Act shall be signed in a single copy in the French language and shall be deposited with the Government of Sweden.

(*b*) Official texts shall be established by the Director General, after consultation with the interested Governments, in such other languages as the Assembly may designate.

(2) This Complementary Act shall remain open for signature at Stockholm until January 13, 1968.

(3) The Director General shall transmit two copies, certified by the Government of Sweden, of the signed text of this Complementary

Act to the Governments of all countries of the Special Union and, on request, to the Government of any other country.

(4) The Director General shall register this Complementary Act with the Secretariat of the United Nations.

(5) The Director General shall notify the Governments of all countries of the Special Union of signatures, deposits of instruments of ratification or accession, entry into force, and all other relevant notifications.

Article 12
Transitional Provision

Until the first Director General assumes office, references in this Complementary Act to the International Bureau of the Organization or to the Director General shall be construed as references to the Bureau of the Union established by the Paris Convention for the Protection of Industrial Property or its Director, respectively.

Part VI
Classification Treaties

1. Nice Agreement Concerning the International Classification of Goods and Services for the Purposes of the Registration of Marks

June 15, 1957, as revised at Stockholm on July 14, 1967, and at Geneva on May 13, 1977

The Nice Agreement Concerning the International Classification of Goods and Services for the Purposes of the Registration of Marks was concluded on June 15, 1957, and entered into effect on April 8, 1961. It was revised at Stockholm in 1967, and at Geneva in 1977.

By creating a uniform system to classify trademarks, the Nice Convention responded to a practical need of the world trademark community.[1] The absence of a worldwide uniform classification system created problems for the international protection of trademarks. For example, when the country of origin and the foreign country had different classification systems, a single registration of a mark in one country might require several registrations in another country.

Under the Nice Agreement, each country may decide what scope to give to the international classification without being bound by the classification system for the protection of a trademark. What the Agreement does require is that a country must indicate for each published and registered mark the class of the international registration (Art. 2).

---

[1]For the current classification system, *see* WORLD INTELLECTUAL PROPERTY ORGANIZATION, INTERNATIONAL CLASSIFICATION OF GOODS AND SERVICES FOR THE PURPOSES OF THE REGISTRATION OF MARKS (NICE CLASSIFICATION) WIPO Pub. No. 500.1(E), 500.2(E) (5th ed. 1987); WORLD INTELLECTUAL PROPERTY ORGANIZATION, LIST OF GOODS AND SERVICES IN ALPHABETICAL ORDER WIPO Pub. No. 500(EF) (5th ed. 1987).

For modifications of the classification system, a committee of experts from each contracting country decides on all such changes in concert with the International Bureau of WIPO (Art. 3).

As of January 1, 1990, the following 34 states were party to the Nice Agreement:

- Algeria
- Australia
- Austria
- Barbados
- Belgium
- Benin
- Czechoslovakia
- Denmark
- Finland
- France
- German Democratic Republic
- Federal Republic of Germany
- Hungary
- Ireland
- Israel
- Italy
- Japan
- Lebanon
- Liechtenstein
- Luxembourg
- Monaco
- Morocco
- Netherlands
- Norway
- Portugal
- Soviet Union
- Spain
- Suriname
- Sweden
- Switzerland
- Tunisia
- United Kingdom
- United States of America
- Yugoslavia

Nice Agreement Concerning the International Classification of Goods and Services for the Purposes of the Registration of Marks, as revised at Geneva, 1977

Article 1

Establishment of a Special Union; Adoption of an International Classification; Definition and Languages of the Classification

(1) The countries to which this Agreement applies constitute a Special Union and adopt a common classification of goods and services for the purposes of the registration of marks (hereinafter designated as "the Classification").

(2) The Classification consists of:

(i) a list of classes, together with, as the case may be, explanatory notes;

(ii) an alphabetical list of goods and services (hereinafter designated as "the alphabetical list") with an indication of the class into which each of the goods or services falls.

(3) The Classification comprises:

(i) the classification published in 1971 by the International Bureau of Intellectual Property (hereinafter designated as "the International Bureau") referred to in the Convention Establishing the World Intellectual Property Organization, it being understood, however, that the explanatory notes to the list of classes included in that publication shall be regarded as provisional and as recommendations until such time as explanatory notes to the list of classes are established by the Committee of Experts referred to in Article 3;

(ii) the amendments and additions which have entered into force, pursuant to Article 4(1) of the Nice Agreement of June 15, 1957, and of the Stockholm Act of July 14, 1967, of that Agreement, prior to the entry into force of the present Act;

(iii) any changes to be made in accordance with Article 3 of this Act and which enter into force pursuant to Article 4(1) of this Act.

Source: Text courtesy of the World Intellectual Property Organization (WIPO).

(4) The Classification shall be in the English and French languages, both texts being equally authentic.

(5)(*a*) The classification referred to in paragraph (3)(i), together with those amendments and additions referred to in paragraph (3)(ii) which have entered into force prior to the date this Act is opened for signature, is contained in one authentic copy, in the French language, deposited with the Director General of the World Intellectual Property Organization (hereinafter designated respectively "the Director General" and "the Organization"). Those amendments and additions referred to in paragraph (3)(ii) which enter into force after the date this Act is opened for signature shall also be deposited in one authentic copy, in the French language, with the Director General.

(*b*) The English version of the texts referred to in subparagraph (*a*) shall be established by the Committee of Experts referred to in Article 3 promptly after the entry into force of this Act. Its authentic copy shall be deposited with the Director General.

(*c*) The changes referred to in paragraph (3)(iii) shall be deposited in one authentic copy, in the English and French languages, with the Director General.

(6) Official texts of the Classification, in Arabic, German, Italian, Portuguese, Russian, Spanish and in such other languages as the Assembly referred to in Article 5 may designate, shall be established by the Director General, after consultation with the interested Governments and either on the basis of a translation submitted by those Governments or by any other means which do not entail financial implications for the budget of the Special Union or for the Organization.

(7) The alphabetical list shall mention, opposite each indication of goods or services, a serial number that is specific to the language in which the said list is established, together with:

(i) in the case of the alphabetical list established in English, the serial number mentioned in respect of the same indication in the alphabetical list established in French, and vice versa;

(ii) in the case of any alphabetical list established pursuant to paragraph (6), the serial number mentioned in respect of the same indication in the alphabetical list established in English or in the alphabetical list established in French.

Article 2
Legal Effect and Use of the Classification

(1) Subject to the requirements prescribed by this Agreement, the effect of the Classification shall be that attributed to it by each country of the Special Union. In particular, the Classification shall

not bind the countries of the Special Union in respect of either the evaluation of the extent of the protection afforded to any given mark or the recognition of service marks.

(2) Each of the countries of the Special Union reserves the right to use the Classification either as a principal or as a subsidiary system.

(3) The competent Offices of the countries of the Special Union shall include in the official documents and publications relating to registrations of marks the numbers of the classes of the Classification to which the goods or services for which the mark is registered belong.

(4) The fact that a term is included in the alphabetical list in no way affects any rights which might subsist in such a term.

Article 3
Committee of Experts

(1) A Committee of Experts shall be set up in which each country of the Special Union shall be represented.

(2)(*a*) The Director General may, and, if requested by the Committee of Experts, shall, invite countries outside the Special Union which are members of the Organization or party to the Paris Convention for the Protection of Industrial Property to be represented by observers at meetings of the Committee of Experts.

(*b*) The Director General shall invite intergovernmental organizations specialized in the field of marks, of which at least one of the member countries is a country of the Special Union, to be represented by observers at meetings of the Committee of Experts.

(*c*) The Director General may, and, if requested by the Committee of Experts, shall, invite representatives of other intergovernmental organizations and international non-governmental organizations to participate in discussions of interest to them.

(3) The Committee of Experts shall:

(i) decide on changes in the Classification;

(ii) address recommendations to the countries of the Special Union for the purpose of facilitating the use of the Classification and promoting its uniform application;

(iii) take all other measures which, without entailing financial implications for the budget of the Special Union or for the Organization, contribute towards facilitating the application of the Classification by developing countries;

(iv) have the right to establish subcommittees and working groups.

(4) The Committee of Experts shall adopt its own rules of procedure. The latter shall provide for the possibility of participation in meetings of the subcommittees and working groups of the Committee of Experts by those intergovernmental organizations referred to in paragraph (2)(*b*) which can make a substantial contribution to the development of the Classification.

(5) Proposals for changes in the Classification may be made by the competent Office of any country of the Special Union, the International Bureau, any intergovernmental organization represented in the Committee of Experts pursuant to paragraph (2)(*b*) and any country or organization specially invited by the Committee of Experts to submit such proposals. The proposals shall be communicated to the International Bureau, which shall submit them to the members of the Committee of Experts and to the observers not later than two months before the session of the Committee of Experts at which the said proposals are to be considered.

(6) Each country of the Special Union shall have one vote.

(7)(*a*) Subject to subparagraph (*b*), the decisions of the Committee of Experts shall require a simple majority of the countries of the Special Union represented and voting.

(*b*) Decisions concerning the adoption of amendments to the Classification shall require a majority of four-fifths of the countries of the Special Union represented and voting. "Amendment" shall mean any transfer of goods or services from one class to another or the creation of any new class.

(*c*) The rules of procedure referred to in paragraph (4) shall provide that, except in special cases, amendments to the Classification shall be adopted at the end of specified periods; the length of each period shall be determined by the Committee of Experts.

(8) Abstentions shall not be considered as votes.

Article 4
Notification, Entry Into Force and Publication of Changes

(1) Changes decided upon by the Committee of Experts and recommendations of the Committee of Experts shall be notified to the competent Offices of the countries of the Special Union by the International Bureau. Amendments shall enter into force six months after the date of dispatch of the notification. Any other change shall enter into force on a date to be specified by the Committee of Experts at the time the change is adopted.

(2) The International Bureau shall incorporate in the Classification the changes which have entered into force. Announcements of those changes shall be published in such periodicals as may be designated by the Assembly referred to in Article 5.

Article 5
Assembly of the Special Union

(1)(*a*) The Special Union shall have an Assembly consisting of those countries which have ratified or acceded to this Act.

(*b*) The Government of each country shall be represented by one delegate, who may be assisted by alternate delegates, advisors, and experts.

(*c*) The expenses of each delegation shall be borne by the Government which has appointed it.

(2)(*a*) Subject to the provisions of Articles 3 and 4, the Assembly shall:

(i) deal with all matters concerning the maintenance and development of the Special Union and the implementation of this Agreement;
(ii) give directions to the International Bureau concerning the preparation for conferences of revision, due account being taken of any comments made by those countries of the Special Union which have not ratified or acceded to this Act;
(iii) review and approve the reports and activities of the Director General of the Organization (hereinafter designed as "the Director General") concerning the Special Union, and give him all necessary instructions concerning matters within the competence of the Special Union;
(iv) determine the program and adopt the biennial budget of the Special Union, and approve its final accounts;
(v) adopt the financial regulations of the Special Union;
(vi) establish, in addition to the Committee of Experts referred to in Article 3, such other committees of experts and working groups as it may deem necessary to achieve the objectives of the Special Union;
(vii) determine which countries not members of the Special Union and which intergovernmental and international non-governmental organizations shall be admitted to its meetings as observers;
(viii) adopt amendments to Articles 5 to 8;
(ix) take any other appropriate action designed to further the objectives of the Special Union;
(x) perform such other functions as are appropriate under this Agreement.

(*b*)With respect to matters which are of interest also to other Unions administered by the Organization, the Assembly shall make its decisions after having heard the advice of the Coordination Committee of the Organization.

(3)(*a*) Each country member of the Assembly shall have one vote.

(*b*) One-half of the countries members of the Assembly shall constitute a quorum.

(*c*) Notwithstanding the provisions of subparagraph (*b*), if, in any session, the number countries represented is less than one-half but equal to or more than one-third of the countries members of the Assembly, the Assembly may make decisions but, with the exception of decisions concerning its own procedure, all such decisions shall take effect only if the conditions set forth hereinafter are fulfilled. The International Bureau shall communicate the said decisions to the countries members of the Assembly which were not represented and shall invite them to express in writing their vote or abstention within a period of three months from the date of the communication. If, at the expiration of this period, the number of countries having thus expressed their vote or abstention attains the number of countries which was lacking for attaining the quorum in the session itself, such decisions shall take effect provided that at the same time the required majority still obtains.

(*d*) Subject to the provisions of Article 8(2), the decisions of the Assembly shall require two-thirds of the votes cast.

(*e*) Abstentions shall not be considered as votes.

(*f*) A delegate may represent, and vote in the name of, one country only.

(*g*) Countries of the Special Union not members of the Assembly shall be admitted to the meetings of the latter as observers.

(4)(*a*) The Assembly shall meet once in every second calendar year in ordinary session upon convocation by the Director General and, in the absence of exceptional circumstances, during the same period and at the same place as the General Assembly of the Organization.

(*b*) The Assembly shall meet in extraordinary session upon convocation by the Director General, at the request of one-fourth of the countries members of the Assembly.

(*c*) The agenda of each session shall be prepared by the Director General.

(5) The Assembly shall adopt its own rules of procedure.

Article 6
International Bureau

(1)(*a*) Administrative tasks concerning the Special Union shall be performed by the International Bureau.

(*b*) In particular, the International Bureau shall prepare the meetings and provide the secretariat of the Assembly, the Committee of Experts, and such other committees of experts and working groups as may have been established by the Assembly or the Committee of Experts.

(*c*) The Director General shall be the chief executive of the Special Union and shall represent the Special Union.

(3) The Director General and any staff member designated by him shall participate, without the right to vote, in all meetings of the Assembly, the Committee of Experts, and such other committees of experts or working groups as may have been established by the Assembly or the Committee of Experts. The Director General, or a staff member designated by him, shall be ex officio secretary of those bodies.

(3)(*a*) The International Bureau shall, in accordance with the directions of the Assembly, make the preparations for the conferences of revision of the provisions of the Agreement other than Article 5 to 8.

(*b*) The International Bureau may consult with intergovernmental and international non-governmental organizations concerning preparations for conferences of revision.

(*c*) The Director General and persons designated by him shall take part, without the right to vote, in the discussions at those conferences.

(4) The International Bureau shall carry out any other tasks assigned to it.

Article 7
Finances

(1)(*a*) The Special Union shall have a budget.

(*b*) The budget of the Special Union shall include the income and expenses proper to the Special Union, its contribution to the budget of expenses common to the Unions, and, where applicable, the sum made available to the budget of the Conference of the Organization.

(*c*) Expenses not attributable exclusively to the Special Union but also to one or more other Unions administered by the Organization shall be considered as expenses common to the Unions. The share of the Special Union in such common expenses shall be in proportion to the interest the Special Union has in them.

(2) The budget of the Special Union shall be established with due regard to the requirements of coordination with the budgets of the other Unions administered by the Organization.

(3) The budget of the Special Union shall be financed from the following sources:

(i) contributions of the countries of the Special Union;
(ii) fees and charges due for services rendered by the International Bureau in relation to the Special Union;
(iii) sale of, or royalties on, the publications of the International Bureau concerning the Special Union;
(iv) gifts, bequests, and subventions;
(v) rents, interests, and other miscellaneous income.

(4)(*a*) For the purpose of establishing its contribution referred to in paragraph (3)(i), each country of the Special Union shall belong to the same class as it belongs to in the Paris Union for the Protection of Industrial Property, and shall pay its annual contributions on the basis of the same number of units as is fixed for that class in that Union.

(*b*) The annual contribution of each country of the Special Union shall be an amount in the same proportion to the total sum to be contributed to the budget of the Special Union by all countries as the number of its units is to the total of the units of all contributing countries.

(*c*) Contributions shall become due on the first of January of each year.

(*d*) A country which is in arrears in the payment of its contributions may not exercise its right to vote in any organ of the Special Union if the amount of its arrears equals or exceeds the amount of the contributions due from it for the preceding two full years. However, any organ of the Special Union may allow such a country to continue to exercise its right to vote in that organ if, and as long as, it is satisfied that the delay in payment is due to exceptional and unavoidable circumstances.

(*e*) If the budget is not adopted before the beginning of a new financial period, it shall be at the same level as the budget of the previous year, as provided in the financial regulations.

(5) The amount of the fees and charges due for services rendered by the International Bureau in relation to the Special Union shall be established, and shall be reported to the Assembly, by the Director General.

(6)(*a*) The Special Union shall have a working capital fund which shall be constituted by a single payment made by each country of the Special Union. If the fund becomes insufficient, the Assembly shall decide to increase it.

(*b*) The amount of the initial payment of each country to the said fund or of its participation in the increase thereof shall be a proportion of the contribution of that country for the year in which the fund is established or the decision to increase it is made.

(*c*) The proportion and the terms of payment shall be fixed by the Assembly on the proposal of the Director General and after it has heard the advice of the Coordination Committee of the Organization.

(7)(*a*) In the headquarters agreement concluded with the country on the territory of which the Organization has its headquarters, it shall be provided that, whenever the working capital fund is insufficient, such country shall grant advances. The amount of those advances and the conditions on which they are granted shall be the subject of separate agreements, in each case, between such country and the Organization.

(*b*) The country referred to in subparagraph (*a*) and the Organization shall each have the right to denounce the obligation to grant advances, by written notification. Denunciation shall take effect three years after the end of the year in which it has been notified.

(8) The auditing of the accounts shall be effected by one or more of the countries of the Special Union or by external auditors, as provided in the financial regulations. They shall be designated, with their agreement, by the Assembly.

Article 8
Amendment of Articles 5 to 8

(1) Proposals for the amendment of Articles 5, 6, 7, and the present Article, may be initiated by any country member of the Assembly, or by the Director General. Such proposals shall be communicated by the Director General to the member countries of the Assembly at least six months in advance of their consideration by the Assembly.

(2) Amendments to the Articles referred to in paragraph (1) shall be adopted by the Assembly. Adoption shall require three-fourths of the votes cast, provided that any amendment to Article 5, and to the present paragraph, shall require four-fifths of the votes cast.

(3) Any amendment to the Articles referred to in paragraph (1) shall enter into force one month after written notifications of acceptance, effected in accordance with their respective constitutional processes, have been received by the Director General from three-fourths of the countries members of the Assembly at the time it adopted the amendment. Any amendment to the said Articles thus accepted shall bind all the countries which are members of the Assembly at the time the amendment enters into force, or which become members thereof at a subsequent date, provided that any amendment increasing the financial obligations of countries of the Special Union shall bind only those countries which have notified their acceptance of such amendment.

Article 9
Ratification and Accession; Entry Into Force

(1) Any country of the Special Union which has signed this Act may ratify it, and, if it has not signed it, may accede to it.

(2) Any country outside the Special Union which is party to the Paris Convention for the Protection of Industrial Property may accede to this Act and thereby become a country of the Special Union.

(3) Instruments of ratification and accession shall be deposited with the Director General.

(4)(*a*) This Act shall enter into force three months after both of the following conditions are fulfilled:

(i) six or more countries have deposited their instruments of ratification or accession;
(ii) at least three of the said countries are countries which, on the date this Act is opened for signature, are countries of the Special Union.

(*b*) The entry into force referred to in subparagraph (*a*) shall apply to those countries which, at least three months before the said entry into force, have deposited instruments of ratification or accession.

(*c*) With respect to any country not covered by subparagraph (*b*), this Act shall enter into force three months after the date on which its ratification or accession was notified by the Director General, unless a subsequent date has been indicated in the instrument of ratification or accession. In the latter case, this Act shall enter into force with respect to that country on the date thus indicated.

(5) Ratification or accession shall automatically entail acceptance of all the clauses and admission to all the advantages of this Act.

(6) After the entry into force of this Act, no country may ratify or accede to an earlier Act of this Agreement.

Article 10
Duration

This Agreement shall have the same duration as the Paris Convention for the Protection of Industrial Property.

Article 11
Revision

(1) This Agreement may be revised from time to time by a conference of the countries of the Special Union.

(2) The convocation of any revision conference shall be decided upon by the Assembly.

(3) Articles 5 to 8 may be amended either by a revision conference or according to Article 8.

Article 12
Denunciation

(1) Any country may denounce this Act by notification addressed to the Director General. Such denunciation shall constitute also denunciation of the earlier Act or Acts of this Agreement which the country denouncing this Act may have ratified or acceded to, and shall affect only the country making it, the Agreement remaining in full force and effect as regards the other countries of the Special Union.

(2) Denunciation shall take effect one year after the day on which the Director General has received the notification.

(3) The right of denunciation provided by this Article shall not be exercised by any country before the expiration of five years from the date upon which it becomes a country of the Special Union.

Article 13
Reference to Article 24 of the Paris Convention

The provisions of Article 24 of the Stockholm Act of 1967 of the Paris Convention for the Protection of Industrial Property shall apply to this Agreement, provided that, if those provisions are amended in the future, the latest amendment shall apply to this Agreement with respect to those countries of the Special Union which are bound by such amendment.

Article 14
Signature; Languages; Depositary Functions; Notifications

(1)(*a*) This Act shall be signed in a single original in the English and French languages, both texts being equally authentic, and shall be deposited with the Director General.

(*b*) Official texts of this Act shall be established by the Director General, after consultation with the interested Governments and within two months from the date of signature of this Act, in the two other languages, Russian and Spanish, in which, together with the languages referred to in subparagraph (*a*), authentic texts of the Convention Establishing the World Intellectual Property Organization were signed.

(*c*) Official texts of this Act shall be established by the Director General, after consultation with the interested Governments, in the Arabic, German, Italian and Portuguese languages, and such other languages as the Assembly may designate.

(2) This Act shall remain open for signature until December 31, 1977.

(3)(*a*) The Director General shall transmit two copies, certified by him, of the signed text of this Act to the Governments of all countries of the Special Union and, on request, to the Government of any other country.

(*b*) The Director General shall transmit two copies, certified by him, of any amendment to this Act to the Governments of all countries of the Special Union and, on request, to the Government of any other country.

(4) The Director General shall register this Act with the Secretariat of the United Nations.

(5) The Director General shall notify the Governments of all countries party to the Paris Convention for the Protection of Industrial Property of:

(i) signatures under paragraph (1);
(ii) deposits of instruments of ratification or accession under Article 9(3);
(iii) the date of entry into force of this Act under Article 9(4)(*a*);
(iv) acceptances of amendments to this Act under Article 8(3);
(v) the dates on which such amendments enter into force;
(vi) denunciations received under Article 12.

2. Locarno Agreement Establishing an International Classification for Industrial Designs

October 8, 1968

The Locarno Agreement Establishing an International Classification for Industrial Designs was signed at Locarno on October 8, 1968. This agreement, with terms virtually identical to those of the Nice Agreement of 1957, on trademark classification, creates a special union within the Paris Union framework.

This agreement brings uniformity to the classification of industrial design to facilitate searches for novelty and priority.

Member countries may use the classification system[1] for whatever purposes the country considers appropriate (Art. 2 para. 1). Each country, however, is required to use the international classification on official documents for deposit, registration, and official publications (Art. 2 para. 3).

The International Bureau of WIPO administers the Agreement (Art. 6) and promulgates amendments or modifications to the classification system as determined by a committee of experts, consisting of representatives from each member state (Art. 3). The Assembly of the Special Union, also made up of representatives from each member state, governs the Special Union (Art. 5).

---

[1]For the current classification system, *see* WORLD INTELLECTUAL PROPERTY ORGANIZATION, INTERNATIONAL CLASSIFICATION FOR INDUSTRIAL DESIGNS (LOCARNO CLASSIFICATION) WIPO Pub. No. 501(E) (5th ed. 1989).

As of January 1, 1990, the following 15 states were party to the Locarno Agreement:

- Czechoslovakia
- Denmark
- Finland
- France
- German Democratic Republic
- Hungary
- Ireland
- Italy
- Netherlands
- Norway
- Soviet Union
- Spain
- Sweden
- Switzerland
- Yugoslavia

Locarno Agreement Establishing an International Classification for Industrial Designs

Article 1

Establishment of a Special Union; Adoption of an International Classification

(1) The countries to which this Agreement applies constitute a Special Union.

(2) They adopt a single classification for industrial designs (hereinafter designated as "the international classification").

(3) The international classification shall comprise:

(i) a list of classes and subclasses;
(ii) an alphabetical list of goods in which industrial designs are incorporated, with an indication of the classes and subclasses into which they fall;
(iii) explanatory notes.

(4) The list of classes and subclasses in the list annexed to the present Agreement, subject to such amendments and additions as the Committee of Experts set up under Article 3 (hereinafter designated as "the Committee of Experts") may make to it.

(5) The alphabetical list of goods and the explanatory notes shall be adopted by the Committee of Experts in accordance with the procedure laid down in Article 3.

(6) The international classification may be amended or supplemented by the Committee of Experts, in accordance with the procedure laid down in Article 3.

(7)(*a*) The international classification shall be established in the English and French languages.

(*b*) Official texts of the international classification, in such other languages as the Assembly referred to in Article 5 may designate, shall be established, after consultation with the interested Governments, by the International Bureau of Intellectual Property (hereinafter designated as "the International Bureau") referred to in the Convention Establishing the World Intellectual Property Organization (hereinafter designated as "the Organization").

Source: Text courtesy of the World Intellectual Property Organization (WIPO).

Article 2
Use and Legal Scope of the International Classification

(1) Subject to the requirements prescribed by this Agreement, the international classification shall be solely of an administrative character. Nevertheless, each country may attribute to it the legal scope which it considers appropriate. In particular, the international classification shall not bind the countries of the Special Union as regards the nature and scope of the protection afforded to the design in those countries.

(2) Each country of the Special Union reserves the right to use the international classification as a principal or as a subsidiary system.

(3) The Offices of the countries of the Special Union shall include in the official documents for the deposit or registration of designs, and, if they are officially published, in the publications in question, the numbers of the classes and subclasses of the international classification into which the goods incorporating the designs belong.

(4) In selecting terms for inclusion in the alphabetical list of goods, the Committee of Experts shall exercise reasonable care to avoid using terms in which exclusive rights may exist. The inclusion of any word in the alphabetical index, however, is not an expression of opinion of the Committee of Experts on whether or not it is subject to exclusive rights.

Article 3
Committee of Experts

(1) A Committee of Experts shall be entrusted with the tasks referred to in Article 1(4), 1(5) and 1(6). Each country of the Special Union shall be represented on the Committee of Experts, which shall be organized according to the rules of procedure adopted by a simple majority of the countries represented.

(2) The Committee of Experts shall adopt the alphabetical list and explanatory notes by a simple majority of the votes of the countries of the Special Union.

(3) Proposals for amendments or additions to the international classification may be made by the Office of any country of the Special Union or by the International Bureau. Any proposal emanating from an Office shall be communicated by that Office to the International Bureau. Proposals from Offices and from the International Bureau shall be transmitted by the latter to the members of the Committee of Experts not later than two months before the session of the Committee at which the said proposals are to be considered.

(4) The decisions of the Committee of Experts concerning the adoption of amendments and additions to be made in the international classification shall be by a simple majority of the countries of the Special Union. Nevertheless, if such decisions entail the setting up of a new class or any transfer of goods from one class to another, unanimity shall be required.

(5) Each expert shall have the right to vote by mail.

(6) If a country does not appoint a representative for a given session of the Committee of Experts, or if the expert appointed has not expressed his vote during the session or within a period to be prescribed by the rules of procedure of the Committee of Experts, the country concerned shall be considered to have accepted the decision of the Committee.

Article 4
Notification and Publication of the Classification and of Amendments and Additions Thereto

(1) The alphabetical list of goods and the explanatory notes adopted by the Committee of Experts, as well as any amendment or addition to the international classification decided by the Committee, shall be communicated to the Offices of the countries of the Special Union by the International Bureau. The decisions of the Committee of Experts shall enter into force as soon as the communication is received. Nevertheless, if such decisions entail the setting up of a new class or any transfer of goods from one class to another, they shall enter into force within a period of six months from the date of the said communication.

(2) The International Bureau, as depositary of the international classification, shall incorporate therein the amendments and additions which have entered into force. Announcements of the amendments and additions shall be published in the periodicals to be designated by the Assembly.

Article 5
Assembly of the Special Union

(1)(*a*) The Special Union shall have an Assembly consisting of the countries of the Special Union.

(*b*) The Government of each country of the Special Union shall be represented by one delegate, who may be assisted by alternate delegates, advisors, and experts.

(*c*) The expenses of each delegation shall be borne by the Government which has appointed it.

(2)(*a*) Subject to the provisions of Article 3, the Assembly shall:

(i) deal with all matters concerning the maintenance and development of the Special Union and the implementation of this Agreement;

(ii) give directions to the International Bureau concerning the preparation for conferences of revision;

(iii) review and approve the reports and activities of the Director General of the Organization (hereinafter designated as "the Director General") concerning the Special Union, and give him all necessary instructions concerning matters within the competence of the Special Union;

(iv) determine the program and adopt the biennial budget of the Special Union, and approve its final accounts;

(v) adopt the financial regulations of the Special Union;

(vi) decide on the establishment of official texts of the international classification in languages other than English and French;

(vii) establish, in addition to the Committee of Experts set up under Article 3, such other committees of experts and working groups as it deems appropriate to achieve the objectives of the Special Union;

(viii) determine which countries not members of the Special Union and which intergovernmental and international non-governmental organizations shall be admitted to its meetings as observers;

(ix) adopt amendments to Article 5 to 8;

(x) take any other appropriate action designed to further the objectives of the Special Union;

(xi) perform such other functions as are appropriate under this Agreement.

(*b*) With respect to matters which are of interest also to other Unions administered by the Organization, the Assembly shall make its decisions after having heard the advice of the Coordination Committee of the Organization.

(3)(*a*) Each country member of the Assembly shall have one vote.

(*b*) One-half of the countries members of the Assembly shall constitute a quorum.

(*c*) Notwithstanding the provisions of subparagraph (*b*), if, in any session, the number of countries represented is less than one-half but equal to or more than one-third of the countries members of the Assembly, the Assembly may make decisions but, with the exception of decisions concerning its own procedure, all such decisions shall take effect only if the conditions set forth hereinafter are fulfilled. The International Bureau shall communicate the said decisions to the countries members of the Assembly which were not represented and shall invite them to express in writing their vote or abstention within a period of three months from the date of the communication. If, at the expiration of this period, the number of countries having thus expressed their vote or abstention attains the number of countries which was lacking for attaining the quorum in the session itself, such decisions shall take effect provided that at the same time the required majority still obtains.

(*d*) Subject to the provisions of Article 8(2), the decisions of the Assembly shall require two-thirds of the votes cast.

(*e*) Abstentions shall not be considered as votes.

(*f*) A delegate may represent, and vote in the name of, one country only.

(4)(*a*) The Assembly shall meet once in every second calendar year in ordinary session upon convocation by the Director General and, in the absence of exceptional circumstances, during the same period and at the same place as the General Assembly of the Organization.

(*b*) The Assembly shall meet in extraordinary session upon convocation by the Director General, at the request of one-fourth of the countries members of the Assembly.

(*c*) The agenda of each session shall be prepared by the Director General.

(5) The Assembly shall adopt its own rules of procedure.

Article 6
International Bureau

(1)(*a*) Administrative tasks concerning the Special Union shall be performed by the International Bureau.

(*b*) In particular, the International Bureau shall prepare the meetings and provide the secretariat of the Assembly, the Committee of Experts, and such other committees of experts and working groups as may have been established by the Assembly or the Committee of Experts.

(*c*) The Director General shall be the chief executive of the Special Union and shall represent the Special Union.

(2) The Director General and any staff member designated by him shall participate, without the right to vote, in all meetings of the Assembly, the Committee of Experts, and such other committees of experts or working groups as may have been established by the Assembly or the Committee of Experts. The Director General, or a

staff member designated by him, shall be ex officio secretary of those bodies.

(3)(*a*) The International Bureau shall, in accordance with the directions of the Assembly, make the preparations for the conferences of revision of the provisions of the Agreement other than Articles 5 to 8.

(*b*) The International Bureau may consult with intergovernmental and international non-governmental organizations concerning preparations for conferences of revision.

(*c*) The Director General and persons designated by him shall take part, without the right to vote, in the discussions at those conferences.

(4) The International Bureau shall carry out any other tasks assigned to it.

Article 7
Finances

(1)(*a*) The Special Union shall have a budget.

(*b*) The budget of the Special Union shall include the income and expenses proper to the Special Union, its contribution to the budget of expenses common to the Unions, and, where applicable, the sum made available to the budget of the Conference of the Organization.

(*c*) Expenses not attributable exclusively to the Special Union but also to one or more other Unions administered by the Organization shall be considered as expenses common to the Unions. The share of the Special Union in such common expenses shall be in proportion to the interest the Special Union has in them.

(2) The budget of the Special Union shall be established with due regard to the requirements of coordination with the budgets of the other Unions administered by the Organization.

(3) The budget of the Special Union shall be financed from the following sources:

(i) contributions of the countries of the Special Union;
(ii) fees and charges due for services rendered by the International Bureau in relation to the Special Union;
(iii) sale of, or royalties on, the publications of the International Bureau concerning the Special Union;
(iv) gifts, bequests, and subventions;
(v) rents, interests, and other miscellaneous income.

(4)(*a*) For the purpose of establishing its contribution referred to in paragraph (3)(i), each country of the Special Union shall belong to the same class as it belongs to in the Paris Union for the Protection of Industrial Property, and shall pay its annual contributions on the basis of the same number of units as is fixed for that class in that Union.

(*b*) The annual contribution of each country of the Special Union shall be an amount in the same proportion to the total sum to be contributed to the budget of the Special Union by all countries as the number of its units is to the total of the units of all contributing countries.

(*c*) Contributions shall become due on the first of January of each year.

(*d*) A country which is in arrears in the payment of its contributions may not exercise its right to vote in any organ of the Special Union if the amount of its arrears equals or exceeds the amount of the contributions due from it for the preceding two full years. However, any organ of the Special Union may allow such a country to continue to exercise its right to vote in that organ if, and as long as, it is satisfied that the delay in payment is due to exceptional and unavoidable circumstances.

(*e*) If the budget is not adopted before the beginning of a new financial period, it shall be at the same level as the budget of the previous year, as provided in the financial regulations.

(5) The amount of the fees and charges due for services rendered by the International Bureau in relation to the Special Union shall be established, and shall be reported to the Assembly, by the Director General.

(6)(*a*) The Special Union shall have a working capital fund which shall be constituted by a single payment made by each country of the Special Union. If the fund becomes insufficient, the Assembly shall decide to increase it.

(*b*) The amount of the initial payment of each country to the said fund or of its participation in the increase thereof shall be a proportion of the contribution of that country for the year in which the fund is established or the decision to increase it is made.

(*c*) The proportion and the terms of payment shall be fixed by the Assembly on the proposal of the Director General and after it has heard the advice of the Coordination Committee of the Organization.

(7)(*a*) In the headquarters agreement concluded with the country on the territory of which the Organization has its headquarters, it shall be provided that, whenever the working capital fund is insufficient, such country shall grant advances. The amount of those advances and the conditions on which they are granted shall be the subject of separate agreements, in each case, between such country and the Organization.

(*b*) The country referred to in subparagraph (*a*) and the Organization shall each have the right to denounce the obligation to grant advances, by written notification. Denunciation shall take effect three years after the end of the year in which it has been notified.

(8) The auditing of the accounts shall be effected by one or more of the countries of the Special Union or by external auditors, as provided in the financial regulations. They shall be designated, with their agreement, by the Assembly.

Article 8
Amendment of Articles 5 to 8

(1) Proposals for the amendment of Articles 5, 6, 7, and the present Article, may be initiated by any country of the Special Union or by the Director General. Such proposals shall be communicated by the Director General to the countries of the Special Union at least six months in advance of their consideration by the Assembly.

(2) Amendments to the Articles referred to in paragraph (1) shall be adopted by the Assembly. Adoption shall require three-fourths of the votes cast, provided that any amendment to Article 5, and to the present paragraph, shall require four-fifths of the votes cast.

(3) Any amendment to the Articles referred to in paragraph (1) shall enter into force one month after written notifications of acceptance, effected in accordance with their respective constitutional processes, have been received by the Director General from three-fourths of the countries members of the Special Union at the time the amendment was adopted. Any amendment to the said Articles thus accepted shall bind all the countries which are members of the Special Union at the time the amendment enters into force, or which become members thereof at a subsequent date, provided that any amendment increasing the financial obligations of countries of the Special Union shall bind only those countries which have notified their acceptance of such amendment.

Article 9
Ratification and Accession; Entry Into Force

(1) Any country party to the Paris Convention for the Protection of Industrial Property which has signed this Agreement may ratify it, and, if it has not signed it, may accede to it.

(2) Instruments of ratification and accession shall be deposited with the Director General.

(3)(*a*) With respect to the first five countries which have deposited their instruments of ratification or accession, this Agreement shall enter into force three months after the deposit of the fifth such instrument.

(*b*) With respect to any other country, this Agreement shall enter into force three months after the date on which its ratification or accession has been notified by the Director General, unless a subsequent date has been indicated in the instrument of ratification or accession. In the latter case, this Agreement shall enter into force with respect to that country on the date thus indicated.

(4) Ratification or accession shall automatically entail acceptance of all the clauses and admission to all the advantages of this Agreement.

Article 10
Force and Duration of the Agreement

This Agreement shall have the same force and duration as the Paris Convention for the Protection of Industrial Property.

Article 11
Revision of Articles 1 to 4 and 9 to 15

(1) Articles 1 to 4 and 9 to 15 of this Agreement may be submitted to revision with a view to the introduction of desired improvements.

(2) Every revision shall be considered at a conference which shall be held among the delegates of the countries of the Special Union.

Article 12
Denunciation

(1) Any country may denounce this Act by notification addressed to the Director General. Such denunciation shall affect only the country making it, the Agreement remaining in full force and effect as regards the other countries of the Special Union.

(2) Denunciation shall take effect one year after the day on which the Director General has received the notification.

(3) The right of denunciation provided by this Article shall not be exercised by any country before the expiration of five years from the date upon which it becomes a member of the Special Union.

Article 13
Territories

The provisions of Article 24 of the Paris Convention for the Protection of Industrial Property shall apply to this Agreement.

Article 14
Signature, Languages, Notifications

(1)(*a*) This Agreement shall be signed in a single copy in the English and French languages, both texts being equally authentic, and shall be deposited with the Government of Switzerland.

(*b*) This Agreement shall remain open for signature at Berne until June 30, 1969.

(2) Official texts shall be established by the Director General, after consultation with the interested Governments, in such other languages as the Assembly may designate.

(3) The Director General shall transmit two copies, certified by the Government of Switzerland, of the signed text of this Agreement to the Governments of the countries that have signed it and, on request, to the Government of any other country.

(4) The Director General shall register this Agreement with the Secretariat of the United Nations.

(5) The Director General shall notify the Governments of all countries of the Special Union of the date of entry into force of the Agreement, signatures, deposits of instruments of ratification or accession, acceptances of amendments to this Agreement and the dates on which such amendments enter into force, and notifications of denunciation.

Article 15
Transitional Provision

Until the first Director General assumes office, references in this Agreement to the International Bureau of the Organization or to the Director General shall be deemed to be references to the United International Bureaux for the Protection of Intellectual Property (BIRPI) or its Director, respectively.

In Witness Whereof, the undersigned, being duly authorized thereto, have signed this Agreement.

Done at Locarno, on October 8, 1968.

ANNEX

List of Classes and Subclasses of the International Classification

Class 1—Foodstuffs, Including Dietetic Foods
01) Bakers' products, biscuits, pastry, macaroni, etc.
02) Chocolates, confectionery, ices
03) Cheeses, butter and other dairy produce and substitutes
04) Butchers' meat (including pork products)
05) Animal foodstuffs
99) Miscellaneous

Class 2—Articles of Clothing, Including Footwear
01) Garments
02) Undergarments, lingerie, corsets, brassières
03) Headwear
04) Footwear (including boots, shoes and slippers)
05) Socks and stockings
06) Neckties, scarves and neckerchiefs
07) Gloves
08) Haberdashery
99) Miscellaneous

Class 3—Travel Goods and Personal Belongings, Not Elsewhere Specified
01) Trunks, suitcases and briefcases
02) Handbags, wallets, pocketbooks, purses, boxes
03) Umbrellas, walking sticks
04) Fans
99) Miscellaneous

Class 4—Brushware
01) Brushes for cleaning and brooms
02) Toilet and clothes brushes
03) Brushes for industry
04) Paint-brushes
99) Miscellaneous

Class 5—Textile Piece-goods Articles, and Other Sheet Material
01) Spun articles
02) Textile fabrics (woven, knitted, etc.)
03) Sheet material
04) Felt
05) Covering sheets (wallpaper, linoleum, etc.)
06) Lace
07) Embroideries
08) Ribbons, braids and other trimmings
09) Leather and substitutes
99) Miscellaneous

Class 6—Furnishing
01) Furniture
02) Mattresses and cushions
03) Curtains (ready-made)
04) Carpets
05) Mats and floor rugs
06) Mirrors and frames
07) Garment hangers
08) Bedspreads
09) Household linen and napery
99) Miscellaneous

Class 7—Household Goods, Not Elsewhere Specified
01) China, glassware, dishes and other articles of a similar nature
02) Cooking utensils and containers
03) Knives, forks and spoons
04) Cooking stoves, toasters, etc.
05) Chopping, mincing, grinding and mixing machines
06) Flat-irons and laundering, cleaning and drying equipment
99) Miscellaneous

Class 8—Tools and Hardware
01) Tools and implements for agriculture, forestry and horticulture
02) Other tools and implements
03) Locks and other hardware fittings
04) Nails, screws, nuts, bolts, etc.
99) Miscellaneous

Class 9—Packages and Containers
01) Bottles, flasks, carboys, demijohns and pots
02) Closing means
03) Drums and casks
04) Boxes and cases
05) Hampers, crates and baskets
06) Bags, wrappers and tubes and capsules
07) Cans
08) Ropes and hooping materials
99) Miscellaneous

Class 10—Clocks and Watches, and Measuring Instruments
01) House clocks
02) Watches and wrist-watches
03) Alarms
04) Other clocks
05) All other chronometrical instruments
06) Dials, hands and all other parts of watches, clocks, and of other chronometrical instruments
07) Geodetic, nautical, acoustic and meteorological articles
08) Instruments for measuring physical sizes, like length, pressure, etc.
09) Instruments for measuring temperature
10) Instruments for measuring electric sizes (voltmeters, etc.)
11) Testing instruments
99) Miscellaneous

Class 11—Articles of Adornment
01) Jewelry
02) Trinkets, table, mantel and wall ornaments, including flower vases
03) Medals and badges
04) Artificial flowers, fruits and plants
05) Festive decorations
99) Miscellaneous

Class 12—Vehicles
01) Vehicles drawn by animals
02) Trolleys, trucks and barrows, hand-drawn
03) Locomotives and rolling-stock for railways and all other rail vehicles
04) Telephone carriers and chair lifts
05) Elevators and hoists
06) Ships and boats
07) Aircraft and space vehicles
08) Motor-cars and buses
09) Lorries and tractors
10) Trailers, including camping or house trailers
11) Motorcycles, scooters, bicycles and tricycles
12) Perambulators and invalid chairs
13) Special vehicles
14) Pneumatic tyres, inner tubes and all other equipment or accessories, not elsewhere specified
99) Miscellaneous

Class 13—Equipment for Production, Distribution and Transformation of Electricity
01) Generators and motors
02) Power transformers, rectifiers, batteries and accumulators
03) Equipment for distribution and control of electric power (conductors, switch-gear, etc.)
99) Miscellaneous

Class 14—Electrical and Electronic Equipment
01) Equipment for the recording and reproduction of sounds or pictures
02) Equipment for the recording, reproduction and retrieval of information
03) Communications equipment (telegraph, telephone, teletype, television and radio)
04) Amplifiers
99) Miscellaneous

Class 15—Industrial and Household Machines
01) Engines (not electrical)
02) Pumps and compressors
03) Agricultural machinery
04) Construction machinery
05) Industrial machines, not elsewhere specified
06) Industrial laundry and cleaning machines
07) Household laundry and cleaning machines
08) Industrial textile sewing, knitting and embroidering machines
09) Household textile sewing, knitting and embroidering machines
10) Industrial refrigeration apparatus
11) Household refrigeration apparatus
12) Food preparation machines
99) Miscellaneous

Class 16—Photographic, Cinematographic and Optical Apparatus

01) Photographic cameras
02) Film cameras
03) Projectors (for slides)
04) Projectors (for films)
05) Photocopying apparatus and enlargers
06) Developing apparatus
07) Accessories
08) Optical articles, such as spectacles, microscopes, etc.
99) Miscellaneous

Class 17—Musical Instruments

01) Keyboard instruments (including electronic and other organs)
02) Wind instruments (including piano accordions)
03) Stringed instruments
04) Percussion instruments
05) Mechanical instruments
99) Miscellaneous

Class 18—Printing and Office Machinery

01) Typewriters and calculating machines, with the exception of electronic machines
02) Typographical machinery
03) Machinery for printing by processes other than typography (excluding photocopying machinery)
04) Characters and type faces
05) Massicots
99) Miscellaneous

Class 19—Stationers' Goods, Desk Equipment, Artists' and Teaching Materials

01) Writing paper and envelopes
02) Desk equipment
03) Calendars
04) Bindings
05) Illustrated cards and other printed matter
06) Materials and instruments for writing by hand
07) Materials and instruments for painting (excluding brushes), for sculpture, for engraving and for other artistic techniques
08) Teaching materials
99) Miscellaneous

Class 20—Sales and Advertising Equipment

01) Automatic vending machines
02) Display and sales equipment
03) Signboards and advertising materials
99) Miscellaneous

Class 21—Games, Toys and Sports Goods

01) Games
02) Toys
03) Gymnastics and sports apparatus and equipment
04) Amusement and entertainment articles
05) Tents
99) Miscellaneous

Class 22—Arms and Tackle for Hunting, Fishing and Vermin Trapping

01) Side arms
02) Projectile weapons
03) Ammunition, fuses and projectiles
04) Hunting equipment (excluding weapons)
05) Fishing rods
06) Reels for fishing rods
07) Baits
08) Other pieces of fishing tackle
09) Traps and articles for vermin destruction
99) Miscellaneous

Class 23—Sanitary, Heating, Ventilation and Air-Conditioning Equipment

01) Fluid and gas-distribution equipment (including pipes and pipe fittings)
02) Sanitary fittings and equipment (baths, showers, wash-basins, lavatories, sanitary units, etc.)
03) Heating equipment
04) Ventilation and air-conditioning
05) Solid fuel
99) Miscellaneous

Class 24—Medical and Laboratory Equipment

01) Equipment for transport and accommodation for patients
02) Hospital and laboratory equipment (for diagnostic, tests, operations, treatment, eye-testing)
03) Medical, surgical, dental instruments
04) Prosthetic articles
05) Material for dressing and nursing
99) Miscellaneous

Class 25—Building Units and Construction Elements

01) Building material and elements, such as bricks, beams, tiles, slates, panels, etc.
02) Windows, doors, blinds, etc.
03) Sections, angles and channels
04) Houses, garages and all other buildings
05) Civil engineering elements
99) Miscellaneous

Class 26—Lighting Apparatus

01) Luminous sources, electrical or not, such as incandescent bulbs, luminous tubes and plates
02) Lamps, standard lamps, chandeliers, wall and ceiling fixtures
03) Public lighting fixtures (outside lamps, stagelighting, floodlights)
04) Torches and hand lamps and lanterns
05) Candles, candlesticks
06) Lamp-shades
99) Miscellaneous

Class 27—Tobacco and Smokers' Supplies
01) Tobacco, cigars and cigarettes
02) Pipes, cigar and cigarette holders
03) Ash-trays
04) Matches
05) Lighters
06) Cigar cases, cigarette cases, tobacco jars and pouches
99) Miscellaneous

Class 28—Pharmaceutical and Cosmetic Articles and Products, Toilet Articles and Apparatus
01) Pharmaceutical articles and products
02) Cosmetic articles and products
03) Toilet articles and beauty parlor equipment
99) Miscellaneous

Class 29—Safety and Protective Devices and Equipment for Human Beings
01) Devices and equipment against fire hazards
02) Devices and equipment for water rescue
03) Devices and equipment for mountain rescue
99) Devices and equipment against other hazards (roads, mines, industries, etc.)

Class 30—Care and Handling of Animals
01) Shelters and pens
02) Feeders and waterers
03) Saddlery
04) Safety and protective devices and equipment for animals
99) Other articles

Class 31—Miscellaneous
All the products not included in the preceding classes.

Resolution
Adopted by the Conference of Locarno on October 7, 1968

(1) A provisional Committee of Experts is hereby set up at the International Bureau. This Committee shall include a representative of each country signatory to the Locarno Agreement Establishing an International Classification for Industrial Designs.

(2) The provisional Committee shall submit to the International Bureau a draft of the alphabetical list of goods and of the explanatory notes mentioned in Article 1(5) of the Agreement. It shall also re-examine the list of classes and subclasses annexed to the Agreement and shall submit to the International Bureau, if necessary, draft amendments and additions to be made to the said list.

3. Strasbourg Agreement Concerning the International Patent Classification

March 24, 1971

The Strasbourg Agreement Concerning the International Patent Classification was adopted on March 24, 1971. It was inspired by the Nice Agreement Concerning the International Classification of Goods and Services for the Purposes of the Registration of Marks and by the Locarno Agreement Establishing an International Classification for Industrial Designs. The Strasbourg Agreement, like the other classification agreements, is administered by WIPO's International Bureau.

The Agreement encourages unification of national patent legislation and serves to provide a uniform foundation for the search of patents. Its international classification system incorporates 8 sections, including 114 classes, and over 46,000 groups and subgroups.[1]

The Agreement requires that member nations apply its international patent classification system, including the symbols of classification, in patents, inventor's certificates, and utility models and certificates (Art. 4).

The Strasbourg Agreement is a special agreement under the Union of Paris and any member country of the Paris Convention may adhere to it.

---

[1]For the current classification system, *see* WORLD INTELLECTUAL PROPERTY ORGANIZATION, INTERNATIONAL PATENT CLASSIFICATION (IPC) WIPO (4th ed. 1984); WORLD INTELLECTUAL PROPERTY ORGANIZATION, OFFICIAL CATCHWORD INDEX, WIPO Pub. No. 463(E) (4th ed. 1984); WORLD INTELLECTUAL PROPERTY ORGANIZATION, CLASS AND SUBCLASS TITLES OF THE INTERNATIONAL PATENT CLASSIFICATION (4th ed. 1984); WORLD INTELLECTUAL PROPERTY ORGANIZATION, REVISION CONCORDANCE LIST WIPO Pub. No. 462(E)/1979 and 462/(E)/1984.

As of January 1, 1990, the following 27 states were party to the Strasbourg Agreement:

Australia	Federal Republic of Germany	Portugal
Austria	Ireland	Soviet Union
Belgium	Israel	Spain
Brazil	Italy	Suriname
Czechoslovakia	Japan	Sweden
Denmark	Luxembourg	Switzerland
Egypt	Monaco	United Kingdom
Finland	Netherlands	United States of America
France	Norway	
German Democratic Republic		

Strasbourg Agreement Concerning the International Patent Classification

Article 1
Establishment of a Special Union: Adoption of an International Classification

The countries to which this Agreement applies constitute a Special Union and adopt a common classification for patents for invention, inventors' certificates, utility models and utility certificates, to be known as the "International Patent Classification" (hereinafter designated as the "Classification").

Article 2
Definition of the Classification

(1)(*a*) The Classification comprises:

(i) the text which was established pursuant to the provisions of the European Convention on the International Classification of Patents for Invention of December 19, 1954 (hereinafter designated as the "European Convention"), and which came into force and was published by the Secretary General of the Council of Europe on September 1, 1968;

(ii) the amendments which have entered into force pursuant to Article 2(2) of the European Convention prior to the entry into force of this Agreement;

(iii) the amendments made thereafter in accordance with Article 5 which enter into force pursuant to the provisions of Article 6.

(*b*) The Guide and the notes included in the text of the Classification are an integral part thereof.

(2)(*a*) The text referred to in paragraph (1)(*a*)(i) is contained in two authentic copies, each in the English and French languages, deposited, at the time that this Agreement is opened for signature, one with the Secretary General of the Council of Europe and the other with the Director General of the World Intellectual Property Organization (hereinafter respectively designated "Director General" and "Organization") established by the Convention of July 14, 1967.

Source: Text courtesy of the World Intellectual Property Organization (WIPO).

(*b*) The amendments referred to in paragraph (1)(*a*)(ii) shall be deposited in two authentic copies, each in the English and French languages, one with the Secretary General of the Council of Europe and the other with the Director General.

(*c*) The amendments referred to in paragraph (1)(*a*)(iii) shall be deposited in one authentic copy only, in the English and French languages, with the Director General.

Article 3
Languages of the Classification

(1) The Classification shall be established in the English and French languages, both texts being equally authentic.

(2) Official texts of the Classification, in German, Japanese, Portuguese, Russian, Spanish and in such other languages as the Assembly referred to in Article 7 may designate, shall be established by the International Bureau of the Organization (hereinafter designated as the "International Bureau"), in consultation with the interested Governments and either on the basis of a translation submitted by those Governments or by any other means which do not entail financial implications for the budget of the Special Union or for the Organization.

Article 4
Use of the Classification

(1) The Classification shall be solely of an administrative character.

(2) Each country of the Special Union shall have the right to use the Classification either as a principal or as a subsidiary system.

(3) The competent authorities of the countries of the Special Union shall include in

- (i) patents, inventors' certificates, utility models and utility certificates issued by them, and in applications relating thereto, whether published or only laid open for public inspection by them, and
- (ii) notices, appearing in official periodicals, of the publication or laying open of the documents referred to in subparagraph (i) the complete symbols of the Classification applied to the invention to which the document referred to in subparagraph (i) relates.

(4) When signing this Agreement or when depositing its instrument of ratification or accession:

(i) any country may declare that it does not undertake to include the symbols relating to groups or subgroups of the Classification in applications as referred to in paragraph (3) which are only laid open for public inspection and in notices relating thereto, and

(ii) any country which does not proceed to an examination as to novelty, whether immediate or deferred, and in which the procedure for the grant of patents or other kinds of protection does not provide for a search into the state of the art, may declare that it does not undertake to include the symbols relating to the groups and subgroups of the Classification in the documents and notices referred to in paragraph (3). If these conditions exist only in relation to certain kinds of protection or certain fields of technology, the country in question may only make this reservation to the extent that the conditions apply.

(5) The symbols of the Classification, preceded by the words "International Patent Classification" or an abbreviation thereof to be determined by the Committee of Experts referred to in Article 5, shall be printed in heavy type, or in such a manner that they are clearly visible, in the heading of each document referred to in paragraph (3)(i) in which they are to be included.

(6) If any country of the Special Union entrusts the grant of patents to an intergovernmental authority, it shall take all possible measures to ensure that this authority uses the Classification in accordance with this Article.

Article 5
Committee of Experts

(1) A Committee of Experts shall be set up in which each country of the Special Union shall be represented.

(2)(*a*) The Director General shall invite intergovernmental organizations specialized in the patent field, and of which at least one of the member countries is party to this Agreement, to be represented by observers at meetings of the Committee of Experts.

(*b*) The Director General may, and, if requested by the Committee of Experts, shall, invite representatives of other intergovernmental and international non-governmental organizations to participate in discussions of interest to them.

(3) The Committee of Experts shall:

(i) amend the Classification;

(ii) address recommendations to the countries of the Special Union for the purpose of facilitating the use of the Classification and promoting its uniform application;

(iii) assist in the promotion of international cooperation in the reclassification of documentation used for the examination of inventions, taking in particular the needs of developing countries into account;

(iv) take all other measures which, without entailing financial implications for the budget of the Special Union or for the Organization, contribute towards facilitating the application of the Classification by developing countries;

(v) have the right to establish subcommittees and working groups.

(4) The Committee of Experts shall adopt its own Rules of Procedure. These shall allow for the possibility of participation of intergovernmental organizations, referred to in paragraph (2)(*a*), which can perform substantial work in the development of the Classification, in meetings of its subcommittees and working groups.

(5) Proposals for amendments to the Classification may be made by the competent authority of any country of the Special Union, the International Bureau, any intergovernmental organization represented in the Committee of Experts pursuant to paragraph (2)(*a*) and any other organization specially invited by the Committee of Experts to submit such proposals. The proposals shall be communicated to the International Bureau which shall submit them to the members of the Committee of Experts and to the observers not later than two months before the session of the Committee of Experts at which the said proposals are to be considered.

(6)(*a*) Each country member of the Committee of Experts shall have one vote.

(*b*) The decisions of the Committee of Experts shall require a simple majority of the countries represented and voting.

(*c*) Any decision which is regarded by one-fifth of the countries represented and voting as giving rise to a modification in the basic structure of the Classification or as entailing a substantial work of reclassification shall require a majority of three-fourths of the countries represented and voting.

(*d*) Abstentions shall not be considered as votes.

Article 6
Notification, Entry into Force and Publication of Amendments and Other Decisions

(1) Every decision of the Committee of Experts concerning the adoption of amendments to the Classification and recommendations of the Committee of Experts shall be notified by the International Bureau to the competent authorities of the countries of the Special Union. The amendments shall enter into force six months from the date of dispatch of the notification.

(2) The International Bureau shall incorporate in the Classification the amendments which have entered into force. Announcements of the amendments shall be published in such periodicals as are designated by the Assembly referred to in Article 7.

Article 7
Assembly of the Special Union

(1)(*a*) The Special Union shall have an Assembly consisting of the countries of the Special Union.

(*b*) The Government of each country of the Special Union shall be represented by one delegate, who may be assisted by alternate delegates, advisors and experts.

(*c*) Any intergovernmental organization referred to in Article 5(2)(*a*) may be represented by an observer in the meetings of the Assembly, and, if the Assembly so decides, in those of such committees or working groups as may have been established by the Assembly.

(*d*) The expenses of each delegation shall be borne by the Government which has appointed it.

(2)(*a*) Subject to the provision of Article 5, the Assembly shall:

(i) deal with all matters concerning the maintenance and development of the Special Union and the implementation of this Agreement;

(ii) give directions to the International Bureau concerning the preparation for conferences of revision;

(iii) review and approve the reports and activities of the Director General concerning the Special Union, and give him all necessary instructions concerning matters within the competence of the Special Union;

(iv) determine the program and adopt the biennial budget of the Special Union, and approve its final accounts;

(v) adopt the financial regulations of the Special Union;

(vi) decide on the establishment of official texts of the Classification in languages other than English, French and those listed in Article 3(2);

(vii) establish such committees and working groups as it deems appropriate to achieve the objectives of the Special Union;

(viii) determine, subject to paragraph (1)(*c*), which countries not members of the Special Union and which intergovernmental and international non-governmental organizations shall be admitted as observers to its meetings, and to those of any committees or working group established by it;

(ix) take any other appropriate action designed to further the objectives of the Special Union;

(x) perform such other functions as are appropriate under this Agreement.

(*b*) With respect to matters which are of interest also to other Unions administered by the Organization, the Assembly shall make its decisions after having heard the advice of the Coordination Committee of the Organization.

(3)(*a*) Each country member of the Assembly shall have one vote.

(*b*) One-half of the countries members of the Assembly shall constitute a quorum.

(*c*) In the absence of the quorum, the Assembly may make decisions but, with the exception of decisions concerning its own procedure, all such decisions shall take effect only if the conditions set forth hereinafter are fulfilled. The International Bureau shall communicate the said decisions to the countries members of the Assembly which were not represented and shall invite them to express in writing their vote or abstention within a period of three months from the date of the communication. If, at the expiration of this period, the number of countries having thus expressed their vote or abstention attains the number of countries which was lacking for attaining the quorum in the session itself, such decisions shall take effect provided that at the same time the required majority still obtains.

(*d*) Subject to the provisions of Article 11(2), the decisions of the Assembly shall require two-thirds of the votes cast.

(*e*) Abstentions shall not be considered as votes.

(*f*) A delegate may represent, and vote in the name of, one country only.

(4)(*a*) The Assembly shall meet once in every second calendar year in ordinary session upon convocation by the Director General and, in the absence of exceptional circumstances, during the same period and at the same place as the General Assembly of the Organization.

(*b*) The Assembly shall meet in extraordinary session upon convocation by the Director General, at the request of one-fourth of the countries members of the Assembly.

(*c*) The agenda of each session shall be prepared by the Director General.

(5) The Assembly shall adopt its own Rules of Procedure.

Article 8
International Bureau

(1)(*a*) Administrative tasks concerning the Special Union shall be performed by the International Bureau.

(*b*) In particular, the International Bureau shall prepare the meetings and provide the secretariat of the Assembly, the Committee of Experts and such other committees or working groups as may have been established by the Assembly or the Committee of Experts.

(*c*) The Director General shall be the chief executive of the Special Union and shall represent the Special Union.

(2) The Director General and any staff member designated by him shall participate, without the right to vote, in all meetings of the Assembly, the Committee of Experts and such other committees or working groups as may have been established by the Assembly or the Committee of Experts. The Director General, or a staff member designated by him, shall be *ex officio* secretary of those bodies.

(3)(*a*) The International Bureau shall, in accordance with the directions of the Assembly, make the preparations for revision conferences.

(*b*) The International Bureau may consult with intergovernmental and international non-governmental organizations concerning preparations for revision conferences.

(*c*) The Director General and persons designated by him shall take part, without the right to vote, in the discussions at revision conferences.

(4) The International Bureau shall carry out any other tasks assigned to it.

Article 9
Finances

(1)(*a*) The Special Union shall have a budget.

(*b*) The budget of the Special Union shall include the income and expenses proper to the Special Union, its contribution to the budget of expenses common to the Unions and, where applicable, the sum made available to the budget of the Conference of the Organization.

(*c*) Expenses not attributable exclusively to the Special Union but also to one or more other Unions administered by the Organization shall be considered as expenses common to the Unions. The share of the Special Union in such common expenses shall be in proportion to the interest the Special Union has in them.

(2) The budget of the Special Union shall be established with due regard to the requirements of coordination with the budgets of the other Unions administered by the Organization.

(3) The budget of the Special Union shall be financed from the following sources:

(i) contributions of the countries of the Special Union;

(ii) fees and charges due for services rendered by the International Bureau in relation to the Special Union;

(iii) sale of, or royalties on, the publications of the International Bureau concerning the Special Union;
(iv) gifts, bequests, and subventions;
(v) rents, interests, and other miscellaneous income.

(4)(*a*) For the purpose of establishing its contribution referred to in paragraph (3)(i), each country of the Special Union shall belong to the same class as it belongs to in the Paris Union for the Protection of Industrial Property, and shall pay its annual contribution on the basis of the same number of units as is fixed for that class in that Union.

(*b*) The annual contribution of each country of the Special Union shall be an amount in the same proportion to the total sum to be contributed to the budget of the Special Union by all countries as the number of its units is to the total of the units of all contributing countries.

(*c*) Contributions shall become due on the first of January of each year.

(*d*) A country which is in arrears in the payment of its contributions may not exercise its right to vote in any organ of the Special Union if the amount of its arrears equals or exceeds the amount of the contributions due from it for the preceding two full years. However, any organ of the Special Union may allow such a country to continue to exercise its right to vote in that organ if, and as long as, it is satisfied that the delay in payment is due to exceptional and unavoidable circumstances.

(*e*) If the budget is not adopted before the beginning of a new financial period, it shall be at the same level as the budget of the previous year, as provided in the financial regulations.

(5) The amount of the fees and charges due for services rendered by the International Bureau in relation to the Special Union shall be established, and shall be reported to the Assembly, by the Director General.

(6)(*a*) The Special Union shall have a working capital fund which shall be constituted by a single payment made by each country of the Special Union. If the fund becomes insufficient, the Assembly shall decide to increase it.

(*b*) The amount of the initial payment of each country to the said fund or of its participation in the increase thereof shall be a proportion of the contribution of that country for the year in which the fund is established or the decision to increase it is made.

(*c*) The proportion and the terms of payment shall be fixed by the Assembly on the proposal of the Director General and after it has heard the advice of the Coordination Committee of the Organization.

(7)(*a*) In the headquarters agreement concluded with the country on the territory of which the Organization has its headquarters, it shall be provided that, whenever the working capital fund is insufficient, such country shall grant advances. The amount of those advances and the conditions on which they are granted shall be the subject of separate agreements, in each case, between such country and the Organization.

(*b*) The country referred to in subparagraph (*a*) and the Organization shall each have the right to denounce the obligation to grant advances, by written notification. Denunciation shall take effect three years after the end of the year in which it was notified.

(8) The auditing of the accounts shall be effected by one or more of the countries of the Special Union or by external auditors, as provided in the financial regulations. They shall be designated, with their agreement, by the Assembly.

Article 10
Revision of the Agreement

(1) This Agreement may be revised from time to time by a special conference of the countries of the Special Union.

(2) The convocation of any revision conference shall be decided by the Assembly.

(3) Articles 7, 8, 9 and 11 may be amended either by a revision conference or according to the provisions of Article 11.

Article 11
Amendment of Certain Provisions of the Agreement

(1) Proposals for the amendment of Articles 7, 8, 9 and of the present Article may be initiated by any country of the Special Union or by the Director General. Such proposals shall be communicated by the Director General to the countries of the Special Union at least six months in advance of their consideration by the Assembly.

(2) Amendments to the Articles referred to in paragraph (1) shall be adopted by the Assembly. Adoption shall require three-fourths of the votes cast, provided that any amendment to Article 7 and to the present paragraph shall require four-fifths of the votes cast.

(3)(*a*) Any amendment to the Articles referred to in paragraph (1) shall enter into force one month after written notifications of acceptance, effected in accordance with their respective constitutional processes, have been received by the Director General from three-fourths of the countries members of the Special Union at the time the amendment was adopted.

(*b*) Any amendment to the said Articles thus accepted shall bind all the countries which are members of the Special Union at the time the amendment enters into force, provided that any amendment increasing the financial obligations of countries of the Special Union shall bind only those countries which have notified their acceptance of such amendment.

(*c*) Any amendment accepted in accordance with the provisions of subparagraph (*a*) shall bind all countries which become members of the Special Union after the date on which the amendment entered into force in accordance with the provisions of subparagraph (*a*).

Article 12
Becoming Party to the Agreement

(1) Any country party to the Paris Convention for the Protection of Industrial Property may become party to this Agreement by:

(i) signature followed by the deposit of an instrument of ratification, or
(ii) deposit of an instrument of accession.

(2) Instruments of ratification or accession shall be deposited with the Director General.

(3) The provisions of Article 24 of the Stockholm Act of the Paris Convention for the Protection of Industrial Property shall apply to this Agreement.

(4) Paragraph (3) shall in no way be understood as implying the recognition or tacit acceptance, by a country of the Special Union, of the factual situation concerning a territory to which this Agreement is made applicable by another country by virtue of the said paragraph.

Article 13
Entry into Force of the Agreement

(1)(*a*) This Agreement shall enter into force one year after instruments of ratification or accession have been deposited by:

(i) two-thirds of the countries party to the European Convention on the date on which the Agreement is opened for signature, and
(ii) three countries party to the Paris Convention for the Protection of Industrial Property, which were not previously party to the European Convention and of which at least one is a

country where, according to the most recent annual statistics published by the International Bureau on the date of deposit of its instrument of ratification or accession, more than 40,000 applications for patents or inventors' certificates have been filed.

(*b*) With respect to any country other than those for which this Agreement has entered into force pursuant to subparagraph (*a*), it shall enter into force one year after the date on which the ratification or accession of that country was notified by the Director General, unless a subsequent date has been indicated in the instrument of ratification or accession. In the latter case, this Agreement shall enter into force with respect to that country on the date thus indicated.

(*c*) Countries party to the European Convention which ratify this Agreement or accede to it shall be obliged to denounce the said Convention, at the latest, with effect from the day on which this Agreement enters into force with respect to those countries.

(2) Ratification or accession shall automatically entail acceptance of all the clauses and admission to all the advantages of this Agreement.

Article 14
Duration of the Agreement

This Agreement shall have the same duration as the Paris Convention for the Protection of Industrial Property.

Article 15
Denunciation

(1) Any country of the Special Union may denounce this Agreement by notification addressed to the Director General.

(2) Denunciation shall take effect one year after the day on which the Director General has received the notification.

(3) The right of denunciation provided by this Article shall not be exercised by any country before the expiration of five years from the date upon which it becomes a member of the Special Union.

Article 16
Signature, Languages, Notification, Depositary Functions

(1)(*a*) This Agreement shall be signed in a single original in the English and French languages, both texts being equally authentic.

(*b*) This Agreement shall remain open for signature at Strasbourg until September 30, 1971.

(*c*) The original of this Agreement, when no longer open for signature, shall be deposited with the Director General.

(2) Official texts shall be established by the Director General, after consultation with the interested Governments, in German, Japanese, Portuguese, Russian, Spanish and such other languages as the Assembly may designate.

(3)(*a*) The Director General shall transmit two copies, certified by him, of the signed text of this Agreement to the Governments of the countries that have signed it and, on request, to the Government of any other country. He shall also transmit a copy, certified by him, to the Secretary General of the Council of Europe.

(*b*) The Director General shall transmit two copies, certified by him, of any amendment to this Agreement to the Governments of all countries of the Special Union and, on request, to the Government of any other country. He shall also transmit a copy, certified by him, to the Secretary General of the Council of Europe.

(*c*) The Director General shall, on request, furnish the Government of any country that has signed this Agreement, or that accedes to it, with a copy of the Classification, certified by him, in the English or French language.

(4) The Director General shall register this Agreement with the Secretariat of the United Nations.

(5) The Director General shall notify the Governments of all countries party to the Paris Convention for the Protection of Industrial Property and the Secretariat General of the Council of Europe of:

(i) signatures;
(ii) deposits of instruments of ratification or accession;
(iii) the date of entry into force of this Agreement;
(iv) reservations on the use of the Classification;
(v) acceptances of amendments to this Agreement;
(vi) the dates on which such amendments enter into force;
(vii) denunciations received.

Article 17
Transitional Provisions

(1) During the two years following the entry into force of this Agreement, the countries party to the European Convention which are not yet members of the Special Union may enjoy, if they so wish,

the same rights in the Committee of Experts as if they were members of the Special Union.

(2) During the three years following the expiration of the period referred to in paragraph (1), the countries referred to in the said paragraph may be represented by observers in the meetings of the Committee of Experts and, if the said Committee so decides, in any subcommittee or working group established by it. During the same period they may submit proposals for amendments to the Classification, in accordance with Article 5(5), and shall be notified of the decisions and recommendations of the Committee of Experts, in accordance with Article 6(1).

(3) During the five years following the entry into force of this Agreement, the countries party to the European Convention which are not yet members of the Special Union may be represented by observers in the meetings of the Assembly and, if the Assembly so decides, in any committee or working group established by it.

4. Vienna Agreement Establishing an International Classification of the Figurative Elements of Marks

Done at Vienna on June 12, 1973

The Vienna Agreement Establishing an International Classification of the Figurative Elements of Marks was completed at Vienna in 1973, and entered into force in 1985.

Similar in purpose and structure to the Nice Agreement Concerning the International Classification of Goods and Services for the Purposes of the Registration of Marks, the Vienna Agreement is a special union under the Paris Union. While the Nice Agreement concerns the classification of words and names, the Vienna Agreement provides a classification system for figurative elements such as images of human beings, animals, plants, landscapes, and geometric figures used as trade symbols. The scope and effect of the agreement is left to each contracting country (Art. 6), and each country may use the system as its principal or secondary system. Contracting countries, however, are required to use the system on official documents and publications relating to registration of the figurative mark.

Like the other classification agreements, the Vienna Agreement has an assembly, a finance system with a budget, and is administered by the International Bureau (Arts. 7, 8, and 9).

A committee of experts is established under the Agreement to decide on the various technical matters and make amendments and additions to the classification system (Art. 5).[1]

As of January 1, 1990, the following five states were party to the Agreement:

France	Sweden
Luxembourg	Tunisia
Netherlands	

[1]For the current classification system, *see* WORLD INTELLECTUAL PROPERTY ORGANIZATION, INTERNATIONAL CLASSIFICATION OF THE FIGURATIVE ELEMENTS OF MARKS (VIENNA CLASSIFICATION), AS AMENDED IN 1985 WIPO Pub. No. 502(E) (2d ed. 1985).

Vienna Agreement Establishing an International Classification of the Figurative Elements of Marks

Article 1
Establishment of a Special Union; Adoption of an International Classification

The countries to which this Agreement applies constitute a Special Union and adopt a common classification for the figurative elements of marks (hereinafter designated as "the Classification of Figurative Elements").

Article 2
Definition and Deposit of the Classification of Figurative Elements

(1) The Classification of Figurative Elements comprises a list of categories, divisions and sections in which the figurative elements of marks are classified, together with, as the case may be, explanatory notes.

(2) The Classification of Figurative Elements is contained in one authentic copy, in the English and French languages, signed by the Director General of the World Intellectual Property Organization (hereinafter designed respectively as "the Director General" and "the Organization") and deposited with him at the time that this Agreement is opened for signature.

(3) The amendments and additions referred to in Article 5(3)(i) shall also be contained in one authentic copy, in the English and French languages, signed by the Director General and deposited with him.

Article 3
Languages of the Classification of Figurative Elements

(1) The Classification of Figurative Elements shall be established in the English and French languages, both texts being equally authentic.

Source: Text courtesy of the World Intellectual Property Organization (WIPO).

(2) The International Bureau of the Organization (hereinafter designated as "the International Bureau") shall establish, in consultation with the interested Governments, official texts of the Classification of Figurative Elements in the languages which the Assembly referred to in Article 7 may designate in accordance with paragraph (2)(*a*)(vi) of that Article.

Article 4
Use of the Classification of Figurative Elements

(1) Subject to the requirements prescribed by this Agreement, the scope of the Classification of Figurative Elements shall be that attributed to it by each country of the Special Union. In particular, the Classification of Figurative Elements shall not bind the countries of the Special Union in respect of the extent of the protection afforded to the mark.

(2) The competent Offices of the countries of the Special Union shall have the right to use the Classification of Figurative Elements either as a principal or as a subsidiary system.

(3) The competent Offices of the countries of the Special Union shall include in the official documents and publications relating to registrations and renewals of marks the numbers of the categories, divisions and sections in which the figurative elements of those marks are to be placed.

(4) The said numbers shall be preceded by the words "Classification of Figurative Elements" or an abbreviation thereof to be determined by the Committee of Experts referred to in Article 5.

(5) Any country may, at the time of its signature or of the deposit of its instrument of ratification or accession, declare that it does not undertake to include the numbers of all or some of the sections in official documents and publications relating to registrations and renewals of marks.

(6) If any country of the Special Union entrusts the registration of marks to an intergovernmental authority, it shall take all possible measures to ensure that that authority uses the Classification of Figurative Elements in accordance with this Article.

Article 5
Committee of Experts

(1) A Committee of Experts shall be set up in which each country of the Special Union shall be represented.

(2)(*a*) The Director General may, and, if requested by the Committee of Experts, shall, invite countries not members of the Special Union which are members of the Organization or party to the Paris Convention for the Protection of Industrial Property to be represented by observers at meetings of the Committee of Experts.

(*b*) The Director General shall invite intergovernmental organizations specialized in the field of marks, of which at least one of the member countries is party to this Agreement, to be represented by observers at meetings of the Committee of Experts.

(*c*) The Director General may, and, if requested by the Committee of Experts, shall, invite representatives of other intergovernmental and international non-governmental organizations to participate in discussions of interest to them.

(3) The Committee of Experts shall:

(i) make amendments and additions to the Classification of Figurative Elements;

(ii) address recommendations to the countries of the Special Union for the purpose of facilitating the use of Classification of Figurative Elements and promoting its uniform application;

(iii) take all the other measures which, without entailing financial implications for the budget of the Special Union or for the Organization, contribute towards facilitating the application of the Classification of Figurative Elements by developing countries;

(iv) have the right to establish subcommittees and working groups.

(4) The Committee of Experts shall adopt its own rules of procedure. The latter shall provide for the possibility of participation in meetings of the subcommittees and working groups of the Committee of Experts by those intergovernmental organizations referred to in paragraph (2)(*b*) which can make a substantial contribution to the development of the Classification of Figurative Elements.

(5) Proposals for amendments or additions to the Classification of Figurative Elements may be made by the competent Offices of any country of the Special Union, the International Bureau, any intergovernmental organization represented in the Committee of Experts pursuant to paragraph (2)(*b*) and any country or organization specially invited by the Committee of Experts to submit such proposals. The proposals shall be communicated to the International Bureau, which shall submit them to the members of the Committee of Experts and to observers not later than two months before the session of the Committee of Experts at which the said proposals are to be considered.

(6)(*a*) Each country member of the Committee of Experts shall have one vote.

(*b*) The decisions of the Committee of Experts shall require a simple majority of the countries represented and voting.

(*c*) Any decision which is regarded by one-fifth of the countries represented and voting as giving rise to a modification of the basic structure of the Classification of Figurative Elements or as entailing a substantial amount of reclassification shall require a majority of three-fourths of the countries represented and voting.

(*d*) Abstentions shall not be considered as votes.

Article 6
Notification, Entry Into Force and Publication of Amendments and Additions and of Other Decisions

(1) Every decision of the Committee of Experts concerning the adoption of amendments and additions to the Classification of Figurative Elements, and the recommendations of the Committee of Experts, shall be notified by the International Bureau to the competent Offices of the countries of the Special Union. The amendments and additions shall enter into force six months after the date of dispatch of the notifications.

(2) The International Bureau shall incorporate in the Classification of Figurative Elements amendments and additions which have entered into force. Announcements of the amendments and additions shall be published in such periodicals as may be designated by the Assembly referred to in Article 7.

Article 7
Assembly of the Special Union

(1)(*a*) The Special Union shall have an Assembly consisting of the countries of the Special Union.

(*b*) The Government of each country of the Special Union shall be represented by one delegate, who may be assisted by alternate delegates, advisors and experts.

(*c*) Any intergovernmental organization referred to in Article 5(2)(*b*) may be represented by an observer in the meetings of the Assembly, and, if the Assembly so decides, in those of such committees or working groups as may have been established by the Assembly.

(*d*) The expenses of each delegation shall be borne by the Government which has appointed it.

(2)(*a*) Subject to the provisions of Article 5, the Assembly shall:

(i) deal with all matters concerning the maintenance and development of the Special Union and the implementation of this Agreement;
(ii) give directions to the International Bureau concerning the preparation for revision conferences;
(iii) review and approve the reports and activities of the Director General concerning the Special Union, and give him all necessary instructions concerning matters within the competence of the Special Union;
(iv) determine the program and adopt the triennial budget of the Special Union, and approve its final accounts;
(v) adopt the financial regulations of the Special Union;
(vi) decide on the establishment of official texts of the Classification of Figurative Elements in languages other than English and French;
(vii) establish such committees and working groups as it deems appropriate to achieve the objectives of the Special Union;
(viii) determine, subject to paragraph (1)(*c*), which countries not members of the Special Union and which intergovernmental and international non-governmental organizations shall be admitted as observers to its meetings, and to those of any committee or working group established by it;
(ix) take any other appropriate action designed to further the objectives of the Special Union;
(x) perform such other functions as are appropriate under this Agreement.

(*b*) With respect to matters which are of interest also to other Unions administered by the Organization, the Assembly shall make its decision after having heard the advice of the Coordination Committee of the Organization.

(3)(*a*) Each country of the Assembly shall have one vote.

(*b*) One-half of the countries members of the Assembly shall constitute a quorum.

(*c*) In the absence of the quorum, the Assembly may make decisions but, with the exception of decisions concerning its own procedure, all such decisions shall take effect only if the conditions set forth hereinafter are fulfilled. The International Bureau shall communicate the said decisions to the countries members of the Assembly which were not represented and shall invite them to express in writing their vote or abstention within a period of three months from the date of the communication. If, at the expiration of this period, the number of countries having thus expressed their vote or abstention attains the number of countries which was lacking for attaining the quorum in the session itself, such decisions shall take effect provided that at the same time the required majority still obtains.

(*d*) Subject to the provisions of Article 11(2), the decisions of the Assembly shall require two-thirds of the votes cast.

(*e*) Abstentions shall not be considered as votes.

(*f*) A delegate may represent, and vote in the name of, one country only.

(4)(*a*) The Assembly shall meet once in every third calendar year in ordinary session upon convocation by the Director General and, in the absence of exceptional circumstances, during the same period and at the same place as the General Assembly of the Organization.

(*b*) The Assembly shall meet in extraordinary session upon convocation by the Director General, at the request of one-fourth of the countries members of the Assembly.

(*c*) The agenda of each session shall be prepared by the Director General.

(5) The Assembly shall adopt its own rules of procedure.

Article 8
International Bureau

(1)(*a*) Administrative tasks concerning the Special Union shall be performed by the International Bureau.

(*b*) In particular, the International Bureau shall prepare the meetings and provide the secretariat of the Assembly, the Committee of Experts and such other committees or working groups as may have been established by the Assembly or the Committee of Experts.

(*c*) The Director General shall be the chief executive of the Special Union and shall represent the Special Union.

(2) The Director General and any staff member designated by him shall participate, without the right of vote, in all meetings of the Assembly, the Committee of Experts and such other committees or working groups as may have been established by the Assembly or the Committee of Experts. The Director General or a staff member designated by him shall be ex officio secretary of those bodies.

(3)(*a*) The International Bureau shall, in accordance with the directions of the Assembly, make the preparations for revision conferences.

(*b*) The International Bureau may consult with intergovernmental and international non-governmental organizations concerning preparations for revision conferences.

(*c*) The Director General and persons designated by him shall take part, without the right to vote, in the discussions at revision conferences.

(4) The International Bureau shall carry out any other tasks assigned to it.

Article 9
Finances

(1)(*a*) The Special Union shall have a budget.

(*b*) The budget of the Special Union shall include the income and expenses proper to the Special Union, its contribution to the budget of expenses common to the Unions administered by the Organization and, where applicable, the sum made available to the budget of the Conference of the Organization.

(*c*) Expenses not attributable exclusively to the Special Union but also to one or more other Unions administered by the Organization shall be considered as expenses common to the Unions. The share of the Special Union in such common expenses shall be in proportion to the interest the Special Union has in them.

(2) The budget of the Special Union shall be established with due regard to the requirements of coordination with the budgets of the other Unions administered by the Organization.

(3) The budget of the Special Union shall be financed from the following sources:

(i) contributions of the countries of the Special Union;
(ii) fees and charges due for services rendered by the International Bureau in relation to the Special Union;
(iii) sale of, or royalties on, the publications of the International Bureau concerning the Special Union;
(iv) gifts, bequests and subventions;
(v) rents, interests and other miscellaneous income.

(4)(*a*) For the purpose of establishing its contribution referred to in paragraph (3)(i), each country of the Special Union shall belong to the same class as it belongs to in the Paris Union for the Protection of Industrial Property, and shall pay its annual contribution on the basis of the same number of units as is fixed for that class in that Union.

(*b*) The annual contribution of each country of the Special Union shall be an amount in the same proportion to the total sum to be contributed to the budget of the Special Union by all countries as the number of its units is to the total of the units of all contributing countries.

(*c*) Contributions shall become due on the first of January of each year.

(*d*) A country which is in arrears in the payment of its contributions may not exercise its right to vote in any organ of the Special Union if the amount of its arrears equals or exceeds the amount of the contributions due from it for the preceding two full years. However, any organ of the Special Union may allow such a country to continue to exercise its right to vote in that organ if, and as long as, it is satisfied that the delay in payment is due to exceptional and unavoidable circumstances.

(*e*) If the budget is not adopted before the beginning of a new financial period, it shall be at the same level as the budget of the previous year, as provided in the financial regulations.

(5) The amount of the fees and charges due for services rendered by the International Bureau in relation to the Special Union shall be established, and shall be reported to the Assembly, by the Director General.

(6)(*a*) The Special Union shall have a working capital fund which shall be constituted by a single payment made by each country of the Special Union. If the fund becomes insufficient, the Assembly shall decide to increase it.

(*b*) The amount of the initial payment of each country to the said fund or of its participation in the increase thereof shall be a proportion of the contribution of that country for the year in which the fund is established or the decision to increase it is made.

(*c*) The proportion and the terms of payment shall be fixed by the Assembly on the proposal of the Director General and after it has heard the advice of the Coordination Committee of the Organization.

(7)(*a*) In the headquarters agreement concluded with the country on the territory of which the Organization has its headquarters, it shall be provided that, whenever the working capital fund is insufficient, such country shall grant advances. The amount of those advances and the conditions on which they are granted shall be the subject of separate agreements, in each case, between such country and the Organization.

(*b*) The country referred to in subparagraph (*a*) and the Organization shall each have the right to denounce the obligation to grant advances, by written notification. Denunciation shall take effect three years after the end of the year in which it was notified.

(8) The auditing of the accounts shall be effected by one or more of the countries of the Special Union or by external auditors, as provided in the financial regulations. They shall be designated, with their agreement, by the Assembly.

Article 10
Revision of the Agreement

(1) This Agreement may be revised from time to time by a special conference of the countries of the Special Union.

(2) The convocation of any revision conference shall be decided by the Assembly.

(3) Articles 7, 8, 9 and 11 may be amended either by a revision conference or according to the provisions of Article 11.

Article 11
Amendment of Certain Provisions of the Agreement

(1) Proposals for the amendment of Articles 7, 8, 9 and of the present Article may be initiated by any country of the Special Union or by the Director General. Such proposals shall be communicated by the Director General to the countries of the Special Union at least six months in advance of their consideration by the Assembly.

(2) Amendments to the Articles referred to in paragraph (1) shall be adopted by the Assembly. Adoption shall require three-fourths of the votes cast, provided that any amendment to Article 7 and to the present paragraph shall require four-fifths of the votes cast.

(3)(*a*) Any amendment to the Articles referred to in paragraph (1) shall enter into force one month after written notifications of acceptance, effected in accordance with their respective constitutional processes, have been received by the Director General from three-fourths of the countries members of the Special Union at the time the amendment was adopted.

(*b*) Any amendment to the said Articles thus accepted shall bind all the countries which are members of the Special Union at the time the amendment enters into force, provided that any amendment increasing the financial obligations of countries of the Special Union shall bind only those countries which have notified their acceptance of such amendment.

(*c*) Any amendment accepted in accordance with the provisions of subparagraph (*a*) shall bind all countries which become members of the Special Union after the date on which the amendment entered into force in accordance with the provisions of subparagraph (*a*).

Article 12
Becoming Party to the Agreement

(1) Any country party to the Paris Convention for the Protection of Industrial Property may become party to this Agreement by:

(i) signature followed by the deposit of an instrument of ratification, or

(ii) deposit of an instrument of accession.

(2) Instruments of ratification or accession shall be deposited with the Director General.

(3) The provisions of Article 24 of the Stockholm Act of the Paris Convention for the Protection of Industrial Property shall apply to this Agreement.

(4) Paragraph (3) shall in no way be understood as implying the recognition or tacit acceptance by a country of the Special Union of the factual situation concerning a territory to which this Agreement is made applicable by another country by virtue of the said paragraph.

Article 13
Entry Into Force of the Agreement

(1) With respect to the first five countries which have deposited their instruments of ratification or accession, this Agreement shall enter into force three months after the fifth instrument of ratification or accession has been deposited.

(2) With respect to any country other than those for which this Agreement has entered into force in accordance with paragraph (1), it shall enter into force three months after the date on which its ratification or accession was notified by the Director General, unless a subsequent date has been indicated in the instrument of ratification or accession. In the latter case, this Agreement shall enter into force with respect to that country on the date thus indicated.

(3) Ratification or accession shall automatically entail acceptance of all the clauses and admission to all the advantages of this Agreement.

Article 14
Duration of the Agreement

This Agreement shall have the same duration as the Paris Convention for the Protection of Industrial Property.

Article 15
Denunciation

(1) Any country of the Special Union may denounce this Agreement by notification addressed to the Director General.

(2) Denunciation shall take effect one year after the day on which the Director General has received the notification.

(3) The right of denunciation provided by this Article shall not be exercised by any country before the expiration of five years from the date upon which it becomes a member of the Special Union.

Article 16
Disputes

(1) Any dispute between two or more countries of the Special Union concerning the interpretation or application of this Agreement, not settled by negotiation, may, by any one of the countries concerned, be brought before the International Court of Justice by application in conformity with the Statute of the Court, unless the countries concerned agree on some other method of settlement. The country bringing the dispute before the Court shall inform the International Bureau; the International Bureau shall bring the matter to the attention of the other countries of the Special Union.

(2) Each country may, at the time it signs this Agreement or deposits its instrument of ratification or accession, declare that it does not consider itself bound by the provisions of paragraph (1). With regard to any dispute between any country having made such a declaration and any other country of the Special Union, the provisions of paragraph (1) shall not apply.

(3) Any country having made a declaration in accordance with the provisions of paragraph (2) may, at any time, withdraw its declaration by notification addressed to the Director General.

Article 17
Signature, Languages, Depositary Functions, Notifications

(1)(*a*) This Agreement shall be signed in a single original in the English and French languages, both texts being equally authentic.

(*b*) This Agreement shall remain open for signature at Vienna until December 31, 1973.

(*c*) The original of this Agreement when no longer open for signature, shall be deposited with the Director General.

(2) Official texts shall be established by the Director General, after consultation with the interested Governments, in such other languages as the Assembly may designate.

(3)(*a*) The Director General shall transmit two copies, certified by him, of the signed text of this Agreement to the Governments of the countries that have signed it and, on request, to the Government of any other country.

(*b*) The Director General shall transmit two copies, certified by him, of any amendment to this Agreement to the Governments of all countries of the Special Union and, on request, to the Government of any other country.

(*c*) The Director General shall, on request, furnish the Government of any country that has signed this Agreement, or that accedes to it, with two copies of the Classification of Figurative Elements, certified by him, in the English or French language.

(4) The Director General shall register this Agreement with the Secretariat of the United Nations.

(5) The Director General shall notify the Governments of all countries party to the Paris Convention for the Protection of Industrial Property of:

(i) signatures under paragraph (1);
(ii) deposits of instruments of ratification or accession under Article 12(2);
(iii) the date of entry into force of this Agreement under Article 13(1);
(iv) declarations made under Article 4(5);
(v) declarations and notifications made in accordance with Article 12(3);
(vi) declarations made under Article 16(2);
(vii) withdrawals of any declarations, notified under Article 16(3);
(viii) acceptances of amendments to this Agreement under Article 11(3);
(ix) the dates on which such amendments enter into force;
(x) denunciations received under Article 15.

Resolution
Adopted by the Diplomatic Conference on the International Classification of the Figurative Elements of Marks on June 8, 1973

1. Pending the entry into force of the Vienna Agreement Establishing an International Classification of the Figurative Elements of Marks, a provisional Committee of Experts is hereby set up at the International Bureau of the World Intellectual Property Organization (WIPO).

2. The provisional Committee shall include a representative of each country having signed or acceded to the said Agreement. Intergovernmental organizations specialized in the field of marks, of which at least one of the member countries has signed or acceded to the Agreement, may be represented by observers. Any country member of WIPO or party to the Paris Convention for the Protection

of Industrial Property which has neither signed nor acceded to the Agreement may, and, if requested by the provisional Committee, shall, be invited by the Director General of WIPO to be represented by observers.

3. The provisional Committee shall reexamine the International Classification of the Figurative Elements of Marks and shall prepare, if necessary, draft amendments or additions to be made to the said Classification.

4. The International Bureau is invited to prepare the work of the provisional Committee.

5. The International Bureau is invited to convene the provisional Committee, after consultation of the countries which have signed or acceded to the Agreement, if amendments or additions are proposed by any such country or by an organization referred to in paragraph 2 above, or if the International Bureau itself intends to propose amendments or additions.

6. The International Bureau is invited to transmit, as soon as the Agreement enters into force, any draft amendments or additions prepared by the provisional Committee to the Committee of Experts set up under Article 5 of the Agreement.

7. The travel and subsistence expenses of members of the provisional Committee and of observers shall be borne by the countries or organizations which they represent.

Part VII
Organizations

1. Convention Establishing the World Intellectual Property Organization

Signed at Stockholm on July 14, 1967

The Convention Establishing the World Intellectual Property Organization was signed at Stockholm on July 14, 1967, and established the most important international organization for the promotion of intellectual property worldwide. WIPO's predecessors were the international bureaus of the Berne and Paris unions, supervised by the Swiss Federal Council and united in an organization called Bureaux Internationaux Réunis pour la Protection de la Propriété Intellectuelle known as BIRPI.

Headquartered in Geneva, WIPO is a specialized agency of the United Nations. The Convention sets forth the tasks given to WIPO. In addition to administering the international unions such as the Berne and Paris conventions, it is to promote the protection of intellectual property on a worldwide scale (Art. 3). WIPO carries this out by publishing the monthly journals *Copyright* and *Industrial Property* and by providing legal and technical assistance as well as educational and training programs in all areas of intellectual property.

The Convention establishes the governmental structure of WIPO. The General Assembly, a representative body having delegates from each member state, appoints the Director General (Art. 6) who is in charge of the International Bureau, the Secretariat of WIPO (Art. 9). The International Bureau is staffed by personnel of diverse nationalities who carry out the day-to-day administration of the unions and the promotional tasks of WIPO.

Membership in WIPO is open to any state that is a member

of any of the unions. Even if it is not a member of a union, a nation can join WIPO if it is a member of the United Nations or other specialized international agencies, or if it is invited by the General Assembly (Art. 5).

As of January 1, 1990, the following 126 states were party to the Convention:

- Algeria
- Angola
- Argentina
- Australia
- Austria
- Bahamas
- Bangladesh
- Barbados
- Belgium
- Benin
- Brazil
- Bulgaria
- Burkina Faso
- Burundi
- Byelorussian SSR
- Cameroon
- Canada
- Central African Republic
- Chad
- Chile
- China
- Colombia
- Congo
- Costa Rica
- Cote d'Ivoire
- Cuba
- Cyprus
- Czechoslovakia
- Democratic People's Republic of Korea
- Democratic Yemen
- Denmark
- Ecuador
- Egypt
- El Salvador
- Fiji
- Finland
- France
- Gabon
- Gambia
- German Democratic Republic
- Federal Republic of Germany
- Ghana
- Greece
- Guatemala
- Guinea
- Guinea-Bissau
- Haiti
- Holy See
- Honduras
- Hungary
- Iceland
- India
- Indonesia
- Iraq
- Ireland
- Israel
- Italy
- Jamaica
- Japan
- Jordan
- Kenya
- Lebanon
- Lesotho
- Liberia
- Libya
- Liechtenstein
- Luxembourg
- Madagascar
- Malawi
- Malaysia
- Mali
- Malta
- Mauritania
- Mauritius
- Mexico
- Monaco
- Mongolia
- Morocco
- Netherlands
- New Zealand
- Nicaragua
- Niger
- Norway
- Pakistan
- Panama
- Paraguay
- Peru
- Philippines
- Poland
- Portugal
- Qatar
- Republic of Korea
- Romania
- Rwanda
- Saudi Arabia
- Senegal
- Sierra Leone
- Somalia

South Africa
Soviet Union
Spain
Sri Lanka
Sudan
Suriname
Swaziland
Sweden
Switzerland
Thailand
Togo
Trinidad and Tobago
Tunisia
Turkey
Uganda
Ukrainian SSR
United Arab Emirates
United Kingdom
United Republic of Tanzania
United States of America
Uruguay
Venezuela
Viet Nam
Yemen
Yugoslavia
Zaire
Zambia
Zimbabwe

Convention Establishing the World Intellectual Property Organization

Article 1
Establishment of the Organization

The World Intellectual Property Organization is hereby established.

Article 2
Definitions

For the purposes of this Convention:

(i) "Organization" shall mean the World Intellectual Property Organization (WIPO);
(ii) "International Bureau" shall mean the International Bureau of Intellectual Property;
(iii) "Paris Convention" shall mean the Convention for the Protection of Industrial Property signed on March 20, 1883, including any of its revisions;
(iv) "Berne Convention" shall mean the Convention for the Protection of Literary and Artistic Works signed on September 9, 1886, including any of its revisions;
(v) "Paris Union" shall mean the International Union established by the Paris Convention;
(vi) "Berne Union" shall mean the International Union established by the Berne Convention;
(vii) "Unions" shall mean the Paris Union, the Special Unions and Agreements established in relation with that Union, the Berne Union, and any other international agreement designed to promote the protection of intellectual property whose administration is assumed by the Organization according to Article 4(iii);
(viii) "intellectual property" shall include the rights relating to:
—literary, artistic and scientific works,

—performances of performing artists, phonograms, and broadcasts,
—inventions in all fields of human endeavor,
—scientific discoveries,
—industrial designs,
—trademarks, service marks, and commercial names and designations,
—protection against unfair competition,
and all other rights resulting from intellectual activity in the industrial, scientific, literary or artistic fields.

Article 3
Objectives of the Organization

The objectives of the Organization are:

(i) to promote the protection of intellectual property throughout the world through cooperation among States and, where appropriate, in collaboration with any other international organization,
(ii) to ensure administrative cooperation among the Unions.

Article 4
Functions

In order to attain the objectives described in Article 3, the Organization, through its appropriate organs, and subject to the competence of each of the Unions:

(i) shall promote the development of measures designed to facilitate the efficient protection of intellectual property throughout the world and to harmonize national legislation in this field;
(ii) shall perform the administrative tasks of the Paris Union, the Special Unions established in relation with that Union, and the Berne Union;
(iii) may agree to assume, or participate in, the administration of any other international agreement designed to promote the protection of intellectual property;
(iv) shall encourage the conclusion of international agreements designed to promote the protection of intellectual property;
(v) shall offer its cooperation to States requesting legal-technical assistance in the field of intellectual property;

(vi) shall assemble and disseminate information concerning the protection of intellectual property, carry out and promote studies in this field, and publish the results of such studies;

(vii) shall maintain services facilitating the international protection of intellectual property and, where appropriate, provide for registration in this field and the publication of the data concerning the registrations;

(viii) shall take all other appropriate action.

Article 5
Membership

(1) Membership in the Organization shall be open to any State which is a member of any of the Unions as defined in Article 2(vii).

(2) Membership in the Organization shall be equally open to any State not a member of any of the Unions, provided that:

(i) it is a member of the United Nations, any of the Specialized Agencies brought into relationship with the United Nations, or the International Atomic Energy Agency, or is a party to the Statute of the International Court of Justice, or

(ii) it is invited by the General Assembly to become a party to this Convention.

Article 6
General Assembly

(1)(*a*) There shall be a General Assembly consisting of the States party to this Convention which are members of any of the Unions.

(*b*) The Government of each State shall be represented by one delegate, who may be assisted by alternate delegates, advisors, and experts.

(*c*) The expenses of each delegation shall be borne by the Government which has appointed it.

(2) The General Assembly shall:

(i) appoint the Director General upon nomination by the Coordination Committee;

(ii) review and approve reports of the Director General concerning the Organization and give him all necessary instructions;

(iii) review and approve the reports and activities of the Coordination Committee and give instructions to such Committee;
(iv) adopt the triennial budget of expenses common to the Unions;
(v) approve the measures proposed by the Director General concerning the administration of the international agreements referred to in Article 4(iii);
(vi) adopt the financial regulations of the Organization;
(vii) determine the working languages of the Secretariat, taking into consideration the practice of the United Nations;
(viii) invite States referred to under Article 5(2)(ii) to become party to this Convention;
(ix) determine which States not Members of the Organization and which intergovernmental and international non-governmental organizations shall be admitted to its meetings as observers;
(x) exercise such other functions as are appropriate under this Convention.

(3)(*a*) Each State, whether member of one or more Unions, shall have one vote in the General Assembly.

(*b*) One-half of the States members of the General Assembly shall constitute a quorum.

(*c*) Notwithstanding the provisions of subparagraph (*b*), if, in any session, the number of States represented is less than one-half but equal to or more than one-third of the States members of the General Assembly, the General Assembly may make decisions but, with the exception of decisions concerning its own procedure, all such decisions shall take effect only if the following conditions are fulfilled. The International Bureau shall communicate the said decisions to the States members of the General Assembly which were not represented and shall invite them to express in writing their vote or abstention within a period of three months from the date of the communication. If, at the expiration of this period, the number of States having thus expressed their vote or abstention attains the number of States which was lacking for attaining the quorum in the session itself, such decisions shall take effect provided that at the same time the required majority still obtains.

(*d*) Subject to the provisions of subparagraphs (*e*) and (*f*), the General Assembly shall make its decisions by a majority of two-thirds of the votes cast.

(*e*) The approval of measures concerning the administration of international agreements referred to in Article 4(iii) shall require a majority of three-fourths of the votes cast.

(*f*) The approval of an agreement with the United Nations under

Articles 57 and 63 of the Charter of the United Nations shall require a majority of nine-tenths of the votes cast.

(*g*) For the appointment of the Director General (paragraph (2)(i)), the approval of measures proposed by the Director General concerning the administration of international agreements (paragraph (2)(v)), and the transfer of headquarters (Article 10), the required majority must be attained not only in the General Assembly but also in the Assembly of the Paris Union and the Assembly of the Berne Union.

(*h*) Abstentions shall not be considered as votes.

(*i*) A delegate may represent, and vote in the name of, one State only.

(4)(*a*) The General Assembly shall meet once in every third calendar year in ordinary session, upon convocation by the Director General.

(*b*) The General Assembly shall meet in extraordinary session upon convocation by the Director General either at the request of the Coordination Committee or at the request of one-fourth of the States members of the General Assembly.

(*c*) Meetings shall be held at the headquarters of the Organization.

(5) States party to this Convention which are not members of any of the Unions shall be admitted to the meetings of the General Assembly as observers.

(6) The General Assembly shall adopt its own rules of procedure.

Article 7
Conference

(1)(*a*) There shall be a Conference consisting of the States party to this Convention whether or not they are members of any of the Unions.

(*b*) The Government of each State shall be represented by one delegate, who may be assisted by alternate delegates, advisors, and experts.

(*c*) The expenses of each delegation shall be borne by the Government which has appointed it.

(2) The Conference shall:

(i) discuss matters of general interest in the field of intellectual property and may adopt recommendations relating to such matters, having regard for the competence and autonomy of the Unions;

(ii) adopt the triennial budget of the Conference;
(iii) within the limits of the budget of the Conference, establish the triennial program of legal-technical assistance;
(iv) adopt amendments to this Convention as provided in Article 17;
(v) determine which States not Members of the Organization and which intergovernmental and international non-governmental organizations shall be admitted to its meetings as observers;
(vi) exercise such other functions as are appropriate under this Convention.

(3)(*a*) Each Member State shall have one vote in the Conference.

(*b*) One-third of the Member States shall constitute a quorum.

(*c*) Subject to the provisions of Article 17, the Conference shall make its decisions by a majority of two-thirds of the votes cast.

(*d*) The amounts of the contributions of States party to this Convention not members of any of the Unions shall be fixed by a vote in which only the delegates of such States shall have the right to vote.

(*e*) Abstentions shall not be considered as votes.

(*f*) A delegate may represent, and vote in the name of, one State only.

(4)(*a*) The Conference shall meet in ordinary session, upon convocation by the Director General, during the same period and at the same place as the General Assembly.

(*b*) The Conference shall meet in extraordinary session, upon convocation by the Director General, at the request of the majority of the Member States.

(5) The Conference shall adopt its own rules of procedure.

Article 8
Coordination Committee

(1)(*a*) There shall be a Coordination Committee consisting of the States party to this Convention which are members of the Executive Committee of the Paris Union, or the Executive Committee of the Berne Union, or both. However, if either of these Executive Committees is composed of more than one-fourth of the number of the countries members of the Assembly which elected it, then such Executive Committee shall designate from among its members the States which will be members of the Coordination Committee, in such a way that their number shall not exceed the one-fourth referred to above, it being understood that the country on the territory of which the

Organization has its headquarters shall not be included in the computation of the said one-fourth.

(*b*) The Government of each State member of the Coordination Committee shall be represented by one delegate, who may be assisted by alternate delegates, advisors, and experts.

(*c*) Whenever the Coordination Committee considers either matters of direct interest to the program or budget of the Conference and its agenda, or proposals for the amendment of this Convention which would affect the rights or obligations of States party to this Convention not members of any of the Unions, one-fourth of such States shall participate in the meetings of the Coordination Committee with the same rights as members of that Committee. The Conference shall, at each of its ordinary sessions, designate these States.

(*d*) The expenses of each delegation shall be borne by the Government which has appointed it.

(2) If the other Unions administered by the Organization wish to be represented as such in the Coordination Committee, their representatives must be appointed from among the States members of the Coordination Committee.

(3) The Coordination Committee shall:

(i) give advice to the organs of the Unions, the General Assembly, the Conference, and the Director General, on all administrative, financial and other matters of common interest either to two or more of the Unions, or to one or more of the Unions and the Organization, and in particular on the budget of expenses common to the Unions;

(ii) prepare the draft agenda of the General Assembly;

(iii) prepare the draft agenda and the draft program and budget of the Conference;

(iv) on the basis of the triennial budget of expenses common to the Unions and the triennial budget of the Conference, as well as on the basis of the triennial program of legal-technical assistance, establish the corresponding annual budgets and programs;

(v) when the term of office of the Director General is about to expire, or when there is a vacancy in the post of the Director General, nominate a candidate for appointment to such position by the General Assembly; if the General Assembly does not appoint its nominee, the Coordination Committee shall nominate another candidate; this procedure shall be repeated until the latest nominee is appointed by the General Assembly;

(vi) if the post of the Director General becomes vacant between two sessions of the General Assembly, appoint an Acting Director General for the term preceding the assuming of office by the new Director General;

(vii) perform such other functions as are allocated to it under this Convention.

(4)(*a*) The Coordination Committee shall meet once every year in ordinary session, upon convocation by the Director General. It shall normally meet at the headquarters of the Organization.

(*b*) The Coordination Committee shall meet in extraordinary session, upon convocation by the Director General, either on his own initiative, or at the request of its Chairman or one-fourth of its members.

(5)(*a*) Each State, whether a member of one or both of the Executive Committees referred to in paragraph (1)(*a*), shall have one vote in the Coordination Committee.

(*b*) One-half of the members of the Coordination Committee shall constitute a quorum.

(*c*) A delegate may represent, and vote in the name of, one State only.

(6)(*a*) The Coordination Committee shall express its opinions and make its decisions by a simple majority of the votes cast. Abstentions shall not be considered as votes.

(*b*) Even if a simple majority is obtained, any member of the Coordination Committee may, immediately after the vote, request that the votes be the subject of a special recount in the following manner: two separate lists shall be prepared, one containing the names of the States members of the Executive Committee of the Paris Union and the other the names of the States members of the Executive Committee of the Berne Union; the vote of each State shall be inscribed opposite its name in each list in which it appears. Should this special recount indicate that a simple majority has not been obtained in each of those lists, the proposal shall not be considered as carried.

(7) Any State Member of the Organization which is not a member of the Coordination Committee may be represented at the meetings of the Committee by observers having the right to take part in the debates but without the right to vote.

(8) The Coordination Committee shall establish its own rules of procedure.

Article 9
International Bureau

(1) The International Bureau shall be the Secretariat of the Organization.

(2) The International Bureau shall be directed by the Director General, assisted by two or more Deputy Directors General.

(3) The Director General shall be appointed for a fixed term,

which shall be not less than six years. He shall be eligible for reappointment for fixed terms. The periods of the initial appointment and possible subsequent appointments, as well as all other conditions of the appointment, shall be fixed by the General Assembly.

(4)(*a*) The Director General shall be the chief executive of the Organization.

(*b*) He shall represent the Organization.

(*c*) He shall report to, and conform to the instructions of, the General Assembly as to the internal and external affairs of the Organization.

(5) The Director General shall prepare the draft programs and budgets and periodical reports on activities. He shall transmit them to the Governments of the interested States and to the competent organs of the Unions and the Organization.

(6) The Director General and any staff member designated by him shall participate, without the right to vote, in all meetings of the General Assembly, the Conference, the Coordination Committee, and any other committee or working group. The Director General or a staff member designated by him shall be ex officio secretary of these bodies.

(7) The Director General shall appoint the staff necessary for the efficient performance of the tasks of the International Bureau. He shall appoint the Deputy Directors General after approval by the Coordination Committee. The conditions of employment shall be fixed by the staff regulations to be approved by the Coordination Committee on the proposal of the Director General. The paramount consideration in the employment of the staff and in the determination of the conditions of service shall be the necessity of securing the highest standards of efficiency, competence, and integrity. Due regard shall be paid to the importance of recruiting the staff on as wide a geographical basis as possible.

(8) The nature of the responsibilities of the Director General and of the staff shall be exclusively international. In the discharge of their duties they shall not seek or receive instructions from any Government or from any authority external to the Organization. They shall refrain from any action which might prejudice their position as international officials. Each Member State undertakes to respect the exclusively international character of the responsibilities of the Director General and the staff, and not to seek to influence them in the discharge of their duties.

Article 10
Headquarters

(1) The headquarters of the Organization shall be at Geneva.

(2) Its transfer may be decided as provided for in Article 6(3)(*d*) and (*g*).

Article 11
Finances

(1) The Organization shall have two separate budgets: the budget of expenses common to the Unions, and the budget of the Conference.

(2)(*a*) The budget of expenses common to the Unions shall include provision for expenses of interest to several Unions.

(*b*) This budget shall be financed from the following sources:

(i) contributions of the Unions, provided that the amount of the contribution of each Union shall be fixed by the Assembly of that Union, having regard to the interest the Union has in the common expenses;

(ii) charges due for services performed by the International Bureau not in direct relation with any of the Unions or not received for services rendered by the International Bureau in the field of legal-technical assistance;

(iii) sale of, or royalties on, the publications of the International Bureau not directly concerning any of the Unions;

(iv) gifts, bequests, and subventions, given to the Organization, except those referred to in paragraph (3)(*b*)(iv);

(v) rents, interests, and other miscellaneous income, of the Organization.

(3)(*a*) The budget of the Conference shall include provision for the expenses of holding sessions of the Conference and for the cost of the legal-technical assistance program.

(*b*) This budget shall be financed from the following sources:

(i) contributions of States party to this Convention not members of any of the Unions;

(ii) any sums made available to this budget by the Unions, provided that the amount of the sum made available by each Union shall be fixed by the Assembly of that Union and that each Union shall be free to abstain from contributing to the said budget;

(iii) sums received for services rendered by the International Bureau in the field of legal-technical assistance;

(iv) gifts, bequests, and subventions, given to the Organization for the purposes referred to in subparagraph (*a*).

(4)(*a*) For the purpose of establishing its contribution towards the budget of the Conference, each State party to this Convention not member of any of the Unions shall belong to a class, and shall pay its annual contributions on the basis of a number of units fixed as follows:

Class A	10
Class B	3
Class C	1

(*b*) Each such State shall, concurrently with taking action as provided in Article 14(1), indicate the class to which it wishes to belong. Any such State may change class. If it chooses a lower class, the State must announce it to the Conference at one of its ordinary sessions. Any such change shall take effect at the beginning of the calendar year following the session.

(*c*) The annual contribution of each such State shall be an amount in the same proportion to the total sum to be contributed to the budget of the Conference by all such States as the number of its units is to the total of the units of all the said States.

(*d*) Contributions shall become due on the first of January of each year.

(*e*) If the budget is not adopted before the beginning of a new financial period, the budget shall be at the same level as the budget of previous year, in accordance with the financial regulations.

(5) Any State party to this Convention not member of any of the Unions which is in arrears in the payment of its financial contributions under the present Article, and any State party to this Convention member of any of the Unions which is in arrears in the payment of its contributions to any of the Unions, shall have no vote in any of the bodies of the Organization of which it is a member, if the amount of its arrears equals or exceeds the amount of the contributions due from it for the preceding two full years. However, any of these bodies may allow such a State to continue to exercise its vote in that body if, and as long as, it is satisfied that the delay in payment arises from exceptional and unavoidable circumstances.

(6) The amount or the fees and charges due for services rendered by the International Bureau in the field of legal-technical assistance shall be established, and shall be reported to the Coordination Committee, by the Director General.

(7) The Organization, with the approval of the Coordination Committee, may receive gifts, bequests, and subventions, directly from Governments, public or private institutions, associations or private persons.

(8)(*a*) The Organization shall have a working capital fund which shall be constituted by a single payment made by the Unions and by each State party to this Convention not member of any Union. If the fund becomes insufficient, it shall be increased.

(*b*) The amount of the single payment of each Union and its possible participation in any increase shall be decided by its Assembly.

(*c*) The amount of the single payment of each State party to this

Convention not member of any Union and its part in any increase shall be a proportion of the contribution of that State for the year in which the fund is established or the increase decided. The proportion and the terms of payment shall be fixed by the Conference on the proposal of the Director General and after it has heard the advice of the Coordination Committee.

(9)(*a*) In the headquarters agreement concluded with the State on the territory of which the Organization has its headquarters, it shall be provided that, whenever the working capital fund is insufficient, such State shall grant advances. The amount of these advances and the conditions on which they are granted shall be the subject of separate agreements, in each case, between such State and the Organization. As long as it remains under the obligation to grant advances, such State shall have an ex officio seat on the Coordination Committee.

(*b*) The State referred to in subparagraph (*a*) and the Organization shall each have the right to denounce the obligation to grant advances, by written notification. Denunciation shall take effect three years after the end of the year in which it has been notified.

(10) The auditing of the accounts shall be effected by one or more Member States, or by external auditors, as provided in the financial regulations. They shall be designated, with their agreement, by the General Assembly.

Article 12
Legal Capacity; Privileges and Immunities

(1) The Organization shall enjoy on the territory of each Member State, in conformity with the laws of that State, such legal capacity as may be necessary for the fulfilment of the Organization's objectives and for the exercise of its functions.

(2) The Organization shall conclude a headquarters agreement with the Swiss Confederation and with any other State in which the headquarters may subsequently be located.

(3) The Organization may conclude bilateral or multilateral agreements with the other Member States with a view to the enjoyment by the Organization, its officials, and representatives of all Member States, of such privileges and immunities as may be necessary for the fulfilment of its objectives and for the exercise of its functions.

(4) The Director General may negotiate and, after approval by the Coordination Committee, shall conclude and sign on behalf of the Organization the agreements referred to in paragraphs (2) and (3).

Article 13
Relations with Other Organizations

(1) The Organization shall, where appropriate, establish working relations and cooperate with other intergovernmental organizations. Any general agreement to such effect entered into with such organizations shall be concluded by the Director General after approval by the Coordination Committee.

(2) The Organization may, on matters within its competence, make suitable arrangements for consultation and cooperation with international non-governmental organizations and, with the consent of the Governments concerned, with national organizations, governmental or non-governmental. Such arrangements shall be made by the Director General after approval by the Coordination Committee.

Article 14
Becoming Party to the Convention

(1) States referred to in Article 5 may become party to this Convention and Member of the Organization by:

(i) signature without reservation as to ratification, or
(ii) signature subject to ratification followed by the deposit of an instrument of ratification, or
(iii) deposit of an instrument of accession.

(2) Notwithstanding any other provision of this Convention, a State party to the Paris Convention, the Berne Convention, or both Conventions, may become party to this Convention only if it concurrently ratifies or accedes to, or only after it has ratified or acceded to:

either the Stockholm Act of the Paris Convention in its entirety or with only the limitation set forth in Article 20(1)(*b*)(i) thereof, or the Stockholm Act of the Berne Convention in its entirety or with only the limitation set forth in Article 28(1)(*b*)(i) thereof.

(3) Instruments of ratification or accession shall be deposited with the Director General.

Article 15
Entry into Force of the Convention

(1) This Convention shall enter into force three months after ten States members of the Paris Union and seven States members of the Berne Union have taken action as provided in Article 14(1),

it being understood that, if a State is a member of both Unions, it will be counted in both groups. On that date, this Convention shall enter into force also in respect of States which, not being members of either of the two Unions, have taken action as provided in Article 14(1) three months or more prior to that date.

(2) In respect to any other State, this Convention shall enter into force three months after the date on which such State takes action as provided in Article 14(1).

Article 16
Reservations

No reservations to this Convention are permitted.

Article 17
Amendments

(1) Proposals for the amendment of this Convention may be initiated by any Member State, by the Coordination Committee, or by the Director General. Such proposals shall be communicated by the Director General to the Member States at least six months in advance of their consideration by the Conference.

(2) Amendments shall be adopted by the Conference. Whenever amendments would affect the rights and obligations of States party to this Convention not members of any of the Unions, such States shall also vote. On all other amendments proposed, only States party to this Convention members of any Union shall vote. Amendments shall be adopted by a simple majority of the votes cast, provided that the Conference shall vote only on such proposals for amendments as have previously been adopted by the Assembly of the Paris Union and the Assembly of the Berne Union according to the rules applicable in each of them regarding the adoption of amendments to the administrative provisions of their respective Conventions.

(3) Any amendment shall enter into force one month after written notifications of acceptance, effected in accordance with their respective constitutional processes, have been received by the Director General from three-fourths of the States members of the Organization, entitled to vote on the proposal for amendment pursuant to paragraph (2), at the time the Conference adopted the amendment. Any amendments thus accepted shall bind all the States which are Members of the Organization at the time the amendment enters into force or which become Members at a subsequent date, provided that

any amendment increasing the financial obligations of Member States shall bind only those States which have notified their acceptance of such amendment.

Article 18
Denunciation

(1) Any Member State may denounce this Convention by notification addressed to the Director General.

(2) Denunciation shall take effect six months after the day on which the Director General has received the notification.

Article 19
Notifications

The Director General shall notify the Governments of all Member States of:

(i) the date of entry into force of the Convention,

(ii) signatures and deposits of instruments of ratification or accession,

(iii) acceptances of an amendment to this Convention, and the date upon which the amendment enters into force,

(iv) denunciations of this Convention.

Article 20
Final Provisions

(1)(*a*) This Convention shall be signed in a single copy in English, French, Russian and Spanish, all texts being equally authentic, and shall be deposited with the Government of Sweden.

(*b*) This Convention shall remain open for signature at Stockholm until January 13, 1968.

(2) Official texts shall be established by the Director General, after consultation with the interested Governments, in German, Italian and Portuguese, and such other languages as the Conference may designate.

(3) The Director General shall transmit two duly certified copies of this Convention and of each amendment adopted by the Conference to the Governments of the States members of the Paris or Berne Unions, to the Government of any other State when it accedes to this Convention, and, on request, to the Government of any other State. The copies of the signed text of the Convention transmitted to the Governments shall be certified by the Government of Sweden.

(4) The Director General shall register this Convention with the Secretariat of the United Nations.

Article 21
Transitional Provisions

(1) Until the first Director General assumes office, references in this Convention to the International Bureau or to the Director General shall be deemed to be references to the United International Bureaux for the Protection of Industrial, Literary and Artistic Property (also called the United International Bureaux for the Protection of Intellectual Property (BIRPI)), or its Director, respectively.

(2)(*a*) States which are members of any of the Unions but which have not become party to this Convention may, for five years from the date of entry into force of this Convention, exercise, if they so desire, the same rights as if they had become party to this Convention. Any State desiring to exercise such rights shall give written notification to this effect to the Director General; this notification shall be effective on the date of its receipt. Such States shall be deemed to be members of the General Assembly and the Conference until the expiration of the said period.

(*b*) Upon expiration of this five-year period, such States shall have no right to vote in the General Assembly, the Conference, and the Coordination Committee.

(*c*) Upon becoming party to this Convention, such States shall regain such right to vote.

(3)(*a*) As long as there are States members of the Paris or Berne Unions which have not become party to this Convention, the International Bureau and the Director General shall also function as the United International Bureaux for the Protection of Industrial, Literary and Artistic Property, and its Director, respectively.

(*b*) The staff in the employment of the said Bureaux on the date of entry into force of this Convention shall, during the transitional period referred to in subparagraph (*a*), be considered as also employed by the International Bureau.

(4)(*a*) Once all the States members of the Paris Union have become Members of the Organization, the rights, obligations, and property, of the Bureau of that Union shall devolve on the International Bureau of the Organization.

(*b*) Once all the States members of the Berne Union have become Members of the Organization, the rights, obligations, and property, of the Bureau of that Union shall devolve on the International Bureau of the Organization.

Appendix

Status of International Conventions

January 1990

Paris Convention for the Protection of Industrial Property

Paris Convention (1883), revised at Brussels (1900), Washington (1911), The Hague (1925), London (1934), Lisbon (1958) and Stockholm (1967), and amended in 1979

(Paris Union)

State	Contribution class	Date on which State became party to the Convention	Latest Act of the Convention to which State is party and date on which State became party to that Act
Algeria	VI	March 1, 1966	Stockholm, April 20, 1975
Argentina	VI	February 10, 1967	*Lisbon: February 10, 1967* Stockholm, Articles 13 to 30: October 8, 1980
Australia	III	October 10, 1925	Stockholm, Articles 1 to 12: September 27, 1975 Stockholm, Articles 13 to 30: August 25, 1972
Austria	IV	January 1, 1909	Stockholm: August 18, 1973
Bahamas	VII	July 10, 1973	*Lisbon: July 10, 1973* Stockholm, Articles 13 to 30: March 10, 1977
Barbados	VII	March 12, 1985	Stockholm: March 12, 1985
Belgium	III	July 7, 1884	Stockholm: February 12, 1975
Benin	S	January 10, 1967	Stockholm: March 12, 1975
Brazil	VI	July 7, 1884	*The Hague: October 26, 1929* Stockholm, Articles 13 to 30: March 24, 1975
Bulgaria	VI	June 13, 1921	Stockholm, Articles 1 to 12: May 19 or 27, 1970 Stockholm, Articles 13 to 30: May 27, 1970
Burkina Faso	S	November 19, 1963	Stockholm: September 2, 1975
Burundi	S	September 3, 1977	Stockholm: September 3, 1977
Cameroon	VII	May 10, 1964	Stockholm: April 20, 1975
Canada	III	June 12, 1925	*London: July 30, 1951* Stockholm, Articles 13 to 30: July 7, 1970
Central African Republic	S	November 19, 1963	Stockholm: September 5, 1978
Chad	S	November 19, 1963	Stockholm: September 26, 1970
China	III	March 19, 1985	Stockholm: March 19, 1985
Congo	VII	September 2, 1963	Stockholm: December 5, 1975
Côte d'Ivoire	VII	October 23, 1963	Stockholm: May 4, 1974
Cuba	VII	November 17, 1904	Stockholm: April 8, 1975
Cyprus	VII	January 17, 1966	Stockholm: April 3, 1984
Czechoslovakia	IV	October 5, 1919	Stockholm: December 29, 1970
Democratic People's Republic of Korea	VII	June 10, 1980	Stockholm: June 10, 1980
Denmark	IV	October 1, 1894	Stockholm, Articles 1 to 12: April 26 or May 19, 1970 Stockholm, Articles 13 to 30: April 26, 1970
Dominican Republic	VI	*July 11, 1890*	*The Hague: April 6, 1951*
Egypt	VII	July 1, 1951	Stockholm: March 6, 1975
Finland	IV	September 20, 1921	Stockholm, Articles 1 to 12: October 21, 1975 Stockholm, Articles 13 to 30: September 15, 1970
France	I	July 7, 1884	Stockholm: August 12, 1975
Gabon	VII	February 29, 1964	Stockholm: June 10, 1975
German Democratic Republic	IV	May 1, 1903	Stockholm, Articles 1 to 12: April 26 or May 19, 1970 Stockholm, Articles 13 to 30: April 26, 1970
Germany, Federal Republic of	I	May 1, 1903	Stockholm: September 19, 1970
Ghana	VII	September 28, 1976	Stockholm: September 28, 1976
Greece	V	October 2, 1924	Stockholm: July 15, 1976
Guinea	S	February 5, 1982	Stockholm: February 5, 1982
Guinea-Bissau	S	June 28, 1988	Stockholm: June 28, 1988
Haiti	S	July 1, 1958	Stockholm: November 3, 1983
Holy See	VII	September 29, 1960	Stockholm: April 24, 1975
Hungary	V	January 1, 1909	Stockholm, Articles 1 to 12: April 26 or May 19, 1970 Stockholm, Articles 13 to 30: April 26, 1970

SOURCE: *Industrial Property,* January 1990. Reproduced with the permission of the International Bureau of the World Intellectual Property Organization (WIPO).

State	Contribution class*	Date on which State became party to the Convention	Latest Act of the Convention to which State is party and date on which State became party to that Act
Iceland	VII	May 5, 1962	*London: May 5, 1962* Stockholm, Articles 13 to 30: December 28, 1984
Indonesia	VI	December 24, 1950	*London: December 24, 1950* Stockholm, Articles 13 to 30: December 20, 1979
Iran (Islamic Republic of)	VI	*December 16, 1959*	*Lisbon: January 4, 1962*
Iraq	VII	January 24, 1976	Stockholm: January 24, 1976
Ireland	IV	December 4, 1925	Stockholm, Articles 1 to 12: April 26 or May 19, 1970 Stockholm, Articles 13 to 30: April 26, 1970
Israel	VI	March 24, 1950	Stockholm, Articles 1 to 12: April 26 or May 19, 1970 Stockholm, Articles 13 to 30: April 26, 1970
Italy	III	July 7, 1884	Stockholm: April 24, 1977
Japan	I	July 15, 1899	Stockholm, Articles 1 to 12: October 1, 1975 Stockholm, Articles 13 to 30: April 24, 1975
Jordan	VII	July 17, 1972	Stockholm: July 17, 1972
Kenya	VI	June 14, 1965	Stockholm: October 26, 1971
Lebanon	VII	September 1, 1924	*London: September 30, 1947* Stockholm, Articles 13 to 30: December 30, 1986
Lesotho	S	September 28, 1989	Stockholm: September 28, 1989
Libya	VI	September 28, 1976	Stockholm: September 28, 1976
Liechtenstein	VII	July 14, 1933	Stockholm: May 25, 1972
Luxembourg	VII	June 30, 1922	Stockholm: March 24, 1975
Madagascar	VII	December 21, 1963	Stockholm: April 10, 1972
Malawi	S	July 6, 1964	Stockholm: June 25, 1970
Malaysia	VII	January 1, 1989	Stockholm: January 1, 1989
Mali	S	March 1, 1983	Stockholm: March 1, 1983
Malta	VII	October 20, 1967	*Lisbon: October 20, 1967* Stockholm, Articles 13 to 30: December 12, 1977
Mauritania	S	April 11, 1965	Stockholm: September 21, 1976
Mauritius	VII	September 24, 1976	Stockholm: September 24, 1976
Mexico	IV	September 7, 1903	Stockholm: July 26, 1976
Monaco	VII	April 29, 1956	Stockholm: October 4, 1975
Mongolia	VII	April 21, 1985	Stockholm: April 21, 1985
Morocco	VI	July 30, 1917	Stockholm: August 6, 1971
Netherlands	III	July 7, 1884	Stockholm: January 10, 1975
New Zealand	V	July 29, 1931	*London: July 14, 1946* Stockholm, Articles 13 to 30: June 20, 1984
Niger	S	July 5, 1964	Stockholm: March 6, 1975
Nigeria	VI	*September 2, 1963*	*Lisbon: September 2, 1963*
Norway	IV	July 1, 1885	Stockholm: June 13, 1974
Philippines	VI	September 27, 1965	*Lisbon: September 27, 1965* Stockholm, Articles 13 to 30: July 16, 1980
Poland	V	November 10, 1919	Stockholm: March 24, 1975
Portugal	IV	July 7, 1884	Stockholm: April 30, 1975
Republic of Korea	VI	May 4, 1980	Stockholm: May 4, 1980
Romania	VI	October 6, 1920	Stockholm, Articles 1 to 12: April 26 or May 19, 1970 Stockholm, Articles 13 to 30: April 26, 1970
Rwanda	S	March 1, 1984	Stockholm: March 1, 1984
San Marino	VI	*March 4, 1960*	*London: March 4, 1960*
Senegal	VII	December 21, 1963	Stockholm, Articles 1 to 12: April 26 or May 19, 1970 Stockholm, Articles 13 to 30: April 26, 1970
South Africa	IV	December 1, 1947	Stockholm: March 24, 1975
Soviet Union	I	July 1, 1965	Stockholm, Articles 1 to 12: April 26 or May 19, 1970 Stockholm, Articles 13 to 30: April 26, 1970
Spain	IV	July 7, 1884	Stockholm: April 14, 1972
Sri Lanka	VII	December 29, 1952	*London: December 29, 1952* Stockholm, Articles 13 to 30: September 23, 1978

State	Contribution class	Date on which State became party to the Convention	Latest Act of the Convention to which State is party and date on which State became party to that Act
Sudan	S	April 16, 1984	Stockholm: April 16, 1984
Suriname	VII	November 25, 1975	Stockholm: November 25, 1975
Sweden	III	July 1, 1885	Stockholm, Articles 1 to 12: October 9, 1970 Stockholm, Articles 13 to 30: April 26, 1970
Switzerland	III	July 7, 1884	Stockholm, Articles 1 to 12: April 26 or May 19, 1970 Stockholm, Articles 13 to 30: April 26, 1970
Syria	VI	*September 1, 1924*	*London: September 30, 1947*
Togo	S	September 10, 1967	Stockholm: April 30, 1975
Trinidad and Tobago	VII	August 1, 1964	Stockholm: August 16, 1988
Tunisia	VII	July 7, 1884	Stockholm: April 12, 1976
Turkey	VI	October 10, 1925	*London: June 27, 1957* Stockholm, Articles 13 to 30: May 16, 1976
Uganda	S	June 14, 1965	Stockholm: October 20, 1973
United Kingdom	I	July 7, 1884	Stockholm, Articles 1 to 12: April 26 or May 19, 1970 Stockholm, Articles 13 to 30: April 26, 1970
United Republic of Tanzania	S	June 16, 1963	*Lisbon: June 16, 1963* Stockholm, Articles 13 to 30: December 30, 1983
United States of America	I	May 30, 1887	Stockholm, Articles 1 to 12: August 25, 1973 Stockholm, Articles 13 to 30: September 5, 1970
Uruguay	VII	March 18, 1967	Stockholm: December 28, 1979
Viet Nam	VII	March 8, 1949	Stockholm: July 2, 1976
Yugoslavia	VI	February 26, 1921	Stockholm: October 16, 1973
Zaire	VI	January 31, 1975	Stockholm: January 31, 1975
Zambia	VII	April 6, 1965	*Lisbon: April 6, 1965* Stockholm, Articles 13 to 30: May 14, 1977
Zimbabwe	VII	April 18, 1980	Stockholm: December 30, 1981

(Total: 100 States)

International Convention for the Protection of New Varieties of Plants

UPOV Convention (1961), as revised at Geneva (1972 and 1978)

(UPOV)

State	Date on which State became party to the Convention	No. of contribution units chosen	Date on which State became party to the Convention of 1961	Date on which State became party to the 1978 Act
Australia	March 1, 1989	1.0	–	March 1, 1989
Belgium	December 5, 1976	1.5	December 5, 1976	–
Denmark	October 6, 1968	1.5	October 6, 1968	November 8, 1981
France	October 3, 1971	5.0	October 3, 1971	March 17, 1983
Germany, Federal Republic of	August 10, 1968	5.0	August 10, 1968	April 12, 1986
Hungary	April 16, 1983	0.5	–	April 16, 1983
Ireland	November 8, 1981	1.0	–	November 8, 1981
Israel	December 12, 1979	0.5	December 12, 1979	May 12, 1984
Italy	July 1, 1977	2.0	July 1, 1977	May 28, 1986
Japan	September 3, 1982	5.0	–	September 3, 1982
Netherlands	August 10, 1968	3.0	August 10, 1968	September 2, 1984
New Zealand	November 8, 1981	1.0	–	November 8, 1981
Poland	November 11, 1989	0.5	–	November 11, 1989
South Africa	November 6, 1977	1.0	November 6, 1977	November 8, 1981
Spain	May 18, 1980	1.0	May 18, 1980	–
Sweden	December 17, 1971	1.5	December 17, 1971	January 1, 1983
Switzerland	July 10, 1977	1.5	July 10, 1977	November 8, 1981
United Kingdom	August 10, 1968	5.0	August 10, 1968	September 24, 1983
United States of America	November 8, 1981	5.0	–	November 8, 1981

(Total: 19 States)

Patent Cooperation Treaty

PCT (Washington, 1970), amended in 1979 and modified in 1984

(PCT Union)

State	Date on which State became party to the Treaty	State	Date on which State became party to the Treaty
Australia	March 31, 1980	Japan	October 1, 1978
Austria	April 23, 1979	Liechtenstein	March 19, 1980
Barbados	March 12, 1985	Luxembourg	April 30, 1978
Belgium	December 14, 1981	Madagascar	January 24, 1978
Benin	February 26, 1987	Malawi	January 24, 1978
Brazil	April 9, 1978	Mali	October 19, 1984
Bulgaria	May 21, 1984	Mauritania	April 13, 1983
Burkina Faso	March 21, 1989	Monaco	June 22, 1979
Cameroon	January 24, 1978	Netherlands	July 10, 1979
Canada	January 2, 1990	Norway	January 1, 1980
Central African Republic	January 24, 1978	Republic of Korea	August 10, 1984
Chad	January 24, 1978	Romania	July 23, 1979
Congo	January 24, 1978	Senegal	January 24, 1978
Democratic People's Republic of Korea	July 8, 1980	Soviet Union	March 29, 1978
		Spain	November 16, 1989
Denmark	December 1, 1978	Sri Lanka	February 26, 1982
Finland	October 1, 1980	Sudan	April 16, 1984
France	February 25, 1978	Sweden	May 17, 1978
Gabon	January 24, 1978	Switzerland	January 24, 1978
Germany, Federal Republic of	January 24, 1978	Togo	January 24, 1978
Hungary	June 27, 1980	United Kingdom	January 24, 1978
Italy	March 28, 1985	United States of America	January 24, 1978

(Total: 43 States)

SOURCE: *Industrial Property*, January 1990. Reproduced with the permission of the International Bureau of the World Intellectual Property Organization (WIPO).

Budapest Treaty on the International Recognition of the Deposit of Microorganisms for the Purpose of Patent Procedure

Budapest Treaty (1977), modified in 1980

(Budapest Union)

State	Date on which State became party to the Treaty	State	Date on which State became party to the Treaty
Australia	July 7, 1987	Japan	August 19, 1980
Austria	April 26, 1984	Liechtenstein	August 19, 1981
Belgium	December 15, 1983	Netherlands	July 2, 1987
Bulgaria	August 19, 1980	Norway	January 1, 1986
Czechoslovakia	August 5, 1989	Philippines	October 21, 1981
Denmark	July 1, 1985	Republic of Korea	March 28, 1988
Finland	September 1, 1985	Soviet Union	April 22, 1981
France	August 19, 1980	Spain	March 19, 1981
German Democratic Republic	July 27, 1989	Sweden	October 1, 1983
Germany, Federal Republic of	January 20, 1981	Switzerland	August 19, 1981
Hungary	August 19, 1980	United Kingdom	December 29, 1980
Italy	March 23, 1986	United States of America	August 19, 1980

(Total: 24 States)

Declarations of Acceptance Filed Under Article 9(1)(*a*) of the Budapest Treaty by Intergovernmental Industrial Property Organizations

International Depositary Authorities Under Article 7 of the Budapest Treaty

Institution	Country	Date status acquired
Agricultural Research Service Culture Collection	United States of America	January 31, 1981
American Type Culture Collection	United States of America	January 31, 1981
Australian Government Analytical Laboratories	Australia	September 30, 1988
Centraalbureau voor Schimmelcultures	Netherlands	October 1, 1981
Collection Nationale de Cultures de Micro-Organismes	France	August 31, 1984
Commonwealth Agricultural Bureau, International Mycological Institute	United Kingdom	March 31, 1983
Culture Collection of Algae and Protozoa	United Kingdom	September 30, 1982
Deutsche Sammlung von Mikroorganismen und Zellkulturen GmbH	Federal Republic of Germany	October 1, 1981
European Collection of Animal Cell Cultures	United Kingdom	September 30, 1984
Fermentation Research Institute	Japan	May 1, 1981
IMET — Nationale Sammlung von Mikroorganismen	German Democratic Republic	August 31, 1989
In Vitro International, Inc.	United States of America	November 30, 1983
Institute of Microorganism Biochemistry and Physiology of the USSR Academy of Science	Soviet Union	August 31, 1987
National Bank for Industrial Microorganisms and Cell Cultures	Bulgaria	October 31, 1987
National Collection of Agricultural and Industrial Microorganisms	Hungary	June 1, 1986
National Collection of Type Cultures	United Kingdom	August 31, 1982
National Collection of Yeast Cultures	United Kingdom	January 31, 1982
National Collections of Industrial and Marine Bacterias Ltd.	United Kingdom	March 31, 1982
USSR Research Institute for Antibiotics of the USSR Ministry of the Medical and Microbiological Industry	Soviet Union	August 31, 1987
USSR Research Institute for Genetics and Industrial Microorganism Breeding of the USSR Ministry of the Medical and Microbiological Industry	Soviet Union	August 31, 1987

(Total: 20 Authorities)

European Patent Organisation (EPO)

Convention on the Grant of European Patents (1973)

(European Patent Convention)

State	Date on which State became party to the Convention
Austria	May 1, 1979
Belgium	October 7, 1977
Denmark	January 1, 1990
France	October 7, 1977
Germany, Federal Republic of	October 7, 1977
Greece	October 1, 1986
Italy	December 1, 1978
Liechtenstein	April 1, 1980
Luxembourg	October 7, 1977
Netherlands	October 7, 1977
Spain	October 1, 1986
Sweden	May 1, 1978
Switzerland	October 7, 1977
United Kingdom	October 7, 1977

SOURCE: *Industrial Property*, January 1990. Reproduced with the permission of the International Bureau of the World Intellectual Property Organization (WIPO).

Madrid Agreement Concerning the International Registration of Marks

Madrid Agreement (Marks) (1891), revised at Brussels (1900), Washington (1911), The Hague (1925), London (1934), Nice (1957) and Stockholm (1967), and amended in 1979

(Madrid Union)

State	Date on which State became party to the Agreement	Latest Act of the Agreement to which State is party and date on which State became party to that Act
Algeria	July 5, 1972	Stockholm: July 5, 1972
Austria	January 1, 1909	Stockholm: August 18, 1973
Belgium	July 15, 1892	Stockholm: February 12, 1975
Bulgaria	August 1, 1985	Stockholm: August 1, 1985
China	October 4, 1989	Stockholm: October 4, 1989
Cuba	December 6, 1989	Stockholm: December 6, 1989
Czechoslovakia	October 5, 1919	Stockholm: December 22 or 29, 1970
Democratic People's Republic of Korea	June 10, 1980	Stockholm: June 10, 1980
Egypt	July 1, 1952	Stockholm: March 6, 1975
France	July 15, 1892	Stockholm: August 12, 1975
German Democratic Republic	December 1, 1922	Stockholm: September 19, or December 22, 1970
Germany, Federal Republic of	December 1, 1922	Stockholm: September 19, or December 22, 1970
Hungary	January 1, 1909	Stockholm: September 19, or December 22, 1970
Italy	October 15, 1894	Stockholm: April 24, 1977
Liechtenstein	July 14, 1933	Stockholm: May 25, 1972
Luxembourg	September 1, 1924	Stockholm: March 24, 1975
Monaco	April 29, 1956	Stockholm: October 4, 1975
Mongolia	April 21, 1985	Stockholm: April 21, 1985
Morocco	July 30, 1917	Stockholm: January 24, 1976
Netherlands	March 1, 1893	Stockholm: March 6, 1975
Portugal	October 31, 1893	Stockholm: November 22, 1988
Romania	October 6, 1920	Stockholm: September 19, or December 22, 1970
San Marino	*September 25, 1960*	*Nice: December 15, 1966*
Soviet Union	July 1, 1976	Stockholm: July 1, 1976
Spain	July 15, 1892	Stockholm: June 8, 1979
Sudan	May 16, 1984	Stockholm: May 16, 1984
Switzerland	July 15, 1892	Stockholm: September 19, or December 22, 1970
Viet Nam	March 8, 1949	Stockholm: July 2, 1976
Yugoslavia	February 26, 1921	Stockholm: October 16, 1973

(Total: 29 States)

Agreement of Madrid for the Prevention of False or Misleading Indications of Source on Goods

Madrid Agreement (Indications of Source) (1891), revised at Washington (1911), The Hague (1925), London (1934) and Lisbon (1958), and supplemented by the Additional Act of Stockholm (1967)

State	Date on which State became party to the Agreement	Latest Act of the Agreement to which State is party and date on which State became party to that Act (see, however, for some States, the Additional Act of Stockholm)	Date on which State became party to the Additional Act of Stockholm
Algeria	July 5, 1972	Lisbon: July 5, 1972	July 5, 1972
Brazil	*October 3, 1896*	*The Hague: October 26, 1929*	—
Bulgaria	August 12, 1975	Lisbon: August 12, 1975	August 12, 1975
Cuba	January 1, 1905	Lisbon: October 11, 1964	October 7, 1980
Czechoslovakia	September 30, 1921	Lisbon: June 1, 1963	December 29, 1970
Dominican Republic	*April 6, 1951*	*The Hague: April 6, 1951*	—
Egypt	July 1, 1952	Lisbon: March 6, 1975	March 6, 1975
France	July 15, 1892	Lisbon: June 1, 1963	August 12, 1975
German Democratic Republic	June 12, 1925	Lisbon: January 15, 1965	April 26, 1970
Germany, Federal Republic of	June 12, 1925	Lisbon: June 1, 1963	September 19, 1970
Hungary	June 5, 1934	Lisbon: March 23, 1967	April 26, 1970
Ireland	December 4, 1925	Lisbon: June 9, 1967	April 26, 1970
Israel	March 24, 1950	Lisbon: July 2, 1967	April 26, 1970
Italy	March 5, 1951	Lisbon: December 29, 1968	April 24, 1977
Japan	July 8, 1953	Lisbon: August 21, 1965	April 24, 1975
Lebanon	*September 1, 1924*	*London: September 30, 1947*	—
Liechtenstein	July 14, 1933	Lisbon: April 10, 1972	May 25, 1972
Monaco	April 29, 1956	Lisbon: June 1, 1963	October 4, 1975
Morocco	*July 30, 1917*	*Lisbon: May 15, 1967*	—
New Zealand	*July 29, 1931*	*London: May 17, 1947*	—
Poland	*December 10, 1928*	*The Hague: December 10, 1928*	—
Portugal	*October 31, 1893*	*London: November 7, 1949*	—
San Marino	*September 25, 1960*	*London: September 25, 1960*	—
Spain	July 15, 1892	Lisbon: August 14, 1973	August 14, 1973
Sri Lanka	*December 29, 1952*	*London: December 29, 1952*	—
Sweden	January 1, 1934	Lisbon: October 3, 1969	April 26, 1970
Switzerland	July 15, 1892	Lisbon: June 1, 1963	April 26, 1970
Syria	*September 1, 1924*	*London: September 30, 1947*	—
Tunisia	*July 15, 1892*	*London: October 4, 1942*	—
Turkey	*August 21, 1930*	*London: June 27, 1957*	—
United Kingdom	July 15, 1892	Lisbon: June 1, 1963	April 26, 1970

(Total: 31 States)

Lisbon Agreement for the Protection of Appellations of Origin and their International Registration

Lisbon Agreement (1958), revised at Stockholm (1967), and amended in 1979

(Lisbon Union)

State	Date on which State became party to the Agreement	Latest Act of the Agreement to which State is party and date on which it became party to Act
Algeria	July 5, 1972	Stockholm: October 31, 1973
Bulgaria	August 12, 1975	Stockholm: August 12, 1975
Burkina Faso	September 2, 1975	Stockholm: September 2, 1975
Congo	November 16, 1977	Stockholm: November 16, 1977
Cuba	September 25, 1966	Stockholm: April 8, 1975
Czechoslovakia	September 25, 1966	Stockholm: October 31, 1973
France	September 25, 1966	Stockholm: August 12, 1975
Gabon	June 10, 1975	Stockholm: June 10, 1975
Haiti	*September 25, 1966*	*Lisbon: September 25, 1966*
Hungary	March 23, 1967	Stockholm: October 31, 1973
Israel	September 25, 1966	Stockholm: October 31, 1973
Italy	December 29, 1968	Stockholm: April 24, 1977
Mexico	*September 25, 1966*	*Lisbon: September 25, 1966*
Portugal	*September 25, 1966*	*Lisbon: September 25, 1966*
Togo	April 30, 1975	Stockholm: April 30, 1975
Tunisia	October 31, 1973	Stockholm: October 31, 1973

(Total: 16 States)

Trademark Registration Treaty

TRT (Vienna, 1973), amended in 1980

(TRT Union)

State	Date on which State became party to the Treaty	State	Date on which State became party to the Treaty
Burkina Faso	August 7, 1980	Soviet Union	August 7, 1980
Congo	August 7, 1980	Togo	August 7, 1980
Gabon	August 7, 1980		

(Total: 5 States)

Source: *Industrial Property*, January 1990. Reproduced with the permission of the International Bureau of the World Intellectual Property Organization (WIPO).

Berne Convention for the Protection of Literary and Artistic Works

Berne Convention (1886), completed at Paris (1896), revised at Berlin (1908), completed at Berne (1914), revised at Rome (1928), at Brussels (1948), at Stockholm (1967) and at Paris (1971), and amended in 1979

(Berne Union)

State	Contribution class	Date on which State became party to the Convention	Latest Act of the Convention to which State is party and date on which State became party to that Act
Argentina	VI	June 10, 1967	*Brussels: June 10, 1967* Paris, Articles 22 to 38: October 8, 1980
Australia	III	April 14, 1928	Paris: March 1, 1978
Austria	VI	October 1, 1920	Paris: August 21, 1982
Bahamas	VII	July 10, 1973	*Brussels: July 10, 1973* Paris, Articles 22 to 38: January 8, 1977
Barbados	VII	July 30, 1983	Paris: July 30, 1983
Belgium	III	*December 5, 1887*	*Brussels: August 1, 1951* *Stockholm, Articles 22 to 38: February 12, 1975*
Benin	S	January 3, 1961	Paris: March 12, 1975
Brazil	VI	February 9, 1922	Paris: April 20, 1975
Bulgaria	VI	December 5, 1921	Paris: December 4, 1974
Burkina Faso	S	August 19, 1963	Paris: January 24, 1976
Cameroon	VI	September 21, 1964	Paris, Articles 1 to 21: October 10, 1974 Paris, Articles 22 to 38: November 10, 1973
Canada	III	*April 10, 1928*	*Rome: August 1, 1931* *Stockholm, Articles 22 to 38: July 7, 1970*
Central African Republic	S	September 3, 1977	Paris: September 3, 1977
Chad	S	*November 25, 1971*	*Brussels: November 25, 1971* *Stockholm, Articles 22 to 38: November 25, 1971*
Chile	VII	June 5, 1970	Paris: July 10, 1975
Colombia	VII	March 7, 1988	Paris: March 7, 1988
Congo	VII	May 8, 1962	Paris: December 5, 1975
Costa Rica	VII	June 10, 1978	Paris: June 10, 1978
Côte d'Ivoire	VI	January 1, 1962	Paris, Articles 1 to 21: October 10, 1974 Paris, Articles 22 to 38: May 4, 1974
Cyprus	VII	February 24, 1964	Paris: July 27, 1983
Czechoslovakia	IV	February 22, 1921	Paris: April 11, 1980
Denmark	IV	July 1, 1903	Paris: June 30, 1979
Egypt	VII	June 7, 1977	Paris: June 7, 1977
Fiji	VII	*December 1, 1971*	*Brussels: December 1, 1971* *Stockholm, Articles 22 to 38: March 15, 1972*
Finland	IV	April 1, 1928	Paris: November 1, 1986
France	I	December 5, 1887	Paris, Articles 1 to 21: October 10, 1974 Paris, Articles 22 to 38: December 15, 1972
Gabon	VII	March 26, 1962	Paris: June 10, 1975
German Democratic Republic	V	December 5, 1887	Paris: February 18, 1978

SOURCE: *Copyright,* January 1990. Reproduced with the permission of the International Bureau of the World Intellectual Property Organization (WIPO).

State	Contribution class	Date on which State became party to the Convention	Latest Act of the Convention to which State is party and date on which State became party to that Act
Germany, Federal Republic of	I	December 5, 1887	Paris, Articles 1 to 21: October 10, 1974 Paris, Articles 22 to 38: January 22, 1974
Greece	VI	November 9, 1920	Paris: March 8, 1976
Guinea	S	November 20, 1980	Paris: November 20, 1980
Holy See	VII	September 12, 1935	Paris: April 24, 1975
Honduras	VII	January 25, 1990	Paris: January 25, 1990
Hungary	VI	February 14, 1922	Paris, Articles 1 to 21: October 10, 1974 Paris, Articles 22 to 38: December 15, 1972
Iceland	VII	September 7, 1947	*Rome: September 7, 1947* Paris, Articles 22 to 38: December 28, 1984
India	IV	April 1, 1928	Paris, Articles 1 to 21: May 6, 1984 Paris, Articles 22 to 38: January 10, 1975
Ireland	IV	October 5, 1927	Paris: January 2, 1990
Israel	VI	*March 24, 1950*	*Brussels: August 1, 1951* *Stockholm, Articles 22 to 38: January 29 or February 26, 1970*
Italy	III	December 5, 1887	Paris: November 14, 1979
Japan	II	July 15, 1899	Paris: April 24, 1975
Lebanon	VI	*September 30, 1947*	*Rome: September 30, 1947*
Lesotho	S	September 28, 1989	Paris: September 28, 1989
Liberia	VII	March 8, 1989	Paris: March 8, 1989
Libya	VI	September 28, 1976	Paris: September 28, 1976
Liechtenstein	VII	*July 30, 1931*	*Brussels: August 1, 1951* *Stockholm, Articles 22 to 38: May 25, 1972*
Luxembourg	VII	June 20, 1888	Paris: April 20, 1975
Madagascar	VI	*January 1, 1966*	*Brussels: January 1, 1966*
Mali	S	March 19, 1962	Paris: December 5, 1977
Malta	VII	September 21, 1964	*Rome: September 21, 1964* Paris, Articles 22 to 38: December 12, 1977
Mauritania	S	February 6, 1973	Paris: September 21, 1976
Mauritius	VII	May 10, 1989	Paris: May 10, 1989
Mexico	IV	June 11, 1967	Paris: December 17, 1974
Monaco	VII	May 30, 1889	Paris: November 23, 1974
Morocco	VI	June 16, 1917	Paris: May 17, 1987
Netherlands	III	November 1, 1912	Paris, Articles 1 to 21: January 30, 1986 Paris, Articles 22 to 38: January 10, 1975
New Zealand	V	*April 24, 1928*	*Rome: December 4, 1947*
Niger	S	May 2, 1962	Paris: May 21, 1975
Norway	IV	April 13, 1896	*Brussels: January 28, 1963* Paris, Articles 22 to 38: June 13, 1974
Pakistan	VI	*July 5, 1948*	*Rome: July 5, 1948* *Stockholm, Articles 22 to 38: January 29 or February 26, 1970*
Peru	VII	August 20, 1988	Paris: August 20, 1988
Philippines	VI	August 1, 1951	*Brussels: August 1, 1951* Paris, Articles 22 to 38: July 16, 1980
Poland	VI	*January 28, 1920*	*Rome: November 21, 1935*
Portugal	V	March 29, 1911	Paris: January 12, 1979
Romania	VI	*January 1, 1927*	*Rome: August 6, 1936* *Stockholm, Articles 22 to 38: January 29 or February 26, 1970*
Rwanda	S	March 1, 1984	Paris: March 1, 1984
Senegal	VI	August 25, 1962	Paris: August 12, 1975
South Africa	IV	October 3, 1928	*Brussels: August 1, 1951* Paris, Articles 22 to 38: March 24, 1975

State	Contribution class	Date on which State became party to the Convention	Latest Act of the Convention to which State is party and date on which State became party to that Act
Spain	II	December 5, 1887	Paris, Articles 1 to 21: October 10, 1974 Paris, Articles 22 to 38: February 19, 1974
Sri Lanka	VII	July 20, 1959	*Rome: July 20, 1959* Paris, Articles 22 to 38: September 23, 1978
Suriname	VII	February 23, 1977	Paris: February 23, 1977
Sweden	III	August 1, 1904	Paris, Articles 1 to 21: October 10, 1974 Paris, Articles 22 to 38: September 20, 1973
Switzerland	III	*December 5, 1887*	*Brussels: January 2, 1956* *Stockholm, Articles 22 to 38: May 4, 1970*
Thailand	VII	July 17, 1931	*Berlin: July 17, 1931* Paris, Articles 22 to 38: December 29, 1980
Togo	S	April 30, 1975	Paris: April 30, 1975
Trinidad and Tobago	VII	August 16, 1988	Paris: August 16, 1988
Tunisia	VII	December 5, 1887	Paris: August 16, 1975
Turkey	VI	*January 1, 1952*	*Brussels: January 1, 1952*
United Kingdom	I	December 5, 1887	Paris: January 2, 1990
United States of America	I	March 1, 1989	Paris: March 1, 1989
Uruguay	VII	July 10, 1967	Paris: December 28, 1979
Venezuela	VII	December 30, 1982	Paris: December 30, 1982
Yugoslavia	VI	June 17, 1930	Paris: September 2, 1975
Zaire	VI	October 8, 1963	Paris: January 31, 1975
Zimbabwe	VII	April 18, 1980	*Rome: April 18, 1980* Paris, Articles 22 to 38: December 30, 1981

(Total: 84 States)

Universal Copyright Convention

Adopted at Geneva (1952), revised at Paris (1971)

State	Date on which State became party to the Convention: Text of 1952	Text of 1971
Algeria	August 28, 1973	July 10, 1974
Andorra	September 16, 1955	–
Argentina	February 13, 1958	–
Australia	May 1, 1969	February 28, 1978
Austria	July 2, 1957	August 14, 1982
Bahamas	December 27, 1976	December 27, 1976
Bangladesh	August 5, 1975	August 5, 1975
Barbados	June 18, 1983	June 18, 1983
Belgium	August 31, 1960	–
Belize	December 1, 1982	–
Brazil	January 13, 1960	December 11, 1975
Bulgaria	June 7, 1975	June 7, 1975
Cameroon	May 1, 1973	July 10, 1974
Canada	August 10, 1962	–
Chile	September 16, 1955	–
Colombia	June 18, 1976	June 18, 1976
Costa Rica	September 16, 1955	March 7, 1980
Cuba	June 18, 1957	–
Czechoslovakia	January 6, 1960	April 17, 1980
Democratic Kampuchea	September 16, 1955	–
Denmark	February 9, 1962	July 11, 1979
Dominican Republic	May 8, 1983	May 8, 1983
Ecuador	June 5, 1957	–
El Salvador	March 29, 1979	March 29, 1979
Fiji	October 10, 1970	–
Finland	April 16, 1963	November 1, 1986
France	January 14, 1956	July 10, 1974
German Democratic Republic	October 5, 1973	December 10, 1980
Germany, Federal Republic of	September 16, 1955	July 10, 1974
Ghana	August 22, 1962	–
Greece	August 24, 1963	–
Guatemala	October 28, 1964	–
Guinea	November 13, 1981	November 13, 1981
Haiti	September 16, 1955	–
Holy See	October 5, 1955	May 6, 1980
Hungary	January 23, 1971	July 10, 1974
Iceland	December 18, 1956	–
India	January 21, 1958	–
Ireland	January 20, 1959	–
Israel	September 16, 1955	–
Italy	January 24, 1957	January 25, 1980
Japan	April 28, 1956	October 21, 1977
Kenya	September 7, 1966	July 10, 1974
Laos	September 16, 1955	–
Lebanon	October 17, 1959	–
Liberia	July 27, 1956	–
Liechtenstein	January 22, 1959	–
Luxembourg	October 15, 1955	–
Malawi	October 26, 1965	–
Malta	November 19, 1968	–
Mauritius	March 12, 1968	–
Mexico	May 12, 1957	October 31, 1975
Monaco	September 16, 1955	December 13, 1974
Morocco	May 8, 1972	January 28, 1976
Netherlands	June 22, 1967	November 30, 1985
New Zealand	September 11, 1964	–
Nicaragua	August 16, 1961	–
Niger	May 15, 1989	May 15, 1989
Nigeria	February 14, 1962	–
Norway	January 23, 1963	August 7, 1974
Pakistan	September 16, 1955	–
Panama	October 17, 1962	September 3, 1980
Paraguay	March 11, 1962	–
Peru	October 16, 1963	July 22, 1985
Philippines	November 19, 1955	–
Poland	March 9, 1977	March 9, 1977
Portugal	December 25, 1956	July 30, 1981
Republic of Korea	October 1, 1987	October 1, 1987
Rwanda	November 10, 1989	November 10, 1989
Saint Vincent and the Grenadines	April 22, 1985	April 22, 1985
Senegal	July 9, 1974	July 10, 1974
Soviet Union	May 27, 1973	–
Spain	September 16, 1955	July 10, 1974
Sri Lanka	January 25, 1984	January 25, 1984
Sweden	July 1, 1961	July 10, 1974
Switzerland	March 30, 1956	–
Trinidad and Tobago	August 19, 1988	August 19, 1988
Tunisia	June 19, 1969	June 10, 1975
United Kingdom	September 27, 1957	July 10, 1974
United States of America	September 16, 1955	July 10, 1974
Venezuela	September 30, 1966	–
Yugoslavia	May 11, 1966	July 10, 1974
Zambia	June 1, 1965	–

SOURCE: *Copyright,* January 1990. Reproduced with the permission of the International Bureau of the World Intellectual Property Organization (WIPO).

International Convention for the Protection of Performers, Producers of Phonograms and Broadcasting Organizations

Rome Convention (1961)

State	Date on which State became party to the Convention	State	Date on which State became party to the Convention
Austria	June 9, 1973	Guatemala	January 14, 1977
Barbados	September 18, 1983	Honduras	February 16, 1990
Brazil	September 29, 1965	Ireland	September 19, 1979
Burkina Faso	January 14, 1988	Italy	April 8, 1975
Chile	September 5, 1974	Japan	October 26, 1989
Colombia	September 17, 1976	Lesotho	January 26, 1990
Congo	May 18, 1964	Luxembourg	February 25, 1976
Costa Rica	September 9, 1971	Mexico	May 18, 1964
Czechoslovakia	August 14, 1964	Monaco	December 6, 1985
Denmark	September 23, 1965	Niger	May 18, 1964
Dominican Republic	January 27, 1987	Norway	July 10, 1978
Ecuador	May 18, 1964	Panama	September 2, 1983
El Salvador	June 29, 1979	Paraguay	February 26, 1970
Fiji	April 11, 1972	Peru	August 7, 1985
Finland	October 21, 1983	Philippines	September 25, 1984
France	July 3, 1987	Sweden	May 18, 1964
Germany, Federal Republic of	October 21, 1966	United Kingdom	May 18, 1964
		Uruguay	July 4, 1977

(Total: 35 States)

SOURCE: *Copyright,* January 1990. Reproduced with the permission of the International Bureau of the World Intellectual Property Organization (WIPO).

Convention for the Protection of Producers of Phonograms Against Unauthorized Duplication of Their Phonograms

Phonograms Convention (Geneva, 1971)

State	Date on which State became party to the Convention	State	Date on which State became party to the Convention
Argentina	June 30, 1973	Hungary	May 28, 1975
Australia	June 22, 1974	India	February 12, 1975
Austria	August 21, 1982	Israel	May 1, 1978
Barbados	July 29, 1983	Italy	March 24, 1977
Brazil	November 28, 1975	Japan	October 14, 1978
Burkina Faso	January 30, 1988	Kenya	April 21, 1976
Chile	March 24, 1977	Luxembourg	March 8, 1976
Costa Rica	June 17, 1982	Mexico	December 21, 1973
Czechoslovakia	January 15, 1985	Monaco	December 2, 1974
Denmark	March 24, 1977	New Zealand	August 13, 1976
Ecuador	September 14, 1974	Norway	August 1, 1978
Egypt	April 23, 1978	Panama	June 29, 1974
El Salvador	February 9, 1979	Paraguay	February 13, 1979
Fiji	April 18, 1973	Peru	August 24, 1985
Finland	April 18, 1973	Republic of Korea	October 10, 1987
France	April 18, 1973	Spain	August 24, 1974
Germany, Federal Republic of	May 18, 1974	Sweden	April 18, 1973
Guatemala	February 1, 1977	Trinidad and Tobago	October 1, 1988
Holy See	July 18, 1977	United Kingdom	April 18, 1973
Honduras	March 6, 1990	United States of America	March 10, 1974
		Uruguay	January 18, 1983
		Venezuela	November 18, 1982
(Total: 43 States)		Zaire	November 29, 1977

SOURCE: ***Copyright,*** **January 1990. Reproduced with the permission of the International Bureau of the World Intellectual Property Organization (WIPO).**

Convention Relating to the Distribution of Programme-Carrying Signals Transmitted by Satellite

Satellites Convention (Brussels, 1974)

State	Date on which State became party to the Convention	State	Date on which State became party to the Convention
Austria	August 6, 1982	Morocco	June 30, 1983
Germany, Federal Republic of	August 25, 1979	Nicaragua	August 25, 1979
Italy	July 7, 1981	Panama	September 25, 1985
Kenya	August 25, 1979	Peru	August 7, 1985
Mexico	August 25, 1979	Soviet Union	January 20, 1989
		United States of America	March 7, 1985
		Yugoslavia	August 25, 1979

(Total: 12 States)

Hague Agreement Concerning the International Deposit of Industrial Designs

Hague Agreement (1925), revised at London (1934) and The Hague (1960), supplemented by the Additional Act of Monaco (1961), the Complementary Act of Stockholm (1967) and the Protocol of Geneva (1975), and amended in 1979

(Hague Union)

State	Date on which State became party to the Agreement	Date on which State became party to the London Act	Date on which State became party to the Hague Act	Date on which State became party to the Complementary Act of Stockholm
Belgium	April 1, 1979	—	August 1, 1984	May 28, 1979
Benin	November 2, 1986	November 2, 1986	November 2, 1986	January 2, 1987
Egypt	*July 1, 1952*	*July 1, 1952*	—	—
France	October 20, 1930	June 25, 1939	August 1, 1984	September 27, 1975
German Democratic Republic	June 1, 1928	June 13, 1939	May 7, 1989	May 7, 1989
Germany, Federal Republic of	June 1, 1928	June 13, 1939	August 1, 1984	September 27, 1975
Holy See	*September 29, 1960*	*September 29, 1960*	—	—
Hungary	April 7, 1984	April 7, 1984	August 1, 1984	April 7, 1984
Indonesia	*December 24, 1950*	*December 24, 1950*	—	—
Italy	June 13, 1987	—	June 13, 1987	August 13, 1987
Liechtenstein	July 14, 1933	January 28, 1951	August 1, 1984	September 27, 1975
Luxembourg	April 1, 1979	—	August 1, 1984	May 28, 1979
Monaco	April 29, 1956	April 29, 1956	August 1, 1984	September 27, 1975
Morocco	*October 20, 1930*	*January 21, 1941*	—	—
Netherlands	April 1, 1979	—	August 1, 1984	May 28, 1979
Senegal	June 30, 1984	June 30, 1984	August 1, 1984	June 30, 1984
Spain	*June 1, 1928*	*March 2, 1956*	—	—
Suriname	November 25, 1975	November 25, 1975	August 1, 1984	February 23, 1977
Switzerland	June 1, 1928	November 24, 1939	August 1, 1984	September 27, 1975
Tunisia	*October 20, 1930*	*October 4, 1942*	—	—

(Total: 20 States)

SOURCE: *Industrial Property,* January 1990. Reproduced with the permission of the International Bureau of the World Intellectual Property Organization (WIPO).

Nice Agreement Concerning the International Classification of Goods and Services for the Purposes of the Registration of Marks

Nice Agreement (1957), revised at Stockholm (1967) and at Geneva (1977), and amended in 1979

(Nice Union)

State	Date on which State became party to the Agreement	Latest Act of the Agreement to which State is party and date on which it became party to that Act
Algeria	July 5, 1972	Stockholm: July 5, 1972
Australia	April 8, 1961	Geneva: February 6, 1979
Austria	November 30, 1969	Geneva: August 21, 1982
Barbados	March 12, 1985	Geneva: March 12, 1985
Belgium	June 6, 1962	Geneva: November 20, 1984
Benin	February 6, 1979	Geneva: February 6, 1979
Czechoslovakia	April 8, 1961	Geneva: February 6, 1979
Denmark	November 30, 1961	Geneva: June 3, 1981
Finland	August 18, 1973	Geneva: February 6, 1979
France	April 8, 1961	Geneva: April 22, 1980
German Democratic Republic	January 15, 1965	Geneva : June 23, 1982
Germany, Federal Republic of	January 29, 1962	Geneva: January 12, 1982
Hungary	March 23, 1967	Geneva: August 21, 1982
Ireland	December 12, 1966	Geneva: February 6, 1979
Israel	April 8, 1961	Stockholm: November 12, 1969, or March 18, 1970
Italy	April 8, 1961	Geneva: February 19, 1983
Japan	February 20, 1990	Geneva: February 20, 1990
Lebanon	*April 8, 1961*	*Nice: April 8, 1961*
Liechtenstein	May 29, 1967	Geneva: February 14, 1987
Luxembourg	March 24, 1975	Geneva: December 21, 1983
Monaco	April 8, 1961	Geneva: May 9, 1981
Morocco	October 1, 1966	Stockholm: January 24, 1976
Netherlands	August 20, 1962	Geneva: August 15, 1979
Norway	July 28, 1961	Geneva: July 7, 1981
Portugal	April 8, 1961	Geneva: July 30, 1982
Soviet Union	July 26, 1971	Geneva: December 30, 1987
Spain	April 8, 1961	Geneva: May 9, 1979
Suriname	December 16, 1981	Geneva: December 16, 1981
Sweden	July 28, 1961	Geneva: February 6, 1979
Switzerland	August 20, 1962	Geneva: April 22, 1986
Tunisia	*May 29, 1967*	*Nice: May 29, 1967*
United Kingdom	April 15, 1963	Geneva: July 3, 1979
United States of America	May 25, 1972	Geneva: February 29, 1984
Yugoslavia	August 30, 1966	Stockholm: October 16, 1973

(Total: 34 States)

Locarno Agreement Establishing an International Classification for Industrial Designs

Locarno Agreement (1968), amended in 1979

(Locarno Union)

State	Date on which State became party to the Agreement	State	Date on which State became party to the Agreement
Czechoslovakia	April 27, 1971	Netherlands	March 30, 1977
Denmark	April 27, 1971	Norway	April 27, 1971
Finland	May 16, 1972	Soviet Union	December 15, 1972
France	September 13, 1975	Spain	November 17, 1973
German Democratic Republic	April 27, 1971	Sweden	April 27, 1971
Hungary	January 1, 1974	Switzerland	April 27, 1971
Ireland	April 27, 1971	Yugoslavia	October 16, 1973
Italy	August 12, 1975		

(Total: 15 States)

SOURCE: *Industrial Property*, January 1990. Reproduced with the permission of the International Bureau of the World Intellectual Property Organization (WIPO).

Vienna Agreement Establishing an International Classification of the Figurative Elements of Marks

Vienna Agreement (1973)

(Vienna Union)

State	Date on which State became party to the Agreement	State	Date on which State became party to the Agreement
France	August 9, 1985	Sweden	August 9, 1985
Luxembourg	August 9, 1985	Tunisia	August 9, 1985
Netherlands	August 9, 1985		

(Total: 5 States)

SOURCE: *Industrial Property*, January 1990. Reproduced with the permission of the International Bureau of the World Intellectual Property Organization (WIPO).

Strasbourg Agreement Concerning the International Patent Classification

Strasbourg Agreement (1971), amended in 1979

(IPC Union)

State	Date on which State became party to the Agreement	State	Date on which State became party to the Agreement
Australia	November 12, 1975	Japan	August 18, 1977
Austria	October 7, 1975	Luxembourg	April 9, 1977
Belgium	July 4, 1976	Monaco	June 13, 1976
Brazil	October 7, 1975	Netherlands	October 7, 1975
Czechoslovakia	August 3, 1978	Norway	October 7, 1975
Denmark	October 7, 1975	Portugal	May 1, 1979
Egypt	October 17, 1975	Soviet Union	October 3, 1976
Finland	May 16, 1976	Spain	November 29, 1975
France	October 7, 1975	Suriname	November 25, 1975
German Democratic Republic	August 24, 1977	Sweden	October 7, 1975
Germany, Federal Republic of	October 7, 1975	Switzerland	October 7, 1975
Ireland	October 7, 1975	United Kingdom	October 7, 1975
Israel	October 7, 1975	United States of America	October 7, 1975
Italy	March 30, 1980		

(Total: 27 States)

SOURCE: *Industrial Property*, January 1990. Reproduced with the permission of the International Bureau of the World Intellectual Property Organization (WIPO).

Convention Establishing the World Intellectual Property Organization

WIPO Convention (1967), amended in 1979

State	Date on which State became member of WIPO	Member also of Paris Union (P) and/or Berne Union (B)	
Algeria	April 16, 1975	P	–
Angola (c)	April 15, 1985	–	–
Argentina	October 8, 1980	P	B
Australia	August 10, 1972	P	B
Austria	August 11, 1973	P	B
Bahamas	January 4, 1977	P	B
Bangladesh (c)	May 11, 1985	–	–
Barbados	October 5, 1979	P	B
Belgium	January 31, 1975	P	B
Benin	March 9, 1975	P	B
Brazil	March 20, 1975	P	B
Bulgaria	May 19, 1970	P	B
Burkina Faso	August 23, 1975	P	B
Burundi	March 30, 1977	P	–
Byelorussian SSR (c)	April 26, 1970	–	–
Cameroon	November 3, 1973	P	B
Canada	June 26, 1970	P	B
Central African Republic	August 23, 1978	P	B
Chad	September 26, 1970	P	B
Chile	June 25, 1975	–	B
China	June 3, 1980	P	–
Colombia	May 4, 1980	–	B
Congo	December 2, 1975	P	B
Costa Rica	June 10, 1981	–	B
Côte d'Ivoire	May 1, 1974	P	B
Cuba	March 27, 1975	P	–
Cyprus	October 26, 1984	P	B
Czechoslovakia	December 22, 1970	P	B
Democratic People's Republic of Korea	August 17, 1974	P	–
Democratic Yemen (c)	December 27, 1989	–	–
Denmark	April 26, 1970	P	B
Ecuador (c)	May 22, 1988	–	–
Egypt	April 21, 1975	P	B
El Salvador (c)	September 18, 1979	–	–
Fiji	March 11, 1972	–	B
Finland	September 8, 1970	P	B
France	October 18, 1974	P	B
Gabon	June 6, 1975	P	B
Gambia (c)	December 10, 1980	–	–
German Democratic Republic	April 26, 1970	P	B

SOURCE: *Industrial Property*, January 1990. Reproduced with the permission of the International Bureau of the World Intellectual Property Organization (WIPO).

State	Date on which State became member of WIPO	Member also of Paris Union (P) and/or Berne Union (B)	
Germany, Federal Republic of	September 19, 1970	P	B
Ghana	June 12, 1976	P	–
Greece	March 4, 1976	P	B
Guatemala (c)	April 30, 1983	–	–
Guinea	November 13, 1980	P	B
Guinea-Bissau	June 28, 1988	P	–
Haiti	November 2, 1983	P	–
Holy See	April 20, 1975	P	B
Honduras	November 15, 1983	–	B
Hungary	April 26, 1970	P	B
Iceland	September 13, 1986	P	B
India	May 1, 1975	–	B
Indonesia	December 18, 1979	P	–
Iraq	January 21, 1976	P	–
Ireland	April 26, 1970	P	B
Israel	April 26, 1970	P	B
Italy	April 20, 1977	P	B
Jamaica (c)	December 25, 1978	–	–
Japan	April 20, 1975	P	B
Jordan	July 12, 1972	P	–
Kenya	October 5, 1971	P	–
Lebanon	December 30, 1986	P	–
Lesotho	November 18, 1986	P	B
Liberia	March 8, 1989	–	B
Libya	September 28, 1976	P	B
Liechtenstein	May 21, 1972	P	B
Luxembourg	March 19, 1975	P	B
Madagascar	December 22, 1989	P	B
Malawi	June 11, 1970	P	–
Malaysia	January 1, 1989	P	–
Mali	August 14, 1982	P	B
Malta	December 7, 1977	P	B
Mauritania	September 17, 1976	P	B
Mauritius	September 21, 1976	P	B
Mexico	June 14, 1975	P	B
Monaco	March 3, 1975	P	B
Mongolia	February 28, 1979	P	–
Morocco	July 27, 1971	P	B
Netherlands	January 9, 1975	P	B
New Zealand	June 20, 1984	P	–
Nicaragua (c)	May 5, 1985	–	–
Niger	May 18, 1975	P	B
Norway	June 8, 1974	P	B
Pakistan	January 6, 1977	–	B
Panama (c)	September 17, 1983	–	–
Paraguay (c)	June 20, 1987	–	–
Peru	September 4, 1980	–	B
Philippines	July 14, 1980	P	B
Poland	March 23, 1975	P	–
Portugal	April 27, 1975	P	B

State	Date on which State became member of WIPO	Member also of Paris Union (P) and/or Berne Union (B)	
Qatar (b)	September 3, 1976	–	–
Republic of Korea	March 1, 1979	P	–
Romania	April 26, 1970	P	B
Rwanda	February 3, 1984	P	B
Saudi Arabia (a)	May 22, 1982	–	–
Senegal	April 26, 1970	P	B
Sierra Leone (c)	May 18, 1986	–	–
Somalia (c)	November 18, 1982	–	–
South Africa	March 23, 1975	P	B
Soviet Union	April 26, 1970	P	–
Spain	April 26, 1970	P	B
Sri Lanka	September 20, 1978	P	B
Sudan	February 15, 1974	P	–
Suriname	November 25, 1975	P	B
Swaziland (c)	August 18, 1988	–	–
Sweden	April 26, 1970	P	B
Switzerland	April 26, 1970	P	B
Thailand	December 25, 1989	–	B
Togo	April 28, 1975	P	B
Trinidad and Tobago	August 16, 1988	P	B
Tunisia	November 28, 1975	P	B
Turkey	May 12, 1976	P	–
Uganda	October 18, 1973	P	–
Ukrainian SSR (c)	April 26, 1970	–	–
United Arab Emirates (b)	September 24, 1974	–	–
United Kingdom	April 26, 1970	P	B
United Republic of Tanzania	December 30, 1983	P	–
United States of America	August 25, 1970	P	B
Uruguay	December 21, 1979	P	B
Venezuela	November 23, 1984	–	B
Viet Nam	July 2, 1976	P	–
Yemen (c)	March 29, 1979	–	–
Yugoslavia	October 11, 1973	P	B
Zaire	January 28, 1975	P	B
Zambia	May 14, 1977	P	–
Zimbabwe	December 29, 1981	P	B

(Total: 126 States)

Bibliography

Industrial Property, Patents, and Trademarks

Books and Monographs

Altman, L. *Callmann on Unfair Competition, Trademarks and Monopolies*. Vol. 4A, 4th ed., Ch. 26, Deerfield, Ill.: Callaghan & Co., 1989.

Bodenhausen, G.H.C. *Guide to the Application of the Paris Convention for the Protection of Industrial Property*. Publication no. 611(E). Geneva: WIPO, 1968.

Chisum, D. *Patents: A Treatise on the Law of Patentability, Validity and Infringements*. New York: Matthew Bender & Co., 1990.

Cooper, I. *Biotechnology and the Law*. Ch. 10. New York: Clark Boardman Co., 1989.

Cornish, W. R. *Intellectual Property: Patents, Copyright, Trademarks and Allied Rights*, 2d ed. London: Sweet & Maxwell, 1989.

Greene, A. *Designs and Utility Models Throughout the World*. New York: Trade Activities, 1983.

Jacobs, A., ed. *Trademarks Throughout the World*. 4th ed. New York: Trade Activities, 1989.

———. *Patents Throughout the World*. 4th ed. New York: Trade Activities, 1989.

Kase, F. J. *Foreign Patents: A Guide to Official Patent Literature*. Dobbs Ferry, N.Y.: Oceana Publications, 1972.

———. *Designs: A Guide to Official Literature on Designs Protection*. Leydon: Sijthoff, 1975.

———. *Dictionary of Industrial Property Terms: Legal and Related Terms: English, Spanish, French, and German*. Alphen aan den Rijn: Sijthoff & Noordhoff, 1980.

Ladas, S. *Patents, Trademarks and Related Rights: National and International Protection*. Cambridge: Harvard University Press, 1975.

Offner, E. *International Trademark Protection.* New York: Fieldston Press. 1965.

Rosenberg, P. *Patent Law Fundamentals.* Vol. II, Ch. 26. New York: Clark Boardman Co., 1989.

Sinnott, J., and J. Baxter. *World Patent Law and Practice.* New York: Matthew Bender & Co., 1968.

Ulmer, E. *Intellectual Property Rights and the Conflict of Laws.* Deventer, the Netherlands: Kluwer, 1978.

———. *International Encyclopedia of Comparative Law.* Vol. 14, Ch. 1. Norwell, Mass.: Kluwer, 1987.

Walton, A. M., and H. I. L. Laddie. *Patent Law of Europe and the United Kingdom.* London: Butterworth & Co., 1978.

White, T. A. Blanco. *Patents for Inventions and the Protection of Industrial Designs.* 5th ed. London: Stevens & Sons, 1983.

White, T. A. Blanco, and Robin Jacob. *Kerley's Law of Trade Marks and Tradenames.* 12th ed. London: Sweet & Maxwell, 1986.

World Intellectual Property Organization. *Guidelines for Drawings Under the Patent Cooperation Treaty (PCT).* Geneva: WIPO, 1977.

———. *Licensing Guide for Developing Countries: A Guide on the Legal Aspects of the Negotiation and Preparation of Industrial Property Licenses and Technology Transfer Agreements Appropriate to the Needs of Developing Countries.* Publication no. 620(E). Geneva: WIPO, 1978.

———. *Industrial Property Glossary.* Publication no. 815(EFSA). Geneva: WIPO, 1979.

———. *PCT Applicant's Guide.* Publication no. 432(E). Geneva: WIPO, 1982.

———. *1883—Paris Convention Centenary—1983. The Paris Convention for the Protection of Industrial Property from 1883 to 1983.* Publication no. 875(E). Geneva: WIPO, 1983.

———. *Background Reading Material on Intellectual Property.* Publication no. 659(E). Geneva: WIPO, 1988.

———. *Guide to the Deposit of Microorganisms under the Budapest Treaty.* Publication no. 661(E). Geneva: WIPO, 1989.

———. *Guide to the International Deposit of Industrial Designs (under the Hague Agreement concerning the International Deposit of Industrial Designs).* Publication no. 623(E). Geneva: WIPO, n.d.

———. *Guide to the International Registration of Marks (under the Madrid Agreement Concerning the International Registration of Marks).* Publication no. 650(E). Geneva: WIPO, n.d.

Articles

Adler, R. "Can Patents Coexist with Breeders' Rights? Developments in U.S. and International Biotechnology Law." *Int'l R. Indus. Prop. & Copyright L.* 17, no. 2 (1986): 185–227.

Ballreich, H., and H. Kunz-Hallstein, "Revision of the Paris Convention: The Principle of Unanimity." *Int'l R. Indus. Prop. & Copyright L.* 9, no. 1 (1978): 21–31.

Bartels, B. "The Advantages of the Patent Cooperation Treaty (PCT) for American Applicants." *J. Pat. Off. Soc'y* 65 (July 1983): 387–403.

Beier, F. K. "The European Patent System." *Vand. J. Transnat'l L.* 14 (Winter 1981): 1–15.

———. "One Hundred Years of International Cooperation—The Role of the Paris Convention in the Past, Present and Future." *Int'l R. Indus. Prop. & Copyright L.* 15, no. 1 (1984): 1–20.

Benson, R. W. "Toward a New Treaty for the Protection of Geographical Indications." *Indus. Prop.* 177 (April 1978): 127–36.

Benson, R. B. "Impact of the Patent Cooperation Treaty (PCT) and the European Patent Convention (EPC) on U.S. Practitioners." *J. Pat. Off. Soc'y* 60 (February 1978): 118–28.

Bogsch, A. "The World Intellectual Property Organization: Its Recent Past and Its Future Plans." *Bull. Copyright Soc'y U.S.A.* 26 (Fall 1979): 194–201.

———. "The First Hundred Years of the Paris Convention for the Protection of Industrial Property." *Indus. Prop.* 23 (July/August 1983): 187–244.

Bruchhausen, K. "Institutions and Procedures Involved in Actions Relating to Community Patents." *Int'l R. Indus. Prop. & Copyright L.* 18, no. 5 (1987): 682–92.

Cabanellas, G. "The Consequences of Stricter Working Requirements for Patentees Under the Paris Conventions." *Int'l R. Indus. Prop. & Copyright L.* 19, no. 2 (1988): 158–84.

Casalonga, A. "The Concept of Inventive Step in the European Patent Convention." *Int'l R. Indus. Prop. & Copyright L.* 10, no. 4 (1979): 412–32.

Clark, G. R. "Patent Cooperation Treaty: Past, Present and Future." *U. Ill. L. F.* 1971, no. 3 (1971): 458–73.

Comment. "United States Position on Revising the Paris Convention: Quid Pro Quo or Denunciation." *Fordham Int'l L. J.* 5, no. 2 (1982): 411–39.

Cornish, W. R. "The Essential Criteria for Patentability of European

Inventions: Novelty and Inventive Step." *Int'l R. Indus. Prop. & Copyright L.* 14, no. 6 (1983): 765–75.

Creel, T. C., and J. Wintringham. "Patent Systems and Their Role in the Technological Advance of Developing Nations." (Symposium on International Law and Technology). *Rutgers Computer Tech. L. J.* 10 (Fall 1984): 255–302.

Dam, K. W. "The Growing Importance of International Protection of Intellectual Property." (Section Symposium: Legal Problems Affecting the Multinational Corporation). *Int'l Law* 216 (Summer 1987): 627–38.

DeVletian, A. "The Protection of Origin and Indications of Source." *Indus. Prop.* 7 (April 1968): 107–16.

———. "The Lisbon Agreement for the Protection of Appellations of Origin and Their International Registration." *Indus. Prop.* 12 (October 1973): 308–14.

———. "The Protection of Appellations of Origin and Indications of Source." *Indus. Prop.* 28 (September 1989): 318–32.

Fernandez-Novoa, C. "The International Protection of Tradenames in Spain—The Application of Article 8 of the Paris Convention by the Spanish Courts." *Int'l R. Indus. Prop. & Copyright L.* 7, no. 4 (1976): 507–18.

Gansser, G. R. "Violations of the Paris Convention for the Protection of Industrial Property." *Int'l R. Indus. Prop. & Copyright L.* 11, no. 1 (1980): 1–26.

Goldman, E. C. "International Trademark Licensing Agreements: A Key to Future Technological Development." *Cal. W. Int'l L. J.* 16 (Winter 1986): 178–204.

Goldsmith, S. D. "Paris Convention Revision—A Problem for U.S. Inventors and Invention Owners." *Prac. Approach Pat. Trademarks & Copyrights* 2 (January 1981): 23–28.

Greengrass, B. "U.P.O.V. and the Protection of Plant Breeders—Past Developments, Future Prospects." *Int'l R. Indus. Prop. & Copyright L.* 20, no. 5 (1989): 622–36.

Haar, P. S. "Revision of the Paris Convention: A Realignment of Private and Public Interests in the International Patent System." *Brooklyn J. Int'l L.* 8 (Winter 1982): 77–108.

Hefter, L. R., and R. L. Stroup. "The International Protection of a Corporation's Trade Names, Trademarks and Service Marks—The Need for a Tailored Registration, Licensing and Enforcement Policy." *Prac. Approach Pat. Trademarks & Copyrights* 1 (April 1980): 169–92.

Llewelyn, D. "International Registration of Trademarks: The Current System and Proposals for Change." *Int'l Bus. Law.* 14 (April 1986) 129.

Le Tallec, G. "The Protocol on Jurisdiction and the Recognition of Decisions in Respect of the Right to the Grant of a European Patent (Protocol on Recognition)." *Int'l R. Indus. Prop. & Copyright L.* 16, no. 3 (1985): 318–25.

Maassal, L. O., and M. E. Turowski. "The Patent Cooperation Treaty After 3.5 Years." *Prac. Approach Pat. Trademarks & Copyrights* 2 (September 1982): 247–72.

McKie, E. F. "Patent Cooperation Treaty: A New Adventure in the Internationality of Patents." *N.C.J. Int'l L. & Com. Reg.* 4 (Spring 1979): 249–60.

Meller, M. N. "The World-Wide Scope of Patenting." *Prac. Approach Pat. Trademarks & Copyrights* 2 (January 1981): 1–22.

Morcom, C. "The Madrid Arrangement—Implications for the Community Trade Mark." *EIPR* 10, 1989: 343–45.

Note. "International Copyright: Domestic Barriers to United States Participation in the Rome Convention on Neighboring Rights." *Ga. J. Int'l Comp. L.* 13, no. 1 (1983): 83–109.

Note. "International Patent Cooperation: The Next Step." *Cornell Int'l L. J.* 16 (Winter 1983): 229–67.

Oddi, A. S. "The International Patent System and Third World Development: Reality or Myth?" *Duke L. J.* (November 1987): 831–78.

Pfanner, K. "The World Intellectual Property Organization." *Int'l R. Indus. Prop. & Copyright L.* 10, no. 1 (1979): 1–19.

———. "Conjunctive Use of the Patent Cooperation Treaty and the European Patent Convention." *Int'l R. Indus. Prop. & Copyright L.* 4, no. 3 (1973): 281–305.

Plaisant, R. "The Revision of the International Treaty Provision Dealing with Appellations of Origin and Indications of Source." *Indus. Prop.* 19 (July/August 1980): 182–88.

Safran, D. A. "Protection of Inventions in the Multinational Marketplace: Problems and Pitfalls in Obtaining and Using Patents." *N.C.J. Int'l L. & Com. Reg.* 9 (Winter 1983): 117–32.

Schuyler, W. E. "Paris Convention for the Protection of Industrial Property—A View of the Proposed Revisions." *N.C.J. Int'l L. & Com. Reg.* 8 (Spring 1983): 155–66.

Sijp, C. "Scope of Protection Afforded by a European Patent." *Int'l R. Indus. Prop. & Copyright L.* 10, no. 4 (1979): 433–50.

Staehelin, J. C. A. "European Patent Grant Procedure In Practice." *Int'l R. Indus. Prop. & Copyright L.* 12, no. 5 (1981): 605–26.

Wagner, H. C. "Patent Law Simplification and the Geneva Patent Convention." *AIPLA Q. L.J.* 14 (Summer 1986): 154–217.

Winner, E. P. "Practical Effects of the Patent Cooperation Treaty and the European Patent Convention on Domestic Technology Management and Patent Practice." *J. Pat. Off. Soc'y* 62 (July 1980): 419–36.

Wolfeld, W. S. "International Patent Cooperation: The Next Step." *Cornell Int'l L.J.* 16 (Winter 1983): 229–68.

World Intellectual Property Organization. "Revision of the Paris Convention." *J. World Trade L.* 16 (March/April 1982): 180–82.

International Classifications

World Intellectual Property Organization. *Revision Concordance List.* Publication no. 462(E). Geneva: WIPO, 1980.

———. *International Patent Classification (IPC) and Official Catchword Index.* 4th ed. Geneva: WIPO, 1984.

———. *Class and Subclass Titles of the International Patent Classification.* 4th ed., Publication no. 463(E). Geneva: WIPO, 1984.

———. *List Indicating Subject Matter Classified Differently According to the Third and Fourth Editions of the International Patent Classification.* Publication no. 462(E). Geneva: WIPO, 1984.

———. *International Classification of the Figurative Elements of Marks (Vienna Classification).* 2d ed., Publication no. 502(E). Geneva: WIPO, 1985.

———. *International Classification of Goods and Services for the Purposes of the Registration of Marks (Nice Classification).* 5th ed., Part I, Publication no. 500.1(E), Part II, Publication no. 500.2(E). Geneva: WIPO, 1987.

———. *List of Goods and Services in Alphabetical Order.* 5th ed., Publication no. 500(EF). Geneva: WIPO, 1987.

———. *International Classification for Industrial Designs (Locarno Classification).* 5th ed., Publication no. 501(E). Geneva: WIPO, 1989.

Records of Diplomatic Conferences

World Intellectual Property Organization. *Records of the Intellectual Property Conference of Stockholm.* Publication no. 311(E). Geneva: WIPO, 1967.

———. *Reports on the Work of the Five Main Committees of the Intellectual Property Conference of Stockholm.* Publication no. 309(E). Geneva: WIPO, 1967.

———. *Records of the Locarno Conference for the Purposes of Setting Up an International Classification for Industrial Designs.* Publication no. 312(E). Geneva: WIPO, 1968.

———. *Records of the Washington Diplomatic Conference on the Patent Cooperation Treaty.* Publication no. 313(E). Geneva: WIPO, 1970.

———. *Records of the Strasbourg Diplomatic Conference on the International Patent Classification.* Publication no. 314(E). Geneva: WIPO, 1971.

———. *Records of the Vienna Diplomatic Conference on the International Classification of the Figurative Elements of Marks.* Publication no. 334(E). Geneva: WIPO, 1973.

———. *Records of the Vienna Diplomatic Conference on the Protection of Type Faces.* Publication no. 333(E). Geneva: WIPO, 1973.

———. *Records of the Vienna Diplomatic Conference on the Trademark Registration Treaty.* Publication no. 317(E). Geneva: WIPO, 1973.

———. *Records of the Conference of Plenipotentiaries of The Hague Union Concerning the International Deposit of Industrial Design.* Publication no. 319(E). Geneva: WIPO, 1975.

———. *Records of the Budapest Diplomatic Conference for the Conclusion of a Treaty on the International Recognition of the Deposit of Microorganisms for the Purposes of Patent Procedure.* Publication no. 332(E). Geneva: WIPO, 1977.

———. *Records of the Diplomatic Conference on the Revision of the Nice Agreement Concerning the International Classification of Goods and Services for the Purposes of the Registration of Marks.* Publication no. 335(E). Geneva: WIPO, 1977.

———. *Records of the Diplomatic Conference for the Conclusion of a Treaty on the International Recording of Scientific Discoveries.* Publication no. 338(E). Geneva: WIPO, 1978.

———. *Records of the Nairobi Diplomatic Conference for the Adoption of a Treaty on the Protection of the Olympic Symbol.* Publication no. 350(E). Geneva: WIPO, 1981.

Copyright and Neighboring Rights

Books and Monographs

Bogsch, A. *The Law of Copyright Under the Universal Copyright Convention.* 3d rev. ed. Leydon: Sijthoff, 1972.

Cornish, W. R. *Intellectual Property: Patents, Copyright, Trademarks and Allied Rights.* 2d ed. London: Sweet & Maxwell, 1989.

Fysh, M. *Russell-Clarke on Copyright in Industrial Designs.* 5th ed. London: Sweet & Maxwell, 1974.

Geller, E., and M. Nimmer, eds. *International Copyright Law and Practice.* New York: Matthew Bender & Co., 1988.

Goldstein, P. *Copyright: Principles, Law and Practice.* Vol. 3, Ch. 16. Boston: Little, Brown & Co., 1989.

Kupferman, T., and M. Foner. *Universal Copyright Convention Analyzed.* New York: Federal Legal Publications, 1955.

Laddie, H., P. Prescott, and M. Vitoria. *The Modern Law of Copyright.* London: Butterworth & Co., 1980.

Leaffer, M. *Understanding Copyright Law.* Ch. 12. New York: Matthew Bender & Co., 1989.

Nimmer, M. *Nimmer on Copyright.* Vol. 13, Ch. 17. New York: Matthew Bender & Co., 1990.

Nondemann, W., K. Vinck, P. Hertin, and G. Meyer. *International Copyright.* Weinheim: VCH, 1990.

Plowman, E. W., and L. C. Hamilton. *Copyright: Intellectual Property in the Information Age.* London: Routledge & Kegan Paul, 1980.

Skone James, E. P., J. F. Mummery, J. E. Rayner James, and A. Latman. *Copinger and Skone James on Copyright.* 12th ed. London: Sweet & Maxwell, 1980.

Stewart, S. *International Copyright and Neighbouring Rights.* 2d ed. London: Butterworth & Co., 1989.

Ulmer, E. *Intellectual Property Rights and the Conflict of Laws.* Deventer, the Netherlands: Kluwer, 1978.

World Intellectual Property Organization. *Guide to the Berne Convention.* Geneva: WIPO, 1978.

———. *WIPO Glossary of Terms of the Law of Copyright and Neighboring Rights.* Geneva: WIPO, 1980.

———. *Guide to the Rome Convention and Phonograms Convention.* Publication no. 617(E). Geneva: WIPO, 1981.

———. *1886—Berne Convention Centenary—1986. The Berne Convention for the Protection of Literary and Artistic Works from 1886 to 1986.* Publication no. 877(E). Geneva: WIPO, 1986.

Articles

Abelman, L. E., and L. L. Berkowitz. "International Copyright Law." *N.Y.L. Sch. L. Rev.* 22, no. 3 (1977): 619–51.

Bloch, M. R. "The Expansion of the Berne Convention and the Universal Copyright Convention to Protect Computer Software and

Future Intellectual Property." *Brooklyn J. Int'l L.* 11 (Spring 1985): 283–323.

Bogsch, A. "The World Intellectual Property Organization: Its Recent Past and Its Future Plans." *Bull. Copyright Soc'y U.S.A.* 26 (Fall 1979): 194–201.

———. "The First Hundred Years of the Berne Convention for the Protection of Literary and Artistic Works." *Copyright* 22 (September 1986): 291–339.

Boytha, G. "Some Private International Law Aspects of the Protection of Authors' Rights." *Copyright* 24 (October 1988): 399–414.

Burger, P. "The Berne Convention: Its History and Key Role in the Future." *J. of Law & Tech.* 3 (Winter 1988): 1–69.

Comment. "A Bird's-Eye View of International Copyright: The Piracy of Satellite Programming and the Public Transmission Right." *Hous. J. Int'l L.* 93 (Autumn 1986): 133–52.

Dam, K. W. "The Growing Importance of International Protection of Intellectual Property." (Section Symposium: Legal Problems Affecting the Multinational Corporation). *Int'l Law.* 21 (Summer 1987): 627–38.

Dawid, H. "Basic Principles of International Copyright." *Bull. Copyright Soc'y U.S.A.* 21 (October 1973): 1–24.

Debois, H. "The Diplomatic Conference for the Revision of the Berne and Geneva Conventions." *R.I.D.A.* 68 (April 1971): 3–67.

———. "The Evolution of Copyright in International Relations Since the Brussels Conference of 1948." *R.I.D.A.* 79 (January 1974): 292–405.

Dietz, A. "Copyright and Satellite Broadcasts." *Int'l R. Indus. Prop. & Copyright L.* 20, no. 2 (1989): 135–50.

Dittrich, R. "The Practical Application of the Rome Convention." *Bull. Copyright Soc'y U.S.A.* 26 (April 1979): 287–307.

———. "On the Interpretation of Article 11 *bis* (1) and (2) of the Berne Copyright Convention." *Copyright* (October 1982): 294–306.

Durrande, S. "The Concept of Publication in the International Conventions." *R.I.D.A.* 111 (January 1982): 73–169.

Fabiani, M. "Copyright and Broadcasting by Satellite." *Copyright* 24 (January 1988): 17–26.

Francon, A. "International Protection of Neighboring Rights." *R.I.D.A.* 79 (January 1974): 407–78.

———. "The Legal Situation Concerning Reprography Internationally and in France." *Int'l R. Indus. Prop. & Copyright L.* 15, no. 6 (1984): 679–85.

Freegard, M. "Direct Broadcasting by Satellite (DBS): The Implications for Copyright." *R.I.D.A.* 136 (April 1988): 62–135.

Geller, P. E. "Copyright Protection in the Berne Union: Analyzing the Issues." *Intell. Prop. J.* 5 (August 1989): 1–50.

Ginsburg, J., and J. M. Kernochan. "One Hundred and Two Years Later: The U.S. Joins the Berne Convention." *Colum.-VLA J. L. & Arts* 13 (1988): 1–36.

Jaszi, P. "A Garland of Reflections on Three International Copyright Topics." *Cardozo Arts and Ent. Law J.* 8, no 1 (1989): 47–72.

Karnell, G. "Photography, A Stepchild of International Conventions and National Laws." *Copyright* 24 (March 1988): 132–45.

Kerever, A. "The Ambiguities of the Brussels Satellite Convention." *R.I.D.A.* 93 (January 1977): 56–75.

Koumantos, G. "Private International Law and the Berne Convention." *Copyright* 24 (October 1988): 415–28.

Laun, M. W. "Improving the International Framework for the Protection of Computer Software." *U. Pitt. L. Rev.* 48 (Summer 1987): 1151–84.

Masouye, C. "The Berne Convention Since Stockholm." *R.I.D.A.* 119 (January 1984): 3–58.

Masouye, P. "The Rome Convention: Realities and Prospects." *Copyright* 21 (September 1985): 296–313.

Ndiaya, N. "The Berne Convention and Developing Countries. (A Conference to Celebrate the Centenary of the Berne Convention, 1886–1986)." *Colum. VLA J.L. & Arts* 11 (Fall 1986): 47–56.

Note. "International Copyright: Domestic Barriers to United States Participation in the Rome Convention on Neighboring Rights." *Ga. J. Int'l Comp. L.* 13 (Winter 1983): 83–109.

Reichman, J. H. "Design Protection in Domestic and Foreign Copyright Law: From the Berne Revision of 1948 to the Copyright Act of 1976." *Duke L.J.* (December 1983): 1143–1264.

Ricketson, S. "The Birth of the Berne Union, (A Conference to Celebrate the Centenary of the Berne Convention, 1886–1986)." *Colum.-VLA J.L. & Arts* 11 (Fall 1986): 9–32.

Ringer, B., and L. I. Flacks. "Applicability of the U.C.C. to Certain Works in the Public Domain in Their Country of Origin." *Bull. Copyright Soc'y U.S.A.* 27 (August 1980): 419–33.

Sandison, H. "The Berne Convention and the U.C.C.—The American Experience." *Colum.-VLA J. L. & Arts* 11 (Fall 1986): 89–120.

Schonherr, F. "On the Interpretation of Article 5(2) of the Berne Convention." *Copyright* 17 (November 1981): 294–98.

Schrader, D. M. "Analysis of the Protocol Regarding Developing

Countries." *Bull. Copyright Soc'y U.S.A.* 17 (Fall 1970): 160–233.

Shute, W. H. "A Bird's-Eye View of International Copyright: the Piracy of Satellite Programming and the Public Transmission Right." *Hous. J. Int. L.* 9 (Autumn 1986): 133–52.

Sobel, L. "The Framework of International Copyright." *Cardozo Arts & Ent. Law J.* 8, no. 1 (1989): 1–26.

Tapper, C. "Copyright in Computer Programs: An International Perspective, (Issue Concerning Intellectual Property)." *Santa Clara High-Tech L.J.* 1 (January 1985): 13–25.

Thompson, E. "Twenty Years of the Rome Convention." *Copyright* 17 (October 1981): 270–76.

Tocups, N. M. "The Development of Special Provisions in International Copyright Law for the Benefit of Developing Countries." *J. Copyright Soc'y U.S.A.* 29 (April 1982): 402–21.

Ulmer, E. "The Revisions of the Copyright Conventions." *Int'l R. Indus. Prop. & Copyright L.* 2, no. 4 (1971): 345–71.

———. "The Convention for the Protection of Producers of Phonograms Against Unauthorized Duplication of their Phonograms." *Int'l R. Indus. Prop. & Copyright L.* 3, no. 2 (1972): 317–34.

———. "Droit de Suite in International Copyright Law." *Int'l R. Indus. Prop. & Copyright L.* 6, no. 1 (1975): 12–28.

———. "Protection of Authors in Relation to the Transmission Via Satellite of Broadcast Programs." 93 *R.I.D.A.* (July 1977): 4–41.

———. "One Hundred Years of the Berne Convention." *Int'l R. Indus. Prop. & Copyright L.* 17, no. 6 (1986): 707–15.

Vaver, D. "The National Treatment Requirements of the Berne and Universal Copyright Conventions." Parts 1, 2. *Int'l R. Indus. Prop. & Copyright L.* 17, nos. 5, 6 (1986): 577–607, 715–33.

Records of Diplomatic Conferences

World Intellectual Property Organization. *Records of the Diplomatic Conference on the International Protection of Performers, Producers of Phonograms and Broadcasting Organisations.* Publication no. 326(E). Rome: WIPO, 1961.

———. *Records of the Diplomatic Conference for the Revision of the Berne Convention for the Protection of Literary and Artistic Works.* Publication no. 315(E). Paris: WIPO, 1971.

———. *Records of the International Conference of States on the*

Protection of Phonograms. Publication no. 318(E). Geneva: WIPO, 1971.

———. *Records of the International Conference of States on the Distribution of Programme-Carrying Signals Transmitted by Satellite*. Publication no. 331(E). Brussels: WIPO, 1974.

———. *Guide to the Rome Convention and to the Phonograms Convention*. Publication no. 617(E). Geneva: WIPO, 1981.

Texts of Laws and Treaties

Bureau of National Affairs, Inc. (BNA) and the United National Educational, Scientific and Cultural Organization (UNESCO). *Copyright Laws and Treaties of the World*. 3 vols. Washington, D.C.: BNA Books, 1956–.

World Intellectual Property Organization. *Industrial Property Laws and Treaties*. Publication no. 609(E). Geneva: WIPO, 1976–.

———. *Copyright and Neighboring Rights Laws and Treaties*. Publication no. 616(E). Geneva: WIPO, 1987–.

Zweigert, K., and J. Kropholler. *Sources of International Uniform Law*. 3 vols. Amsterdam: Sijthoff & Noordoff, 1973 and 1979.

Index

Berne Convention for the Protection of Literary and Artistic Works (Paris Act) 339–377

Administrative provisions 355–368
acceptance and entry into force of act 362–364
countries in the Union 362–363
countries outside the Union 363–364
effect of and WIPO Convention 364
amendments 361–362
applicability to certain territories 365
application of convention 367
assembly, nature and description of 355–357
denunciation 367
developing countries, special provisions regarding 355
disputes 366
duration of convention 367
earlier provisions, closing of 366–367
executive committee, nature and description of 357–358
final clauses 367
languages of act 367
notification 367
registration 367
signature 367
finances of Union 359–361
International Bureau, nature and description of 358–359
reservations 364–365
revisions 362
transitory provisions 368
Appendix 368–377
applications and 376–377
faculties open to developing countries 368–370
licenses, provisions common to 374–376
right of reproduction, limitations on 372–374
right of translation, limitations on 370–372
alternative possibilities for 376
Editor's introduction 339–341
Introductory provisions 342
establishment of a Union 342
Substantive provisions 342–354
adaptation, arrangement, other alterations, right of 350
broadcasting and related rights 349–360
cinematographic and related rights 351
special provisions 351–352
control of circulation, presentation, and exhibition of works 353–354
copies, infringing 351
criteria for eligibility for protection 343–344
criteria of eligibility for protection of cinematographic works, works of architecture and certain artistic works 344
dramatic works, rights in 349
droit de suite 352
entry into force 354
literary works, rights in 350
moral rights 346
musical works, rights in 349
possible limitation of protection of certain works 342
possible restriction of protection in respect of certain works of nationals of certain countries outside the Union 345–346

protected rights, right to enforce 352–353
protected works, nature and description of 342–343
protection greater than resulting from convention 354
recording, right of 350–351
limitations 350–351
reproduction, right of 348
rights guaranteed, nature and description of 344–345
special agreements among countries of the Union 354
term of protection 346–347
translation, right of 347–348
works, other free uses of 348–349

Budapest Treaty on the International Recognition of the Deposit of Microorganisms for the Purposes of Patent Procedure 125–140

Administrative provisions 134–137
assembly 134–135
International Bureau 136
regulations 136–137
Editor's introduction 125–126
Final provisions 138–140
becoming party to the treaty 138
denunciation of the treaty 139
deposit of the treaty 139–140
entry into force of the treaty 138
notifications 140
registration of the treaty 140
signature and languages of the treaty 139
transmittal of copies 140
Introductory provisions 127–128
definitions 127–128
establishment of a Union 127
Revision and amendment 137–138
amendment of certain provisions of the treaty 137–138
revision of the treaty 137
Substantive provisions 128–134
acquisition of the status of international depositary authority 131–132
export and import restrictions 130
intergovernmental industrial property organizations 133–134
new deposit 129–130
recognition and effect of the deposit of microorganisms 128–129
status of international restrictions 130–131
termination and limitation of the status of international depositary authority 132–133

Convention Establishing the World Intellectual Property Organization 563–581

Administrative provisions 568–580
amendments 579–580
becoming a party to the convention 578
conferences 570–571
Coordination Committee 571–573
denunciation, right of 580
entry into force 578
finances 575–577
General Assembly 568–570
headquarters 574
International Bureau 573–574
legal capacity 577
notifications 580
privileges and immunities 577
relations with other organizations 578
reservations 579
Editor's introduction 563–565
Final provisions 580
Substantive provisions 566–568
definitions 566–567
establishment of WIPO 566
functions 567–568
membership 568
objectives 567
Transitional provisions 581

Convention for the Protection of Producers of Phonograms Against Unauthorized Duplication of Their Phonograms (Geneva Convention) 430–436

Administrative procedures 434–436
denunciation, right of 435–436
entry into force 435
International Bureau 434
languages 436
ratification and accession 435
reservations 435
signatures 434–435
Editor's introduction 430–431
Substantive procedures 432–434

compulsory licenses, conditions of 433
definitions 432
duration of protection 433
implementation of convention 432
notice 433
notification 434
protection 432

Convention Relating to the Distribution of Programme-Carrying Signals Transmitted by Satellite (Brussels Convention) 437–443

Administrative provisions 441–443
denunciation, right of 442
deposits 441–442
entry into force 442
languages of 443
reservations 441
signatures 443
Editor's introduction 437–438
Substantive provisions 439–441
contracting states, obligations of 439–440
definitions 439
domestic law and convention 441
measures 440–441
signals 440

European Patent Convention (With Protocols) 141–226

Appeals procedure 184–187
decision in respect of appeals 186
decision or opinion of the Enlarged Board of Appeal 186–187
decisions subject to appeal 184–185
examination of appeals 186
interlocutory revision 185
persons entitled to appeal and to be parties to appeal proceedings 185
time limit and form of appeal 185
Application for European patents 171–177
filing and requirements of the European patent application 171–175
abstract 175
claims 175
date of filing 174
designation of contracting states 173–174
designation of the inventor 174
disclosure of the invention 174
European divisional applications 172
filing of application 171–172
forwarding of application 172–173
renewal of fees 175
requirements of application 173
unity of invention 174
priority 175–177
claiming priority 176–177
effect of priority right 177
priority right 175–176
Common provisions governing procedure 187–193
amendments 192
basis of decisions 187
examination by the European Patent Office of its own motion 187
further processing of the European patent application 190–191
information concerning national patent applications 192
notification 190
observations by third parties 188
oral proceedings 188
reference to general principles 193
restitutio in integrum 191–192
taking of evidence 188–189
termination of financial obligations 193
time limits 190
unity of the European patent application or European patent 189–190
Editor's introduction 141–142
Final provisions 212–218
accession 212–213
denunciation 216
disputes between contracting states 216
duration between contracting states 215
duration of convention 215
entry into force 214–215
financial rights and obligations of former contracting states 217
implementing regulations and protocols 212
initial contribution 215
languages of the convention 217
preservation of acquired rights 216–217
reservations 213–214
revision 215–216
signature and ratification 212

territorial field of application 214
transmission and notifications 217–218
General and institutional provisions 143–162
Administrative Council 153–157
attendance of observers 154
board 153–154
chairmanship 153
competence of the Administrative Council in certain cases 155–156
languages of the Administrative Council 155
meetings 154
membership 153
staff, premises, and equipment 155
voting rights 156
voting rules 156
weighting of votes 156–157
European Patent Office 146–153
appointment of senior employees 146–147
boards of appeal 150–151
direction 146
disputes between the Organisation and the employees of the European Patent Office 147
duties of office 147
examining divisions 149
exclusion and objection 152
independence of the members of the boards 151–152
languages of the European Patent Office 147–148
legal division 150
opposition divisions 150
procedure, departments charged with 148–149
receiving section 149
search divisions 149
technical opinion 152–153
European Patent Organisation 144–145
legal status 144
liability 145
privileges and immunities 145
seat 144
sub-offices of the European Patent Office 144–145
Financial provisions 157–162
accounting period 160
advances 159
appropriations for unforeseeable expenditure 160
auditing of accounts 161–162
authorization for expenditure 160
budget 159–161
implementation of 161
cover for expenditure 157
financial regulations 162
level of fees 158–159
Organisation's own resources 157
preparation and adoption of the budget 160
provisional budget 161
renewal fees, payment of 158
rules relating to fees 162
General provisions 143–144
European law for the grant of patents 143
European patent 143
European Patent Organisation 144
territorial effect 143
Impact on national law 198–201
conversion into a national patent application 198–199
formal requirements for conversion 199
request for the application of national procedure 198
submission and transmission of the request 199
miscellaneous effects 201
national utility models and utility certificates 201
renewal fees for European patents 201
revocation and prior rights 200
grounds for revocation 200
rights of earlier date or same date 200
Information to the public or official authorities 193–196
administrative and legal cooperation 195
exchange of information 195
exchange of publications 196
inspection of files 194
periodical publications 194
register of European patents 193
International application pursuant to the Patent Cooperation Treaty 204–208
application of the Patent Cooperation Treaty 204
European Patent Office as a designated office 205–206
European Patent Office as an elected office 207

European Patent Office as an international preliminary examining authority 206–207
European Patent Office as an international searching authority 206
European Patent Office as a receiving office 204–205
filing and transmittal of the international application 205
international search report 207–208
publication of the international application 208
Opposition procedure 182–184
costs 184
examination of the opposition 182–183
grounds for opposition 182
intervention of the assumed infringer 184
opposition 182
publication of a new specification of the European patent 183
revocation or maintenance of the European patent 183
Procedure up to grant 177–181
European search report 179
examination as to formal requirements 178–179
examination of the European patent application 180–181
examination on filing 177–178
extension of the period within which requests for examination may be filed 180
publication of a specification of the European patent 181
publication of European patent application 179
refusal or grant 181
request for examination 179–180
Protocols 219–226
Representation 196–198
general principles 196
professional representatives 197–198
Special agreements 201–204
cover for expenditure for carrying out special tasks 202–203
European patent application as an object of property 203
joint designation 203–204
renewal fees for unitary patents 203
representation before special departments 202
select committee of the Administrative Council 202
special departments of the European Patent Office 202
unitary patents 201
Substantive provisions 163–171
applying for and obtaining European patents 165–166
entitlement to file a European patent application 165
multiple applicants 165
persons not having right to a European patent 166
right of inventor to be mentioned 166
right to a European patent 165–166
effect of European patent and the European patent application 167–170
authentic text of European patent application 170
effect of revocation of the European patent 169
equivalence of European filing with national filing 168
extent of protection 169–170
rights conferred by European patent 167
rights conferred by European patent application after publication 168–169
term of the European patent 167
translation of the specification of the patent 167–168
European patent application as an object of property 170–171
assignment 171
contractual licensing 171
law applicable 171
transfer and constitution of rights 170–171
patentability 163–165
exceptions to patentability 163–164
industrial application 165
inventive step 165
nonprejudicial disclosures 165
novelty 164
patentable inventions 163
Transitional provisions 208–212
Administrative Council during a transitional period 208–209
appointment of employees during a transitional period 209
first accounting period 209–210
professional representatives during a transitional period 210–212
progressive expansion of the field of activity of the European Patent Office 210

The Hague Agreement Concerning the International Deposit of Industrial Designs, 1960 471–487

Administrative provisions 480–487
accession 484
amending of regulations 484
applicability of 1925 or 1934 Acts 486
applicability of protection accorded by national laws and by copyright treaties 482
application of agreement under national law 484
certified copies 487
denunciation, right of 485
entry into force 484–485
fees 480
fees belonging to contracting states 480–481
International Design Committee 483
principles governing fixation of amounts of fees belonging to the International Bureau 482
protocol 486–487
ratification 484
regional groups 486
regulations 481
reserve fund 482–483
revisions 485–486
signature 484, 487
territories 485
Editor's introduction 471–472
Protocol 487
Substantive provisions 473–480
contents of application 475
date of registration 476
deferral of publication 476
definitions 473–474
deposit, renunciation of 479
establishment of Union 473
form of deposit 474–475
International Bureau, deposit with 474
international deposits, right to make 474
international design notice 480
international design register 475–476
marking 480
ownership, changes in 479
priority, right of 477
protection, duration of 478–479
public access to archives 476
publication 476
refusal of legal effect by national offices 476–477
registered deposits, legal effect of 476
remedies against refusal 477
renewal of deposit 478

Hague Agreement Concerning the International Deposit of Industrial Designs, of November 6, 1925, Complementary Act of Stockholm of July 14, 1967 488–496

Administrative provisions 491–496
accession 494
amendments 492–494
automatic acceptance of certain provisions 495
entry into force 494–495
finances 491–492
International Bureau 490–491
ratification 494
signature 495–496
transitional provision 496
Substantive provisions 488–490
assembly 488–490
definitions 488

International Convention for the Protection of New Varieties of Plants (UPOV) 53–75

Administrative provisions 63–75
acceptance 69
accession 69
auditing of accounts 66
closing of earlier texts 69–70
contracts, joint utilization of examination services 68–69
Council, composition of 63
decisions of Council 65
different texts, relation between states bound by 70
duration and denunciation of 73
entry into force 69–70
exceptional rules 71–72
finances 66–67
implementation 68
languages, depository functions 73
language used 68
meetings and the status of observers 63
officers of Council 64
organs of the convention 63
preservation of 72
ratification of convention 69
recommendations to Articles 4 and 5 74–75
regulations, financial and administrative 64

requirement of novelty 72
reservations 72
revision of convention 67–68
rules of procedure 64
sessions of Council 64
signature 69
special agreements 68
species and 70–71
communications concerning 70–71
information to be published 70–71
territories 71
tasks of Council 64–65
Union, office of 65–67
voting 63
Editor's introduction 53–54
Substantive provisions 55–63
applications 60–61
botanical genera, protection of 56–57
constitution of convention 55
national treatment 55–56
priority, right of 61
protection 57–61, 63
conditions required 58–59
nullity and forfeiture of 60
period of 59
provisional 59
restrictions 59–60
rights of 57–58
scope of 58
protection, forms of 55
purpose of convention 55
reciprocity 55–56
scope convention 57–58, 63
conditions required 58–59
period of 59
seat of 55
varieties 55–62
denomination of 61–62
official examination of 59
provisional protection of 59

International Convention for the Protection of Performers, Producers of Phonograms and Broadcasting Organisations (Rome Convention) 415–429

Administrative provisions 424–429
denunciation, right of 425
depositary functions 424, 428–429
disputes, resolution of 427
entry into force 425
Intergovernmental Committee 427
languages 428
notification and 425
ratification and accession 424
reservations 427
revisions 426
Editor's introduction 415–416
Substantive provisions 417–424
contracting states 423–424
rights and 424
special agreements and 424
definitions 417–418
denouncing 422–423
fixation, criterion of 423
and Article 7 423
national treatment, definition of 417
broadcasting organizations and 419
nonperformers and 420
performers and 418
phonograms and 418–419
producers and 420–421
protection and 419–420
phonograms 421
protection, term of 421, 422, 424
exceptions to 422

Lisbon Agreement for the Protection of Appellations of Origin and Their International Registration 278–290

Administrative provisions 280, 282–290
amendments 287
denunciation 289
entry into force 288–290
international bureau, 284–285
languages 289–290
notification and accession 288
signatures 289–290
Special Union of 282–289
finances of 285–286
Union for the Protection of Industrial Property 280
Editor's introduction 278–279
Substantive provisions 280–282, 288
appellation of origin 280–282
definition of 280
protection of 282
registration of 281–282
protection 280, 282
ratification 288
registration 280
revision 288

Locarno Agreement Establishing an International Classification for Industrial Design 513–530

Administrative provisions 517–530
classes and subclasses of international classification 525–530

denunciation, right of 523
entry into force 523
finances 520–522
force and duration of agreement 523
International Bureau 519–520
languages 524
notifications 524
ratification and accession 522–523
resolution 530
revisions 523
signature 524
Special Union, assembly of 517–519
territories 524
transitional provision 524
Editor's introduction 513–514
Substantive provisions 515–517
amendments, notification and publication of 517
classifications, notification and publication of 517
Committee of Experts 516
establishment of Union 515
international classification adoption of 515
use and legal scope of 516

Madrid Agreement Concerning the International Registration of Marks (With Protocol) 229–269

Administrative provisions 238–249
accession 246–247
amendments 246
application of earlier acts 248–249
assembly of Union 242–243
common office for several contracting countries 241
denunciation, right of 248
depositary functions 249
entry into force 247–248
fees 238–239
finances 244–246
International Bureau 243–244
international mark, transfer of 240
assignment of 241
languages 249
national register, changes in 239–240
Paris Convention, reference to 241, 248
ratification 246
renunciation 239
signature 249
Editor's introduction 229–231
Protocol 251–269
administrative provisions 258–269
agreement, safeguard of 263
amendments 266
assembly 264–265
becoming a member of protocol 266
common office of contracting states 262
denunciation, right of 267–268
depositary functions 269
entries, copies of 258
entry into force 267
fees for international registration 259–261
finances 265–266
International Bureau 265
languages 269
ownership, change in of International Registration 261
recordals, fees for 262
recording of international registration 261–262
signature 268
transformation of international registration 263
substantive provisions 251–259
dependence of international registration 258
independence of international registration 258–259
international application 252–254
international registration, effects of 254–255
mark, legitimacy of 257–258
membership in Madrid Union 251
protection, securing of, international registration 251–252
refusal or invalidation of international registration 255–257
renewal of international registration 259
replacement by international registration 255
territorial effect 254
territorial extension, request for 254
validity of international registration 258
Substantive provisions 232–238
anticipation, searches for 236–237
copies of entries in international register 236–237
country of origin, definition of 232
establishment of Union 232
filing of marks at international bureau 232
international register, extracts from 237

international registration 233–235, 237
legitimacy of use of certain elements of mark 236
national offices, refusal by 235
Paris Convention, reference to 232
protection, termination of 237
renewal of international registration 238
territorial extension, request for 234
territorial limitation 234
Transitional provisions 250

Madrid Agreement for the Prevention of False or Misleading Indications of Source on Goods 270–277

Editor's introduction 270–271
Madrid, Agreement of 272–274
marks, false or misleading 272–274
prohibition of 272
sanctions 272
seizure of 272
and Custom authorities 272–273
ratification of act 273–274
Stockholm, Additional Act of 275–277
depositary functions, transfer of 275
entry into force 276
Paris Convention and 275
ratification of 275
signature 275
transitional provision 277

Nice Agreement Concerning the International Classification of Goods and Services for the Purposes of the Registration of Mark 499–512

Administrative provisions 503–512
accession 510
amendment of articles 509
assembly 505–506
Committee of Experts 503–504
denunciation, right of 511
depositary functions 512
duration 510–511
entry into force 504, 510
finances 507–509
International Bureau 506–507
languages 512
notifications 504, 512
Paris Convention 511
publication of changes 504
ratification 510
revision 511
signature 511
Editor's introduction 499–500
Substantive provisions 501–503
adoption of international classification 501
definitions 501–502
establishment of Union 501
languages of classification 502
legal effect and use of classification 502–503

Paris Convention for the Protection of Industrial Property 17–49

Administrative provisions 35–49
accession by countries of the Union 44
accession by countries outside the Union 45
accession to earlier acts 46
amendment of articles 42–43
assembly of the Union 35–38
consequences of ratification or accession 46
denunciation, right of 47
depositary functions 49
disputes 48
earlier acts, application of 47–48
entry into force by countries of the Union 44–45
entry into force by countries outside the Union 45–46
Executive Committee 38–39
finances 40–42
implementation of convention on domestic level 47
International Bureau 39–40
languages 48–49
ratification 44
revision of articles 43
signature 48
special agreements 43
special national industrial property services 35
territories 46
Editor's introduction 17–19
Substantive provisions 20–35
establishment of Union 20
false indications 33–34
remedies 34
right to sue 34
seizure of goods 33
industrial designs 21–23, 25–27, 35
failure to work 25
importation of articles 25
marking 26

period of grace 26
protection of 27
right of priority 21–23
temporary protection of certain international exhibitions 35
inventors' certificates 21–23, 26
marking 26
period of grace 26
right of priority 21–23
marks 21–23, 25–34
assignment of 30
collective marks 32
conditions, of registration 27
different forms 25–26
failure to use 25
independence of protection of same mark in different countries 27
marking 26
nature of goods to be marked 32
period of grace 26
prohibitions 28–30
protection of 30–31
registration of 32
remedies 34
right of priority 21–23
right to sue 34
seizure on importation of goods unlawfully bearing a mark or trade name 33
service marks 31
temporary protection of certain international exhibitions 35
use by co-proprietors 25–26
well-known marks 27–28
patents 22–27, 35
compulsory licenses 25
division of application 22–23
failure to work or insufficient working 25
importation of articles 25
importation of products manufactured by a process patented in the importing country 27
independence of patents obtained for same invention in different countries 24
marking 26
mention of inventor in patent 24
patentability in case of restrictions of sale 24–25
patented devices forming part of vessels, aircraft, or land vehicles 26
period of grace 26
restoration 26
right of priority 21–23
temporary protection of certain international exhibitions 35
trade names 33–34
remedies 34
right to sue 34
seizure on importation of goods unlawfully bearing a mark or trade name 33
unfair competition 34
remedies 34
right to sue 34
utility models 21–23, 26, 35
marking 26
period of grace 26
right of priority 21–23
temporary protection of certain international exhibitions 35
transitional provisions 49

Patent Cooperation Treaty 76–124

Administrative provisions 109–117
assembly 109–111
Committee for Technical Cooperation 113–115
Executive Committee 111–112
finances 115–116
International Bureau 113
regulations 116–117
Common provisions 105–107
delay in meeting certain time limits 107
incorrect translation of the international application 106
regional patent treaties 106
right to practice before international authorities 107
seeking certain kinds of protection 105
seeking two kinds of protection 105–106
time limits 106
Disputes 117–118
Editor's introduction 76–78
Final provisions 119–124
becoming a party to the treaty 119
denunciation 122–123
depositary functions 123
entry into force 119–120
gradual application 122
notifications 123–124
reservations 120–121
signature and languages 123
International application and international search 81–97

amendment of claim, description and drawings 95
amendment of claims before International Bureau 89–90
applicant 83–84
availability of copy of the international application 85
claims 81–82
communication to designated offices 90
confidential nature of international application 96–97
copy, translation, and fee to designated offices 91–92
defects in the international application 86
delaying of national procedure 92–93
description 81
drawings 82
effects of international publication 95–96
filing date and effects of international application 84–85
international application 81
international publication 90–91
international search 86–87
international searching authority 87–88
international search reports 89
national requirements 93–95
opportunity to correct before designated offices 93
possible loss of effect in designated states 92
priority, claiming 83
procedure before international searching authority 88–89
receiving office 84
request 81–82
review by designated offices 92–93
transmittal of international application 85
International preliminary examination 97–105
amendment of claims, description, and drawings 104
confidential nature of international preliminary examination 102
copy, translation, and fee to elected offices 103–104
delaying of national examination and other processing 104
demand for international preliminary examination 97–98
international preliminary examination 98–99
international preliminary examination report 101
international preliminary examining authority 98
procedure before international preliminary examining authority 99–100
results of national examination 105
transmittal, translation, and communication of the international preliminary examination report 101–102
withdrawal of demand or election 102
Introductory provisions 79–81
definitions 79–81
establishment of a Union 79
Revision and amendment 118–119
amendment of certain provisions of treaty 118–119
Technical services 107–109
patent information services 107–108
relations with other provisions of the treaty 109
technical assistance 108–109

Strasbourg Agreement Concerning the International Patent Classification 531–545

Administrative provisions 537–544
amendments 541–542
assembly of Special Union 537–538
becoming a party to agreement 542
denunciation, right of 543
depositary functions 544
duration of agreement 543
entry into force 542–543
finances 539–541
International Bureau 538–539
languages 544
notification 544
revisions 541
signature 544
Editor's introduction 531–532
Substantive provisions 533–537
adoption of international classification 533
amendments, publication of 537
Committee of Experts 535–536
definition of the classification 533–534
entry into force 537
establishment of Union 533
languages of the classification 534
notification 536
use of the classification 534–535
Transitional provisions 544–545

Trademark Registration Treaty 291–336

Administrative provisions 325–330
  assembly 325–326
  finances 327–329
  International Bureau 326–327
  regulations 329
  search service 330
Editor's introduction 291–292
Final provisions 331–336
  becoming party to treaty 331–332
  denunciation of treaty 334–335
  depositary functions 335
  entry into force of treaty 334
  notifications 336
  reservations to treaty 334
  settlement of disputes 335–336
  signature and languages of treaty 335
  transitional provisions 332–334
Introductory provisions 293–295
  abbreviated expressions 293–295
  establishment of Union 293
Revision and amendment 330–331
  amendment of provisions 330–331
  revision of Treaty 330
Substantive provisions 295–325
  goods and services 311–312
    limitation of 311–312
  international application 295–297, 299–302
    contents of 296–297
    defects and 299–302
    later designation and (see also *later designation*) 298–299
    right to file 295
  International Bureau 322–325
    correction of errors 324–325
    representation and 322–323
  International Register of Marks 295
  international registration 295–296, 299, 304–311
    effects of 304–305
      cancellation of 307
      refusal of 305–307
    fees and 313–314
    Madrid Agreement and 319–320
      preservation of rights and 319–320
      preservation of right to use 320
    ownership of 295–296, 308–310, 325
      change in 308–310
      name change and 310–311
      notification of 325
      right of 295–296
    priority claim and 323
    publication and notification of 304
    renewal of 312–313
    term of 312–313
  later designation 318–319
    declining of 302–304
      avoiding effects of 303–304
    priority claim and 323
    publication and notification of 304
    recording of 302–303
      effects of 304–305
  national registration 318–319
    international registration and 321
    preservation of rights and 318–319
  national requirements 314–318
  recording of marks 318
  regional marks 321–322
  time limits, delay in meeting 323

Treaty on the Intellectual Property in Respect of Integrated Circuits 455–468

Administrative provisions 462–467
  amendments 463–464
  assembly 462–463
  becoming party to treaty 466
  denunciation, right of 467
  depositary functions 467
  disputes, settlement of 464–466
  entry into force 466–467
  International Bureau 463
  reservations 464
  safeguards 464
  signature 467
  texts of treaty 467
Editor's introduction 455–456
Substantive provisions 457–462
  definitions 457–458
  disclosure 461–462
  duration of protection 462
  establishment of Union 457
  exploitation 461
  legal form of protection 459
  national treatment 459
  registration 461–462
  scope of protection 459–461
  subject matter of treaty 458

Treaty on the International Registration of Audiovisual Works 444–454

Administrative provisions 448–451
  assembly 448–449
  finances 450–451

International Bureau 449–450
regulations 451
Editor's introduction 444–445
Final provisions 452–454
becoming a party to treaty 452
denunciation, right of 453
entry into force 453
notifications 454
reservations 453
signature and languages 454
Revisions and amendments 451–452
amendments 452
revision of treaty 451–452
Substantive provisions 446–447
audiovisual work, definition of 446
establishment of Union 446
international register 446–447
legal effect of 447

Universal Copyright Convention (And Protocols) 378–394

Administrative provisions 385–389
Berne Union and relations to UCC 388
copies and notification 389
denunciation, right of 387
entry into force 385
giving effect to the convention 386
Inter-American Copyright Convention, relations to 388
Intergovernmental Copyright Committee 386
International Court of Justice, jurisdiction of 387
languages of the convention 387–388
non-self-governing territories 387
relations to other treaties 388–389
reservations to convention 389
revisions 386
signature of and adhesion to convention 385
Appendix 389–390
documents of Geneva Conference 389–390
documents of Intergovernmental Copyright Committee 390
Editor's introduction 378–380
Preamble 381
Protocols 391–394
conditional adherence to convention 393
stateless persons and refugees, extension of convention to 391
works of intergovernmental organizations, extension of convention to 392
Substantive provisions 381–385
definition of "publication" 385
application of definition and other provisions 385
duration of protection 382–383
basic rule 382
minimum terms 382–383
rule of the shorter term 383
field of application of convention and national treatment 381
eligibility under the provisions of the convention 381
national treatment 381
formalities 381–382
published works 381–382
unpublished works 382
obligation of states to protect copyright 381
public domain 385
right to translate 383–384
exclusive right of translation 383
compulsory license 384

Universal Copyright Convention as Revised at Paris and Protocols Annexed Thereto, 1971 395–414

Administrative provisions 406–410
accession 406–407
Berne Convention and UCC 409
copyright conventions and UCC 410
denunciation, right of 408–409
deposits 406
dispute resolution 409
entry into force 407
Intergovernmental Committee 407–408
International Court of Justice 409
languages 409
ratification 406–407
registration 409–410
reservations 409
Appendix 411
Protocols 413–414
stateless persons and refugees, extension of convention to 413
works of intergovernmental organizations, extension of convention to 414
Resolution 411–412
Substantive provisions 395–406
broadcasting rights 398
duration of protection 396–397

field of application of the convention and national treatment 395
formalities 395–396
licenses 400–406
notification 399–400
obligation of states to protect copyright 395–406
publication, definition of 406
public domain works 406
reproduction rights 397–398
translation rights 398–399

Vienna Agreement Establishing an International Classification of the Figurative Elements of Marks 546–560

Administrative provisions 551–560
amendments 556
assembly of Special Union 551–553
becoming a party to agreement 556–557
denunciation, right of 557–558
depositary functions 559
disputes 558
duration 557
entry into force 557
finances 554–555
International Bureau 553–554
languages 558
notifications 559
resolution 559–560
revisions 555–556
signature 558
Editor's introduction 546–547
Substantive provisions 548–551
additions, publication of 551
adoption of international classification 548
amendments, publication of 551
Committee of Experts 549–551
definition of classification 548
deposit of classification 548
entry into force 551
establishment of Union 548
languages of classification 548–549
notification 551
use of classification of figurative elements 549

About the Author

Marshall A. Leaffer is a professor of intellectual property law at the University of Toledo and a past lecturer at the Université de Paris. His experience in the practice of trademark, copyright, and related areas of intellectual property law include attorney positions with the U.S. Copyright Office; U.S. Patent and Trademark Office; Hazeltine, Lake & Waters in New York; and American Home Products Corporation.

Professor Leaffer received his Master of Laws degree in trade regulation from New York University Law School, his J.D. and B.A. from University of Texas, and his M.A. from the University of Illinois.